INTRODUCTION TO
PSYCHOLOGY

MARK GARRISON
KENTUCKY STATE UNIVERSITY

GLENCOE
Macmillan/McGraw–Hill

Lake Forest, Illinois   Columbus, Ohio   Mission Hills, California   Peoria, Illinois

Send all inquiries to:
Glencoe Division, Macmillan/McGraw-Hill
936 Eastwind Drive
Westerville, OH 43081

Library of Congress Cataloging-in-Publication Data

Garrison, Mark (Mark David)
    Introduction to psychology/Mark Garrison.
        p. cm.
    Includes bibliographical references and index.
    ISBN 0-02-800140-0 (soft)
    1. Psychology   I. Title
BF121.G385   1992
150--dc20   91-29429
                                            CIP

1 2 3 4 5 6 7 8 9 10 VH 00 99 98 97 96 95 94 93 92 91

Preface

It has taken a good part of the twentieth century for us to realize that psychology is as much a part of the basic skills we need for living and working as it is a field of academic study. This book provides students with an introduction to the fundamental concepts of psychology and the scientific research underlying the science. It also helps students understand how these concepts and principles affect their thought processes, behaviors, and relationships with others.

There is ample evidence of the need for an understanding of basic psychological principles and their applications. As faceless technologies grow in the workplace, employers look increasingly for employees with excellent human relations skills. The increasing complexity of life, in general, makes it important that everyone develop the self-understanding and inner resources that promote satisfying work and interpersonal relationships.

Introduction to Psychology provides comprehensive coverage of this dynamic field. The text includes summaries of the fundamental research and theories. Great care has been taken to familiarize students with the ways in which all aspects of psychology influence their lives. In addition to providing many examples involving work, school, and other settings, the text encourages students to bring their own experience to bear on the concepts presented.

Organization/Content

Chapter 1, Introducing Psychology, defines psychology as an empirical science. The chapter gives students a context for their study by providing an account of the philosophical origins of psychology and by describing the major subfields that fall under the general category of psychology.

The textbook is then organized into the following seven units, each corresponding to a major subfield of study:

- **Unit 1, Learning and Cognitive Processes,** gives students some insight into how they learn, memorize, and think. They are encouraged to think about their own thought processes and are given practical applications related to study and to learning various skills.

- **Unit 2, The Workings of Mind and Body,** deals with perception and the senses, motivation and emotion, and altered states of consciousness. This unit summarizes the latest research on the way our mental activities and physiological functions interact as we perceive and react to our surroundings.

- **Unit 3, The Life Span,** focuses on developmental psychology as it examines life from infancy through old age. The three chapters in this unit survey the intellectual, social, and psychological demands we are faced with at every stage of life.

- **Unit 4, Personality and Individuality,** discusses the psychology of personality and the use of various psychological tests. Students are presented with sample questions from psychological tests along with helpful tips on how to prepare to take these tests and alleviate anxiety.

- **Unit 5, Adjustment and Breakdown,** deals with issues such as stress and the way it affects people during crucial life experiences. The chapter also provides an overview of neuroses and psychoses and the different forms of therapeutic intervention that may be needed to help the affected individual adjust to life's challenges.

- **Unit 6, Human Relations,** focuses on the social aspect of our lives. By examining many different dimensions of human relations, this unit helps students analyze and understand social interactions in varying forms.

- **Unit 7, Psychological Research,** discusses research methods, statistical evaluation, and the latest trends in research.

Two appendixes are included at the end of Unit 7. One appendix provides detailed instructions on writing a research paper that conforms to American Psychological Association standards. The second appendix presents an overview of various career options in the field of psychology.

Learning Aids

Units and chapters are designed to facilitate learning. Each chapter begins with a chapter outline that provides an overview of the topics to be discussed. Key terms are in boldface type within the text and are repeated in the review section at the end of the chapter. End-of-chapter review pages include a summary and objective review questions along with activities and projects that enable students to apply the concepts.

   Throughout the book, marginal features expand on the theories presented in the chapters.

- **Using Psychology** illustrates real-world applications of research. Among the topics discussed are the uses of computer-assisted instruction, the influence of mood on memory, and the influence of peer groups.

- **Psychology Update** discusses topics of current research such as the training of dolphins by the U.S. Navy to detect undersea mines.

- **Fact or Fiction** confirms or dispels some common beliefs about phenomena such as an alcoholic's ability to drink socially and the effect of smell on memory.

- **More About** provides additional information about key psychological topics, including the functions of dreams and the differences in men's and women's emotional expression.

- **Psychology and You** uses concrete examples to illustrate how psychology applies to students' lives. One of these features discusses the effective study technique of SQ3R.

Teaching Aids

Introduction to Psychology is supported by a comprehensive ancillary package, which consists of the following:

- The **Study Guide** provides the student with a comprehensive tool for checking comprehension of the essential material covered in the textbook. In addition to objective questions and an overview of chapter objectives and key terms, students are exposed to application activities that will test critical thinking skills and the ability to apply theoretical concepts to their own lives.

- The **Instructor's Resource Manual** provides a comprehensive teaching support tool. This manual contains lecture outlines and teaching strategies for the textbook and the ancillaries. Additional discussion topics, classroom demonstrations, and extension activities are included for each chapter. Also included is an answer key to textbook questions.

- **Readings in Psychology** is a student reader of recent, relevant journal articles and case studies that expand on research topics discussed in the text. Students will find this book useful in understanding how theory is applied to real-world situations.

- A **Testbank** (IBM), consisting of approximately 1,000 objective and applied questions of varying levels of difficulty, is available with this program.

- Thirty-two **Transparencies** provide instructors with opportunities to discuss illustrations in detail.

CONTENTS

CHAPTER *1* Introducing Psychology   2

Why Study Psychology?   5
Overview of Psychology   7
A Brief History of Psychology   10
Psychology as a Profession   15
Chapter 1 Review   18

UNIT 1

Learning and Cognitive Processes

CHAPTER *2* Learning: Principles and Applications   22

Classical Conditioning   23
Operant Conditioning   29
Factors That Affect Learning   37
Learning Strategies   38
Learning Complicated Skills   40
Modeling   42
Chapter 2 Review   50

CHAPTER *3* Memory and Thought   52

Taking Information In   53
Storing Information   56
Retrieving Information   60
Central Processing of Information   69
Chapter 3 Review   76

UNIT 2

The Workings of Mind and Body

CHAPTER 4 Body and Behavior   **80**

The Nervous System   **81**
How Psychologists Study the Brain   **89**
The Endocrine System   **95**
The Relationship Between Humans and Animals   **96**
Heredity and Environment   **101**
Chapter 4 Review   **104**

CHAPTER 5 Sensation and Perception   **106**

Sensation   **108**
The Senses   **114**
Perception   **120**
Extrasensory Perception   **126**
Chapter 5 Review   **129**

CHAPTER 6 Motivation and Emotion   **132**

Biological Motives   **133**
Social Motives   **139**
Emotion   **145**
Chapter 6 Review   **154**

CHAPTER 7 Altered States of Consciousness   **156**

Sleep and Dreams   **158**
Hypnosis   **163**
Hallucinations   **165**
Near-Death Experiences   **166**
Psychoactive Drugs   **167**
Biofeedback   **174**
Meditation   **175**
Chapter 7 Review   **178**

UNIT 3

The Life Span

CHAPTER 8 Infancy and Childhood   **182**

What Causes Development?   183
The Beginning of Life   185
Cognitive Development   188
The Development of Language   193
Emotional Development   197
Socialization   202
Chapter 8 Review   215

CHAPTER 9 Adolescence   **218**

Views of Adolescence   219
Personal Development   222
Social Development   234
Difficulties in the Transition from
Late Childhood to Early Adolescence   239
Chapter 9 Review   240

CHAPTER 10 Adulthood and Old Age   **242**

Adulthood   243
Old Age   253
Death and Dying   257
Chapter 10 Review   262

UNIT 4

Personality and Individuality

CHAPTER 11 Personality Theory   **266**

What Personality Theories Try to Do   268
Psychoanalytic Theories   270
Behavioral Theories   277
Humanistic Psychology   279
Trait Theories   284
Chapter 11 Review   287

CHAPTER *12* Psychological Testing   290

Basic Characteristics of Tests   292
Intelligence Testing   295
Measuring Abilities and Interests   299
Test-Taking Strategies   303
Personality Testing   307
Situational Testing   309
Chapter 12 Review   311

UNIT 5

Adjustment and Breakdown

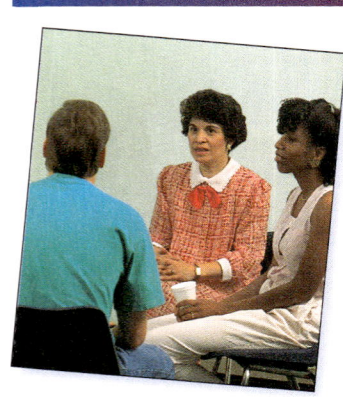

CHAPTER *13* Stress and Conflict   316

Sources of Stress   318
Reactions to Stress   324
Coping with Stress   333
Chapter 13 Review   338

CHAPTER *14* Adjustment in Society   340

Love and Marriage   342
Parent-Child Relationships   348
College Life   352
The Work Experience   355
Chapter 14 Review   360

CHAPTER *15* Disturbance and Breakdown   362

What Is Abnormal Behavior?   364
DSM-III-R: New Ways to Categorize Mental Illness   367
Further Aspects of Classification   371
Neurosis   372
Psychosis   378
Personality Disorders   384
Substance Abuse Disorders   385
Chapter 15 Review   389

CHAPTER *16* Therapy and Change   **392**

What Is Psychotherapy?   **393**
Kinds of Psychotherapy   **397**
Does Psychotherapy Work?   **409**
Organic Therapy   **411**
Mental Institutions   **413**
Community Mental Health   **415**
Chapter 16 Review   **420**

UNIT 6

Human Relations

CHAPTER *17* Human Interaction   **424**

Needing Other People   **425**
Choosing Friends   **427**
Personal Relationships   **432**
How People Perceive One Another   **437**
What Are Groups?   **440**
How Groups Are Held Together   **442**
Interactions Within Groups   **443**
Group Conflict Versus Cooperation   **450**
Chapter 17 Review   **453**

CHAPTER *18* Attitudes and Social
                  Influence   **456**

Where Attitudes Come From   **457**
Attitude Formation   **459**
Prejudice   **461**
Cognitive Consistency and Changing Attitudes   **466**
Attitudes and Actions   **468**
Persuasion   **470**
Social Influence   **477**
Chapter 18 Review   **483**

UNIT 7

Psychological Research

CHAPTER 19 Research Methods 488

Gathering Data 489

Traps in Doing Psychological Research
and How to Avoid Them 497

Conclusions 499

Chapter 19 Review 500

CHAPTER 20 Statistical Evaluation 502

Descriptive Statistics 503

Inferential Statistics 511

Statistics and You 513

Chapter 20 Review 514

CHAPTER 21 Psychology: Approaching the
Twenty-First Century 516

Biological Psychology 517

Psychology and the New Stressors of Life 520

Psychology and Work 523

War and Peace 528

Chapter 21 Review 531

APPENDIX A How to Write a
Research Paper 533

Choosing a Topic 533

Creating a Preliminary Outline 534

Doing Research at the Library 535

Taking Notes and Revising the Outline 537

Writing the Paper 539

Formatting the Paper 539

APPENDIX *B* Careers in Psychology   **543**

    What Is a Psychologist?   **543**

    Specialty Areas in Psychology   **545**

    **Applications of Psychology to
    Careers and Professions**   **548**

    Glossary   **551**
    Bibliography   **565**
    Photo Credits   **588**
    Index   **589**

Figure 1.1 Studying psychology can help you gain a perspective on your own behavior.

Objectives: *After studying this chapter, you should be able to*
- describe the range of topics covered in an introductory course in psychology.
- list the aims of an introductory course in psychology.
- explain what psychology is and describe basic methods of research.
- explain the three most important areas of study in psychology.
- summarize the specialized fields within psychology.

Introducing Psychology

What is it that fascinates psychologists about ordinary behavior? What exactly do they study? One way to answer this question is to look at a slice of life through a psychologist's eyes.

Ruth, a college student, decides to have lunch at the school cafeteria. She walks to the cafeteria, gets in line, chooses tuna salad and orange juice, and pays at the counter. She then looks around for someone to sit with. She doesn't see any close friends, so she goes to a table by herself, sits down, and begins to eat.

A few minutes later, Gary, a young man in Ruth's English class, comes over to join her. When Ruth looks up at him, she no longer feels like eating. She thinks Gary is very good looking, but he never speaks to Ruth unless he's missed a class and wants to borrow her notes. She greets him coolly, but Gary sits down anyway and begins to tell a long, rambling story about *A Visit from the Little Green People,* the horror movie on TV he stayed up to watch last night. Meanwhile, Ruth remembers that Gary missed this morning's English class and catches him eyeing her notebook.

Ruth fantasizes dumping her lunch on Gary's neatly groomed hair, but instead she gets up to leave. Gary attempts a casual smile and asks to borrow her notes. Now Ruth is more than annoyed. Although her English notebook is in plain sight, she tells him curtly that she is sorry but she has left her notes in the library—to which, as a matter of fact, she must return right away. As she leaves the cafeteria, she glances back and sees Gary still sitting at the table. He looks depressed. Suddenly, she feels a bit depressed herself.

This is a simple story, but from a psychologist's point of view, the behavior was complex. First of all, Ruth decided to have lunch because of her *physiological* (physical) *state*—she was hungry. She may also have

Why Study Psychology?
Insight • Practical Information

Overview of Psychology
Defining Psychology • The Scientific Basis of Psychology • The Goals of Psychology

A Brief History of Psychology
Psychology as a Discipline • Psychology as the Study of Unconscious Processes • Psychology as the Study of Individual Differences • Psychology as the Study of Observable Behavior

Psychology as a Profession
What Is a Psychologist? • Specialty Fields in Psychology

Figure 1.2
Where we might see two people sitting and talking, a psychologist might see a sequence of complex behaviors.

been motivated by *cognitive* (factual) elements—she knew she must eat now because she had classes scheduled for the next few hours. When she entered the cafeteria, she *perceived* sensory stimuli different from those outside, but she paid little attention to the new sights, sounds, and smells, except to note that the food smelled good and the line was mercifully short. She went through the line and paid for her food—*learned behavior* not too different from that of a hungry rat that runs a maze for a food reward.

Ruth looked for a *social group* to join, but found none to which she belonged. She sat alone until Gary joined her. He felt free to do so because in most schools there is an informal rule, or *norm*, that students who have a class together may approach each other socially. (This rule usually does not apply to members of a looser group, such as commuters who ride the same bus.) Ruth *remembered* how Gary had behaved toward her in the past and realized that he was about to follow the same note-borrowing routine. This triggered the *emotional* reaction of anger. However, she did not dump her food on his head as a two-year-old might have done, but acted in a way that was more appropriate to her stage of *development*. We can assume that her response was characteristic of her *personality:* she told the young man that she didn't have the notes (even though he had seen them) and left.

In the example above, if such situations occurred often, and if they were always followed by depression, either student's behavior could indicate psychological *disturbance*. If Gary always relied on others for help and manipulated people to get his way, his behavior might be a sign of disorder. So might Ruth's, since she interprets simple requests as demands but finds herself unable either to meet or refuse the request in a direct way. However, in this context, neither student's behavior seems *abnormal*.

Viewed in this way, an apparently simple event raises many questions about why people behave and feel as they do. How is their behavior influenced by their physiological states? What motivates them to choose one action instead of another? Nearly all of the topics covered in this book are reflected in a psychologist's perception of this brief story.

WHY STUDY PSYCHOLOGY?

Many people are attracted to the study of psychology because they think they will gain a better understanding of people. You may be studying psychology for more specific and personal reasons. As you read this book, you will discover new ways of looking at yourself and of interpreting the behavior of other people. The daily events you might ordinarily take for granted may now become fuel for thought. Two things you will gain by learning about psychology are insight into behavior and new practical information on how to deal with situations in everyday life.

Insight

Psychology can provide useful insight into your own and other people's behavior. For example, suppose a young man is convinced that he is hopelessly shy and doomed forever to feel uncomfortable in groups. Then he learns through studying social psychology that different kinds of groups tend to have different effects on their members. He thinks about this for a while and notes that, although he is miserable at parties, he feels fine at meetings of a special task force at work and with members of the volleyball team he belongs to. (In technical terms, he is much more uncomfortable in unstructured social groups than in structured, task-oriented groups.) Realizing that he is uncomfortable only in some groups brings relief. He is not paralyzingly shy; he just does not like unstructured groups. He is not alone in his feelings.

There is something to learn about each of us in *Introduction to Psychology*. You, too, may find that because of something you read in one chapter or another, you see yourself in a new way.

Of course, you must be careful in applying your new insight. Few people are more obnoxious than the individual who has had one psychology course and proceeds to terrorize family, friends, and strangers with an analysis of every action. Many puppies and kittens have become the unlucky targets of a psychology student's newly learned training methods.

"A little learning is a dangerous thing," according to an old cliché, but the more psychology you study, the more respect you will gain for the complexity and diversity of human behavior. An introductory psychology course is just one investment in a lifelong process of education about yourself and others.

Practical Information

Some of the chapters in this book include material that has a practical application in everyday life. You will learn concrete and detailed ways to carry out a number of useful procedures psychologists have developed.

For example, Chapter 2 describes the systematic way of dispensing rewards and punishments that psychologists call *shaping* (Figure 1.3). You will definitely find this useful if you ever have to train a puppy, and you may find yourself wondering how you are shaping the behavior of people around you. Perhaps you have two friends who are always happy to join you for coffee or a movie but who never bring any money along. You have loaned them money many times and, just as many times, they have failed to pay you back. You know they can afford to pay their share, and you have told them so repeatedly. They are good friends, however, so you end up paying their way again and again. In doing so, you are rewarding or reinforcing an undesirable behavior pattern. Is that what you really want to do?

Chapter 3 includes a description of several *mnemonic devices,* or memory aids, that will help you retain information by rote. The poem beginning "Thirty days has September," which helps many people remember the number of days in each month, is an example. With mnemonic devices, you usually associate each item on a list with something easier to remember, such as a mental picture, rhyme, or phrase. Although this may require time and effort, memory experts have shown that it is worth the trouble. The techniques described may help you memorize almost any list of words or numbers—the names of the presidents of the United States and their dates in office, the authors and titles of important works in psychology, the batting averages of major league baseball players, telephone numbers, shopping lists, and so on.

In reading the chapter on child development, you may recall similar experiences you had in your own childhood. The chapter on disturbance

Figure 1.3
Kissing is a response that is subject to shaping. Here the response is emitted tentatively and would probably be repeated only after a considerable time if it produced no result. The kiss is reinforced, however, and immediately the response increases in frequency and in vigor.

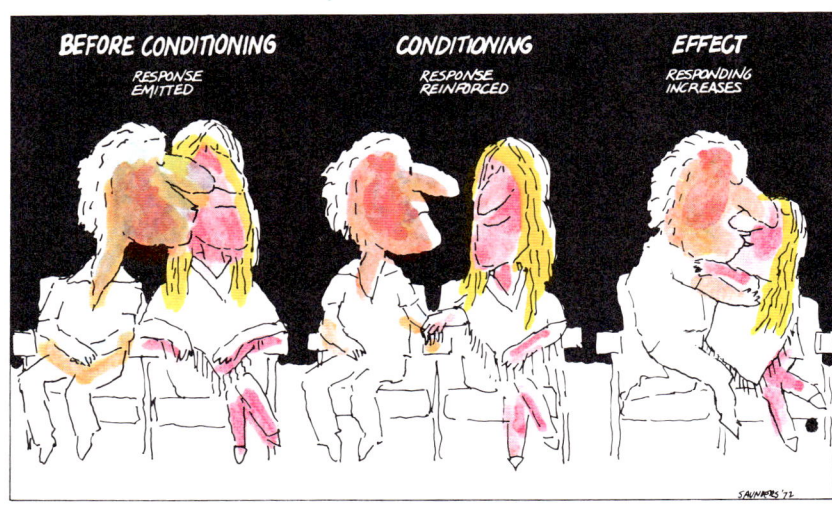

and breakdown may help you understand difficult periods in your own life and in the lives of those around you. Chapter 16 will tell you about the different kinds of therapy available to people who are experiencing severe or chronic difficulties. Of course, you should not jump to conclusions on the basis of this introduction to psychology. It takes a trained professional to diagnose and treat developmental and psychological problems (as Chapter 16 explains).

OVERVIEW OF PSYCHOLOGY

Defining Psychology

Psychology is the study of human behavior and mental processes. It covers everything that people think, feel, and do. Psychologists differ in how much importance they place on specific types of behavior. For example, some psychologists believe that you should study only behavior that you can see, observe, or measure directly. Ruth's behavior of selecting and paying for her food, choosing a table, and refusing to lend her notes to Gary are all examples of behaviors that are observable. Some psychologists believe that our fantasies, thoughts, and feelings are also important kinds of human behavior, even though these behaviors are not directly observable. Ruth may infer or guess that Gary is sad by the expression on his face, but she cannot directly observe his emotional reaction.

While psychologists may differ on which kinds of human behavior are important, they do agree that the study of behavior must be systematic. The use of a systematic method of asking and answering questions about why people think, act, and feel as they do reduces the chances of coming to false conclusions about behavior. Consider the old story of the blind men and the elephant. A long time ago three very wise but blind men were out on a journey when they came across a sleeping elephant. Because they could not see the elephant, they did not know what was blocking their way so they set about to discover what they could about the obstacle. As it happened, each man put his hands on a different section of the elephant, examining it in great detail and with much thought. The first man, having felt the elephant's trunk, described a creature that was long, wormlike, and quite flexible. "No, no! You must be mistaken," said the second man who was seated on the back of the elephant, "This creature is wide, very round, and does not move very much." The man who was holding one of the elephant's tusks added his description of a small, hard, pointed creature. Each of these men was correct in his description of what he felt, but, in order to understand the elephant fully, they needed to combine their accumulated knowledge. The study of human behavior is similar. Many different approaches are necessary to understand the complex richness of human behavior.

We each like to think we understand people. We spend time observing others (and ourselves) and form conclusions about people in general from

Many different approaches are necessary to understand the complex richness of human behavior.

our daily interactions. Sometimes the conclusions we draw, however, are not accurate because we are not systematic in our "study" of people. Check the accuracy of some of your conclusions by responding true or false to the statements in Figure 1.4. Then compare your answers with the correct ones found at the end of this chapter (page 18).

The Scientific Basis of Psychology

Psychologists rely on the *scientific method*. This means that they reach their conclusions by identifying a specific problem or question, formulating a hypothesis, collecting data through observation and experiment, and analyzing the data.

By asking specific, well-defined questions, psychologists can gain insight into the behavior pattern they are studying. Asking a precise question about a limited aspect of behavior is basic to psychological research. Forming a *hypothesis* to explain the behavior is also a basic method of research. A **hypothesis** is an "educated guess"—the researcher has some evidence for suspecting a specific answer. In a hypothesis, researchers state what they expect to find in such a way that their theory can be tested. A psychologist might, for example, make the following hypothesis: People who have similar opinions on important issues in their lives are more likely to be attracted to each other than people who have very different opinions. The psychologist would then test the hypothesis in a way that would enable him or her to collect data. A survey might be conducted, for example, or questionnaires sent out. Finally, the psychologist would analyze the data (see Chapter 19). The hypothesis might turn out to be wrong—that is,

Figure 1.4

Test your intuitions about human behavior by answering true or false to the statements below. Turn to page 16 for the answers.

1. The behavior of most lower animals—insects, reptiles and amphibians, most rodents, and birds—is instinctive and unaffected by learning.
2. For the first week of life, a baby sees nothing but a gray blur regardless of what he or she "looks at."
3. A child learns to talk more quickly if the adults around the child habitually repeat the word he or she is trying to say, using proper pronunciation.
4. The best way to get a chronically noisy schoolchild to settle down and pay attention is to punish him or her.
5. Slow learners remember more of what they learn than fast learners.
6. Highly intelligent people— "geniuses"—tend to be physically frail and socially isolated.
7. On the average, you cannot predict from a person's grades at school and college whether he or she will do well in a career.
8. Most national and ethnic stereotypes are completely false.
9. In small amounts, alcohol is a stimulant.
10. LSD causes chromosome damage.
11. The largest drug problem in the United States, in terms of the number of people affected, is marijuana.
12. Psychiatry is a subdivision of psychology.
13. Most mentally retarded people are also mentally ill.
14. A third or more of the people suffering from severe mental disorder are potentially dangerous.
15. Electroshock therapy is an outmoded technique rarely used in today's mental hospitals.
16. The more severe the disorder, the more intensive the therapy required to cure it; for example, schizophrenics usually respond best to psychoanalysis.
17. Quite a few psychological characteristics of men and women appear to be inborn; in all cultures, for example, women are more emotional and sexually less aggressive than men.
18. No reputable psychologist "believes in" such irrational phenomena as ESP, hypnosis, or the bizarre mental and physical achievements of Eastern yogis.

the researcher may find that there are no differences between the two groups.

There are many hypotheses, but real answers to general questions are arrived at only by general agreement on the part of the experts after years of research on many different aspects of a problem.

The Goals of Psychology

As psychologists go about their systematic and scientific study of people, they have several goals. Overall, psychologists seek to do four things—describe, explain, predict, and control behavior.

The first task for any scientist or psychologist is to gather information about the behavior being studied and to present what is known. For example, we described Ruth's behavior in the cafeteria. A psychologist, however, would not be content with simply stating the facts; he or she would also be interested in explaining why people behave as they do. Such an explanation often goes beyond what can be observed to include ideas about why people react in certain ways.

Psychologists present their ideas in the form of hypotheses, which can be grouped together into theories. A theory represents past hunches or trial explanations about the facts observed. Psychological theories are tentative; they are always on trial because they are subject to change as more information about people and their behaviors is gathered. Theories do, however, allow us to fulfill the first two goals of psychology—to describe and explain observed behavior.

The third goal of psychology is to be able to predict, as a result of accumulated knowledge, what people will think, feel, or do in certain situations. By studying descriptive accounts linking certain behaviors together, psychologists can predict certain events.

Finally, psychologists seek to go beyond description, explanation, and prediction to influence or control behavior in helpful ways. Although many psychologists are involved in doing basic research to find out more about human behavior, other psychologists are more interested in discovering ways to use what is already known about people to benefit others. Some psychologists are interested in both **basic science,** or research, and **applied science,** or practical applications of the principles discovered in basic science research.

Psychologists who are studying the ability of infants to perceive visual patterns are doing basic research. They would not be concerned with the implication their findings might have on the design of a crib. Psychologists studying rapid eye movement in sleep research are also involved in basic science. If they discover that one individual has a sleep disturbance, they will try to understand and explain the situation, but they will not try to correct it. That is a job for applied scientists, such as clinical psychologists. An example of a psychologist involved in applying psychological principles rather than discovering them is a consultant to a toy manufacturer.

Why is this distinction important? The reason is that the transfer of findings from basic to applied science can be tricky. The following example illustrates this.

Psychologists seek to go beyond description, explanation, and prediction to influence or control behavior in helpful ways.

Figure 1.5
This engraving depicts a forest scene, doesn't it? If you answer yes, it may be because you looked only at the "framed area." If we had said, "Look at the muddy road," you would have seen that the forest is simply a reflection in a puddle. The same thing happens in psychology. Attending to one theoretical view prevents a researcher from seeing others.

Psychologists doing basic research have found that babies raised in institutions such as orphanages are seriously retarded in their physical, intellectual, and emotional development. Wayne Dennis (1960), among others, traces this to the fact that these babies have nothing to look at but a blank, white ceiling and white crib cushions, and are handled only when they need to be fed or changed. However, we have to be very careful not to apply this finding too broadly. Because children who lack stimulation tend to develop poorly, we can't conclude that by providing children with maximum stimulation—playing with them continually, having music piped into their rooms, surrounding them with fancy toys—we can guarantee that they will grow up emotionally sound and intellectually superior. On the contrary, it appears that most babies do best with a medium level of stimulation (White, 1969). In basic science, we are provided with specific findings: what happened in one study conducted at one time and in one place. To generalize these specific findings into a list of general rules (as the blind wise men did) would be misleading.

Introduction to Psychology focuses on psychology as a basic research science. The research findings provide the foundations on which practical applications are built. However, we give you some idea of the range of applications in psychology by including many subsections (in yellow) called "Using Psychology."

A BRIEF HISTORY OF PSYCHOLOGY

Even though psychology is one of the newer sciences, the study of human behavior began with the ancient Greek philosophers. In the fifth and sixth centuries B.C., they began to study human behavior and decided that people's lives were dominated not so much by the gods as by their own minds: people were rational.

These early philosophers attempted to interpret the world they observed around them in terms of human perceptions—objects were hot or cold, wet or dry, hard or soft, and these qualities influenced people's experience of them. Although the Greek philosophers did not rely on systematic study, they did set the stage for the development of the science of psychology through their reliance on observation as a means of knowing about people.

Much later, seventeenth-century philosophers introduced the idea of *dualism*, the concept that the world is divided into two elements (in this case, mind and matter). The mind accounted for our thoughts and feelings. Matter referred to our physical being, our bodies. Mind and matter were believed to be completely independent of each other. Furthermore, since the mind was believed to be part of God's domain, it was not subject to the same kind of investigation as the more material aspects of life. The mind was studied by theologians, while matter was studied by other scholars in universities.

The French philosopher René Descartes helped mold current psychological study when he wrote that there was a link between mind and body. He reasoned that the mind controlled the body's movements, sensations, and perceptions. His approach to understanding human behavior was based on the assumption that the mind and body influence each other to create a person's experiences. Exactly how this interaction takes place is still being studied today.

Toward the end of the seventeenth century, the British philosopher John Locke contributed yet another important concept to the foundation for modern psychology. Locke believed in the concept of *empiricism*, that all knowledge is obtained through observation and experience. He said that infants come into this world with blank minds, with no experiences. The term he used to describe the mind of the human infant was *tabula rasa* (Latin for blank tablet). Whatever experiences a person has in life are written into this blank tablet. Knowledge, then, is the result of a buildup of experiences. Locke's ideas have influenced education as well as psychology.

Psychology as a Discipline

The establishment of psychology as a separate, formal field of study began in 1879 in Leipzig, Germany, when Wilhelm Wundt started his Laboratory of Psychology. Wundt is often called the founder of psychology as a science. Although he was trained in physiology—the study of how the body works—his real interest was in the study of the human mind. In his laboratory, he modeled his research on the mind after that in other natural sciences he had studied. Wundt developed a method of self-observation called **introspection** to collect information about the mind. In carefully controlled situations, trained subjects reported their thoughts, and Wundt tried to map out the basic structure of thought processes. Wundt's experiments were very important historically, not so much because he ad-

Psychology as the Study of Physiological Processes. In addition to the ways psychology has been studied in the past, some psychologists today also focus on the physiological bases of behavior. Psychologists who subscribe to the physiological perspective contend that behavior can be best understood by looking at its biological or physical causes. *Physiological psychologists* (also called *biopsychologists*) believe that most or all psychological events are the result of a underlying biological or chemical processes. Many physiological psychologists do research on the functioning of the nervous system, study how brain cells communicate with each other, and explore the relationship between hormones and behavior.

Physiological psychologists often conduct research on animals in order to understand basic physiological processes. These results can then be applied to the study of more complicated behavior of human beings. Recent successes in treating problems such as depression and schizophrenia with drugs lend support to the physiological position that to understand human behavior we must understand its underlying physiological processes.

vanced our understanding of the mind, but because his work attracted many students who carried on the tradition of psychological research.

A close rival for the honor of founder of psychology is the American psychologist William James. James, the first American psychologist, was more involved in writing than research. (His brother, Henry James, was a great American writer.) In his text *Principles of Psychology* (1890), James speculated that thinking, feeling, learning, remembering—all of the activities of the mind—serve one major function, to help us survive as a species. Rather than focusing on the structure of the mind as Wundt did, James focused on the functions of the conscious mind. Although James did not produce any significant experimental findings, his writings and theories are still influential. In Chapter 6, you will learn more about James' ideas on motivation and emotion.

Psychology as the Study of Unconscious Processes

While the first psychologists were interested in understanding the conscious mind, Sigmund Freud, a physician who practiced in Vienna until 1938, was more interested in the unconscious mind. He believed that our conscious experiences are only the tip of the iceberg, that beneath the surface are primitive biological urges that are in conflict with the requirements of society and morality. According to Freud, these unconscious motivations and conflicts are responsible for much human behavior. He thought that they were responsible for many medically unexplainable physical symptoms that troubled his patients.

Freud used a new method for indirectly studying unconscious processes. In this technique, known as *free association*, a patient said everything that came to mind—no matter how absurd or irrelevant it seemed—without attempting to produce logical or meaningful statements. The person was instructed not to edit or censor the thoughts. Freud's role, that of *psychoanalyst*, was to be objective; he merely sat and listened, then interpreted the associations (Figure 1.6). Free association, Freud believed, revealed the operation of unconscious processes. Freud also believed that dreams are expressions of the most primitive unconscious urges. To learn more about these urges, he developed *dream analysis*—basically an extension of free association—in which the patient applied the same technique to his or her dreams (Freud, 1940).

While working out his ideas, Freud took careful, extensive notes on all his patients and treatment sessions. He used these records, or case studies, to develop and illustrate a comprehensive theory of personality—that is, of the total, functioning person (Hall and Lindzey, 1978). Freud's theory of personality will be discussed in Chapter 11.

In many areas of psychology today, Freud's view of unconscious motivation remains a powerful and controversial influence. Modern psychologists may support, alter, or attempt to disprove it, but most have a strong opinion about it. The technique of free association is still used by psychoanalysts, and the method of intensive case study is still a major tool for investigating behavior.

Figure 1.6
Sigmund Freud in his Vienna office, 1938.

Psychology as the Study of Individual Differences

Sir Francis Galton, a nineteenth-century English mathematician and scientist, wanted to understand how heredity (inherited traits) influences a person's abilities, character, and behavior (Figure 1.7). Galton (1869) traced the ancestry of various eminent people and found that greatness runs in families. (This was appropriate, since Galton himself was considered a genius and his family included at least one towering intellectual figure, a cousin named Charles Darwin.) He therefore concluded that genius or eminence is a hereditary trait. This conclusion was like the blind men's ideas about the elephant. Galton did not consider the possibility that the tendency of genius to run in eminent families might be a result of the exceptional environments and socioeconomic advantages that also tend to run in such families.

Figure 1.7
Sir Francis Galton, who invented procedures for testing abilities and characteristics that are still used in modern personality and intelligence tests.

The data Galton used were based on his study of biographies. However, not content to limit his inquiry to indirect accounts, he went on to invent procedures for directly testing the abilities and characteristics of a wide range of people. These tests were the primitive ancestors of the modern personality tests and intelligence tests that virtually everyone who reads this book has taken at some time. Galton also devised statistical techniques that are still in use today.

Although Galton began his work shortly before psychology emerged as an independent discipline, his theories and techniques quickly became central aspects of the new science. In 1883 he published a book, *Inquiries into Human Faculty and Its Development,* that is regarded as having defined the beginnings of individual psychology. Galton's writings raised the issue of whether behavior is determined by heredity or environment—a subject that has become the focus of controversy, especially in recent years. Gal-

PSYCHOLOGY
UPDATE

Psychology in China. Psychology in modern China lags far behind the United States, but the roots of psychological testing can be traced to the ancient Chinese. Several thousand years ago, the Chinese developed and used written tests to evaluate abilities in areas such as law and poetry.

In more recent times, Chinese psychologists seeking training often came to the United States. After World War II, the People's Republic of China was established and communist rule predominated. Because of China's communist orientation, psychology came under the influence of Soviet ideology. Pavlovian psychology became the standard, and Chinese psychologists were required to learn Russian.

Chinese psychologists attempted to establish their own identity in the 1960s but suffered a setback during the repressive Cultural Revolution, when psychology was removed from university curricula. Many psychologists were sent to labor farms, and some even committed suicide. There are now more than 2,000 psychologists in China. These psychologists are encouraged to study practical issues, especially in education.

ton's influence can also be seen in the current widespread use of psychological tests.

Psychology as the Study of Observable Behavior

The pioneering work of Russian physiologist Ivan Pavlov, who won the Nobel Prize in 1904, charted another new course for psychological investigation. In a now-famous experiment, Pavlov rang a tuning fork each time he gave a dog some meat powder. The dog would naturally salivate the moment it saw the meat powder. After Pavlov repeated the procedure several times, the dog would salivate when it heard the tuning fork, even if no food appeared. It had been conditioned to associate the sound with the food.

The concept of the conditioned reflex—a response (salivation) elicited by a stimulus (the tuning fork) other than the one that first produced it (food)—was used by psychologists as a new tool, as a means of exploring the development of behavior. Using this tool, they could begin to account for behavior as the product of prior experience. This enabled them to explain how certain acts and certain differences among individuals were the result of learning.

Psychologists who stressed investigating observable behavior became known as *behaviorists*. Their position, as formulated by American psychologist John B. Watson (1924), was that psychology should concern itself *only* with the observable facts of behavior. Watson further maintained that all behavior, even apparently instinctive behavior, is the result of conditioning and occurs because the appropriate stimulus is present in the environment.

Although it was Watson who defined and solidified the behaviorist position, it was B. F. Skinner, another American psychologist, who refined and popularized it. Skinner attempted to show how, in principle, his laboratory techniques might be applied to society as a whole. In his classic novel *Walden Two* (1949), he portrayed his idea of Utopia—a small town in which conditioning, through rewarding those who display behavior that is considered desirable, rules every conceivable facet of life.

Skinner exerted great influence on both the general public and the science of psychology. His book *Beyond Freedom and Dignity* (1971) became a best-seller (Figure 1.8), and a number of Walden Two communities were set up in various parts of the country. In addition, many people toilet-train their children, lose weight, quit smoking, and overcome phobias by using Skinner-inspired methods.

Skinner has been widely criticized, for many people are convinced that his "manipulative" conditioning techniques are a means of limiting personal freedom. He has also been heartily applauded as a social visionary. In any event, his theories and methods have been highly influential in psychology. Behaviorist-inspired techniques compete with more traditional psychotherapy for use in the treatment of various psychological disorders. The techniques of *reinforcement*, or controlled reward and punishment, have become increasingly popular in education, and Skinner's teaching machine was the forerunner of modern computerized programmed instruction. Moreover, a vast number of today's psychologists use Skinner's research methods to obtain precise findings in their laboratory experiments.

Humanistic psychology developed as a reaction to the behavioral movement. Humanistic psychologists, notably Abraham Maslow, Carl Rogers, and Rollo May, describe human nature as active and creative rather than passively reacting to external stimuli. Unlike behaviorists, humanists feel that the human mind is able to influence and change the world in which it functions.

PSYCHOLOGY AS A PROFESSION

What Is a Psychologist?

Perhaps the best way to answer this question is to ask who is not a psychologist. Although your parents may tell you they know a lot about human behavior and may have been studying your behavior all your life, they are not psychologists because of it. Psychologists are people who have been trained to observe and analyze behavior patterns, to develop theories on behavior, and to apply what they know to influence behavior. Just as there are many different branches of medicine, there are many different fields of psychology. The principle ones are described below.

People often confuse the terms "psychologist" and "psychiatrist." These are different professions. **Psychiatry** is a specialty of medicine. After a psychiatry student completes medical school, he or she continues training in psychiatric medicine and learns to treat people with disturbed behavior. Psychiatrists work mainly in hospitals and have their own private practices; unlike psychologists, they can prescribe drugs to treat their patients. Sometimes, a psychiatrist works with a psychologist in testing, evaluating, and treating patients. Unlike psychologists, most psychiatrists are not involved in much research; they focus their efforts primarily on helping their patients deal with emotional difficulties.

Specialty Fields in Psychology

Psychology today covers an enormous range of specialty fields. Psychologists are employed in advertising, education, and criminology. Some psychologists are studying death, art, and robots. Psychological themes and terminology have become part of everyday life, and of novels, films, and television programs.

In the process of expanding its scope, psychology has been divided into a number of subfields. Clinical and *counseling psychology* are the most popular. Specialists in this field are usually referred to as *psychotherapists*. Clinical psychologists help people deal with their personal problems. They

Figure 1.8
Behaviorist B. F. Skinner has influenced large numbers of people with his techniques of conditioning behavior by rewards and punishments.

FACT or FICTION

Forensic psychologists apply psychology to legal issues.

Fact. *Forensic psychology* is a relatively new but growing area of psychology. It attempts to apply psychological principles to the legal system. A forensic psychologist might provide testimony as an expert witness in a trial, be employed to counsel inmates at a correctional facility, or have a job working with police authorities assisting them in solving criminal cases.

Answers to Figure 1.4
All of the statements in Figure 1.4 are false. As you read the different chapters in this book, you will learn more about the correct answers to these statements and the research that psychologists have conducted to prove these theories false.

Figure 1.9
(Opposite) Psychologists at work. (a) One to one therapy. (b) An automated instructional system designed by educational psychologists. (c) Administering a standard intelligence test. (d) A therapist working with a mentally disturbed child. (e) Space vehicles designed with the help of psychologists. (f) Doing research on sleep and dreaming. (g) Videotaping a family interaction for later use in family therapy. (h) Brain research: an experiment in chemical stimulation of the brain.

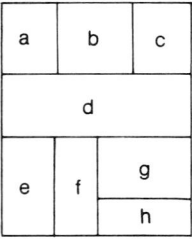

work mainly in private offices, mental hospitals, prisons, and clinics. Some specialize in giving and interpreting personality tests designed to determine whether a person needs treatment and, if so, what kind. Counseling psychologists usually work in schools or industrial firms, advising and assisting people. Your school may have a special type of counseling psychologist, known as a school psychologist, who is trained to help young people with their problems.

A large number of specialists study *personality psychology, social psychology*, and *developmental psychology*. These psychologists are usually involved in basic rather than applied science. Personality psychologists study personality development and traits and devise personality tests. Social psychologists study groups and the way they influence individual behavior. Some are particularly interested in public opinion and devote much of their time to conducting polls and surveys. Most developmental psychologists focus on children from birth to about age fifteen. In recent years, however, some have been leaning toward the "life-cycle" or "cradle-to-grave" approach—that is, studying development as something that continues from birth to old age.

Educational psychology deals with topics related to teaching children and young adults, such as intelligence, memory, problem solving, and motivation. Specialists in this field are concerned with evaluating teaching methods, devising tests, and developing new instructional devices for films and television.

Community psychology is a relatively new area of community mental health. A psychologist who specializes in this area may work in a mental health or social welfare agency operated by the state or local government or by a private organization. A community psychologist may help design, run, or evaluate a mental health clinic in a remote area.

Industrial psychology is another area of specialization. Industrial psychologists have developed methods to boost production, improve working conditions, place applicants in jobs for which they are best suited, train people, and reduce accidents.

Finally, about a fourth of all psychologists are engaged in *experimental psychology*. These psychologists do everything from testing how electrical stimulation of a certain area of a rat's brain affects its behavior, through studying how disturbed people think, to observing how different socio-economic groups vote in elections. They are basic scientists rather than applied scientists.

What psychologists think about, what experiments they have done, and what this knowledge means form the subject of this book. Psychology is dedicated to answering some of the most interesting questions of everyday life: What happens during sleep? How can bad habits be broken? Is there a way to measure intelligence? Why do crowds sometimes turn into mobs? Do dreams mean anything? How does punishment affect a child? Can memory be improved? What causes psychological breakdowns? In trying to answer such questions, psychology ties together all that has been discovered about human behavior and feelings in order to look at the total human being. The picture is far from complete, but much of what is known will be found in the chapters that follow.

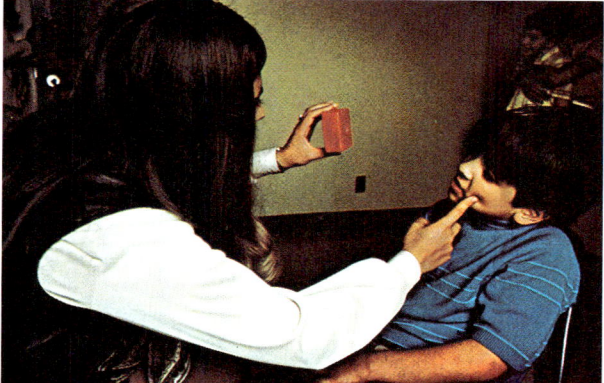
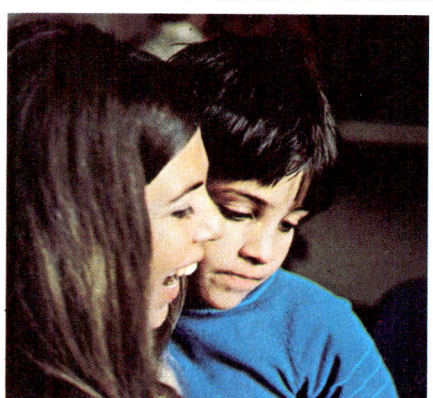

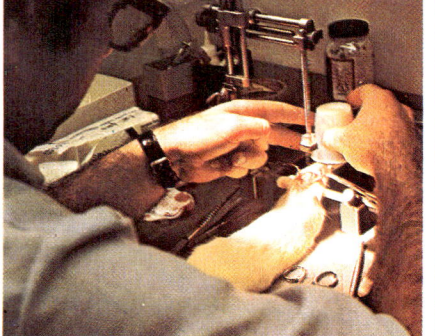
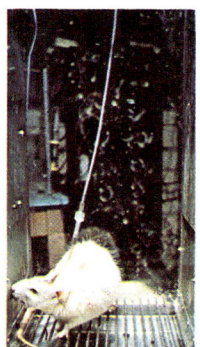

KEY TERMS

- *applied science*
- *basic science*

- *hypothesis*
- *introspection*

- *psychiatry*
- *psychology*

SUMMARY

1. The primary focus of psychology is the complexity of everyday behavior.

2. An apparently simple and ordinary meeting in a college cafeteria illustrates most of the topics psychologists study: physiological states, perception, cognition, motivation, memory, learned behavior, development, social groups, emotions, personality disturbances.

3. From this introduction to psychology, you may gain insights, practical information, and an objective test of your beliefs.

4. The first step in psychological research is generating testable ideas. These usually take the form of hypotheses: statements about what a researcher expects to find put in such a way that they can be proved or disproved.

5. Science thrives on debate. The results of a single study should not be mistaken for "the final answer" or for authoritative advice on how to handle everyday situations.

6. The study of human behavior had its origins with the Greek philosophers. In the seventeenth century, the concept of dualism developed, introducing the idea that the mind and body were two independent elements of the human being. René Descartes believed that the mind and body interacted. John Locke developed the philosophy of empiricism, which held that knowledge was obtained through observation and experience, rather than inborn. Wilhelm Wundt is referred to as the founder of the study of psychology as a science. He analyzed the way the mind functions by studying sensation through introspection, or self-observation. William James, the first American psychologist, concluded that all the activities of the mind function to help the species survive.

7. Sigmund Freud believed that we act the way we do as a result of primitive unconscious urges.

8. Sir Francis Galton was one of the first to study systematically how one individual differs from the next, and today's psychological tests can be traced back to his work.

9. Ivan Pavlov, John Watson, and B. F. Skinner are three key figures in behaviorism, which studies the way learning shapes our observable behavior.

10. Psychology is subdivided in practice as well as in theory. Major areas of specialization in psychology today include clinical and counseling psychology; personality, social, and developmental psychology; educational psychology; industrial psychology; and experimental psychology.

REVIEW QUESTIONS

1. How did Greek philosophers set the stage for the development of the science of psychology?

2. What are some advantages of learning about psychology?

3. What is the first step in psychological research?

4. What are the four goals of psychology?

5. Would a psychologist working as an occupational counselor be involved in applied or basic science?

6. Who established the idea of empiricism and the tabula rasa?

7. What was the main focus of the work of William James?

8. Who established the first psychology laboratory and is considered the founder of psychology as a science?

9. What type of motivations did Freud study? By what methods?

10. What did Sir Francis Galton want to understand? What area of psychology developed from his work?

11. What is the name given to psychologists who investigate observable behavior? Name three of these psychologists.

12. Who influenced the formation of communities based on learning, or conditioning, principles? What was the name given to these communities?

13. Summarize John Watson's view of the proper realm of psychology.

14. Define humanistic psychology and explain why it developed.

15. What are the most popular subfields of psychology?

16. What type of psychologist usually works in schools? What type might work in a factory?

ACTIVITIES

1. Write your own definition of psychology. Is your definition different from one you would have written before reading the chapter? Put the definition in a safe place and take it out and read it at the end of the course to see if you still agree with it.

2. How is psychology involved in your life? Make a list of all the ways in which psychology affects your life. (Hint: Traffic signs and classroom interiors are often designed by psychologists.) Keep in mind the different specialties of psychology you read about in the chapter.

3. Psychology is generally thought of as a benevolent science and is expected to produce happier people, accident-free and more productive workers, and greater understanding of interpersonal relationships. However, well-meaning people throughout history have also applied what they considered to be sound "psychologi-cal" techniques that have actually tormented or totally destroyed their intended beneficiaries. Can you see any possibilities today where psychological knowledge could be used against the best interests of an individual or society?

4. Much of psychology is, in effect, an attempt to articulate the nature of human behavior. Make a list of characteristics or behavioral tendencies that you think apply to all people. Compare your list with those of other students in the class. Do you think there are any characteristics or "laws," comparable to established laws in physics, that are universally true for all of us?

5. Make a list of various professions or occupations. List the ways a psychologist might contribute to better functioning within the occupation or profession. What kind of psychologist do you think would be most helpful in performing each job?

UNIT 1

Learning and Cognitive Processes

CHAPTER *2*
Learning: Principles and Applications

CHAPTER *3*
Memory and Thought

Figure 2.1 Skill at a sport is learned behavior, as is almost everything else human beings do.

Objectives: *After studying this chapter, you should be able to*
- describe the principles and techniques of classical conditioning.
- outline the principles and techniques of operant conditioning.
- identify factors that affect the process of learning.
- discuss the application of the principles of learning to human behavior.

Learning: Principles and Applications

Learning is basic to our understanding of human behavior. It is involved in nearly all aspects of life. As young infants, we learn to hold ourselves upright, to walk, and to use our hands. Later, we learn to run, to play baseball, and to use a can opener. We learn to read, to write, to memorize information to help us pass an exam. We learn how to get people to give us what we want by asking, bargaining, being nice, or pouting. We even learn to be afraid of the dentist or of taking exams, and then we learn to overcome these fears. We also learn how to learn. **Learning** can be defined as a relatively permanent change in behavior that results from experience.

Not all of the behaviors that we learn are acquired in the same way. Furthermore, the same behavior can be learned in different ways. For example, we may learn to fear the dentist because we associate the dentist with the experience of pain. We may have acquired a fear of the dentist because every time we express our fears, our parents or friends give us special attention and comfort. We may never have gone to the dentist, but we may have learned to fear him or her by watching someone else's reaction to a dentist. These examples represent the three basic types of learning that have been studied by psychologists: *classical conditioning, operant conditioning,* and *modeling.*

CLASSICAL CONDITIONING

Like many great discoveries, Ivan Pavlov's discovery of the principle of classical conditioning was accidental. Around the turn of the century, this Russian scientist had been studying the process of digestion. Pavlov wanted to understand how a dog's stomach prepares to digest food when something is placed in the dog's mouth. Then he noticed that the mere sight

Classical Conditioning
Pavlov's Experiment
• General Principles of Classical Conditioning
• Classical Conditioning and Human Behavior

Operant Conditioning
Reinforcement • Schedules of Reinforcement • Signals
• Aversive Control

Factors That Affect Learning
Feedback • Transfer • Practice

Learning Strategies
Learning to Learn
• Helplessness and Laziness

Learning Complicated Skills
Combining Responses: Chaining

Modeling
Using Psychology: Behavior Modification • Computer-Assisted Instruction • Token Economies • Self-Control
• Improving Your Study Habits

or smell of food was enough to start a dog salivating. Pavlov became fascinated with these "psychic secretions" that occurred before food was actually presented, and decided to investigate how they worked.

Pavlov's Experiment

Pavlov (1927) began his experiments by ringing a tuning fork and then immediately placing some meat powder on the dog's tongue. He chose the tuning fork because it was a **neutral stimulus**—that is, one that had nothing to do with the response (salivation). After only a few times, the dog started salivating as soon as it heard the sound, even if food were not placed in its mouth (Figure 2.2). Pavlov went on to demonstrate that any neutral stimulus will cause an unrelated response if it is presented regularly just before the stimulus (here, food) that normally induces that response (salivation).

Pavlov distinguished among the different elements of his experiment as follows. He used the term "unconditioned" to refer to natural stimuli and to automatic, involuntary responses. Such responses include blushing, shivering, being startled, or salivating. In the experiment, food was the **unconditioned stimulus (UCS):** a stimulus that leads to a certain response without previous training. (A dog doesn't have to be taught to salivate when it smells meat.) Food normally causes salivation. This is an **unconditioned response (UCR):** a response that occurs naturally and automatically when the unconditioned stimulus is presented.

Under normal conditions, the sound of a tuning fork would not cause salivation. The dog had to be taught, or *conditioned*, to associate this sound with food. An ordinarily neutral stimulus that, after training, leads to a response such as salivation is termed a **conditioned stimulus (CS).** The salivation it causes is a **conditioned response (CR).** A conditioned response is learned. A wide variety of stimuli may serve as conditioned stimuli for salivation: the sight of food or an experimenter entering the room, the sound of a tone, a flash of light. Controlling an animal's or a person's

Figure 2.2
The apparatus Pavlov used to study conditioned salivation in dogs. The harness held the dog steady, while the tube leading from the dog's mouth deposited saliva on an arm connected to the recorder on the left. Drops of saliva moved the pen, making a permanent record of the salivation response to such stimuli as food and sights or sounds associated with food.

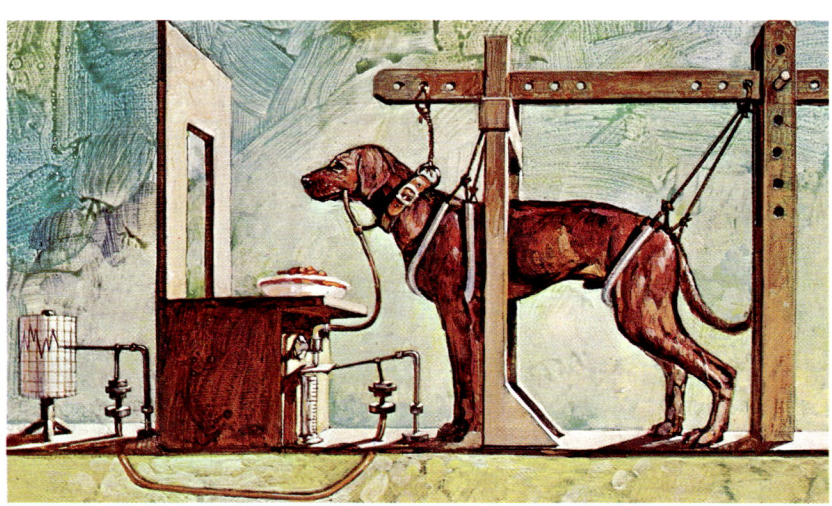

responses in this way so that an old response becomes attached to a new stimulus is called **classical conditioning**. A number of different reflex responses that ordinarily occur automatically can be conditioned to occur whenever the correct conditioned stimulus occurs. These include responses produced by the glands, such as salivation or weeping, and responses of our internal muscles, such as those of the stomach. In general, these responses are controlled by the autonomic nervous system and are very much involved in our emotions, as we will see in Chapter 4, "Body and Behavior."

General Principles of Classical Conditioning

Acquisition of a classically conditioned response generally occurs gradually. With each pairing of the artificial, conditioned stimulus with the natural, unconditioned stimulus, the learned response is strengthened. In Pavlov's experiment, the more frequently the turning fork was paired with the food, the more often the tone elicited salivation (the conditioned response). The timing of the association between the conditioned stimulus (the tone) and the unconditioned stimulus (food) also influences learning. Pavlov tried several different conditioning procedures in which he varied the time between the conditioned stimulus and the unconditioned stimulus. Sometimes he presented the tone before the food was presented. Other times, he presented the tone at the same time as the food. Generally, he found that classical conditioning was more reliable and effective when the conditioned stimulus was presented just before the unconditioned stimulus. He found that presenting the CS about a second before the UCS gave the best results.

In the same set of experiments, Pavlov also explored the phenomena of *generalization* and *discrimination*. **Generalization** occurs when an animal responds to a second stimulus similar to the original conditioned stimulus. When Pavlov conditioned a dog to salivate at the sight of a circle (the CS), he found that the dog would salivate when it saw an oval as well. The dog had generalized its response to include a similar stimulus. Pavlov was later able to do the opposite, to teach the dog to respond only to the circle by always pairing meat powder with the circle but never pairing it with the oval. He thus taught the dog a **discrimination:** the ability to respond differently to different stimuli.

Generalization and discrimination are complementary processes and are part of our everyday life. For example, assume a person has come to associate the sound of a dentist's drill (CS) with a nervous reaction (CR). After several exposures to a dentist's drill, the person may find that he or she has generalized this uncomfortable feeling to the sound of other, nondental drills. Later, the person may learn to discriminate between the sound of a dentist's drill and other drills.

A classically conditioned response, like any other behavior, is subject to change. Pavlov discovered that if he stopped presenting food after the sound of the tuning fork, the sound gradually lost its effect on the dog. After he repeatedly struck the tuning fork without giving food, the dog no longer associated the sound with the arrival of food—the sound of the

The Case of Little Albert

John B. Watson and Rosalie Rayner (1920) showed how conditioning could be used on a human infant. They experimented with a well-adjusted eleven-month-old child named Albert. They presented Albert with many objects, including a rat, a rabbit, blocks, a fur coat, and a hairy Santa Claus mask. Albert showed no fear of any of these objects—they were all neutral stimuli for the fear response.

Watson and Rayner decided that they would attempt to condition Albert to fear rats. They began by placing a furry white rat in front of him. Albert would reach out to touch it and, each time he did, one of Watson's assistants would sound a metal bar with a hammer behind Albert's head. The first time the metal bar was struck, Albert fell forward and buried his head in a pillow. The next time he reached for the rat and the bar was struck, Albert began to whimper. The noise, the unconditioned stimulus, brought about a natural, unconditioned response, fear. After only a few such pairings, the rat became a *conditioned stimulus* that elicited a *conditioned response*, fear.

After Watson and Rayner conditioned Albert to fear rats, they presented him with a rabbit. Albert now reacted fearfully to the rabbit. The researchers found that the degree of fear Albert felt toward other neutral stimuli depended upon how much they resembled the furry white rat. His conditioned fear response had generalized to include the rabbit. Other furry white objects, such as the fur coat and Santa Claus mask, also caused Albert to cry and try to escape whenever Watson and Rayner presented them, although the response was not so great as when the rabbit was presented.

One of the most frequent criticisms of Watson and Rayner's experimental demonstration of a conditioned fear in Little Albert was that they were successful in teaching a previously healthy, well-adjusted child to be fearful. Apparently, the researchers knew at least one month ahead of time that Albert would be leaving the study and yet they made no attempt to extinguish his conditioned fears (Harris, 1979). Ethical researchers today would not repeat the Little Albert study, because of the potential psychological harm to the young child.

One of Watson's students, Mary Cover Jones (1924, 1974), developed an extinction procedure to reduce people's existing fears. Peter was a boy who was extremely fearful of rabbits. Jones helped Peter eliminate his fear by extinction and by pairing the feared object (the rabbit) with pleasant experiences such as eating ice cream or receiving special adult attention.

tuning fork was no longer able to elicit the salivation response. Pavlov called this effect **extinction** because the conditioned response had gradually died out.

Even though a classically conditioned response may be extinguished, this does not mean that the person has completely unlearned the conditioned response. After a period of time in which the conditioned stimulus is not presented, the previously extinguished conditioned response may reappear when the conditioned stimulus is presented again. This *spontaneous recovery* does not bring the conditioned response back to its full strength before extinction, however. For example, the amount of salivation

Pavlov's dog produced during spontaneous recovery was much less than the amount produced during the conditioning period. Furthermore, presenting the tone several times without food resulted in gradual loss of the salivation response.

A good example of extinction and spontaneous recovery is the following. Every time you are in the shower and the water pressure drops, the water suddenly turns very hot. You learn to associate the normally neutral stimulus of a drop in water pressure with your automatic startle reaction to the hot water surge. Even after you finally repair your plumbing so that hot water no longer follows a drop in water pressure, it may take several showers before you no longer react to a water pressure change. You eventually extinguish the startle reaction. Then you go away for a period of time. When you return, you again react with a startle whenever the water pressure changes. You have had a spontaneous recovery of your conditioned startle reaction. Then, after several showers without any hot water assaults, you no longer have a reaction.

Classical Conditioning and Human Behavior

Classical conditioning was discovered in learning experiments with animals, but, as we have seen, the principles of classical conditioning apply to human learning as well.

Using the principle of classical conditioning, a practical solution to the problem of bedwetting was discovered by O. Hobart Mowrer and his wife Mollie (1938). One reason bedwetting occurs is that children do not wake up during the night when they have a full bladder. Instead, they wet the bed while they are sleeping. The Mowrers developed a device known as the *bell and pad*. It consists of two metallic sheets perforated with small holes and attached by wires to a battery-run alarm. The thin, metal sheets are placed under the child's bed sheets. When the sleeping child moistens the sheet with the first drops of urine, the circuit closes, causing the alarm to go off and wake the child. The child can then use the bathroom. The alarm is the unconditioned stimulus which produces the unconditioned response of waking up. The sensation of a full bladder is the conditioned stimulus which, before conditioning, did not produce wakefulness. After several pairings of the alarm (UCS) and the full bladder (CS), the child is able to awaken to the sensation of a full bladder without the help of the alarm. This technique has proved to be a very effective way of treating bedwetting problems.

To identify the elements in this conditioning example and compare them to Pavlov's experiment, see Figure 2.3.

Taste Aversions. Suppose you go out on a date to a fancy restaurant. You may decide to try an expensive appetizer you've never had, such as snails. Then suppose that, after dinner, you go on to a concert and become violently ill. You will probably develop a taste aversion—you will never be able to look at another snail without becoming at least a little nauseated.

TWO EXAMPLES OF CLASSICAL CONDITIONING

Figure 2.3
The classical conditioning procedure involves three phases—before, during, and after training. The learner responds to the neutral stimulus (the CS) with a conditioned response.

		Stimulus	*Response*
Pavlov's Experiment			
	BEFORE CONDITIONING	Tone (neutral stimulus) →	Does not produce response of salivation
		Food (UCS) ⟶	Salivation (UCR)
	DURING CONDITIONING	Tone (CS) and Food (UCS) ⟶	Salivation (UCR)
	AFTER CONDITIONING	Tone (CS) ⟶	Salivation (CR)
Mowrer's Experiment			
	BEFORE CONDITIONING	Full bladder (neutral stimulus) ⟶	Does not produce response of wakening
		Alarm (UCS) ⟶	Awakening (UCR)
	DURING CONDITIONING	Full bladder (CS) and Alarm (USC) ⟶	Awakening (UCR)
	AFTER CONDITIONING	Full bladder (CS) ⟶	Awakening (CR)

Your nausea reaction to snails is an example of classical conditioning. What makes this type of conditioning particularly interesting to learning theorists is that, when people or other animals become ill, they seem to decide, "It must have been something I ate," even if they haven't eaten for several hours. In the above situation, it is unlikely that the concert hall in which you were sick will become the conditioned stimulus. Nor will other stimuli from the restaurant—the wallpaper pattern or the type of china used. What's more, psychologists can even predict which part of your meal will be the conditioned stimulus: you will probably blame a new food, one that you haven't had before. Thus, if you get sick after a meal of salad, steak, and snails, you will probably learn to hate snails, even if they are really not at fault.

John Garcia and R. A. Koelling (1966) first demonstrated this phenomenon with rats. The animals were placed in a cage with a tube containing flavored water. Whenever a rat took a drink, lights would flash and clicks would sound. Then the rats were divided into two groups. Some rats were given an electric shock after they drank. All these rats showed traditional classical conditioning: the lights and the sounds became conditioned stimuli, and they tried to avoid them in order to avoid a shock. Other rats were not shocked, but were injected with a drug that made them sick after they drank and the lights and sounds occurred. These rats developed an aversion not to the lights or the sounds but only to the taste of the flavored water.

This special relationship between food and illness was used in a study (Gustavson *et al.*, 1974) that made coyotes hate the taste of lamb by giving them a drug to make them sick when they ate sheep. This is an important application because sheep farmers in the western United States would like to eliminate the coyotes that threaten their flocks, while naturalists are opposed to killing the coyotes. The experimenters realized that coyotes could be trained to eat other kinds of meat, and thus learn to coexist peacefully with sheep.

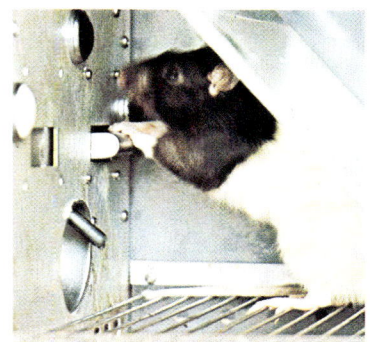

Figure 2.4
A rat pressing a bar in a Skinner box. The Skinner box is an artificial environment in which lights, sounds, rewards, and punishments can be delivered and controlled and in which some of the animal's behaviors, such as bar pressing, can be recorded by automatic switches.

OPERANT CONDITIONING

Suppose a dog is wandering around the neighborhood, sniffing trees, checking garbage cans, looking for a squirrel to chase. A kind person sees the dog and tosses a bone out of the kitchen door to it. The next day, the dog is likely to stop at the same door on its rounds, if not go to it directly. The kind person produces another bone, and another the next day. The dog becomes a regular visitor.

Suppose a child is unhappy because his younger sister seems to be capturing their mother's attention. He begins to pout and act aggressively toward his sister. Right away his mother stops attending to the younger sister to reprimand him. Even though the mother's attention is negative, the boy seems to like it; a short time later, he is back again harassing his sister and earning another reprimand from his mother.

Both stories are examples of **operant conditioning**—that is, learning from the consequences of behavior. The term "operant" is used because the subject (the wandering dog and the boy in our examples) *operates* on or causes some change in the environment, producing a result that influences whether it will operate in the same way in the future. Depending on the effect of the operant behaviors, the learner will repeat or eliminate these behaviors—to get rewards or avoid punishment.

Operant conditioning differs from classical conditioning in two important ways. First, in order for operant conditioning to occur, the learner must behave in a way that produces some consequences. The control of the learning is in the hands of the learner. If the learner takes no action, no operant conditioning can occur.

A second difference between operant and classical conditioning concerns the kinds of behavior that are acquired. In classical conditioning, the most effective learning occurs with automatic, reflexive behavior. Operant conditioning is not limited to reflexive responses, but may involve the acquisition of a wide range of voluntary behaviors.

Reinforcement

B. F. Skinner (1974) is the psychologist most closely associated with operant conditioning. He and his colleagues believed that most behavior is influenced by one's history of rewards and punishments. Suppose you want to teach a dog to shake hands. One way would be to give the animal a pat on the head or a biscuit every time it lifts its paw up to you. The biscuit or pat is called a positive reinforcer. In this example, the dog will get the message and shake hands again to get another reward. **Reinforcement** can be defined as a stimulus or event that affects the likelihood that a behavior will be repeated. The nature of the reinforcement depends on the effect it has on the learner. Examples of reinforcers that people respond to are social approval, money, and extra privileges.

Your dog will stop shaking hands when you forget to reward it for the trick and withdraw reinforcement. Extinction will occur, but it will take time. In fact, for a while after you stop rewarding it, the dog will probably become impatient, bark, and paw even more insistently than it did before.

Figure 2.5
Practice is an important part of learning to play a musical instrument. Beginners spend many hours practicing scales and simple tunes. Once they master the basics, they can move on to more complicated arrangements.

Schedules of Reinforcement

One important factor in operant conditioning is the type and frequency of reinforcement. You might suppose that behavior would best be acquired by reinforcing every response. This is called a *continuous schedule* of reinforcement. However, the best results are not obtained from a continuous schedule. When positive reinforcement occurs only intermittently or on a partial schedule, the responses are generally more stable and more persistent.

Consider, for example, two vending machines in the cafeteria. You have found that the first machine always delivers the candy bar you have selected. You have never lost any money in it, and you have always received a positive reinforcement (your candy bar). The second machine is unreliable. Sometimes you get your candy bar after you put your money in. At other times you get nothing: no candy bar, no money returned. Now, suppose one day you find that the first, reliable machine does not give you your candy bar. From which machine would you continue to try to get a reinforcement (candy bar)? You would probably not choose the first, more reliable machine, because you would assume that you would not get a candy bar from it no matter how long you tried. You would probably continue to try the second vending machine, because you know that sometimes it works and sometimes it doesn't. You would not consider it unusual when it failed to work, and you would expect that, after a few tries, it would give you your selection.

This example shows how intermittent reinforcement causes responses to be generally more stable and persistent than a continuous schedule of reinforcement.

Although intermittent reinforcement may be arranged in a number of ways, four basic methods, or schedules, have been studied in the laboratory. Schedules of reinforcement may be based either on the *number* of correct responses that the organism makes between reinforcements (*ratio* schedules) or on the *amount of time* that elapses before reinforcement is made available (*interval* schedules). In either case, reinforcement may appear on a regular, or fixed, schedule or on an irregular, or variable, schedule. The four basic schedules result from the combination of these four possibilities. People respond differently to each type.

In a **fixed-ratio schedule,** reinforcement depends on a specified quantity of responses, such as rewarding every fourth response. The student who receives a good grade after completing a specified amount of work and the typist who is paid by the number of pages completed are on fixed-ratio schedules. People tend to work hard on fixed-ratio schedules, pausing briefly after each reward. However, if the amount of work or number of responses to be completed before the next reward is great, the student or pieceworker is likely to show low morale and few responses at the beginning of each new cycle because there is a long way to go before the next reinforcement.

A **variable-ratio schedule** requires that an average number of responses be made for each reinforcement. Instead of the fixed number of responses being set, as in the fixed-ratio schedule, the number of responses needed for a reinforcement changes from one time to the next. Slot machines are a good example of a variable-ratio schedule. They are set to pay off after a varying number of attempts. Gamblers often overlook this feature of slot machines and continue to deposit coins at a steady high rate, believing (mistakenly) that the more they do so, the sooner they will hit the jackpot. Casino operators encourage this response by giving out free tokens to newcomers. Yet the casino operators also control the variable ratio for the jackpot. Generally, people on variable-ratio schedules of reinforcement tend to work or respond at a steady high rate.

On a **fixed-interval schedule,** reinforcement is available after a predetermined time. Reinforcement can occur after a certain number of minutes, hours, or days, but the time interval is always the same. People who are reinforced under a fixed-interval schedule are likely to decrease responding right after a reinforcement, but as the end of the interval draws near again, their rate of response may increase rapidly. Workers who are paid every Thursday may be more motivated to come to work on Thursday morning (payday) than on Friday (the day after payday). Absenteeism is generally much lower on payday.

On a **variable-interval schedule,** the time at which a reinforcer will be available varies throughout the conditioning procedure. An example of a variable-interval reinforcement would be a call from a prospective employer that you knew would come at some point, but you did not know when. You would probably jump up to answer the phone for hours so that no one in the family would answer it first, even though you did not know whether an individual call was going to be the reinforcer (the call from the employer). No matter how long you continued your answering behavior, you could not increase the likelihood of hearing his or her voice. You would continue your answering behavior because you knew that it would pay off eventually. Similarly a pigeon (such as the one in Figure

Figure 2.6
This pigeon is showing signs of emotional upset common in extinction of an operantly conditioned response. The bird was trained to obtain food from the square hole by pecking at the key in the round hole. When the experimenter switched off the circuit that made the arrangement work, the bird pecked the key for a while and then, finding no food, began to jump around and flap its wings.

2.6) that is on a variable-interval schedule tends to peck at the key much more regularly than an animal on a fixed-interval schedule, because the amount of time it will take to be reinforced is unknown.

In summary, ratio schedules are based on events, while interval schedules are based on time. In general, responses are learned better and are more resistant to extinction when reinforced on a variable rather than on a fixed schedule. However, to be effective, the reinforcement (including punishment) must be consistent for the same type of behavior even though it does not have to follow every time. Most reinforcers in human relationships are on a variable schedule because of the complexity of behavior and because we cannot predict how people will interact.

Signals

In operant conditioning, stimuli that are associated with receiving rewards or punishment become **signals** for particular behaviors. For example, we learn to cross a street only when the traffic light is green and to answer the phone only when it rings. These signals simply indicate that if you cross the street or answer the phone, a reinforcer is likely to follow in the form of safe arrival on the other side of the street or of a voice on the phone.

Just as organisms generalize among and discriminate between conditioned stimuli in classical conditioning, they also generalize among and discriminate between stimuli that serve as signals in operant conditioning. For example, the child who has been rewarded for saying "doggie" every time he or she sees the family's basset hound may generalize and say "doggie" when he or she sees a sheep, a cow, or a horse. These animals are similar enough to the hound for them to become signals that "doggie" will produce a reward. Discrimination results when "doggie" fails to produce a reward in these other cases. The child learns to confine the use of the word to dogs and to respond differently when seeing sheep, cattle, or horses.

Because signals are guides to future rewards and punishments, they often become rewards or punishers in themselves. In such cases, the signal is called a **conditioned reinforcer** because without the conditioning process, it would be like a neutral stimulus having no positive or negative value to a person. With conditioning, almost any stimulus can acquire almost any value.

One experimenter (Wolfe, 1936) demonstrated this with chimpanzees. Poker chips have no value for chimps—they aren't edible and they aren't very much fun to play with. This experimenter, however, used operant conditioning to teach chimps to value poker chips as much as humans value money. He provided the animals with a "Chimp-O-Mat" that dispensed peanuts or bananas, which are **primary reinforcers**, or natural rewards. (Chimps like these foods.) To obtain food, the chimps had to pull down on a heavily weighted bar to obtain poker chips, then insert the chips in a slot in the machine (Figure 2.7). In time, the poker chips became conditioned reinforcers. Their value was evident from the fact that the

Figure 2.7
Using the Chimp-O-Mat to "buy" peanuts and bananas with poker chips obtained by pulling down on a heavily weighted bar. Through operant conditioning, this chimp had learned to value something that was neither edible nor fun to play with.

chimpanzees would work for them, save them, and sometimes try to steal them from one another.

There is no need to look only to animals for examples of this phenomenon. Smiles have little value for newborn babies, and words of approval have no meaning. In time, however, babies learn that these expressions and sounds mean that an adult is about to pick them up, cuddle them, perhaps feed them (primary reinforcers). The smiles and sounds of approval signal a reward. In time, children begin to value smiles, praise, and other forms of social approval in and of themselves.

Aversive Control

People often use the word "reinforcement" to refer only to the pleasant consequences of behavior. Psychologists, however, use it to refer to anything that increases the frequency of a behavior. Unpleasant or aversive consequences (as opposed to pleasant ones) influence much of our everyday behavior. **Aversive control** refers to this type of conditioning, or learning. There are two ways in which unpleasant events, or aversive stimuli, can affect our behavior: as negative reinforcers or as punishers.

Negative reinforcement.   In **negative reinforcement,** a painful or unpleasant stimulus is removed or is not applied at all if a certain kind of
behavior occurs. The removal of unpleasant consequences increases the
frequency of a behavior (Figure 2.8). There are two types of negative
reinforcement learning that psychologists have studied in detail: *escape
conditioning* and *avoidance conditioning.* In **escape conditioning,** the behavior a person engages in causes an unpleasant event to stop. Consider
the case of a child who hates liver and is served it for dinner—a thoroughly
repulsive experience. She whines about the food and gags while eating it.
At this point, her mother removes the liver. The gagging and whining
behavior has been thus negatively reinforced, and the child is likely to
gag and whine in the future when given an unpleasant meal. This kind
of learning is called escape conditioning because the behavior has enabled
the child to escape the liver meal.

In **avoidance conditioning,** the person's behavior has the effect of preventing an unpleasant situation from happening. In our example, if the
girl's past whining and gagging behavior had stopped the mother from
even serving the liver, we would identify the situation as avoidance conditioning; the child would have avoided the unpleasant consequences in
advance.

Punishment.   The most obvious form of aversion control is not negative
reinforcement, but punishment. If you want to stop a dog from pawing
at you when it wants attention, you should link your attention to it with
a punishment such as a smack on the rump with a newspaper. Such
actions are called **punishers.**

As with reinforcers, the events or actions that serve as punishers depend
on their effect on the learner. In the opening example on operant conditioning, the mother's reprimands that were meant to be punishers were
actually reinforcers because of the effect they had on the boy, who wanted

Figure 2.8
A rat makes the correct choice in a
trial on the Lashley jump stand.
Learning is rapid in this apparatus
because an incorrect choice
produces aversive consequences:
The rat bumps its nose on the
closed door (horizontally striped in
this case) and falls into the net
below.

Figure 2.9
An analysis of the relationship between the behavior of a child and the behavior of his parents. (from left to right and from top to bottom) The child is about to engage in a positively reinforcing activity (playing in the mud), but his parents are emitting a behavior (forbidding him to play in the mud). He punishes their forbidding behavior with an aversive stimulus (a violent tantrum). Their forbidding behavior decreases in strength and they give in. The parents' giving-in behavior is now negatively reinforced by the removal of the aversive tantrum. The child's tantrum is positively reinforced by playing in the mud. The results of this conditioning process are that tantrums are now more likely, forbidding is less likely, and giving in is more likely. The new behavior may generalize to a new yet similar situation.

attention. Perhaps sending him to his room every time he harassed his sister would have been an appropriate punisher; this unpleasant stimulus would have prevented him from repeating the behavior.

In punishment, an unpleasant consequence occurs and decreases the frequency of the behavior that produced it. Negative reinforcement and punishment operate in opposite ways: in negative reinforcement, escape or avoidance behavior is *repeated*, and in punishment, behavior that is punished is *not repeated*.

Psychologists have found several disadvantages in using aversive stimuli to change behavior. For one thing, aversive stimuli can produce unwanted side effects such as rage, aggression, and fear. Then, instead of having to change only one problem behavior, there may be two or more. For example, children whose parents rely on spanking to control disobedience may also have to deal with the problem of their children's increased aggressiveness toward other children.

A second problem with aversive stimuli is that people learn to avoid the person delivering the aversive consequences. In the cases of parents or teachers who punish often, children learn to stay away from them. One consequence of this is that parents and teachers have less opportunity to correct the children's inappropriate behavior. Also, punishment is likely to suppress rather than eliminate behaviors.

FACTORS THAT AFFECT LEARNING

Studies of more complex forms of learning have revealed that several factors can help or hinder the process. Among them are feedback, transfer, and practice.

Feedback

Finding out the results of an action or performance is called **feedback.** Without feedback, you might repeat the same mistakes so many times that you develop a skill incorrectly—you would never learn what you were doing wrong. Even if you were performing correctly, you would not be receiving reinforcement for continuing. If, for example, you always wore earplugs while you practiced the piano, you would never know just how bad your version of "Chopsticks" sounded.

Transfer

Often a skill that you have already learned can help you to learn a new skill. If you have learned to play the saxophone, it will be much easier for you to learn to play the clarinet. You can **transfer** skills you already have such as reading notes and converting them into responses of your lips, tongue, and fingers to the clarinet. When previously learned responses help you learn a new task, it is called *positive* transfer.

When a previously learned task hinders learning, *negative* transfer has occurred. An American may find driving in England to be more difficult than it is for an Englishman who is learning to drive. In England the steering wheel is on the opposite side of the car, and people drive on the opposite side of the road. The learned skill of driving American style makes it difficult to perform the necessary new mental and motor tasks. An American's responses are often the exact opposite of what is needed.

Practice

Practice, the repetition of a task, helps to bind responses together. It is the key element that makes for smooth and fluent movement from response to response.

Because practice takes time, psychologists have been interested in determining how to use that time most efficiently. They have found that whatever type of skill a person is learning, it is usually better to space out practice rather than do it all at once.

It is possible to practice by imagining oneself performing a skill. Athletes imagine themselves making golf swings over and over again or mentally shooting free throws in basketball to improve their performance. Psychologists call such effort *mental practice*. Although it is not as effective as the real thing, it is better than nothing at all.

LEARNING STRATEGIES

It would be difficult to solve problems if people had to relearn the solution process each time a problem occurred. Fortunately, when you learn to solve one problem, some of the problem-solving experiences may transfer to other, similar problems. Once you learn certain strategies for solving problems and learning tasks, you will usually have an easier time on your next attempts. (Such problem-solving strategies are also discussed in Chapter 3.) Strategies are affected by their consequences just as less complex reasons are. If a strategy works, the person or animal is likely to use it again. Many learned principles for dealing with life are valuable; others may actually be handicaps.

Learning to Learn

Harry Harlow (1949) has shown that animals can learn to learn—they can learn to use strategies for solving similar problems and tasks. He gave a monkey the problem of finding a raisin under one of two wooden lids, one red and one green (Figure 2.10). The raisin was always hidden under the green lid. Because the experimenter kept changing the position of the lids, the monkey took a while to realize that color was important, not location.

When the monkey had learned to always pick the green lid, the experimenter changed the problem. Now the monkey had to choose between triangular and circular lids. The raisin was always placed under the circular lid, and the experimenter again changed the location of the lids on each trial. As before, it took several tries for the monkey to learn that the shape of the lid, not its location, indicated where the raisin would be. After doing a number of problems like these, the monkey began to learn that the difference between the two lids always contained the key to the problem. Eventually the monkey could solve any similar two-choice problem with, at most, one error.

The learning of strategies and principles is extremely important in human behavior. In school you practiced such skills as reading books, writing essays, and taking tests. In many cases the particular things you learned will prove to be less important and useful than what you have learned about learning generally. Learning to extract information from a book, for example, will be helpful whether the book is about physics, grammar, or cooking. Just as Harlow's monkey acquired a general method for quickly solving particular problems, you are acquiring a general strategy for learning particular pieces of information.

Helplessness and Laziness

Psychologists have shown that general learning strategies can affect a person's relationship to the environment. For example, if a person has numerous experiences in which his actions have no effect on his world, he may learn a general strategy of helplessness or laziness.

Martin Seligman did a number of experiments to show how learned helplessness developed in animals. He strapped dogs into a harness from which they could not escape, and then gave them a series of shocks at irregular intervals. After days of shock treatment, the dogs were unharnessed. Now they could escape the shocks or avoid them entirely simply by jumping over a hurdle into a safe compartment. More than half the dogs failed to learn to jump. When several dogs that had not been shocked were also tested, almost all of them quickly learned to jump to safety. Apparently, many of the dogs in the first group had learned to stand and endure the shocks, resigned to the fact that any effort to escape would be useless.

Later experiments showed that people reacted in the same way. In the first stage of one study (Hiroto, 1974), some college students were able to turn off an unpleasant loud noise, while others had no control over it. Later, all were placed in a situation in which they merely had to move a lever to stop a similar noise. Only the ones who had control over the noise in the first place learned to turn it off. The others did not even try.

It is not hard to see how these results can apply to everyday situations. In order to be able to try hard and to be full of energy, people must learn that their actions *do* make a difference. If rewards come without effort, a person never learns to work (learned laziness). If pain comes no matter how hard one tries, a person gives up (learned helplessness).

Seligman believes that learned helplessness is one major cause of depression. He has revised his theory (Abramson, Seligman, and Teasdale, 1978; Miller and Seligman, 1982) so that it is now somewhat more detailed than his earlier theory, which was based primarily on animal studies. He reasons that, when people are unable to control events in their lives, they generally respond in one of the following ways. They may be less motivated to act and thus stop trying. They may have trouble learning to bring about new outcomes or may stop thinking. They may experience a lowered sense of self-esteem and think negatively about themselves. They may also feel depressed.

Seligman identified three important elements of helplessness: *stability*, *globality*, and *internality*. Stability refers to the person's belief that the state of helplessness results from a permanent characteristic. For example, a student who fails a math test can decide that the problem is either temporary ("I did poorly on this math test because I was sick") or *stable* ("I never have done well on math tests and never will"). Similarly, the person can decide that the problem is either specific ("I'm no good at

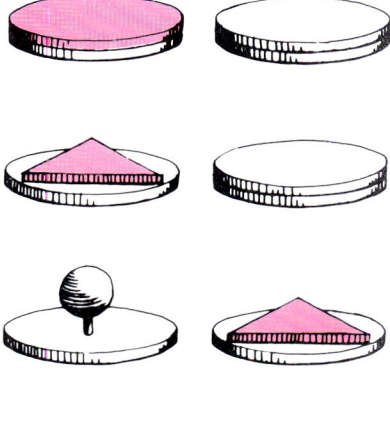

Figure 2.10
Harry Harlow presented monkeys with pairs of lids like those shown here and required them to learn strategies for determining which lid in each pair covered a morsel of food. After being presented with a few hundred such problems, the monkeys learned to use the same strategy for dealing with each new pair.

▲▲▲▲▲

**PSYCHOLOGY
UPDATE**

Shaping Complicated Behaviors in Animals. Psychologists have used shaping to condition very complicated behavior patterns in animals. Pigeons have been taught to play Ping-Pong and play songs on a small piano. During World War I, the British trained sea gulls to detect enemy submarines in the English Channel. To train them, the British sent their own submarines out in the Channel while dropping food on the surface. Soon the sea gulls would follow submarines from the air without the presence of food, and the sighting of sea gulls over the Channel became a signal of the possible presence of German subs.

During World War II, B. F. Skinner was involved in a project that trained pigeons to guide missiles to enemy targets. The pigeons were gradually reinforced for pecking at images of enemy targets projected on a screen. Although these "top gun" pigeons were quite accurate, they were never actually used in real combat.

More recently, the U.S. Navy has trained dolphins to detect enemy divers and locate undersea mines. Also, sea lions have been taught to recover antisubmarine rockets so that the Navy can evaluate the rockets' performance.

math tests") or *global* ("I'm just dumb"). Both stability and globality focus on the student—on *internal* reasons for failure. The student could have decided that the problem was external ("This was a bad math test") instead of internal. People who attributed an undesirable outcome to their own inadequacies will probably experience depression along with guilt and self-blame. Those who attribute their problems to their own inadequacies and see these personal shortcomings as enduring traits that apply to all situations are likely to suffer from severe depression.

The revision of Seligman's theory is important because it is a good example of several new trends in behaviorism. As learning theorists begin to study people rather than animals, they are finding that some of the old behavior models are too simple because they focus simply on what people *do*. What people *think* is also important.

LEARNING COMPLICATED SKILLS

When you acquire a skill such as knitting, photography, shooting a basketball, or talking persuasively, you learn more than just a single new stimulus-response relationship. You learn a large number of them, and you learn how to put them together into a large, smooth-flowing unit. Psychologists have devoted considerable attention to how new responses are acquired and to how they are put together in complex skills.

Shaping is a process in which reinforcement is used to sculpt new responses out of old (Figure 2.11). An experimenter can use this method to teach a rat to do something it has never done before and would never do if left to itself. He can shape it, for example, to raise a miniature flag. The rat is physically capable of standing on its hind legs and using its mouth to pull a miniature-flag–raising cord, but at present it does not do so. The rat probably will not perform this unusual action by accident, so the experimenter begins by rewarding the rat for any action similar to the wanted responses, using reinforcement to produce successive, or closer and closer, approximations of the desired behavior.

Imagine the rat roaming around on a table with the flag apparatus in the middle. The rat inspects everything and finally sniffs at the flagpole. The experimenter immediately reinforces this response by giving the rat a food pellet. Now the rat frequently sniffs the flagpole, hoping to get another pellet, but the experimenter waits until the rat lifts a paw before he gives it another reward. This process continues, with the experimenter reinforcing close responses and then waiting for even closer ones. Eventually, he has the rat on its hind legs nibbling at the cord. Suddenly the rat seizes the cord in its teeth and yanks it. Immediately the rat is rewarded, and it begins pulling rapidly on the cord. A new response has been shaped.

Shaping has been used to teach language skills to impaired children.

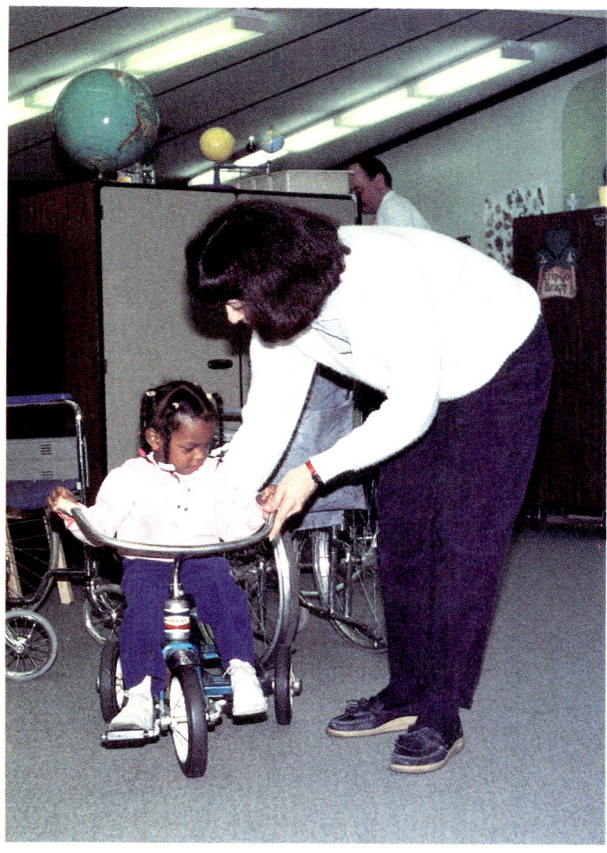

Figure 2.11
Psychologists shape behavior by using reinforcement to sculpture new responses out of old ones. Th s instructor is shaping behavior as she teaches this disabled preschooler to ride a tricycle.

Psychologists at first reward the children for simple sounds, such as "bah." Later the children are only rewarded for complete words, such as "beans," and later for complete sentences, such as "Beans, please." Many such children have successfully learned to use some language by this method (Lovaas *et al.*, 1967).

Combining Responses: Chaining

In order to learn a skill, a person must be able to put various new responses together. Responses that follow one another in a sequence are put together in **response chains.** Each response produces the signal for the next one. For example, to hammer a nail into a board, you would have to put together the following chain of responses: pick up the hammer, pick up the nail, position the nail, swing the hammer, hit the nail, swing the hammer, hit the nail, and so on until the nail is completely sunk in. Each hit of the nail is a signal that you are striking it correctly, and the nail's being flush with the board's surface is a signal that no further responses are required.

In learning, chains of responses are organized into larger *response patterns*. For example, the complex skill of swimming has three major chains that are combined to make up the whole swimming pattern: an arm-stroking chain, a breathing chain, and a leg-kicking chain (Figure 2.12). After much practice, you no longer have to think about the different steps involved. The behavior takes on a rhythm of its own: the chains of responses flow naturally as soon as you dive into the water.

It is often necessary to learn simple responses before mastering the complex pattern. If you cannot hit a nail with a hammer, you certainly cannot build a house. Therefore, before a person can learn to perform a particular skill, he or she must learn all the subordinate skills that make the larger skill possible.

MODELING

Up to this point it would seem that there are two types of learning: emotional responding, conditioned by the close association of neutral and unconditioned stimuli; and operant responses, learned either by reward or punishment. However, the informal observations you have been making all your life concerning learning probably suggest to you that there is more to learning than this—that, in fact, we most often learn by imitating others. This is especially true of social responses—when we learn how to behave in a new situation by watching how others behave. When you go to a concert for the first time, you may be very hesitant about where to go, when to enter (especially if you are late), when to clap, how to get a better seat after the first intermission, and so on. So you observe others, follow them, and soon you are an "old hand."

Figure 2.12
In learning a skill, responses that follow one another in sequence are put together in chains, and the chains are then organized into response patterns. The complex skill of swimming has three major parts: arm stroke, breathing, and leg kicking.

Figure 2.13
A modern technique in teaching is computer-
assisted instruction (CAI). Computers ask the
student a question, get a response, and tell the
student if the answer is right or wrong.

There are several advantages to this system of instruction over conventional classroom methods. The learner has
immediate feedback about whether he or she understands
the material. The learner reviews only material he or she
does not understand. There is constant incentive to learn
because of many positive reinforcements. This method also
avoids aversive aspects of classroom learning, including a
sense of failure for wrong answers in class or on tests. The
student can progress at an individual rate, depending on
how well rather than how fast he or she learns.

In most variations of CAI, the student can "talk" with
the computer by typing in various comments or writing
on the screen with a special pen. In the *branching* system
of information delivery, the student can choose between
paths of instruction after she or he makes a response. The
paths can be remedial or supplementary. If the student
responds incorrectly, she or he is taken back to the original
question that led to the path she or he was on. There is
also a simpler, *linear*, system in which such choices are not
included.

After completing a course taught by CAI, the student is either given a letter grade automatically (according to how much of the course was completed) or takes a test to see how much information was retained.

Almost every study comparing this method of instruction with conventional classroom methods has shown it to be superior in student retention of the material. The only problem sometimes experienced with CAI is that students may not finish the courses when there is no set timetable of instruction. Other disadvantages are expense and lack of human interaction.

Several principles of learning psychology are at work in CAI. The student is learning complex material through a response chain. She or he is reinforced constantly on a fixed schedule. Knowledge is being shaped in a systematic and predictable way. The student is able to have a dialogue with the instructor on every point, which is impossible for a class of students in a conventional setting.

Token Economies

Psychologists tried an experiment with a group of extremely disenchanted boys in Washington, D.C. In fact, the boys had been labeled "uneducable" and placed in the National Training School. The experimenters used what is known as a **token economy** to motivate the boys. The youngsters received points for good grades on tests. They could "cash" these points in for such rewards as snacks, lounge privileges, or items in a mail-order catalog. In other words, they created a system that worked like the Chimp-O-Mat, discussed earlier. Within a few months, a majority of the students showed a significant increase in IQ scores (an average gain of twelve and a half points). The boys continued to improve in the months that followed, showing that they were, indeed, educable (Cohen and Filipczak, 1971).

In another experiment teachers used a token economy to teach preschoolers in a Head Start program to write, and compared their scores on writing tests with those achieved by children who did not participate in a token economy. The youngsters who received tokens, which they could exchange for food, movies, and other rewards, improved dramatically. Equally important, they seemed to be developing a very positive attitude toward school. The youngsters who did not receive tokens made very little progress (Miller and Schneider, 1970).

Thus, in token economies, people are systematically paid

to act appropriately. In the real world, behaviorists argue, the rewards are just as real; they are simply less systematic. In overcrowded mental hospitals, for example, the only way some patients can get attention is by "acting crazy." Most staff members simply don't have time to bother with people who are not causing trouble. Since attention from the staff is reinforcing for these patients, in effect people are rewarded for undesirable behavior. By systematically rewarding only desirable behavior, token economies have been set up in prisons, mental hospitals, halfway houses, and classrooms. (See also Chapter 16.)

Self-Control

In token economies, a researcher sets up an elaborate system of reinforcers to get people to act the way he or she wants. One of the most important new trends in behavior modification is a growing emphasis on asking people to set up personal systems of rewards and punishments to shape their own thoughts and actions.

In the past, behaviorists limited their studies to observable behavior (Chapter 1), and made little attempt to observe or change the way people thought. Then, as more learning researchers began to study humans (instead of focusing exclusively on animals), it became obvious that what people *do* is only part of the story. As we described above, for example, Martin Seligman recently expanded his theory of learned helplessness to try to explain why some people develop long-lasting depressions while others seem to get over them. Part of the difference, Seligman argues, is based on what people *think*—that is, how they interpret their failures.

As in any application of behavior modification, the first step in self-control is to define the problem. A person who smokes too much would be encouraged to actually count how many cigarettes he smoked every hour of the day and note what kinds of situations led him to smoke. (After a meal? When talking to friends? Driving to work?) Similarly, a person who had a very poor opinion of herself would have to define the problem more concretely. She might begin by counting the number of self-deprecating remarks she made and thoughts she had. Researchers have found that just keeping track of behavior in this way often leads a person to start changing it.

The next step may be to set up a single behavioral contract. One soda lover who had trouble studying decided that she would only allow herself a Pepsi after she studied for half an hour. Her cola addiction remained strong, but her study time increased dramatically under this system. A behavioral contract simply involves choosing a reinforcer (buying a new shirt, watching a favorite TV program) and making it contingent on some unpleasant but necessary act (getting to work on time, washing the kitchen floor). These contracts are most likely to succeed if you also use successive approximations—starting with an easy task and gradually making it more difficult. For example, you might begin by studying ten minutes before rewarding yourself, and gradually increase it to an hour.

Behavior modifiers are now developing and testing many other techniques to help people learn to control themselves.

Improving Your Study Habits

One psychologist designed a program to help students improve their study habits and tried it on a group of volunteers. The students were told to set a time when they would go to a small room in the library they had not used before, taking only the materials they wanted to study. They were then to work for as long as they remained interested—and *only* for as long as they were interested. As soon as they found themselves fidgeting, daydreaming, becoming drowsy or bored, they were to make the decision to stop studying. There was only one condition. They had to read one more page, or solve one more simple problem, before they left. Even if this made them want to study longer, they were instructed to hold to their decision to leave the library, go for a cup of coffee, call a friend, or do whatever they wanted to do.

The next day they were asked to repeat the same procedure, adding a second page to the amount they read between the time they decided to leave and the time they actually left the library. The third day they added a third page, and so on. Students who followed this procedure found that in time they were able to study for longer periods than before, that they were studying more effectively, and that they didn't mind studying so much.

Why did this procedure work? Many students force themselves to study. One common technique is to go to the library to avoid distractions. The result may be hours spent staring at a book without really learning anything. Repeated failures to get anything accomplished and sheer

Figure 2.14
The library need not become a conditioned aversive stimulus if you learn how to build positive reinforcement into your studying routine.

discomfort turn studying into a dreaded chore. The library becomes a conditioned aversive stimulus—you hate it because you've spent so many uncomfortable hours there. The procedure was designed to change these feelings.

Requiring students to leave as soon as they felt distracted helped to reduce the negative, punishing emotions associated with studying. The students stopped when these feelings began. Studying in a new place removed the conditioned aversive stimulus. Thus, aversive responses were not conditioned to the subject matter or the room, as they are when students force themselves to work.

Second, the procedure made use of successive approximations. The students began by reading just one page after they became bored, and only gradually increased the assignment. This also reduced the aversive response to studying. The task no longer seemed so difficult.

Finally, when they left their work, the students received two kinds of positive reinforcement. They had the satisfaction of knowing they had followed the procedure and had completed an assignment (namely, one more page), and they were free to do something they enjoyed. Thus they rewarded or reinforced themselves for however much studying they did (Fox, 1966). You might try this procedure.

CHAPTER REVIEW

SUMMARY

1. Learning is a lasting change in behavior that results from experience.

2. Classical conditioning was discovered by Ivan Pavlov. In this form of learning, a previously neutral stimulus comes to elicit a response because it has been paired with a stimulus that already elicited a response. Extinction of a classically conditioned response occurs when the conditioned stimulus is no longer associated with the unconditioned stimulus.

3. Operant conditioning occurs when an organism's activities are either reinforced or punished. Any consequence that increases the likelihood of a behavior is called a reinforcer. Extinction occurs when a behavior decreases in frequency because it is no longer reinforced.

4. Different schedules of reinforcement produce different patterns of behavior. When reinforcement depends on number of responses (ratio schedules), the organism tends to respond faster than it does if reinforcement depends on time (interval schedules). When responses are reinforced on a regular basis (fixed schedules), the organism will tend to pause after a reward. If reinforcers appear irregularly (variable schedules), the organism will keep going at a steady rate. Intermittently reinforced responses disappear more slowly during extinction than do continuously reinforced ones.

5. Signals are stimuli that come to be associated with getting rewards or punishments. Organisms have the ability to generalize among and discriminate between signals. A signal becomes a conditioned reinforcer when the signal itself serves as a reward or punisher.

6. Aversive control means using unpleasant influences on behavior. In punishment, the unpleasant event comes as a consequence of a response and the response decreases in frequency. In avoidance and escape conditioning, the response has the effect of removing the unpleasant event. In negative reinforcement, the frequency of a response that terminates an unpleasant event increases.

7. Factors that influence learning include feedback, transfer, and practice.

8. Organisms can learn to learn by discovering certain strategies. A strategy for solving problems or learning tasks can be applied to subsequent, similar situations. Organisms learn strategies of laziness or helplessness if they experience situations in which their behavior has no consequences.

9. To learn a complicated skill, a person must acquire and coordinate a number of new responses. The learning of skills may be facilitated by

imitation and shaping. To learn a skill, one must put new responses together in chains, which are then organized into response patterns.

10. Modeling is a kind of learning that results from imitation.

11. Behavior modification involves the systematic application of learning principles to change people's actions and feelings. Two examples are the personalized system of instruction and token economies. It is also possible to change one's own habits through reinforcement.

REVIEW QUESTIONS

1. What type of learning is involved when an old response becomes attached to a new stimulus? What terms did Pavlov use for each of the following elements in his experiments with dogs: food, the dog's salivation response at the sight of food, the sound of the tuning fork, the animal's salivation response to the sound of the tuning fork? What term did he use to explain the effect of repeatedly striking the tuning fork without providing food?

2. Who is the psychologist closely associated with operant conditioning? Which type of conditioning emphasizes that the stimulus elicits the response?

3. What are positive consequences called? What are negative consequences called? Name two ways to have a behavior repeated and two ways to prevent a behavior from being repeated.

4. Name the four schedules of reinforcement.

5. What are some examples of primary reinforcers? What type of reinforcer is money?

6. Aversive stimuli can be used in two ways. What are they? How are they different?

7. How did Martin Seligman develop learned helplessness in animals? A person who has learned helplessness is more likely to be depressed. If a person feels helpless and depressed after taking an exam, what two things is this person likely to be thinking about?

8. What is the process in which a person is reinforced for closer and closer approximations of the desired behavior? What is the name of the sequence in which one response produces the signal for the next response?

9. What are the three types of modeling?

ACTIVITIES

1. Businesses often use conditioning techniques in their advertisements. They associate the name of their product with pleasant tunes or exciting scenes, so that the name alone will elicit conditioned relaxation or excitement. Describe an ad that uses these techniques.

2. Which of the schedules of reinforcement do your instructors generally use in conducting their classes? How would your classes be different if they used the other schedules? Give examples for your answers and justify your reasoning.

3. In the experiment on learned helplessness, the animals who were unable to change their situation for long periods of time seemed unable or unwilling to change when the possibility was presented to them. What implications do such experiments have for humans? Can you think of situations in your life that have had the effect of learned helplessness?

4. Select some particular subject of study that you find difficult or unpleasant. Whenever you sit down to study this subject, play one of your favorite records or tapes as you study. In time, the favorable feelings toward this music may become associated with the subject of study, making it easier to learn and remember.

Figure 3.1 No mysteries are more fundamental than how we think, remember, solve problems, and create ideas.

Objectives: *After studying this chapter, you should be able to*
- explain the concept of information processing.
- identify and discuss different types of memory systems.
- explain the different theories of memory.
- describe the units of thought and the basic kinds of thinking.
- define problem solving and describe problem-solving strategies.

Memory and Thought

Is anything more complex than the human mind?

Consider all the material stored in your memory: your social security number, the capital of South Dakota, "The Star Spangled Banner," your first love's phone number, the major generals of the Civil War, the starting lineup for the Boston Red Sox, your best friend in first grade, and so on. What kind of incredible filing system allows you to instantly recover a Beatles song or your favorite recipe? How does all that information fit in your head?

Going beyond memory, how do we think? How do we solve problems? How do we create ideas? No mysteries are more fundamental, and researchers are just beginning to investigate human thought. Psychologists refer to all cognitive and mental activities—from memorizing lists of numbers to writing poems and inventing new technologies—as *information processing*. This involves three steps: input, central processing, and output. **Input** is the information people receive from their senses. **Central processing** is the storing (in memory) and sorting (by thought) of this information in the brain. **Output** refers to the ideas and actions that result from processing.

Taking Information In
Selective Attention • Feature Extraction

Storing Information
Sensory Storage • Short-Term Memory • Long-Term Memory • Memory and the Brain

Retrieving Information
Recognition • Using Psychology: Eyewitness Testimony • Recall • Forgetting • Using Psychology: Mood and Memory • Improving Memory

Central Processing of Information
Thinking • Problem Solving • Creativity

TAKING INFORMATION IN

Information is any event that reduces uncertainty. For example, when a traffic light changes from red to green, it provides you with information—it reduces your uncertainty about whether you should step on the gas. Information is transmitted through the senses in many forms—voices, musical sounds, sweet tastes, pungent odors, colorful images, rough textures, painful stings. At any given moment a confusing array of sights, sounds, smells, and other sensations compete for your attention. If you accepted all these inputs, you would be completely overwhelmed. Two processes help people to narrow sensory inputs to a manageable number: selective attention and feature extraction.

Selective Attention

The ability to pick and choose among the various available inputs is called **selective attention.** For example, if you are at a large party where the music is turned up and everyone is talking, you can focus on a friend's voice and ignore all other sounds. In a way, selective attention is like tuning in a specific television channel.

Unlike a television dial, however, selective attention does not completely block out the other programs or stimuli. You may be listening attentively to what a friend is saying, but at the same time you are unconsciously monitoring information that is coming in over other channels. If your name is mentioned in a conversation going on three feet away, you will notice it and tune into that input. If someone strolls by dressed in a

Figure 3.2
The ''filter model'' of how we listen to the input to only one ear at a time during shadowing. (After Broadbent, 1958.)

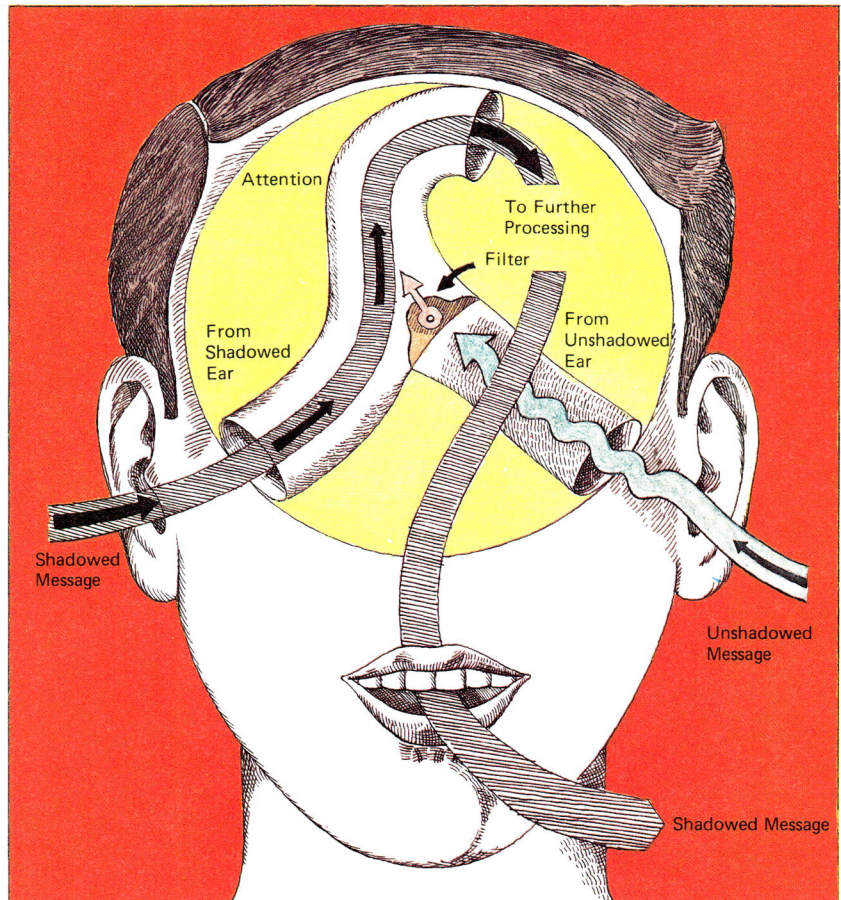

bathing suit, snorkel, and fins, you will notice him. The "cocktail-party phenomenon," as selective attention is sometimes called, allows you to concentrate on one thing without tuning out everything else that is happening.

In laboratory experiments, researchers have shown how selective attention affects the brain (Hernández-Peón, 1961). For example, if people are asked to pay attention to an auditory stimulus, the brain waves that record their response to sound will get larger. While this is happening, the brain waves that record their response to what they see will get smaller because they are not paying close attention to visual stimuli. If the same people are asked to pay attention to visual stimuli, the reverse occurs: visual brain waves increase while auditory brain waves decrease. A similar experiment has shown that a certain kind of brain wave diminishes but does not disappear when people are given a problem to solve or are drawn into conversation. Such experiments seem to indicate that the brain somehow evaluates the importance of the information that comes in over different channels. Top-priority information is allowed to reach the highest brain centers, whereas unimportant information is suppressed (Figure 3.2).

What makes one input more important than another? Information leading to the satisfaction of such needs as hunger and thirst has top priority. (A person who is very hungry, for example, will pay more attention to his dinner than to the dinner-table chitchat.) We also give priority to inputs that are strange and novel, such as an individual who comes to a party dressed for snorkeling. A third director of attention is interest: the more interested you are in something, the more likely you are to notice it. For example, most people "tune in" when they hear their name mentioned; we're all interested in what other people have to say about us. Likewise, if you become interested in chess, you will suddenly begin to notice newspaper articles about chess, chess sets in store windows, and references to chess moves in everyday speech (for example, "stalemate"). These inputs are not new. They were there last year and the year before, but you simply weren't interested enough to notice them.

Figure 3.3
Can you spot the hidden faces in this picture? To find them, it is necessary for you to extract those features that define a human face from a large amount of irrelevant and misleading information.

Feature Extraction

Selective attention is only the first step in narrowing down input. The second step is to decide which aspects of the selected channel you will focus on. This process, called **feature extraction,** involves locating the outstanding characteristics of incoming information (Figure 3.3). If you want to identify the make of a car, you look for certain features—the shape of the fenders, the proportion of height to length, and so on. For the most part, you ignore such features as color, upholstery, and tires, which tell you little about the make of the car. Similarly, when you read, you focus on the important words, skimming over such words as "the," "and," or "for example."

Being able to extract the significant features of an input helps a person to identify it and compare it to other inputs. For example, you are able to distinguish faces from one another and, at the same time, see resemblances. You may notice that all the members of a family have similar

noses, yet you are able to recognize each person on the basis of other features.

Obviously, feature extraction depends to some extent on experience—on knowing what to look for. This is especially true where fine distinctions must be made. It takes considerable expertise to distinguish an original Rembrandt from a skillful forgery. Most of us cannot distinguish between two accomplished pianists playing the same concerto, but an expert who knows what to listen for can.

Like selective attention, feature extraction is an evaluative process. If you are reading a novel for pleasure, you may look for the "juicy" parts. If you're reading a historical biography to prepare for an exam, you'll probably still look for the juicy parts. When you don't find any, you go ahead and concentrate on the other facts.

STORING INFORMATION

In order to be used, the inputs that reach the brain must be registered, held onto, perhaps "filed" for future reference. We call the storage of inputs **memory.** Psychologists distinguish among three kinds of memory, each of which has a different purpose and time span. **Sensory storage** holds information for only an instant; **short-term memory** keeps it in mind for about twenty seconds; **long-term memory** stores it indefinitely.

Sensory Storage

The senses—sight, hearing, and so on—seem to be able to hold an input for a fraction of a second before it disappears. For example, when you watch a movie, you do not notice the gaps between frames. The actions seem smooth because each frame is held in sensory storage until the next frame arrives.

Sperling (1960) demonstrated this phenomenon in an ingenious experiment. He used a tachistoscope (a device that presents a picture for a very brief time) to present a group of letters to people for a twentieth of a second. Previous studies had shown that if you present a stimulus like this

```
T   D   R
S   R   N
F   Z   K
```

people will usually be able to tell you four or five of the letters. Sperling believed that people took a mental photograph of the letters, and were able to read back only a few before the picture faded. He told the people in his experiment that after he flashed the letters on the tachistoscope screen, he would present a tone. Upon hearing a high tone, the subjects were to tell him the top row, a medium tone the middle row, and a low tone the bottom row. Once people learned this system, they were indeed able to remember any row of letters. Thus, he proved that the subject retains a brief image of the whole picture so that he or she can still read off the items in the correct row *after* the picture has left the screen.

The information held momentarily by the senses has not yet been narrowed down or analyzed. It is like a short-lived but highly detailed photograph or tape recording. However, by the time information gets to the next stage—short-term memory—it has been analyzed, identified, and simplified so that it can be conveniently stored and handled for a longer time.

Short-Term Memory

The things you have in your conscious mind at any one moment are being held in short-term memory. Short-term memory does not necessarily involve paying close attention. You have probably had the experience of listening to someone only partially and then having that person accuse you of not paying attention. You deny it, and, in order to prove your innocence, you repeat to him, word for word, the last words he said. You can do this because you are holding the words in short-term memory. Usually, however, the sense of what he was saying does not register on you until you repeat the words out loud. Repeating the words makes you pay attention to them. This is what psychologists mean by rehearsal.

Rehearsal. To keep information in short-term memory for more than a few seconds, you have to repeat it to yourself, in your mind or out loud. When you look up a telephone number, for example, you can remember the seven digits long enough to dial them *if* you repeat them several times. If you are distracted or make a mistake in dialing, the chances are you will have to look the number up again. It has been lost from short-term memory.

Psychologists have measured short-term memory by seeing how long a subject can retain a piece of information without rehearsal. The experimenter shows the subject a card with three letters on it, such as CPQ. However, at the same time the experimenter makes the subject think about something else in order to prevent her from rehearsing the letters. For example, she might ask the subject to start counting backward by threes from 798 as soon as she flashes the card. If the subject performs this task for only a short time, she will usually remember the letters. But if she is kept from rehearsing for more than eighteen seconds, the information is forgotten. Thus, short-term memory seems to last for less than twenty seconds without rehearsal.

Chunking. Short-term memory is limited not only in its duration, but in its capacity as well. It can hold only about seven unrelated items, If, for example, someone quickly reels off a series of digits to you, you will be able to keep only about seven or eight of them in your immediate memory. Beyond that number, confusion among them will set in. The same would be true if the unrelated items were a random set of words. We may not notice this limit to our capacity because we usually do not have to store so many unrelated items in our immediate memory. Either the items are

> **Short-term memory can hold only about seven unrelated items.**

Figure 3.4
Glance quickly at the left figure in this pair, then look away. How many dots did you see? Now do the same with the right figure. You were probably more sure and more accurate in your answer for the right figure because the organization of the dots into a small number of chunks makes it easier to process the information.

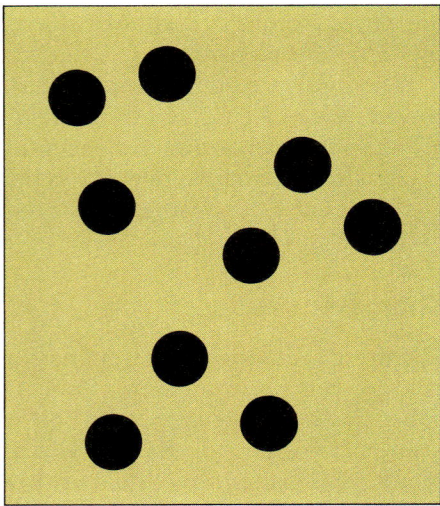

related (as when we listen to someone speak) or they are rehearsed and placed in long-term memory.

The most interesting aspect of this limit, discovered by George Miller (1956), is that it involves about seven items of any kind. Each item may consist of a collection of many other items, but if they are all packaged into one "chunk" then there is still only one item. Thus we can remember about seven unrelated sets of initials, such as COMSAT, DDT, SST, or the initials of our favorite radio stations, even though we could not remember all the letters separately. This occurs because we have connected, or "chunked," them together previously, so that DDT is one item, not three.

One of the tricks of memorizing a lot of information quickly is to chunk together the items as fast as they come in. If we connect items in groups, we have fewer to remember. For example, we remember new phone numbers in two or three chunks (555–6794 or 555–67–94) rather than as a string of seven digits (5–5–5–6–7–9–4). As Figure 3.4 illustrates, we use chunking to remember visual as well as verbal inputs.

Even with chunking, short-term memory is only a temporary device. It contains information labeled "of possible interest." If the information is worth holding onto, it must be transferred to long-term memory.

Long-Term Memory

Long-term memory is where we store information for future use. It can be thought of as a kind of filing cabinet or storage bin for names, dates, words, and faces. When we say someone has a good memory, we usually mean he or she can recall a great deal of this type of information. But long-term memory also contains representations of countless experiences and sensations. You may not have thought about your childhood home for years, but you can probably still visualize it.

Long-term memory involves all the processes we have been describing. Suppose a person goes to see a play. As the actors say their lines, the sounds flow through sensory storage. Selective attention screens out other sounds, and feature extraction turns sounds into words. These words accumulate in short-term memory and form meaningful phrases and sentences.

The viewer attends to the action and changing scenery in much the same way. Together, they form chunks in her memory. An hour or two later, she will have forgotten all but the most striking lines, but she has stored the *meaning* of the lines and actions in long-term memory. The next day, she may be able to give a scene-by-scene description of the play. Throughout this process, the least important information is dropped and only the essentials are retained (Figure 3.5). A month or two later, the woman may remember only a brief outline of the plot and perhaps a few particularly impressive moments. In time she may not remember anything about the play. Other, more recently stored items block access to earlier memories or may even replace them. But if she sees the play again, she will probably recognize the lines of the play and anticipate the actions. Although it has become less accessible, it is still stored in long-term memory.

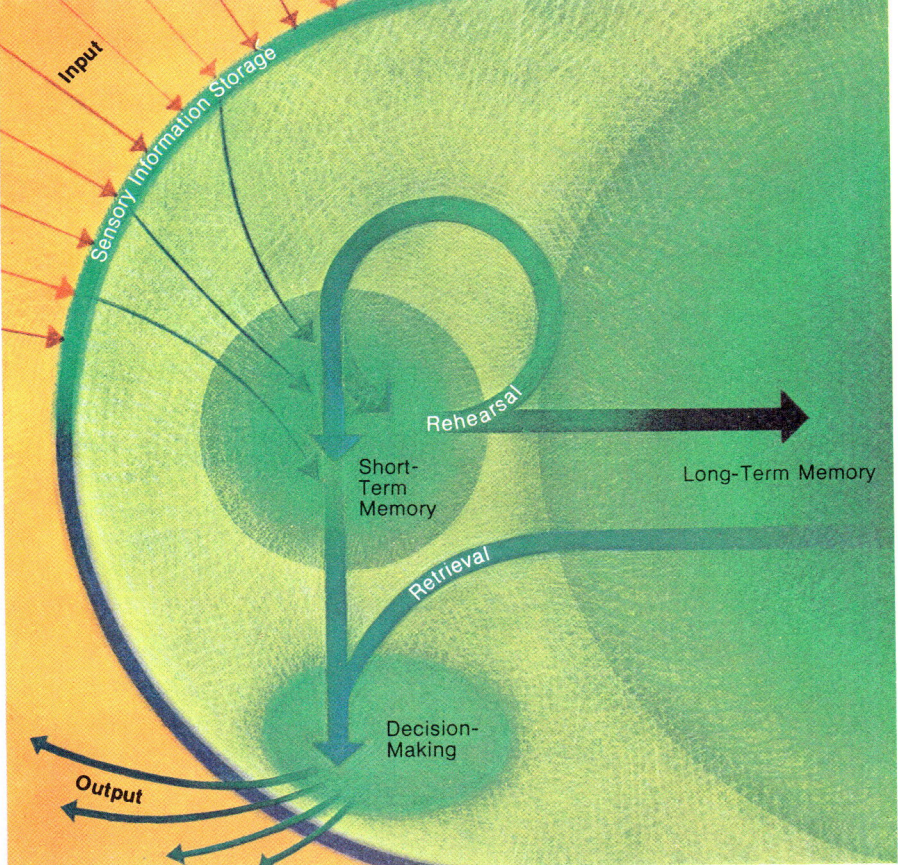

Figure 3.5
The flow of information processing. Input to the senses is stored temporarily, and some of it is passed on into short-term memory. Information may be kept in short-term memory by rehearsal or it may be passed on to long-term memory. Material stored in both short- and long-term memory is used in making decisions. The decision process results in outputs such as talking, writing, or moving.

Memory and the Brain

What happens in the brain when something is stored in long-term memory? This question is highly controversial. Although psychologists agree that some physiological changes must occur in the brain, they do not know what these changes are.

Some researchers believe that memory is due to changes in the form of protein molecules in the brain. In one experiment, a number of mice were trained to run through a maze, avoiding alleys where they would receive an electric shock. Then the mice were injected with a chemical known to disrupt protein production in the brain. Afterward, the mice could no longer remember the safe way out of the maze (Flexner, 1967). Recently, researchers (Flood, Bennett, and Orme, 1975) have been able to control the amount of "amnesia" in mice by injecting varying amounts of the chemical for certain time periods after the training task. The more of the protein-blocking chemical the mice receive, the more forgetful they become. One theory is that senility in the aged may be related to the end of protein production in the brain.

Another theory focuses on chemical-electrical changes in the brain. It may be that memory develops when the characteristics of the synapses change chemically. (As explained in Chapter 5, synapses are the gaps between nerve cells.) When something is learned, some pathways in the brain are facilitated and others inhibited. To date, it is impossible to say which of these theories is closer to the truth.

To complicate matters further, there is some controversy about just where memories are located in the brain. Karl Lashley (1929) argued that no one cell, or group of cells, can be removed to destroy a memory. Indeed, he found that he had to destroy most of the upper part of a rat's brain to erase the memory of a problem it had learned to solve. As a result, many psychologists believe that the same memories may be stored in several parts of the brain, so that destroying one area simply removes one copy. More recently, Richard Thompson (1976) and others have questioned Lashley's view. They believe that more sophisticated physiological techniques may be able to identify specific learning pathways.

All these ideas remain highly speculative. Many psychologists believe, however, that a better understanding of the processes underlying memory will be reached in the near future.

RETRIEVING INFORMATION

Stored information is useless unless it can be retrieved from memory. Once you've forgotten to send a card for your mother's birthday, it's not very consoling to prove that you have the date filed away in your brain. We've all experienced the acute embarrassment of being unable to remember a close friend's name. There are few things in life more frustrating than having a word "on the tip of your tongue," but just not being able to remember it.

The problem of memory is to store many thousands of items in such a way that you can find the one you need when you need it. The solution to **retrieval** is organization. Since human memory is extraordinarily efficient, it must be extremely well organized. Psychologists do not yet know how it is organized, but they are studying the processes involved in retrieval for clues.

Recognition

Human memory is organized in such a way as to make recognition quite easy—people can say with great accuracy whether or not something is familiar to them. If someone asked you the name of your first-grade teacher, for example, you might not remember it. But chances are that you would recognize the name if you heard it. Similarly, a multiple-choice test may bring out knowledge that a student might not be able to show on an essay test. The ability to recognize suggests that much more information is stored in memory than one might think.

The process of **recognition** provides insight into how information is stored in memory. We can recognize the sound of a particular musical instrument (say, the piano) no matter what tune is being played on it. We can also recognize a tune no matter what instrument is playing it. This pattern of recognition indicates that a single item of information may be "indexed" under the several "headings" so that it can be reached in a number of ways. Thus, "the attractive teller at the Five Cents Savings Bank" might be indexed under "Five Cents Savings Bank," "service people," "potential friends," "blondes," and possibly under several other headings as well. The more categories an item is filed in, the more easily it can be retrieved.

USING PSYCHOLOGY

Eyewitness Testimony

One situation in which recognition is extremely important (sometimes a matter of life or death) is in the courtroom. It is very convincing to a judge or jury when an eyewitness points to someone in the room and says, "That's the one who did it."

A psychologist who is deeply involved in the issue of eyewitness testimony is Elizabeth Loftus. She has shown (1974) that even after it had been proved that the eyesight of a witness was too poor for her to have seen a robber's face from where she stood at the scene of a robbery, the jury was still swayed by her testimony.

Lawyers can cite many cases of people falsely accused by eyewitnesses whose testimonies later proved to be inaccurate. In one such case, fourteen eyewitnesses agreed that the defendant had robbed a California supermarket

---

Selective Memory Problems. Memory problems can sometimes take a surprising twist. One example is the peculiar condition known as *prospagnosia*, in which the patient is unable to recognize familiar faces—even his or her own mirror image. People who have this condition can still perceive other aspects of faces, however, such as whether a person's expression is happy or sad.

Prospagnosia usually results from a stroke or head injury, and it illustrates how remarkably narrow or selective memory problems can sometimes be.

As another example of a selective problem, consider the case of a 34-year-old man who suffered a stroke. Afterwards, he regained his previous abilities—except that he found it nearly impossible to name common fruits and vegetables. He could, however, pick out the objects if the names were read to him. Selective problems such as these suggest that memories are organized into categories. Somehow, an individual category may become disconnected from the memory system as a whole.

and shot a policeman. However, later evidence proved that he was nowhere near the scene of the crime.

Elizabeth Loftus (1974) has done a fascinating series of experiments showing that when people are asked to recall the details of auto accidents, they, too, are likely to distort the facts. After groups of college students saw a filmed accident, she asked some of them, "About how fast were the cars going when they hit each other?" The average estimate was 34 miles per hour. When she substituted the word "smashed" for "hit" in the above question, another group of students remembered the cars as going significantly faster—41 miles per hour.

Figure 3.6

Three sketches of the "Son of Sam" killer show that eyewitnesses have different memories of his appearance.

Loftus (1979, 1980) has also found that a person's memory of an event can be distorted in the process of remembering it. Shocking events, such as those involving violence, can disrupt our ability to form a strong memory. Without a strong, clear memory of the event, the eyewitness is more likely to incorporate misinformation into the recall. For example, if a police officer asks a witness to describe the gun used in a robbery, the witness may recall a gun even though the robber never revealed a weapon.

Defense attorneys are well aware of the effects that leading questions can have on people's memories. Expert testimony by psychologists on the nature of human memory and on the factors that influence the accuracy of an identification may be needed to convince jurors to be more critical in their appraisal of eyewitness testimony. Even after being cautioned by experts on human memory, however, jurors still tend to believe that the eye is a camera and that recall is like a videotape.

Recall

More remarkable than the ability to recognize information is the ability to recall it. **Recall** is the active reconstruction of information. Just think about the amount of recall involved in a simple conversation. Each person uses hundreds of words involving all kinds of information, even though each word and bit of information must be retrieved separately from the storehouse of memory.

Recall involves more than searching for and finding pieces of information, however. It involves a person's knowledge, attitudes, and expectations. This was demonstrated in the following experiment. The researcher showed a group of young children a bottle of colored water, tilted as shown in Figure 3.7. The children were then asked to draw what they had seen from memory. Most of their drawings did not look at all like the original arrangement. However, six months later, when the same children were asked to draw the bottle they had seen, many did much better (Figure 3.8). Apparently they now had a better idea of what the tilted bottle *should* look like (Inhelder, 1969).

Because of this process of reconstruction, memories may change over time. They may be simplified, enriched, or distorted, depending on the individual's experiences and attitudes. This is why we sometimes make mistakes in memory. One type of mistake is called **confabulation:** a person "remembers" information that was never stored in memory. Confabulation generally occurs when an individual remembers parts of a situation and fills in the gaps by making up the rest. This is precisely what eyewitnesses to a crime often do—they fill in the holes in their memory with reasonable guesses, without even being aware that they are doing it.

Some people do not need to reconstruct information, because they have an **eidetic memory,** usually referred to as a "photographic memory." People with eidetic memories can remember with amazing accuracy all the details of a photograph, or pages of a text, or an experience on the basis of short-term exposure. There is some controversy about just how common

Memories may be simplified, enriched, or distorted over time.

Figure 3.7
Children between the ages of five and seven were shown a bottle half filled with colored water and suspended at an angle, such as is shown in this drawing. After each child had seen this arrangement he was asked to draw it from memory. Some of the results of this experiment are shown in Figure 3.8a, b.

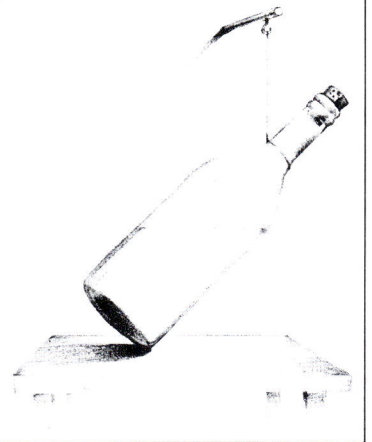

Figure 3.8
Drawings produced by children who had been shown an arrangement like that depicted in Figure 3.7. (a) The five- to seven-year-old children were not too successful in reproducing this arrangement from memory. (b) A drawing done by one of these children six months later. Even though the child had had half a year to forget what he had seen, his reproduction of the arrangement actually improved because he had developed a better idea of what bottles look like and of how water behaves.

photographic memory is. Several researchers have suggested that it is more common in children than in adults.

The Mind of a Mnemonist.   One of the best documented cases of a man with an astounding memory is presented in A. R. Luria's delightful book *The Mind of a Mnemonist* (1968). In the 1920s, a newspaper reporter came to Luria's laboratory to participate in a memory experiment. The Russian psychologist was amazed to learn that S. (as he called the reporter) could easily repeat lists of thirty, fifty, or seventy numbers after he heard them once. He could repeat them backward and forward with equal ease. And when Luria asked him for some of the same lists more than fifteen years later, S. still remembered them.

Perhaps as a result of Dr. Luria's tests, S. began another career as a professional mnemonist: he would repeat complicated lists supplied by people in the audience. How did he do it? Every word or number would conjure up rich visual images which S. easily remembered. For example, in one performance the audience provided him with the following nonsensical formula:

$$N \cdot \sqrt{d^2 \, x \, \dfrac{85}{vx}} \quad \cdot \quad \sqrt[3]{\dfrac{276^2 \cdot 86x}{n^2v \cdot 264}} \, n^2b \, = \quad sv \, \dfrac{1{,}624}{32^2} \cdot r^2 \, s.$$

S. was able to repeat this perfectly after studying it for a few minutes. He later told Dr. Luria a story he made up to help remember the formula:

"Neiman *(N)* came out and jabbed at the ground with his cane (.). He looked up at a tall tree which resembled the square root sign ($\sqrt{}$), and thought to himself: 'No wonder the tree has withered and begun to expose its roots. After all, it was here when I built these two houses' *(d²)*" (49). And so on.

But being a professional mnemonist is not all roses. One of S.'s biggest problems was learning to forget. His brain was cluttered with old lists of words, numbers, and letters. Even when he tried to relax, his mind would be flooded with vivid images from the past. S. also had trouble reading: every word brought a sea of images, and he had trouble focusing on the underlying meaning of a passage. Partly because of these problems, Dr. Luria wrote, "S. struck one as a disorganized and rather dull-witted person" (65).

Forgetting

Everyone experiences a loss of memory from time to time. You're sure you've seen that person before but can't quite place her. You have the word on the tip of your tongue, but. . . . When information that once entered long-term memory cannot be retrieved, it is said to be forgotten. Forgetting may involve decay, interference, or repression.

Some inputs may fade away, or decay, over time. Items quickly decay in sensory storage and short-term memory, as indicated above. It is not

Remembering High School Classmates

Few of us will ever forget our high school days, with all their glory and pain. But how many of us will remember the names and faces of the members of our high school class ten, twenty, thirty, and even forty years after graduation? According to one study, apparently more of us than you might think.

To find out just how long our long-term memory is, researchers showed nearly 400 high school graduates, ranging in age from seventeen to seventy-four, pictures from their high school yearbooks. Here are some of the surprising results:

- 35 years after graduation, people could identify the faces of 9 out of 10 of their classmates. The size of the high school made no difference in their response.
- 15 years after graduation, subjects could recall 90 percent of their classmates' names.
- Name recall began to fade to between 70 and 80 percent by the time people reached their late thirties.
- Women generally had better memories for names and faces than men.

Researchers explain these amazing results by looking to the way we collect this information in the first place. Our storehouse of names and faces is built over our four-year high school career, and continual repetition helps cement this knowledge in our memories for decades.

So if you're afraid that you are going to forget all the classmates you left behind, take heart. They will probably be part of your memory for a very long time.

For more details, see Harry P. Bahrick, Phyllis O. Bahrick, and Roy P. Wittinger, "Those Unforgettable High School Days," *Psychology Today*, December, 1974.

certain, however, whether long-term memories can ever decay. We know that a blow to the head or electrical stimulation of certain parts of the brain can cause loss of memory. The memories lost are the most recent ones, however; older memories seem to remain (see box). The fact that apparently forgotten information can be recovered through meditation, hypnosis, or brain stimulation suggests that at least some memories never decay. Rather, interference or repression causes people to lose track of them.

Interference refers to a memory being blocked or erased by previous or subsequent memories. This blocking is of two kinds: proactive and retroactive. In **proactive interference** an earlier memory does the blocking. In **retroactive interference** a later memory does the blocking. Suppose you move to a new home. You now have to remember a new address and

phone number. At first you may have trouble remembering them because the memory of your old address and phone number gets in the way (proactive interference). Later, you know the new information, but have trouble remembering the old data (retroactive interference).

It may be that interference actually does erase some memories permanently. In other cases the old data have not been lost. The information is in your memory somewhere, if only you could find it. According to Sigmund Freud, sometimes blocking is no accident. A person may subconsciously block memories of an embarrassing or frightening experience. This kind of forgetting is called **repression.** The material still exists in the person's memory, but it has been made inaccessible because it is so disturbing. (We discuss repression further in Chapter 11.)

USING PSYCHOLOGY

Mood and Memory

In 1968, Sirhan Sirhan assassinated Robert Kennedy in a Los Angeles hotel. Sirhan was in a highly agitated state when he killed Kennedy. When questioned about it immediately afterward, he had no recollection of the event. A hypnotist was called in. The hypnotist re-created the events of the murder. As Sirhan listened, he became agitated and recalled more and more details of the murder. Sometimes while he was in a trance he described events aloud; at other times he recorded his memories by writing them down automatically, without being aware of what he was writing (Bower, 1981). In his non-hypnotized state, Sirhan was never conscious of these memories and even denied that he had committed the murder.

Sirhan Sirhan's case is a dramatic example of *state-dependent memory*. The theory of this type of memory is based on the assumption that events learned in a certain emotional state can be remembered better when one is put back into the same state.

To learn more about the influence of mood on memory, psychologist Gordon Bower conducted a series of laboratory experiments. In one study, he hypnotized a group of subjects and made them feel happy. While they were in that happy state, he gave them a list of words to learn. At another session, he hypnotized them again, but put them in a sad mood and gave them a different list of words to learn. Later, the subjects were hypnotized again and were asked to recall one of the lists they had been given previously. Bower found that the subjects who tried to recall a list in the same mood as that in which they learned it could remember more of the words than subjects who tried to recall the list they had learned while in the other mood.

Bower also had subjects keep daily records of the emotional events in their lives. Later, he hypnotized them and asked them to recall the incidents they had recorded. Bower found that subjects who were placed in a sad mood recalled more unpleasant events in their daily lives than subjects who were hypnotized to be in a happy mood. Also, subjects recalled more unpleasant events from their childhood when they were in a sad mood than they recalled happy events when in a happy mood.

One explanation for this mood-dependent recall offered by Bower is that mood serves as a cue for retrieving information. When a memory is stored, it is associated with a specific emotion as well as with specific actions or people. The emotional state later functions as a marker in our memory of the specific event. When we are in the same mood, we are more likely to be able to find the memory thus marked.

There are some practical implications of Bower's research. First, if you want to maximize your recall of material, one way to do so is to recall the material in a circumstance or emotional context similar to the one in which the material was learned. For example, if you match a mood of tension while studying for an exam with a tense mood while taking an exam, you can expect to do better in recalling the studied material. Often, students are relaxed while studying for an exam, but anxious while taking it—a bad match for recall, according to Bower.

Improving Memory

Techniques for improving memory are based on efficient organization of the things you learn and on chunking information into easily handled packages. Meaningfulness, association, lack of interference, and degree of original learning all influence your ability to retrieve data from memory.

The more meaningful something is, the easier it will be to remember. For example, you would be more likely to remember the six letters DFIRNE if they were arranged to form the word FRIEND. Similarly, you remember things more vividly if you associate them with things already stored in memory or with a strong emotional experience. As pointed out earlier, the more categories a memory is indexed under, the more accessible it is. If an input is analyzed and indexed under many categories, each association can serve as a trigger for the memory. If you associate the new information with strong sounds, smells, tastes, textures, and so on, any of these stimuli could trigger the memory. The more senses you use when

PSYCHOLOGY UPDATE

SQ3R. "SQ3R" is an effective study method that can be applied to textbooks. It involves five steps. Step one is to *Survey*. When beginning a chapter, read through the section headings quickly to see what is going to be covered. Next comes *Question*. Change each section heading into a question. This helps you keep in mind what is to be learned. For example, the title of the adjacent section in this book is "Improving Memory." You might, therefore, pose the question, "How can memory be improved?" Step three is to *Read* the chapter. As you do, try to answer the questions you posed. In step four, *Recite*, either write brief notes covering the highlights of the reading or recite the main points out loud. Finally, *Review* the main points by asking the questions again and then writing or reciting the answers. By the time you finish doing all four steps, you should have learned much about the text, partly because, by using the SQ3R method, you have actively thought about the material.

trying to memorize something, the more likely it is that you will be able to retrieve it. This is a key to improving your memory.

For similar reasons, a good way to protect a memory from interference is to *overlearn* it—to keep on rehearsing it even after you think you know it well. Another way to prevent interference while learning new material is to avoid studying similar material together. Instead of studying history right after political science, study biology in between. Still another method is to space out your learning. Trying to absorb large amounts of information at one sitting results in a great deal of interference. It is far more effective to study a little at a time.

Mnemonic Devices.   **Mnemonic devices** are techniques for using associations to memorize information. The ancient Greeks memorized speeches by mentally walking around their homes or neighborhoods and "placing" each line of a speech in a different spot. Once they made the associations, they could recall the speech by mentally retracing their steps and "picking up" each line. A more familiar mnemonic device is the rhyme we use to recall the number of days in each month ("Thirty days has September"). Another is the phrase "Every Good Boy Does Fine," in which the first letters of the words are the same as the names of the musical notes on the lines of a staff (E, G, B, D, and F); the notes between the lines spell FACE.

Figure 3.9
Here is a mnemonic device for remembering that Picasso (which sounds like "pickax") was a Cubist. Often, the sillier the mental picture, the better it is for retrieving the information you have trouble remembering.

Another useful mnemonic device is to form mental pictures containing the information you want to remember—the sillier the better. Suppose you have trouble remembering the authors and titles of books, or which artists belong to which schools of painting. To plant the fact in your mind that John Updike wrote *Rabbit, Run*, you might picture a RABBIT RUNning UP a DIKE. To remember that Picasso was a Cubist, picture someone attacking a giant CUBE with a PICKAX (which sounds like Picasso) (Lorayne and Lucas, 1974: 166–169) (Figure 3.9).

Mnemonic devices are not magical. Indeed, they involve extra work—making up words, stories, and so on. But the very effort of trying to do this may help you to remember things.

CENTRAL PROCESSING OF INFORMATION

If storage and retrieval were the only processes we used to handle information, human beings would be little more than glorified cameras and projectors. But, in fact, we are capable of doing things with information that make the most complex computers seem simple by comparison. These processes—thinking and problem solving—are most impressive when they show originality or creativity.

Thinking

Thinking may be viewed as changing and reorganizing the information stored in memory in order to create new information. By thinking, humans are able to put together any combination of words from memory and create sentences never devised before—such as this one.

Units of Thought.   The processes of thought depend on several devices or units of thought: images, symbols, concepts, and rules.

The most primitive unit of thought is an **image,** a mental representation of a specific event or object. The representation is not usually an exact copy; rather, it contains only the highlights of the original. For example, if an adult tries to visualize a grandmother who died when he was seven, he would probably remember only a few details—perhaps the color of her hair or a piece of jewelry that she wore.

A more abstract unit of thought is a **symbol,** a sound or design that represents an object or quality. The most common symbols in thinking are words: every word is a symbol that stands for something other than itself. An image represents a specific sight or sound, but a symbol may have a number of meanings. The fact that symbols differ from the things they represent enables us to think about things that are not present, to range over the past and future, to imagine things and situations that never were or will be. Numbers, letters, and punctuation marks are all familiar symbols of ideas that have no concrete existence.

When a symbol is used as a label for a class of objects or events with certain common attributes, or for the attributes themselves, it is called a

Figure 3.10
This problem was devised by psychologist Edward De Bono, who believes that conventional directed thinking is insufficient for solving new and unusual problems. His approach to problem-solving requires use of nondirected thinking in order to generate new ways of looking at the problem situation. The answer to this problem is provided in Figure 3.15.

An old money-lender offered to cancel a merchant's debt and keep him from going to prison if the merchant would give the money-lender his lovely daughter. Horrified yet desperate, the merchant and his daughter agreed to let Providence decide. The money-lender said he would put a black pebble and a white pebble in a bag and the girl would draw one. The white pebble would cancel the debt and leave her free. The black one would make her the money-lender's, although the debt would be canceled. If she refused to pick, her father would go to prison. From the pebble-strewn path they were standing on, the money-lender picked two pebbles and quickly put them in the bag, but the girl saw he had picked up two black ones. What would you have done if you were the girl?

concept. "Animals," "music," "liquid," and "beautiful people" are examples of concepts based on the common attributes of the objects and experiences belonging to each category. Thus the concept "animal" separates a group of organisms from such things as automobiles, carrots, and Roquefort cheese. Concepts enable us to chunk large amounts of information. We do not have to treat every new piece of information as unique since we already know something about the class of objects or experiences to which the new item belongs.

The fourth and most complex unit of thought is a **rule,** a statement of a relation between concepts. The following are examples of rules: a person cannot be in two places at the same time; mass remains constant despite changes in appearance.

Images, symbols, concepts, and rules are the building blocks of mental activity. They provide an economical and efficient way for people to represent reality, to manipulate and reorganize it, and to devise new ways of acting. A person can think about pursuing several different careers, weigh their pros and cons, and decide which to pursue without having to try them all.

Kinds of Thinking.   People think in two distinct ways. The first, called **directed thinking,** is a systematic and logical attempt to reach a specific goal, such as the solution of a problem. This kind of thinking depends heavily on symbols, concepts, and rules. The other type, called **nondirected thinking,** consists of a free flow of thoughts through the mind, with no particular goal or plan, and depends more on images (Figure 3.10).

Nondirected thinking is usually rich with imagery and feelings. Daydreams, fantasies, and reveries are typical examples. People often engage in nondirected thought when they are relaxing or trying to escape from boredom or worry. This kind of thinking may provide unexpected insights into one's goals and beliefs. Scientists and artists say that some of their best ideas emerge from drifting thoughts that occur when they have set aside a problem for the moment.

In contrast, directed thinking is deliberate and purposeful. It is through directed thinking that we solve problems, formulate and follow rules, and set, work toward, and achieve goals.

Problem Solving

One of the main functions of directed thinking is to solve problems—to bridge the gap, mentally, between a present situation and a desired goal. The gap may be between hunger and food, a column of figures and a total, lack of money and bills to pay, or cancer and a cure. In all these examples, getting from the problem to the solution requires some directed thinking.

Strategies. Problem solving depends on the use of strategies, or specific methods for approaching problems. One strategy is to break down a complex problem into a number of smaller, more easily solved problems. For example, it is the end of the semester and your life is falling apart. You don't even have time to tie your shoelaces. You solve the problem by breaking it down into small pieces: studying for a science exam; finishing that overdue paper; canceling your dinner date; scheduling regular study breaks to maintain what's left of your sanity; and so on.

For some problems, you may work backward from the goal you have set. Mystery writers often use this method: They decide how to end the story ("who did it") and then devise a plot leading to this conclusion.

Another problem may require you to examine various ways of reaching a desired goal. Suppose a woman needs to be in Chicago by 11:00 A.M. on July 7 for a business conference. She checks train departures and arrivals, airline schedules, and car-rental companies. The only train to Chicago that morning arrives at 5:00 A.M. (too early), and the first plane arrives at 11:30 A.M. (too late). So she decides to rent a car and drive.

To determine which strategy to use in a particular situation, most of us analyze the problem to see if it resembles a situation we have experienced in the past. A strategy that worked in the past is likely to work again. The more unusual the problem, the more difficult it is to devise a strategy for dealing with it.

Set. There are times when certain useful strategies become cemented into the problem-solving process. When a particular strategy becomes a habit, it is called a **set**—you are "set" to treat problems in a certain way. For example, a chess player may always attempt to control the four center

Figure 3.11
Given the materials pictured here, how would you go about mounting the candle vertically on a wooden wall in such a way that it can be lit? This problem was formulated by Carl Duncker to test how well people are able to overcome functional fixedness. The solution is presented in Figure 3.15.

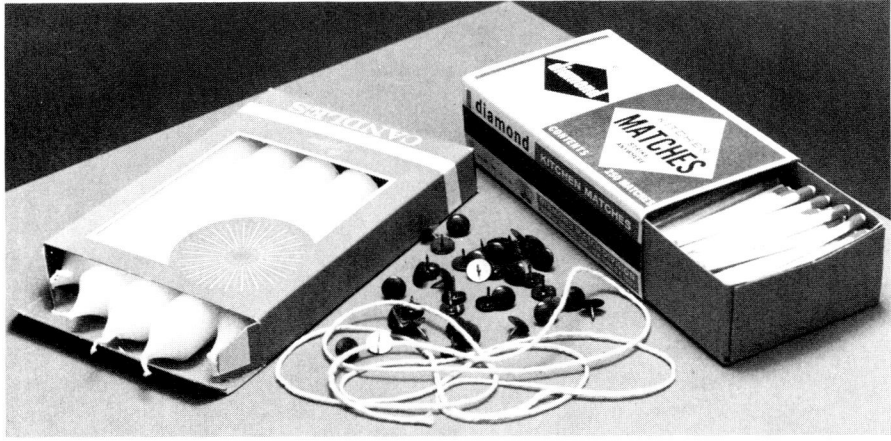

squares of the chessboard. Whenever her opponent attacks, she responds by looking for ways to regain control of those four squares. She has a "set" for this strategy. If this set helps her to win, fine. Sometimes, however, a set interferes with problem solving, and then it is called *rigidity*. You probably know the old riddle, "What is black, white, and read all over? A newspaper." When you say the riddle, the word "read" sounds like "red," which is why some people cannot guess the answer. "Read" is heard as part of the black and white set—it is interpreted as being a color. If you asked, "What is read by people every day and is black and white?" the correct answer would be obvious. And boring.

One form of set that can interfere with problem solving is functional fixedness—the inability to imagine new functions for familiar objects. In experiments on functional fixedness, people are asked to solve a problem that requires them to use a familiar object in an unfamiliar way (Duncker, 1945). Because they are set to use the object in the usual way, people tend to pay attention only to the features of the object that relate to its everyday use (see Figure 3.11). They respond in a rigid way.

Another type of rigidity occurs when a person makes a wrong assumption about a problem. In Figure 3.12, for example, the problem is to connect the dots with four straight lines without lifting your pencil. Most people have trouble solving this puzzle because they falsely assume that they must stay within the area of the dots.

People trying to solve the kind of problem shown in Figure 3.13 experience a third kind of rigidity. Most people look for direct methods of solving problems and do not see solutions that require several intermediate steps.

Rigidity can be overcome if the person realizes that his or her strategy is not working and looks for other ways to approach the problem. The more familiar the situation, the more difficult this will be. Rigidity is less likely to occur with unusual problems.

Figure 3.12
Connect these dots with four straight lines without lifting your pencil. The solution appears in Figure 3.15.

Creativity

Creativity is the ability to use information in such a way that the result is somehow new, original, and meaningful. All problem solving requires

Figure 3.13
How would you go about solving this problem: Eight soldiers need to cross a river, but the only way to cross is in a small boat in which two children are playing. The boat can carry at most two children or one soldier. How do the soldiers get across? You'll find the answer in Figure 3.15.

some creativity. Certain ways of solving problems, however, are simply more brilliant or beautiful or efficient than others. Psychologists do not know exactly why some people are able to think more creatively than others, although they have identified some of the characteristics of creative thinking—including flexibility and the ability to recombine elements to achieve insight.

Flexibility.   Flexibility is, quite simply, the ability to overcome rigidity. Psychologists have devised a number of ingenious tests to measure flexibility. One test is shown in Figure 3.14. The individual is asked to name a word that the three words in each row have in common. To do this, a person must be able to think of many different aspects of each of these words. Another test of flexibility is to ask people how many uses they can imagine for a single object, such as a brick or a paper clip. The more uses a person can devise, the more flexible he or she is said to be. Whether such tests actually measure creativity is debatable. Nevertheless, it is obvious that inflexible, rigid thinking leads to unoriginal solutions, or no solutions at all.

Recombination.   When the elements of a problem are familiar but the required solution is not, it may be achieved by **recombination,** a new mental rearrangement of the elements. In football and basketball, for example, there are no new moves—only recombinations of old ones. Such recombination seems to be a vital part of creativity. Many creative people say that no truly great poem, no original invention, has ever been produced by someone who has not spent years studying his or her subject. The creative person is able to take the information that he or she and others have compiled and put it together in a totally new way. The brilliant philosopher and mathematician Sir Isaac Newton, who discovered the laws of motion, once said, "If I have seen further, it is by standing on the shoulders

Figure 3.14
A test devised to measure flexibility in thinking. The task is to name a single word that all three words on a line have in common. For example, the answer to the first item is "foot." (The other answers are given in Figure 3.15.)

1.	stool	powder	ball
2.	blue	cake	cottage
3.	man	wheel	high
4.	motion	poke	down
5.	line	birthday	surprise
6.	wood	liquor	luck
7.	house	village	golf
8.	card	knee	rope
9.	news	doll	tiger
10.	painting	bowl	nail
11.	weight	wave	house
12.	made	cuff	left
13.	key	wall	precious
14.	bull	tired	hot
15.	knife	up	hi
16.	handle	hole	police
17.	plan	show	walker
18.	hop	side	pet
19.	bell	tender	iron
20.	spelling	line	busy

of giants." In other words, he was able to recombine the discoveries of the great scientists who had preceded him to uncover new and more far-reaching truths.

Another result of brilliant recombination is Samuel Taylor Coleridge's unusual poem "Kubla Khan." Scholars have shown that almost every word and phrase came directly from Coleridge's past readings and personal experiences. Coleridge recombined these elements during a period of non-

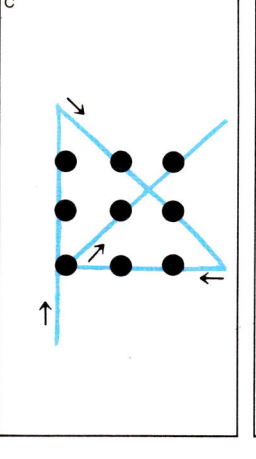

c

1.	foot	11.	light
2.	cheese	12.	hand
3.	chair	13.	stone
4.	slow	14.	dog
5.	party	15.	jack
6.	hard	16.	man
7.	green	17.	floor
8.	trick	18.	car
9.	paper	19.	bar
10.	finger	20.	bee

Figure 3.15
Solutions to the problems presented in the chapter. Note that in each case the solution requires breaking certain habits of thought. (a) In the De Bono money-lender problem, it is difficult to imagine that control of the situation can be taken out of the hands of the powerful money-lender. (b) Solving the Duncker candle problem requires one to look at the matchbox and candle box as more than containers to be discarded. The presence of the useless piece of string usually serves to confuse problem solvers. (c) As the text points out, the solution to this problem is blocked if the person avoids going beyond the boundaries of the dots. (d) The answers to the test of flexibility require that the individual ignore common associations and look for unusual ones. (e) The first steps in solution of the river problem. Once the solver discovers the first step in the problem's solution, he or she may become further bogged down if he doesn't realize the lengthy cyclical nature of the process required.

Figure 3.16
Most of us have experienced insight or the "aha" experience at some time. Can you recall the most recent time you experienced frustration, abandoned the task for a while, and suddenly the solution seemed to come out of nowhere?

directed thinking—drug-induced sleep. He awoke with the entire poem in his mind, but was only able to commit part of it to paper before he was interrupted by a knock at his door. When·Coleridge went back to his poem, it had vanished from his mind.

Insight.   The sudden emergence of a solution by recombination of elements is called **insight**. Insight usually occurs when problems have proved resistant to all problem-solving efforts and strategies. The scientist or artist reaches a point of high frustration and temporarily abandons the task. But the recombination process seems to continue on an unconscious level. When the person is absorbed in some other activity, the answer seems to appear out of nowhere. This sudden insight has appropriately been called the "aha" experience.

Certain animals appear to experience this same cycle of frustration, temporary diversion (during which time the problem "incubates"), and then sudden insight. For example, Wolfgang Köhler (1925) placed a chimpanzee in a cage where a cluster of bananas was hung out of its reach. Also in the cage were a number of wooden boxes. At first the chimpanzee tried various unsuccessful ways of getting at the fruit. Finally it sat down, apparently giving up, and simply stared straight ahead for a while. Then suddenly it jumped up, piled three boxes on top of one another, climbed to the top of the pile, and grabbed the bananas.

CHAPTER REVIEW

KEY TERMS

- central processing
- chunking
- concept
- confabulation
- creativity
- directed thinking
- eidetic memory
- feature extraction
- image
- input

- insight
- long-term memory
- memory
- mnemonic devices
- nondirected thinking
- output
- proactive interference
- recall
- recognition
- recombination

- repression
- retrieval
- retroactive interference
- rule
- selective attention
- sensory storage
- set
- short-term memory
- symbol

SUMMARY

1. Information processing involves three steps: input from the senses, central processing (memory, thought), and output (ideas or actions).

2. Two processes that help narrow down inputs are selective attention and feature extraction. Selective attention is the ability to pick and choose among various incoming channels, focusing on some and ignoring others. Channels are chosen when they help satisfy needs, are unusual, or relate to one's interests. Feature extraction is the ability to respond to specific characteristics of a given input and to ignore others.

3. The shortest form of memory is sensory storage, which lasts less than a second. Next is short-term memory, which retains information for about twenty seconds. Items stored in short-term memory are quickly forgotten if they are not rehearsed or transferred to long-term memory.

4. Long-term memory contains information that has some significance. One theory is that memory is due to changes in the form of protein molecules in the brain. Another theory focuses on chemical-electrical changes in the brain.

5. Retrieval is essential if memory is to be useful. Retrieval takes two forms: recognition and recall. Recall is an active reconstructive process that may give rise to such errors as confabulation, in which memories are reconstructed in-

correctly. Recognition simply means deciding whether you've seen or heard something before.

6. Forgetting may be caused by decay, interference, or repression. Decay is the fading away of a memory. Interference occurs when new or old information blocks or erases the memory of a related piece of information. In repression, access to information has been blocked.

7. Information is stored better and is more easily retrieved when (a) it is organized into meaningful chunks; (b) it has many paths, or associations, leading to it; and (c) it has been overlearned.

8. Thinking is the process of reorganizing and rearranging the information in memory to produce new information or ideas. The units of thought are images, symbols, concepts, and rules.

9. Thinking may be directed or nondirected. Directed thinking is deliberate and purposeful, as in problem solving and decision making. Nondirected thinking is looser and more passive, as in daydreaming and reverie.

10. Problem solving is bridging the gap between a present situation and a desired goal by means of specific strategies. When strategies become habits, they can lead to failure rather than success. This difficulty is called rigidity.

11. Creativity is the ability to manipulate information to produce something new, original, and meaningful. Flexibility and the ability to re- combine elements to achieve insight seem to be important aspects of creativity. Insight often occurs after a person has abandoned a task.

REVIEW QUESTIONS

1. Describe the three steps involved in information processing.

2. What are the two processes that help people narrow sensory inputs?

3. What inputs are more important than others?

4. Name the three types of memory. How long is information retained in each type?

5. List two strategies for expanding the limits of short-term memory.

6. What are the two theories that explain the activities in the brain when something is stored in long-term memory?

7. Identify the two types of interference that block memory.

8. What factors influence a person's ability to retrieve data from memory?

9. List the four units of thought in order of increasing complexity.

10. Explain how a problem-solving strategy can interfere with problem solving.

11. What are three characteristics of creative thinking?

ACTIVITIES

1. Try this simple learning task on your friends. Give them a list of numbers to memorize: 6, 9, 8, 11, 10, 13, 12, 15, 14, 17, 16. Tell some of them simply to memorize the material. Tell others that there is an organizational principle behind the sequence that can be used to help memorize the list. In the sequence above, the principle is "plus 3, minus 1."

2. Try to remember what you were doing on your last birthday. As you probe your memory, verbalize the mental steps you are going through. What does this exercise tell you about your thought processes?

3. Solve this problem. A sloppy man has twenty blue socks and twenty brown ones in his drawer. If he reaches for a pair of socks in the dark, how many must he pull out to be sure he has a matched pair? How long did it take you to solve the problem? Can you identify what steps you went through in your mind in order to solve it?

4. Relax and engage in nondirected thinking—let your thoughts wander. Things may come into your mind that you thought you had forgotten or that you didn't know you knew. Or reflect on a recent dream. Where might the various images have come from? You may begin to see the vast amount of information you have stored in your brain.

5. You and your friends can test the way your memories are organized by playing a popular game called Categories. Make a grid with five columns and five rows, and put a category, such as fruits or furniture, at the top of each column. Now pick five random letters, and assign one to each row. Give yourself five minutes to think of an item starting with each letter for each category and fill in the boxes in the grid. (Example: If your letters are A, G, P, O, and B, your entries under "fruit" might be apple, grape, peach, orange, and banana.)

UNIT 2

The Workings of Mind and Body

CHAPTER 4
Body and Behavior

CHAPTER 5
Sensation and Perception

CHAPTER 6
Motivation and Emotion

CHAPTER 7
Altered States of Consciousness

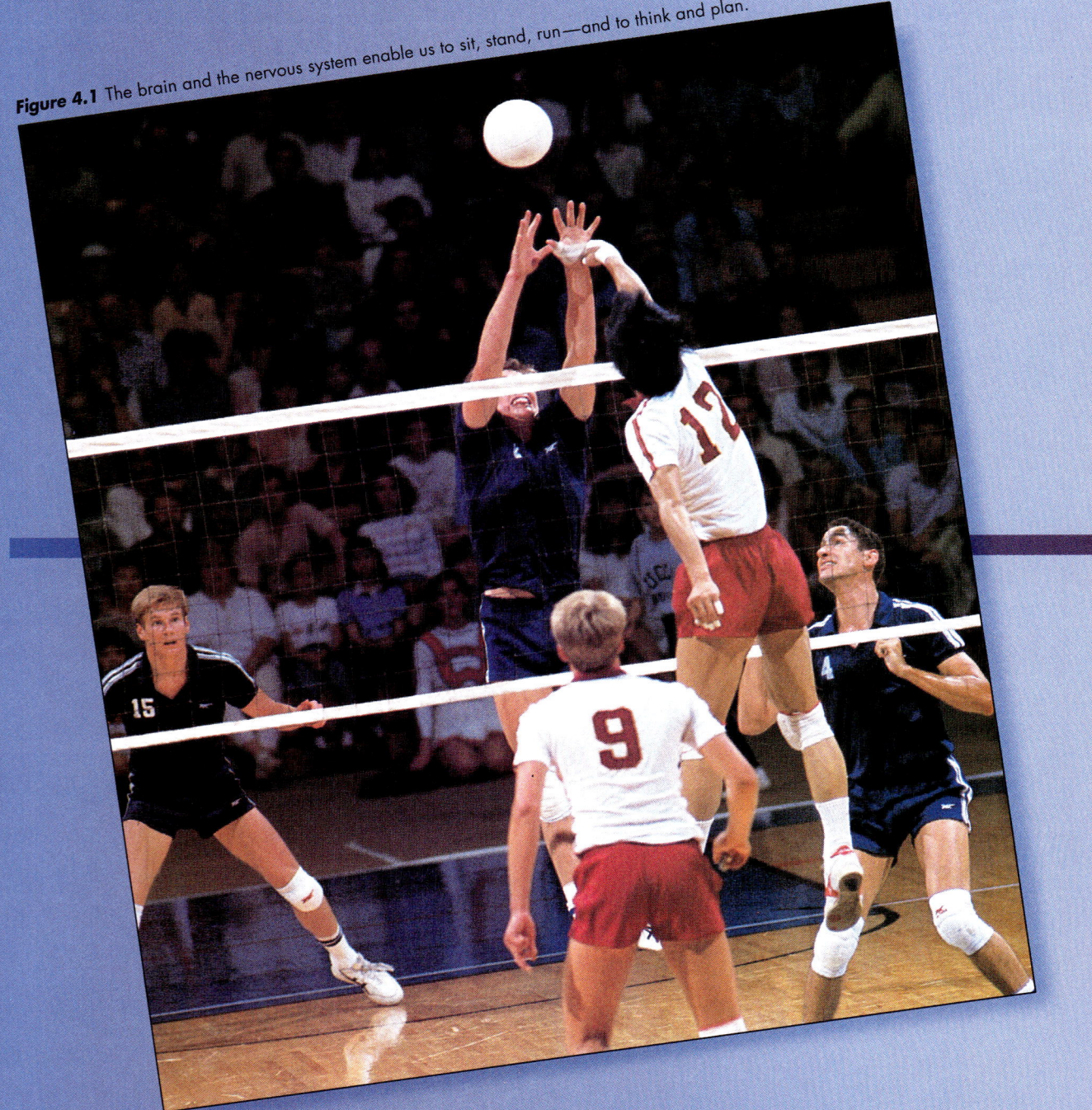

Figure 4.1 The brain and the nervous system enable us to sit, stand, run—and to think and plan.

Objectives: *After studying this chapter, you should be able to*
- identify the parts of the nervous system and explain their function.
- describe the structures of the human brain and discuss methods of studying the brain.
- describe the endocrine system and explain its function.
- identify and describe the disciplines of ethology and sociobiology.
- summarize research on the effects of heredity and environment on human behavior.

Body and Behavior

You are your brain. Your pleasant personality, your wry sense of humor, and your favorite color are all coded in the 13 billion nerve cells of your brain. Ordinarily, we pay no attention to our biological nature. But your reliance on the physical properties of the nervous system would become painfully obvious if you were involved in a car accident that damaged your brain: your personality, your memories, and even your sense of humor might be affected.

The Greek physician Hippocrates was the first to notice that head injuries often disturbed thought and behavior. In the twenty-five centuries since his observations, many attempts have been made to explain how this mass of soggy, gray tissue could create the theory of relativity, the Sistine Chapel ceiling, and a trade treaty between two nations. But the mind remains a mystery to itself.

Some of the most exciting developments in psychology are going on in the brain sciences, and this chapter will help you to understand the newspaper and magazine articles reporting new discoveries that you will probably be reading for the next twenty-five years. In addition to describing the organization of the nervous system, we will discuss studies of lower animals and the possible role of genes in complex human behavior.

The Nervous System
How the Nervous System Works • The Hemispheres of the Brain

How Psychologists Study the Brain
Recording • Stimulation • Lesions • Using Psychology: Psychosurgery

The Endocrine System

The Relationship Between Humans and Animals
The Evolution of Behavior • Ethology • Sociobiology

Heredity and Environment

THE NERVOUS SYSTEM

In some ways, the nervous system is like the telephone system in a city. Messages are constantly traveling back and forth. As in a telephone system, the messages are basically electrical. They travel along prelaid cables,

Once a neuron begins to "fire," it can be stopped if the original stimulation is weak.

Fiction. Transmission between neurons or nerve cells occurs when the cells are stimulated past a minimum point and emit a signal. The neuron is said to "fire." The firing of neurons occurs in line with the all-or-none principle, which states that when a neuron fires it does so at full strength. If a neuron is not stimulated past the minimum level, it does not fire at all.

linked with one another by relays and switchboards. In the body, the cables are **nerve fibers.** The relays are **synapses,** the gaps that occur between individual nerve cells. The switchboards are special cells that are found along the lines of communication (called *interneurons*) and the networks of nerve cells found in the brain and spinal cord. One major difference is that a telephone system simply conveys messages, while the nervous system actively helps to run the body.

The brain monitors what is happening inside and outside the body by receiving messages from **receptors**—cells whose function is to gather information. The brain sifts through these messages, combines them, and sends out orders to the **effectors**—cells that work the muscles and internal glands and organs. For example, receptors in your eye may send a message to the brain such as "Round object. Size increasing. Distance decreasing rapidly." Your brain instantly connects this image with information from memory to identify this object as a baseball. Almost simultaneously your brain orders the effectors in your arms to position themselves so you don't get beaned in right field.

How the Nervous System Works

Messages to and from the brain travel along the nerves, which are strings of long, thin cells called **neurons** (see Figure 4.2). Chemical-electrical signals travel down the neurons much as flame travels along a firecracker fuse. The main difference is that the neuron can "burn" over and over

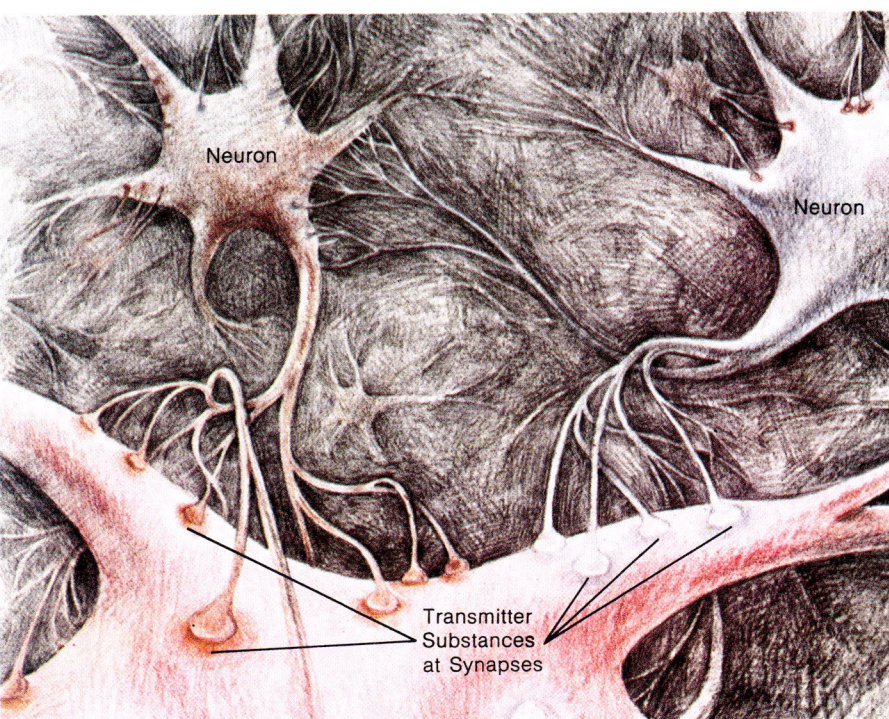

Figure 4.2
A few of the billions of neurons in the human body, shown tens of thousands of times bigger than they really are. Neurons connect with each other at the synapses, where chemical substances cross the gap from one nerve cell to another. In that way, messages can travel through the body.

again, hundreds of times a minute.

Each neuron is long and thin, with branching or brushlike extensions (Figure 4.2). One end receives the message and the other, which can be as much as three feet long, transmits the electro-chemical impulse to the next neuron. The next neuron picks up chemicals called **neurotransmitters** from across the synapse (gap). The neurotransmitters can excite the next neuron or stop it from transmitting (inhibition). The neurotransmitters are like the valves in a water system that allow flow in only one direction.

The intensity of activity in each neuron depends on how many other neurons are acting on it. Each individual neuron is either ON or OFF, depending on whether the majority of neurons acting on it are exciting it or inhibiting it. The actual destination of nerve impulses produced by an excited neuron, as they travel from one neuron to another, is limited by what tract in the nervous system they are on. Ascending tracts carry sensory impulses to the brain; descending tracts carry motor impulses from the brain.

Some of the actions that your body takes in response to impulses from the nerves are voluntary acts, such as lifting your hand to turn a page (which actually involves many impulses to many muscles). Others are involuntary acts, such as changes in the heartbeat, in the blood pressure, or in the size of the pupils. The term **somatic nervous system** refers to the part of the nervous system that controls voluntary activities. The term **autonomic nervous system** refers to the part of the nervous system that controls involuntary activities—those that ordinarily occur "automatically," such as heartbeat, stomach activity, and so on.

The autonomic nervous system itself has two parts: *sympathetic* and *parasympathetic*. The **sympathetic nervous system** prepares the body for dealing with emergencies or strenuous activity. It speeds up the heart to hasten the supply of oxygen and nutrients to body tissues. It constricts some arteries and relaxes others so that blood flows to the muscles, where it is most needed in emergencies and strenuous activity. It increases the blood pressure and suspends some activities, such as digestion. In contrast, the **parasympathetic nervous system** works to conserve energy and to enhance the body's ability to recover from strenuous activity. It reduces the heart rate and blood pressure and helps bring the body back to normal.

All of this takes place automatically. Receptors are constantly receiving messages (hunger, the need to swallow or cough) that alert the autonomic nervous system, via the *thalamus* in the brain, to carry out routine activities. Imagine how difficult it would be if you had no autonomic nervous system and had to think about it every time your body needed to digest a sandwich or perspire.

Structurally, the nervous system is divided into two parts (Figure 4.3): the brain and **spinal cord** (the **central nervous system (CNS)**); and smaller branches of nerves that reach the other parts of the body (the **peripheral nervous system (PNS)**). More than three-fourths of the body's neurons are in the brain, which weighs about 3 pounds. The nerves of the peripheral system that branch out from the spinal column are about as thick as a pencil. Those in the extremities, such as the fingertips, are invisibly small. All parts of the nervous system are protected in some way: the brain by

Figure 4.3
The central nervous system (CNS) and the peripheral nervous system (PNS) in the human body.

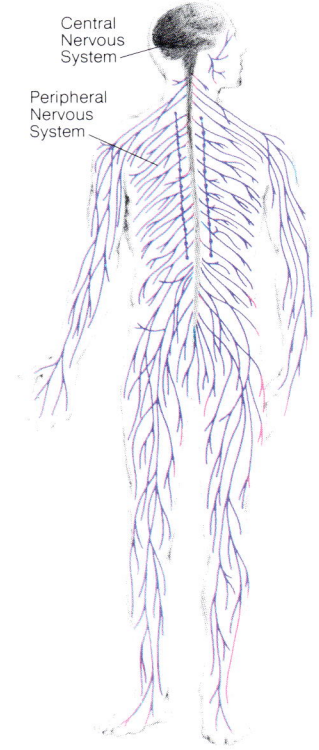

Central Nervous System

Peripheral Nervous System

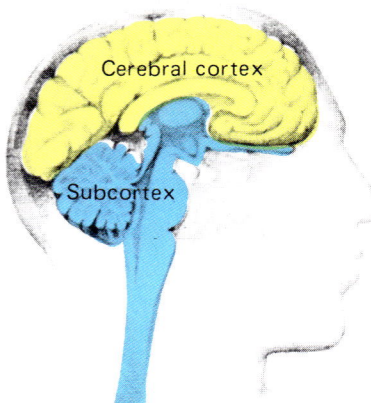

Figure 4.4
A cross section of the human brain, showing the subcortex, or "old brain," and the cerebral cortex, or "new brain."

the skull and several layers of sheathing; the spinal cord by the vertebrae; and the peripheral nerves by layers of sheathing. The bony protection of the spinal cord is vital. An injury to the spinal cord could prevent the transmittal of messages from the brain to the muscles, and could result in paralysis.

The spinal cord extends into the brain through a widening called the *brainstem.* Generally, this part of the brain and the other physically "lower" sections of the brain control "lower" functions (such as sleeping, chewing, and salivation) that we share with all other animals. The correct name for this part of the brain is the **subcortex.** It is often referred to as the "old brain" because it is thought to have evolved millions of years ago in our prehuman ancestors. At the back and bottom of the old brain is the **cerebellum.** This structure looks somewhat like a miniature version of the brain as a whole. One of its main functions is to control posture and balance.

The "higher" thinking processes are housed in the "new brain." The outer layer of the new brain consists of the **cerebral cortex.** The inner layer is the **cerebrum.** The cerebral cortex and cerebrum surround the subcortex as a halved peach surrounds the pit (Figure 4.4). The cerebral cortex gives you the ability to learn and store complex and abstract information, and to project your thinking into the future. It is your cerebral cortex that allows you to see, read, and understand this sentence. The

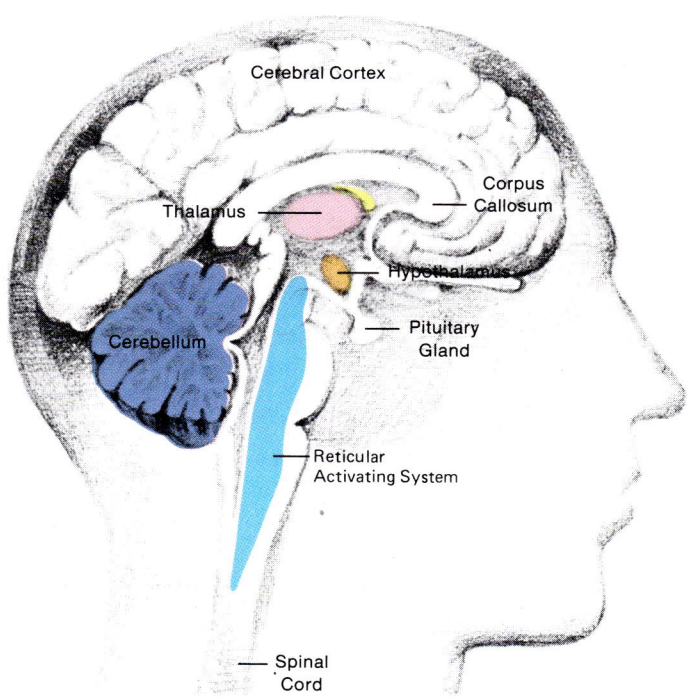

Figure 4.5
The structures of the subcortex. (This illustration shows the brain as it would appear if it were sliced exactly in half from front to back.)

cortex, or bark, of the cerebrum is the site of most conscious thinking processes, yet it is less than a half-inch thick.

Precisely which areas of the cerebral cortex control which activities is not completely known, but information is being gathered and brain maps are being made. To help them describe the location of certain activities, scientists refer to sites on different **lobes,** or regions, of the brain (Figure 4.6). The information that is available is based on observations of people and laboratory animals with brain or nerve damage. Scientists have also gathered information by stimulating parts of the brain during surgery (this is painless), and by conducting tests that measure the activity in different areas of the brain.

Some areas of the cortex receive information from the skin senses and from muscles. The amount of brain tissue connected to any given body part is based on the sensitivity of that area, not on its size (Figure 4.7). For example, the highly developed sense of touch in the hand involves a much larger brain area than that of the relatively insensitive calves. The part of the cortex that receives information is called the **somatosensory cortex.** The **motor cortex** sends information to control body movement. The motor cortex is also divided according to need: the more sophisticated the movements have to be (such as those used in speaking), the bigger the brain area involved. The *association areas* mediate between the other two and do the actual synthesizing of information.

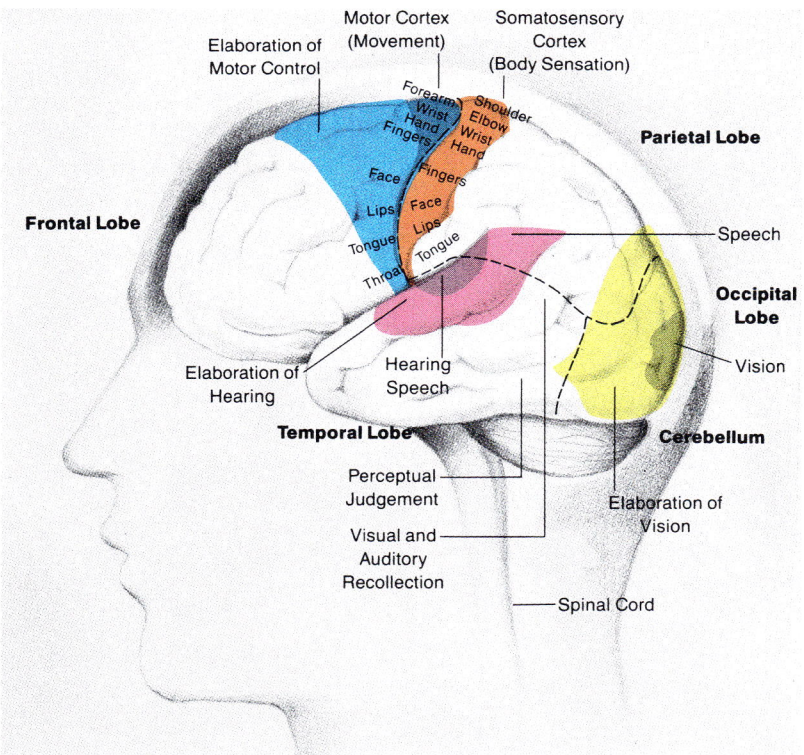

Figure 4.6
An external view of the brain from the side. Most of the areas exposed here are parts of the "new" brain. The functions of the cerebral cortex are not fully understood; areas whose behavioral importance is known are indicated.

Figure 4.7
Two views of the same half of the brain, sliced in half between the parietal and frontal lobes (along the groove that separates the somatosensory cortex from the motor cortex). The areas of greatest sensitivity (left) and motor control (right) are listed. The funny little men depict how the body would look if areas of greatest sensitivity and motor control were proportionate in the body to their size in the brain.

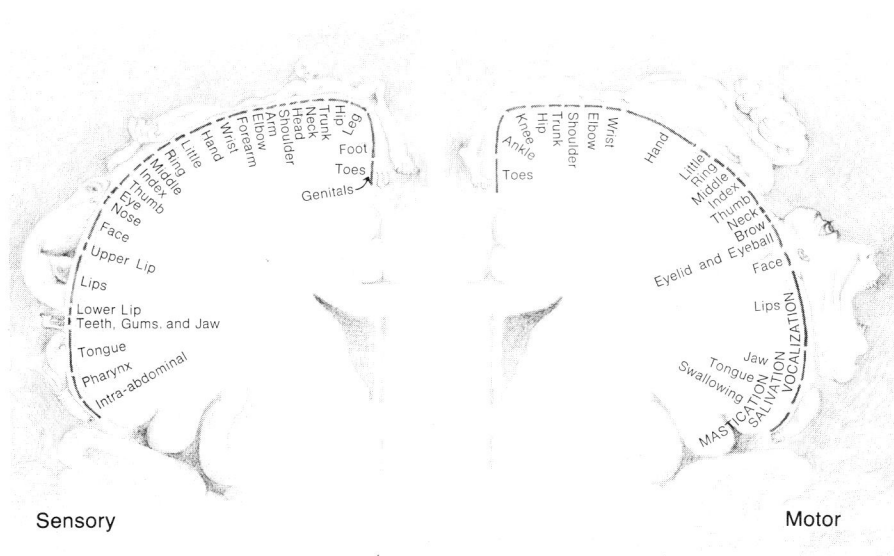

Sensory   Motor

Figure 4.8
This drawing was adapted from one of the sketches made by the doctor who attended Phineas Gage. It shows the path taken by the iron stake that was propelled through Gage's skull.

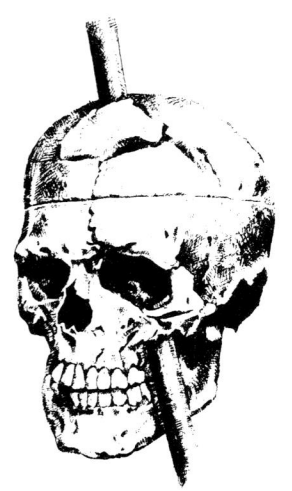

The brain processes a vast number of incoming and outgoing messages every second, but not all of them reach the cerebral cortex. Some parts of the lower brain (such as the **reticular activating system** and the **thalamus**) filter out all but the most important messages. Exactly how the parts of the brain process so much information is being studied. It seems that patterns of stimuli and appropriate responses are stored in the memory so that when a pattern of incoming impulses is screened by the lower parts of the brain, they are compared to other, previous patterns. This is an ongoing process.

The brain's ability to process many experiences at once make it so superior to the most sophisticated computer that scientists can never hope to match its capabilities. They are still trying to determine the different functions and interactions of the parts of the brain. Some studies suggest that the **frontal lobes** control creativity and personality: they enable people to be witty, sensitive, or easygoing. Evidence for this theory is provided by the case of Phineas Gage. A quarryman, he was injured in an explosion in the mid-1800s. The force of the blast drove an iron stake through Gage's head, damaging the frontal lobes (Figure 4.8). Remarkably, Gage survived and was back at work in a few months. The accident did not impair his bodily functions or his memory or skills. However, Gage's personality changed dramatically. This once trustworthy and dependable man became childish, fitful, impatient, and capricious. Later studies of large numbers of people with similar brain damage suggest that planning future action, emotional control, and the ability to pay attention depend on the frontal lobes.

The Hemispheres of the Brain

The cortex is divided into two hemispheres that are roughly mirror images of each other. (Each of the four lobes is present in both hemispheres.) The two hemispheres are connected by a band of nerves called the **corpus callosum,** which carries messages back and forth between the two. Each hemisphere is connected to half of the body in a crisscrossed fashion. The motor cortex of the left hemisphere of the brain controls most of the right side of the body; the right hemisphere motor cortex controls most of the left side of the body. Thus a stroke that causes damage to the right hemisphere will result in numbness or paralysis on the left side of the body. Researchers have also found a number of more subtle differences between the sides of the brain: in right-handed people, the left hemisphere controls language, while the right hemisphere is involved in spatial tasks.

Many psychologists became interested in differences between the cerebral hemispheres when "split brain" operations were tried on epileptics like Harriet Lees. For most of her life Ms. Lees's seizures were mild and could be controlled with drugs. However, at age twenty-five they began to get worse, and by thirty Lees was having as many as a dozen violent seizures a day. An epileptic seizure involves massive electrical activity that begins in one hemisphere and spreads to the other. To enable this woman to live a normal life, doctors decided to sever the corpus callosum so that seizures could not spread.

The operation was a success—Lees has not had a seizure since. But psychologists were even more interested in the potential side effects of this dramatic operation. Despite the fact that patients who had this operation now had "two separate brains," they seemed remarkably normal. Researchers went on to develop a number of ingenious techniques to try to detect subtle effects of the operation. To understand the procedures, you need to know a little about brain anatomy. For example, the left half of each eye is connected to the right hemisphere and the right half of each eye is wired to the left hemisphere. To get a message to only one hemisphere at a time, the researchers asked each split-brain patient to stare at a dot while they briefly flashed a word or a picture on one side of the dot. If the word "nut" was flashed to the right of the dot, it went to the left hemisphere. The patient could usually read it quite easily under these circumstances, because the left hemisphere controls language for most right-handed people.

But when the same word was flashed to the right hemisphere (left side of each eye), the patient was not able to repeat it. For an ordinary person, the word "nut" would quickly go from one side of the brain to the other via the corpus callosum. Since this patient's corpus callosum had been cut, however, the message could not get from the nonverbal right hemisphere to the verbal left. Even more amazing was the fact that the patient really did recognize the word: with her left hand (which is also connected to the right hemisphere), she could pick out a nut from a group of objects hidden behind a screen. But even after she correctly picked out the nut and held it in her hand, still she could not remember the word!

In another experiment, a picture of a nude woman was flashed to the right hemisphere (left side of each eye) of another split-brain patient (Figure 4.9). This woman laughed but said she saw nothing. Only her left hemisphere could speak and it did not see the nude; but the right hemisphere, which did see the nude, produced the laugh. When the woman was asked why she laughed, she acted confused and couldn't explain it.

Planning the future, controlling emotions, and paying attention seem to depend on the frontal lobes of the brain.

Figure 4.9
The presentation of a visual stimulus to a single hemisphere of a person who has undergone split-brain surgery. The patient reacts with amusement to the picture of the nude woman flashed on the left side of the screen but is unable to say why.

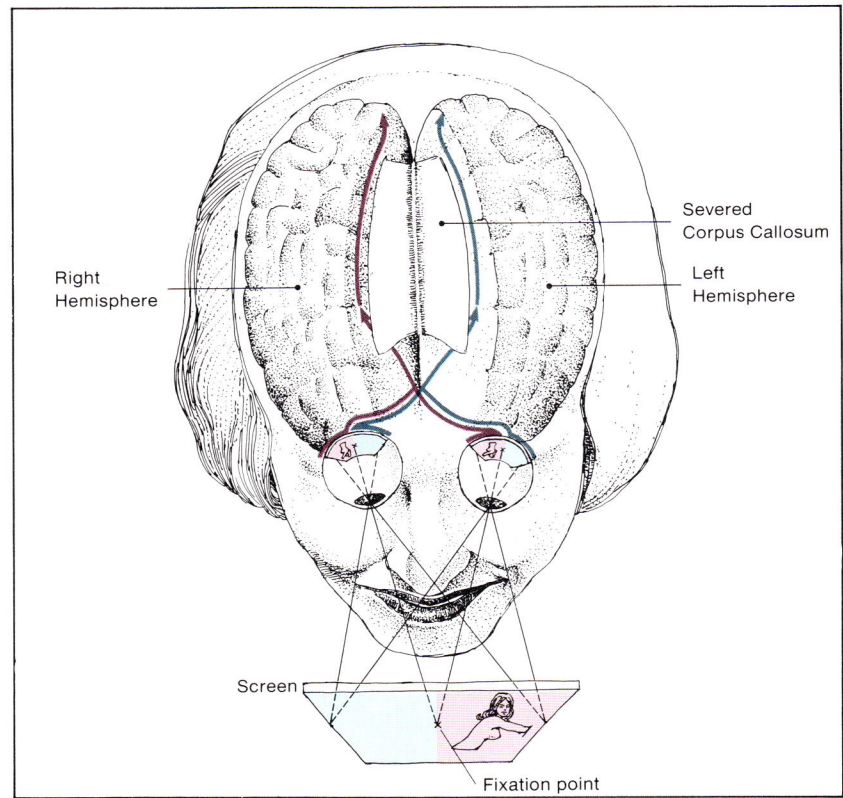

Right-handed children are genetically predisposed to develop verbal left hemispheres, but the actual specialization develops over the years. If a child suffers damage to the left hemisphere, the right hemisphere will take over the function of speech. The child may learn more slowly than other children, but he or she will learn to speak. However, almost all adults who suffer damage to the left hemisphere have extreme difficulty speaking—if they can speak at all. The effects of right-hemisphere damage are less clear, but they probably include problems with spatial abilities.

Though this specialization of labor is particularly relevant for people with brain damage, it also involves normal people. One group of studies, for example, has looked at the brain waves (or EEG—see below) of right-handed people as they perform verbal and spatial tasks. The EEG shows greater activity in the right hemisphere for spatial tasks like memorizing geometrical designs, remembering faces, or imagining an elephant in a swing. But when the same people were asked to perform verbal tasks— writing a letter in their heads, thinking of words that begin with "t," and listening to boring passages from the *Congressional Record*—their EEG showed relatively greater activity in the left hemisphere (Hassett, 1978). Even more interesting, and far easier to observe, is the fact that normal people tend to move their eyes in a certain way depending on which hemisphere they are using (see box).

Which Way Do the Eyes Move?

Did you know that the direction your eyes move when you think about a question may indicate which side of the brain you are using for the answer?

Ask a friend the following four questions, and secretly watch whether she first looks to the right or the left as she considers each:

1. Make up a sentence using the words "code" and "mathematics."
2. Picture the last automobile accident you saw. In which direction were the cars going?
3. What does the proverb "Easy come, easy go" mean?
4. Picture and describe the last time you cried.

Questions 1 and 3 are verbal, nonemotional questions; a right-handed person should use the left hemisphere to answer and, as a result, tend to look to the right. Questions 2 and 4 are spatial-emotional questions that require the right hemisphere and should, on the average, yield more eye movements to the left than the right.

For more details, see G. E. Schwartz, R. Davidson, and F. Maer, "Right Hemisphere Laterali-zation for Emotion in the Human Brain: Interactions with Cognition," *Science*, 190 (1975): 286–288.

These clear differences between the hemispheres apply primarily to right-handed people. Some left-handers have the opposite pattern of cerebral dominance—language is found in the right hemisphere. More commonly, lefties have less dramatic differences between the halves of the brain.

One by-product of all the research on cerebral dominance has been to increase interest in the phenomenon of handedness. About nine out of ten people prefer to use their right hand, and this seems to be a distinctly human characteristic with a long history. Even the people pictured in Egyptian tomb paintings usually use their right hand (Figure 4.10). Jeannine Herron (1976) has argued that left-handers are a discriminated-against minority. Teachers often try to get young children to use their right hands. The French word for left is *gauche*, which in English means clumsy or socially inept, as in "left-handed compliment." There is no scientific basis, Herron argues, for believing that right-handed is better.

About nine out of ten people are right-handed.

HOW PSYCHOLOGISTS STUDY THE BRAIN

Mapping the brain's mountains, canyons, and inner recesses has supplied scientists with fascinating information about the role of the brain in behavior. Psychologists who do this kind of research are called physiological

Figure 4.10
An Egyptian tomb painting showing people at work, using their right hands.

psychologists. Among the methods they use to explore the brain are recording, stimulation, and lesioning.

Recording

By inserting wires called **electrodes** into the brain, it is possible to detect the minute electrical changes that occur when neurons fire (Figure 4.11). The wires are connected to electronic equipment that amplifies the tiny voltages produced by the firing neurons. Even single neurons can be monitored. For example, two researchers placed tiny electrodes in the sections of cats' and monkeys' brains that receive visual information. They found that different neurons fired, depending on whether a line, an edge, or an angle was placed before the animal's eyes (Hubel and Wiesel, 1962).

The electrical activity of whole areas of the brain can be recorded with an **electroencephalograph (EEG).** Wires from the EEG machine are taped to the scalp so that millions upon millions of neurons can be monitored at the same time (Figure 4.12). Psychologists have observed that the overall electrical activity of the brain rises and falls rhythmically and that the

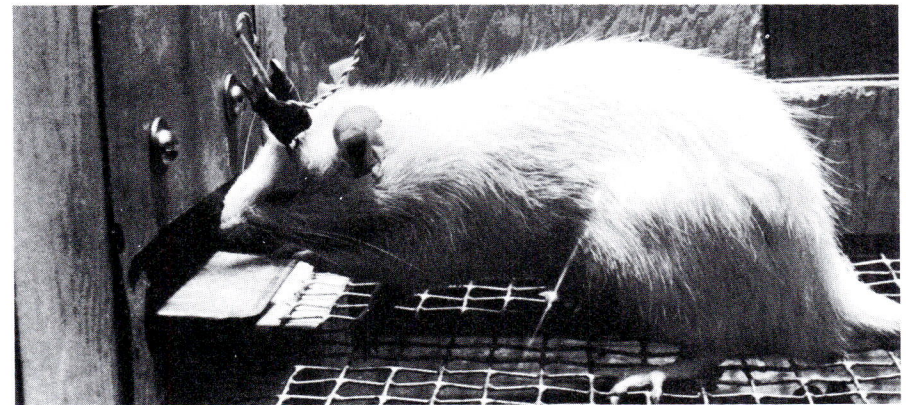

Figure 4.11
This rat has an electrode implanted in an area of its "old" brain. Each time the animal presses the lever, a tiny pulse is delivered to its brain. The extremely high rates of lever-pressing performed by animals with such implants indicate that a "pleasure center" is probably being stimulated by the electricity.

pattern of the rhythm depends on whether a person is awake, drowsy, or asleep (as illustrated in Chapter 7). These rhythms, or brain waves, occur because the neurons in the brain tend to increase or decrease their amount of activity in unison.

EEGs can be used to monitor the brain disorder that causes epilepsy. When an epileptic seizure occurs, abnormal electrical activity begins in a small piece of damaged brain tissue. It then spreads to neighboring areas of the brain. By monitoring brain waves on an EEG, doctors can determine what kind of surgical procedure (if any) would reduce violent seizures. Another test has been developed that measures brain activity by revealing the amount of glucose consumed by neurons in the brain. This technique, called a *positron emission tomography* (*PET*) scan, can be used to locate tumors and seizure activity.

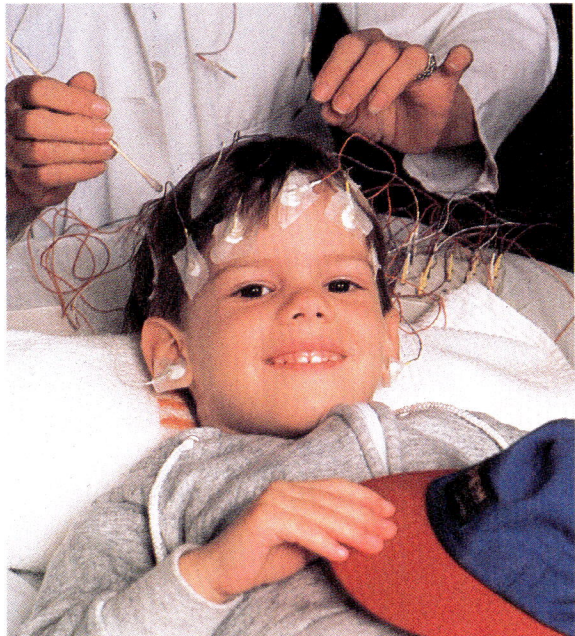

Figure 4.12
Measuring brain waves using an electroencephalograph (EEG) machine.

Stimulation

Electrodes may be used to set off the firing of neurons as well as to record it. Brain surgeon Wilder Penfield stimulated the brains of his patients during surgery to determine what functions the various parts of the brain perform. In this way he could localize the malfunctioning part for which surgery was required, for example, for epilepsy. When Penfield applied a tiny electric current to points on the temporal lobe of the brain, he could trigger whole memory sequences. During surgery, one woman heard a familiar song so clearly that she thought a record was being played in the operating room (Penfield and Rasmussen, 1950).

Using the stimulation technique, other researchers have shown that there are "pleasure" and "punishment" centers in the brain. One research team implanted electrodes in certain areas of the "old brain" of a rat, then placed the rat in a box equipped with a lever that the rat could press. Each time the rat pressed the lever, a mild electrical current was delivered to its brain. When the electrode was placed in the rat's "pleasure" center, it would push the lever several thousand times per hour (Olds and Olds, 1965) (see Figure 4.11).

Scientists have used chemicals as well as electricity to stimulate the brain. In this method, a small tube is implanted in an animal's brain so that the end touches the area to be stimulated (Figure 4.13). Chemicals can then be delivered through the tube to the area of the brain being studied. Such experiments have shown that different chemicals in the hypothalamus can affect hunger and thirst in an animal.

Stimulation techniques have aroused great medical interest. They have been used with terminal cancer patients to relieve them of intolerable pain without using drugs. A current delivered through electrodes implanted in certain areas of the brain seems to provide a sudden temporary relief (Delgado, 1969). Furthermore, some psychiatrists have experimented with similar methods to control violent emotional behavior in otherwise uncontrollable patients.

Figure 4.13
The technique for stimulating the inside of a rat's brain with chemicals. (a) The rat is prepared for brain surgery. (b) A small funnel at the top of a tiny tube is permanently implanted in the rat's skull. The other end of the tube is deep inside the brain. (c) A small amount of some chemical that affects the nervous system is passed into the tube in a solution of water.

a

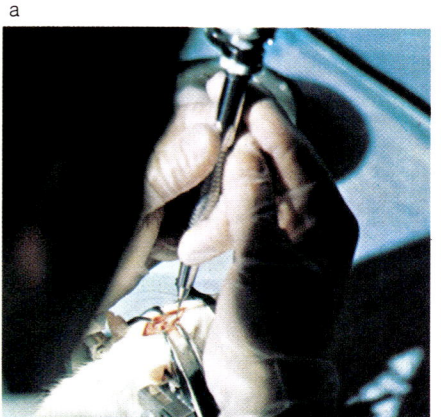

b

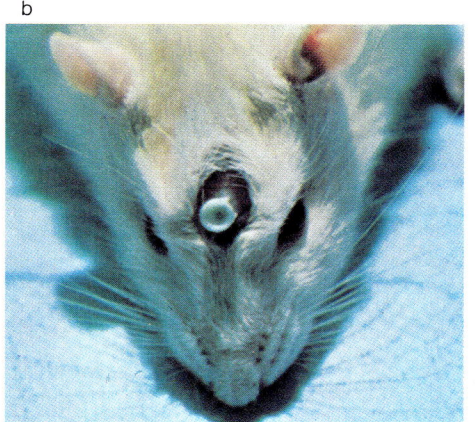

c

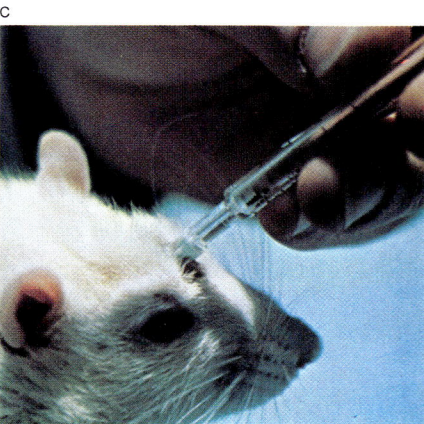

The Courts and Psychosurgery

In 1973, a Michigan court made an important decision which limited psychosurgery.

L.S., a criminal who had been charged with first-degree murder and rape, had been confined to a Michigan mental hospital for eighteen years when he agreed to have brain surgery to try to make him less violent. Legal services lawyer Gabe Kaimowitz brought suit to prevent the operation.

Both L.S. and his parents had given written consent for the operation. But it became clear in court that neither completely understood the implications of the procedure. Furthermore, L.S. suspected that he might be released earlier if he went along with the operation.

The court ruled that the operation should not be done even though L.S. had said he wanted it. Involuntarily confined patients, the court said, simply cannot give legally adequate consent to experimental high-risk procedures like psychosurgery. Thus, the legal status of certain types of psychosurgery is now in doubt.

For more details, see Carol Wade Offir, "The Movement to Pull Out the Electrodes," *Psychology Today,* 7 (May 1974): 69–70.

Lesions

Scientists sometimes create lesions by cutting or destroying part of an animal's brain. If the animal behaves differently after the operation, they assume that the destroyed brain area is involved with that type of behavior. For example, in one classic lesion study, two researchers removed a certain area of the subcortex (or "old brain") from rhesus monkeys. Normally, these animals are aggressive and vicious. After the operation they became less fearful and at the same time less violent (Kluver and Bucy, 1937). The implication was that this area of the brain controlled aggression. Subsequent researchers have learned that the relations revealed by this type of research are far more subtle and complex than people first believed.

USING PSYCHOLOGY

Psychosurgery

We have already discussed the use of lesions in treating violent epileptic seizures (by severing the corpus callosum). Experiments with animals suggested to some researchers that it might be possible to treat certain behavioral problems with similar operations. Brain surgery aimed at changing people's thoughts and actions is called **psychosurgery.**

PSYCHOLOGY UPDATE

Brain Damage: The Role of Glutamate. Strokes or head injuries often cause brain damage. Within several minutes, brain cells begin to die. Since this process happens so quickly, it had been thought that little could be done to prevent permanent brain damage. However, recent research by neuroscientists suggests otherwise. They contend that although brain cells that are directly on the site of the injury die quickly, adjacent cells are damaged and die by a chemical process that occurs hours after the initial event. This chemical process revolves around glutamate—an excitatory chemical in the brain. Usually, only small amounts of glutamate are released and stimulate adjacent neurons. However, a stroke or head injury disrupts the brain's chemical balance and results in large amounts of glutamate being released. A chain reaction of overstimulation begins in cells near the initial injury. These overstimulated cells are damaged and ultimately die. This may be why a brain-injured person's condition continues to worsen for hours after the initial injury. Scientists are currently looking for ways to reduce this flow of glutamate in order to reduce brain damage.

The first great wave of psychosurgery was from about 1935 to 1955. A number of studies had showed that monkeys were less upset by frustration after portions of the frontal lobe of their brains were destroyed. A similar operation, called a prefrontal lobotomy, was tried on about 50,000 mental patients in the United States and Great Britain. These operations often seemed to help people who had serious mental problems. But they also had some undesirable side effects.

After the frontal lobes were destroyed, many patients lost the ability to deal with new information or pursue goals. For example, a woman who was a very innovative cook before her operation had trouble with new recipes afterward. Even more distressing was the fact that when she went out food shopping, she would sometimes get distracted and would forget why she had left the house (Valenstein, 1973: 298). But it is hard to draw a firm conclusion about the overall effects of frontal lobotomies. After reviewing all the available evidence, Elliot Valenstein wrote: "There is certainly no grounds for either the position that all psychosurgery necessarily reduces people to a 'vegetable status' or that it has a high probability of producing miraculous cures. The truth, even if somewhat wishy-washy, lies in between these extreme positions. There is little doubt, however, that many abuses existed" (Valenstein, 1973: 315). But the matter became academic in the mid-1950s because new drugs were introduced that became the treatment of choice in mental hospitals.

Within the last fifteen years, however, new operations have been introduced, and people have become interested in psychosurgery once again. Instead of destroying large portions of the frontal lobes, these operations used sophisticated techniques to destroy very small areas of tissue deep inside the brain. These operations quickly became controversial, particularly when they were used to change people who had a history of violent behavior. (Michael Crichton's best-selling novel *The Terminal Man* gave a fictional account of one such operation that went wrong.) In recent years, psychosurgeons have operated on about 400 people per year in the United States.

Public attention brought psychosurgery into the courts and the political arena. In 1974, Congress appointed the eleven-member National Commission for the Protection of Human Subjects of Biomedical and Behavioral Research to study several controversial areas. In October 1976, they released their report on psychosurgery. At this time, public and scientific opinion was generally opposed to psychosurgery. The commission's conclusions were, in the words of one reporter

(Culliton, 1976), "surprisingly favorable." They did not approve the older technique of frontal lobotomy, but they did say that some of the newer operations seemed to work. For example, an operation called a cingulotomy (destruction of a major subcortical structure) seems to be very helpful for some people who suffer from pain and severe depression.

The complexity of these operations on the brain and the philosophical issues raised by the idea of changing the way people act by changing their brains guarantees that psychosurgery will remain controversial for some time to come.

THE ENDOCRINE SYSTEM

The nervous system is one of two communication systems for sending information to and from the brain. The second is the endocrine system. The **endocrine system** sends chemical messages called **hormones.** The hormones are produced in the endocrine glands and are distributed by the blood and other body fluids. (The names and locations of these glands are shown in Figure 4.14.) The hormone messages are like letters in a postal system. They can circulate throughout the bloodstream, but they can be delivered only to a specific address: the particular organ of the body that they influence. The endocrine glands are also called ductless glands because they release hormones directly into the bloodstream. In contrast, the *duct glands,* or *exocrine glands,* release their contents through small holes, or ducts, onto the surface of the body. Examples of duct glands are sweat glands and tear glands.

Under the direction of the **hypothalamus** in the brain, the **pituitary gland** acts as the "master gland." The pituitary gland secretes a large number of hormones, many of which control the output of hormones by other endocrine glands. The hypothalamus monitors the amount of hormones in the blood and sends out messages to correct imbalances.

What do these hormone messages tell the body to do? They carry messages to organs involved in regulating and storing nutrients so that, despite changes in conditions outside the body, cell metabolism can continue on an even course. They also control growth and reproduction, including ovulation and lactation (milk production) in women.

The **thyroid gland** produces the hormone thyroxin. Thyroxin stimulates certain chemical reactions that are important for all tissues of the body. Too little thyroxin makes people feel lazy and lethargic; too much makes them overactive. The adrenal glands become active when a person is angry or frightened. They release adrenalin into the bloodstream. The adrenalin causes the heartbeat and breathing to increase. These and other changes help a person feel the extra energy he or she needs to handle a difficult situation.

Through the combined action of the nervous and endocrine systems,

Figure 4.14
The endocrine glands.

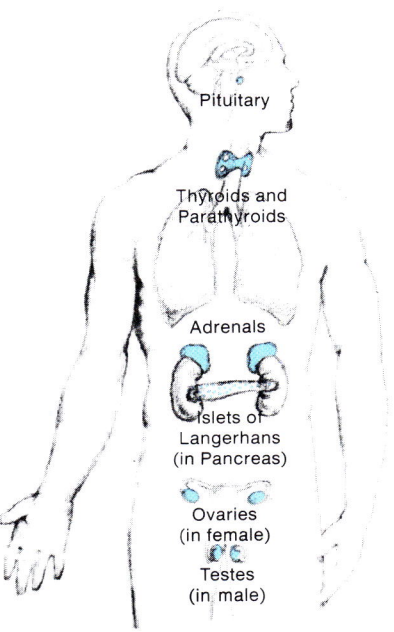

the brain monitors and controls most human behavior. In the next chapter we will see how the endocrine system influences behavior we normally attribute to psychological causes—emotion and motivation.

THE RELATIONSHIP BETWEEN HUMANS AND ANIMALS

Much of the research described in this chapter has been done primarily with lower animals. Researchers often study animals because they cannot perform a risky operation on a human being without a better reason than scientific inquiry. The research that has been done on humans has either occurred as a part of some necessary medical operation or has involved observing people who have suffered an injury by accident.

It is now commonly accepted that the study of animals can help in the study of human beings, even though direct experiments on humans would be even more useful if they could be done. Animal studies are especially valuable in medicine and physiology. Drugs. vaccines, and new forms of surgery are regularly tested on animal subjects. The reason such research is considered useful is that human beings are believed to have evolved from more primitive animal origins, and their bodies are therefore similar to the bodies of other animals.

The Evolution of Behavior

What many people often do not realize is that evolution applies not only to anatomy and physiology but also to behavior. Charles Darwin, the biologist who in 1859 published his theory of evolution, believed that all animal

Figure 4.15
There are many similarities between human behavior and animal behavior. At this penguin gathering, for example, there are penguins in pairs and by themselves. Some are aloof, some are enjoying the sunshine, and some are simply observing the scene.

species are related to one another. Consequently, the structure of their bodies and their behavior patterns can be distinguished and compared just as one may compare a child's nose or his temper to that of his father. The bones in a bird's wing are different but comparable to the bones in a human arm; the way birds flock together can be compared to the way humans gather in groups (Figure 4.15). And just as the parts of a chimpanzee's brain can be compared to a human's, so can a chimpanzee's ability to solve problems be compared to human thinking ability.

Darwin's theory does not mean that humans do not possess unique qualities, but it does make it possible to think of humans as members of a particularly complex, interesting species instead of as totally different from other animals.

Ethology

One of the major outgrowths of Darwin's theory of evolution is **ethology,** the study of the natural behavior patterns of all species of animals from a biological point of view. They attempt to understand how these patterns have evolved and changed, and how they are expressed in humans. Ethologists call these natural patterns **species-specific behaviors,** behaviors that are characteristic of a particular animal species. By observing animals in their natural environment, ethologists hope to discover the links between a species' surroundings and its behaviors.

Ethologists have found that the behavior and experience of more primitive animals (such as insects or fish) are less flexible, or more stereotyped, than the behavior of higher animals, such as apes or humans. Stereotyped behaviors consist of patterns of responses that cannot change readily in response to changes in the environment. They work well only if the environment stays as it was when the behavior pattern evolved.

For example, when a horse is confronted with danger and requires a quiet escape, it is impossible for it to tiptoe away. Its escape behavior consists of only three patterns: walking, trotting, and galloping. Each pattern is a distinct series of movements that vary little from one horse to another, and all normal horses display these patterns. These are called **fixed action patterns** because they are inflexible—an animal can react to certain situations only in these ways.

Fixed action patterns are one kind of **instinct**—a behavior pattern that is inborn rather than learned. People often misuse the word "instinct" to refer to behaviors that become automatic after long practice. A professional baseball player may be described as "instinctively" making the right play, for example. But ethologists use the term "instinct" to refer only to those abilities that seem to be inherited.

Ethologists have found that animals are born with special sensitivities to certain cues in the environment (as well as with special ways of behaving). These cues are called sign stimuli. For example, Niko Tinbergen showed that the male stickleback, a small fish, will attack a model of another stickleback if it has a red belly. Even if the model is distorted, as in Figure 4.16, the male will still attack. Yet if it sees a very lifelike model of a stickleback without a red belly, the male will leave it alone. In this case, the

Figure 4.16
The bright red belly of the male stickleback is a sign stimulus for attack from other sticklebacks. They will attack red-bellied models like the ones below before they will respond to a realistic model of a stickleback that does not have a red belly.

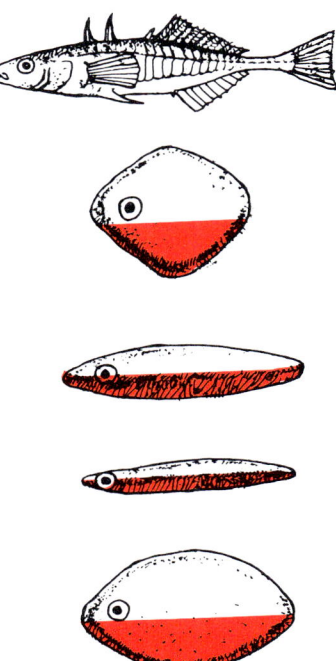

Using Ethology to Study Human Behavior.

Human ethology is the study of human behavior as it naturally occurs. Ethologists make comparisons between human and animal behaviors as part of their investigations.

One study investigated whether people crossing the street looked both ways before they crossed. When males and females crossed together, males looked both ways more often than females. Human ethologists see a similarity between this finding and the behavior of monkey and baboon troops living in the wild, whose adult males serve as lookouts. A human ethologist might say that humans have exchanged "cheetahs for Chevrolets" as the focus of their lookout behaviors.

Basketball fans know that Michael Jordan sticks out his tongue when he is attempting a difficult shot. Similarly, it has been found that expert billiard players stick out their tongues more often when making hard shots than when attempting relatively easy shots. According to ethologists, a tongue display acts as a nonverbal signal that interaction is not desired. For humans, the tongue displays seem to indicate that the person does not want to be interrupted because of the need to concentrate in a difficult situation.

sign stimulus that triggers attack is the color red. In other species other sign stimuli can trigger certain behaviors.

Do sign stimuli occur in humans? Although instincts are less common and less powerful in human behavior, there is evidence that some stereotyped behaviors exist. For example, Konrad Lorenz found that a "parental instinct" seems to be aroused by the appearance of the human baby. When he compared human infants to other young animals, he noticed that they all seem to display a similar set of sign stimuli which appear to stir up parental feelings. Short faces, prominent foreheads, round eyes, and plump cheeks all seem to arouse the parental response.

Sociobiology

Closely related to ethology is another new discipline that studies the hereditary basis of social behavior in animals and humans to determine whether these behaviors are inherited from remote ancestors. This science, known as **sociobiology,** draws on the findings of biology, anthropology, and psychology. It has attracted a great deal of attention, and an even greater amount of controversy. In 1975, Harvard zoologist Edward O. Wilson published *Sociobiology: A New Synthesis*, in which he defined the new discipline as "the systematic study of the biological basis of all social behavior" (1975a: 595). Wilson surveyed the social behavior of all known primates and suggested that certain traits humans share with almost all other primates—prolonged maternal care of offspring, for instance, and male dominance over females—may have been passed along to us in our genes.

Sociobiologists regard their discipline as the last phase of the revolution begun by Charles Darwin. It tries to fill a major gap in Darwin's theory of natural selection: nature's goal is individual survival and reproduction, yet several traits of humans and other animals seem to work directly against this goal. Soldier ants will fight to the death, thus contributing to saving their group from invaders. A bird will often call out a warning to other birds that a predator is nearby, though the warning call itself alerts the enemy to that particular bird's whereabouts and risks the bird's life. Dolphins have been known to band together and support a stricken companion on the surface of the water where it can breathe (Wilson, 1975b). And, of course, among humans, parents die rescuing their children from fires, and soldiers throw themselves suicidally on grenades to save their buddies.

Sociobiologists fit all these acts of self-sacrifice into nature's economy. They explain that altruism itself favors genetic gain: the individual risks itself, but the result of this behavior is that other individuals who share its genes may survive (Figure 4.17). The soldier ant, which is sterile, protects its queen, which then lives to produce more of the soldier ant's kind. The bird who calls a warning in effect also protects its kind, and this increases the chance that its genes will survive, as does the behavior of the mother who saves her baby. The battlefield hero dies confident that the nation will keep his family safe to reproduce—and thus to perpetuate his own genes. The noted British biologist J. B. S. Haldane once joked that he would give his life for his two brothers, each of whom shares about half his genes, or for eight cousins (cited in *Time*, August 1, 1977, 56).

Figure 4.17
Sociobiologists explain firefighters risking their lives to save others as yet another aspect of natural selection: the individual risks itself, but the species survives.

Sociobiology seeks to explain other social behaviors, even aggression, in terms of genetic advantage. The bully who kicks sand in the ninety-seven-pound weakling's face is actually sending a message to the weakling's girl friend: "I have good genes. You ought to mate with me."

The idea that genes determine human social behavior has been so controversial that Wilson has been picketed and even had water thrown in his face at the otherwise sedate 1978 meeting of the American Association for the Advancement of Science. Some critics, notably Richard Lewontin, Stephen Gould, and other members of the Harvard-based Sociobiology Study Group, have expressed fear that sociobiology can be used to support the political, economic, and legal status quo. According to the logic of sociobiology, these must have been determined by our genes (reported in Wade, 1976).

Other critics point out that there is no hard evidence that specific genes exist for altruism, aggression, or other social behaviors, but only theories and guesswork (Washburn, 1978). They also point out that animals may behave very selfishly indeed. Among the lions of the Serengeti plain in East Africa, lionesses have been observed driving their own cubs away from food if the catch was small; many of these cubs have died of starvation. Of

Figure 4.18 A baboon troop in the wild. Although many people believe that primate males dominate females, relations between the sexes are actually quite complicated.

1,400 herring gull chicks studied during one period, 23 percent were killed by attacks from adults of their own species as they strayed from the nest (Marler, 1976).

Along the same lines, anthropologists have repeatedly contested the popular belief that human males are innately aggressive and dominant over females. The supporters of this argument often cite studies of baboons that document male aggression and dominance over females. Opponents point out that the baboons observed in these studies were in a game park, an abnormal environment that exposed them to a heavy concentration of predators (especially human ones) and to a high level of tension. Among baboon troops that live undisturbed in the forest, however, it is female baboons who determine the troop's movements. Males exhibit very little aggression and little dominance (Pilbeam, 1972).

If baboon behavior can vary so widely in different environments, it is even more likely that human behavior will do so. Genes may very well be an important component of human social behavior, but they cannot entirely determine it. If the children of two great athletes are never permitted to exercise, their genes will never make them athletes. Indeed, the flexibility of human social behavior, the extreme differences in various cultures and in different contexts, is almost uniquely human (Pilbeam, 1972). Only human beings construct cultures, passing on large and growing accumulations of learning from generation to generation and thereby to a certain extent overcoming the slow process of genetic evolution. Only human beings exhibit a wide variety of culturally determined behaviors, such as wearing black to funerals in some countries and white in others.

The question of the extent to which heredity does determine human social behavior is far from settled. But Wilson and some other sociobiologists believe that humankind is flexible and must be so, and that genetic inclinations need not always be obeyed and sometimes should not be. Evolution takes place so slowly that we may still be inheriting behavior patterns that were adaptive in prehistoric times but that are no longer useful in our radically different world. In the Stone Age it may well have been important to raise as many healthy children as possible; on today's crowded planet it is not. When humans lived in hunter-gatherer societies, it might have been necessary to wage war against all foreigners in order to survive; now war could mean the end of humankind (Wilson, 1975b). The major contribution of sociobiology has been to remind us that genes do count, but that human beings have the capacity to learn a wide range of behaviors and to unlearn those that cease to be adaptive.

HEREDITY AND ENVIRONMENT

People often argue about whether human behavior is instinctive (due to heredity) or learned (due to environment). Do people learn to be good athletes, or are they born that way? Do people learn to do well in school, or are they born good at it? Do people learn to be homosexual, or are they born that way? The reason for the intensity of the argument may be that many people assume that something learned can probably be changed, whereas something inborn will be difficult or impossible to change. This is wrong. Whenever psychologists investigate a particular case, they find that the issue is not that simple. Inherited factors and environmental conditions always act together in complicated ways. Asking whether heredity or environment is responsible for something turns out to be like asking "What makes a cake rise, baking powder or heat?" Obviously, an interaction of the two is responsible.

Inherited factors and environment always act together in complicated ways.

The argument over the nature-nurture question has been going on for centuries. Sir Francis Galton, a cousin of Charles Darwin, was one of the first to preach the importance of nature in the modern era. In 1869 he published *Hereditary Genius*, a book in which he analyzed the families of over 1,000 eminent politicians, religious leaders, artists, and scholars. He found that success ran in the families and concluded that heredity was the cause.

But most psychologists have emphasized the importance of the environment. The tone was set by John Watson, the father of behaviorism, who wrote in 1930: "Give me a dozen healthy infants, well-formed, and my own specified world to bring them up in and I'll guarantee to take any one at random and train him to become any type of specialist I might select—doctor, lawyer, artist, merchant-chief, and, yes, even beggarman and thief, regardless of his talents, penchants, tendencies, abilities, vocations, and race of his ancestors" (Watson, 1930: 104).

Watson's view now seems a bit extreme. Recent studies that directly looked for evidence of genetic influence on human traits have focused on three general areas: cognitive abilities (like IQ), mental illness, and personality. The argument over IQ (see Chapter 12) has been particularly loud and long, but each of the other areas is also controversial.

One way to find out whether a trait is inherited is to study twins. Identical twins develop from a single fertilized egg (thus, they are called monozygotic) and share the same genes. Fraternal twins develop from two fertilized eggs (thus, dizygotic), and their genes are no more similar than those of brothers or sisters.

Figure 4.19
Because identical twins share the same genes as well as the same environment, studying them is one way to find out whether a trait is inherited or learned.

Obviously, twins growing up in the same house share the same general environment. But identical twins who grow up together also share the same genes. So, if identical twins prove to be more alike on a specific trait than fraternal twins do, it probably means that genes are important for that trait.

For example, many twin studies have been done on the inheritance of mental disease. Schizophrenia is the most common form of serious mental illness and affects about 1 percent of the world population (see Chapter 15). Studies have shown that if one twin becomes schizophrenic, the other twin is three to six times more likely to become schizophrenic if he is an identical twin rather than a fraternal twin (Rosenthal, 1970). Thus, schizophrenia is at least partly genetic. However, it is also clear that in many cases, one identical twin develops schizophrenia and the other does not. Thus, environmental factors are also important.

There are several other ways of studying the nature-nurture problem in humans. In a few cases, identical twins have been separated at birth by adoption agencies or whatever. These twins show the effects of the same genes in different environments. Although such cases are relatively rare, they are extremely important from a scientific point of view. It is also possible to see whether adopted children more closely resemble their biological parents (thus suggesting the importance of genes) or their adoptive parents (emphasizing the influence of environment). Although many such studies are going on, the nature-nurture question will probably continue to be controversial, at least until people gain a more sophisticated understanding of how heredity and environment interact to produce behavior.

Psychologists at the University of Minnesota have been studying identical twins who were separated at birth and reared in different environments (Holden, 1980). One of the researchers, Thomas Bouchard, reports that despite very different social, cultural, and economic backgrounds, the twins shared many common behaviors. For example, in one set of twins (both named Jim), both had done well in math and poorly in spelling while in school, both worked as deputy sheriffs, vacationed in Florida, gave identical names to their children and pets, bit their fingernails, had identical smoking and drinking patterns, and liked mechanical drawing and carpentry. These similarities and others suggest that heredity may contribute to behaviors that we normally associate with experience.

Many researchers now believe that many of the differences among people can be explained by considering heredity as well as experience. Contrary to popular belief, the influence of genes on behavior does not mean that nothing can be done to change the behavior. Although it is true that it is difficult and undesirable to change the genetic code that may direct behavior, it is possible to alter the environment in which the genes operate. The genetic disorder phenylketonuria (PKU) is a case in point. PKU is a single gene defect which, if undetected and untreated, results in severe mental retardation. A simple blood test at birth (Figure 4.20) can reveal the presence of PKU, which afflicts about 1 in 20,000 whites (it is rare among blacks). Afflicted infants can be placed on a special diet until the brain develops and is no longer in danger. Thus, although PKU is inherited, its effects can be changed by controlling the environment.

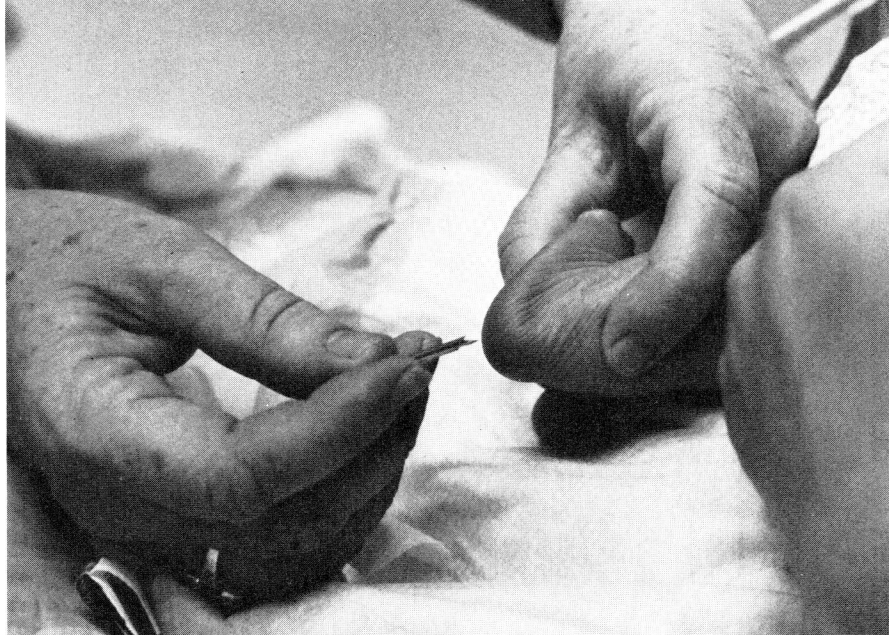

Figure 4.20
The test for PKU, a simple prick on the heel, is now given automatically to all newborns, since early detection can prevent the ravages of this congenital disease.

CHAPTER REVIEW

KEY TERMS

KEY TERMS

- autonomic nervous system
- central nervous system (CNS)
- cerebellum
- cerebral cortex
- cerebrum
- corpus callosum
- effectors
- electrode
- electroencephalograph (EEG)
- endocrine system
- ethology
- firing
- fixed action patterns

- frontal lobes
- hormones
- hypothalamus
- instinct
- lobes
- motor cortex
- nerve fibers
- neurons
- neurotransmitters
- parasympathetic nervous system
- peripheral nervous system (PNS)
- pituitary gland
- psychosurgery

- receptors
- reticular activating system
- sociobiology
- somatic nervous system
- somatosensory cortex
- species-specific behavior
- spinal cord
- subcortex
- sympathetic nervous system
- synapses
- thalamus
- thyroid gland

SUMMARY

1. Messages are constantly traveling back and forth in the body through the nervous system to the brain. The spinal cord, a part of the nervous system, transmits most of the messages back and forth between the body and the brain. The messages to and from the brain are communicated by chemical-electrical signals traveling down long, thin cells called neurons.

2. The autonomic nervous system plays a key role in the physiology of emotion. One of its components, the sympathetic nervous system, prepares the body for dealing with emergencies or strenuous activities. The parasympathetic nervous system, the other part of the autonomic nervous system, works to conserve energy and to enhance the body's ability to recover from strenuous activity.

3. The brain is composed of the cerebral cortex and the subcortex. The subcortex guides a person's biological needs and animal instincts. The cerebral cortex enables a person to read and solve problems. The brain processes vast amounts of information every second. Scientists believe that it compares patterns of stimuli and responses stored in its memory with new stimuli.

4. The cortex is divided into two hemispheres, each containing four lobes. For right-handed people, the left hemisphere is more involved with verbal thoughts while the right hemisphere is involved with spatial relations.

5. Recording, stimulation, and lesions are three techniques psychologists use to study the brain. Psychosurgery is brain surgery aimed at changing a person's thoughts or actions.

6. The endocrine or hormone system is a chemical system of communication between the body and the brain. Through the combined action of the nervous and endocrine systems, the brain monitors and controls human behavior.

7. Studies of animal behavior have revealed that many species respond to their environments in terms of fixed action patterns—that is, they can react to certain situations only in set ways. Such automatic responses play a minor role in human behavior.

8. Sociobiologists look for the biological basis of social behavior. For example, they believe that altruism is based on an animal's desire to insure that its genes are passed on to the next generation.

9. All human behavior is based on the interaction of heredity and environment. The comparison of identical and fraternal twins can help discover the influence of genes on a specific trait.

CHAPTER REVIEW

1. Explain how messages travel to and from the brain through the nervous system. What are the neurotransmitters?

2. What are the two types of nervous system? Which system does the spinal cord belong to?

3. Describe the functions of the somatic nervous system and the autonomic nervous system.

4. What are the two parts of the autonomic nervous system? Which part uses up energy in the body?

5. What part of the cortex receives information?

6. What is the task of the thalamus?

7. What two parts of the lower brain work to filter out all but the most important messages before they reach the cerebral cortex? Give a possible explanation for the brain's ability to process large amounts of information.

8. What is one of the main functions of the cerebellum?

9. Name the four lobes of the cerebral cortex. What is the main function of each?

10. The cortex of the brain is divided into the left and the right hemispheres. Which side of the body does each hemisphere control? What kinds of tasks does each hemisphere control in right-handed people? What is the function of the corpus callosum?

11. What are the three methods used to explore the brain?

12. What is the name of the chemical system of communication between the body and the brain? How are the messages of this system transmitted? Which gland is the center of control for this system? What other gland helps in regulating general bodily activity?

13. What is the study of the natural behavior patterns of animals from a biological point of view?

14. How do ethologists use the term *instinct*?

15. What is the name of the science that studies the hereditary basis of social behavior? What is the major contribution of this science?

16. One way to find out whether a trait is inherited is to compare the behavior of identical and fraternal twins. Explain how this works.

ACTIVITIES

1. Can you observe species-specific behaviors in cats, dogs, or any other animals you see regularly? If you have an animal that you can observe carefully, try to identify fixed action patterns that are common to the animal's species. Do they exist in any form in yourself?

2. What aspects of your personality, your way of acting, and your appearance are most obviously the result of heredity? Which seem to be more related to your environmental upbringing? What factors make it difficult to decide whether hereditary or environmental factors are of greatest influence?

3. Ask several of your friends (individually) to perform some mental task, such as multiplying 31 by 24 in their heads, or counting the number of letters in a simple phrase (such as "early to bed"). Observe which way their eyes shift as they begin to think about the problem. If their eyes shift to the right, they are doing the counting in the left hemisphere of the cortex, and vice versa.

Figure 5.1 Through our senses—sight, sound, touch, taste, and smell—we perceive the world around us.

Objectives: After studying this chapter, you should be able to
- describe the field of study known as psychophysics.
- explain the concepts of threshold, Weber's law, and signal detection.
- describe the sense organs and explain their functions.
- explain the principles involved in perception.
- discuss the general psychological attitude toward ESP.

Sensation and Perception

In the next few seconds, something peculiar will start happening to the material youa rereading. Iti soft ennotre alized howcom plext heproces sofrea ding is. Afe w sim plerear range mentscan ha veyoucomp lete lycon fused!

As you can see, your success in gathering information from your environment, interpreting this information, and acting on it depends considerably on its being organized in ways you expect.

Your knowledge of the external world—and of your internal state as well—comes entirely from chemical and electrical processes occurring in the nervous system, particularly in the brain. Physical change in the external or internal environment triggers chemical, electrical, and mechanical activity in sense receptors. After complex processing in the nervous system, a pattern of activity is produced in certain areas of the brain. You experience this electrical activity as a **sensation**—awareness of colors, forms, sounds, smells, tastes, and so on. Usually you experience some meaningful whole—you see Woody Allen, hear Paul McCartney's voice, smell an old, dirty sock—rather than a collection of sensations. The organization of sensory information into meaningful wholes is known as **perception**.

This process can be seen in the act of eating. When someone puts two hamburgers in front of you, receptors in your eyes send a message to the brain: the all-beef patties are stacked together in the sesame seed bun, along with some lettuce. Receptors in your nose may tell you there's ketchup and cheese inside, while other receptors in your mouth send messages about pickles and some mysterious sauce. As you grasp this gourmet delight in your hands, receptors in your fingers tell you that the roll is soft and warm. And the brain combines all these inputs into one unified perception: it's a Big Mac.

Sensation
Threshold • Using Psychology: Subliminal Advertising • Sensory Differences and Ratios • Sensory Adaptation • Motivation and Signal-Detection Theory

The Senses
Vision • Hearing • Smell and Taste • The Skin Senses • Balance • Body Sensations

Perception
Principles of Perceptual Organization • Figure-Ground Perception • Perceptual Inference • Learning to Perceive • Depth Perception • Constancy • Illusions

Extrasensory Perception

107

Avoiding Motion Sickness. One sensation you may be familiar with is "motion sickness." This condition occurs when a person's body is in motion and the inner ear becomes overstimulated or confused. Here are some things you can do to avoid motion sickness:

When you are flying try to position yourself where there is the least movement. Airline passengers sitting next to the wings have the smoothest ride. Recline your seat if possible. Avoid large meals, but try to take frequent small amounts of fluids and simple foods.

If you are riding in a car, avoid reading. You are less likely to get sick if you watch the ground or the horizon. The visual input helps you maintain equilibrium. One reason that small children are especially prone to motionsickness is that they cannot see out of the car and so they lose visual contact with their environment.

In this chapter we will look at each of these steps more closely, focusing on how each organ converts physical changes into chemical-electrical signals to the brain and how perceptions are built from this information. In the last section we will discuss the possibility of gaining information without the known senses—through the process of extrasensory perception.

SENSATION

The world is filled with physical changes—an alarm clock sounds; the flip of a switch fills a room with light; you stumble against a door; steam from a hot tub billows out into the bathroom, changing the temperature and clouding the mirror. All these changes result in sensations—of loudness, brightness, pain in the elbow you bump, heat, tastes, smells, and so on. Any aspect of or change in the environment to which an organism responds is called a stimulus. An alarm, an electric light, and an aching muscle are all stimuli for human beings.

A stimulus can be measured in some physical way—by its size, its duration, its intensity, its wavelength, and so on. A sensory experience can also be measured (at least, indirectly). But a sensory experience and a stimulus are not the same. For example, the same English muffin (stimulus) might taste (sensory experience) one way if you had just eaten and quite a different way if you hadn't eaten anything for a week. On the other hand, the same sensory experience (flashing lights, for example) might be produced by different stimuli (a blow to the head or a fireworks display).

Psychologists are interested in the relationship between physical stimuli and sensory experiences. In vision, for example, the sensation of color corresponds to the wavelength of the light, whereas brightness corresponds to the intensity of this stimulus.

What is the relationship between color and wavelength? How does changing a light's intensity affect one's sensation of its brightness? The psychological study of such questions is called **psychophysics.** The goal of psychophysics is to develop a quantified relationship between stimuli from the world (such as frequency and intensity) and the sensory experiences (such as pitch and loudness) produced by them.

Threshold

In order to establish laws about how people sense the external world, psychologists first try to determine how much of a stimulus is necessary for a person to sense it at all. How much energy is required for someone to hear a sound or to see a light? How much of a scent must be in the room before one can smell it? How much pressure must be applied to the skin before a person will feel it?

To answer such questions, a psychologist might set up the following experiment. First, a person (the subject) is placed in a dark room and is instructed to look at the wall. He is asked to say "I see it" when he is able to detect a light. The psychologist then uses an extremely precise machine that can project a low-intensity beam of light against the wall. The experimenter turns on the machine to its lowest light projection. The subject says nothing. The experimenter increases the light until finally the subject responds, "I see it." Then the experimenter begins another test in the opposite direction. He starts with a clearly visible light and decreases its intensity until the light seems to disappear. Many trials are completed and averaged. The **absolute threshold**—the smallest amount of energy that will produce a sensation—is defined as the amount of energy that a subject can see about half the time.

Interestingly enough, thresholds determined in this way are not as absolute as psychologists first believed. The point at which the person says "I see it" may vary with the instructions he is given ("Say you see it only if you're absolutely certain" versus "If there's any doubt, say you see it") or even the order in which the stimuli are presented.

Under ideal conditions, the senses have very low absolute thresholds. That is, sensations will be experienced with very small amounts of stimulation. For example, the eardrum registers a sound if it moves as little as 1 percent of the diameter of a hydrogen molecule. If the ear were any more sensitive, you might hear the sound of air molecules bumping into each other (Geldard, 1972). Similarly, the eye is about as sensitive as it could possibly be.

If the ear were any more sensitive, you might hear the sound of air molecules bumping into each other.

USING PSYCHOLOGY

Subliminal Advertising

On September 12, 1957, an advertising executive held a press conference to announce a revolutionary breakthrough in marketing techniques: **subliminal advertising.** The word "subliminal" comes from the Latin: *sub* ("below") and *limen* ("threshold"). The words "Eat Popcorn" and "Coca-Cola" had been flashed on a movie screen in a New Jersey theater on alternate nights for six weeks, according to the executive. Although the flashes were so brief (1/3,000 of a second, once every five seconds) that none of the moviegoers even seemed to notice them, popcorn sales rose 18.1 percent and Coca-Cola sales went up 57.7 percent.

The public response to this announcement was long, loud, and hysterical. In a TV interview, Aldous Huxley predicted that it would be possible to manipulate people politically with this technique "by about 1964" (quoted in Brown, 1963: 184). Congressmen called for FCC regulations, while several state legislatures passed laws banning subliminal ads.

Meanwhile, more test results began to appear. When the man who made the original claims staged another test for the FCC a few months later, the results were equivocal. Later, WTWO-TV in Bangor, Maine, flashed the words "If you have seen this message, write WTWO" on the screen for 1/60 of a second every day for a week. Nobody wrote. A Seattle radio station experimented with auditory subliminal ads. During regular programming, a very low whisper in the background repeated "TV's a bore" and "Isn't TV dull?" (These experimenters had planned to add the message "TV causes eye cancer," but decided they'd better not risk it.) There is no reason to believe that these ads had any effect.

British television got into the act by flashing the message "Pirie breaks world record" during a ballet program. At the end of the show, an announcer asked the 4.5 million viewers to write to the station if they had noticed anything unusual. Four hundred thirty replies were received; 20 of them repeated the message verbatim and another 134 were close to being right.

The idea for subliminal ads was a natural outgrowth of a long series of controversial studies on *subliminal perception*—the ability to notice stimuli that affect only the unconscious mind. Most of these earlier studies involved presenting verbal or visual material at intensities that were considered too low for people to perceive. However, a more critical look at the studies revealed several flaws in the way they were designed and carried out. For example, the original New Jersey study was done by nonpsychologists working for the Subliminal Projection Company. No attempt was made to assess or control factors other than the subliminal message that might have influenced the purchase of Coke or popcorn. The temperature in the theater or the length of the movie might have contributed to the increase in sales. Unfortunately, the study was not presented in enough detail to be evaluated by scientists.

Even if it is possible for people to perceive information at very low levels of intensity, there is not much evidence that these weak, often limited, messages would be more powerful than conscious messages in influencing people. The idea may be appealing to some advertising executives looking for a way to increase sales. There is a growing consensus among psychologists who have done controlled studies, however, that subliminal advertising does not work.

Sensory Differences and Ratios

Another type of threshold is the **difference threshold** or just noticeable difference. This refers to the smallest change in a stimulus that will produce a change in sensation. So to return to our example of the person tested in a dark room, a psychologist would test for the difference threshold by gradually increasing the intensity of a visible light beam until the person says, "Yes, this is brighter than the light I just saw." With this technique, it is possible to identify the smallest increase in light intensity that will be noticeable to the human eye.

Psychologists also have found that a particular sensory experience depends more on *changes* in the stimulus than on the absolute size or amount of the stimulus. For example, if you put a three-pound package of food into an empty backpack, the sensation of weight will be greatly increased. But if you add the same amount to a hundred-pound backpack, the sensation will hardly increase at all. This is because the sensation produced by the added weight reflects a proportional change—and three pounds does not provide much change in a one-hundred-pound load.

In psychophysics, this idea is known as **Weber's law:** the larger or stronger a stimulus, the larger the change required for an observer to notice that anything has happened to it (to experience a just noticeable difference) (Weber, 1834).

The amount of stimulus change necessary to produce some increase in sensory experience is different for different cases, but it is almost always proportional. Suppose, for example, that you have a glass of unsweetened lemonade. In order to make it sweet, you add two spoonfuls of sugar. Now to make the lemonade taste "twice as sweet," you must add six spoonfuls—three times the original amount of sugar. Then you discover that in order to make the lemonade "four times as sweet," you must add a total of eighteen spoonfuls (Figure 5.2). Each time the sweetness doubles, the amount of sugar triples (see Stevens, 1962).

Figure 5.2
A change in sensory experience is proportional to the amount of physical change. In this case, each time the amount of sugar triples, the sweetness of the lemonade doubles.

PSYCHOLOGY
UPDATE

Seeing in the Dark. Certain workers, such as radar operators, sometimes need to keep their eyes adapted to darkness, even when they take a rest break in a well-lit room. They can do this by wearing goggles that admit only red light. The red goggles work because, as described in the text, the eye has two kinds of receptor cells, called rods and cones. It is the cones that allow us to see colors. Since the red light admitted by the goggles stimulates only the cones, the adaptation level of the rods is not affected. It is, in fact, as if the rods were still in darkness.

When the worker returns to a dim room and removes the goggles, the rods will be highly sensitive and night vision will be good. Though the cones are now light-adapted, they will not interfere with vision unless the perception of color becomes especially important.

Phantom Limb Pain

Every night Andy woke covered in a cold, soaking sweat. The pain that filled his left hand was more than he could bear. It felt like a razor-sharp scalpel was being jabbed deeper and deeper into the palm of his hand. No one had prepared him for this pain—not even the doctors who had amputated his left hand two years before.

The *phantom limb pain* we've just described is one of the most bizarre phenomenons in medicine. It may take the form of tingling feelings, warmth, coldness, heaviness, or intense pain in a limb that is no longer there.

About one-third of all amputees report phantom limb pain, which in most cases continues for about a year. But as doctors and some unfortunate amputees know, pain may last for decades.

Evidence suggests that phantom limb pain has no single cause. Irritation of the stump, abnormal sympathetic nervous system activity, and emotional disturbance may all play a role. But no one is sure exactly how these factors contribute to the pain or how to rid an amputee of the agony he feels in a limb that is no longer there.

For more details, see Ronald Melzack, *The Puzzle of Pain;* New York: Basic Books, 1973.

By experimenting in this way with variations in sounds, temperatures, pressures, colors, tastes, and smells, psychologists are learning more about how each sense responds to stimulation. Some senses produce huge increases in sensation in response to small increases in energy. For example, the pain of an electric shock can be increased more than eight times by doubling the voltage. On the other hand, the intensity of a light must be increased many times to double its brightness.

Sensory Adaptation

Psychologists have focused on people's responses to changes in stimuli because they have found that the senses are tuned to change: they are most responsive to increases and decreases, to new events rather than to ongoing, unchanging stimulation. This is because our senses have a general ability to adapt, or adjust themselves, to a constant level of stimulation. They get used to a new level and respond only to changes away from it.

A good example of this process of adaptation is the increase in visual sensitivity that you experience after a short time in a darkened movie theater. At first you see only blackness, but after a while your eyes adapt to the new level, and you can see seats, faces, and so on. Adaptation occurs for the other senses as well. Receptors in your skin adapt to the cold water when you go for a swim; disagreeable odors in a lab seem to disappear after a while; street noises cease to bother you after you've lived in a city for a time. Without sensory adaptation, you would feel the constant pressure of the clothes on your body, and other stimuli would seem to be bombarding all your senses at the same time.

Motivation and Signal-Detection Theory

Sensory experience does not depend on stimulus alone, however. A person's ability to detect a stimulus also depends on motivation. The individual does not simply receive a signal passively. Rather, the individual's perceptual system makes a decision as to its presence, though the decision-making process is usually entirely unconscious.

Thus the nervous new radar operator may see blips on his screen when there are none while the overrelaxed veteran may not notice the unexpected. To use a more complex example, if you've been thinking a lot about your old boyfriend, you may think you see him walking down the street when it's really somebody else. On the other hand, you probably wouldn't expect to meet your dentist at a baseball game, and you might not notice him if he showed up there. Thus, feelings, expectations, and motivation influence whether or not you experience a sensation.

Signal-detection theory studies the mathematical relations between motivation, sensitivity, and sensation (Green and Swets, 1966). Detection thresholds involve recognizing some stimulus against a background of noise. A radar operator must be able to detect an airplane on a radar screen even when the plane's blip is faint and difficult to distinguish from blips

Figure 5.3
Air controllers must be able to detect an airplane on the radar screen even when the plane's blip is faint and difficult to distinguish from blips caused by natural phenomena such as flocks of birds or bad weather.

caused by flocks of birds or bad weather, which can produce images that are like visual "noise" (Figure 5.3). Consider radar operators watching a screen in wartime during a storm. How do they decide whether a blip on the screen is an enemy plane or a patch of noise? If they were to call out massive armed forces for every blip, they would create chaos. But if one bomber was mistakenly identified as noise, the results could be disastrous. The radar operator's judgment will be influenced by many factors, and different operators appear to have different sensitivities to blips. Moreover, a specific individual's apparent sensitivity seems to fluctuate, depending on the situation. For example, being watched by a superior will probably affect the operator's performance, as will fatigue or other distractions.

In studying the difficulties faced by radar operators, psychologists have reformulated the concept of absolute threshold to take into account the many factors that affect detection of minimal stimuli. As a result, the signal-detection theory abandons the idea that there is a single true absolute threshold for a stimulus. Instead it adopts the notion that the stimulus, here called a signal, must be detected in the face of noise, which can interfere with detection of the signal. Thus signal detection is similar to standing in a noisy bus terminal, listening for the announcement of your bus departure time over the loudspeaker. Although the volume of the loudspeaker remains constant, you will have more or less difficulty in detecting your "signal," depending on the amount of noise in the bus terminal.

THE SENSES

Although people are thought to have five senses, there are actually more. In addition to vision, hearing, taste, smell, and touch, there are several skin senses and two "internal" senses: *vestibular* and *kinesthetic*.

Each type of sensory receptor takes some sort of external stimulus—light, chemical molecules, sound waves, pressure—and converts it into a chemical-electrical message that can be understood by the brain. So far we know most about these processes in vision and hearing. The other senses have received less attention and are more mysterious in their functioning.

Figure 5.4

The process of vision. (a) A cross-section of the human eye, showing the passage of light. Note that the retina receives an inverted image of the external world, although people are never aware of this inversion. The place where the optic nerve leaves the eye is called the blind spot because it is the only spot on the retina where no sensation takes place. (b) The cell structure of the retina. Note that the light-sensitive cells (the rods and cones) are those furthest from the light, not the closest as one might expect. Light arriving at the retina must pass through various other cells before striking the rods and cones, which convert it into nervous impulses. The impulses then pass through these other cells to be coded and organized before traveling over the optic nerve to the brain.

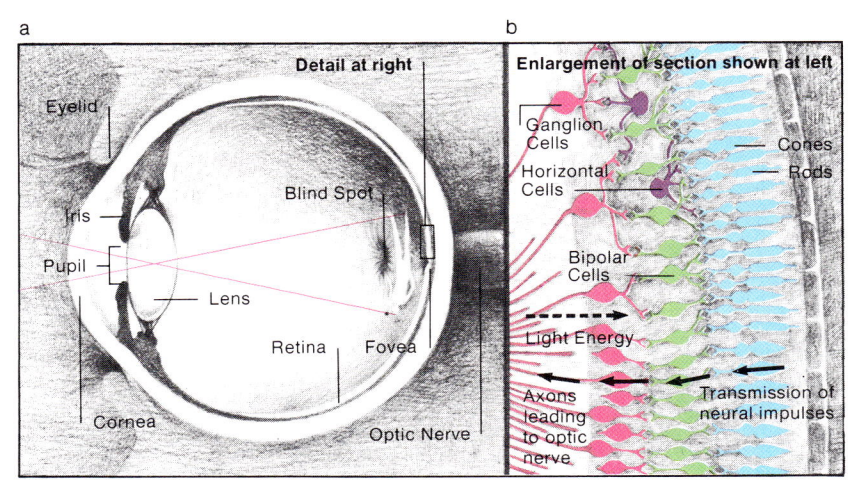

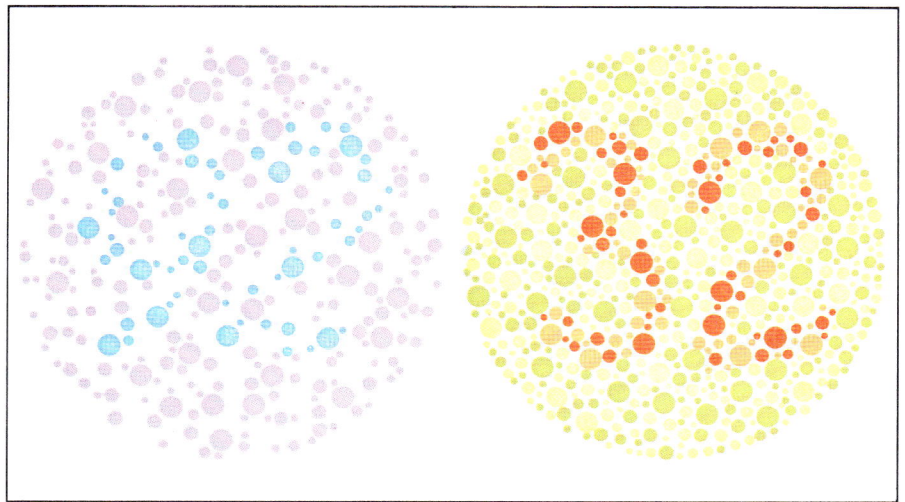

Figure 5.5
A test for color blindness. You should be able to see numerals in the dot patterns that make up these two figures. If you cannot distinguish the numerals in the circle on the left, you may be yellow-blue color-blind. If you cannot see those on the right, you may be red-green color-blind. Color-blind people use brightness differences to distinguish objects that most other people distinguish by color. In this test the dots are carefully equated for brightness, so the only way to see the numerals is to see the color differences. Due to the limitations of color printing, the illustration here may not pick up all cases of color blindness. (The Dvorine Pseudo-Isochromatic Plates.)

Vision

Vision is the most studied of all the senses, reflecting the high importance we place on our sense of sight. Vision provides a great deal of information about one's environment and the objects in it—the sizes, shapes, and locations of things, and their textures, colors, and distances.

How does vision occur? Light enters the eye through the **pupil** (see Figure 5.4a) and reaches the **lens,** a flexible structure that focuses light on the **retina**. The retina contains two types of light-sensitive receptor cells: **rods** and **cones** (see Figure 5.4b). These cells are responsible for changing light energy into chemical and electrical impulses, which then travel over the **optic nerve** to the brain.

Cones require more light than rods before they begin to respond; they work best in daylight. Rods are sensitive to much lower levels of light than cones and are particularly useful in night vision. There are many more rods (75 to 150 million) than there are cones (6 to 7 million), but only cones are sensitive to color. Rods and cones can be compared to black-and-white and color film. Color film takes more light and thus works best in daylight; sensitive black-and-white film works not only in bright light but in shadows, dim light, and other poor lighting conditions.

Color Blindness.   When some or all of a person's cones do not function properly, he or she is said to be **color-blind.** There are several kinds of color blindness; most color-blind people do see *some* colors (Figure 5.5). For example, some people have trouble distinguishing between red and green. Other people are able to see red and green but cannot distinguish between yellow and blue. A very few people are totally color-blind. They depend on their rods, so to them the world looks something like black-and-white television programs—nothing but blacks and whites and shades of gray.

Color blindness affects about 8 percent of American men and less than 1 percent of American women. It is believed to result from a hereditary defect in the cones. This defect is carried in the genes of women whose vision is usually normal. These women pass the color-blindness genes on to their sons, who are born color-blind (see Wald, 1964).

Figure 5.6
To experience stereoscopic depth perception, take a tall, thin piece of cardboard and place it perpendicular to the page on the line that marks the separation of the two pictures. Then, with the edge of the cardboard resting between your eyes (as shown in the drawing), look at the left photo with your left eye and the right photo with your right eye and try to let the two images come together as one. (It helps to concentrate on the white dot.) If you are successful in fusing the images, the scene will suddenly jump out in depth. This process of binocular fusion contributes continuously to your ability to perceive depth.

Binocular Fusion and Stereopsis.   Because we have two eyes, located about 2.5 inches apart, the visual system receives two images. But instead of seeing double, we see a single image, probably a composite of the views of two eyes. The combination of the two images into one is called **binocular fusion.**

Not only does the visual system receive two images, but there is a difference between the images on the retinas. This difference is called **retinal disparity.** You can easily observe retinal disparity by bringing an object such as an eraser close to your eyes. Without moving it, look at the eraser first with one eye, then with the other. You will see a difference in the two images because of the different viewpoint each eye has. When you open both eyes you will no longer see the difference, but will instead see the object as solid and three-dimensional, if you have good binocular vision. **Stereopsis** refers to the phenomenon of seeing depth as a result of retinal disparity (Figure 5.6).

Figure 5.7
The hearing process. Sound vibrations in the air strike the eardrum and set in motion a chain of three bones—the malleus (hammer), the incus (anvil), and the stapes (stirrup). The stapes strikes another drum on the cochlea—a long, coiled, fluid-filled tube with a skin-like membrane running down the middle of it. The vibrations on this membrane stimulate hair-like cells that in turn stimulate the adjacent sensory nerve cells. The snail-like cochlea in this picture is also shown in cross section, with wavy pink lines representing the electrical impulses that will travel to the brain.

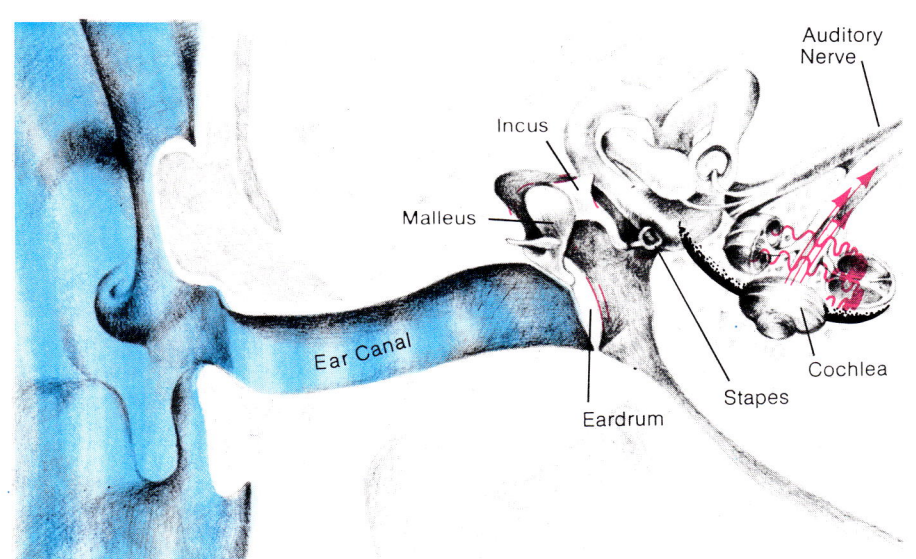

Hearing

Hearing depends on vibrations of the air, called sound waves. Sound waves from the air pass through various bones and fluids (shown in Figure 5.7) until they reach the inner ear, which contains tiny hairlike cells that move back and forth (much like a field of wheat waving in the wind). These hair cells change sound vibrations into chemical-electrical signals that travel through the **auditory nerve** to the brain.

The sensation of loudness depends on the strength of the vibrations in the air. This strength, or energy, is measured in **decibels.** The sounds we hear range upward from zero decibels, the softest sound the human ear can detect, to about 140 decibels, which is roughly as loud as a jet plane taking off. Any sound over 110 decibels can damage hearing, and any sound that is painful when you first hear it *will* damage your hearing if you hear it often enough. Figure 5.8 lists the decibel levels of some common sounds.

Pitch depends on sound frequency, or the rate of the vibration of the medium through which the sound is transmitted. Frequencies range from low to high: low frequencies produce deep bass sounds; high frequencies produce shrill squeaks. If you hear a sound composed of a combination of different frequencies, you can hear the separate pitches even though they occur simultaneously. For example, if you strike two keys of a piano at the same time, your ear can detect two distinct pitches.

Sounds are located through the interaction of the two ears. When a noise occurs on your right, for example, the sound comes to both ears, but it reaches your right ear a fraction of a second before it reaches the left. It is also slightly louder in the right ear. These differences often tell you which direction it is coming from.

Smell and Taste

Smell and taste are known as the chemical senses because their receptors are sensitive to chemical molecules rather than to light energy or sound waves. For you to smell something, the smell receptors in your nose must come into contact with the appropriate molecules. These molecules enter your nose in vapors, which reach a special membrane in the nasal passages on which the smell receptors are located. These receptors send messages about smells over the **olfactory nerve** to the brain.

For you to taste something, appropriate chemicals must stimulate receptors in the taste buds on your tongue. Taste information is relayed to the brain along with data about the texture and temperature of the substance you have put in your mouth.

Some scientists have proposed that all smells are made up of six qualities: flowery, fruity, spicy, resinous, putrid, and burned (Henning, 1916). Other scientists have come up with a similar scheme for taste, which they say is composed of four primary qualities, shown in Figure 5.9: sour, salty, bitter, and sweet (Beebe-Center, 1949).

Much of what is referred to as taste is actually produced by the sense of smell, however. You have undoubtedly noticed that when your nose is blocked by a cold, foods usually taste bland.

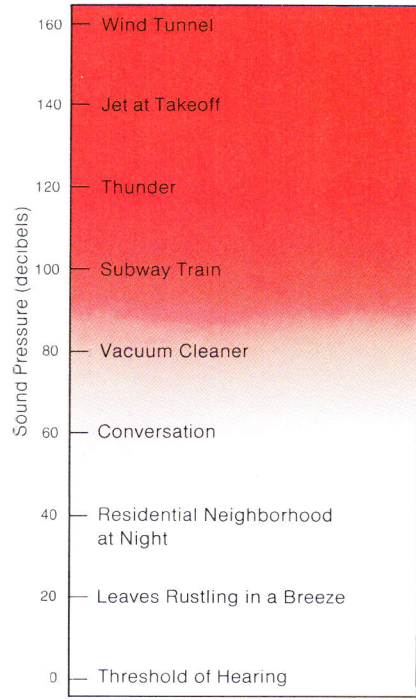

Figure 5.8
The decibel ratings for various common sounds. Sound actually becomes painful at about 130 decibels. Decibels represent ratios: A 20-decibel difference between two sounds indicates that one sound is ten times more intense than the other. Thus a vacuum cleaner puts ten times as much pressure on your eardrums as conversation does.

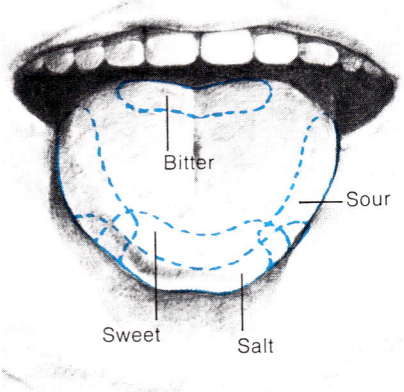

Figure 5.9
A map of the human tongue, indicating the areas that seem more sensitive to one kind of stimulation than to others. Interestingly, it is possible to be taste-blind as well as color-blind: A chemical called phenylthiocarbamide (PTC) tastes extremely bitter to some people and is quite tasteless to others.

Sex and Smell

Many animals communicate by means of odors, as any dog owner whose pet has gone into heat knows. Is it possible that people too communicate by scents? No one knows for sure, but there have been some fascinating studies suggesting that this may be the case.

Martha McClintock tested the "old wives' tale" that women's menstrual cycles synchronize when they live together. She found that the menstrual cycles of college roommates and friends did indeed become more similar as the school year progressed. She believed that pheromones—scented chemical messengers—were the cause.

Richard Michael has shown that female rhesus monkeys secrete certain substances that seem to make them more sexually attractive. In 1974, he reported that human females secrete the same chemical. But so far, no one has been able to prove that the odor increases human sexual desire.

For more details, see James Hassett, "Sex and Smell," *Psychology Today,* 11 (March 1978), pp. 40–45.

Sensations of warmth, cold, and pressure also affect taste. Try to imagine eating cold chicken soup or drinking a hot Pepsi, and you will realize how important temperature is to the sense of taste. Now imagine the textural differences between a spoonful of pudding and a crunchy chocolate bar, and you will see how the texture of food also influences taste.

The chemical senses seem to play a relatively unimportant role in human life when compared to their functions in lower animals. Insects, for example, often depend on smell to communicate with one another, especially in mating. In humans, smell and taste have become more a matter of esthetics than of survival (see box).

The Skin Senses

Receptors in the skin are responsible for providing the brain with at least four kinds of information about the environment: pressure, warmth, cold, and pain.

Sensitivity to pressure varies from place to place in the skin. Some spots, such as your fingertips, are densely populated with receptors and are, therefore, highly sensitive. Other spots, such as the middle of your back, contain relatively few receptors. Pressure sensations can serve as protection. For example, feeling the light pressure of an insect landing on your arm warns you of the danger of being stung.

Some skin receptors are particularly sensitive to hot or cold stimuli. In order to create a hot or cold sensation, a stimulus must have a temperature greater or less than the temperature of the skin. If you plunge your arm into a sink of warm water on a hot day, you will experience little or no sensation of its heat. If you put your arm in the same water on a cold day, however, the water will feel quite warm.

Many kinds of stimuli—scratches, punctures, severe pressure, heat, and cold—can produce pain. Their common property is real or potential injury to bodily tissues. Pain makes it possible for you to prevent damage to your body—it is an emergency system that demands immediate action.

Because pain acts as a warning system for your body, it does not easily adapt to stimulation—you rarely get "used to" pain. Pain tells you to avoid a stimulation that is harmful to you. Without this mechanism, you might "adapt" to a fire when you stand next to it. After a few minutes you would literally begin to cook, and your tissues would die.

Balance

The body's sense of balance is regulated by the **vestibular system** inside the inner ear. Its prominent feature is the three semicircular canals, as shown in Figure 5.10. When your head starts turning, the movement causes the liquid in the canals to move, bending the endings of receptor hair cells. The cells connect with the vestibular nerve, which joins the auditory nerve with the brain.

The stimuli for vestibular responses include movements such as spinning, falling, and tilting the body or head. Overstimulation of the vestibular sense by such movements can result in dizziness and "motion sickness," as you probably have experienced by going on amusement-park rides or by spinning around on a swivel stool. Although you are seldom directly aware of your sense of balance, without it you would be unable to stand or walk without falling or stumbling.

Body Sensations

Kinesthesis is the sense of movement and body position. It cooperates with the vestibular and visual senses to maintain posture and balance. The sensation of kinesthesis comes from receptors in and near the muscles, tendons, and joints. When any movement occurs, these receptors immediately send messages to the brain.

Without kinesthetic sensations, your movements would be jerky and uncoordinated. You would not know what your hand was doing if it were behind your back, and you could not walk without looking at your feet. Furthermore, complex physical activities, such as surgery, piano playing, and acrobatics, would be impossible.

Another type of bodily sensation comes from receptors that monitor internal body conditions. These receptors are sensitive to pressure, temperature, pain, and chemicals inside the body. For example, a full stomach stretching these internal receptors informs the brain that the stomach has ingested too much.

Little is known about pain from the interior of the body except that it seems to be deep, dull, and much more unpleasant than the sharply localized pain from the skin. In some cases, internal pain receptors may send inaccurate messages. They may indicate, for example, that a pain is located in the shoulder when in reality the source of irritation is in the lower stomach. Such sensation of pain in an area away from the actual source is called **referred pain.**

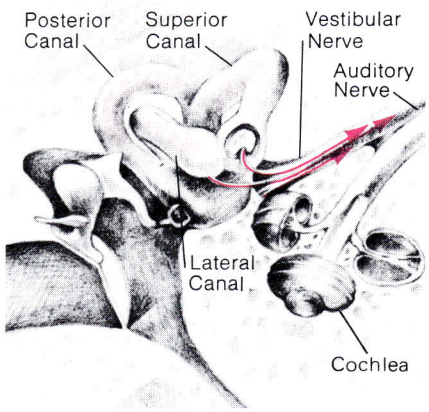

Figure 5.10
The vestibular system. The organs of balance consist of three semicircular canals at right angles to one another, filled with a freely moving fluid. Continuous motion in a straight line produces no response in this system, but starting, stopping, turning, speeding up, or slowing down makes the fluid in at least one of the canals move, stimulating the hair cells attached to the canal walls. These hair cells convert the movement into electrical impulses that are sent to the brain via the auditory nerve.

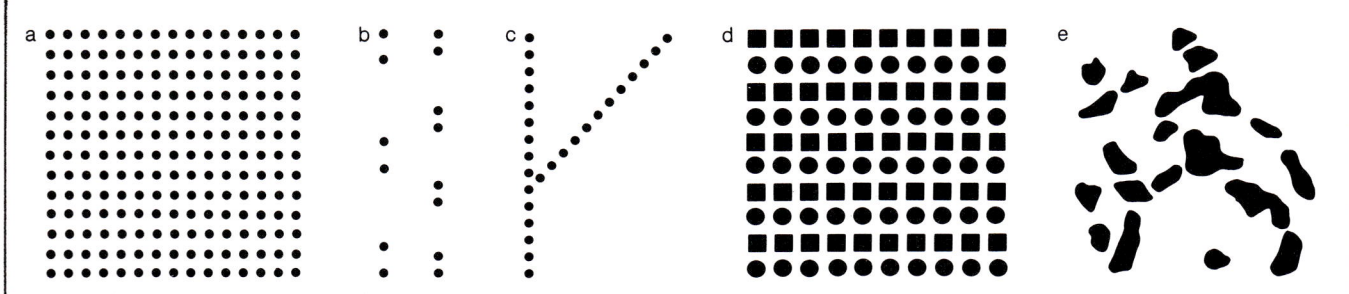

Figure 5.11
Principles of perceptual organization. Human beings see patterns and groupings in their environments rather than disorganized arrays of bits and pieces. For example, it is impossible to look at the array of dots in (a) without seeing shifting patterns of squares and lines. In (b), elements that are close to one another seem to belong together. However, as (c) shows, continuity can be more important: Although the bottom dot in the inclined series is closer to the vertical series, it is not seen as belonging to the vertical row. It is seen as a continuation of the inclined row and therefore as part of it. (d) Similar elements seem to belong to one another and therefore one sees the array as a set of horizontal rows rather than vertical columns, as one might if all the elements were the same. In (e) a principle known as closure is demonstrated. The breaks are ignored; what is seen is a "whole."

PERCEPTION

People do not usually experience a mass of colors, noises, warmths, and pressures. Rather we see cars and buildings, hear voices and music, and feel pencils, desks, and close friends. We do not merely have sensory experiences; we perceive objects. The brain receives information from the senses and organizes and interprets it into meaningful experiences—unconsciously. This process is called perception.

Principles of Perceptual Organization

Through the process of perception, the brain is always trying to build "wholes" out of the confusion of stimuli that bombards the senses. The "whole" experience that comes from organizing bits and pieces of information into meaningful objects and patterns is called a **Gestalt.** Here, the whole is greater than the sum of the parts. ("Gestalt" is a German word meaning pattern or configuration.)

Gestalt psychologists have tried to identify the principles the brain uses in constructing perceptions (Koffka, 1963). Some of the principles they have discovered are demonstrated in Figure 5.11. For example, they have found that people tend to see dots in patterns and groups. Thus when you look at Figure 5.11a, you see shifting patterns of lines and rectangles, not just an array of dots. Two principles that people use in organizing such patterns are proximity and similarity. If the elements of the pattern are close to one another or are similar in appearance, they tend to be perceived as belonging to one another. These principles are demonstrated in Figures 5.11b, c, and d.

The Gestalt principles of organization help to explain how people group their sensations and fill in gaps in order to make sense of the world. In music, for instance, you tend to group notes on the basis of their closeness to one another in time—you hear melodies, not single notes. Similarity and continuity are also important. They allow you to follow the sound of a particular voice or instrument even when many other sounds are occurring. For example, you can follow the sound of a bass guitar through a song.

Figure-Ground Perception

One form of perceptual organization is the division of experience into figure and ground. Look at Figure 5.12. What do you see? Sometimes the figure looks like a white vase against a black background. At other times it appears to be two black faces against a white background.

Figure-ground perception is the ability to discriminate properly between figure and ground. When you look at a three-dimensional object against the sky, you have no trouble distinguishing between the object and its background. It is when something is two-dimensional, as in Figure 5.12, that you may have trouble telling the figure from the ground. Nevertheless, such figure-ground perceptions give clues as to the nature of perception. The fact that a single pattern can be perceived in more than one way demonstrates that we are not passive receivers of stimuli.

Figure and ground are important in hearing as well as in vision. When you follow one person's voice at a noisy meeting, that voice is a figure and all other sounds become ground. Similarly, when you listen to a piece of music, a familiar theme may "leap out" at you: the melody becomes the figure, and the rest of the music merely background.

Perceptual Inference

Often we have perceptions that are not based entirely on current sensory information. When you hear barking as you approach your house, you assume it is your dog—not a cat or a rhinoceros or even another dog. When you take a seat in a dark theater, you assume it is solid and will hold your weight even though you cannot see what supports the seat. When you are driving in a car and see in the distance that the road climbs up a steep hill, then disappears over the top, you assume the road will continue over and down the hill, not come to an abrupt halt (Figure 5.13).

This phenomenon of filling in the gaps in what our senses tell us is known as perceptual inference (Gregory, 1970). Perceptual inference is

Figure 5.12
What did you see the first time you looked at this famous illustration? Whatever you saw, you saw because of your past experiences and current expectations. People invariably organize their experience into figure and ground. Whatever appears as figure receives the attention, is likely to be remembered, and has a distinctness of form that is lacking in the vague, formless ground. But, as this figure shows, what is meaningless ground one minute may become the all-important figure the next.

Figure 5.13
Perceptual inference: Even though you cannot see it, you assume that the road will continue beyond the slight rise—not stop abruptly at the limits of your vision from the car.

largely automatic and unconscious. We need only a few cues to inform us that a noise is our dog barking or that a seat is solid. Why? Because we have encountered these stimuli and objects in the past and know what to expect from them in the present. Perceptual inference thus sometimes depends on experience. On the other hand, we are probably born with some of our ability to make perceptual inferences. For example, experimenters have shown that infants just barely able to crawl will avoid falling over what appears to be a steep cliff—thus proving that they perceive depth (Gibson and Walk, 1960). (See Figure 5.14.)

Learning to Perceive

In large part, perceiving is something that people *learn* to do. For example, infants under one month will smile at a nodding object the size of a human face, whether or not it has eyes, a nose, or other human features. At about

Figure 5.14
The visual cliff apparatus. A human infant of crawling age (about six months) will usually refuse to cross the glass surface over the "deep" side even if his mother is on the other side and is urging the child to join her. The infant is perfectly willing to cross the "shallow" side to reach his mother, however. Even though the child can feel the hard solid glass surface beneath him, he refuses to venture out over an edge that appears to be a sudden drop.

Figure 5.15
A cut-away view of the apparatus used to show that active involvement is necessary for perceptual learning. Both kittens are receiving roughly the same visual input as they move in relation to the vertical stripes painted on the walls of the cylinder, but one kitten is producing the changes in what it sees by its own muscular movements. The other kitten sees similar changes because of the way it is harnessed to the first kitten, but what it sees has nothing to do with its own movements. This second kitten was found not to have developed the ability to see depth in this situation, while the active kitten developed depth perception normally.

twenty weeks, however, a blank oval will not make most babies smile, but a drawing of a face or a mask will. The baby has learned to distinguish something that looks like a person from other objects. Babies twenty-eight weeks and older are more likely to smile at a female than a male face. By thirty weeks most smile more readily when they see a familiar face than when they see someone they do not know. But it takes seven or eight months for babies to learn to recognize different people (Ahrens, 1954).

Experiments show that people and animals must be actively involved in their environments to develop perception. An experiment with newborn kittens demonstrates this. A number of kittens were raised in the dark until they were ten weeks old. Then they were divided into two groups: actives and passives.

For three hours a day an active kitten and a passive kitten were linked together, as shown in Figure 5.15. The kittens were harnessed in such a way that every action of the active kitten moved the passive kitten an equal distance, forward, backward, up, down, and from side to side. The visual stimulation for the two kittens was approximately the same, but the active animal produced its *own* changes in stimulation (by walking, for example). The other kitten was merely a passive receiver of stimulation. When the kittens were tested later, the passive one was not able to discriminate depth—to judge how close or far away various objects were. But the active kitten developed this ability normally. Not until the passive kitten had been allowed to live normally for two days—to move around in a visual environment of its own—did it develop normal depth perception (Held and Hein, 1963).

Experiments with human beings have also shown that active involvement in one's environment is important for accurate perception. People who have been blind from birth and who have had their sight restored by

By feeling people's faces, blind people can visualize how they look.

Fiction. Visualization is based on the memory of things we have seen. If a person has been blind since birth, he or she has no such memories.

Depth perception develops in infancy.

an operation (which is possible in only a few cases) have visual sensations, but initially they cannot tell the difference between a square and a circle or see that a red cube is like a blue cube (Valvo, 1971). In fact some had difficulty making such simple distinctions six months after their vision was restored.

Not all such cases end happily. Gregory (1978) tells the story of S. B., a man who had his sight restored at the age of fifty-two. Before the operation this man had lived an active and productive life. He liked making things in a shed in his garden, and sometimes rode a bicycle with a friend holding his shoulder to guide him. Immediately after the cornea transplant, he could only see a blur, but his sight improved rapidly. He had some trouble judging distance—for example, he thought his hospital window was about 6 feet from the ground when it was really about 60. But he recognized objects by sight that he had learned by touch. He had little trouble learning to tell time—for years he had used a watch with large raised numerals.

But S. B. never learned to completely trust his new sense. When he was blind, he would blithely cross the busiest streets with only his cane to guide him. Later, he was terrified by traffic and never felt comfortable crossing the street. After the initial thrill wore off, S. B. gradually became rather depressed by how drab the world was. Flaking paint and blemishes on things disturbed him. His depressions gradually became deeper and more general, and he died a few years after the operation.

Depth Perception

Depth perception—the ability to recognize distances and three-dimensionality—develops in infancy. If you place a baby on a large table, he or she will not crawl over the edge. The baby is able to perceive that it is a long distance to the floor. Psychologists test depth perception in infants with a device called the visual cliff, shown in Figure 5.14 (Gibson and Walk, 1960).

People use many cues to perceive depth. One is the information provided by retinal disparity, as discussed earlier in the chapter. Another is **motion parallax**—the apparent movement of objects that occurs when you move your head from side to side or when you walk around. You can demonstrate motion parallax by looking toward two objects in the same line of vision, one near you and the other some distance away. If you move your head back and forth, the near object will seem to move more than the far object. In this way, motion parallax gives you clues as to which objects are closer than others.

You are probably familiar with many other cues to distance. Nearby objects sometimes obscure parts of objects that are farther away. The more distant an object is, the smaller its image. Continuous objects such as railroad tracks, roads, rows of trees, and the walls of a room form converging lines, another cue to distance.

Constancy

When we have learned to perceive certain objects in our environment, we tend to see them in the same way, regardless of changing conditions. You probably judge the whiteness of the various portions of these pages to be fairly constant, even though you may have read the book under a wide range of lighting conditions. The light, angle of vision, distance, and, therefore, the image on the retina all change, but your perception of the object does not. Thus despite changing physical conditions, people are able to perceive objects as the same by the processes of size, shape, and brightness **constancy** (Figure 5.16).

An example of size constancy will illustrate how we have an automatic system for perceiving an object as being the same size whether it is far or near. A friend walking toward you does not seem to change into a giant even though the images inside your eyes become larger and larger as she approaches. To you, her appearance stays the same size because even though the size of your visual image is increasing, you are perceiving an additional piece of information: distance is decreasing. The enlarging eye image and the distance information combine to produce a perception of an approaching object that stays the same size.

Distance information compensates for the enlarging eye image to produce size constancy. If information about distance is eliminated, your perception of the size of the object begins to correspond to the actual size of the eye image. For example, it is difficult for most people to estimate the size of an airplane in the sky because they have little experience judging such huge sizes and distances. Pilots, however, can determine whether a flying plane is large and far away or small and close because they are experienced in estimating the sizes and distances of planes.

Illusions

Illusions are perceptions that are misrepresentations of reality. For example, look at the lines in Figure 5.17. Which lines are longer? Measure the

Figure 5.16
This figure can be used to demonstrate two striking features of vision. Stare steadily at the lowest right-hand star for about forty-five seconds, or until the colors start to shimmer. Then stare at a blank piece of paper. After a second or two you should see a *negative afterimage* of this figure in which the flag shows the normal colors. This occurs because the receptors for green, black, and yellow become fatigued, allowing the complementary colors of each to predominate when you stare at the white paper. Since these complements are, respectively, red, white, and blue, you see a normal American flag. Now shift your glance to a blank wall some distance away. Suddenly the flag will appear huge. This happens because of the principle of constancy—the brain interprets the same image as large when it is far away (apparently on the wall) and small when it is close (apparently on a piece of paper in your hand).

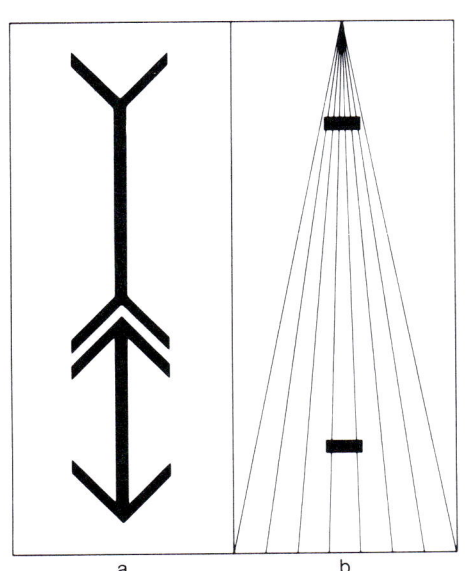

a   b   c

Figure 5.17
The Muller-Lyer illusion (a) and the Ponzo illusion (b) are two of the most famous illusions in psychology. The lines between the arrow heads in (a) are exactly the same length, as are the heavy black lines in (b). Some psychologists believe that the reason these lines appear to be different in length is that the brain interprets the diagrams in (a) and (b) as though they are scenes such as that in (c).

Figure 5.18
These two women appear to be a giant and a midget in an ordinary room. In fact, they are ordinary-sized women in a very peculiar room. This room, the true design of which is shown in the accompanying diagram, was constructed by psychologist Adelbert Ames. Again, the illusion is produced by tricking the brain into accepting an unusual situation as usual.

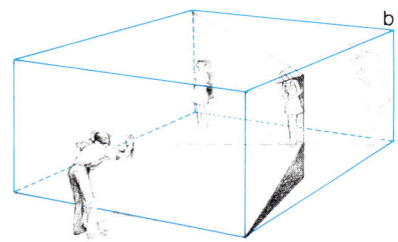

lengths of the pairs of lines with a ruler, then look again. Do the lines *look* as long now that you *know* they are the same? For most people, the answer is no.

A possible explanation of this type of illusion is that even though the patterns are two-dimensional, your brain treats them as three-dimensional. These illusions have features that usually indicate distance in three-dimensional space. The top line in Figure 5.17a, for example, can be thought of as the far corner of a room; the bottom line is like the near corner of the building. In Figure 5.17b and c the converging lines create the illusion of distance so that the lower bar looks nearer and shorter than the upper bar. This "perceptual compensation" seems to be unconscious and automatic.

Figure 5.18 shows two women in a room. The sizes of the women look dramatically different because you perceive the room as rectangular. In fact, the ceiling and walls are slanted so that the back wall is both shorter and closer on the right than on the left. But even when you know how this illusion was achieved, you still accept the peculiar difference in the women's sizes because the windows, walls, and ceiling appear rectangular. Your experience with rectangular rooms overrides your knowledge of how this trick is done.

EXTRASENSORY PERCEPTION

In this chapter, we have discussed the perception of tangible and measurable aspects of our environment. But humans are rarely content with un-

Figure 5.19
Dr. J. B. Rhine of Duke University administering an ESP test to two subjects using a special deck of cards.

derstanding only what can be seen and directly measured. We are fascinated by things that can't be seen, easily explained, or often even verified—flying saucers, atoms, genes, and extrasensory perception.

Extrasensory perception (ESP)—receiving information about the world through channels other than the normal senses—is a hotly debated topic. Many people are convinced that ESP exists because of an intense personal experience that can never be scientifically validated. For instance, we all have some fears before traveling, and we imagine the worst: our plane will crash, our train will be derailed, or we will have an automobile accident. These events almost never happen, and we easily forget about our frightening premonitions. However, if the improbable should actually take place, our premonitions turn into compelling evidence for the existence of precognition. Such coincidences sometimes become widely publicized evidence supporting paranormal phenomena, and we may quickly forget all the occasions when our premonitions were completely wrong. However, if we are truly interested in validating the existence of ESP, we must keep track of the frequency of its failures as well as its successes.

Scientists have been investigating ESP since the turn of the century. Probably the most famous **parapsychologist** (as these researchers into the supernatural are called) is J. B. Rhine. Around 1930, Rhine began a series of precise statistical tests of ESP. In tests of telepathy, for example, a "sender" focuses one at a time on each of twenty-five cards in a special deck. (The deck includes five cards for each of five different symbols.) A "receiver" locked in a distant room states which card he thinks the sender is focusing on. With luck alone, the receiver will guess about five cards correctly, sometimes a few more, sometimes a few less. Yet thousands of tests have shown that some people consistently respond above the average.

Some ESP researchers have concluded that these people are receiving information through senses or other channels we do not know about.

The results found in these studies are indeed statistically unlikely, but in other ways they are not nearly as impressive. For example, in one recent study (described in Chance, 1976), Charles Tart screened 1,500 college students and found 25 who seemed to have ESP. The students were shown a machine that randomly turned on one of four lights. They had to guess which light would come on next. They guessed nearly 7,500 times, and were right 26.8 percent of the time. Since one would expect people without ESP to be right only 25 percent of the time (one out of four), and since they guessed so many times, the result was statistically significant: the odds were more than 2,500 to 1 against this performance occurring by chance. These are impressive odds, but they are not particularly impressive results. This minimal ESP would not be particularly useful for playing the stock market or a football pool.

And there is one more problem with Tart's experiment. Unsupervised undergraduates collected the data. Many studies have shown that experimenters who believe in ESP tend to make errors supporting their belief, just as skeptics make errors showing that it does not exist. Another problem is that of intentional fraud. It would not be the first time a student falsified data to please his professor or get a good grade. And there have been several rather spectacular cases of fraud in ESP research.

Another reason many scientists do not accept the results of experiments supporting ESP is that the findings are highly unstable. One of the basic principles of scientific research is that one scientist should be able to replicate another scientist's results. Not only do different ESP experiments yield contradictory findings, but the same individual seems to show ESP on one day but not on the next. Proponents of ESP argue that this type of research cannot be consistently replicated because the special abilities are stifled in a laboratory situation. They say that ESP responses are best generated in highly emotional or relevant situations. Laboratory experiments that test people's ability to sense which symbols appear on cards are irrelevant to most people's lives and far from being highly emotional, and are usually a boring way to spend an afternoon. According to this viewpoint, it is remarkable that ESP has been reported to appear in the laboratory setting at all.

Although ESP may indeed be a very fragile phenomenon, the inability to replicate results and the difficulty of verifying ESP events are crucial problems. Many will remain skeptical about the existence of ESP until these problems are solved. However, such skepticism has often been overcome in the past. For example, just a century or so ago, the suggestion that many diseases were caused by invisible organisms was greeted with disbelief. Only after the work of Pasteur and other researchers proved that a clear relationship existed between these organisms and illness, was the "germ theory" of disease accepted. Perhaps the development of appropriate techniques for testing ESP could similarly lead to establishing the existence of paranormal phenomena—and perhaps they won't.

CHAPTER REVIEW

KEY TERMS

- absolute threshold
- adaptation
- auditory nerve
- binocular fusion
- color blindness
- cones
- constancy
- decibel
- difference threshold
- extrasensory perception (ESP)
- figure-ground perception
- Gestalt
- illusions
- kinesthesis
- lens
- motion parallax
- olfactory nerve
- optic nerve
- parapsychology
- perception
- perceptual inference
- pitch
- psychophysics
- pupil
- referred pain
- retina
- retinal disparity
- rods
- sensation
- signal-detection theory
- stereopsis
- stimulus
- subliminal advertising
- vestibular system
- Weber's law

SUMMARY

1. Our information about the outside world comes in through our senses. The sense organs convert stimuli in the environment into chemical-electrical activity that travels to the brain. This process results in sensation.

2. Psychophysics is the study of the relationship between physical stimuli and the sensory experiences they produce. The smallest amount of energy that will produce a sensation is called an absolute threshold. The smallest change in a stimulus that produces a change in sensation is called the difference threshold.

3. Experiencing a sensation depends more on changes in the stimulus than on the absolute size or amount of the stimulus. Sensory adaptation occurs when a stimulus continues without changing. Motivation can influence whether or not certain stimuli will be detected.

4. The chief stimulus in vision is light. The rods and cones in the retina of the eye convert light energy to chemical impulses that travel over the optic nerve to the brain. Cones respond to color and work best in daylight. Rods are more sensitive to brightness but do not detect color. Color blindness results when cones are absent or mal-

functioning. Binocular fusion, the combination of images from both eyes, is accompanied by stereopsis, the three-dimensional interpretation of the world. This is made possible by retinal disparity, which is the difference between the images in the two eyes.

5. The stimuli for hearing are sound waves, which are converted to chemical-electrical impulses by hair cells in the inner ear. These messages reach the brain via the auditory nerve.

6. Smell and taste are chemical senses. Receptors in the nose and on the tongue respond to contact with molecules. Most taste sensations involve the sense of smell to some extent.

7. Skin receptors respond to pressure, warmth, cold, and pain. These sensations play an important role in warning the brain of possible external dangers.

8. Internal bodily sensations include balance, kinesthesis, and internal sensitivity to pressure, temperature, pain, and chemicals.

9. Perception is the process of creating meaningful wholes out of information from the senses. Perceptual wholes are called Gestalts. Psychologists study such phenomena as figure-ground

relationships, perceptual inference, perceptual development, depth perception, constancy, and illusions to determine how perception works.

10. There has been a great deal of research on extrasensory perception, but the topic is still controversial.

1. What is the difference between an absolute threshold and a difference threshold?

2. What is the current view of the ability of subliminal advertising to influence a person's behavior?

3. What psychological principle explains why you are more likely to notice when a single light bulb burns out in a room with three lamps than when a single light bulb burns out in a sports arena?

4. Which sense has received the most research? Why?

5. What cues do we use to determine distance and depth in vision? What cues do we use to determine direction of sounds?

6. What four kinds of information do we receive from our skin?

7. Which sensory system regulates our sense of balance? What causes dizziness?

8. What sources of sensory information would a person use when dancing?

9. Gestalt psychologists have identified several principles that we use in organizing our perceptions. What are some of these principles?

10. What experimental evidence suggests that we are born with the ability to make perceptual inferences? What evidence is there that perception is the result of interaction with the environment?

11. If you took two books of the same size and placed one at the far end of the room and the other on a table in front of you, you would conclude that they are the same size, even though the farther one creates a smaller image on your retina. Why do you perceive them as the same size?

12. How do psychologists currently feel about the available evidence for the existence of ESP?

1. Hold a pencil about twelve inches in front of your face. Look at it with your left eye closed, then with your right eye closed. Notice how the pencil seems to jump around. What happens when you look at the pencil with both eyes? What principle does this experiment demonstrate?

2. Fill three bowls with water—hot water in one, cold in another, and lukewarm in the third. Put one hand in the cold water and the other in the hot water and leave them there for thirty seconds. Now put both hands in the lukewarm water at the same time. What do you feel? How does this demonstrate the principle of sensory adaptation?

3. Get a fresh potato and peel it. Do the same with an apple. Now have a friend close his eyes and

smell a fresh onion while he takes a bite of each one. Can he tell which food is which without his sense of smell? Try this experiment with various people, using different foods that have similar textures.

4. If sensation consists entirely of electrical signals in the brain that are subject to interpretation by perception, does everyone experience the world differently? Animals have different sensory apparatus than humans—do they live in a different perceptual world?

5. Have a friend stand with her back to you. Touch various parts of her back with one pencil or with two pencils held close together. Each time you touch her back, ask her how many points she felt. Now touch the points to her hand and arm, again asking how many points she feels. What are your results? What accounts for the results?

6. To demonstrate the information shown in Figure 5.9, prepare solutions of salt water (salt), lemon juice (sour), baking soda (bitter), and sugar water (sweet). Dab each solution on various points on your tongue, and see if you can verify which area of the tongue is predominately sensitive to each of these major tastes.

7. Perform the following experiment to test one kind of sensory adaptation. Write a sentence while looking at your writing in a mirror. Do this until it begins to feel natural. Then write the sentence normally. Does normal writing now feel strange?

8. Try the following experiment to demonstrate an illusion of the sense of touch. Stretch a foot-square piece of chicken wire tautly over a frame. Blindfold your subject(s) and ask him or her to hold the thumb and forefinger of his or her hand to lightly touch each side of the chicken wire. Slide the wire rapidly back and forth between his or her fingers. Ask your subject to report the sensation he or she feels. Most people believe that they feel a continuous slippery or oily surface. This illusion will probably be stronger if the subject does not know in advance the actual nature of the material that he or she is feeling.

9. Station yourself behind a window or glass door (to eliminate sounds and smells that you might give off) and stare intently at someone who has his or her back toward you. Pick someone who is within a ten-yard range and who is not engaged in any particular activity at the moment. Does the person turn around and look at you? If so, how long does it take him or her to "sense" your presence? How can you explain this phenomenon? Can you develop a "control" procedure to see how long it takes someone to turn around when you're not looking at his or her back?

10. To illustrate the importance of two retinal images for depth perception, try out the following demonstration with the help of a friend. You will need to construct a pendulum using a 3- to 4-foot piece of string with a weight attached. Secure your pendulum to the middle of the top part of a door frame. With the door open, set the pendulum in motion swaying back and forth parallel to the door frame. Now have your friend stand in front of the doorway while wearing a patch over one eye. Ask your friend to describe the motion of the pendulum. In what direction does he or she think the pendulum is moving? Now have your friend switch the patch from one eye to the other. Ask him or her to describe the pendulum movement again. What differences are there in the two descriptions? Explain these differences.

11. Close your eyes and gently press on your eyeballs. What sensation do you experience? Do you "see" anything? How can you explain the fact that you have visual experiences in the absence of light rays?

12. Put on a backpack that has been filled with ten pounds of materials. Arrange a series of objects that differ in weight from very light (a piece of paper) to medium weight (a paperback book) to heavy (a pound of candy or a two-pound weight). Have a friend insert these objects into the backpack one at a time, in increasing order of weight. Be sure you cannot see which object is being placed in the pack. After each object is placed in the pack, give a report of the perceived difference in weight. At what point do you notice the difference in the weight of the pack? Explain your experience with weight perception by referring to the concept of difference thresholds.

13. To appreciate the importance of visual sensations in your daily life, try doing some of your daily activities while blindfolded. You will need the help of a friend who can serve as your watchdog to prevent injury. While you are blindfolded, notice your sensations of taste, sound, and touch. How is your use of these sensations different from what it normally is? What signals do you use to guide your walking? In what ways do you rely on your past experiences to help you "see" while wearing the blindfold?

Objectives: *After studying this chapter, you should be able to*
- explain the physiological basis of motivation.
- explain drive reduction theory and discuss its critiques.
- summarize the study of social motives.
- summarize the various physiological theories of emotion.
- summarize the cognitive theories of emotion.

CHAPTER
6

Motivation and Emotion

Why do people climb Mount Everest and cross the Atlantic in a balloon? Why do some people spend every waking moment memorizing batting averages while others don't know the difference between the New York Yankees and the Boston Red Sox? And, as the song asks, why do fools fall in love?

Although all psychology is concerned with what people do and how they do it, research on motivation and emotion focuses on the underlying why of behavior.

BIOLOGICAL MOTIVES

We see Ruth studying all weekend while the rest of us hang out, and since we know she wants to go to law school, we conclude that she is "motivated" by her desire to get good grades. We see Harold working after classes at a job he doesn't like, and since we know he wants to buy a car, we conclude that he is "motivated" to earn money for the car. Conceptions of motivation in psychology are in many ways similar to those expressed in everyday language; since motivation cannot be observed directly, psychologists, like the rest of us, infer motivation from goal-directed behavior.

Some behavior is determined by the physiological state of the organism. Like other animals, human beings have certain survival needs. The nervous system is constructed in such a way that dramatic variations in blood sugar, water, oxygen, salt, or essential vitamins lead to changes in

Biological Motives
The Physiology of Motivation
• Drive Reduction Theory
Social Motives
McClelland and the Need for Achievement • Maslow's Hierarchy of Needs
Emotion
Expressing Emotions: Innate and Learned Behavior
• Physiological Theories
• Using Psychology: Lie Detection • Cognitive Theories

Anorexia Nervosa and Bulemia. Anorexia nervosa and bulemia are serious eating disorders. Both syndromes are found mostly in young females. They very rarely occur in males.

A person suffering from anorexia nervosa stops eating to the point of starvation. The disorder is typically associated with extreme dieting. Symptoms of anorexia include body weight at least 15 percent below normal, an extreme fear of gaining weight, and a perception that one's body is too heavy or out of shape. Psychologists estimate that 1 out of 250 women between 12 and 18 years of age are anorexic. Up to 10 percent of anorexics die within 10 years.

Bulemia is a more common eating disorder. It is characterized by alternating periods of uncontrolled eating followed by purging—self-induced vomiting, taking of laxatives, or fasting. This is why bulemia is also referred to as binge–purge syndrome. Bulemia can result in ulcers, tooth decay, and electrolyte imbalance, which may cause heart problems. It has been estimated that about 4.5 percent of female college students suffer from bulemia.

behavior designed to return the body to a condition of chemical balance. The first part of this section discusses the role of such physiological factors in motivating behavior.

But many human motives, such as Ruth's desire to get into law school or Harold's desire to buy a car, do not have a simple physiological basis. Although not all psychologists would be able to agree on an explanation of these behaviors, none would say that they were the result of physiological deficits. The rest of this section discusses some approaches to analyzing the motivational bases of these kinds of human activities.

The Physiology of Motivation

All organisms, including humans, have built-in regulating systems that work like thermostats to maintain body temperature, the level of sugar in the blood, the production of hormones, and so on. As we saw in Chapter 4, when the level of thyroxin in the bloodstream is low, the pituitary gland secretes a thyroxin-stimulating hormone. When the thyroxin level is high, the pituitary gland stops producing this hormone. Similarly, when your body temperature drops below a certain point, you start to shiver, your blood vessels constrict, and you put on more clothes. All these activities reduce heat loss and bring body temperature back to the correct level. If your body heat rises above a certain point, you start to sweat, your blood vessels dilate, and you remove clothes. These processes cool you.

The tendency of all organisms to correct imbalances and deviations from their normal state is known as **homeostasis.** Several of the drives that motivate behavior are homeostatic—hunger, for example.

Hunger.   What motivates people to seek food? Often you eat because the sight and smell of, say, pizza tempts you into a store. Other times you eat out of habit (you always have lunch at 12:30) or to be sociable (a friend invites you out for a snack). But suppose you are working frantically to finish a term paper. You don't have any food in your room, so you ignore the fact that it is dinner time and you keep working. But at some point your body will start to demand food. You'll feel an aching sensation in your stomach. What produces this sensation? What makes you feel hungry?

Your body requires food to function. When you miss a meal, your liver releases stored sugar into your bloodstream to keep you going. After a time, however, this supply runs out and the hypothalamus begins to act.

The hypothalamus, as indicated above, is a structure at the base of the brain that regulates food intake. It not only tells us when we need to eat, it also tells us when to stop eating. How does it work? The hypothalamus is laced with blood vessels that make it extremely sensitive to levels of sugar in the blood. It also has numerous connections to the brain that are capable of raising or lowering the level of certain chemicals in the brain (Ahlskog and Hoebel, 1973). Experiments have shown that this is what makes us crave food or feel too full to eat more.

If the portion of the hypothalamus called the **lateral hypothalamus (LH)** is stimulated with electrodes, a laboratory animal will begin eating, even if it has just finished a large meal. Conversely, if the LH is removed

a

b

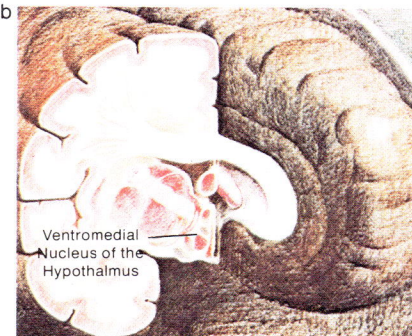

Ventromedial
Nucleus of the
Hypothalmus

Figure 6.2
(left) The fat rat. (right) A drawing showing the part of the human brain that corresponds to the part lesioned in the rat. The view is from the front of the brain, with one half shown in cross section. (See Figure 4.5, page 84.)

surgically, an animal will stop eating and eventually die of starvation if it is not fed artificially. Thus the LH provides the "go" signals: it tells you to eat.

If a different portion of the hypothalamus called the **ventromedial hypothalamus (VMH)** is stimulated, an animal will slow down or stop eating altogether, even if it has been kept from food for a long period. However, if the VMH is removed, the animal will eat everything in sight until it becomes so obese it can hardly move (Figure 6.2). This indicates that the VMH provides the "stop" signals: it tells you when you have had enough food.

The level of sugar in the blood is not the only thing that causes the hypothalamus to act. If your stomach is empty, the muscles in the stomach walls contract periodically (producing hunger pangs). These contractions activate the LH, which sends "go" or "eat" signals to other areas of your brain. When your stomach is full, the VMH sends "stop" signals, even though the energy from the food you have just eaten has not yet reached your bloodstream (digestion takes time). In addition, the hypothalamus responds to temperature. The LH, or "go" signal, is more active in cold temperatures; the VMH, or "stop" signal, more active in warm temperatures (presumably because people and other animals need to eat more in cold weather).

In summary, the hypothalamus "interprets" at least three kinds of information: the level of sugar in the blood, the amount of food in the stomach, and body temperature. These determine whether the hypothalamus will tell you (via chemical changes in the brain) to eat or stop eating.

Obesity. Like the rats whose VMHs are destroyed, many people have trouble keeping their hips from looking like the Goodyear blimp. Stanley Schachter (1971) and his colleagues at Columbia University have done a number of ingenious studies which show that obese people respond to external cues—they eat not because they are hungry, but because they see something good to eat or their watches tell them it's time.

Obese people eat not because they are hungry, but because they see something tempting or their watches say it's time.

To prove this, Schachter first set up a bogus taste test in which people were asked to rate five kinds of crackers. He was really not interested in how these people rated the crackers on his elaborate questionnaires. Schachter simply wanted to see how many crackers normal and overweight people would eat. Each person was asked to skip lunch, so they all came to the test hungry. Some were told that the taste test required a full stomach; they were given as many roast beef sandwiches as they wanted. The rest stayed hungry. Schachter's theory predicted that normal people eat because they're hungry while obese people eat whether they are hungry or not. This was true. People of normal weight ate more crackers than overweight people did when both groups were hungry, and fewer crackers after they had eaten the roast beef.

In another study, Schachter put out a bowl of peanuts which people could eat while they sat in a waiting room. Sometimes the nuts were still in their shells, and sometimes they weren't. Fat people ate the nuts only when they didn't have to bother taking the shells off. Thus, again, they ate simply because food was there. People of normal weight were equally likely to try a few nuts whether they were shelled or not. In still another study, Schachter found that fat college freshmen were more likely to cancel dormitory food contracts than normal freshmen. Why? The overweight were more concerned with the taste of their food, and they simply couldn't stand the institutional fishcakes and spaghetti.

In summary, Schachter argues that overweight people respond to external cues (for example, the smell of cookies hot from the oven) while normal people respond to internal cues (the stomach contractions of hunger). His work shows that, for people, even physiological needs like hunger are influenced by complex factors.

Drive Reduction Theory

Drive reduction theory, which dominated psychological thinking in the 1940s and early 1950s, emerged from the work of experimental psychologist Clark Hull and his associates (1943). Hull traced motivation back to basic physiological needs. According to Hull, when an organism is deprived of something it needs (such as food, water, or sex) it becomes tense and agitated. To relieve this tension it engages in more or less random activity. Thus biological needs *drive* an organism to act.

If one of these random behaviors reduces the drive, the organism will begin to acquire a habit; that is, when the drive is again felt, the organism will first try the same response again. Habits channel drives in certain directions. In short, **drive reduction theory** states that physiological needs drive an organism to act in either random or habitual ways until its needs are satisfied.

Hull and his colleagues suggested that all human motives—from the desire to acquire property to striving for excellence and seeking affection or amusement—are extensions of basic biological needs. For example, people develop the need for social approval because as infants they were fed and cared for by a smiling mother or father. Gradually, through generalization and conditioning, the need for approval becomes important in itself. Approval becomes a learned drive.

Losing Weight

If you want to lose weight, begin by keeping detailed records of everything you eat for a week or two. Get a good book on nutrition and analyze your eating habits, particularly the number of calories you consume on an average day. Forget about miracle diets that promise you can have as many cheesecakes as you want. The only people who benefit from miracle diets are the writers who get rich from books about them.

Once you figure out what you are eating and what you should be eating, all that's left is the hard part—doing something about it. Set up a system of rewards for sticking to your diet and punishments for sneaking off for hot fudge sundaes. Continue to monitor what and when you eat and chart your progress.

Some therapists believe you should not start a major weight-reduction program when the rest of your life is a mess. Of course, if your life is always a mess, this may be one place to start.

For more details, see R. L. Williams and J. D. Long, *Toward a Self-Managed Life Style,* 2nd ed. Boston: Houghton Mifflin, 1979.

Drive reduction theory dominated psychologists' thinking for over a decade. However, the results of experiments conducted in the late 1950s suggested that Hull and his colleagues had overlooked some of the more important factors in human—and animal—motivation.

Figure 6.3
What motivates a hard-driven executive? Researchers suggest a variety of factors may be involved, including the desire to lead others, to earn more money, and to gain recognition and praise.

Figure 6.4
The monkeys in Harlow's classic experiment on the determinants of mother love spent most of their time with the terrycloth mother even though they fed from the wire mother. The terrycloth mother was also a security base when they were frightened.

Figure 6.5
This monkey worked hard for the privilege of watching an electric train, but it would be difficult to say what drive is reduced as a result.

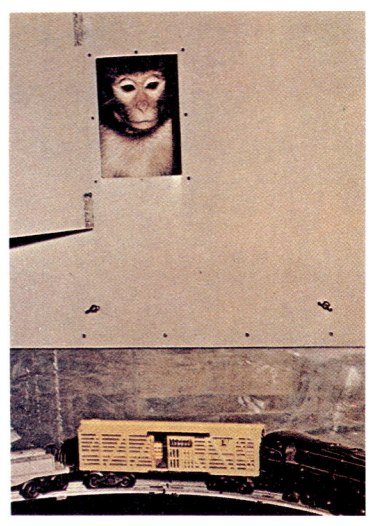

According to drive reduction theory, infants become attached to their mothers because mothers usually relieve such drives as hunger and thirst. Harry Harlow (among others) doubted that this was the only or even the main source of an infant's love for its mother. Harlow decided to challenge drive reduction theory with an experiment. He took infant monkeys away from their mothers and put them alone in cages with two surrogate "mothers" made of wire (Figure 6.4). One of the wire mothers was equipped with a bottle. If drive reduction theory were correct, the monkeys would become attached to this figure, because it was their only source of food. The other wire mother was covered with soft cloth but could not provide food and relief from hunger. In test after test, the small monkeys preferred to cling to the cloth mother, particularly when strange, frightening objects were put into their cages (Harlow and Zimmerman, 1959).

Thus one of the factors that many drive theorists overlooked is that some experiences (such as hugging something or someone soft) are inherently pleasurable. Although they do not seem to reduce biological drives, these experiences serve as incentives or goals for behavior. Another factor that drive theorists overlooked was the pleasure humans and related animals derive from stimulation or arousal (Figure 6.5). Just think about how dogs love to be petted or how children love horror movies and rides at amusement parks that are designed to terrify them. In the end, then, a drive *for* stimulation looked as plausible as a drive to *reduce* stimulation.

Many psychologists concluded that there could be no general theory of motivation of the type Hull suggested. Instead of a drive reduction theory, we are left with a list of unlearned, innate drives that include hunger and thirst, but also curiosity, contact with soft things, and many others.

What Motivates People To Take Unnecessary Risks?

Fifty . . . forty-nine . . . forty-eight . . . forty-seven. . . . The skydiver counted the seconds till it would all be over. There was no chance he would get out of this fall alive . . . no chance his chute would open. As he pulled the cord and felt the chute snap open above his head, only one thought ran through his mind: he would live to try it again.

What motivates skydivers and others to take such risks? Psychologists Richard Solomon and John Corbit believe the answer lies in the emotional responses the risk-taker experiences before, during, and after the feat:

1. The skydiver is terrified the first time he jumps. When he lands, his terror is quickly replaced by a stunned feeling that lasts only a few minutes. This in turn is replaced by normal composure.
2. After several jumps, the skydiver is no longer terrified; instead he feels anxious before the jump. But the main change is in the way he feels afterward. The exhilaration lasts for many hours.
3. This "afterglow" motivates the skydiver to jump again.

According to Solomon and Corbit, another response pattern may also be working at the same time. They propose that the central nervous system automatically opposes highly emotional responses in order to reduce the intensity of these feelings. Thus, after we've taken part in a risky activity for a while, we do not experience the extreme highs and lows we did at first. And we are more willing to take risks we found nearly impossible to take in the beginning.

For more details, see Richard L. Solomon and John D. Corbit, "An Opponent-Process Theory of Motivation," *Psychological Review*, 81 (1974): 119–145.

Figure 6.6
Needs identified by Henry Murray in his formulation of a theory of human personality. Murray distinguishes between a class of primarily physical needs and a—much larger—class of psychological needs.

n Acquisition
(to gain possessions and property)

n Conservance
(to collect, repair, clean, and preserve things)

n Order
(to arrange, organize, put away objects)

r. Construction
(to organize and build)

r. Achievement
(to overcome obstacles, to exercise power, to strive to do something difficult as well and as quickly as possible)

r. Recognition
(to excite praise and commendation)

r. Defendance
(to defend oneself against blame or belittlement)

r. Dominance
(to influence or control others)

n Autonomy
(to resist influence or coercion)

n Aggression
(to assault or injure)

n Affiliation
(to form friendships and associations)

n Rejection
(to snub, ignore, or exclude)

n Nurturance
(to nourish, aid, or protect)

n Succorance
(to seek aid, protection, or sympathy)

n Play
(to relax, amuse oneself, seek diversion and entertainment)

n Cognizance
(to explore)

SOCIAL MOTIVES

Many psychologists have concentrated their research on social motives rather than on the unlearned, biological motives we have been discussing. Social motives are learned from our interactions with other people.

In Chapter 11 we will discuss the theories of several psychologists who sought to explain the development of personality. One such psychologist was Henry Murray, whose theory of personality identifies sixteen basic needs (see Figure 6.6). Note that most of these are social motives rather than biological needs (see Murray *et al.,* 1934). Lists such as these are sometimes forgotten shortly after they appear in print, because in itself such a list is not very useful. Murray's list has not been forgotten, however. In fact, hundreds of studies have been performed on just one of these needs, the need for achievement.

McClelland and the Need for Achievement

One reason the achievement motive has been so well researched is that David McClelland became interested in finding some quantitative way of measuring social motives (McClelland *et al.,* 1953). Once he did this, he believed he could search for a technique of changing motivation, because he could then have a method of measuring whether a change had occurred. McClelland concentrated his research on the need for achievement because he felt that techniques for increasing this motive might be very useful in improving the lives of millions of people.

McClelland's main tool for measuring achievement motivation was the Thematic Apperception Test (TAT). This test consists of a series of pictures. Subjects are told to make up a story that explains each picture. Tests of this sort are called projective tests, and we will describe them in detail in Chapter 12. At this point, it is only important to know that there are no right

Figure 6.7
A picture of the sort that might be used in the measurement of the need for achievement. Examples of stories that would be scored from fairly high to low are given below. The portions of the stories printed in italics are the kinds of themes considered to reflect the need for achievement.

This guy is just getting off work. These are all working guys and they don't like their work too much either. The younger guy over on the right knows the guy with the jacket.

Something bad happened today at work—*a nasty accident that shouldn't have happened.* These two guys don't trust each other *but they are going to talk* about it. *They mean to put things to rights. No one else much cares,* it seems.

The guy with the jacket is *worried.* He feels that *something has to be done. He wouldn't ordinarily talk to* the younger man *but now he feels he must.* The young guy is ready. He's *concerned* too but doesn't know what to expect.

They'll both realize after talking that you never know where your friends are. *They'll both feel better* afterward because they'll feel they have someone they can rely on next time there's trouble.

Harry O'Silverfish has been working on the Ford assembly line for thirteen years. Every morning he gets up, eats a doughnut and cup of coffee, takes his lunch pail, gets in the car, and drives to the plant. It is during this morning drive that his mind gets filled with *fantasies of what he'd like to be doing* with his life. Then, about the same time that he parks his car and turns off his ignition, he also *turns off his mind—* and it remains turned off during the whole working day. In the evenings, he is *too tired and discouraged to do much* more than drink a few beers and watch TV.

But this morning Harry's mind didn't turn off with the car. He had witnessed a car accident on the road—in which two people were killed—soon after leaving home. Just as he reaches the plant gate, Harry suddenly turns. Surprised, he discovers that he has made *a firm decision* never to enter that plant again. He knows that *he must try another way* to live before he dies.

These are hard-hats. It's the end of the shift. There is a demonstration outside the plant and the men coming out are looking at it. Everyone is just walking by. They are not much interested. One person is *angry and wants to go on strike,* but this does not make sense to anyone else. He is out of place. Actually he is not really angry, he is just bored. He looks as though he might do a little dance to amuse himself, which is more than the rest of them do. *Nothing will happen* at this time *till more people join* this one man in his needs.

or wrong answers. Since the test questions are ambiguous, the answers a person gives are believed to reflect his or her unconscious desires. Each story is "coded" by looking for certain kinds of themes and scoring these themes according to their relevance to various types of needs, such as achievement. Coding has by now been refined to the point where trained coders agree about 90 percent of the time.

McClelland noted first that hungry subjects tended to include more stories about getting food than subjects who were not hungry. Next he performed an analogous test for the need for achievement: he created a group of subjects who were "deprived" of achievement. He did this by giving them a series of tests designed so that they did poorly and knew it. They were allowed to try again and still did poorly. Then he administered the TAT, saying that it was being used to look for creative, intelligent group leaders. As a control, he gave the TAT to another group with a "relaxed" set of instructions, encouraging them to write stories that pleased them. Then he analyzed the stories to see how they differed. In addition, the TAT stories of all kinds of known successful achievers were studied and compared to those of control groups. (Figure 6.7 shows an example of how need for achievement might be measured.)

Based on these tests, McClelland developed a scoring system for the TAT. For example, a story would be scored high in achievement imagery if the main character was concerned with standards of excellence and a high level of performance, with unique accomplishments (such as inventions and awards), or with the pursuit of a long-term career or goal.

In later studies, people who scored high and low in achievement on the TAT were compared in a variety of situations. For example, it was found that high achievers were able to solve anagrams (unscrambling and rearranging letters into meaningful words) faster than those less interested in achievement (Kolb, 1973). More significantly, McClelland followed up the careers of some students at Wesleyan University who had been tested with the TAT in 1947. He wanted to see which students had chosen entrepreneurial work—that is, work in which they had to initiate projects on their own. He found that eleven years after graduation, 83 percent of the entrepreneurs (business managers, insurance salesmen, real estate investors, consultants, and so on) had scored high in achievement, but only 21 percent of the nonentrepreneurs had scored that high (McClelland, 1965).

Next, McClelland checked to see whether the achievement motive had any real effects on society (1961). He and his associates studied the children's literature of England, Spain, and ancient Athens, scoring it for achievement in the same manner as they would a TAT story. They found that, in general, high levels of achievement motivation appeared fifty to one hundred years before improvements in the economic situation of each country.

Encouraged by this finding, McClelland and others then set about devising a training course in achievement motivation. The trainees in this course learned to score their own TAT stories and to recognize achievement themes in them. They also rewrote their stories again and again, attempting to include more achievement themes in them. Then they discussed everyday life situations and case histories with other members of the group, focusing on achievement themes. Group members also played a business game designed to give them quick feedback for decision making and problem solving.

Success with this program has been reported after applying it in such diverse places as Spain, Mexico, Italy, India, and poverty areas of Kentucky (McClelland and Winter, 1969). For example, a group of seventy-six men running small businesses in Indian villages was given the training and was later compared to a similar group not given the training. The trained groups showed significant and large increases in entrepreneurial activity (such as starting new businesses or gaining large increases in salary), while the untrained group did not change.

McClelland does not believe we should all train ourselves as high achievers. In fact, he has said that such persons are not always the most interesting, and they are usually not artistically sensitive (McClelland and Harris, 1971). They would also be less likely to value intimacy in a relationship. Studies have shown that high achievers prefer to be associated with experts who will help them achieve instead of with more friendly people.

One interesting feature of the research on achievement motivation is that virtually all of the major studies used males as their subjects. The generalizations regarding the factors that influence the desire for achievement apply to men but not to women. Research has revealed that women have a more complex set of motives for achievement and success.

Fear of Success.   McClelland's work has inspired a wide variety of research on other aspects of motivation. Matina Horner (1970, 1972) asked eighty-nine men to write a story beginning with the line, "After first term finals, John finds himself at the top of his medical school class." Substituting the name Anne for John in the opening line, she also asked ninety women to write a story. Ninety percent of the men wrote success stories. However, over sixty-five percent of the women predicted doom for Anne.

Some of the women feared for Anne's social life. They described her as undatable or unmarriageable, and suggested that she would be socially isolated if she excelled in her studies and career. Some wrote about the guilt and despair she would experience if she continued to succeed. And some refused to believe the opening line. It was impossible for Anne to be first in her class; there must be some mistake.

On the basis of this study Horner identified another dimension of achievement motivation, the *motive to avoid success*. Females in our society are (or were) raised with the idea that being successful in all but a few careers is odd and unfeminine. Thus a woman who is a success in medicine, law, and other traditionally male occupations must be a failure as a woman. It might have been all right for Anne to pass her exams, but the fact that she did better than all the men in her class made the female subjects anxious.

Horner discovered that bright women, who had a very real chance of achieving in their chosen fields, exhibited a stronger fear of success than did women who were average or slightly above average. (Expecting success made them more likely to avoid it, despite the obvious advantages of a

Being a mother might be quite satisfying for one woman, but not for another.

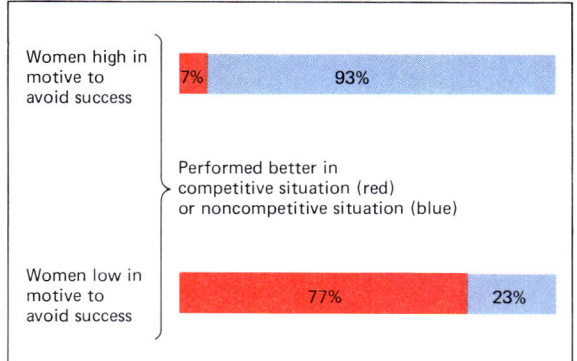

Women high in
motive to
avoid success

7%   93%

Performed better in
competitive situation (red)
or noncompetitive situation (blue)

Women low in
motive to
avoid success

77%   23%

Figure 6.8
Data from Horner's experiment on
the motive to avoid success in
women. (After Horner, 1970)

rewarding career.) This seemed to confirm Horner's belief that success involves deep conflicts for women (see Figure 6.8).

Many other researchers then set out to verify Horner's findings. They quickly found that the picture was more complicated than Horner's study seemed to suggest. For one thing, it's very hard to define success. Being a mother might be quite satisfying for one woman, but a sign of failure for someone who would have preferred a career. Also, it is often hard to tell whether a person who doesn't try something is more afraid of success or failure.

It is important to remember that much of the earlier research into people's need for achievement or fear of success was done at a time when traditional sex role stereotypes were more accepted than they are now. In the 1970s, we began to see a change in the way males and females were treated. These changes have resulted in a different set of learned motives for men and women. In any case, many different tests of people's attitudes toward success have been invented as a result of Horner's work, and psychologists are beginning to understand the many issues involved in getting ahead in our society. Tresemer (1976b: 215) wrote that researchers are now asking: "When does a person avoid success, and, by the way, what do you mean by success?"

Maslow's Hierarchy of Needs

Abraham Maslow, one of the pioneers of humanistic psychology, believes that *all* human beings need to feel competent, to win approval and recognition, and to sense that they have achieved something. He places achievement motivation in the context of a hierarchy of needs all people share.

Maslow's scheme, shown in Figure 6.9, incorporates all the factors we have discussed so far in this chapter, and goes a step further. He begins with biological drives, including the need for physical safety and security. In order to live, people have to satisfy these **fundamental needs.** If people are hungry, most of their activities will be motivated by the drive to acquire food, and they will not be able to function on a higher level.

Figure 6.9
Maslow's hierarchy of needs. According to Maslow, it is only after satisfying the lower levels of needs that a person is free to progress to the ultimate need of self-actualization.

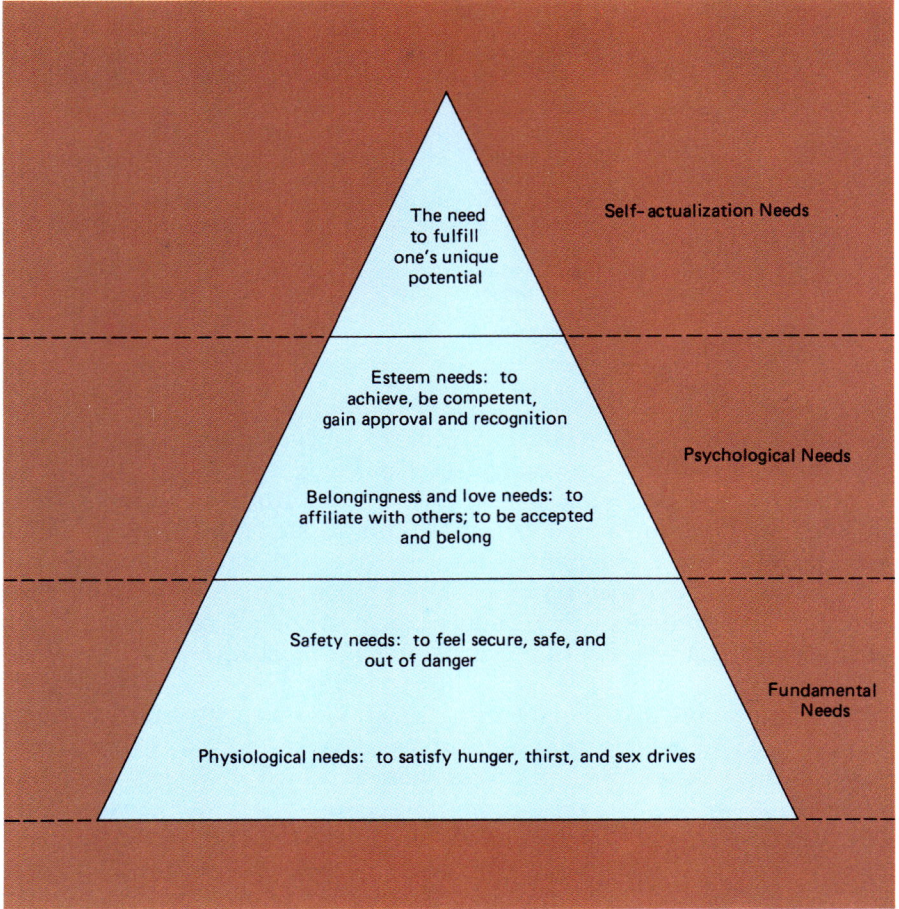

The second level in Maslow's hierarchy consists of **psychological needs:** the need to belong and to give and receive love, and the need to acquire esteem through competence and achievement. Maslow suggests that these needs function in much the same way that biological needs do, and that they can be filled only by an outside source. A lack of love or esteem makes people anxious and tense. There is a driven quality to their behavior. They may engage in random, desperate, and sometimes neurotic or maladaptive activities to ease their tensions. Unless these needs are satisfied, a person will be unable to move on. Most of his or her behavior will be motivated by unfulfilled psychological needs. Thus an unusually intelligent woman who does not feel loved may avoid success in the hope of being accepted as one of the crowd.

Self-actualization needs are at the top of Maslow's hierarchy. These may include the pursuit of knowledge and beauty, or whatever else is required for the realization of one's unique potential. Maslow believes that although relatively few people reach this level, we all have these needs. To be creative in the way we conduct our lives and use our talents, we must first satisfy our fundamental and psychological needs. The satisfaction of these needs motivates us to seek self-actualization.

Maslow thus adds to motivation theory the idea that some needs take precedence over others and the suggestion that achieving one level of satisfaction releases new needs and motivations. (We discuss Maslow's theory in more detail in Chapter 11.)

EMOTION

It is difficult to draw a clear line between motives and emotions. We saw that when a person needs food, the stomach contracts, the level of sugar in the blood drops, neural and endocrine systems are thrown slightly off balance, and taste buds become more sensitive. We saw that when a person is frightened, heart and breathing rates quicken, energy level rises, the senses mobilize, and blood rushes away from the stomach into the brain, heart, and other muscles. Of course, a poet might diagnose a pounding heart, loss of appetite, and heightened awareness of the moonlight and scented breezes as love. Why, if all three involve identifiable physiological changes, do we call hunger a biological drive, and fear and love emotions?

It depends on whether we are describing the source of our behavior or the feelings associated with our behavior. When we want to emphasize the needs, desires, and mental calculations that lead to goal-directed behavior, we use the word "drive" or "motivation." When we want to stress the feelings associated with these decisions and activities, we use the word "emotion" or "affect."

Clearly, the two are intertwined. We frequently explain our motives in terms of emotions. Why did you walk out of the meeting? I was angry. Why do you go to so many parties? I enjoy meeting new people and love to dance. Why did you lend your notes to someone you don't particularly like? I felt guilty about talking behind her back. Why did you apply for a summer job overseas? The idea of flying to Saudi Arabia excites me—and so on.

As these examples demonstrate, emotions push and pull us in different directions. Sometimes emotions function like biological drives: our feelings energize us and make us pursue a goal. Which goal we pursue may be determined by our social learning experiences. Other times we do things because we think they will make us feel good: anticipated emotions are the incentive for our actions. The consequences of striving for one goal or another also evoke emotions.

Expressing Emotions: Innate and Learned Behavior

In *The Expression of the Emotions in Man and Animals* (1872), Charles Darwin argued that all people express certain basic feelings in the same ways. Without knowing a person's language, you can tell whether he or she is amused or infuriated just by looking at that person's face.

Recent studies indicate that Darwin was right. One group of re-

FACT or FICTION

A person who is in a good mood is more likely to be helpful.

Fact. Positive emotional states are associated with greater helping. It has been found that the "glow of good will" occurs even when being in a good mood is caused by a minor event. Thus, people who find change left in phone booths or have cookies placed on their study tables in the library are more generous when asked for help.

Photograph Judged						
Judgment	Happiness	Disgust	Surprise	Sadness	Anger	Fear
Culture			**Percent Who Agreed with Judgment**			
99 Americans	97	92	95	84	67	85
40 Brazilians	95	97	87	59	90	67
119 Chileans	95	92	93	88	94	68
168 Argentinians	98	92	95	78	90	54
29 Japanese	100	90	100	62	90	66

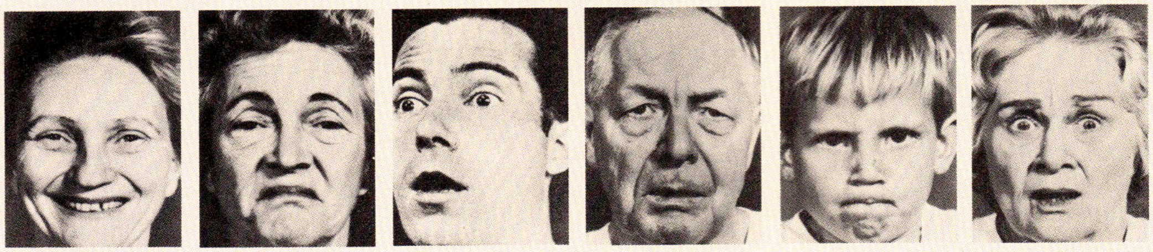

Figure 6.10
The data in this table show that there is substantial agreement among the members of different cultures about the meaning of various facial expressions. The muscular movements that produce these expressions are probably innate human responses. (After Ekman, Friesen, and Ellsworth, 1972)

searchers selected a group of photographs they thought depicted surprise, anger, sadness, and happiness. Then they showed the photographs to people from five different cultures and asked them to say what the person in each photograph was feeling. The results of this experiment are shown in Figure 6.10. The overwhelming majority of the subjects identified the emotions as the researchers expected they would. Was this simply because they had met Americans, or at least seen American television shows and movies, and so learned how to "read" our facial expressions? Apparently not. A second study was conducted in a remote part of New Guinea, with people who had had relatively little contact with outsiders and virtually no exposure to mass media. They too were able to identify the emotions being expressed (Ekman, Friesen, and Ellsworth, 1972).

These studies imply that certain basic facial expressions are **innate**—that is, part of our biological inheritance. Observations of children who were born blind and deaf lend support to this view. These youngsters could not have learned how to communicate feelings by observing other people. Still, they laugh like other children when they're happy, pout and frown to express resentment, clench their fists and teeth in anger (see Goodenough, 1932).

Psychologist Carroll Izard and his colleagues (Trotter, 1983) developed a coding system for assessing emotional states in people. By noticing changes in different parts of the face, such as the eyebrows, eyes, and mouth, they have been able to identify ten different emotional states. For example, anger is indicated when a person's eyebrows are sharply lowered and drawn together, and the eyes narrowed or squinted. Izard has used his coding system to study emotional expressions in infants. Trained coders watching videotaped segments of an infant's face assess the emotional state of the baby. This technique is especially useful for studying emotions in young children who cannot verbally report what they are feeling. Izard's work also enables psychologists to study how effectively parents are able to read their babies' faces and figure out what they are feeling. Not only are parents watching their babies, but the reverse is also true. Babies spend a lot of time watching their parents. Infants have many opportunities to learn about and express emotions by using the parents' faces as models.

Learning is an important factor in emotional expression. James Averill (1983) believes that many of our everyday emotional reactions are the result of social expectations and consequences. He believes that emotions are responses of the whole person and that we cannot separate an individual's physical or biological experience of emotions from that person's thoughts or actions associated with those emotions. We learn to express and experience emotions in the company of other people and we learn that emotions can serve different social functions. Parents, for example, modify their children's emotions by responding angrily to some outbursts, by being sympathetic to others, and on occasion by ignoring their youngsters. In this way, children are taught which emotions are considered appropriate in different situations and which emotions they are expected to control.

Learning explains the differences we find among cultures once we go beyond such basic expressions as laughing or crying. For example, in Victorian English novels, women closed their eyes, opened their mouths with a gasp, and fainted when they were frightened or shocked. In Chinese novels, men fainted when they became enraged. Medical records from the period indicate that Chinese men did indeed faint from anger (Klineberg, 1938). What these findings suggest is that all of us are born with the capacity for emotion and with certain basic forms of expression, but that when, where, and how we express different feelings depend in large part on learning.

Analyzing facial expressions helps us to describe emotions, but it does not tell us where emotions come from. Some psychologists believe emotions derive from physical changes; others, that emotions result from mental processes.

Physiological Theories

In *Principles of Psychology,* a classic work published in 1890, William James attempted to summarize the best available literature on human behavior, motivations, and feelings. When it came to drawing up a catalogue of human emotions, James gave up; he felt there were too many subtle variations, too many personal differences. But he was struck by the fact that nearly every description of emotions he read emphasized bodily changes. James's observations of his own and other people's emotions confirmed this point. We associate feelings with sudden increases or decreases in energy, muscle tension and relaxation, and sensations in the pit of our stomach.

The James-Lange Theory.   After much thought James concluded that we use the word "emotion" to describe our visceral or "gut" reactions to the things that take place around us. In other words, James (1890) believed that emotions are the perception of certain internal bodily changes.

> My theory . . . is that *the bodily changes follow directly the perception of the exciting fact, and that our feeling of the same changes as they occur IS the emotion.* Commonsense says, we lose our fortune, are sorry and weep; we meet a bear, are frightened and run; we are insulted by a rival, are angry and strike. . . . [T]he more rational statement is that we feel sorry because we cry, angry because we strike, afraid because we tremble. . . . Without the bodily states following on the perception, the latter would be . . . pale, colorless, destitute of emotional warmth.

In a sense, James was putting the cart before the horse. Other psychologists had assumed that emotions trigger bodily changes; James argued that the reverse is true. Because Carl Lange came to the same conclusion about the same time, this position is known as the **James-Lange theory** (Lange and James, 1922). Izard's (1972) theory of emotions bears a striking resemblance to the James-Lange theory. He believes that our conscious experience of emotion results from the sensory feedback we receive from the muscles in our faces. You can check this out by noticing the difference in your emotional experience when you smile for two minutes as opposed to when you frown for two minutes. According to Izard's view, if you continue to frown, you will experience an unpleasant emotion.

The Cannon-Bard Theory.   Techniques for studying bodily changes improved over the next three decades, and evidence that contradicted the James-Lange theory began to grow. For example, the physiological changes that occur during emotional states also occur when people are not feeling angry or sad—or anything. In fact, injecting a drug that produces physiological arousal of the body does not necessarily produce changes in emotions. (If James and Lange had been correct, such physiological changes would always produce emotions.) Also the internal state of the body changes only slowly. "Gut" reactions could not produce the rushes of emotion we all experience from time to time. Indeed, if bodily changes were the seat of emotion, we would all be rather dull.

In 1929, Walter B. Cannon published a summary of the evidence against the James-Lange theory. Cannon argued that the thalamus (part of the lower brain) is the seat of emotion—an idea Philip Bard (1934) expanded and refined. According to the **Cannon-Bard theory,** certain experiences activate the thalamus, and the thalamus sends messages to the cortex (or

Figure 6.11
Taking a lie detector test: the polygraph measures sweating of the skin, breathing, blood pressure, and heart rate.

higher brain) and to the body organs. (More sophisticated experiments showed that the thalamus is not involved in emotional experience, but the hypothalamus is.) Thus, when we use the word "emotion," we are referring to the *simultaneous* burst of activity in the brain and "gut" reactions. In Cannon's words, "The peculiar quality of emotion is added to simple sensation when the thalamic processes are aroused" (1929).

Cannon also emphasized the importance of physiological arousal in many different emotions. He was the first to describe the "fight or flight" reaction of the sympathetic nervous system that prepares us for an emergency. Some of the signs of physiological arousal are measured in one of the most famous applications of psychological knowledge: lie detection.

USING PSYCHOLOGY

Lie Detection

Most of us associate lie detection with shifty-eyed criminals accused of murdering their grandmothers. But in reality, American industry uses the lie detector far more often than the police do. No one knows exactly how many polygraph tests (**polygraph** is another name for a lie detector) are given each year, but one psychologist (Lykken, 1974) places the number at several million. Companies use these tests for everything from finding out whether a job applicant has ever

Men, Women, and Lying. A psychologist who has conducted research on conflict between men and women has found that many women get upset about men's lack of emotional expression.

Women seem to express emotions more often than men. This may explain another research finding: Men are better liars than women. One study found that videotapes of male college students instructed to lie were seen as sincere. However, women's lies were more easily detected.

Why are women worse liars than men? One possibility has to do with women being better at expressing their emotions than men. Since women appear to be better at expressing themselves and do so more often than men, they may find it more difficult when required to hide what they truly feel. Men, on the other hand, tend to limit their emotional expressions. They also believe that the expression of most emotions is controllable. Thus, expressing an emotion that one does not feel may come more easily for many males.

been in trouble to seeing who's got his or her hand in the till at the local hamburger stand.

The first modern "lie detector" was invented by Leonarde Keeler, a member of the Berkeley, California, police force in the 1920s. As you can see in Figure 6.11, a polygraph includes electrodes for measuring the electrical resistance of the skin (often called the GSR, this is a measure of sweating), a tube that is tied around the chest to measure breathing, and an inflatable cuff that measures blood pressure and heart rate. There is no single physiological change that always goes along with a lie. Rather, the lie-detection expert looks for general signs of the activation of the sympathetic nervous system: an irregular breathing pattern, high heart rate and blood pressure, and increased sweating (indicated by decreases in the electrical resistance of the skin). Lie detection is an art rather than a science, so the technique is only as good as the man who uses it (Hassett, 1978).

Surprisingly, almost all of the people who become lie-detection experts have backgrounds not in psychology but in law enforcement. The way they cross-question a person is at least as important as the machine itself. To illustrate this point, polygraphers sometimes tell an old tale about a medieval prince who wanted to find out which of his servants had stolen some food. He called all his servants together and announced that he had a sacred donkey in the next room. The donkey would bray only when the guilty man pulled his tail. One by one, the servants went by themselves into a dark room with the donkey, pulled his tail, and returned to the prince. Finally, the last man returned and still the ass had not made a sound. The prince then told the servants to hold out their hands. He had covered the donkey's tail with soot. Only the guilty man had been afraid to pull the tail, and so only his hands were clean (Sternbach, Gustafson, and Colier, 1962). Similarly, some experts say that if a person believes in the lie detector, it can be used to make him or her tell the truth. Indeed, many people confess during an hour-long interview that usually takes place before the machine is even plugged in.

The polygrapher tries to develop three different kinds of questions for the actual tests. Some are nonemotional (for example "Is your name Richard Nixon?"); some are emotional but not relevant to the investigation ("Have you ever lied to your parents?"); a few are related specifically to the investigation. The theory is that everyone will react emotionally to the last two categories, but only the guilty party will respond *more* to questions about the crime. It is important that the questions be as specific as possible. A polygrapher would not ask "Did you ever steal anything?" but rather "Did you ever steal more than one hundred dollars from the E-Z Credit Furniture Store?"

How effective are lie detectors? It's hard to say. Like all good businesspeople, polygraph experts advertise their successes and forget about their failures. In one review of many criminal cases (Orlansky, 1965), the lie detector was proved wrong about 2 percent of the time. But this figure is misleading. If a lie detector test says a suspect is innocent, the police often won't bother to look for more evidence. So it's very hard to know when it's wrong. And even if the figure were as low as 2 percent, that's not going to help you if you're one of the people the lie detector lies about.

Overall, the ability of polygraphs to detect the arousal often associated with lying is quite impressive. But lie detectors do make mistakes. For this reason, the results of polygraph tests are not ordinarily allowed as evidence in a court of law. When, if ever, they should be used in industry is a political question rather than one that psychologists are specially qualified to answer.

Cognitive Theories

Cognitive theorists believe that bodily changes and thinking *work together* to produce emotions. Physiological arousal is only half of the story. What you feel depends on how you interpret your symptoms. And this, in turn, depends on what is going on in your mind and in your environment.

The Schachter-Singer Experiment.   Stanley Schachter and Jerome Singer designed an experiment to explore this (1962). They told all their subjects they were testing the effects of vitamin C on eyesight. In reality, most received an adrenalin injection. One group was told that the "vitamin" injection would make their hearts race and their bodies tremble (which was true). Another group was deliberately misinformed: the injection would make them numb. A third group was not told anything about how their bodies would react to the shot. And a fourth group received a neutral injection that did not produce any symptoms. Like the third group, these subjects were not given any information about possible side effects.

After the injection, each subject was taken to a reception room to wait for the "vision test." There they found another person who was actually part of the experiment. The subjects thought the stooge had had the same injection as theirs. With some subjects, the stooge acted wild and crazy— dancing around, laughing, making paper airplanes with the questionnaire they'd been asked to fill out. Other subjects had to fill out a long and

> **Cognitive theorists believe bodily changes and thinking work together to produce emotions.**

offensive questionnaire that asked, for example: "With how many men (other than your father) has your mother had extramarital relationships? 4 and under ___; 5–9 ___; 10 and over ___." The stooge for this group acted quite angry.

Subjects from the first group, who had been told how the injection would affect them, watched the stooge with mild amusement. So did subjects who had received the neutral injection. However, those from the second and third groups, who either had no idea or an incorrect idea about the side effects, joined in with the stooge (Figure 6.12). If the stooge was euphoric, so were they; if he was angry, they became angry.

What does this experiment demonstrate? That internal components of emotion (such as those adrenalin produces) affect a person differently, depending on his or her interpretation or perception of the social situation. When people cannot explain their physical reactions, they take cues from their environment. The stooge provided cues. But when people knew that their hearts were beating faster because of the adrenalin shot, they did not feel particularly happy or angry. The experiment also shows that internal changes are important—otherwise the subjects from the neutral group would have acted in the same way as those from the misinformed groups. Perception and arousal *interact* to create emotions.

Arnold's Theory.   According to Magda Arnold, everyday emotions can be analyzed into a series of stages (Figure 6.13). In the first, you *perceive* a person, object, or event. It may take place in your imagination, as when you think about something you expect to happen in the future or replay a scene from your past.

The next stage is *appraisal*. You decide whether what is happening will

Figure 6.12
Two of the conditions in Schachter and Singer's experiment on emotion. (a) A subject is misled about the effects he should expect from an adrenalin injection. Placed with a stooge who joyfully flies airplanes around the room, he attributes his state of arousal to a similar mood in himself and joins in. (b) A subject is told exactly what to expect from the injection. Although placed in the same situation as the first subject, he recognizes his physical sensations as the product of the injection and is not affected by the actions of the stooge.

1. Observation: "There are fighter planes coming up."
2. Appraisal: "There is danger; they may catch up with me and hit the plane."
3. Fear (not attended to because the pilot is fully occupied evading the fighter planes).
4. Physiological changes: increase in heart rate; tremor; and fatigue, which becomes cumulative until the mission is finished.
5. Awareness of these changes (will be delayed until the necessity for action is past and attention is free to notice the physiological state).
6. Secondary estimate: "I am chronically tired, trembling, irritable--I must be ill."
7. Secondary emotion: fear of illness, heart disease, and so on.
8. Physiological changes: reinforcement of fatigue, tremor, and so on, increasing the malaise.

Figure 6.13
Magda Arnold's theory of emotion describes a continuous process of reaction and appraisal. This figure shows how a person may respond immediately and effectively in a dangerous situation and later misinterpret the aftereffects.

help you, hurt you, or have no effect on you. Suppose you see one of your instructors walking toward you. If you have nothing special to gain and nothing to fear from her, you do not react emotionally. You say hello, chat for a moment, and walk on.

However, if you have been cutting class and suspect that the instructor is going to ask for an explanation, or if you know that she was impressed with a term paper you wrote and will probably compliment you, you will react—physiologically and emotionally. Your heart begins to beat a little faster, and you feel nervous or excited (depending on whether you cut classes or wrote an excellent paper). These are the third and fourth stages: *bodily change* and *emotion*.

In most cases, emotion and bodily change occur at the same time. However, in some situations you skip from stage three (bodily changes) to stage five, which is *action*. You see a car rushing toward you, adrenalin pours into your system, and you jump back without stopping to think. Only after you've leaped to safety do you sense your heart pounding and experience the emotion of fright (Arnold, 1960, 1970). (See also the discussion of stress in Chapter 13.)

In fact, other emotion researchers believe that emotion may play an important role in our survival as human beings and in our ability to achieve goals, precisely because it spurs us to action. Take the example of the car rushing toward you. If you do not jump out of the way, you may not live to see another day. On less extreme levels, emotions may serve to help us achieve difficult goals. Suppose you want your own car, but your parents say no. You may feel angry with them, or embarrassed because all your friends have cars. These emotions may spur you to get a job to earn money for a car, or to explore other options with your parents. Either way, you are responding to an emotion by acting to achieve a goal.

Emotions and physical changes are interwined. It will probably be many years before we understand all the complex ways in which the two interact in human behavior.

CHAPTER REVIEW

KEY TERMS

- *Cannon-Bard theory*
- *drive reduction theory*
- *fundamental needs*
- *homeostasis*

- *innate behavior*
- *James-Lange theory*
- *lateral hypothalamus (LH)*
- *polygraph*

- *psychological needs*
- *self-actualization needs*
- *ventromedial hypothalamus (VMH)*

SUMMARY

1. Several of the physiological drives that motivate behavior are homeostatic. That is, they represent a need to correct deviations from the normal state.

2. Drive reduction theory states that physiological needs drive an organism to act in either random or habitual ways until its needs are satisfied. But drive reduction theory overlooks the fact that some experiences are inherently pleasurable, and that even though they do not reduce biological drives, they still provide incentives or goals for behavior.

3. Social needs also motivate behavior. One of these, the need for achievement, has been intensively studied by David McClelland. He and his associates devised a method for measuring achievement motivation. They also developed achievement training programs that have been successful cross-culturally.

4. McClelland's work inspired a wide variety of research on other aspects of motivation. One researcher, Matina Horner, discovered another dimension of achievement motivation: the motive to avoid success. Although Horner believed that this was more of a problem for women than men, other researchers have questioned this.

5. Abraham Maslow believed that all people want to feel competent, to win approval and recognition, and to sense they have achieved something. According to his theory, there is a hierarchy of needs: fundamental needs, psychological needs, and self-actualization needs. Some needs take precedence over others, and the achievement of one level of satisfaction releases new needs and motivations.

6. Emotions and motivations are intertwined.

7. All of us are born with the same basic capacity for emotion. When and where we express different feelings depend in large part on learning.

8. Investigation of where emotions come from brought cognitive theorists to the conclusion that bodily changes and thinking *work together* to produce emotions.

9. Internal sensations affect each person differently, depending on mental interpretation and the social situation.

10. According to Magda Arnold, there are four stages in the development of emotion: perception, appraisal, bodily change, and emotion. The stage following this is action.

REVIEW QUESTIONS

1. What physiological processes determine whether or not we "feel hungry"? How do normal-weight and overweight people differ in their sensitivity to these cues?

2. Explain why each of the following is or is not consistent with Hull's drive reduction theory: hunger, curiosity, the need for oxygen, taking risks.

3. How did McClelland measure a person's need for achievement? What kind of person has a high need for achievement?

4. What explanation is given for the finding that women have a greater motive to avoid success? Why might this difference disappear in the future?

5. According to Maslow's hierarchy of needs, which needs must be satisfied first? Which needs are satisfied after all others?

6. What research evidence suggests that our expression of emotions is universal across different societies and cultures and may be innate? What evidence suggests that emotions are affected by learning?

7. How does the Cannon-Bard theory of emotion differ from the James-Lange theory?

8. You are driving a car and a small child steps into the street a third of a block in front of the car's path. Use Arnold's theory of emotion to explain your response.

ACTIVITIES

1. Try going without bread in your meals for several days a week. Do you find that you are beginning to think about bread more often, even dream about it? Are you becoming more aware of advertisements for bread? Compare your experience with the description of drive reduction behavior in this chapter.

2. Write down several activities or behaviors you do when your time is your own. In which level of Maslow's hierarchy of needs would you place each of these activities or behaviors; that is, what really motivates you to engage in each of them? Perhaps you will discover a different kind of motive, one that doesn't seem to fit in with Maslow's set. Check the chapter on personality and the Maslow readings to see whether or not it might fit. If none of the activities on your list seems to be motivated by self-actualization, can you imagine activities that would be, and that you might enjoy doing?

3. With a partner or as a group, select ten emotions to express. Then play a variation of charades, with one person attempting to convey each of these emotions by facial expression alone. Are some emotions harder to convey than others? Are there consistent differences in interpretation between individuals? How important do you think context (the social situation in which the facial expression occurs) is in perceiving other people's emotions?

4. Recall the four stages of development of an emotion, described in this chapter. Then observe them in yourself, at a time when you are entering an emotional state. If possible, you should take notes, at least "mental notes," to enable you to view yourself with some objectivity even while you are having the emotion. To induce the emotion you might go to a movie that you know will be scary or sad. Or you might attend a religious service or mystical ritual of some sort if that affects you.

5. If you are interested in the achievement motive, you might try the story-writing techniques described in this chapter. Try writing stories with and without achievement themes. Supposedly, those who deliberately attempt to include themes related to the three aspects of achievement motivation will increase their own ability to achieve; at least, such an exercise makes a person more aware of achievement.

6. Collect the fantasies of people in your class. Each person should write several stories or fantasies, possibly around a set of ambiguous pictures. Names should not be placed on fantasies (so as to insure privacy), but each person should mark male or female on the fantasy. Then compare the fantasies of men and women for the achievement motive. Are there differences? Do you think there have been changes in this factor in the last few years?

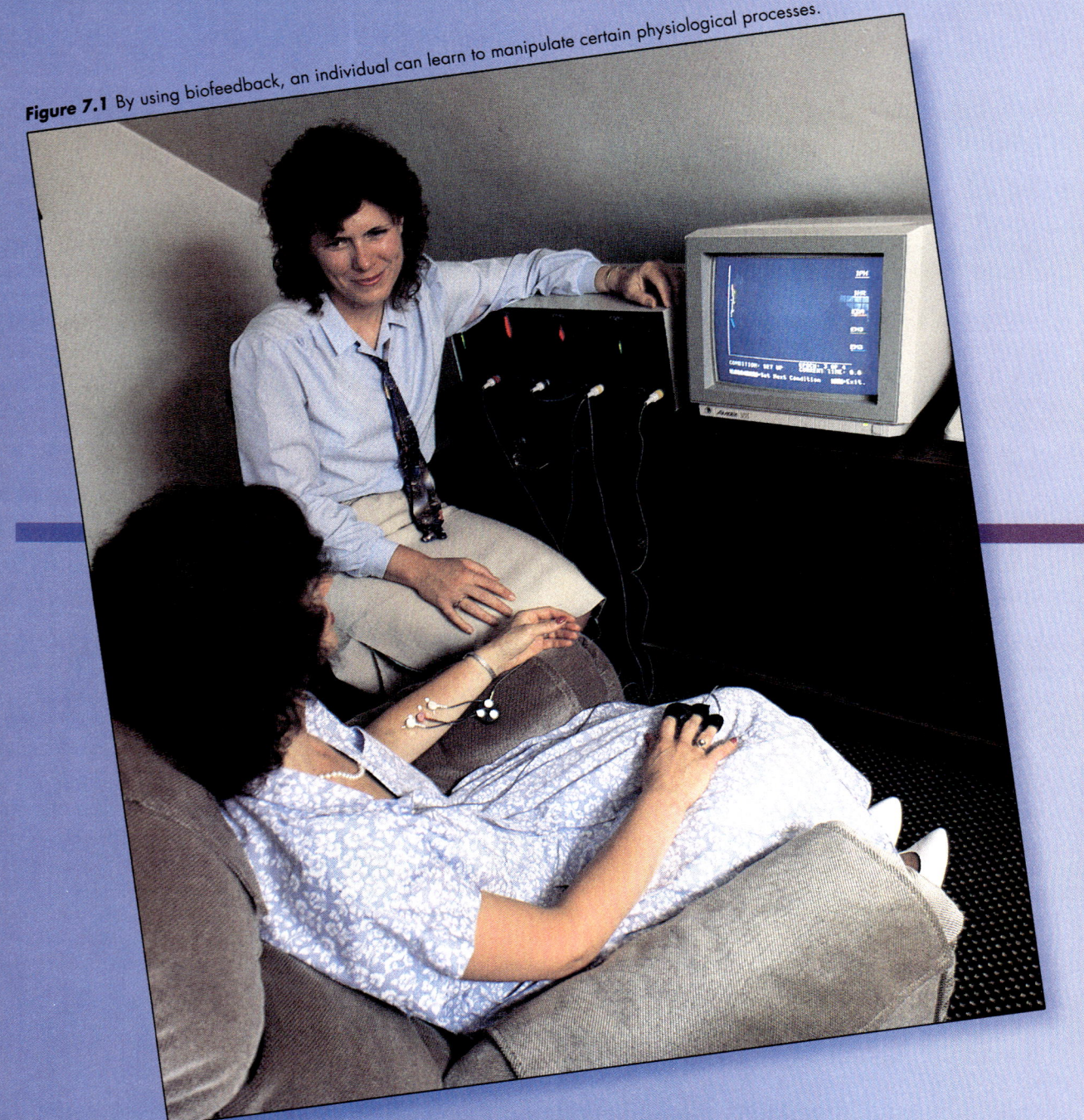

Figure 7.1 By using biofeedback, an individual can learn to manipulate certain physiological processes.

Objectives: After studying this chapter, you should be able to
- describe the research into sleep and dreaming.
- define altered states of consciousness, such as hypnosis and hallucination.
- describe out-of-body and near-death experiences.
- discuss the effects of drug states and such substances as marijuana and alcohol.
- describe research into such techniques as biofeedback and meditation.

Altered States of Consciousness

As you read this sentence, you are conscious of the words on this page. Or maybe your awareness is drifting to that attractive classmate sitting across from you in the library. In either case, everything you think and feel is part of your conscious experience.

You might expect, then, that normal states of **consciousness** would be one of the most active areas of research in psychology. But this is not the case. Although some of the earliest researchers defined psychology as the study of conscious experience, consciousness proved to be a difficult topic to analyze scientifically. Behaviorism—with its emphasis on studying only what people do, not what they think or feel—became popular partly because studying consciousness had proved to be so difficult. Psychobiologist Roger Sperry (1976: 9) has called consciousness "one of the most truly mystifying unknowns remaining in the whole of science."

But a related area that *has* been the subject of a great deal of research in recent years is the study of altered states of consciousness. An altered state of consciousness involves a change in mental processes, not just a quantitative shift (such as feeling more or less alert). Sensations, perceptions, and thought patterns actually change. The most obvious and familiar example is sleep. People spend about a third of their lives in this altered state of consciousness. Other examples include daydreams, hallucinations, delirium, hypnotic states, being drunk or "high" on drugs, and the heightened awareness people experience during various forms of meditation (Tart, 1972).

In the past twenty years, psychologists have begun to examine altered states of consciousness by having people sleep, undergo hypnosis, or take drugs during laboratory experiments. In the laboratory, researchers can observe changes in behavior and measure changes in breathing, pulse rate, body temperature, and brain activity. (Brain activity, or "waves," can be recorded with a device known as an electroencephalograph, or EEG.) The

Sleep and Dreams
Stages of Sleep • How Much Sleep? • Sleep Disorders • Dreams • Why We Dream

Hypnosis

Hallucinations
Out-of-Body Experiences

Near-Death Experiences

Psychoactive Drugs
Marijuana • Hallucinogens • Cocaine • Alcohol

Biofeedback

Meditation
Using Psychology: Lowering Blood Pressure

Figure 7.2
Everything we think and feel is part of our conscious experience. This girl, for instance, may be conscious of several things—the sound of the rain on the window, the look of a tree bending in the wind, her mother standing next to her, and voices in a nearby room.

Figure 7.3
This woman is doing a yoga exercise. Yoga stretches and tones muscles, but it is also a mental discipline that allows practitioners to achieve an altered state of consciousness.

subjects' own reports of how they feel or what they remember supplement these data. What have psychologists learned about these phenomena? We begin with sleep.

SLEEP AND DREAMS

Most people think of sleep as a state of unconsciousness, punctuated by brief periods of dreaming. This is only partially correct. Sleep is a state of *altered* consciousness, characterized by certain patterns of brain activity.

Although sleep is a major part of human and animal behavior, it has been extremely difficult to study until recently. A researcher cannot ask a sleeping person to report on the experience without first waking the person. This problem was solved with the development of the EEG machine for recording the electrical activity of the brain. By observing sleeping subjects and by recording their brain and body responses, researchers have discovered two different types of sleep patterns—*quiet sleep* and *active sleep*. There are four different stages of quiet sleep.

Stages of Sleep

As you begin to fall asleep, your body temperature declines, your pulse rate drops, and your breathing grows slow and even. Gradually, your eyes close and your brain briefly emits alpha waves, as observed on the EEG, which are associated with the absence of concentrated thought and with relaxation (Figure 7.4). Your body may twitch, your eyes roll, and brief visual images flash across your mind (although your eyelids are shut) as you enter Stage I sleep, the lightest level of sleep.

In Stage I sleep, your muscles relax and your pulse slows a bit more, but your breathing becomes uneven and your brain waves grow irregular. This phase lasts for about ten minutes. At this point, your brain waves begin to fluctuate between high and low voltages—a pattern that indicates you have entered Stage II sleep. Your eyes roll slowly from side to side. Some thirty minutes later, you drift down into a deeper level of Stage III sleep, and low voltage waves (called delta waves) begin to sweep your brain every second or so.

Stage IV is the deepest sleep of all; it is difficult to waken a sleeper in this stage. Large, regular delta waves indicate you are in a state of oblivion. If you are awakened by a loud noise or sudden movement, you may feel disoriented. Talking out loud, sleepwalking, and bed-wetting—all of which may occur in this stage—leave no trace on memory. Deep sleep is important to your physical and psychological well-being. Perhaps this is why people who are able to sleep only a few hours at a time descend rapidly into Stage IV and remain there for most of their nap.

On an average night, however, Stage IV sleep lasts only an hour or an hour and a half. You then climb back through Stages III and II to Stage I. At this point, something curious happens. Although your muscles are even more relaxed than before, your eyes begin to move rapidly. You have en-

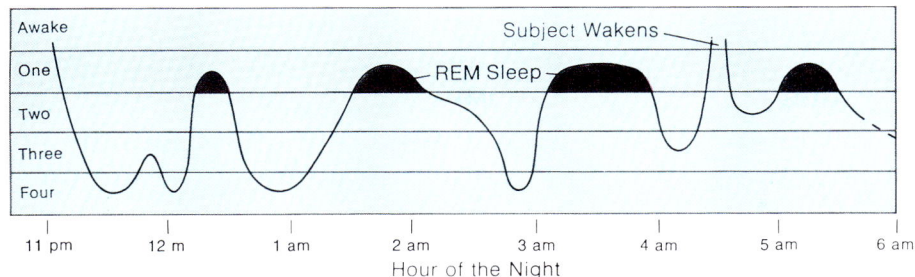

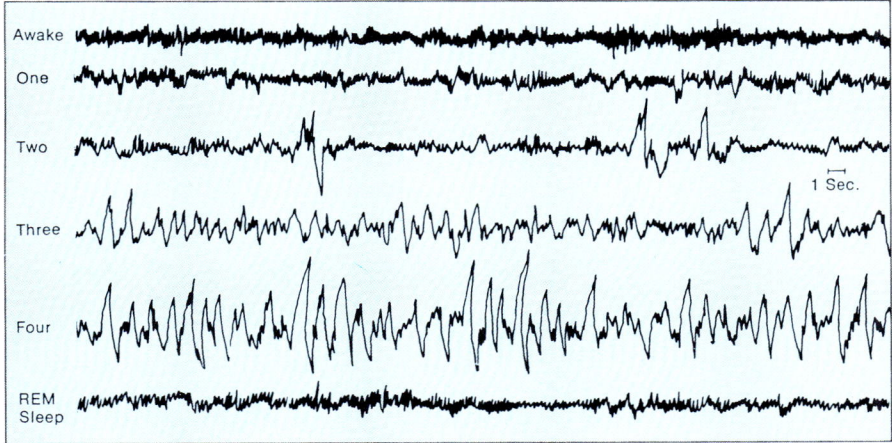

Figure 7.4
(top) A diagram showing the passage of a sleeper through the various stages of sleep over a seven-hour period. (bottom) The patterns of electrical activity (EEGs) in the brain that correspond to the various stages of sleep. The EEG pattern shown for being awake is one that occurs when the person is resting quietly with eyes closed.

tered a more active type of sleep characterized by rapid eye movement. This is called **REM sleep**. Your pulse rate and breathing become irregular, and the levels of adrenal and sexual hormones in your blood rise—as if you were in the middle of an intensely emotional or physically demanding activity. Often, your face or fingers twitch and the large muscles in your arms and legs are paralyzed. Your brain sends out waves that closely resemble those of a person who is fully awake. For this reason, REM sleep is called active sleep. Stages I through IV are sometimes referred to as NREM (non-REM) or quiet sleep because of the absence of rapid eye movement and because of the slower pattern of brain waves. It is during REM sleep that almost all dreaming normally takes place.

REM sleep lasts for about ten minutes, after which you retrace the descent to Stage IV. You go through this cycle every ninety minutes or so. Each time the period of Stage IV sleep decreases and the length of REM sleep increases—until you eventually wake up. But at no point does your brain become inactive.

How Much Sleep?

The amount of sleep a person needs in order to function effectively varies considerably from individual to individual and from time to time within a person's life. Sixteen-year-olds spend an average of ten to eleven hours asleep each night. Students in graduate school average eight hours a night. Newborns spend an average of sixteen to eighteen hours a day sleeping, almost half of it in REM sleep (Dement, 1976). Unless deprived of REM sleep, adults average about 25 percent of their sleeping time in REM sleep and 75 percent in NREM sleep. Although the amount of sleep a person needs may vary, it does appear that everyone sleeps and that both types of sleep are important to normal functioning.

Sleep Disorders

Most of us experience normal sleep patterns. But some people have problems associated with sleep. The three main sleep disorders are insomnia (discussed in the box below), sleep apnea, and narcolepsy.

Sleep apnea occurs when a person stops breathing during sleep, usually for ten seconds or more. The person then wakes up to start breathing again. Some people with this disorder may wake up suddenly during the night without knowing why. Others may awaken so briefly that they have

Insomnia

Everyone has had a sleepless night at one time or other—a night where nothing you do brings the calm, soothing peace you want. Some people have sleep problems like this all the time, and they rarely get more than an hour or two of uninterrupted sleep a night. To help these insomniacs, psychologists Richard R. Bootzin and Perry M. Nicassio have developed a behavior modification program to strengthen the bed as a cue for sleep and weaken it as a cue for sleep-interfering activities.

They suggest that insomniacs follow these instructions:

1. Lie down to sleep only when you feel sleepy.
2. Don't use the bed for any activity other than sleep. That means no eating, reading, watching television, listening to the radio, or worrying in bed. The only exception is sexual activity.
3. If after you're in bed for about ten minutes you find that you can't sleep, get up and go into another room. This will help you associate your bed with falling asleep quickly and dissociate it with tossing and turning. Return to your bed when you feel sleep coming on.
4. Repeat step 3 if you still can't sleep. Get out of bed as many times as necessary during the night.
5. Get up at the same time every morning no matter how little sleep you had the night before. This will help you develop a consistent sleep pattern.
6. Don't nap during the day.

Laboratory studies have shown the effectiveness of these techniques in helping insomniacs fall asleep and stay asleep. If you have a problem, they may work for you.

For more details, see Richard R. Bootzin, *Behavior Modification and Therapy: An Introduction.* Cambridge, Mass.: Winthrop, 1975.

no memory of it in the morning. One common form of this disorder, called **obstructive sleep apnea**, is caused by the collapse of the upper airways during sleep (Guilleminault, 1987). People with this problem are often fitted with an apparatus to wear over their faces while they sleep. This apparatus helps keep air flowing through the airways, thereby minimizing bouts of apnea. Sleep apnea is found most often in obese males (Jamieson, 1988) who have high blood pressure.

While an insomniac and a person with sleep apnea lose sleep, a person with **narcolepsy** may fall asleep at any moment. These episodes, which usually last less than thirty minutes, are beyond the person's control. The narcoleptic often falls asleep during monotonous activities, such as long drives. One form of narcolepsy can be brought on by such bursts of emotion as laughter (Mitler, Nelson, and Hajdukovic, 1987). In these instances, the person may become paralyzed, unable to move, but may still be aware of his or her surroundings. Hallucinations may also precede narcoleptic attacks. Narcolepsy is frequently treated with amphetamines, drugs that stimulate the central nervous system.

Dreams

We call the mental activity that takes place during sleep dreaming. Everybody dreams, although most people are able to recall only a few, if any, of their dreams. Sleep researchers sometimes make a point of waking subjects at regular intervals during the night to ask them about their dreams. The first few dreams are usually composed of vague thoughts left over from the day's activities. A subject may report that she was watching television, for example. As the night wears on, dreams become longer and more vivid and dramatic, especially dreams that take place during REM sleep. Since the amounts of time spent in REM sleep increase during the night, the last dream is likely to be the longest and the one people remember when they wake up. Researchers have found that, after people have been deprived of REM sleep, they subsequently increase the amount of time they spend in REM sleep. Thus it appears that a certain amount of dreaming each night is necessary (Dement, 1976).

The Content of Dreams.   When people are awakened randomly during REM sleep and asked what they had just been dreaming, the reports generally are commonplace, even dull (Hall and Van de Castle, 1966). The dreams we remember and talk about "are more coherent, sexier, and generally more interesting" than those collected in systematic research (Webb, 1975: 140).

Researchers who have recorded the contents of thousands of dreams have found that most—even the late-night REM adventures—occur in such commonplace settings as living rooms, cars, and streets. Most dreams involve either strenuous recreational activities or passive events such as sitting and watching, not work or study. A large percentage of the emotions experienced in dreams are negative or unpleasant—anxiety, anger, sadness, and so on. Contrary to popular belief, dreams do not occur in a split second; they correspond to a realistic time scale.

Everybody dreams, but most people can recall very few of their dreams.

Figure 7.5
A sleep experiment. In recent years psychologists have done much research on sleep in order to increase our knowledge of the various states of consciousness.

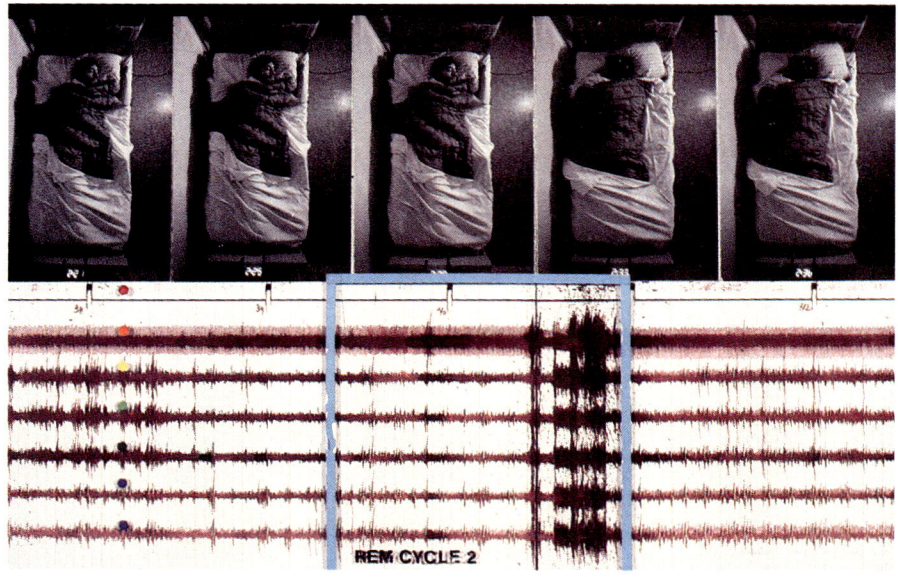

REM CYCLE 2

Anxious people have more nightmares.

Fiction. Anxious people have about the same number of nightmares as emotionally stable people.

Often we incorporate our everyday activities and some night events into our dreams. Some sleep researchers have attempted to manipulate the content of a person's dreams by exposing the dreamer to either a light water spray, or a flashing light, or a five-second tone. They found that the water was incorporated into 42 percent of the dreams, the light into 23 percent, and the tone into 9 percent (Dement and Wolpert, 1958). Some people maintain that their creative ideas or inspiration come from dreaming. Samuel Taylor Coleridge, for example, is said to have composed his poem *Kubla Khan* while dreaming.

Only a small proportion of dreams are negative enough to be considered nightmares. Nightmares often have such a frightening quality that we awaken in the middle of them. The sense of dread in nightmares may be related to the intensity of brain activity and to the stimulation of those parts of the brain responsible for emotional reactions. The emotional reaction of dread may then influence the content of the dream. For example, you may dream that you are about to open a door and you experience a sense of dread. Once you are emotionally aroused in the dream, you may create images in the dream to justify your feelings.

Why We Dream

Although dreams may contain elements of ordinary, waking reality, these elements are often jumbled in fantastic ways. The dreamer may see people in places they would never go, wander through strange houses with endless doors, find her- or himself transported backward in time. The dreamer may be unable to speak—or able to fly. What do these distortions mean?

Dream interpretations have been discovered dating back to 5,000 years before Christ. Sigmund Freud was the first in the modern era to argue that dreams are an important part of our emotional lives.

Freud believed that no matter how simple or mundane, dreams may contain clues to thoughts and desires the dreamer is afraid to acknowledge or express in his or her waking hours. Indeed, he maintained that dreams are full of hidden meanings and disguises.

Freud believed that the symbolism of dreams is a private language that each individual has invented for himself or herself. These symbols vary greatly from person to person. Suppose that a dreamer sees herself standing naked among fully clothed strangers. For one person, this dream may symbolize a desire to show her true self to people, without pretense. For another person, the dream may symbolize a fear of having her inadequacies exposed in public. In his work with patients, Freud tried to break through the disguise of dream imagery and discover the true desires and wishes of the dreamer.

However, some social scientists are skeptical of dream interpretations. Nathaniel Kleitman, one of the pioneers who discovered REM sleep, wrote in 1960: "Dreaming may serve no function whatsoever." According to this view, the experience of a dream is simply an unimportant by-product of stimulating certain brain cells during sleep. McCarley (1978), for example, argues that the common experience of feeling paralyzed in a dream simply means that brain cells that inhibit muscle activity were randomly stimulated. Still other researchers propose that dreaming is a form of mental housecleaning (see "More About The Function of Dreams").

HYPNOSIS

Hypnosis is a form of altered consciousness in which a person becomes highly suggestible and does not use his critical thinking ability. By allowing the hypnotist to guide and direct him, a person can be made conscious of things he is usually unaware of and unaware of things he usually notices. (The subject may recall in vivid detail an incident he had forgotten, or feel no pain when his hand is pricked with a needle.)

Hypnosis does not put the subject to sleep, as many people believe. A hypnotic trance is quite different from sleep. In fact, the subject becomes highly receptive and responsive to certain internal and external stimuli. He is able to focus his attention on one tiny aspect of reality and ignore all other inputs. The hypnotist induces a trance by slowly persuading the subject to relax and to lose interest in external distractions. Whether this takes a few minutes or much longer depends on the purpose of the hypnosis and the method of induction.

Psychologists who use hypnosis stress that the relationship between the hypnotist and subject involves cooperation, not domination. The subject is not under the hypnotist's "power" and cannot be forced to do things against his will. Rather, the person is simply cooperating with the hypnotist by becoming particularly responsive to the hypnotist's suggestions. *Together* they try to solve a problem or to learn more about how the subject's mind works. Anyone can resist hypnosis by simply refusing to open his or

The Function of Dreams. Contrary to the view that dreams serve no function, a new theory suggests that dreams are the brain's way of "unlearning" or removing certain unneeded memories. In other words, dreams are a form of mental housecleaning.

Such mental housecleaning might be necessary because it is not useful to remember every single detail of your life. Instead we tend to remember *important* things and somehow forget the rest. If the theory is correct, then those things that need to be forgotten are included in dreams, and the very act of dreaming somehow helps to erase them.

This idea has been proposed by Francis Crick, Nobel Prize winner and co-discoverer of DNA. Crick believes that if it were not for the helpful effects of dreams, evolution could not have produced the highly refined human brain. He theorizes that a brain so complex as ours could not work properly without a cleaning-up mechanism.

Figure 7.6
A hypnotist, drawn by Daumier, a famous nineteenth-century French painter and caricaturist.

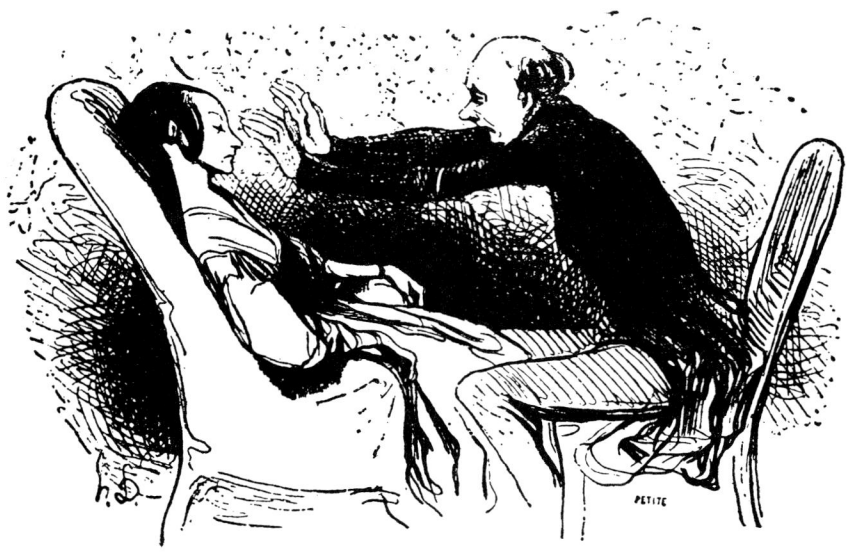

her mind to the hypnotist, and people under hypnosis cannot be induced to do things they would not do when "awake" unless they want to.

Hypnotists can also suggest things for their subjects to remember when the trance is over, a phenomenon known as **posthypnotic suggestion**. For example, the hypnotist might suggest that after the person is awakened she will be unable to hear the word "psychology." When she comes out of the trance, the subject may report that some people around her are speaking strangely. They seem to leave out some words occasionally, especially when they are talking about topics involving the taboo word "psychology." The subject is not aware that part of her consciousness has been instructed to block out that word. Posthypnotic suggestion has been found to be particularly helpful in changing unwanted behaviors, such as smoking or overeating.

Psychologists do not agree about the nature of hypnosis. Some, like Theodore Barber (1965), argue that hypnosis is not a special state of consciousness. If people are simply given instructions and told to try their hardest, they will be able to do anything that hypnotized people can do. Barber has shown that unhypnotized people can hold a heavy weight at arm's length for several minutes; they can lie stiff as a board with only one chair under their shoulders and another under their feet to support them; they can even stick needles through their hands.

Others, like Ernest Hilgard (1977), believe that there is something special about the hypnotic state. People who are hypnotized are very suggestible; they go along with the hypnotist and do not initiate activities themselves; and they can more easily imagine and remember things. Hilgard believes that consciousness includes many different aspects that may become separated, or dissociated, during hypnosis. This view is called neodissociation theory.

Another explanation of hypnosis is based on the importance of suggestibility in the hypnotic induction. According to some theorists (Sarbin and Coe, 1972, 1979), hypnotized people behave as they do because they have accepted the role of a hypnotized subject. We expect that hypnotized individuals will forget certain things when told or will recall forgotten material, and we play the role. Many stage hypnotists entertain their audiences with dramatic hypnotic demonstrations by carefully selecting volunteers who appear most willing to play the role (Bowers, 1976).

Whether hypnosis is a special state of consciousness or not, it does reveal that people often have potential abilities that they don't use. Continued study may help us to understand where these abilities come from and how to use them better.

HALLUCINATIONS

Hallucinations are sensations or perceptions that have no direct external cause—seeing, hearing, smelling, tasting, or feeling things that do not exist.

Hypnosis, meditation, certain drugs, withdrawal from a drug to which one has become addicted, and psychological breakdown may produce hallucinations. (We discuss the hallucinations associated with drug withdrawal and mental breakdowns in Chapter 15.) But they also occur under "normal" conditions. People hallucinate when they are dreaming and when they are deprived of the opportunity to sleep. Periods of high emotion, concentration, or fatigue may also produce false sensations and perceptions. For example, truck drivers on long hauls have been known to swerve suddenly to avoid stalled cars that do not exist. Even daydreams involve mild hallucinations.

Interestingly enough, it seems that hallucinations are very much alike from one person to the next. Soon after taking a drug that causes hallucinations, for example, people often see many geometric forms in a tunnellike perspective. These forms float through the field of vision, combining with each other and duplicating themselves. While normal imagery is often in black and white, hallucinations are more likely to involve color.

Out-of-Body Experiences

> Suddenly my sight cleared and I was looking at the back of myself and the dogs from a position eight or ten feet behind myself and about a foot higher than my height. My physical self had no sight or other senses and it was exactly as if I was simply walking along behind someone, except that someone was me. . . . (Blackmore, 1982: 9)

Have you ever experienced the feeling that you had left your body and were looking at a scene from a completely different perspective? An **out-of-body experience** (OBE), also called a metachoric experience, is a type of hallucination in which a person's entire perceptual world changes. In an OBE, a person reports leaving his or her body to look at a scene from a completely different and very real perspective. Although out-of-body experiences are not common, they are not entirely rare either. One study of 200 hospital patients (Olson, 1988) found 31 people who reported having experienced an OBE during their lifetimes. Some people can even induce an out-of-body experience (Irwin, 1988).

What type of person is likely to have an OBE? Spanos and Moretti (1988) found that such people were more easily hypnotized than others. In fact, Irwin (1988) has suggested that hypnosis can be used to induce these experiences. Blackmore (1987) found that people having OBEs were more likely to recall dreams from an observer's perspective than from their own, and Stanford (1987) reports that they spent more time reading and being read to as children. Further research is needed to fully understand these experiences.

NEAR-DEATH EXPERIENCES

A man is dying and, as he reaches the point of greatest physical distress, he hears himself pronounced dead by his doctor. He begins to hear an uncomfortable noise, a loud ringing or buzzing, and at the same time feels himself moving very rapidly though a long dark tunnel. After this, he suddenly finds himself outside of his own physical body, but still in the immediate physical environment, and he sees his own body from a distance, as though he is a spectator. He watches the resuscitation attempt from this unusual vantage point and is in a state of emotional upheaval. (Moody, 1976: 21–23, as cited in Blackmore, 1982)

This man is having what is called a **near-death experience**. It is similar to the out-of-body experience, but it is initiated by either a close brush with death or at least the belief that death is near (Stevenson, Cook, and Mc-Clean-Rice, 1990). It is not surprising that people should report unusual perceptual experiences at such times. It is somewhat surprising, though, that their reports should have so many characteristics in common.

Many people who have had a near-death experience describe a sort of tunnel, through which they travel to another place or experience a different perspective. The tunnel may represent a transition between life and death or it could be a flashback to birth memories. People often report meeting deceased loved ones in this tunnel or at the end of it. An 8-year-old boy who nearly drowned said he was comforted by two of his family's pets who had died (Serdahely, 1990).

Whatever the sensations may be, almost everyone who has a near-death experience is changed significantly by the event (Roberts and Owen, 1988). Many report increased anxiety or religious conversion, while others experience a heightened self-awareness (Raft and Andresen, 1986). Bauer (1985) has found that more people report changing for the better than for the worse. The changes are so significant that those who have had near-death experiences often talk about "returning" from them. Some have reported that this return is akin to culture shock (Furn, 1987). Others believe they came back from the near-death experience for a specific purpose (Geraci, 1987).

Many explanations have been put forth for near-death experiences. Physiological approaches suggest factors such as neurochemical imbalances (Morse, Venecia, and Milstein, 1989) or disruptions in blood and oxygen levels in the brain (Saavendra-Aguilar and Gomez-Jeria, 1989). In a review of the literature, Roberts and Owen (1988) conclude that the near-death experience is a complex phenomenon with many causes.

PSYCHOACTIVE DRUGS

The drugs of interest for the study of consciousness are those that interact with the central nervous system to alter a person's mood, perception, and behavior. These are called **psychoactive drugs**. They range from the caffeine in coffee and in cola drinks to powerful consciousness-altering substances like marijuana, alcohol, amphetamines, and LSD (see Table 7.1).

Marijuana

Marijuana has been used as an intoxicant among Eastern cultures for centuries. In some societies it is legally and morally acceptable whereas alcohol is not. Before 1960, marijuana use in the United States was common only among members of certain subcultures, such as jazz musicians and artists in big cities. By 1960, however, college students had discovered marijuana, and its use became widespread for almost two decades. Recent studies, however, have shown that marijuana use among adolescents has been declining since 1979.

The active ingredient in marijuana is a complex molecule called tetrahydrocannabinol (THC), which occurs naturally in the common weed *Cannabis sativa,* or Indian hemp. Marijuana is made by drying the plant; hashish is a gummy powder made from the resin exuded by the flowering tops of the female plant. Both marijuana and hashish are usually smoked, but they can also be cooked with food and eaten.

The effects of the drug vary somewhat from person to person and also seem to depend on the setting in which the drug is taken. But, in general, most sensory experiences seem greatly augmented—music sounds fuller; colors look brighter; smells are stronger; foods have stronger flavors; and other experiences are more intense than usual. Users may feel elated, the world may seem somehow more meaningful, and even the most ordinary events may take on an extraordinary significance. A person who is high on marijuana may, for example, suddenly become aware of the mystical implications of a particular painting. The sense of time is greatly distorted. A short sequence of events may seem to last for hours. Users may become so obsessed with an object that they sit and stare at it for many minutes.

As many users of marijuana have discovered, however, the drug can heighten unpleasant as well as pleasant experiences. If a person is in a frightened, unhappy, or depressed mood to begin with, the chances are excellent that taking the drug will blow the negative feelings out of proportion, so that the user's world, temporarily at least, becomes very upsetting.

Table 7.1 / Drugs Used for Mind-Alteration

Name of Drug or Chemical	Duration of Action (Hours)	Habituation Potential (Psychological Dependence)	Tolerance Potential (Leading to Higher Dose)	Addiction Potential (Physical Dependence)
Alcohol	2–4	High	Yes	Yes
Nicotine	1–2	High	Yes	Yes
Depressants Barbiturates (Amytal, Nembutal, phenobarbital, Seconal) Quaaludes	4–6	High	Yes	Yes
Valium/Librium	4–6	Moderate	Yes	Yes
Narcotics (opium, heroin, morphine, codeine, percodan, demerol, cough syrup)	4–6	High	Yes	Yes
Stimulants (amphetamines, Benzedrine, Methedrine, Dexedrine, Ritalin, preludin)	4–8	High	Yes	Yes
Caffeine	2–4	Moderate	Yes	Yes
Hallucinogens LSD	10–12	Degree unknown	Unknown	Unknown
Psilocybin	6–8	Degree unknown	Unknown	Unknown
Mescaline	12–14	Degree unknown	Unknown	Unknown
PCP	Variable	High	Yes	Yes
Inhalants (hydrocarbons, nitrous oxide, chlorohydrocarbons)	1–2	Moderate	Unknown	Unknown
Cocaine (crack)	1–2	High	Yes	Yes
Antidepressants Lithium Dibenzapines (tofranil, elavil) MAO inhibitors	8–12	Low	No	No
Marijuana (cannabis)	2–4	Moderate	Possible	Possible
Hashish	2–4	Moderate	Possible	Possible

Usual Short-Term Effects	Usual Long-Term Effects
CNS depressant; relaxation (sedation); sometimes euphoria; drowsiness; impaired judgment, reaction time, coordination, and emotional control; frequent aggressive behavior	Diversion of energy and money from more creative and productive pursuits; habituation; possible obesity with chronic excessive use; irreversible damage to brain and liver; addiction; DTs; death
CNS stimulation; relaxation; constriction of blood vessels; impaired breathing	Cancer; heart and blood vessel disease; respiratory diseases; habituation
CNS depressants; sleep induction; relaxation (sedation); sometimes euphoria; drowsiness; impaired judgment, reaction time, coordination, and emotional control; relief of anxiety-tension; lethargy; suppression of hallucinations	Irritability, weight loss, addiction with severe withdrawal illness; drowsiness; blurred vision; jaundice; habituation; possible death
CNS depressants; sedation; euphoria; relief of pain; apathy; impaired intellectual functioning and coordination	Constipation; loss of appetite and weight; temporary impotence or sterility; habituation; addiction with unpleasant and painful withdrawal illness; death
CNS stimulants; increased alertness, reduction of fatigue; loss of appetite; insomnia; sometimes euphoria; increased respiration and heart rate	Restlessness, insomnia, irritability, weight loss; paranoia; gastric irritation; habituation; death
Effects are unpredictable but can include intense visual imagery; increased sensory awareness; feeling of consciousness expansion; anxiety; rapid mood changes; nausea; increased pulse rate and blood pressure; very violent behavior with PCP	Sometimes precipitates or intensifies an already existing psychosis. Other effects include panic reaction; distorted judgment and perception; flashbacks; possible brain damage and genetic damage
Euphoria, shortness of breath, nausea, headache, dizziness, fainting	Unknown
CNS stimulant; often elevates mood; increased heart rate and respiration; drying of the nose; laxative; depression and fatigue after effects wear off	Restlessness; irritability; destruction of nasal walls; habituation; diversion of energy and money; weight loss; paranoia; death
Relief of depression (elevation of mood); stimulation	Basically the same as tranquilizers
Distortion of thoughts and perception; short-term memory loss; impaired coordination; panic reaction; increased appetite; hallucination in larger doses	Impaired judgment; apathy; temporary sterility and infertility; brain damage; lung cancer; possible genetic damage; habituation

Cases have been reported in which marijuana appears to have helped bring on psychological disturbances in people who were already unstable before they used it.

Psychologists have investigated the relationship between marijuana use and lifestyle and personality factors. Much of the research has focused on adolescent marijuana users. A longitudinal study of almost 700 students that began tracking students before marijuana use found that those who did come to use the drug tended to have lower achievement in school, increased deviant behavior, and greater rebelliousness. Marijuana use also appeared to interfere with adolescents' relationships with their parents (Brook, Gordon, Brook, and Brook, 1989). In comparing marijuana users to nonusers, another study (Rob, Reynolds, and Finlayson, 1990) found that users were twice as likely to come from broken homes and three times as likely to have had sexual intercourse. Also, use of other drugs was found almost exclusively in the marijuana users group. However, marijuana use alone cannot be cited as the single cause of the problems noted, because it is often combined with other contributing factors, such as the use of other illicit drugs (Kleinman, Wish, Deren, and Rainone, 1988).

Research has also been conducted on the physical effects of marijuana use. Some studies have suggested that heavy and prolonged use of marijuana may impair reproductive functioning. Other studies suggest that marijuana use is more damaging to the lungs than cigarette use. Although there is no direct evidence that marijuana use causes lung cancer, the tar in marijuana smoke has been shown to produce tumors in laboratory animals.

Hallucinogens

Hallucinogens—so-called because their main effect is to produce hallucinations—are found in plants that grow throughout the world, and have been used for their effects on consciousness since earliest human history (Schultes, 1976). These drugs are also called psychedelic ("mind-manifesting") because they are seen as demonstrating the ways in which the mind has the potential to function.

Among the more common hallucinogenic plants are belladonna, henbane, mandrake, datura (jimson weed), one species of morning-glory, peyote, many kinds of mushrooms, and also cannabis. While we still do not know the exact chemical effects of hallucinogens on the brain, some contain chemical compounds that seem to mimic the activity of certain neurotransmitters, the chemical messengers that regulate brain-cell activity.

LSD.   The best-known and most extensively studied of the hallucinogens, **LSD (lysergic acid diethylamide)** is also the most potent; in fact, it is one of the most powerful drugs known. LSD, which is a synthetic substance, is 100 times stronger than psilocybin, which comes from certain mushrooms, and 4,000 times stronger than mescaline, which comes from peyote. A dose of a few millionths of a gram has a noticeable effect; an average dose of 100 to 300 micrograms produces a "trip" that lasts from six to fourteen hours.

Figure 7.7
South American Indian in a drug trance during a religious ceremony. In this culture, hallucinogens are used to heighten the religious experience.

During an LSD trip a person can experience any number of mood states, often quite intense and rapidly changing. The person's "set"—expectations, mood, beliefs—and the circumstances under which he or she takes LSD can affect the experience, making it euphoric or terrifying.

As measured by the ability to perform simple tasks, LSD impairs thinking, even though users may feel they are thinking more clearly and logically than ever before. Panic reactions are the most common of LSD's unpleasant side effects. Those who experience panic and later describe it often say that they felt trapped in the experience of panic and were afraid that they would never get out or that they would go mad.

PCP (phencyclidine). Considered a hallucinogen, **PCP** is also a central nervous system depressant capable of producing symptoms not normally expected from either a depressant or a hallucinogen (Frier, 1989). PCP, or angel dust, is one of the most widely used recreational drugs among adolescents. The average age of first use is 14 years (Young, 1987). Controlled laboratory studies have shown that high doses of PCP can produce numbness, light-headedness, dizziness, loss of muscle coordination, and psychotic or violent behavior (Pradhan, 1984). Some users are attracted to PCP because of the apparent loss of control it brings on (Fram and Stone, 1986).

Designer Drugs.   The hallucinogens that are known as **designer drugs** are defined as "illegally manufactured psychoactive compounds that are chemically manipulated for the consumer" (Stanford, 1988). These drugs are usually a variation on existing drugs. Each "batch" is produced by different individuals and may therefore vary greatly in terms of strength and purity. This makes it difficult to evaluate the effects and potential dangers of these drugs.

Use of MDMA, one of the more common designer drugs, is on the rise (Beck, 1986). It is related to both amphetamines and mescaline, and its street name is "ecstasy." One study of undergraduates who used MDMA recreationally (Peroutka, Newman, and Harris, 1988) revealed that the most common pleasurable effect was a heightened sense of "closeness" with other people. Less pleasurable effects included excessively rapid heart rate, dry mouth, and teeth grinding. Twenty percent of the users reported visual hallucinations. Unpleasant side effects were most common the day after use. These included muscle aches, fatigue, depression, and difficulty concentrating. Two-thirds of the frequent users reported that with successive doses of MDMA the pleasurable effects decreased and the unpleasant effects increased.

Cocaine

A drug whose use has increased dramatically in the past decade is cocaine. Cocaine is a stimulant: it produces feelings of alertness, confidence, and well-being. As its effects wear off, however, users experience anxiety and depression.

Cocaine was once considered a fairly harmless recreational drug with little potential for dependence. Its use tended to be limited by its high price. In recent years, however, as larger quantities of the drug were produced, and as a cheaper form of the drug—crack—became available, its use has spread.

Studies now indicate that cocaine is indeed addictive. Users can become so dependent on the drug that they will go to any lengths to obtain supplies. Crack is particularly addictive: addiction can occur after only a few uses. Today, crack addiction—and its attendant social problems—is widespread in many of our inner cities.

Experts indicate that while detoxification is an important step in treatment for crack addiction, it cannot be the only step (Wallace, 1989). This is one reason why Holden (1989) explores the use of ethnography as a research technique. This method involves close observation: the observer effectively immerses himself in the world of the drug user in order to develop a holistic understanding of the person. Effective treatment programs have many dimensions and look at such things as social skills and the person's ability to adapt to and integrate with the adult world (Alexander, 1987).

Figure 7.8
The effects of cocaine, like other crugs, vary from person to person.

Alcohol

The most widely used and abused mind-altering substance in the United States is alcohol. The consumption of alcohol is encouraged by advertisements and by social expectations and traditions. The immediate effect of alcohol is a general loosening of inhibitions. Despite its seeming stimulating effect, alcohol is actually a depressant that serves to inhibit the brain's normal functions. When people drink, they often act without the social restraint or self-control they normally apply to their behavior.

In small doses, alcohol use can have a temporarily pleasant effect. The effects of alcohol consumption, however, depend on the amount and frequency of drinking. As the amount consumed increases within a specific time, the drinker's ability to function diminishes. The person experiences slurred speech, blurred vision, and an impairment in judgment and memory. Permanent damage to the brain and liver and a change in personality can result from prolonged heavy use of alcohol.

Recent studies have suggested that not all of the early effects of drinking are the result of the alcohol alone. People expect to feel a certain way when they drink. In one study, men who were led to believe they were drinking alcohol when they were, in fact, drinking tonic water, became more aggressive. They also felt more sexually aroused and were less anxious in social situations (Marlatt and Rohsenow, 1981). The effects and treatment of alcohol abuse are discussed more fully in Chapter 15.

BIOFEEDBACK

Biofeedback involves learning to control your internal physiological processes with the help of feedback from these physiological states. For example, you can be hooked up to a biofeedback machine so that a light goes on every time your heart rate goes over 80 (Figure 7.9). You could then learn to keep your heart rate below 80 by trying to keep the light off. How would you do it? When researcher David Shapiro (1973) asked a participant in one of his experiments how he changed his heart rate, the subject asked in return, "How do you move your arm?"

However people do it, biofeedback has been used to teach people to control a wide variety of physiological responses, including brain waves

Figure 7.9
Subject practicing biofeedback.

(EEG), heart rate, blood pressure, skin temperature, and sweat-gland activity (Hassett, 1978a). The basic principle of biofeedback is simple: feedback makes learning possible. Biofeedback involves using machines to tell people about very subtle, moment-to-moment changes in the body. People can then experiment with different thoughts and feelings while they watch how each affects their bodies. In time, most people can learn to change their physiological processes.

In the 1960s, researchers began experimenting with biofeedback to cure medical and stress-related conditions like high blood pressure, migraine headaches, and tension headaches. At first, many biofeedback cures were reported in the press. But psychologists were suspicious that these miraculous cases had more to do with the power of suggestion than with biofeedback itself. (Doctors are very familiar with the fact that patients often improve when they believe in a treatment.)

Therefore, more careful studies were started to see what medical conditions could be helped by biofeedback. Some of the best-documented biofeedback cures involve special training in muscular control. Tension headaches often seem to result from constriction of the frontalis muscle in the forehead. Thomas Budzynski and others (1973) used biofeedback to teach people to relax this specific muscle. The practice went on for several weeks while other people were given similar treatments without biofeedback. Only the biofeedback group improved significantly.

Biofeedback has more potential for treating physical disease than for spiritual well-being.

MEDITATION

In the 1960s, psychologists began to study **meditation**, focusing attention on an image or thought with the goal of clearing one's mind and producing an "inner peace." In one of the first experiments, people were simply asked to concentrate on a blue vase.

The participants soon reported that the color of the vase became very vivid and that time passed quickly. The people could not be distracted as easily as they normally might. Some people felt themselves merging with the vase. Others reported that their surroundings became unusually beautiful. All the meditators found the experience pleasant. After twelve sessions they all felt a strong attachment to the vase and missed it when it was not present during the next session (Deikman, 1963).

Other researchers went on to show that when people meditated, their physiological state changed. The most famous of these studies was done by Robert Keith Wallace at UCLA (1970). He measured the brain waves (EEG), heart rate, oxygen consumption, and sweat-gland activity of fifteen people as they practiced Transcendental Meditation. (Transcendental Meditation is a Westernized version of yoga meditation techniques that was developed by the Maharishi Mahesh Yogi.) For two twenty-minute periods each day, meditators sit in a comfortable position and repeat a special word—called a *mantra*—over and over again. Wallace found that when people did this, electrical measurements of their bodies proved that they were deeply relaxed.

Further studies suggested that the regular practice of meditation was not only physically relaxing (Woolfolk, 1975), but also led to changes in behavior such as decreased drug use (Benson and Wallace, 1972). Dr. Leon Otis recently warned that a few people who meditate develop anxiety, depression, and other problems (Hassett, 1978c). But researchers generally agree that most people can benefit from the sort of systematic relaxation that meditation provides.

There is some controversy over how meditation techniques differ and what their specific effects are. In his best-selling book *The Relaxation Response*, Herbert Benson (1975) argues that most forms of meditation produce the same result, which he called the "relaxation response." Four basic elements are required to elicit the relaxation response: a quiet environment, a comfortable position, a "mental device" (such as a word that is repeated over and over again, or a physical object that the meditator concentrates on), and a passive attitude. Although not all psychologists agree that the relaxation response is entirely different from sleep or that all relaxation yields the same physical pattern, most do believe that Benson's technique can be helpful for many people.

USING PSYCHOLOGY

Lowering Blood Pressure

One out of every three American adults has high blood pressure. More than 90 percent of these cases are diagnosed as essential **hypertension**—a euphemism that means nobody really knows what is causing it. Traditionally, physicians have treated this problem with pills. But now doctors are shifting their emphasis from pills to people. Patients with high blood pressure are being taught to relax, often with the help of meditation and biofeedback (Hassett, 1978b).

Blood pressure is the force of the blood moving away from the heart, pushing against the artery walls. It changes from instant to instant, peaking as the heart beats and blood spurts through the arteries, and gradually decreasing to a minimum just before the next beat. Blood pressure is expressed as two numbers: systolic pressure (the maximum value when the heart beats) over diastolic pressure (the minimum pressure between beats). It is measured in millimeters of mercury (abbreviated mmHg), a standard unit of force. Normal blood pressure is somewhere around 120/80 mmHg.

Blood pressure varies constantly and increases under stress. Visiting the dentist, taking an examination, even drinking a cup of coffee (a mild stimulant) will increase your blood pressure temporarily. Strong emotions, particularly suppressed anger, will also raise blood pressure.

When blood pressure goes up and stays up, the medical condition is called hypertension. Definite hypertension refers to a blood pressure greater than 160/95. Hypertension is called the silent killer because it usually produces no pain, no other symptoms or warnings before causing severe damage to the cardiovascular system or other organs. But a killer it is. It is a primary cause of stroke (blood-vessel damage in the brain) and, like smoking and high cholesterol levels, increases the risk of heart attacks and coronary-artery disease.

After researchers discovered that normal people could raise and lower blood pressure with the help of biofeedback, it was but a small step to the idea that hypertensives could be taught to lower their blood pressure. In 1971, Harvard researchers Herbert Benson, David Shapiro, Bernard Tursky, and Gary Schwartz reported in *Science* that they had done just that. Five essential hypertensives had learned to lower their systolic pressure over the course of several weeks of training. Since then, others have found that biofeedback can be used to reduce both systolic and diastolic blood pressure.

Even in the first study, however, there were hints that biofeedback's effects don't always last after the subject leaves the laboratory. Gary Schwartz, for example, noticed that one man had a puzzling pattern of successes and failures. Five days a week, this hypertensive man faithfully attended training sessions, collecting $35 every Friday for his success in lowering his systolic pressure. When he returned each Monday morning, however, his blood pressure was high. After several weeks of this, Schwartz asked the patient for an explanation. It seemed that Saturday nights the man took his biofeedback earnings to the race track, gambled, and lost both his money and his controlled level of blood pressure.

So it was clear from the start that biofeedback was not a magical cure, only part of the answer. Since blood-pressure biofeedback requires complex and expensive equipment, it wasn't practical to use it with large numbers of patients. Other researchers therefore experimented with teaching hypertensives to relax their muscles, using a simpler form of biofeedback. This too led to lower blood pressure.

Herbert Benson has experimented with meditation as a partial treatment for high blood pressure, and again it has been successful. Finally, one group of researchers (Surwit, Shapiro, and Good, 1978) directly compared the effects of blood-pressure biofeedback, muscle-tension biofeedback, and meditation. All three reduced blood pressure, and there were no significant differences among the groups.

CHAPTER REVIEW

KEY TERMS

- biofeedback
- consciousness
- designer drugs
- hallucination
- hallucinogens
- hypertension
- hypnosis

- LSD
- marijuana
- MDMA
- meditation
- narcolepsy
- near-death experience
- obstructive sleep apnea

- out-of-body experience
- PCP
- posthypnotic suggestion
- psychoactive drugs
- REM sleep
- sleep apnea

SUMMARY

1. The most common altered state of consciousness is dreaming. People are mentally active throughout the night, although the degree of activity varies with each stage in the sleep cycle.

2. The stage of sleep in which vivid dreams occur is called REM sleep. Dreams may symbolically depict significant emotional problems and disturbances that are part of a person's daily experiences.

3. Hypnosis may be an altered state of consciousness in which a subject becomes highly receptive to the suggestions of another person. He or she does so willingly and cannot be made to do anything he or she would not normally do while awake.

4. Hallucinations—sensations or perceptions that have no direct external cause—may occur during drug states or after sleep deprivation. During an out-of-body experience, a person's entire perceptual world changes.

5. A near-death experience occurs when a person has a close brush with death or believes death is near. Almost everyone who has a near-death experience is changed by it.

6. Psychoactive drugs interact with the central nervous system to alter a person's mood, perception, and behavior. The effects of marijuana vary from person to person. LSD, PCP, and MDMA are the most common hallucinogens—drugs that alter awareness and produce hallucinations.

7. Use of cocaine has increased, especially since crack became available. Treatment programs for crack addiction must be multidimensional.

8. Biofeedback involves learning to control your physiological state with the help of machines that give you feedback about bodily processes.

9. Meditation is a state of consciousness involving high levels of concentration—a drug-free "high" for many people. Experienced meditators are able to achieve a high state of relaxation with greatly reduced anxiety.

REVIEW QUESTIONS

1. Describe each of the four stages of sleep. During which stage is it most difficult to awaken someone? During which stage do we dream and display REM?

2. What were Sigmund Freud's main beliefs about dreams? What did he think dreams were based on? How did Nathaniel Kleitman's beliefs about dreams differ from those of Freud?

3. What happens when someone is hypnotized? What does Barber say about hypnosis being an altered state of consciousness? How does Hilgard view hypnosis?

4. What are hallucinations? How does an out-of-body experience differ from other hallucinations?

5. What are the typical characteristics of a near-death experience?

6. Which psychoactive drugs are depressants? Which are stimulants?

7. Describe the relationship between marijuana use and lifestyle and personality factors.

8. What are the typical reactions caused by LSD?

9. What are some health problems that biofeedback can potentially help?

10. What are the basic elements of the relaxation response?

11. What is the most widely used and abused mind-altering substance in the United States?

ACTIVITIES

1. What behaviors do you perform automatically? Pick one of your automatic behaviors and pay close attention to how you perform it. What are the individual parts that make up the behavior? How does consciously thinking about the behavior affect your performance of it?

2. Keep track of your dreams for at least a week. Dreams are difficult to remember, so keep a paper and pencil by your bed. When you wake up after a dream, keep your eyes closed and try to remember it in your mind. Then write it down, including as much detail as you can. Also write down any ideas you may have about what the dream means and any feelings you may have about the dream. After you have kept track of your dreams for several days, ask yourself: Am I able to consciously control my dreams in any way? Am I better able to understand myself by examining my dreams?

3. One way of becoming aware of your consciousness is through meditation. Meditation is not concentration in the normal sense of the word. It is opening up one's awareness to the world at the present. Try the following for ten to fifteen minutes a day. Find a quiet spot without distractions. Listen quietly without making any generalizations on what you hear. Listen for the sounds without naming them. After each period, write down your observations. Which sounds did you "hear" for the first time?

4. Hypnosis is a form of suggestibility. You may discover which of your friends is susceptible to hypnosis by doing the following test in hypnosis. Have your subjects place a coin in their open palm. Repeatedly suggest to them that they feel the palm slowly turning over, until the coin falls out of the palm. You may be surprised at the results.

5. Pick any word and say it one hundred times. What happens?

6. Have you ever hallucinated a sight or sound— perhaps when you were very tired or upset? What did you experience? Why do you suppose you created this particular hallucination?

7. Read the daily newspaper over a two-week period. Keep a record of the articles that are about psychoactive drugs. Organize the articles according to the drug categories presented in Table 7.1. Which drugs are most in the news? Are there drugs publicized that are not listed in the table? Do the articles discuss drug use, drug production, drug distribution, or drug treatment? What conclusions can you draw from these articles? Do they tell you anything about the frequency of drug use or what society thinks is important about drugs?

The Life Span

CHAPTER *8*
Infancy and Childhood

CHAPTER *9*
Adolescence

CHAPTER *10*
Adulthood and Old Age

Figure 8.1 We change faster and learn more in childhood than we ever will again.

Objectives: *After studying this chapter, you should be able to*
- identify the concept of nature/nurture interaction in human development.
- outline the psychological research into cognitive development.
- discuss the development of language and related research.
- cite the studies of emotional development.
- summarize the major theories of socialization.

182

Infancy and Childhood

The young child lives in a strange world of wonders and delights. An empty box is as fascinating to an infant as the gift that comes in it. Mommy and Daddy are the source of all life's great pleasures, and many of its pains. Each day there is something new to be learned.

It is hard to believe that all of us were once only two feet tall and were taking our first steps. Just a year or two after that, we spent our days intently playing house, cops and robbers, and doctor. Most of the events from our early lives are long forgotten, but we changed faster and learned more in childhood than we ever will again.

Developmental psychology is the study of the changes that occur as people grow up and grow old. It covers the entire life cycle, from conception to death. What does the newborn know? How does the infant respond in the early years of life? How do people learn to walk and talk, to think and feel? How do people develop their unique personalities? These are some questions developmental psychologists seek to answer.

In this chapter we describe the many different psychological processes humans experience from infancy through childhood. In the next chapters we will look at adolescence, adulthood, and old age.

WHAT CAUSES DEVELOPMENT?

Psychologists have long been concerned with what influences human development. Why does one child excel in math and another in music? Why does Matthew start walking at eleven months and Alexa at fourteen months? Are these differences due to nature—what a child is born with? Or are they a result of nurturing—what each of us experiences in our environment? What is traditionally called the nature/nurture controversy is a central issue in developmental psychology (see Chapter 4 for a historical perspective).

What Causes Development?
The Beginning of Life
Cognitive Development
How Knowing Changes
• Stages of Cognitive Development
The Development of Language
Can Animals Use Language?
• How Children Acquire Language
Emotional Development
Experiments with Animals
• Human Attachment • Using Psychology: Child Abuse
Socialization
Freud's Theory of Psychosexual Development
• Erikson's Theory of Psychosocial Development
• Social Learning • Theories of Development • Using Psychology: Children and Television • The Cognitive-Developmental Approach

Figure 8.2
Some stages of motor development in infants. Although some infants reach each stage ahead of others, the order of the stages is the same for all infants. The colored bars show age ranges for the development of each stage. The far left side of the bar is the age by which 25 percent have mastered this movement; the far right side is the age by which 90 percent have mastered it. The point on the bar where orange meets purple is the age by which half of the infants have mastered the movement.

Most contemporary psychologists agree that neither nature nor environment alone determines development. Rather, each of us is the product of the interaction between what we have inherited biologically and what we experience in the world. This interaction is the key to development.

In his classic study of the development of walking in orphanage-reared children in Iran, Wayne Dennis (1960) demonstrated the importance of the nature/nurture interaction. While most children begin walking at about one year of age, most of the orphans did not walk until well after two years of age (see Figure 8.2). What makes Dennis's findings particularly interesting is that he does not blame late walking on malnutrition or some other biological cause. Rather Dennis cites the children's lack of opportunity to lie in a prone position or to be propped on a pillow by a caring adult as the reason for their delayed walking. Furthermore, because the children were made to lie on their backs, they did not creep or crawl before walking. Instead, they slid on the floor on their backsides. This finding shows that the sequence of motor development as shown in Figure 8.2 depends in part on the child's environment. It is not a universal progression.

Researchers have also found that if nature and environment influence development, then the timing of this interaction is crucial. In other words, there are **critical periods** or times when specific environmental influences

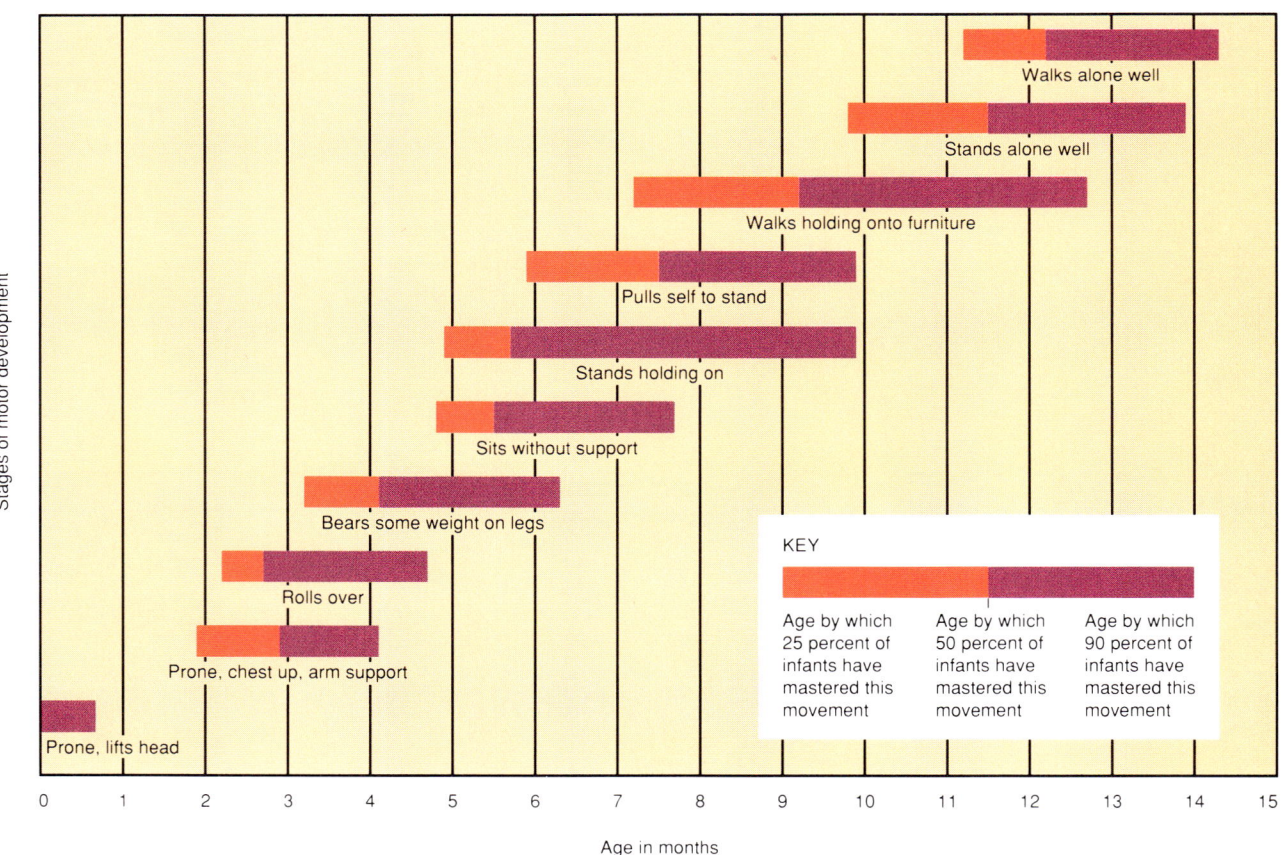

KEY

| Age by which 25 percent of infants have mastered this movement | Age by which 50 percent of infants have mastered this movement | Age by which 90 percent of infants have mastered this movement |

Stages of motor development

Walks alone well
Stands alone well
Walks holding onto furniture
Pulls self to stand
Stands holding on
Sits without support
Bears some weight on legs
Rolls over
Prone, chest up, arm support
Prone, lifts head

0 1 2 3 4 5 6 7 8 9 10 11 12 13 14 15

Age in months

are most likely to affect development. For example, in the 1950s and 1960s the drug thalidomide was prescribed for pregnant women to help alleviate nausea and insomnia. However, when many of these women gave birth, it was discovered that this drug caused birth defects. Specifically, it stopped the growth of arms and/or legs so that feet and hands grew directly from the affected infants' bodies. Further research revealed that the drug only caused birth defects if taken between the thirty-eighth and fiftieth day of pregnancy—the critical period for thalidomide. A mother-to-be who took the drug after the fiftieth day did not endanger her infant (Steinberg, Belsky, and Meyer, 1991).

Critical periods have also been described in terms of animals. Konrad Lorenz, a student of animal behavior, discovered that infant geese experience a critical period when they become attached to their mothers. This process is called **imprinting**. A few hours after they struggle out of their shells, goslings are ready to start waddling after the first thing they see. Whatever that first object is, the goslings stay with it and treat it as though it were their mother from that time on. Usually, of course, the first thing they see is the mother goose; however, Lorenz found that if he substituted himself or some moving object like a green box being dragged along the ground, the goslings would follow that (Figure 8.3). From this early experience with their mother—or mother substitute—the goslings form their idea of what a goose is. If they have been imprinted with a human being instead of a goose, they will prefer the company of human beings to other geese and may even try to mate with humans later in life.

Psychological changes during a critical period have traditionally been regarded as permanent. However, some psychologists prefer to use the term **sensitive period** to mean a specific time that individuals are most receptive to certain environmental influences. Change during a sensitive period is not necessarily permanent. An infant's early attachment to its mother or care giver occurs during a sensitive period. We will discuss the consequences of this attachment later in this chapter.

Finally, although sensitive periods are generally acknowledged, timing is not an important factor in all developmental changes. That is, humans are able to acquire a variety of abilities at almost any age. For example, we can learn how to read at just about any age beyond five years. However, the skills we can learn at any age are still limited by our biological endowment. For example, humans cannot learn to fly at any age. As you read through this chapter, you will recognize many concepts and examples that illustrate the interaction of nature and environment in the developmental process.

Figure 8.3
Konrad Lorenz and the baby geese imprinted on him instead of a mother goose.

THE BEGINNING OF LIFE

Development begins long before an infant is born. Expectant mothers can feel strong kicking inside them during the later stages of pregnancy, and it is common for a fetus (an unborn child) to suck its thumb, even though it has never suckled at its mother's breast or had a bottle.

Figure 8.4
(a) The strength of the grasping reflex is demonstrated in a baby only a few days old. (b) This infant is responding to a touch on the cheek by opening his mouth and turning his head. The response is called the rooting reflex.

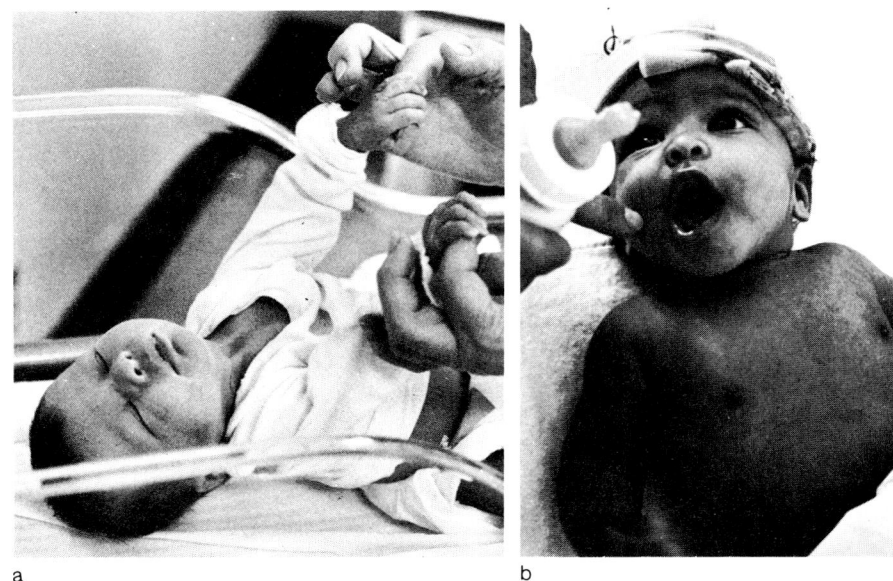

a   b

Birth puts staggering new demands on a baby's capacity to adapt and survive. Newborns go from an environment in which they are totally protected from the world to one in which they are assaulted by lights, sounds, touches, and extremes of temperature. Infants are capable of certain coordinated movement patterns, called reflexes, that can be triggered by the right stimulus (Figure 8.4). The **grasping reflex**, for example, is a response to a touch on the palm of the hand. Infants can grasp an object, such as a finger, so strongly that they can be lifted into the air. We suspect this reflex is left over from an earlier stage in human evolution, when babies had to cling to their apelike mothers' coats while their mothers were climbing or searching for food.

Also vital is the **rooting reflex**. If an alert newborn is touched anywhere around the mouth, he will move his head and mouth toward the source of the touch. In this way the touch of his mother's breast on his cheek guides the baby's mouth toward her nipple. The sucking that follows contact with the nipple is one of the baby's most complex reflexes. The baby is able to suck, breathe air, and swallow milk twice a second without getting confused. This is at least as difficult as learning to walk and chew gum at the same time.

Besides grasping and sucking, newborns look at their bodies and at their surroundings. Their waking time is divided between two distinct states called active awake and quiet alert. In the active awake state, newborns move actively but do not appear to be attending to or focusing on anything specific. In the quiet alert state, they remain relatively motionless and seem to gaze intently at the objects around them. Over the course of the first several months of life, these two states of arousal gradually fuse together into one state which we call the waking state.

How do newborn infants, lying in a hospital nursery, perceive the world? Do they see a roomful of stable objects and hear distinct sounds? Or is the sensory world of newborns an ever-changing chaos of meaningless shapes and noises—as William James put it, "one great booming, buzzing confusion"?

These are difficult questions to answer. How does one measure the capabilities of newborn infants who cannot speak or understand the questions of curious psychologists? One reasonable approach is to take advantage of the things babies *can* do. And what they can do is suck, turn their heads, look at things, cry, smile, and show signs of surprise or fright. The vigor of a baby's sucking, the patterns of eye movements, and expressions of pleasure and displeasure are all closely tied to how the baby is being stimulated. By measuring these behaviors, it is possible to infer how the infant perceives the world. For example, researchers can show a baby two different visual patterns. If the baby prefers one more than the other by consistently looking at it, this is an indicator that the baby can discriminate between the two. In fact, recent research indicates that newborns experience all the senses: they can see, hear, taste, and smell as well as touch. Some of the senses, however, undergo developmental change as the infant grows. In particular, newborns have relatively poor visual capabilities.

Ethnic Differences in Infants

It probably won't surprise you to learn that different breeds of puppies show striking differences in temperament and behavior. Young beagles, for example, are irrepressibly friendly; wire-haired terriers are tough and aggressive. But it probably will raise both your eyebrows to discover that newborn infants belonging to different ethnic groups start out life with different sets of responses that seem to relate more to their genes than to their individual personalities.

To learn just how important ethnic differences are in the way we respond, psychologist Daniel G. Freedman studied the responses of newborn Chinese and Caucasian babies. His results show that in many ways Chinese and Caucasian babies behave like two different breeds.

Here are some examples of the differences Dr. Freedman found. The Chinese babies were far more adaptable than the Caucasians. They cried less easily and were easier to console. In addition, they seemed comfortable in almost any position they were placed in, while the Caucasian infants tossed and turned until they were satisfied. When a cloth was briefly placed against the babies' noses, the Caucasian infants responded with a fight; they immediately turned their faces or swiped at the cloth with their hands. The Chinese babies adapted to the cloth's presence in the simplest possible way—by breathing through their mouths. As Dr. Freedman points out, "It was as if the old stereotypes of the calm, inscrutable Chinese and the excitable, emotionally changeable Caucasian were appearing spontaneously in the first forty-eight hours of life."

For more details, see Daniel G. Freedman, "Ethnic Differences in Babies," *Human Nature*, January 1979.

PSYCHOLOGY UPDATE

Drugs and Pregnancy. A child's mental and emotional development can be seriously affected by the mother's lifestyle, even before the child is born. The use of alcohol, tobacco, or other drugs by a mother-to-be has been linked to a number of developmental problems.

Children born to women who drink large amounts of alcohol during pregnancy may suffer from *fetal alcohol syndrome*. This condition is characterized by mental retardation, poor motor development, and unusual facial features such as a flat nose and widely spaced eyes.

A woman who smokes during pregnancy reduces the amount of oxygen that reaches her unborn child. This can have an adverse effect on the baby in terms of physical growth, intellectual development, and mental health.

The use of crack or other psychoactive drugs during pregnancy causes a range of developmental problems, not the least of which is that babies born to drug users may themselves be addicted to the drug by the time they are born.

However, by six months their sight is fairly well developed. Their vision continues to undergo small improvements beyond that age. We now know that for the infant the world is a place where mysteries continue to unfold as senses develop.

COGNITIVE DEVELOPMENT

Imagine this scene in the sandbox at the local playground. Lucy wants Max to give her his truck. Max doesn't let go of the truck so Lucy hits him on the head with her sand shovel. Her mother says, "Stop that. You wouldn't like it if Max hit you on the head, would you? So don't do it to him." What is Lucy's response? That depends on her age. If Lucy is three years old, she may very well become frightened and say, "I don't want Max to hit me." She may even hit Max again, because despite what her mother has said, Max has still not given her the truck. For her, hitting Max has nothing to do with how Max behaves toward her. However, if Lucy is six years old, she most likely will stop hitting Max. She understands the relationship between her behavior and that of Max, and she can also see herself in Max's place.

Why and how does Lucy's cognition or thinking change with age? Is she simply stupid at three and smarter at six? Or do our minds develop as we grow? These are the kinds of questions that the Swiss psychologist Jean Piaget set out to answer more than fifty years ago. Through his research, he developed a very comprehensive and influential theory of cognitive or intellectual development.

Piaget spent years observing, questioning, and playing games with babies and young children—including his own. He concluded that younger children aren't "dumb" in the sense of lacking a given *amount of information*. Rather, they think in a different *way* than older children and adults; they use a different kind of logic. A seven-year-old is completely capable of answering the question, "Who was born first, you or your mother?" but a four-year-old isn't (Chukovsky, 1963). Cognitive development involves quantitative changes (growth in the *amount* of information) as well as qualitative changes (differences in the *manner* of thinking). Most importantly, it involves children actively shaping their own intellectual abilities through their interaction with the world around them.

How Knowing Changes

Understanding the world involves the construction of *schemes,* or plans for knowing. Each of us is an architect and engineer in this respect, constructing intellectual schemes, applying them, and changing them as necessary. When we put a scheme into action, we are trying to understand something. In the process of **assimilation**, we try to fit the world into our scheme. In that of **accommodation**, we change our scheme to fit the characteristics of the world.

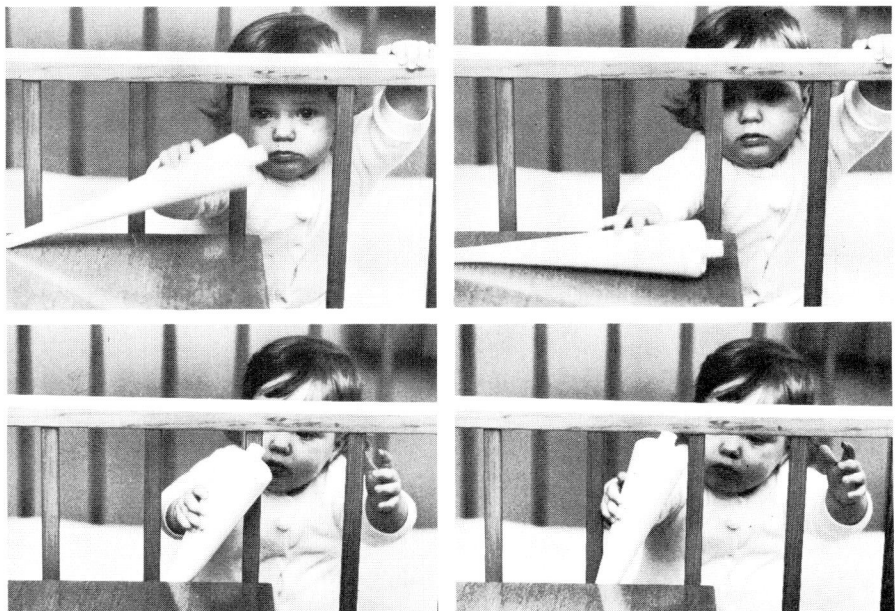

Figure 8.5
(from left to right and top to bottom) This child possesses a scheme for grasping objects and pulling them to her that does not adequately match the features of the environment she is now trying to assimilate. Her scheme will not get the toy through the bars of the playpen. An accommodation—the addition of turning to grasping and pulling—achieves a state of equilibrium.

According to Piaget, newborns have a set of ready-made responses. They respond to bright lights by blinking, to objects in their hands by grasping, to a sudden loss of support by throwing out their arms and legs, and to an object in the mouth by sucking. These reflexes let babies understand things. In grasping a block, babies assimilate it to their grasping scheme after accommodating it—changing their grasp to fit it.

Assimilation and accommodation work together to produce intellectual growth. When events do not fit into existing schemes, new and grander schemes have to be created. The child begins to see and understand things in a new light. Progressive changes in the way a baby conceives objects illustrate this.

Stages of Cognitive Development

Piaget described the changes that occur in children's understanding in four stages of cognitive development (Table 8.1). During the *sensorimotor stage*, the young infant uses schemes that primarily involve his or her body and sensations. The *preoperational stage* emerges when the child begins to use mental images or symbols to understand things. By the third, *concrete operational stage*, children are able to use logical schemes, but their understanding is limited to concrete objects or problems. In the *formal operational stage*, individuals are able to solve abstract problems. According to Piaget, a person's development through these four stages depends on both the maturation of his or her nervous system and on the kinds of experiences he or she has had. Everyone goes through the stages in the same order, but not necessarily at the same age.

Table 8.1 / Piaget's Stages of Cognitive Development

SENSORIMOTOR STAGE (birth to two years): Thinking is displayed in action, such as the grasping, sucking, and looking schemes. Child gradually learns to discover the location of hidden objects at about eighteen months, when the concept of object permanence is fully understood.

PREOPERATIONAL STAGE (two to six years): Beginning of symbolic representation. Language first appears; child begins to draw pictures that represent things. Child cannot represent a series of actions in his or her head in order to solve problems.

CONCRETE OPERATIONAL STAGE (six to twelve years): Ability to understand conservation problems. Ability to think of several dimensions or features at same time. Child can now do elementary arithmetic problems, such as judging the quantity of liquid containers and checking addition of numbers by subtraction.

FORMAL OPERATIONAL STAGE (twelve years to adulthood): Thinking becomes more abstract and hypothetical. The individual can consider many alternative solutions to a problem, make deductions, contemplate the future, and formulate personal ideals and values.

Sensorimotor Stage.   During the sensorimotor stage, a baby's understanding of things lies totally in the here and now. The sight of a toy, the way it feels in her hands, the sensation it produces in her mouth are all she knows. She does not imagine it, picture it, think of it, remember it, or even forget it. How do we know this?

When an infant's toy is hidden from her, she acts as if it has ceased to exist (Figure 8.6). She doesn't look for it; she grabs whatever else she can find and plays with that. Or she may simply start crying. At about eight months, however, this pattern begins to change. When you take the baby's toy and hide it under a blanket—while she is watching—she will search for it under the blanket. However, if you change tactics and put her toy behind your back, she will continue to look for it under the blanket—even if she was watching you the whole time.

You can't fool a twelve- to eighteen-month-old baby quite so easily. A child this age watches closely and searches for the toy in the last place she saw you put it. But suppose you take the toy, put it under the blanket, conceal it in your hands, and then put it behind your back. A twelve-month-old

Figure 8.6
This infant of about six months cannot yet understand that objects have an existence of their own, away from her presence. (a) The infant gazes intently at a toy elephant. (b) When the elephant is blocked from view, she gives no indication that she understands the toy still exists. This thinking pattern changes by age two, as shown in Figure 8.7.

a

b

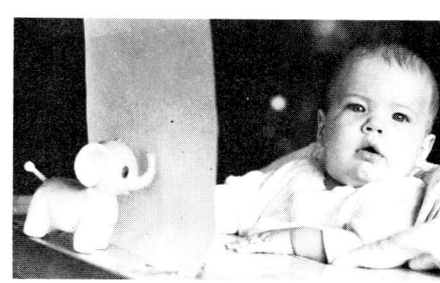

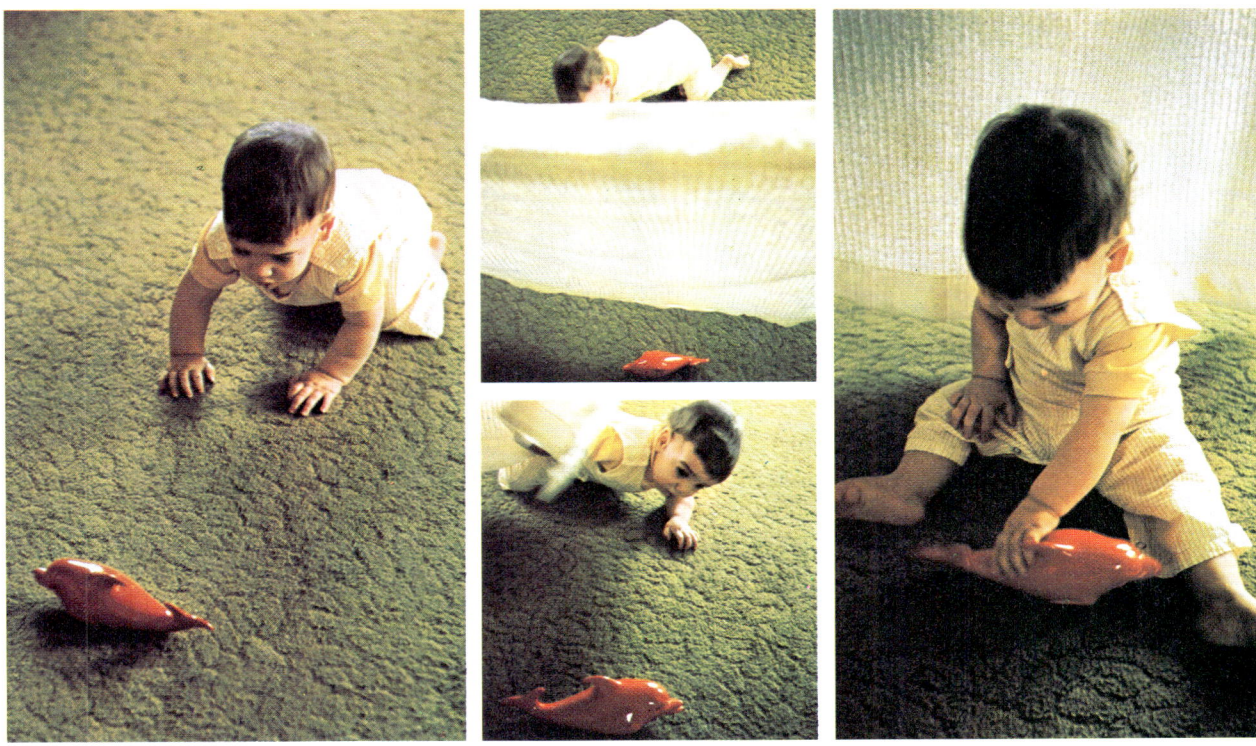

Figure 8.7
By the age of two, a child realizes that the disappearance of an object does not mean that it no longer exists. In fact, if an object is concealed, a child will search for it because he or she knows it still exists somewhere.

will act surprised when she doesn't find the toy under the blanket—and keep searching there. An eighteen- or twenty-four-month-old will guess what you've done and walk behind you to look (Figure 8.7). She knows the toy must be somewhere (Ginsburg and Opper, 1969: 50–56). She has developed a new scheme, **object permanence**, which might be expressed as "Things continue to exist even though I cannot see or touch them."

This is a giant step in intellectual development and a major accomplishment of the sensorimotor stage. The child has progressed from believing that her own actions created the world to realizing that people and objects are independent of her actions. The child now conceives of a world of which she is only a part.

The achievement of object permanence suggests that a child has begun to engage in what Piaget calls **representational thought**. Now, children can begin to picture (or represent) things in their minds. At fourteen months of age, Piaget's daughter demonstrated this. When she was out visiting another family, she happened to witness a child throwing a temper tantrum. She had never had a tantrum herself, but the next day she did—screaming, shaking her playpen, and stamping her feet as the other child had. She had formed so clear an image of the tantrum in her mind that she was able to create an excellent imitation a day later (Ginsburg and Opper, 1969: 65). To Piaget, this meant that his daughter was using symbols.

Soon, in the *preoperational stage,* she would learn to use a much more complex system of symbols—spoken language.

Preoperational Stage. The use of representational thought expands in a variety of areas during the preoperational stage. Language abilities increase rapidly. To communicate through language, a child must have a working understanding of symbols. At three years of age, a child can offer you a "pretend" piece of cake and discuss how it tastes with you. The child knows what cake is without seeing it and can even "play with" the concept of it. Children in this stage also begin to draw pictures of what they see in the world, and they begin to count.

The preoperational stage is a time of transition. The child consolidates the cognitive progress of the sensorimotor stage and begins moving toward the more logical thinking of concrete operations. The three-year-old has difficulty distinguishing what is real from what he sees. For example, a person in a Santa Claus costume *is* Santa Claus. By the age of six, the child has usually figured out that he is only Santa's helper, a person in costume. Taken in by the way things look, the child also has difficulty explaining why things happen. In recent years, however, researchers have found that in certain situations children as young as three may be able to distinguish between what is real and what they actually see or feel (Steinberg, Belsky, and Meyer, 1991).

Concrete Operational Stage. When children develop a working knowledge of the world, they are said to be in the concrete operational stage. They develop skills in the trial-and-error approach to problem solving. But in general, their thinking is extremely concrete. During this stage, most children begin to understand what Piaget calls **conservation**, the principle that a given quality does not change when its appearance is changed. For example, if you have two identical short, wide jars filled with water and you pour the contents of one of these jars into a tall, thin jar, a child under five will say that the tall jar contains more water than the short one. If you pour the water back into the short jar to show the amount has not changed, the child will still maintain that there was more water in the tall container. Children under five do not seem to be able to think about two dimensions (height and width) at the same time. That is, they do not understand that a change in width is made up for by a change in the height of the tall glass (Figure 8.8).

Within two years, the same child will tell you that the second jar contains the same amount of water as the first. If you ask why, he may say because the short jar is fatter than the tall jar—indicating that he is able to coordinate his perceptions of height and width. Or he may point out that if you poured the water back into the short jar, it would be the same—indicating that he is able to think in reverse, to retrace the steps of the experiment. Younger children generally cannot do this.

Another type of conservation experiment begins when a child is shown two identical balls of clay. Then, the child watches the experimenter flatten one ball and roll it into the shape of a sausage. Again, the young child be-

lieves that the amount of clay has changed. The older child conserves. That is, she recognizes that the amount of clay is unaffected by the change in appearance.

Whereas Piaget maintained that conservation could not be understood until at least the age of five, many contemporary psychologists disagree. If the task is designed properly, researchers have found that even three- and four-year-olds understand the basic logic of conservation (Gelman and Baillergeon, 1983).

Formal Operational Stage.   The final stage of cognitive development occurs around the age of twelve when adolescents develop adult thinking patterns. For a complete explanation of formal operational thinking, see Chapter 9 under the heading "Changes in Thinking."

Figure 8.8
The girl taking part in this demonstration thinks there is more water in the tall beaker; she has not yet acquired conservation. Although she has seen the liquid poured from one beaker to another, she bases her decision on the height of the column of water and ignores its diameter.

THE DEVELOPMENT OF LANGUAGE

We use language everyday in a variety of situations. It is this "ordinariness," the fact that humans acquire and use language despite vast differences in environment, education, and individual intelligence, that makes human language ability so extraordinary. Children acquire language at a relatively immature time in their lives. They combine words in new ways on a daily basis. For example, let's say three-year-old Dana sees an elephant for the first time. Dana says, "The elephant is hungry. He is eating lunch." Dana knew all these words before talking about the elephant but has never uttered these exact sentences before. These are original sentences expressing thoughts the instant they come to mind. When you stop to think about it, this is an amazing accomplishment, yet it happens all the time. How is this possible?

Many theorists have tried to answer this question. The behaviorist B. F. Skinner claimed that children are conditioned to learn language. Their parents reinforce and model good grammar and vocabulary use. According to Skinner, this is how children learn to speak. However, Noam Chomsky, among others, has criticized this theory. Chomsky maintains that conditioning could never teach children all the rules of language they obviously use quite easily. He suggests that we are born with a special language learning mechanism in our brains called the language acquisition device (LAD). One way to determine whether humans have a unique, biologically based ability to learn language is to see whether other species can be taught humanlike languages. If they can, then the LAD theory may not be correct.

Can Animals Use Language?

For the most part researchers working with animals focus on two major aspects of language. First, they want to know whether animals can use signs or symbols to represent objects. Since animals cannot mimic human speech, researchers try to teach them to use sign language or to press buttons with symbols of objects on them. The second major language issue that animal researchers deal with is whether animals can use grammar, the rules for organizing symbols or words in new combinations to produce meaningful utterances. Grammatical rules are what make the sentence "The rhinoceros roared at the boy" mean the same thing as "The boy was roared at by the rhinoceros." On the surface, these sentences appear different because the word position is changed. But on a deeper level, we know that the first is an active sentence and the second a passive transformation of it. It may be in our ability to use such grammatical rules that we surpass the simpler language of the chimpanzee.

Many psychologists have tried to teach chimpanzees to use language. One husband-and-wife team, the Gardners, raised a baby chimp named

Figure 8.9
Washoe at about five years of age. She is shown here using the American Sign Language sign for "hat."

Washoe in their home and taught her to use the American Sign Language for deaf people (Figure 8.9). At three-and-one-half years of age, Washoe knew eighty-seven signs for words like "food," "dog," "toothbrush," "gimmee," "sweet," "more," and "hurry."

Making these signs at the appropriate times would not be enough to be called language, though. According to the Gardners, Washoe's remarkable achievement was that some of her signs had abstract meanings and that she could put signs together in new ways to produce new meanings. For example, she learned the sign for "more" (putting her fingertips together over her head) because she loved to be tickled and wanted more. But she was not simply doing something like a dog does when it rolls over to be tickled; she was able to use the same sign later in entirely new circumstances—asking for more food or more hair brushing.

Whether Washoe and several other chimpanzees in similar experiments have actually acquired human language is a controversial issue. Some researchers disagree with the Gardners; they maintain that the chimpanzees have acquired very little language, perhaps the ability of a nine- or ten-month-old child. Herbert Terrace (1979), who worked with Nim Chimpsky, a chimpanzee, found that Nim could put together what appeared to be longer and longer sentences. However, upon closer observation, he found that these long utterances were not really examples of the use of grammar. Rather, they were basically repetitive strings of phrases.

The strongest case for language acquisition was made by Savage-Rumbaugh and her colleagues (1986). They tried to teach Matata, a pygmy chimpanzee, to pick out symbols on a keyboard to express language. Unfortunately, Matata had difficulty learning many of the symbols. But she had brought a baby chimp, Kanzi, with her to all her lessons. One day Kanzi, whom researchers had not attempted to teach, started picking out symbols on the keyboard. Like a human child, he seems to have learned language simply by being exposed to it. For example, he touches the key for "chase" and runs around. He can also understand spoken complicated sentences, such as "Go get the lettuce in the microwave." No other primate has ever done this (Golden, 1991). Has the case of Kanzi proved that animals can acquire language like humans? More research with Kanzi and other animals is needed to answer this question fully.

How Children Acquire Language

There are several steps in learning language. First, one must learn to make the signs; then, one must give them meaning; and finally, one must learn grammar. Each child takes these steps at his or her own rate. Crying is the child's earliest vocalization. When crying lessens, the child starts making mostly cooing sounds, which develop into a babble or string of sounds.

Late in the first year, the strings of babbles begin to sound more like the language that the child hears. Children imitate the speech of their parents and their older brothers and sisters and are greeted with approval whenever they say something that sounds like a word. In this way children learn to speak their own language, even though they could just as easily learn any other.

Until recently it was thought that this early stage of language development concerned sound production only. However, a new study has shown that deaf babies of deaf parents begin to "babble" in sign language at the same age as hearing babies babble vocally. This finding indicates that the development of language is separate from the development of speech. Just as a Chinese baby learns Chinese and a French baby learns French, deaf babies of parents who sign learn sign language. Similarly, just as speaking parents reinforce familiar sounds in speaking infants, deaf parents reinforce correct signing by their children. This study also supports the notion that language development involves cognitive development or brain development whether or not speech accompanies it (Angier, 1991).

The leap to using sounds as symbols occurs at about twelve months of age. The first attempts at saying words are primitive, and the sounds are incomplete: "Ball" usually sounds like "ba," and "cookie" may even sound like "doo-da." The first real words usually refer to things the infant can see or touch. Often they are labels or commands ("dog!" "cookie!").

By the time children are two years old, they have a vocabulary of at least fifty words. Beginning at about two years of age, children learn five to eight new words each day. Toward the end of the second year, children begin to express themselves more clearly by joining words into two-word phrases (Figure 8.10).

But at age two, a child's grammar is still unlike that of an adult. Children use what psychologists call **telegraphic speech**—for example, "Where my apple?" and "Daddy fall down." They leave out words but still get the message across. As psychologists have discovered, two-year-olds already understand certain rules (Brown, 1973). They keep their words in the same order adults do. Indeed, at one point they overdo this, applying grammatical rules too consistently. For example, the usual rule for forming the

Figure 8.10
A two-year-old's telegraphic speech: the two-word phrases leave out words but still get the message across.

past tense of English verbs is to add "ed." But many verbs are irregular: "go" / "went," "come" / "came," "swim" / "swam," "fall" / "fell." At first children learn the correct form of the verb: "Daddy went yesterday." But once children discover the rule for forming past tenses, they replace the correct form with sentences like "Daddy *goed* yesterday." Although they have never heard adults use this word, they construct it in accordance with the rules of grammar that they have extracted from the speech they hear.

By the age of four or five children have mastered the basics of the language. Their ability to use words will continue to grow with their ability to think about and understand things.

EMOTIONAL DEVELOPMENT

While children are developing their ability to use the body, to think and to express themselves, they are also developing emotionally. They begin to become attached to specific people and to care about what they think and feel. In most cases, a child's first relationship is with the mother. This early attachment or relationship can affect a child's later emotional development. Research with animals has shed light on some of the factors involved in early parent/child attachment.

Experiments with Animals

Earlier in this chapter, we discussed Konrad Lorenz's experiments with geese. His work showed how experience with a mother—whether real or a substitute—can determine an infant bird's entire view of itself and others. An American psychologist, Harry Harlow, went on to study the relationship between mother and child in a species closer to humans, the rhesus monkey. His first question was: What makes the mother so important? He tried to answer this question by taking baby monkeys away from their natural mothers as soon as they were born, as described in Chapter 6. To review: Harlow raised the monkeys with two surrogate, or substitute, mothers. Each monkey could choose between a mother constructed of wood and wire and a mother constructed in the same way but covered with soft, cuddly terry cloth. In some cages, the cloth mother was equipped with a bottle; in others, the wire mother was.

The results were dramatic. The young monkeys became strongly attached to the cloth mother, whether she gave food or not, and for the most part ignored the wire mother. If a frightening object was placed in the monkey's cage, the baby monkey would run to the terry-cloth mother for security, not to the wire mother. It was the touching that mattered, not the feeding.

In another set of experiments, Harlow discovered that monkeys raised without real mothers grew up with serious emotional problems. As adults, they did not seem to know how to play or defend themselves or even mate,

Figure 8.11
One of Harry Harlow's series of experiments with monkeys showed the importance of early peer contact for normal development.

although they tried. In fact, when frightened by a strange human they often attacked their own bodies instead of making threatening signs of aggression as normal monkeys do.

The monkeys who had cloth mothers with bottles grew up more normally than the others, but even they were not well adjusted to normal monkey life. A partially adequate substitute for a mother turned out to be peers—other baby monkeys. Infant monkeys who played with other monkeys like themselves grew up fairly normally even if they never saw their mothers. To grow up completely normally, however, both mother *and* peers were necessary (Figure 8.11). It seems that interactions with mother and peers allow the baby to see and learn from the behavior of other monkeys. The silent surrogate provided no such opportunities.

Human Attachment

An infant begins to develop a strong attachment to its mother by the age of six months.

Just as animals develop early attachments that shape their emotional development, so do human infants. Up to six or seven months of age, most infants are indiscriminate. They respond to strangers as readily as they respond to their mothers and other familiar people; they will coo or whine at just about anyone. At six months, however, they begin to develop a strong attachment to their mothers (or whoever is caring for them). In fact, at about eight months many babies rather suddenly develop an intense fear of strangers—crying, hiding against their mothers, and showing other signs of distress when someone they do not know or remember approaches them. Separation anxiety, which appears at ten to twelve months, is further proof of attachment. Children do not remain exclusive for long, however. By eighteen months of age, nearly all babies have developed attachments to their fathers, siblings, grandparents, or other care givers who play an active role in their lives (Maccoby and Masters, 1970).

The quality of the attachment relationship children have with their care givers varies. Most of us have witnessed mothers trying to encourage their children to play on their own in new surroundings such as a relative's home. How do the children react? Do they readily start to examine objects in the room? Do they desperately hold onto their mothers? Do they cry? And what factors influence their reaction?

Mary Ainsworth sought to answer these questions. She studied mothers and children in the type of situation described. What she found were three basic types of attachment (Table 8.2). According to Ainsworth, securely attached children are able to leave a parent without fuss to explore new situations. They are also easily and quickly comforted if they are upset in a new situation and will soon leave the parent again. The child who has an anxiously resistant attachment has difficulty leaving the parent in a new situation. This child may cling and become distressed at the prospect of separation. However, when the parent tries to comfort this child, the child may pull away and become inconsolable. Finally, the child who has an anxiously avoidant attachment to the parent will easily separate. However, when the parent returns, the child will avoid contact with the parent (Sroufe, Cooper, and Marshall, 1988).

Table 8.2 / Patterns of Attachment

Secure Attachment
A. Care giver is a secure base for exploration
    1. readily separate to explore toys
    2. affective sharing of play
    3. affiliative to stranger in mother's presence
    4. readily comforted when distressed (promoting a return to play)
B. Active in seeking contact or interaction upon reunion
    1. if distressed,
        a. immediately seek and maintain contact
        b. contact is effective in terminating distress
    2. if not distressed,
        a. active greeting behavior (happy to see care giver)
        b. strong initiation of interaction

Anxious/Resistant Attachment
A. Poverty of exploration
    1. difficulty separating to explore, may need contact even prior to separation
    2. wary of novel situations and people
B. Difficulty settling upon reunion
    1. may mix contact seeking with contact resistance (hitting, kicking, squirming, rejecting toys)
    2. may simply continue to cry and fuss
    3. may show striking passivity

Anxious/Avoidant Attachment
A. Independent exploration
    1. readily separate to explore during preseparation
    2. little affective sharing
    3. affiliative to stranger, when care giver absent (little preference)
B. Active avoidance upon reunion
    1. turning away, looking away, moving away, ignoring
    2. may mix avoidance with proximity
    3. avoidance more extreme on second reunion
    4. no avoidance of stranger

Source: Adapted from Ainsworth et al. *Patterns of Attachment.* Hillsdale, NJ: Erlbaum, 1978.

    Research has shown that attachment is important to later emotional development. The securely attached child is more independent, more cooperative, less rigid, and basically happier than other children. This is contrary to earlier beliefs that the parent must "push the child out of the nest" to encourage independence. Research supports the need for parents to provide a secure base; only then will the child feel confident enough to venture out alone. Independent exploration is crucial to a child's emotional and intellectual growth.

    Today, when more than 50 percent of mothers with children under the age of five work outside the home, the issue of attachment has also become central to the controversy over whether day care is harmful to children.

Figure 8.12
A one-year-old clings to his mother: at this age, attachment to the mother or steady care giver is strong and exclusive.

Some psychologists maintain that day care for children under one year of age is detrimental to their secure attachment and will negatively affect their emotional development. Others have found that the quality of day care is the key to determining possible harm. For example, a child with one steady care giver can form a secure attachment. In contrast, a child placed in a large group with many different care givers may never feel secure. Still other psychologists maintain that group day care can be beneficial, particularly to older children, who have shown greater socialization skills than those not in day care. It is clear that parents must carefully consider their day-care options. Further research needs to be done to understand fully the effects of day care.

USING PSYCHOLOGY

Child Abuse

While many parents cope with their life stresses and provide a warm and safe environment for their children, an alarming number of cases are reported in which children are physically, sexually, or psychologically abused or neglected by their parents or stepparents (Parke and Lewis, 1980). *Child abuse* includes the physical or mental injury, sexual abuse, negligent treatment, or mistreatment of children under the age of eighteen by adults entrusted with their care.

Accurate statistics are difficult to compile, since many incidents of child abuse go unreported. One estimate, however, is that in 1982 one out of every forty-three American children under the age of fourteen was abused (*New York Times*, 1983). Abuse can range from such hideous acts as beating, burning, and scalding to less intense but damaging violent spankings and verbal abuse.

Child abuse is viewed as a social problem resulting from a variety of causes. Many abusive parents were themselves mistreated as children, suggesting that these parents may have learned an inappropriate way of caring for children. Some parents still believe in "spare the rod and spoil the child" (if you do not spank children, they will be spoiled). Such parents tend to use the harsh physical discipline that they saw their own parents using. Many abusive parents have little patience with their children. Often they have unrealistic expectations of them.

Overburdened and stressed parents are more likely to abuse their children, particularly children who are troublesome. Low-birthweight infants and hyperactive or mentally retarded children have a higher than normal incidence of abuse. One reason for this higher incidence may be that such children are less responsive and more difficult to care for, thus making greater demands on the parents (Belsky, 1980). Social-cultural stresses such as unemployment and lack of contact with family, friends, and groups in the community are also associated with child abuse.

The most effective way of treating child abuse is to prevent future incidents. Parent education for abusive parents allows them to learn new ways of dealing with their children. Many state social welfare agencies not only provide assistance to abusive parents in managing their children but also have programs to identify families at risk for child abuse. Families that are experiencing severe economic, psychological, or

Abusive parents abuse all their children.

Fiction. Studies indicate that abusive parents often focus on only one child. That child usually has had physical or behavioral problems from an early age. And while that one child may be grossly maltreated, more "normal" siblings may not be abused by the parents at all.

marital strains are viewed as high-risk families. By providing information about resources and a support system for these families, communities may reduce the incidence of child abuse. Such support services as employment and educational opportunities for both parents and children, support groups for parents, child care facilities, homemaker services, and hotlines help reduce child abuse (Parke and Slaby, 1983).

One especially troubling form of child abuse is sexual abuse. While more than 90 percent of those who abuse children are men, women have also been known to participate in individual or organized sexual abuse of children. Perhaps the most devastating effect of sexual abuse is that the child is often tricked into participating in the activity but later believes the act to be his or her fault. If the offender is someone the child knows well, the child not only experiences the trauma and stress of abuse but is also forced to keep the incident a secret for fear of getting the grownup in trouble. Often, parents and other usually responsible adults unintentionally dismiss the sexually abused child's attempts to tell about the incident because the idea of sexual abuse is too horrifying for them to accept.

SOCIALIZATION

Learning the rules of behavior of the culture in which you are born and grow up is called **socialization**. To live with other people, a child has to learn what is considered acceptable and unacceptable behavior. This is not as easy as it sounds. Some social rules are clear and inflexible. For example, you are not permitted to have sexual relations with members of your immediate family. However, most social rules leave room for individual decisions, so that sometimes there seems to be a "gray area" between right and wrong.

Learning what the rules are, when to apply and when to bend them, is only part of socialization. Every society has ideas about what is meaningful, valuable, beautiful, and worth striving for. Every society classifies people according to their family, sex, age, skills, personality characteristics, and other criteria. Every culture has notions about what makes individuals behave as they do. In absorbing these notions, a child acquires an identity as a member of a particular society, a member of different social categories (such as male or female), a member of a family—and an identity as an individual. This is a second dimension of socialization.

Figure 8.13
Learning the difference between acceptable and unacceptable behavior is part of socialization.

Finally, socialization involves learning to live with other people and with yourself. Anyone who has seen the shock on a two-year-old's face when another child his age takes a toy he wants, or the frustration and humiliation a four-year-old experiences when she discovers she can't hit a baseball on the first try, knows how painful it can be to discover that other people have rights and that you have limitations.

In the pages that follow we examine several theories about how the child becomes socialized. We begin with Freud's theory of psychosexual development, which has been a major influence on our understanding of socialization.

Freud's Theory of Psychosexual Development

Freud believed that all children are born with powerful sexual and aggressive urges that must be tamed. In learning to control these impulses, children acquire a sense of right and wrong. They become "civilized." The process—and the results—are different for boys and girls.

In the first few years of life boys and girls have similar experiences. Their erotic pleasures are obtained through the mouth, sucking at their mother's breast. Weaning is a period of frustration and conflict—it is the child's first experience with not getting what he wants. Freud called this the **oral stage** of development. Later the anus becomes the source of erotic pleasure, giving rise to what Freud called the **anal stage**. The child enjoys holding in or pushing out his feces until he is required, through toilet training, to curb this freedom.

The major conflict comes between the ages of three and five, when children discover the pleasure they can obtain from their genitals. As a consequence, they become extremely aware of the differences between themselves and members of the opposite sex. In this **phallic stage**, according to Freud, the child becomes a rival for the affections of the parent of the opposite sex. The boy wants to win his mother for himself and finds himself in hostile conflict with his father. The girl wants her father for herself and tries to shut out her mother. These struggles take place on an unconscious level; generally the child and the parents do not have any clear awareness that it is going on.

Freud called this crisis the **Oedipal conflict**, after Oedipus, the king in Greek tragedy who unknowingly killed his father and married his mother. Freud believed that the boy's feelings for his mother create intense conflicts. The boy finds that he hates his father and wishes him gone or dead. But his father is far stronger than he is. The boy fears that his father will

Figure 8.14
Socialization is a process that begins almost immediately after birth. Through it, children learn how to behave with others and how to use certain behaviors to get their own way.

see how he feels and punish him, perhaps by castrating him. (A parent telling the child that masturbation is nasty, or perhaps that it will make him sick, merely confirms his fears.) To prevent this horrible punishment, the boy buries his sexual feelings and tries to make himself "good." He tries to become as much like his father as possible so that his father will not want to hurt him. He satisfies himself with becoming *like* the person who possesses his mother, instead of trying to possess her himself. In this process, which is called **identification** with the aggressor, the boy takes on all his father's values and moral principles. Thus, at the same time that he learns to behave like a man, he **internalizes** his father's morality. His father's voice becomes a voice inside him, the voice of conscience.

Freud believed that in girls the Oedipal conflict takes a different form. The girl finds herself in the similarly dangerous position of wanting to possess her father and to exclude her mother. To escape punishment and to possess the father vicariously, she begins to identify with her mother. She feels her mother's triumphs and failures as if they were her own, and she internalizes her mother's moral code. At the same time, the girl experiences what Freud called penis envy. Whereas the boy is afraid of being castrated, the girl suspects that her mother has removed the penis she once had. To make up for this "deficiency," she sets her sights on marrying a man who is like her father and develops the wish to have babies.

Freud believed that at about age five children enter a **latency stage**. Sexual desires are pushed into the background, and children busy themselves with exploring the world and learning new skills. This process of redirecting sexual impulses into learning tasks is called **sublimation**. Although children this age often avoid members of the opposite sex, sexual interest reappears in adolescence. The way in which a person resolves the Oedipal conflict in childhood influences the kind of relationships he or she will form with members of the opposite sex throughout life. Ideally, when one reaches the **genital stage**, one derives as much satisfaction from giving pleasure as from receiving it.

Today relatively few psychologists believe that sexual feelings disappear in childhood, that all young girls experience penis envy, or that all young boys fear castration. Freud was attempting to set off a revolution in our thinking about childhood. Like many revolutionaries, he probably overstated the case. Yet the idea that children have to learn to control powerful sexual and aggressive desires and the belief that such early childhood experiences can have a long-term effect on adult personality and behavior would be difficult to deny. (We shall return to Freud in the chapter on personality theories.)

Erikson's Theory of Psychosocial Development

To Erik Erikson, socialization is neither so sudden nor so emotionally violent. Erikson takes a broader view of human development than Freud in terms of both time and scope. Although he recognizes the child's sexual and aggressive urges, he believes that the need for social approval is just as important (hence his term, psychosocial development). And although he

---

Table 8.3 / Erikson's Stages of Psychosocial Development

Approximate Age	*Crisis*
0–1	TRUST VS. MISTRUST: If an infant is well cared for, she will develop faith in the future. But if she experiences too much uncertainty about being taken care of, she will come to look at the world with fear and suspicion.
1–2	AUTONOMY VS. DOUBT: Here the child learns self-control and self-assertion. But if he receives too much criticism, he will be ashamed of himself and have doubts about his independence.
2–5	INITIATIVE VS. GUILT: When the child begins to make her own decisions, constant discouragement or punishment could lead to guilt and a loss of initiative.
5–Puberty	INDUSTRY VS. INFERIORITY: The child masters skills and takes pride in his competence. Too much criticism of his work at this stage can lead to long-term feelings of inferiority.
Adolescence	IDENTITY VS. ROLE CONFUSION: The teenager tries to develop her own separate identity while "fitting in" with her friends. Failure leads to confusion over who she is.
Early Adulthood	INTIMACY VS. ISOLATION: A person secure in his own identity can proceed to an intimate partnership in which he makes compromises for another. The isolated person may have many affairs or even a long-term relationship but always avoids true closeness.
Middle Age	GENERATIVITY VS. STAGNATION: A person who becomes stagnated is absorbed in herself and tries to hang onto the past. Generativity involves a productive life that will serve as an example to the next generation.
Later Adulthood	INTEGRITY VS. DESPAIR: Some people look back over life with a sense of satisfaction and accept both the bad and the good. Others face death with nothing but regrets.

---

believes that childhood experiences have a lasting impact on the individual, he sees development as a lifelong process.

We all face many "crises" as we grow from infancy to old age, as we mature and people expect more from us. Each of these crises represents an issue that everyone faces. The child—or adolescent or adult—may develop more strongly in one way or another, depending on how other people respond to his or her efforts.

For example, the two-year-old is delighted with his newfound ability to walk, to get into things, to use words, and to ask questions. The very fact that he has acquired these abilities adds to his self-esteem. He's eager to use them. If the adults around him applaud his efforts and acknowledge his achievements, he begins to develop a sense of autonomy, or independence. However, if they ignore him except to punish him for going too far or being a nuisance, the child may begin to doubt the value of his achievements. He may also feel shame because the people around him act as if his new desire for independence is bad.

This is the second of eight stages in Erikson's theory. Each stage builds on the preceding one. A child who has learned to trust the world is better equipped to seek autonomy than one who is mistrustful; a child who has achieved autonomy takes initiative more readily than one who doubts himself; and so on. The basic question in each stage is whether the individual will find ways to direct his needs, desires, and talents into socially acceptable channels and learn to think well of himself.

Erikson's eight crises are outlined in Table 8.3. We will refer to this theory as we continue our discussion of the life cycle in the next chapter.

Social Learning Theories of Development

Both Freud and Erikson stress the emotional dynamics of social development. Their theories suggest that learning social rules is altogether different from learning to ride a bicycle or to speak a foreign language. Many psychologists disagree. They believe children learn the ways of their social world because they are rewarded for conforming and because they copy older children and adults in anticipation of future rewards. In other words, social development is a matter of reinforcement and imitation.

Reinforcement. Adults—especially parents and teachers—have the power to reward and punish. Consciously and unconsciously they use praise, smiles, and hugs to reward a child for behaving in ways they consider good and for expressing attitudes that support their own. They tend to ignore or to be hostile toward the expression of opinions that are contrary to their own and toward behavior of which they disapprove.

Sex role training provides obvious examples of this. At home and in school, boys are encouraged to engage in athletics and to be assertive. Girls are discouraged from doing these things but are rewarded for being helpful and nice, looking neat, and acting cute. Even the rewards children receive are usually sex-typed. How many girls receive footballs or tool kits as presents? How many boys get dolls or watercolor sets?

These are some of the ways in which adults use reinforcement to shape a child's development. Children gradually learn to behave in the way that leads to the greatest satisfaction, even when no one is watching. To avoid punishment and gain rewards from those around them, they learn to reward and punish themselves. A child may criticize herself for making a mistake that has led to punishment in the past. The mistake may be a moral one—lying, for example. A boy may learn to be hard on himself for showing sensitivity, because in the past his tears and blushes were met with humiliating laughter.

This is not to say that children always do as they are told. Adults also teach youngsters how to get away with misbehavior—for example, by apologizing or by giving a present to someone they have wronged. In this way, some children learn that they may receive praise instead of punishment for bad conduct.

Imitation. A second way in which children learn social rules is by observing other people. When youngsters see another child or an adult being

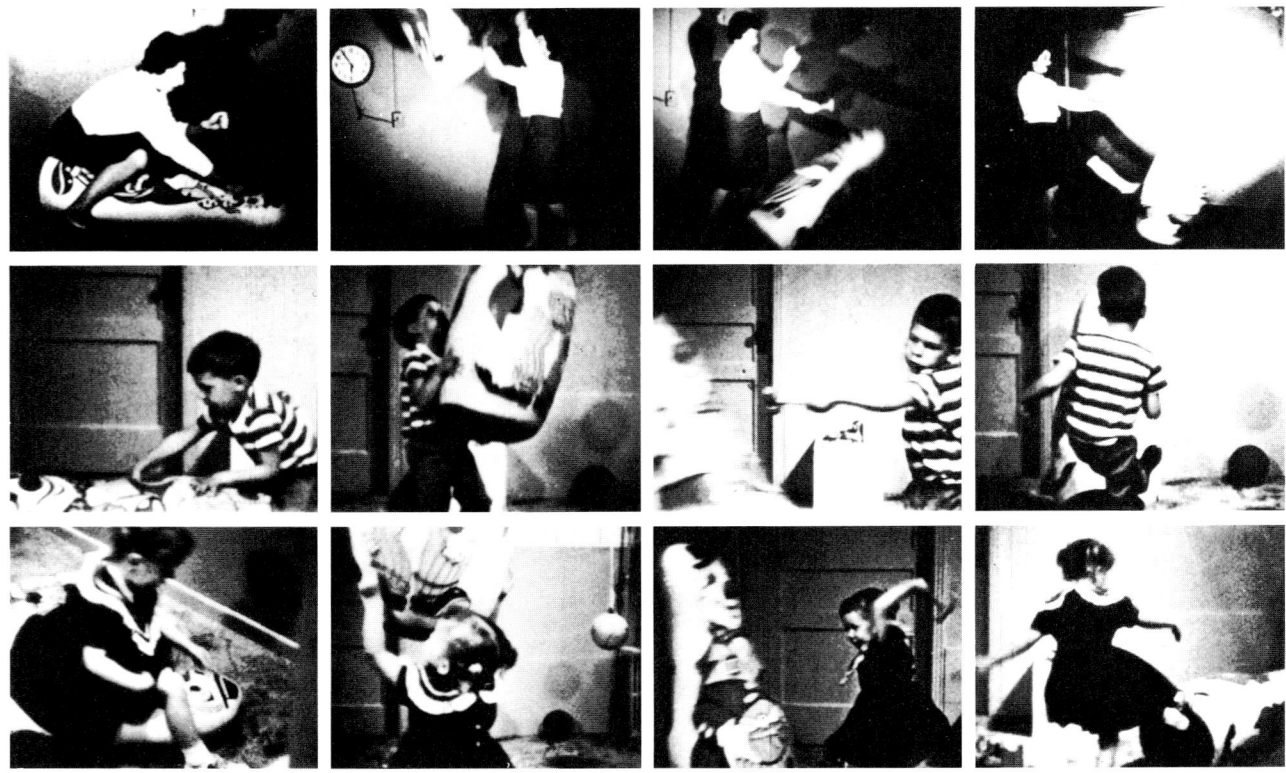

Figure 8.15
Imitation of aggression in children. (top row) Frames from one of the films psychologist Albert Bandura showed to children. (bottom two rows) Behavior of children who watched the film and were given a chance to play with similar objects.

congratulated for behaving in certain ways or expressing certain attitudes, they are likely to imitate that person in the hope of obtaining rewards themselves.

Albert Bandura's experiments indicate that children are very quick indeed to imitate other people's behavior (Bandura and Walters, 1963). Bandura's basic technique is to show children movies of a person reacting to a situation. He then puts the children in the same situation to see how they behave.

In one experiment Bandura showed a film of a frustrated adult taking out her anger on a "Bobo" doll (Figure 8.15). The woman assaulted the doll—yelling, kicking, and punching it with all her might. After the film, children who had been deliberately frustrated with broken promises and delays were led to a room that contained an identical doll. Taking their cue from the film, they launched furious attacks—imitating the actress's behavior down to the last kick.

Later Bandura added two different endings to the film. In one the actress was praised and given candy and soft drinks after she had attacked the doll. In the other she was severely scolded for her behavior. Most of the children who saw the second version learned from the actress's experience and did not attack the doll so they would not be punished. What this suggests is that conditioning and modeling work together. Children do not imitate everything they see, only the behavior that seems to bring rewards.

USING PSYCHOLOGY

Children and Television

Today, more than 95 percent of American families have at least one television set—some have two or more—and children spend a significant amount of time watching TV. One estimate is that children under two spend an average of two and a half hours a day watching television. This amount increases to four hours a day for children eight to ten years old (Liebert, Sprafkin, and Davidson, 1982). By the time you graduate from high school, you will have spent an estimated 15,000 hours in front of the TV. Clearly, television is an important force in children's lives. In what specific ways does television viewing affect children's development? This question has generated much debate and numerous research studies.

Perhaps the most controversial and studied issue is the effect of watching television violence and aggression on children's behavior. The results of research studies support the view that violence on television leads to aggressive behavior in children. By observing highly attractive models engaging in a variety of aggressive and physically violent behaviors, children are encouraged to act in a similar way.

The extent to which children imitate aggressive acts on TV is influenced by the age of the child. The most sensitive time for children to learn aggressive behaviors from TV is when they are eight to nine years old (Eron et al., 1983). Also, if children are already predisposed to aggressive behaviors, they are more likely to imitate aggression seen on TV. When parents watch aggressive or violent shows with their children and discuss the events afterward, the negative effects seem to be reduced and the positive effects enhanced.

When children watch television, they are forming beliefs about what the world is like. Their views of reality, including their views of how people act toward one another, are influenced by the characters they see portrayed on television. Often, adult TV themes include negative motives, such as jealousy, revenge, corruption, and violence. While adults may view these programs as entertainment and not base conclusions about their social world on them, children do not have the cognitive sophistication to separate television "reality" from everyday experience.

Another potent way in which television affects social behavior is through the presentation of sex role models and ethnic stereotypes. Girls who consistently see women portrayed

Figure 8.16

as helpless victims or housewives are likely to accept this view of women as part of their sex role. Recent concerns over the racial, ethnic, and sex role stereotypes on television have resulted in a more representative depiction of people on television. However, commercials still seem flagrantly to reinforce limiting social stereotypes.

Special attention has been given to the format of children's television programs. Programs are carefully produced to capture and hold the viewer's attention. The format of commercial television programs, particularly children's shows, contains rapid-fire, action-packed sequences that are highlighted by audio and visual special effects. Children's attention is especially guided by the television format of cartoons (Wright and Huston, 1983). Children spend countless hours, particularly on Saturday morning, watching the humorous (and often violent and aggressive) adventures of cartoon characters. The faster the pace of the program, the more receptive children are to it.

On the positive side, TV has a rich and largely untapped potential for educating and enhancing children's development (Singer and Singer, 1983). Television is an excellent vehicle for presenting new information about the world beyond the child's or adult's immediate experience. Also, some of the more recent children's programs have attempted to help children deal more effectively with their fears. For example, by watching a television character overcome a fear of animals, children are able to deal more effectively with similar fears.

In 1982, the United States government conducted a review of studies on the impact of television on social behavior (Pearl et al., 1982). On the basis of over twenty years of research and 3,000 scientific studies, the reviewers concluded:

> Television can no longer be considered a casual part of daily life, an electronic toy. Research findings have long since destroyed the illusion that television is merely innocuous entertainment. While the learning it provides is mainly incidental rather than direct and formal, it is a significant part of the total acculturation process (Pearl, 1982, 1: 87).

The use of educational programs is an important issue for psychologists, educators, and parents. The American Psychological Association has released a statement supporting the view that exposure to violence on television promotes aggressive behavior. With more responsible attitudes toward TV programs, we can use them as a vehicle for education.

The Cognitive-Developmental Approach

Theorists who emphasize the role of cognition or thinking in development view the growing child quite differently. Social learning theory implies that the child is essentially passive—a piece of clay to be shaped. The people who administer rewards and punishments and serve as models do the shaping. Cognitive theorists see the *child* as the shaper. Taking their cue from Piaget, they argue that social development is the result of the child's acting on the environment and trying to make sense out of his experiences. The games children play illustrate this.

Play.   Children's games are serious business. When left to their own devices, youngsters spend a great deal of time making up rules. This enables them to learn for themselves the importance of agreeing on a structure for group activities. Children can relax and enjoy themselves without fear of rejection as long as they do not break the rules. The world of play thus becomes a miniature society, with its own rules and codes.

Another function of most games is to teach children about aspects of adult life in a nonthreatening way. In young children's games, it is the experience of playing, not winning, that counts. Children can learn the dimensions of competition of various kinds, including testing themselves

Figure 8.17
Children's games are not just fun: seeing the need for and making rules, trying on adult roles, and learning the dimensions of competition are all part of the developmental process.

Imaginary Playmates

There's nothing new about polka dot elves, pink teddy bears, and other imaginary playmates; children have had them since childhood began. But there's a lot new in our understanding of the role these invisible, mysterious friends play in the normal development of children.

When Dr. Jerome L. Singer and Dr. Dorothy G. Singer studied a group of three- and four-year-olds, they found a number of striking differences between children with imaginary playmates and those without. Here are some of their findings:

- Imaginary playmates are more common than you might think; more than half the children had them.
- Children with imaginary playmates are less aggressive and more cooperative than other children.
- They are rarely bored and have a rich vocabulary, far advanced for their age.
- They watch fewer hours of television than other children, and the programs they watch have fewer cartoons and less violence.
- They have a greater ability to concentrate than other children.

Above all, imaginary playmates are true companions to children. They are always there to listen and talk, to be supportive and forever loyal. They seem to fill a gap in children's lives and are especially important to children who are first-born or who have no brothers or sisters. They are an adaptive mechanism that helps children get through the boring times of life.

Instead of worrying that imaginary playmates are a sign of insecurity and withdrawal, we should all look in wonderment at how creative and adaptive a healthy child can be.

For more details, see Maya Pines, "Invisible Playmates," *Psychology Today,* September 1978.

against their outer limits, but they will not be hurt by comparison as they may be in win-or-lose situations.

Much of children's play involves **role taking**. Youngsters try on such adult roles as mother, father, teacher, storekeeper, explorer, and rock star. Role taking allows them to learn about different points of view firsthand. Suppose a child plays a mother opposite another child who plays a whiny, disobedient baby. When she finds herself totally frustrated by the other child's nagging, she begins to understand why her mother gets mad. You can't cook even a pretend meal when the baby keeps knocking over the pots and pans.

Moral Development.   Lawrence Kohlberg's studies show just how important being able to see other people's points of view is to social development in general and to moral development in particular. Kohlberg (1968) studied the development of moral reasoning—deciding what is right and what

Kohlberg and Bias. Not everybody agrees with Kohlberg. Critics accuse him of being overly influenced by Western culture. They say that he sees moral reasoning through the eyes of someone brought up in Europe or the United States. Children from other cultures, they say, do not necessarily follow Kohlberg's six stages of moral development.

For example, we are raised to believe that we are responsible for ourselves and for our families and that we must make our own decisions. Other cultures, in contrast, place the community first and the individual second. Thus, a child from an Israeli kibbutz or from a Chinese village would look at Heinz's situation in a different way. The child might say that Heinz should consult his community before making a decision. Or the child might ask why the community is not helping Heinz in the first place.

Although it seems that children throughout the world go through Kohlberg's first stages, their later stages of moral development may be influenced by their particular culture.

is wrong—by presenting children of different ages with a series of moral dilemmas. For example:

> In Europe, a woman was near death from cancer. One drug might save her, a form of radium that a druggist in the same town had recently discovered. The druggist was charging $2,000, ten times what the drug cost him to make. The sick woman's husband, Heinz, went to everyone he knew to borrow the money, but he could only get together about half of what it cost. He told the druggist that his wife was dying and asked him to sell it cheaper or let him pay later. But the druggist said no. The husband got desperate and broke into the man's store to steal the drug for his wife. Should the husband have done that? Why?

At every age, some children said that the man should steal, some that he should not. What interested Kohlberg, however, was how the children arrived at a conclusion. He wanted to know what sort of reasoning they used. After questioning about a hundred children, Kohlberg identified six stages of moral development.

In stage one, children are totally egocentric. They do not consider other people's points of view and have no sense of right and wrong. Their main concern is avoiding punishment. A child in this stage will say that the man should steal because people will blame him for his wife's death if he does not, or that he should not steal because he might get caught and go to prison.

Children in stage two have a better idea of how to "work the system" to receive rewards as well as to avoid punishment. Youngsters at this level interpret the Golden Rule as "help someone if he helps you, and hurt him if he hurts you." They are still egocentric and premoral, evaluating acts in terms of the consequences, not in terms of right and wrong.

In stage three, children become acutely sensitive to what other people want and think. A child in this stage will say that the man in the story should steal because people will think he is cruel if he lets his wife die, or that he should not steal because people will think he is a criminal. In other words, children want social approval in stage three, so they literally and rigidly apply the rules other people have decreed.

In stage four, a child is less concerned with the approval of others. The key issue here is "law and order"—a law is seen as a moral rule and is obeyed because of a strong belief in established authority. Many people remain at the fourth stage of moral development for their whole lives.

In the remaining two stages, people begin to broaden their perspective. The stage-five person is primarily concerned with whether a law is fair or just. He believes that laws must change as the world changes. The important question is whether a given law is good for society as a whole. Stage six involves an acceptance of ethical principles that apply to everyone, like the Golden Rule: "Do unto others as you would have them do unto you." Such moral "laws" are more important than any written law.

To reach the highest levels of moral development, a child must first be able to see other people's points of view. But this understanding is no guarantee that a person will respect the rights of others. Thus, cognitive abilities influence moral development, but there is far more to morality than simple understanding.

CHAPTER REVIEW

KEY TERMS

- accommodation
- anal stage
- assimilation
- conservation
- critical periods
- developmental psychology
- genital stage
- grasping reflex

- identification
- imprinting
- internalize
- latency stage
- object permanence
- Oedipal conflict
- oral stage
- phallic stage

- representational thought
- role taking
- rooting reflex
- sensitive period
- socialization
- sublimation
- telegraphic speech

SUMMARY

1. Developmental psychology is the study of the changes that occur as people mature.

2. Each of us is the product of the interaction between nature (what we have inherited biologically) and nurturing (what we experience in the world). There are critical periods or times when specific environmental influences are most likely to affect development. Yet timing is not an important factor in all developmental changes.

3. At birth an infant is capable of certain coordinated movement patterns that can be triggered by the right stimulus. One of these, the grasping reflex, is a response to a touch on the palm. Another, the rooting reflex, involves the movement of the infant's head toward the source of any touch near his or her mouth.

4. An infant's waking time is divided between two distinct states—active awake and quiet alert. Over the first several months of life these states fuse together into the waking state.

5. Psychologists infer how the infant perceives the world by measuring the capabilities of newborn infants. Research has shown that all the senses function at birth, but some undergo developmental changes as the infant grows.

6. Swiss psychologist Jean Piaget formulated a comprehensive theory of intellectual development. Cognitive development involves changes in the amount of information we have as well as in the way we think.

7. The four stages of cognitive development are the sensorimotor stage, preoperational stage, concrete operational stage, and formal operational stage. Piaget believed everyone goes through the same stages, but not necessarily at the same age.

8. In order to acquire language, children spend the first year of life practicing sounds, then imitating the speech they hear around them. In the second year they use sounds as symbols, and their first real words usually refer to something they can see or touch. By four or five years of age, children have usually mastered the basics of their native language.

9. While children learn to use their bodies, to think, and to express themselves, they also develop emotionally. They begin to form attachments to people; their first relationship is usually with their mothers. By eighteen months of age nearly all babies have developed attachments to their fathers, siblings, grandparents, or anyone else playing an active role in their lives.

10. There are three basic types of attachment. Securely attached children are able to leave a parent without fuss to explore new situations. A child with an anxiously resistant attachment has difficulty leaving the parent in a new situation. The child with an anxiously avoidant at-

tachment will easily separate but will avoid the parent when he or she returns.

11. Some overburdened parents react to unemployment, lack of support groups, and other stresses by abusing their children physically or verbally. Another trauma for children is sexual abuse. Community resources can be used to help prevent child abuse.

12. Socialization involves learning the rules of behavior of the culture in which a child is born and will grow up.

13. The theories of Sigmund Freud and Erik Erikson stress the emotional dynamics of social development. According to both Freud and Erikson, children must learn to control the sexual and aggressive urges they are born with, but Erikson would add that the need of children for social approval is just as important to their social development.

14. Social learning theorists give much less emphasis to the emotional dynamics of social development. They argue that children learn appropriate social behavior through reinforcement and imitation.

15. Children spend a significant amount of time watching television. Research studies support the view that watching violence on television leads to aggressive behavior in children. Children's views of reality are influenced by what they see on TV. On the positive side, television has a rich potential for educating children and enhancing their development.

16. Cognitive theorists argue that social development is more than just the result of the child being shaped by rewards and punishments. These psychologists see the *child* as the shaper. They argue that social development results from the child acting on the environment, trying to make sense out of his or her experiences.

17. Lawrence Kohlberg has observed that the moral development of a child progresses in six stages. Essentially, each stage represents an advance in the child's ability to take the roles of other people. At stage one, the child is egocentric and has no sense of right or wrong. At each successive stage, the child's awareness of other people and society increases, until at stages five and six he or she is finally able to develop universal ethical principles based on ideals of reciprocity and human equality.

REVIEW QUESTIONS

1. What are the two factors that interact to shape development?

2. What behaviors do newborn babies display?

3. How do psychologists infer how newborn infants perceive the world?

4. Describe the two processes that Piaget cited as the basis for intellectual development in children.

5. Describe the concept of object permanence.

6. What is the principle of conservation and when do children acquire it?

7. How do children learn to talk?

8. How are the first six months of life different from the second six months in terms of a child's emotional and interpersonal development?

9. What is socialization? Why is it so important to development?

10. How do Freud's and Erikson's theories of development differ?

11. What role does play assume in the development of children?

12. Describe Kohlberg's stages of moral development.

CHAPTER REVIEW

1. Observe an infant under eighteen months of age, keeping a log of the baby's activities. Compare your notes with the developmental descriptions in this chapter. How closely does the baby follow the norm? What differences did you note?

2. Talk with children who are under five years old, paying particular attention to their grammar. What kinds of errors do they make? What kinds of grammatical rules do they already seem to know?

3. Do you and your parents share the same religious beliefs? Political orientation? Feelings about violence? Attitudes toward sex? Goals for living? Opinions about money? Views on drugs? Do you have similar tastes in clothing colors and styles? Music? Pets? Housing? Furniture? Foods? Cars? Entertainment? After asking yourself these questions, determine how well your beliefs, opinions, and tastes agree with those of your parents. How important do you think your early social training was for what you believe, think, and like?

4. What happens when a boy plays with G. I. Joe dolls? How does this behavior fit into the concept of modeling? Is this behavior liberating to boys, or does it feminize their behavior? Explain your answer. What would be the effect of girls playing football? Explain the difference(s) between your answers about boys and girls.

5. How are sex roles communicated to people in American society? Look carefully through magazines and newspapers, watch television commercials, and listen to the radio. What activities, interests, worries, virtues, weaknesses, physical characteristics, and mannerisms are presented as attributes of typical men and women? Are sex roles portrayed differently in different media? Are there various stereotypes within each sex?

6. Write a brief autobiography. What are the events that you feel have been the most significant in your life? What have been the main influences on your social and emotional development?

7. Ask children of different ages the following questions: Where does the sun go at night? Could you become a girl (a boy) if you wanted to? Does your brother (sister) have any brothers (sisters)? What makes leaves fall off trees? If you find some of their theories interesting, it is easy to think of many other questions.

8. Observe a father with an infant one or two years old for signs of emotional attachment. An infant day-care center, a church nursery, a pediatrician's waiting room, or a play area in a shopping mall are good places to locate a father-child pair. Ideally, you want to find a place where the toddler is allowed some freedom to move about while in the presence of the father. How often does the child make contact with his or her father? Does the child move away and explore? How does the infant respond to unfamiliar people or objects? Besides physical contact, in what ways do the father and child stay in contact with each other? If the father happens to leave for a moment, what is the infant's reaction?

9. Child abuse is a growing concern in our culture; everyday examples of the problem can be found in your local newspapers, in magazines, or on television news reports. Keep a record of these accounts for a period of time. What kinds of abuse are being reported? How old are the children involved? Who are the abusers? What legal action was taken? How was the abuse detected? What state or local agencies are involved with the care of the children?

10. Watch children's television programs on a Saturday morning. Notice both the programs and the commercials. What kinds of behavior do the characters on television model for the young viewers? What do the programs and commercials teach children about how to get along with others, about aggression, sex roles, and food? What are the differences between the behavior of cartoon characters and live characters? Do you think television is good for children? Explain your reasoning.

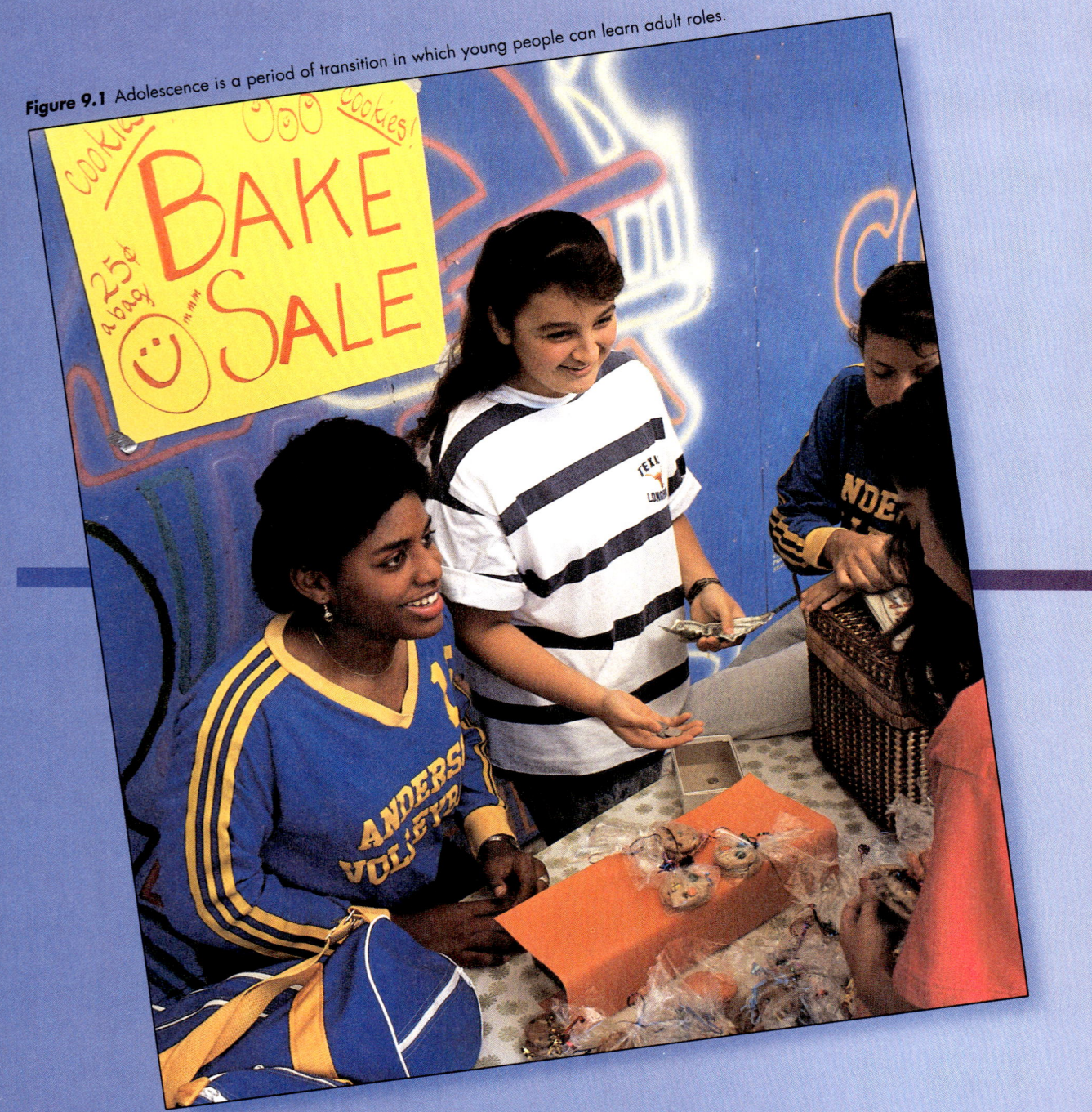

Figure 9.1 Adolescence is a period of transition in which young people can learn adult roles.

Objectives: After studying this chapter, you should be able to
- define adolescence.
- describe the physical, cognitive, and ideological changes that characterize adolescence.
- describe research related to the sexual attitudes and roles of adolescents.
- discuss the social development of the adolescent and the role of peers and family.

CHAPTER 9

Adolescence

Adolescence is the transition period between childhood and adulthood during which people reach a new stage of their psychosocial development. In some societies adolescence is not recognized as a separate stage of life; individuals move directly from childhood to adulthood (see Mead, 1961). In our own society, however, adolescence is looked upon as a time of preparation for adult responsibilities (Hall, 1904). These new burdens must be assumed just at the time when young people are undergoing complex physical and emotional changes that afffect them both personally and socially.

Because so much is happening in these years, psychologists have focused a great deal of attention on the period of adolescence. Though we cannot report on all of that research here, we can highlight some important psychological findings concerning the personal and social development of teenagers and the difficulties they may experience. But first we will turn our attention to some widely held views of the adolescent years.

VIEWS OF ADOLESCENCE

What is it like to be adolescent? Are the years between late childhood and early adulthood the best that life has to offer—a carefree time to act on ideals unburdened by practical concerns? Or is that period a time of crisis, rebellion, and unhappiness? The answer seems to depend on whom you ask. Adults, adolescents themselves, and psychologists give different answers.

Views of Adolescence
How Adults View Adolescence • How Adolescents View Themselves • Theories of Adolescence

Personal Development
Physical Changes • Changes in Thinking • Moral Development • Personality Changes and Identity Formation • Sexuality: Attitudes and Roles • Using Psychology: Teenage Depression and Suicide

Social Development
The Family • The Peer Group

Difficulties in the Transition from Late Childhood to Early Adolescence

How Adults View Adolescence

Every adult has lived through the experience of adolescence. However, the past teenage years of most adults do not always help them understand the concerns and difficulties of today's adolescents. Adults vary in their attitudes toward teenagers in general and certain adults have conflicting feelings about them.

Many adults admire and even idealize young people. Youth is valued in our culture. The values, music, fashions, and activities of young people are heavily promoted in the mass media. Through dress, cosmetics, consumer purchases, and a variety of physical activities, adults attempt to look and feel as healthy and active as adolescents. Adults who love sports admire young athletes. Studies have shown that adults dedicated to such social issues as nuclear disarmament, world hunger, and improving the environment admire young people who are active in trying to achieve progress in these areas (Rice, 1978).

Older people who live and work directly with teenagers often value the influence young people have in their lives. Teenagers help keep them connected to a larger world outside their own experience.

On the other hand, many studies have shown that some adults feel threatened by youth. Most parents are in their forties when they watch their teenage children develop physically into maturity and are themselves beginning to see the decline of their own bodies. This situation can produce negative feelings, particularly when the adults see themselves outperformed by younger people. They may regret the loss of their own youth and envy those who are still young.

While advertising contributes to a "cult of youth," the news and popular press often portray teenagers in a negative light. Young people are often depicted as disruptive or disturbed—the stories of teenage crime and misconduct are the most sensational and thus the ones the average person is likely to notice. In truth, most adolescents go through their teenage years without extreme storm and stress.

One of the reasons that negative images of adolescents surface is that different generations sometimes hold different ideas of morality. On controversial issues such as sexual activity or the use of nuclear weapons, the views of younger people may contrast with those of their parents, whose experiences have been different.

Also, adolescents may provoke a negative reaction from their parents by displaying traits that their parents see as a reflection of themselves that they would prefer not to see. For example, parents who are insecure about their academic abilities may feel uncomfortable if they see the same pattern emerging in their teenage children.

For one reason or another, some adults do view adolescents in an exaggerated light—either good or bad. Some idealize youth by remembering only its positive aspects. Others look on adolescence with horror, seeing only its burdens of stress, tension, conflict, or dependency. Studies have shown that some adults can see younger people only as antisocial, destructive, dirty, and unreliable (Majeras, 1976). However, most adults probably do not hold extreme views, just as most young people do not fit into either extreme stereotype.

How Adolescents View Themselves

Does the overly idealized view of adolescence on the one hand and the overly negative view on the other affect the way the young see themselves? According to many psychologists, the answer is yes. Adolescents tend to regard themselves the way they think others see them. Adult stereotypes serve as a mirror for them, and they take society's reflections as authentic models for their own behavior (Anthony, 1969). Therefore, depending on the views of the adults with whom he or she interacts, an adolescent will tend to either overidealize or hold a negative image of himself or herself.

Theories of Adolescence

The contradictory views of society at large are reflected not just in the behavior of adolescents but in the theories of psychologists. Controversy concerning the nature of adolescent experience has raged ever since 1904, when G. Stanley Hall presented his pioneering theory of adolescence. Hall, who thought in evolutionary terms, saw the adolescent as representing a transitional stage in our evolutionary development from beast to human. Being an adolescent for Hall was something like being a fully grown animal in a cage, an animal who sees freedom but doesn't know quite when he or she be freed or how he or she will handle it. Thus, the adolescent was portrayed as existing in a state of great "storm and stress," as a marginal being, confused, troubled, and highly frustrated.

Through the years many psychologists and social scientists have supported Hall's theories, but there have been others who strongly disagreed. The latter theorists regard adolescence as a relatively smooth period of growth that is in no way discontinuous with the period of childhood that precedes and the period of young adulthood that follows.

Figure 9.2
The experience of adolescence varies widely among different cultures. These boys in New Guinea are undergoing the last stage of a puberty rite. When they complete the ritual and emerge from this hut, they will be adults of their tribe.

One major proponent of this theory was Margaret Mead. In a series of classic anthropological studies in the late 1920s and early 1930s, Mead (1961) found that in some cultures adolescence is a highly enjoyable time of life and not at all marked by storm and stress.

Other studies conducted since then have tended to support Mead. They point to a relative lack of conflict in the lives of adolescents and a smooth, continuous development out of childhood.

Though adolescence may not be as crisis-ridden as some psychologists think, few would deny that there is at least some stress during that period. Great physical, mental, and emotional changes occur during adolescence. As psychologist Robert Havighurst (1972) has pointed out, every adolescent faces challenges, in the form of developmental tasks that must be mastered. Among the tasks that Havighurst lists are the following:

1. Accepting one's physical make-up and acquiring a masculine or feminine sex role
2. Developing appropriate relations with agemates of both sexes
3. Becoming emotionally independent of parents and other adults
4. Achieving the assurance that one will become economically independent
5. Deciding on, preparing for, and entering a vocation
6. Developing the cognitive skills and concepts necessary for social competence
7. Understanding and achieving socially responsible behavior
8. Preparing for marriage and family
9. Acquiring values that are harmonious with an appropriate scientific world picture

Though the tasks present a challenge, adolescents generally handle it well. Most face some stress but find ways to cope with it.

There are, of course, exceptions. A small percentage of young people experience storm and stress throughout their adolescent years. Another small group confronts the changes all adolescents experience with no stress at all. Perhaps the only safe generalization is that development through adolescence is a highly individual and varied matter.

The pattern of development a particular adolescent displays depends upon a great many factors. The most important of these include the individual's adjustment in childhood, the level of adjustment of his or her parents and peers, and the changes that occur during adolescence. It is to these changes that we now turn.

PERSONAL DEVELOPMENT

Becoming an adult involves much more than becoming physically mature, though that is an important part of the process. The transition from childhood to adulthood also involves changes in patterns of reasoning and moral thinking, and adjustments in personality and sexual behavior. Though the process is complex, most adolescents cope reasonably well with their changing circumstances.

Physical Changes

Physical Growth.   **Puberty,** or sexual maturation, is the biological event that marks the end of childhood. Hormones trigger a series of internal and external changes. These produce different growth patterns in boys and girls.

At about the age of ten, girls rather suddenly begin to grow. Before this growth spurt fat tissue develops, making the girl appear chubby. The development of fat tissue is also characteristic of boys before their growth spurt. But whereas boys quickly lose it, progressing into a "string bean" or lean and lanky phase, girls retain most of this fat tissue as they begin to spurt, and even add to it (Faust, 1977).

Once their growth spurt begins, females can grow as much as two or three inches a year. During this period, a girl's breasts and hips begin to fill out, and she develops pubic hair. Between ten and seventeen she has her first menstrual period, or **menarche.** Another year or so will pass before her periods become regular and she is capable of conceiving a child. Yet most societies consider menarche the beginning of womanhood.

At about twelve, boys begin to develop pubic hair and larger genitals. Within a year or two they become capable of ejaculation. Though their growth spurt begins later than that of girls, it lasts about three years longer. Once their growth spurt begins, boys grow rapidly and fill out, developing the broad shoulders and thicker trunk of an adult man. They also acquire more muscle tissue than girls and develop a larger heart and lungs. Their voices gradually deepen. Hair begins to grow on their faces and later on their chests.

The rate and pattern of sexual maturation varies so widely that it is difficult to apply norms or standards to puberty. In general, however, girls begin to develop earlier than boys and for a year or two may tower over male agemates.

The period of adolescent growth can be an awkward one for both boys and girls because of **asynchrony**—the condition of uneven growth or maturation of bodily parts. For example, the hands or feet may be too large or small for the rest of the body. As the adolescent grows older, however, the bodily parts assume their correct proportions.

Reactions to Growth.   In general young people today are better informed than they were two or three generations ago. Most do not find the signs of their sexual maturation upsetting. Nevertheless, the rather sudden bodily changes that occur during puberty make all adolescents somewhat self-conscious. This is particularly true if they are early or late to develop. Adolescents desperately want to be accepted by their peers, to conform to ideals of how a male or female their age should act, dress, and look. In one study, over half of the adolescent girls and a third of the boys spontaneously expressed concern about their appearance (Dwyer and Mayer, 1968–1969).

Studies also suggest a relation between the way young men and women see their bodies and the way they feel about themselves (McCandless, 1960). Most adolescents, and especially girls, tend to evaluate themselves in terms of their culture's body ideal. For example, in our culture, long legs, a

Figure 9.3
The physiological changes of puberty bring a new kind of self-awareness that did not exist in childhood.

sleek figure, and well-developed breasts are thought of as desirable for women, and girls are very concerned about approximating this ideal (Wiggins, Wiggins, and Conger, 1968).

Youths of both sexes are particularly sensitive about any traits they possess that appear to be sex-inappropriate. For example, boys tend to be very shy about "underdeveloped" genitalia, lack of pubic hair, or "fatty breasts," whereas girls are likely to be disturbed by "underdeveloped" breasts, dark facial hair, or visible muscles.

Individual differences in growth significantly affect the personality of young adolescents. For example, research indicates that boys who mature early have an advantage. They become heroes in sports, leaders in formal and informal social activities. Other boys look up to them; girls have crushes on them; adults tend to treat them as more mature. As a result they are generally more self-confident and independent than other boys. Late-maturing boys, whose high-pitched voices and less-than-ideal physiques may make them feel inadequate, tend to be withdrawn or rebellious (Dwyer and Mayer, 1968–1969).

Variations in the rate of development continue to have an effect on males even into their thirties. Those who matured earlier have been found to have a higher occupational and social status than those who matured later (Ames, 1957). The correlation weakens, however, as males enter their forties (Jones, 1965).

With girls the pattern is somewhat different. Girls who mature early may feel embarrassed rather than proud of their height and figure at first. Some begin dating older boys and become bossy with people their own age. Late-maturing girls tend to be less quarrelsome and to get along with their peers more easily. In their late teens, girls who matured early may be more popular and have a more favorable image of themselves than girls who matured slowly. However, the differences between early maturers and late maturers do not seem to be as pronounced among girls as they are among boys (Dwyer and Mayer, 1968–1969).

Why does physical growth have such powerful psychological effects, especially for boys? According to one widely held theory, the psychological reactions to physical growth may be the result of a **self-fulfilling prophecy.** For example, the boy who believes he does not meet his culture's physical ideal may think less of himself and not pursue success as doggedly as the next person. His belief actually helps bring about the failure he feared.

Changes in Thinking

During adolescence, the thinking patterns characteristic of adults emerge. Jean Piaget has described this as "formal operational" thinking (Piaget and Inhelder, 1969). From about age eleven or twelve, most people's thinking becomes more abstract and less concrete. For example, the adolescent can consider the answer to a hypothetical question like, "What would the world be like if people lived to be 200?" He or she can entertain such hypothetical possibilities in a way that a young child cannot. This ability expands the adolescent's problem-solving capacity. A teenage boy who discovers that his car's engine has a knock can consider a number of possible causes and systematically test out various auto parts until he finds the root of the problem. This is the same ability that a scientist must have to conduct experiments.

With comprehension of the hypothetical comes the ability to understand abstract principles. Not only is this capacity important for studying higher-level science and mathematics, but it leads the adolescent to deal with such abstractions in his or her own life as ethics, conformity, and phoniness. It allows for introspection—examining one's own motives and thoughts. One adolescent is quoted as saying, "I found myself thinking about my future, and then I began to think about why I was thinking about my future, and then I began to think about why I was thinking about why I was thinking about my future."

These new intellectual capacities also enable the adolescent to deal with overpowering emotional feelings through **rationalization.** After failing a test, for example, an individual may rationalize that it happened "because I was worried about the date I might be going on next week." An eight-year-old is too tied to concrete reality to consider systematically all the reasons why he or she might have failed.

Do all adolescents fully reach the stage of formal operational thinking at the same age? As you might suspect, just as there are variations in sexual maturity, so there are variations in cognitive maturity. In general, the rate of mental growth varies greatly both among individual adolescents and among social classes in this country. One study showed that less than half of the seventeen-year-olds tested had reached the stage of formal operational thinking (Higgins-Trenk and Gaite, 1971). Another study indicated that this type of thinking was more common among upper- and middle-class adolescents than working- and lower-class youth (Dulit, 1972).

Differences have also been noted among nations. Formal operational thinking is less prevalent in some societies than in others, probably because of differences in the amount of formal education available. People who cannot read and write lack the tools to separate thought from concrete reality and hence never reach a more advanced level of thinking (Greenfield and Bruner, 1966).

For those who do reach that level, the change in thinking patterns is usually accompanied by changes in personality and social interactions as well. For example, adolescents tend to become very idealistic. This is related to the fact that, for the first time, they can imagine the hypothetical—how things might be. When they compare this to the way things are, the world seems a sorry place. As a result, they can grow rebellious. Some adolescents even develop a "messianic complex" and believe they can save the world from evil. In addition, they typically become impatient with what they see as the adult generation's failures. They don't understand why, for example, a person who feels a job compromises his or her principles doesn't just quit. In other words, adolescents tend to be somewhat unrealistic about the complexities of life. But at the same time, their idealism can help keep older adults in touch with ways in which the world could be improved.

Moral Development

Besides experiencing physical and cognitive changes, some adolescents, though by no means all, also go through important changes in their moral thinking. You'll recall that, according to Lawrence Kohlberg (whose theory was reviewed in Chapter 8), moral reasoning develops in stages. Young children in the early stages of their moral development are very egocentric. They consider an act right or wrong depending on whether or not it elicits punishment (Stage 1) or on whether it has positive or negative consequences for themselves (Stage 2). At later stages they judge an action by whether or not it is socially approved (Stage 3) or is sanctioned by established authority (Stage 4).

Many people never get beyond the last stage, and their moral thinking remains quite rigid. But for those who do, adolescence and young adulthood are usually the periods of the most profound development. Individuals who progress to Stage 5 become concerned with whether a law is fair or just. They believe that the laws must change as the world changes and are never absolute. Individuals who reach Stage 6, on the other hand, accept absolute ethical principles, such as the Golden Rule, that they have worked through for themselves. Such moral laws apply to everyone, cannot be broken, and are more important than any written law.

Reaching higher levels of moral thinking involves the ability to abstract—to see a situation from another's viewpoint. That is why such moral development tends to occur in adolescence, when individuals gain the capacity for formal operational thinking. But not all adolescents who display such thinking simultaneously show higher levels of moral reasoning. In fact, only about one in ten do (Kohlberg and Gilligan, 1971). Thus, formal thought, while necessary for higher moral development, does not guarantee it.

Overall, psychologists agree that a person's moral development depends on many factors, especially the kind of relationship the individual has with his or her parents. Evidence shows that during high school, adolescent moral development does not progress much. However, after high school, when the individual spends more time away from home and is therefore less under the influence of parents, more pronounced changes in moral development occur.

Personality Changes and Identity Formation

The changes adolescents undergo affect many facets of their existence, so it is hardly surprising that cumulatively they have a shaping influence on personality. Psychologists who have studied personality changes in adolescence have focused on the concept of identity. One psychologist in particular, Erik Erikson, has shown that the establishment of identity is key to adolescent development. His theory of how individuals arrive at an integrated sense of self has inspired a great deal of argument, both pro and con. Because his views have been so influential, we turn our attention now to his theory and the studies that support and challenge it.

Erikson's Theory of the Identity Crisis. According to Erikson, building an identity is a task that is unique to adolescence. Children are aware of what other people (adults and peers) think of them. They know the labels others apply to them (good, naughty, silly, talented, brave, pretty, and the like). They are also aware of their biological drives and of their growing physical and cognitive abilities. Children may dream of being this or that person and act these roles out in their play. But they do not brood about who they are or where they are going in life. Children live in the present; adolescents begin to think about the future.

To achieve some sense of themselves, adolescents must go through what Erikson termed an **identity crisis**—a time of storm and stress during which they worry intensely about who they are (1968). Several factors contribute to the onset of this crisis, including the physiological changes and cognitive developments we have described as well as awakening sexual drives and the possibility of a new kind of intimacy with the opposite sex. Adolescents begin to see the future as a reality, not just a game. They know they have to confront the almost infinite and often conflicting possibilities and choices that lie ahead. In the process of reviewing their past

Children live in the present; adolescents begin to think about the future.

and anticipating their future, they begin to think about themselves. The process is a painful one, full of inner conflict, because they are torn by the desire to feel unique and distinctive on the one hand and to "fit in" on the other. Only by resolving this conflict do adolescents achieve an integrated sense of self.

Erikson's theory finds support in the work of another psychologist, James Marcia. According to Marcia (1966), Erikson is correct in pointing to the existence of an adolescent identity crisis. That crisis arises because individuals must make commitments on such important matters as occupation, religion, and political orientation. Using the categories of "crisis" and "commitment," Marcia distinguished four adolescent personality types: (1) *identity moratorium adolescents*, who have not experienced a crisis or made a commitment on any of the important matters facing them; (2) *identity foreclosure adolescents*, who have not had a crisis but have made a commitment based not on their own choice, but on the suggestion of others; (3) *identity confused* or *diffused adolescents*, who are in a continual search for meaning, commitment, and self-definition and thus experience life as a series of ongoing crises, and (4) *identity achievement adolescents,* who have experienced crises, considered many possibilities, and freely committed themselves to occupations and other important life matters.

These categories must not be too rigidly interpreted. It is possible for an individual to make a transition from one category to another, and it is also possible for the same individual to belong to one category with respect to religious commitment and to another with regard to political orientation or occupational choice. Marcia's main contribution is in clarifying the sources and nature of the adolescent identity crisis.

Criticism of Erikson's Theory.   Although Erikson and Marcia insist that all adolescents experience an identity crisis, not all psychologists agree. The term "crisis" suggests that adolescence is a time of nearly overwhelming stress. It also implies that the adolescent transition to maturity requires a radical break with childhood experience. As we noted earlier, many psychologists believe that adolescence is not so strife-ridden and constitutes a relatively smooth transition from one stage of life to the next.

One of the reasons Erikson may have arrived at his view is that he focused his study on disturbed adolescents who sought clinical psychiatric treatment. When adolescents attending school are selected at random and studied, critics point out, most show no sign of crisis and appear to be progressing rather smoothly through adolescence (Haan and Day, 1974).

Other Viewpoints.   Psychologists and social scientists seeking an alternative to Erikson's theory have offered several other explanations of adolescent identity formation. Albert Bandura (1964), for example, starts with the premise that crisis is not the normal state of affairs for adolescents. When crises develop—as they do in only about 10 percent of all adolescents—the cause is generally a change in the external circumstances of an individual's life rather than a biological factor. Thus, a divorce in the family or a new set of friends may trigger teen-age rebellion and a crisis, but no internal biological clock dictates those events.

Human development, in Bandura's view, is one continuous process. At all stages, including adolescence, individuals develop by interacting with others. Because of Bandura's emphasis on interaction in understanding adolescence and all other phases of human development, his approach is usually referred to as the **social learning theory** of development (Bandura, 1977).

Margaret Mead, mentioned earlier in this chapter, also stresses the importance of the social environment in adolescent identity formation. On the basis of her studies in Samoa (1961), for example, she concluded, like Bandura, that human development is more a continuous process than one marked by radical discontinuity. In that remote part of the world, adolescents are not expected to act any differently than they did as children or will be expected to act as adults. The reason is that children in Samoa are given a great deal of responsibility: They do not suddenly go from being submissive in childhood to being dominant later in life. Mead also points out that in Samoa, as in other non-industrial societies, children have sex roles similar to those of adults and therefore do not experience the onset of sexuality as a traumatic experience or an abrupt change. The identity crisis, then, is by no means a universal phenomenon.

Personality development in adolescence is a complex phenomenon. No one theory can do justice to all that is involved in the process. Erikson's emphasis on the adolescent's need for his or her own identity is an important contribution to understanding adolescent development. By focusing on individual psychology, however, he tended to ignore the influence of society and culture on the young. The studies of Bandura and Mead provide needed correctives. Thus, to arrive at a balanced picture of personality change and identity formation in adolescence, we must call upon all viewpoints.

Sexuality: Attitudes and Roles

As we noted earlier, adolescence is accompanied by puberty, when individuals mature sexually. The physical changes that occur are accompanied by changes in behavior. Adolescence is also the time when an individual develops attitudes about sex and expectations about the sex role he or she will fill.

Sexual Attitudes.   Most of us have heard the term "sexual revolution" but has one actually occurred in the last decade or so? In terms of behavior, the answer is "probably not." Although middle- and upper-class girls who attend college seem to be more sexually active than college girls were twenty years ago, sexual behavior in other social categories is about the same today as it was then. In terms of attitudes, however, there has been a change. For example, the majority of young people believe it is morally acceptable for an engaged couple to have sexual intercourse; the majority of adults do not.

Attitudes affect the way we feel about sex and the way we respond sexually. Around the world there are wide variations in what youngsters are told about sex and how they respond. In some societies children are kept in the dark about sex until just before they are married, whereas in

Figure 9.4
While the sexual behavior of adolescents has not changed significantly over the past twenty years, there has been a major shift in their sexual attitudes.

others preadolescent children are encouraged to engage in sexual play, even intercourse, in the belief that such play will foster mature development.

In the United States, because of our "Puritan" past, many people still identify sex with sin except within marriage and with the intent of reproducing. This view is being challenged, however, by those who view sex as a source of pleasure as well as a means of perpetuating the species.

Today, girls' attitudes toward such sexual matters as premarital intercourse and pornography are still more conservative than boys', though this gap between the sexes is smaller than originally thought (Zubin and Money, 1973). Other variations among adolescents today with respect to attitudes have been noted. For example, older adolescents are less conservative than younger ones, and, in recent years, more affluent and educated adolescents (especially girls) have become more "liberated" in their attitudes (and behaviors) than their less affluent and educated counterparts.

Sex Roles.   Sex identity and sex role are two different, though closely related, aspects of our sexual lives. **Sex identity** results from biological inheritance. Thus, if one has a vagina, one's sex identity is female; if a penis, male. Sex identity includes genetic traits we have inherited, and may include perhaps some sex-linked behaviors as well. An obvious example of a sex-linked behavior is the erection of the penis during sexual excitement.

A person's **sex role,** in contrast, is defined partly by genetic makeup but mainly by the society and culture in which the individual lives. The sex role is a standard of how a person with a given sex identity is supposed to behave. For example, in the United States, men were traditionally viewed as dominant, competitive, and emotionally reserved; women were viewed as submissive, cooperative, and emotionally responsive. These traits were considered appropriate for the different sexes.

Sex roles tell us how we are expected to behave, look, think, and feel in order to be considered by others, and to consider ourselves, "masculine" or "feminine." For example, in the past, a woman who repaired telephone lines might be considered by many people to be "unfeminine." Why? Because she does not conform to the traditional sex role requirement that women are not supposed to perform physical labor.

Sex roles vary from one society to another, and they can change over time within a given society. Sex roles give social meaning to sex identity. However, not all societies agree on the roles the sexes should assume. Indeed, anthropologists have found that some societies reverse the roles that we traditionally give to men and women, while others assign to both sexes what we might consider "masculine" or "feminine" roles. Not only do sex roles vary among societies, but they may change radically within a society, as we are witnessing today in America.

Characteristics that have been encouraged in American men are ruggedness, forcefulness, independence, strength, dominance, and aggressiveness—traits necessary to be the breadwinner in the family. In contrast, women have been encouraged to be meek, passive, sensitive, dependent, and affectionate—characteristics suitable for being a helpmate and child rearer. These sex-role stereotypes have their roots deep in a time in our history when a division of labor was necessary for survival. Today, however, modern technology and birth control have freed women from duties associated with child rearing and childbearing for a large part of their lives. Sharp sex role divisions are no longer necessary or appropriate, especially in the labor force. New concepts of what it means to be "masculine" and "feminine" are becoming more widely accepted.

Partly because of the changing technology and partly as a result of affirmative action and other social and political movements, young people today have a much broader definition of what is appropriate behavior for men and women. Many people not only accept men who are to be emotionally and physically involved in the care of their children and take responsibility for other domestic duties, but expect these behaviors from them. Likewise, many women today are involved in occupations that, in the past, were reserved for men. Some of the symbols used to distinguish the sexes such as "wearing the pants" are completely obsolete. Similarly, many traditionally feminine symbols such as hair dyes and cosmetics are available to men.

Given these changing standards of acceptable sex roles, psychologist Sandra Bem argues that people should accept new **androgynous** roles—that is, roles that involve a flexible combination of traditionally male and female characteristics. She began her research by asking college students how desirable they considered various characteristics for a man and for a woman. Not surprisingly, she found that traits such as ambition, self-reliance, independence, and assertiveness were considered to be desirable for men. It was desirable for women to be affectionate, gentle, understanding, and sensitive to the needs of others.

These and other traits were then listed in a questionnaire called the

Bem Sex Role Inventory. Bem asked people to rate how each of these traits applied to them on a scale from one (never or almost never true) to seven (always or almost always true). In one early report (Bem, 1975), she described the results for 1,500 Stanford undergraduates: about 50 percent stuck to "appropriate" sex roles (masculine males or feminine females), 15 percent were "cross-sex typed" (women who described themselves in traditionally male terms, or men who checked feminine adjectives), and 36 percent were androgynous people who checked off both male and female characteristics when they described themselves.

In later studies, Bem found that the androgynous people were indeed more flexible. Such women were able to be assertive when it was required (so could traditional males, but traditional females could not). Such people were also able to express warmth, playfulness, and concern (as could traditional females, but traditional males could not). In our complex world, Bem argues, androgyny should be our ideal: there is no room for an artificial split between "woman's work" and "a man's world."

Androgyny is becoming an accepted ideal in our culture. One consequence of this shift is that adolescents who are developing into adults have more choices in the way they define themselves in life. In some ways, this shift toward more freedom in sex roles has resulted in greater personal responsibility. No longer limited by rigid sex role stereotypes, young people are challenged to define themselves according to their talents, temperaments, and values. At the same time, not all people within the culture accept the more androgynous sex roles. Older people, especially, may still define themselves and others in terms of more traditional and rigid sex role standards.

USING PSYCHOLOGY

Teenage Depression and Suicide

Each year more than one million teenagers run away from home. More than a million teenage girls in the United States get pregnant each year. It is estimated that more than 1.3 million American teenagers have serious drinking problems. These statistics highlight the seriousness of teenage depression. Many teenagers who feel helpless and hopeless use alcohol or other drugs, run away, become pregnant, or kill themselves. Suicide is second only to accidents as a cause of death among adolescents. Many accidents may, in fact, be disguised suicides.

According to Kathleen McCoy (1982), the phenomenon of teenage depression is much more widespread than most parents or educators suspect. To many grownups who see adolescence as the best years of life, depression and youth may seem incongruous.

What events trigger depression in adolescents? One major event is the loss of a loved one through death, divorce, separation, or family relocation. The adolescent may experience grief, guilt, panic, and anger as a reaction to a loss. If the youth is not able to express these feelings in a supportive atmosphere, depression may result.

Another related source of teenage depression is the breakdown of the family unit, often as a result of separation and divorce. Family members may be in conflict with each other and thus unable to communicate well. Adolescents may be thus deprived of the emotional support they need.

Unlike depressed adults, who usually look and feel sad or "down," depressed teenagers may appear to be extremely angry. They often engage in rebellious behavior such as truancy, running away, drinking, using drugs, or being sexually promiscuous. Often, depressed teenagers appear intensely hyperactive and frantic, traits that are often mistaken for normal behavior in teenagers. McCoy urges parents and educators to be aware of the warning signals of teenage depression and suicide. One warning signal is a change in the intensity and frequency of rebellious behavior. Others are withdrawal from friends, engaging in dangerous risk-taking, talking about suicide, and excessive self-criticism. Often the greatest danger of suicide occurs after a depression seems to be lifting.

The best way to deal with teenage depression is to communicate with the teenager about his or her problems. Sometimes, a caring, listening parent can help the youth deal with his or her concerns. In other cases, parents and their teenage child may need professional help. This is particularly true when few channels of communication have been established within the family.

Suicide attempts are made more frequently among females, but are more often fatal among males. One of the reasons that males more often "succeed" in committing suicide is that they are apt to use more violent means such as shooting, stabbing, or hanging themselves. Females are more likely to take a drug overdose, which is a slower process and can be more readily reversed if the person is found in time.

Some teenagers attempt suicide as a cry for help or attention or as a way of manipulating others rather than out of a desire to die. A suicide attempt may be designed to punish a former boyfriend or girlfriend or to call attention to a drug problem the teenager cannot deal with alone.

FACT or FICTION

Publicizing teenage suicides helps prevent more suicides.

Fiction. In the mid-1980s, leaders in communities around the country believed that talking publicly about teenage suicides as they occurred would stop other teens from taking their own lives. Unfortunately, the opposite occurred. Publicizing suicides seems to encourage more. Psychologists are trying to understand why this happens.

SOCIAL DEVELOPMENT

Adolescent development is multifaceted. In addition to the personal development just described, the adolescent also experiences changes in his or her social relationships. No longer a child though not yet an adult, the teenager must find a new role in the family—one that parents are not always ready to accept. He or she must also adjust to new, often more intense relationships with peers. The influence of family and peers on adolescent development has been the subject of much research, which is worth reviewing here.

The Family

One of the principal developmental tasks for adolescents is becoming independent of their families. Unfortunately, the means of achieving this status are not always clear, either to the adolescents or to their parents. First, there are mixed feelings on both sides. Some parents have built their life styles around the family and are reluctant to let the child go. Such parents know they will soon have to find someone else on whom to shift their emotional dependence. Also, parents whose children are old enough to leave home sometimes have to wrestle with their own fears of advancing age. Many parents worry about whether their children are really ready to cope with the harsh realities of life—and so do adolescents. At the same time that young people long to get out on their own and try themselves against the world, they worry a lot about failing there. This internal struggle is often mirrored in the adolescent's unpredictable behavior, which parents may interpret as "adolescent rebellion." Against this background of uncertainty, which is almost universal, there are various family styles of working toward autonomy.

The way in which adolescents seek independence and the ease with which they resolve conflicts about becoming adults depend in large part on the parent-child relationship.

In **authoritarian families** parents are the "bosses." They do not feel that they have to explain their actions or demands. In fact, such parents may feel the child has no right to question parental decisions.

In **democratic families** adolescents participate in decisions affecting their lives. There is a great deal of discussion and negotiation in such families. Parents listen to their children's reasons for wanting to go somewhere or do something, and make an effort to explain their rules and expectations. The adolescents make many decisions for themselves, but the parents retain the right to veto plans of which they disapprove.

In **permissive** or **laissez-faire** families children have the final say. The parents may attempt to guide the adolescents, but give in when the children insist on having their own way. Or the parents may simply give up their child-rearing responsibilities—setting no rules about behavior, making no demands, voicing no expectations, virtually ignoring the young people in their house.

What Adolescents Need and Want from Their Parents

Much as teenagers may wish it, the perfect parents probably do not exist. Every family's circumstances and personalities practically guarantee that there will be at least occasional clashes between parents and their adolescent offspring. Yet both parents and teenagers can benefit from having a general idea of the qualities adolescents need and want from their parents. This knowledge can help parents meet their children's needs, and it provides a yardstick against which teenagers can measure their expectations of their parents to see how realistic those expectations are. Several studies have revealed a number of qualities that adolescents most need and want in their parents.

1. Teenagers want parents to take an interest in their activities and to be available when they need help and support. One disappointed high school basketball player expressed this view very clearly:

I'm the star player on the school basketball team, but never once has either parent come to see me play. They're either too busy or too tired or can't get a baby sitter for my younger sister. The crowds cheer for me, the girls hang around my locker, some kids even ask me for my autograph. But it doesn't mean much if the two most important people in my life don't care.

2. Parents should listen to what their teenaged children say, and should try to understand their point of view.
3. Similarly, parents should communicate with their children, exchanging ideas and talking *with* their teenagers, not *at* them.
4. Parents should love and accept adolescents as they are. Too often, teenagers feel rejected and worthless because they cannot meet their parents' too-high expectations of them.
5. Parents should trust their children and respect their privacy. Teenagers especially resent parents who open their mail, read their diaries, or eavesdrop on their phone conversations.
6. Parents should allow their children to learn to be independent by giving them leeway in such areas as choice of friends and clothing. Teenagers especially want their parents to grant them autonomy in gradually increasing amounts as they learn to handle it.
7. Parents should be neither too strict nor too permissive. Once family rules are established—preferably in a democratic way—parents should be consistent in enforcing them.
8. Parents should do their best to provide a positive emotional climate in the home. A prevailing mood of affection, cheerfulness, and optimism is much more beneficial to all family members than an atmosphere of marital unhappiness, fear, depression, and hostility.
9. Parents should set a good example for their adolescent children. By this teenagers mean that parents should "practice what they preach" and not be afraid to admit it when they make mistakes.

For more details, see F. P. Rice, *The Adolescent: Development, Relationships, and Culture,* 2nd ed. Boston: Allyn and Bacon, 1978, pp. 410–419.

Figure 9.5
The style of parent-child relationship—authoritarian, democratic, or permissive—plays a large part in determining how adolescents gain independence and make the transition to adulthood.

Numerous studies suggest that adolescents who have grown up in democratic families are more autonomous, in the sense of having more confidence in their own values and goals than other young people do. They are also more independent, in the sense of wanting to make their own decisions (with or without advice). There are several reasons for this.

First, the child is able to assume responsibility gradually. He or she is not denied the opportunity to exercise judgment (as in authoritarian families) or given too much responsibility too soon (as in permissive families). Second, the child is more likely to identify with parents who love and respect him or her than with parents who treat him or her as incompetent or who seem indifferent. Finally, through their behavior toward the child, democratic parents present a model of responsible, cooperative independence for the growing person to imitate.

Children raised in authoritarian families lack practice in negotiating for their desires and exercising responsibility. They tend to resent all authority, to rebel without cause. Children raised in permissive families tend to feel unwanted and to doubt their own self-worth. They often do not trust themselves or others (Conger, 1973: 208–215).

Although the style parents adopt in dealing with their children influences adolescent development, it would be wrong to conclude that parents are solely responsible for the way their children turn out. Adolescents themselves may contribute to the style parents embrace, with consequences for their own personal development. Parents may adopt a laissez-faire attitude simply because they find that style the easiest way to cope with a teenager who insists on having his or her own way. Adolescents experiencing rapid physical and emotional changes may force their parents to make major adjustments to them.

Conflict between adolescents and parents, even in democratic families, is not uncommon. Quarrels can arise over many issues, including church attendance, choice of friends, performance of home chores, use of time, and attitude toward studies. In general, the more authoritarian a family, the more frequent such conflicts tend to be. But other factors affect the frequency of arguments. The sex of the adolescent is one such factor, with girls reporting more conflict with family members than boys. The size of the family is another. Large middle-class families, for example, experience more conflict than smaller ones (Edwards and Branberger, 1973: 105).

Despite the sometimes strained relations in families, the home environment does have a shaping influence on such important decisions as occupational choice. Sociologists have found, for example, that adolescents from high-status families tend to select high-status occupations much more frequently than those from lower-class families (Elder, 1968). This fact may be explained in large part by the kind of feedback parents in different social classes tend to give their children. The parents of the high achievers may have fostered in their children the kind of self-confidence necessary for success (Rosenberg and Simmons, 1972).

Thus far in this section we have emphasized the relationship between the adolescent and his or her parents, but there is also a flow of influence between the adolescent and other family members, especially siblings. Older siblings, for example, serve as role models for the adolescent. Younger siblings allow the adolescent to assume the role of surrogate parent, and thus to learn an array of adult roles and responsibilities. In general, siblings learn from one another—through play, sharing secrets and experiences, and through fighting—how to negotiate relationships with others and thereby to get along better in the larger world.

The Peer Group

The people all adolescents can trust not to treat them like children are their peers. Teenagers spend much of their time with friends—they need and use each other to define themselves.

High schools are important as places for adolescents to get together. And they do get together in fairly predictable ways. Most schools contain easily recognizable and well-defined sets, or crowds. And these sets are arranged in a fairly rigid hierarchy—everyone knows who belongs to which set and what people in that set do with their time. Early in adolescence the sets are usually divided by sex, but later the sexes mix. Sets usually form along class lines. Some school activities bring teenagers of different social classes together, but it is the exception rather than the rule that middle-class and lower-class adolescents are close friends, though recent evidence suggests that interclass friendships may be increasing (Hraba and Grant, 1970; Proshansky and Newton, 1968).

Besides class, what determines whether an adolescent will be accepted by a peer group? Many studies have shown that personal characteristics are very important. Well-liked peers tend to be well-groomed, good-looking, outgoing, neat, fun, and adept at making others feel accepted. Unpopular peers are seen by others as irresponsible, sloppy, childish, shy, and lonely, among other negative characteristics (Hartup, 1970; Harrocks and Benimoff, 1967).

Belonging to a *clique* (a group within a set) is very important to most adolescents and serves several functions. Most obviously, perhaps, it ful-

Adolescents need and use the peer group to define themselves.

fills the need for closeness with others. But, in addition, it gives the adolescent a means of defining himself or herself, a way of establishing an identity. The group does this by helping the individual achieve self-confidence, develop a sense of independence from family, clarify values, and experiment with new roles (Rogers, 1977). By providing feedback, clique members not only help define who an individual is but also who he or she is not: group membership separates an adolescent from others who are not in his or her set.

Of course, there are drawbacks to this kind of social organization. One of the greatest is the fear of being disliked, which leads to **conformity**—the "glue" that holds the peer group together. A teenager's fear of wearing clothes that might set him or her apart from others is well known. But group pressures to conform may also lead young people to do more serious things that run contrary to their better judgment.

Despite their tendency to encourage conformity, peer groups are not always dominant in an adolescent's life. Both parents and peers exercise considerable influence in shaping adolescent behavior and attitudes. Peers tend to set the standards on such matters as fashion and taste in music (Munns, 1972). Their advice on school-related issues may also be considered more reliable than parental counsel (Brittain, 1963, 1969).

When it comes to basic matters, however, involving marriage, religion, or educational plans, adolescents tend to accept their parents' beliefs and to follow their advice (Chand, Crider, and Willets, 1975; Kandel and Lesser, 1969). Only in a few areas touching basic values—for example, drug use or

Figure 9.6
Most adolescents spend much of their time with a peer group, which is a source of self-identity as well as a source of social pressure to conform.

sexual behavior—are there differences. Even here the differences are not fundamental and represent only a difference in the strength with which the same basic belief is held (Lerner and Knapp, 1975).

Peer groups, then, do not pose a threat to parental authority. Even though parents spend less time with their adolescent children as the latter mature, their influence is still strong. Adolescents of both sexes tend to choose friends with values close to those of their parents (Bandura, 1964; Douvan and Adelson, 1966). Thus, generational conflict is not nearly so pronounced as some would have us believe.

DIFFICULTIES IN THE TRANSITION FROM LATE CHILDHOOD TO EARLY ADOLESCENCE

As we have seen in this chapter, adolescence is a time of transition. There are many developmental tasks to be mastered, but adolescence is not distinct from other periods of life in this respect. As Havighurst (1972) has pointed out, every stage of life brings with it unique challenges specific to that stage, be it old age, early childhood, or adolescence.

When a person has mastered the tasks of adolescence, he or she is an adult, but not a "mature" adult, for the developmental stage of adulthood spans many years and the end of adolescence is just the beginning of this long journey. The graduate-adolescent is a "young" adult heading toward "middle" adulthood, the phase before mature adulthood. The young adult will find that he or she now has new tasks to master unique to this stage of life.

Given the great array of profound changes the adolescent must cope with involving his or her mind, body, emotions, and social relationships, it is natural and normal that most adolescents should experience some *temporary* psychological difficulties. The great majority, however, adjust fairly quickly. Mental illness and suicide are relatively rare among adolescents (though the rates of both have been increasing over the past several decades). Thoughts about mental illness and death, however, are quite common among otherwise healthy adolescents.

Research shows that only about 20 percent of adolescents have problems so severe that they can't function well in social situations or at school (Masterson, 1967). This troubled minority often "acts out" problems in one of several ways. Acts of juvenile delinquency, running away from home, unwanted pregnancies, alcohol and drug abuse, and underachievement at school are typical.

Unfortunately, troubled adolescents do not simply "outgrow" their problems, but carry them into later life if they are not treated (Jones, 1974; Masterson, 1967). Adults, therefore, should be concerned about troubled teenagers. It is important to note, however, that abnormal behavior should be seen as a more intense form, or a more extreme degree, of normal behavior. It should not be considered a different *kind* of behavior. For example, teenagers who experiment with drugs—or even become drug abusers—need understanding; by not labeling the teenaged drug abuser "strange" or "different," we can better meet his or her psychological needs.

PSYCHOLOGY and YOU

Teenagers and Work. By high school graduation, more than 80 percent of students have had some kind of job. Most take low-skilled jobs that provide an opportunity to make some extra money. While most people tend to believe that any kind of job experience is good, research indicates that such work can, in fact, be harmful.

One reason for this is that students who work evenings or weekends have less time to study. If you work, you need to set time aside for school work. Another is that students might gain a false impression of the workplace from their work experience. The jobs they take tend to be low-paying, boring, and unchallenging. You need to remember that while you are still in high school you have few skills to offer. A higher education, and some training, will open doors to better jobs.

Finally, working while still in school can create false ideas about money. Most students work to pay for luxury items such as brand-name clothes or concert tickets. There's a danger that they will experience "premature affluence" because what they earn is spending money; they don't have to pay for necessities such as food and rent. Realizing that spending money may, in fact, be less available when you take a full-time job will help you avoid this trap.

CHAPTER REVIEW

KEY TERMS

- androgynous
- asynchrony
- authoritarian families
- conformity
- democratic families

- identity crisis
- laissez-faire families
- menarche
- permissive families
- puberty

- rationalization
- self-fulfilling prophecy
- sex identity
- sex role
- social learning theory

SUMMARY

1. Adults vary in their attitudes toward adolescents. Some adults admire and even idealize young people. Others feel threatened by, or jealous of, youth. One reason for the negative attitudes is that different generations sometimes have different ideas of morality.

2. Adolescents tend to regard themselves in the way that the adults with whom they interact view them.

3. The study of adolescence has been marked by two major theoretical orientations or viewpoints—the "storm and stress" theory and what may be called the "continuous growth" theory. The former sees adolescence as a highly turbulent time of development that is discontinuous with childhood, while the latter sees adolescence as a rather smooth progression out of childhood and into adulthood.

4. During adolescence there are certain developmental tasks the adolescent must master that are unique to this stage of life. Studies have shown that most adolescents successfully master their developmental tasks.

5. In addition to the developmental tasks the adolescent must master, he or she must experience, accept, and cope with the radical physical, mental, emotional, social, and, for some, identity changes beginning with puberty and continuing throughout most of the teenage years.

6. The adolescent's reaction to growth tends to be highly idiosyncratic, as is the rate and pattern of growth itself. Cultural definitions of ideal body type can affect an adolescent's self-image, and this, in turn, can affect his or her success in later life.

7. During adolescence individuals become capable of what Piaget calls concrete operational thinking. Though there are individual, class, and cultural differences, many adolescents can comprehend the hypothetical and understand abstract principles.

8. Because of their maturing thought processes, adolescents are capable of mature moral thinking—of formulating principles based on the ability to see another person's viewpoint.

9. The personality changes that adolescents experience have to do with the formation of identity. Erikson believes that adolescents achieve their identity by going through a series of crises, but others maintain that such crises are rare and that social influences are of prime importance in the shaping of identity.

10. Adolescent sexual attitudes today are different from those of past generations. The strict division between traditional sex roles, which are largely learned, is in the process of breaking down.

11. Parents vary in the styles they adopt in dealing with their children. Adolescents raised in democratic families tend to develop the most self-confidence and ability to assume responsibility.

12. Conflict is present in even the best parent-adolescent relationships. Even so, parents have a

profound and lasting influence on adolescents. The influence flows both ways, however, and adolescents also affect other family
members.

13. Competing with the family for the attention of
the adolescent is the peer group. Adolescents
typically feel a commitment to both family and
peer group. Which group is more influential at
a given time depends on the nature of the issue.
Peer groups serve many important functions
for the adolescent.

14. About 20 percent of adolescents have severe
psychological problems. The best approach in
helping troubled adolescents is not to set them
apart by drawing a sharp distinction between
normal and abnormal behavior.

REVIEW QUESTIONS

1. What are two views that adults have towards
adolescents?

2. What are four reasons that may explain why
some adults view adolescents in a negative light?

3. What is Stanley Hall's theory of adolescence?
Does the research of Margaret Mead support his
position?

4. Do early maturing adolescent boys have a more
positive view of themselves than late maturers?
Is this difference the same for early and late maturing girls? Why does physical growth affect
how persons feel about themselves?

5. What does Piaget mean by "formal operational"
thinking? How does this change in cognitive
ability affect an adolescent?

6. According to Kohlberg, what are the fifth and
sixth stages of moral development? What other
change is necessary in order for persons to
achieve these advanced stages of moral development?

7. Based on Erikson's concept of identity crisis,
what are the four adolescent personality types
presented by Marcia? According to Bandura,
what percentage of adolescents go through an
identity crisis and what is its cause?

8. How does sex role differ from sexual identity?
When Sandra Bem discusses androgyny, is she
talking about sex role or sexual identity?

9. What are the three types of family interaction
patterns? Which style would you use if you
wanted your children to act independently and
have confidence in their personal decisions?

10. In what areas do adolescents tend to follow the
beliefs and advice of their parents?

11. What percentage of adolescents have a very difficult time mastering the developmental tasks
of this period in their lives? Are these persons
"different" from other adolescents who have
less difficulty?

ACTIVITIES

1. Write five words or phrases that, in your opinion, characterize adolescence. Ask an adult (for
example, a parent) to write five words or phrases, also. What are the similarities and differences? In your opinion, what are some reasons
for the differences?

2. Pretend you are a high school psychology
teacher. Tell what you would plan to teach in
the course, reasons for your selections, and
how you would plan to teach this material.
Would you use an experiential or a cognitive
approach? Which topics of importance to adolescents would you specifically include?

3. Erikson and Marcia insist that all adolescents
experience an identity crisis. Do you agree?
What identity crises have you experienced?

Figure 10.1 People who plan for their later years are more likely to enjoy them.

Objectives: *After studying this chapter, you should be able to*
- identify and describe the changes that occur during adulthood.
- summarize findings on social and personality development in adults.
- cite research on the aging process and on the part of the life cycle known as old age.
- identify and describe the five stages of coming to terms with death and summarize the controversy over an individual's right to die.

Adulthood and Old Age

In the preface to *The Seasons of a Man's Life* (1978), Yale researcher Daniel Levinson writes: "Young adults often feel that to pass 30 is to be 'over the hill,' and they are given little beyond hollow clichés to provide a fuller sense of the actual problems and possibilities of adult life at different ages. The middle years, they imagine, will bring triviality and meaningless comfort at best, stagnation and hopelessness at worst. . . . Adults hope that life begins at 40—but the great anxiety is that it ends there. The result of this pervasive dread about middle age is almost complete silence about the experience of being adult."

As much as middle age is dreaded, old age is looked on with even greater fear and misunderstanding. Whereas in some cultures reaching old age is thought of as a blessing, in ours it is awaited with anxiety. Everyone wants to look and act young. Gray hair must be dyed, faces lifted.

Much of our fear of aging is rooted in stereotypes of what it is to grow older. Middle age, it is thought, is a time of deterioration, both physically and mentally. Many believe that sexual life declines markedly. In old age the process of deterioration only accelerates.

But these are not true pictures of aging. Indeed, the positive side of adult life is one of the best-kept secrets in our society. By undermining some of the stereotypes about growing older, we hope to convey a true image of adult life.

Adulthood
Physical Changes • Intellectual Changes • Social and Personality Development

Old Age
Changes in Health • Changes in Life Situation • Changes in Mental Functioning

Death and Dying
Using Psychology: Hospices • The Right to Die

ADULTHOOD

What is middle age like? For one thing, it is a period of great paradox. There is change and sameness, success and failure, crisis and stability, joy and sadness. Middle age can be a time when a person matures fully into what he or she is. Or it can be a time when life closes in and what was once possibility is now limitation. How each person reacts depends on circumstances and one's general outlook on life.

243

The Cohort Effect. Suppose you were asked to measure the performance of trains at various points along a busy route. How would you go about it?

You might adopt a *longitudinal* approach. You would board a train and stay with it for its entire journey, recording your observations along the way. Alternatively, you might employ a *cross-sectional* strategy. You would ask observers stationed at key points to report on the performance of various trains that pass by.

Psychologists who study the behavior of people as they progress through adulthood and old age face a similar task. Since this "journey" can last decades, few researchers adopt a purely longitudinal approach. Instead, most conduct cross-sectional studies in which they can measure different age-groups, or *cohorts*, together at one time.

Unfortunately, people from different cohorts usually have different experiences in a number of important areas, including education, nutrition, career opportunities, and social values. Their different backgrounds make it difficult to determine how age affects human abilities, attitudes, and even health.

Until quite recently psychologists knew little about adulthood. In the past, more emphasis was placed on childhood and adolescence, and relatively little attention was given to the study of middle age. Today, however, a growing number of psychologists are studying adult psychology. Many approach adulthood from a **life events perspective** (Evans, 1985). According to this perspective, adult development is more closely linked to significant events than it is to the passage of time. Examples of significant events or developmental tasks of adulthood are helping teenage children become responsible and satisfied adults, taking on adult social and civic responsibility, performing well in an occupation, finding satisfying leisure activities, relating to one's husband or wife as a person, adjusting to the physical changes of middle age, and relating to one's aging parents (Havighurst, 1972). Supporting the life events perspective, Hancock (1985) found that a woman's development is usually affected more significantly by the course of her relationships than by her age.

If you recall the developmental tasks of adolescence discussed in Chapter 9 (and some of your own experiences), you may recognize similarities between the years of adulthood and the adolescent years. During both periods, bodily changes require psychological adjustments; relating well to others is an important goal (whether to parents, peers, or spouses); and meeting new responsibilities requires a good deal of effort. Teenagers often think they have nothing in common with their parents. But the tasks of adolescence and adulthood are similar enough that they can form the basis for improved communication between generations. In addition, understanding the problems and changes that accompany growing older can be good preparation for a time of life we all must enter.

Physical Changes

In general, human beings are at their physical peak between the ages of eighteen and twenty-five. This is the period when we are strongest, healthiest, and have the quickest reflexes. One has only to think of the average age of professional athletes or dancers to verify this.

For most adults, the process of physical decline is slow and gradual. Strength and stamina begin to decline in the late twenties. A twenty-year-old manages to carry four heavy bags of groceries; a forty-year-old finds it easier to make two trips. In middle age, appearance changes. The hair starts to turn gray and perhaps to thin out. The skin becomes somewhat dry and inelastic; wrinkles appear. In old age, muscles and fat built up over the years break down, so that people often lose weight, become shorter, and develop more wrinkles, creases, and loose skin.

With time the senses require more and more stimulation. During their forties most people begin having difficulty seeing distant objects, adjusting to the dark, and focusing on printed pages, even if their eyesight has always been good. Many experience a gradual or sudden loss of hearing in their later years. In addition, reaction time slows. If an experimenter asks a young person and an older person to push a button when they see a light flash on, the older person will take longer to do so.

There also may be differences in the way men and women age physically. In a recent study of sixty-nine men and women between the ages of eighteen and eighty, Ruben Gur and his associates discovered a dramatic difference in brain deterioration based on gender (*New York Times*, 1991). Using advanced technology to scan the brain (see Chapter 21), they found that men's brains deteriorate two to three times faster than women's brains. Furthermore, the degeneration of men's brains occurs mostly on the left side, the center of speech, language abilities, and logical thinking. In contrast, both sides of women's brains seem to age evenly. Does this difference in brain deterioration mean that men and women behave differently as they age? This is a question that psychologists will try to answer in the future.

Health Problems.   Some of the changes we associate with growing older are the result of the natural processes of aging. Others result from diseases and from simple disuse and abuse. Two of the most common health problems of middle age—heart disease and cancer—are related to obesity and smoking. Obesity can cause heart attacks and lead to hypertension and diabetes. In fact, for someone who is 30 percent overweight, the chance of dying during middle age is increased by 40 percent (Turner and Helms, 1979). Heavy smoking is related to cancer of the mouth, throat, and lungs and to respiratory and heart problems. It increases the possibility of cardiovascular disease, which is the leading cause of death during middle age (U.S. Department of Health, Education, and Welfare, 1971). The nonsmoker, on the other hand, encounters only half the health problems of the heavy smoker. A person who eats sensibly, exercises, avoids cigarettes, drugs, and alcohol, and is not subjected to severe emotional stress will look and feel younger than someone who neglects his or her health.

Menopause.   Between the ages of forty-five and fifty, a woman's production of sex hormones is sharply reduced. This biological event is called **menopause**. The woman stops ovulating (producing eggs) and menstruating and therefore cannot have any more children. However, menopause does not cause any reduction in a woman's sexual drive or sexual enjoyment.

Many women experience some degree of discomfort during menopause. However, the irritability and severe depression some women experience with "the change of life" appear to have an emotional rather than a physical origin.

A recent study shows that the negative effects of menopause are greatly exaggerated. Half of the women interviewed said they felt better, more confident, calmer, and freer after menopause than they had before. They no longer had to think about their periods or getting pregnant. Their relations with their husbands improved; they enjoyed sex as much as or more than they had before. Many said the worst part of menopause was not knowing what to expect (Neugarten et al., 1963).

In fact, it seems that the attitudes of the woman and of the society in which she lives offer the best prediction of how severe a woman's menopausal symptoms will be. A woman living in an environment that values her as she gets older is likely to have a more positive experience than a woman who has been made to feel that menopause is somehow a mark against her womanhood (Papalia and Olds, 1989).

Sexual Behavior.   Is there sex after forty? According to one study, most college students believe their parents have intercourse no more than once a month; one-fourth of the students in the study believed that their parents had had intercourse only once or not at all in the last year (Pocs et al., 1977). In general, young people are uncomfortable with the idea that older people have sexual lives.

Despite younger people's beliefs, studies have shown that sexual activity does not automatically decline with age. Indeed, as sex researchers William Masters and Virginia Johnson (1970) point out, there is no physiological reason for stopping sexual activity with advancing age. Most older people who have an available partner maintain quite vigorous sex lives. Those who are inactive cite boredom with a partner of long standing, poor physical condition or illness (such as heart disease), or acceptance of the stereotype of loss of sex drive with aging.

It is true that there are changes in sexuality during adulthood. A man reaches his sexual peak in his late teens. From that time on, his sexual responsiveness declines. But the decline is very gradual and, except for the self-doubt it sometimes causes, does not usually interfere with normal sexual functioning. Kinsey measured this gradual decline of frequency of orgasm per week for males from age sixteen on but found that even at age seventy almost 70 percent of the males were still sexually active (Kinsey et al., 1948). Women reach their sexual peak later than men; in addition, the decline in their sexual responsiveness occurs later. When it does occur, it is probably less than in men (Botwinick, 1978).

More so than age, then, good physical and mental health seem to be the key factors affecting sexual activity. Adults can and do continue to enjoy a healthy sex life. Sex after forty is not only possible, it is a fact of life.

Figure 10.2
Sexual interest and activity do not suddenly cease at a certain age: as more and more studies show, those who have partners and remain active, productive people also continue to enjoy active sex lives.

Intellectual Changes

People are better at learning new skills and information, solving problems that require speed and coordination, and shifting from one problem-solving strategy to another in their mid-twenties than they were in adolescence (Baltes and Schaie, 1974). These abilities are considered signs of intelligence; they are the skills intelligence tests measure.

At one time many psychologists thought that intellectual development reached a peak in the mid-twenties and then declined. The reason was that people do not score as high on intelligence tests in middle age as they did when they were younger. Further investigation revealed that some parts of these tests measure speed, not intelligence (Bischof, 1969). As indicated above, a person's reaction time begins to slow after a certain age. Intelligence tests usually "penalized" adults for this fact.

One intelligence test, the Wechsler, takes this into account by testing two very different sorts of abilities. On the verbal portion, which measures facility with words and stored information, older people show little decline. However, on the performance parts of the test, which measure speed of reaction in performing tasks, their scores are lower. On the basis of such tests researchers have concluded that overall decline in abilities is not great and is hardly apparent until about age fifty or later (Botwinick, 1978).

Even with a decline in speed, people continue to acquire information and to expand their vocabularies as they grow older. The ability to comprehend new material and to think flexibly improves with the years. This is particularly true if a person has had higher education, lives in a stimulating environment, and works in an intellectually demanding career. One researcher studied more than 700 individuals who were engaged in scholarship, science, or the arts. Although the patterns varied from profession to profession, most of the subjects reached their peaks of creativity and productivity in their forties (Dennis, 1966).

Social and Personality Development

As we mentioned earlier, studies have just begun to focus on middle age. There is evidence to suggest that an individual's basic character—his or her style of adapting to situations—is relatively stable over the years. But researchers are also convinced that personality is flexible and capable of changing as an individual confronts new tasks.

Many studies support the first point. A number of researchers have given the same attitude and personality tests to individuals in late adolescence and again ten or fifteen years later. Many of the subjects believed that they had changed dramatically. But the tests indicated they had not. The degree of satisfaction they expressed about themselves and about life in general in their middle years was consistent with their earlier views. Confident young people remained confident; self-haters, self-hating; passive individuals, passive—unless something upsetting had happened to them, such as a sudden change in economic status (Kimmel, 1974).

Like adolescents, adults must cope with new situations and developmental tasks.

Despite the stability of character, people do face many changes in their lifetimes and adjust accordingly. Adults encounter new developmental tasks, just as adolescents do. They too must learn to cope with problems and deal with new situations. Learning the skills needed to cope with change seems to occur in stages for both adult males and females. One researcher who has studied personality development in males, Daniel Levinson, has developed a theory concerning the cycle of changes men go through.

Levinson's Theory of Male Development.   The work of Daniel Levinson and his colleagues at Yale was not well known until 1976, when it was popularized in a national best-seller by Gail Sheehy entitled *Passages: Predictable Crises of Adult Life*. During his research, Levinson interviewed four groups of men between the ages of thirty-five and forty-five: ten were executives, ten were hourly workers in industry, ten were novelists, and ten were university biologists.

A life structure was developed for each man on the basis of these interviews. Each life structure was an account of the major periods of the man's life as determined by his activities, his associations, and his relationships. A careful analysis of these life structures revealed a pattern that seemed to apply to almost all the men sampled.

The model of adult development for men that Levinson and his colleagues proposed is shown in Figure 10.3. The three major eras are early adulthood (from about age seventeen to about age forty), middle adulthood (forty to sixty), and late adulthood (beginning at about sixty). Between these eras are important transition periods at ages thirty, forty, fifty, and sixty, which last approximately five years. Levinson's research focused on the early adult era and the mid-life transition. The following discussion concentrates on what he learned about these stages.

Entering the adult world. From about age twenty-two to age twenty-eight, the young man is considered, both by himself and by society, to be a novice in the adult world—not fully established as a man, but no longer an adolescent. During this time he must attempt to resolve the conflict between the need to explore the options of the adult world and the need to establish a stable life structure. He needs to sample different kinds of relationships, to keep choices about career and employment open, to explore the nature of the world now accessible to him as an adult. But he also needs to begin a career and to establish a home and family of his own. The first life structure, then, may have a tentative quality. The young man may select a career or a job but not be committed to it. He may form romantic attachments and may even marry during this period; but the life structure of early adulthood often lacks a full sense of stability or permanence.

The age-thirty crisis. Some years ago the motto of the rebellious, politically oriented young people who sought to change American society was "Never trust anyone over thirty." Levinson's data reveal that the years between twenty-eight and thirty-three are indeed often a major transition period. The thirtieth birthday can truly be a turning point; for most men in Levinson's sample, it could be called "the age-thirty crisis." During this transitional period the tentative commitments that were made in the first

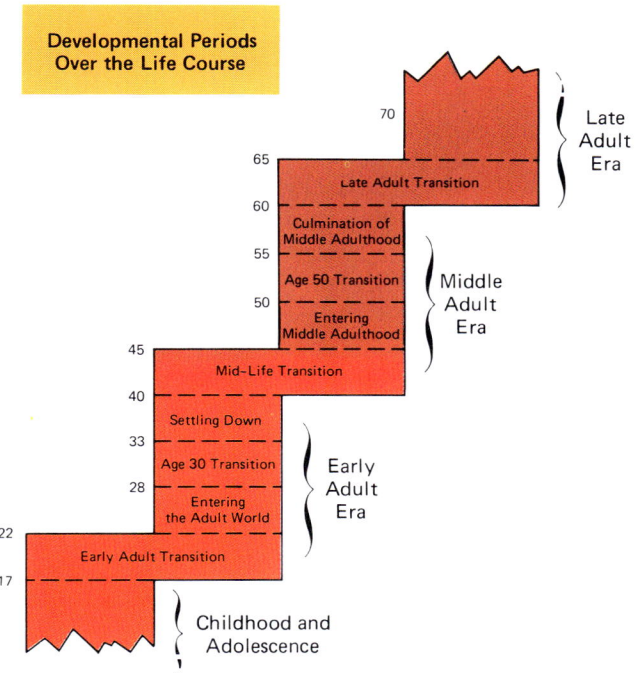

**Developmental Periods
Over the Life Course**

70

Late
Adult
Era

65

Late Adult Transition

60

Culmination of
Middle Adulthood

55

Age 50 Transition

Middle
Adult
Era

50

Entering
Middle Adulthood

45

Mid–Life Transition

40

Settling Down

33

Age 30 Transition

Early
Adult
Era

28

Entering
the Adult World

22

Early Adult Transition

17

Childhood and
Adolescence

Figure 10.3
A model of the developmental sequence of a man's life proposed by Levinson. The scheme emphasizes that development is an ongoing process that requires continual adjustment.

life structure are reexamined, and many questions about the choices of marriage partner, career, and life goals are reopened, often in a painful way. The man feels that any parts of his life that are unsatisfying or incomplete must be attended to now, because it will soon be too late to make major changes.

Settling down. The questioning and searching that are part of the age-thirty crisis begin to be resolved as the second adult life structure develops. Having probably made some firm choices about his career, family, and relationships, the man now begins actively carving out a niche in society, concentrating on what Levinson calls "making it" in the adult world. The man attempts to move up the ladder of prestige and achievement in his chosen career or profession and to be a full-fledged member of adult society.

Levinson found that near the end of the settling-down period, approximately between the ages of thirty-six and forty, there is a distinctive phase that he has labeled "becoming one's own man." Whereas earlier the young man had looked to an older, more experienced man as a mentor, someone who would share his experience and wisdom, the relationship with the mentor is often fundamentally changed, or even broken off, in the process of becoming one's own man. Now it is time to become fully independent. During this period the man strives to attain the seniority and position in the world that he identified as his ultimate goal at the beginning of the settling-down period.

The mid-life transition. At about age forty the period of early adulthood comes to an end and the mid-life transition begins. From about age forty to age forty-five, the man begins again to ask questions, but now the questions concern the past as well as the future. He may ask: "What have I done with my life?" "What have I accomplished?" "What do I still wish to accomplish?" At age thirty the man had primarily looked ahead toward goals, but at the mid-life transition he is in a position to assess his accomplishments and to determine whether or not they have been satisfying. During this transition, he begins to develop yet another life structure that will predominate during the period of middle adulthood.

During this period, the man often experiences a resurgence of interest in sex. In part this may be a result of his general reevaluation of his life to this point. In addition, he and his wife may have more time together alone, without the pressures of caring for small children. At the same time, however, his marriage may be at a low point (Rollins and Feldman, 1970) if he and his wife have developed different interests over the years of their marriage. Thus, the man's relationship with his wife—whether good or bad—is likely to be an important factor in the mid-life transition.

Often a successful mid-life transition is accompanied by the man's becoming a mentor for a younger man. This event signals the attainment, in Erik Erikson's terms, of generativity. By **generativity**, Erikson means the desire to use one's accumulated wisdom to guide future generations—directly, as a parent, or indirectly. The opposite—**stagnation**—can also occur. A man may choose to hang on to the past, perhaps by having an affair with a younger woman to recapture his youth. Or he may become preoccupied with his health or bitter about the direction his life has taken.

Figure 10.4
Mentor and protégé: the desire to transmit one's knowledge and experience to the next generation is a sign of what Erikson calls the "generativity" resolution of the crisis of middle age. The opposite resolution—stagnation—results in self-absorption, bitterness, and looking backward.

The mid-life transition has been the most discussed aspect of Levinson's work. About 80 percent of the men in his sample experienced the mid-life transition as a moderate to severe crisis, characterized by the questioning of virtually every aspect of their lives. But it is a period of questioning from which a new life structure must emerge.

Middle adulthood. The late forties is a time when true adulthood can be achieved. The man who finds satisfactory solutions to his life crisis reaches a period of stability. He understands and tolerates others; he displays a sensitivity and concern for other individuals as people. He is able to strike a balance between the need for friends and the need for privacy.

For the man who is not as fortunate, this period can be a time of extreme frustration and unhappiness. Instead of generativity, there is stagnation; instead of change and improvement, there is a mood of resignation to a bad situation. The job is only a job. The individual may feel cut off from family and friends. The future holds no promise. By avoiding this life crisis, he is only inviting a later appearance of it, at age fifty, with more crushing force (Rogers, 1979).

Those who successfully adjust to middle age can find it a most gratifying period. The difficult early adulthood years are behind them; now they are looked to for leadership and expertise. In their work, marriage, and personal lives, they are happier than ever before.

Female Development.   While there have been far more studies conducted among men than among women, some researchers have focused their attention on women's mid-life development. Sheehy's best-selling book, mentioned earlier, is one of them. Working with Levinson's basic theories, Sheehy interviewed 115 people who described their experiences as adults. The author discovered a major difference between men and women in how they can best rebuild their lives at mid-life. Throughout their lives, most women have traditionally served others in their roles as wife and mother. So although generativity may be a goal for many men, it may not be the ideal solution for some women who have reached mid-life.

Career versus family. Until recently, both men and women in industrial societies felt that women had to make an either-or choice between home and career. Most women chose the former. The traditional roles of wife and mother, while satisfying for many, proved to be unfulfilling for others. For some women, staying at home to care for the children makes it difficult to feel involved in the world. Other women sense a loss of self-worth in being defined by their husband's role. They want to be thought of as more than simply "the wife of an attorney."

To solve this problem, Sheehy believes, women must overcome their dependency on their spouses. Returning to work or to school may give a woman the missing sense of personal identity. Today, more and more women are realizing that they do not have to choose between career and family. Women now have more opportunities than ever to become independent and self-fulfilled human beings.

The "empty nest" syndrome. A significant event in many women's lives is the departure from home of the last child. Contrary to popular belief, this event need not be traumatic. In fact, many women find that the period

Figure 10.5
Many women experience what is called the "empty nest" syndrome when grown children leave home and the twenty-four-hour-a-day job in which they have been absorbed for probably two decades is suddenly over. Some women find new careers; others return to those they gave up when the children were born. For many, however, this is a period of stress and readjustment.

after the children are grown is one of the happiest of their lives. If they have not already done so, they may return to an interrupted career or start a new one (Stevens-Long, 1979). Women working outside the home seem to cope better than full-time homemakers with their children leaving home (Adelmann et al., 1989).

Of course, not all women experience the same sense of new freedom. Psychologists have found that a stable marriage makes a difference. If a woman has a warm relationship with her husband, she may find the adjustment easier because of his support. Conversely, if the woman is widowed or divorced, the transition can be much more difficult. How well her children adjust to their new independence can also affect a mother's happiness at this time (Harkins, 1978).

A relatively recent trend opposite to the empty nest syndrome is called the **crowded nest syndrome** (Schnaiberg and Goldenberg, 1989). This syndrome occurs when grown children move back into their parents' home. When this happens, the parent-child relationship must be reassessed (Shehan, Berardo, and Berardo, 1984). This reassessment can be problematic. Sometimes the returning child has problems such as a failed marriage or history of drug abuse. It may be that parents have gotten used to their freedom and resent the child's return. Adult children returning home can be a positive experience, but all of those involved must be ready to make adjustments.

Depression in mid-life. In her book *Unfinished Business*, Maggie Scarf (1980) draws attention to another difference between men and women in their mid-life development. Statistically, women are from two to six times more likely than men to suffer from depression. Depression can affect people of all ages, but it is most common among middle-aged women. In a survey conducted in New Haven (Boyd and Weissman, 1981), 7 percent of the women compared with 2.9 percent of the men aged forty to sixty-five years old suffered from depression. Scarf believes that the reason for this difference in rate of depression is cultural. She views depression as the byproduct of a traditional feminine sex-role stereotype. Early in life, young girls have been taught and encouraged to define themselves as worthwhile through their relationships with other people. They feel good when they establish connections with people and are taught to look to others for approval and to be dependent.

Thus, during the early years of a woman's life, she may derive a sense of personal worth from her roles of daughter, lover, wife, and mother. These relationships change as children grow, parents die, or marriages fail. Some women begin to experience a sense of loss and personal worthlessness. They may see themselves as failures compared with their husbands, who have experienced successes in their careers. Some women in their fifties find that the nature of their marriage changes when they no longer have to focus their attention on the needs of their children. The prospect of giving up the traditional role of a dependent wife for a more independent role may be unsettling for a while, especially for those women who have spent a lifetime living according to a sex-role stereotype. Once those women become accustomed to their new role, however, many find that they enjoy the freedom that middle adulthood brings.

OLD AGE

The fear of growing old is probably one of the most common fears in our society. We are surrounded with indications that aging and old age are negative—or at best something to ridicule. Birthday cards make light of aging; comedians joke about it. Advertisements urge us to trade in older products for the newer, faster model. We retire older workers—whether or not they want to retire—and replace them with younger people. Many of us do not even want to use the word "old"; instead, we refer to "golden agers," "senior citizens," and the like.

Many of our attitudes about aging are based on the **decremental model of aging**, which holds that progressive physical and mental decline is inevitable with age. In other words, chronological age is what makes people "old." In fact, there are great differences in physical condition among the elderly, depending on their genetic makeup and environment. Many of us know people who are eighty and look and act fifty, and vice versa. The prevalence of the decremental view in our society can be explained in part by ignorance and a lack of contact with older people. The result is a climate of prejudice against the old. One researcher, Butler, has coined the word **ageism** to refer to this prejudice. As with racism and sexism, ageism feeds on myths rather than facts.

Young people tend to believe that the old suffer from poor health, live in poverty, and are frequent victims of crime. But the elderly seldom see these as personal problems, though, interestingly, they tend to think of them as problems for other older people (Harris, 1975).

The notion that the aged tend to withdraw from life and sit around doing nothing is also very common. But this too is a false picture. Dr. Benjamin Spock, Ronald Reagan, and Jessica Tandy are good examples of active older Americans, and many lesser known older people follow their lead. In fact, the majority of older Americans work or wish to work either for pay or as volunteers.

FACT or FICTION

The elderly need more sleep than younger adults.

Fiction. Studies show that as people progress from adulthood to old age, their need for sleep generally decreases. However, sleep efficiency declines rapidly with age. Sleep in elderly people is more disrupted and fragmented, so they need to spend more time in bed and take naps to get their required sleep. To the casual observer, the elderly appear to sleep longer.

Figure 10.6
Many of our society's stereotyped attitudes about the elderly are not valid. Old people do not always become senile; they are not necessarily resistant to change; and they are not useless.

Alzheimer's Disease. Alzheimer's disease is a common affliction among the elderly. Although extremely rare in people under fifty, Alzheimer's strikes roughly 2 percent of those over sixty-five and more than 10 percent of those over eighty.

Alzheimer's is a neurological disease marked by a gradual deterioration of cognitive functioning. Early signs of the disease include frequent forgetting, poor judgment, increased irritability, and social withdrawal. Eventually, Alzheimer's patients lose their ability to comprehend simple questions and to recognize friends and loved ones. Ultimately, they require constant supervision and custodial care. Rarely do patients die from the disease itself, but their weakened state leaves them vulnerable to a variety of other potentially fatal problems.

Little is known about the cause of Alzheimer's. Some recent research suggests a genetic component, though this is not conclusive.

At present there is no cure for the disease. Many patients and their caretakers (usually their families) are offered supportive therapy that helps them learn to accept the relentless progression of the disease and the limitations it imposes on its victims.

Changes in Health

Most people over sixty-five are in reasonably good health. Physical strength and the five senses do decline, of course, but 80 percent of the elderly are able to carry out their normal activities. (Fifteen percent are unable to do so, and 5 percent are in institutions.) For the most part, the health of an older person is related to his or her health when younger. Good health in adolescence and adult life carries over into old age.

All people, young and old, are subject to disease, though. About 40 percent of the elderly have at least one chronic disease (a permanent disability as opposed to an acute or temporary disability more common with younger people). The four most prevalent chronic diseases—heart disease, hypertension, diabetes, and arthritis—tend to afflict women more than men. In general, the major causes of death among the old are heart disease, strokes, and cancer.

The quality of health care for the elderly remains by and large inferior to that of the general population. The elderly in the lower socioeconomic class tend not to take care of themselves or to seek out treatment when needed. Many doctors prefer to administer to younger patients with acute diseases rather than to older patients with long-term chronic conditions that can only be stabilized, not cured. Some doctors hold stereotypical views of the aged that can lead to misdiagnosis and improper treatment.

More than one million old people who are no longer able to care for themselves live in institutions. Unfortunately, too many of these nursing homes have inadequate facilities. As more and more people each year reach late adulthood, it is paramount that there be a general overhaul of health care treatment and facilities for the elderly.

Changes in Life Situation

For younger people, transitions in life—graduation, marriage, parenthood—are usually positive and create a deeper involvement in life. In late adulthood, transitions—retirement, widowhood—are often negative and reduce responsibilities and increase isolation. Perhaps the most devastating transition is the loss of a spouse. Over 50 percent of women and 20 percent of men are widowed by the age of fifty-six. And by the age of eighty, one-third of men and seven out of ten women are alone (Stevens-Long, 1979). All too often, the person loses not just a spouse but the support of friends and family, who cannot cope with the widowed person's grief or feel threatened by the survivor's new status as a single person.

The loss of self-esteem that comes with retirement and a diminished role in the community, or the grief over the loss of a spouse, can bring on a deep depression. Suicide rates among the elderly continue to be high in the United States (McIntosh and Hubbard, 1988) and in other countries such as Germany (Erlemeir, 1988) and Australia (Hassan and Carr, 1989). Of this group, white males have the highest suicide rate. One reason for this may be that a white male who has defined himself by his career and its prestige may find retirement and aging particularly difficult (Papalia and Olds, 1989). Many elderly people who attempt suicide do so through nonviolent means, including self-starvation or noncompliance with medical reg-imens, such as taking too much or too little medicine. This phenomenon is called **silent suicide**. These silent suicides are often ruled natural deaths. Thus, there are probably even more suicides among the elderly than are re-ported (McIntosh and Hubbard, 1988). Warning signs for suicide among those who are seventy-five and older include diminished physical energy, odd behavior, the appearance of problems with daily functioning, persis-tent refusal of food and liquids, lack of strong family support, loneliness, social isolation, and withdrawal (Brant and Osgood, 1990).

Unfortunately, the elderly receive only 2 percent of the available psychi-atric services. To some extent, this is a result of societal attitudes toward old people. The adjustment and emotional problems of the old are often viewed by mental health personnel as natural and unavoidable results of aging. The same symptoms in younger people would more likely receive at-tention and treatment (Butler, 1963).

Emotional Development.   There is a commonly held belief that as people age, they change emotionally. Accordingly, some people become "crotchety" or "ornery," while others "mellow" with age. Is this true? Psychologists (Malatesta and Kalnok, 1984) have found that one aspect of emotion, **emo-tional experience**, what we actually feel inside ourselves at any time, re-mains stable throughout adult life. However, **emotional expression**, how we externalize our emotions, may change. As we develop, we learn that in certain situations we should not express how we feel. For example, if some-one has promised you fifty-yard-line tickets to a football game and later tells you they are all sold out, you might feel angry or disappointed. These feel-ings constitute your emotional experience and are likely to stay the same as you get older. However, how you express these feelings will change. A younger person, concerned with convention, would probably mask these feelings with a "Thanks for trying" response. In contrast, an elderly person is likely to be less concerned with **display rules**, societal conventions or what other people think. As a result, an elderly man might express his emo-tions more openly and yell at the person who has disappointed him. Thus, the way people express their emotions does change with age.

Life Review Process.   At some point during old age, people begin to re-view their lives. This process can be rational and systematic or dreamlike in nature (Fitch, 1985). In general, the elderly stop thinking in terms of fresh starts or new directions. Rather, they are concerned with evaluating the decisions they have made in life that have brought them to the present point. The life review process can become all-consuming and take on an importance that makes the "here and now" seem irrelevant. This review helps the elderly get their lives in order. They think through significant re-lationships, justify decisions, and "make peace" with those, living or dead, with whom they may have had conflicts. This task can be so engrossing that the person may seem disoriented while engaging in it. The life review process may also be emotionally draining, causing anxiety, guilt, and even depression. Naomi Feil (1985) has suggested that conventional attempts to reorient people during this process are not constructive. Instead, she says,

Growing Old in Japan

The Japanese view of aging is markedly different from that in the United States. In contrast to the old in America, the elderly in Japan occupy a position of honor. In part, this respect for age is based on ancient social and religious traditions not readily adaptable to our culture. But there are specific Japanese programs and practices that we might well import.

Old people in the United States may not be given much respect because they often lack status. Strongly encouraged to leave their jobs at sixty-five, many then occupy the lower rungs of the economic ladder. In Japan the able-bodied continue to work or to help their families in the home. In addition, they are guaranteed a minimum income, receive free annual health examinations, and are eligible for completely free medical care after age seventy. We could benefit by following Japan's lead here, especially in providing more job opportunities for the aged.

We Americans might also profit by copying the Japanese example of fully integrating the elderly in our daily lives. In Japan 75 percent of the old live with their children, as opposed to only 25 percent in the United States. For those who do live alone, the Japanese have established programs to assure that they receive daily visits or calls. To encourage the active involvement of all older citizens in social activities, the government subsidizes Elders Clubs and sports programs. Through these programs the aged supply each other with mutual support and gain a sense of self-pride.

For more details, see Erdman Palmore, "What Can the USA Learn from Japan about Aging?" in S. H. Zarit (ed.), *Readings in Aging and Death: Contemporary Perspectives.* New York: Harper & Row, 1977.

we must validate the feelings that are being confronted by helping the person express emotions and thoughts. Individuals going through this life review process need an empathetic and nonjudgmental listener.

Financial Resources. Most of the elderly have incomes of only half their preretirement income. Although the public believes that the lack of money is a major problem for the old, only 15 percent of the elderly find it a personal problem (Kalish, 1977). Yet even though the percentage is smaller than many of us may have thought, it still indicates that lack of money is a problem for many of the elderly. Those who are living alone and without family are in the most precarious position. Of course, many old people do not stop working because they want to; quite frequently workers who are forced to retire would rather continue working. Societal prejudice against hiring and retaining people over the normal retirement years will no doubt change as the life span of the general population increases.

Changes in Mental Functioning

As people age, there are also changes in many of the mental functions they use, although there is much less decline in intelligence and memory than people assume. If you compare measures of intellectual ability for a group of elderly people with similar measures for younger people, you might see a difference—namely, that older people do not score as well on intellectual tests. However, the older group of people will most likely be less educated and less familiar with taking tests than younger people. Furthermore, there are many different types of mental skills and abilities that combine to produce intellectual functioning, and these abilities do not develop at the same rate or time across the life span.

John Horn (1979) has proposed two types of intelligence, *crystallized* and *fluid* intelligence. Crystallized intelligence refers to the ability to use accumulated knowledge and learning in appropriate situations. This ability increases with age and experience, showing no decline in older adulthood. Fluid intelligence is the ability to solve abstract relational problems and to generate new hypotheses. This ability is not tied to schooling or education and gradually increases in development as the nervous system matures. As people age and their nervous systems decline, so does their fluid intelligence. A decline in the nervous system affects reaction time, visual motor flexibility, and memory. Thus, older people may not be as good at problems that require them to combine and generate new information or ideas. However, with practice, the elderly can enhance their abilities to master fluid-intelligence tasks (Baltes, Sowarka, and Kliegl, 1989).

The ability of older people to remember and think clearly may also vary with their environment. B. F. Skinner maintained that older people do not receive as much reinforcement from the environment for their mental and verbal behaviors as younger people do and so decline in their performance (Skinner and Vaughn, 1983). As they age, elderly people become less motivated to use their mental faculties. Recognizing the ways in which one's thinking is influenced by the circumstances of aging is a necessary first step toward changing these circumstances.

At age seventy-nine, Skinner wrote a book entitled *Enjoy Old Age* in which he suggested some practical ways to change one's environment to increase mental performance. One technique he used to improve his memory of new ideas was to carry a pocket notebook in which he wrote down a thought as he had it. Later, he did not have to search his memory, but merely flipped open his notebook for recall. To avoid the embarrassment and unpleasantness of not remembering a person's name, he suggested appealing graciously to age and accepting this shortcoming. He recommended that to avoid getting sidetracked in a discussion by an interruption, the older person should rehearse or make mental notes of what is to be said. Just as physical abilities decline with physical fatigue, mental abilities decline with mental fatigue. Skinner suggested that older people should protect themselves from mental fatigue by taking leisurely breaks in their mental activity and by working fewer hours a day on thought-related tasks.

DEATH AND DYING

Should terminally ill patients be told they are going to die? What are the consequences for the family, the hospital staff, and the patient if the patient is informed? What if the patient is not informed? In their book *Awareness of Dying* (1965), Barney Glaser and Anselm Strauss look at these issues and their effects on dying patients, their families, and hospital staffs. Very often physicians decide not to tell patients that they are dying. Glaser and Strauss have called this *closed awareness*; the staff and family are aware of a patient's condition but the patient is not. Doctors often prefer this alternative because it minimizes demands on them. The patient's family and friends frequently support this decision because they are unable to confront the fact of death. Even when they are not informed, however, some patients begin to suspect that their illness is terminal. At this point, *suspected awareness*, they try to find out from the staff or their families whether their suspicions are correct.

If the patient does discover the seriousness of the illness, the hospital staff has two alternatives. They may pretend with the patient that neither knows that the disease is terminal *(mutual pretense awareness)*, or they may openly acknowledge its gravity and perhaps even discuss the condition with the patient *(open awareness)*. Nurses often prefer to be completely frank with patients from the start to avoid the distrust that sometimes develops when patients suspect they are dying but cannot discover the truth. The trend today is to inform patients of their condition, with the hospital staff given some discretion as to how much information to reveal.

Once patients have been informed of their condition, they must then cope with a truth that few of us want to face. Elisabeth Kübler-Ross (1969) has done some pioneer work on how the terminally ill react to their impending death. Her investigations have made a major contribution to the new field of **thanatology**—the study of death and dying. Based on interviews with 200 dying patients, she has identified five stages of psychological adjustment. The first stage is *denial*. People's most common reaction to learning that they have a terminal illness is shock and numbness, followed by denial. They react by saying, "No, it can't be happening to me." They may assert that the doctors are incompetent or the diagnosis mistaken. In extreme cases, people may refuse treatment and persist in going about business as usual. Most patients who use denial extensively throughout their illness are people who have become accustomed to coping with difficult life situations in this way. Indeed, the denial habit may contribute to the seriousness of a condition. For example, a person might refuse to seek medical attention at the onset of the illness, denying that it exists.

During the second stage, *anger*, the reaction of dying people is "Why me?" They feel anger—at fate, at God, at the powers that be, at every person who comes into their life. They resent the healthy, particularly those who must care for them. They are angry at others for perceiving them as dying. At this stage, they are likely to alienate themselves from others, for no one can relieve the anger they feel at their shortened life span.

During the stage of *bargaining*, people change their attitude and attempt to bargain with fate. For example, a woman may ask God for a certain amount of time in return for good behavior. She may promise a change of ways, even a dedication of her life to the church. She may announce that she is ready to settle for a less threatening form of the same illness and begin to bargain with the doctor over the diagnosis. This stage is relatively short and is followed by the stage of *depression*.

USING PSYCHOLOGY

Hospices

Death is one of the few taboos left in twentieth-century America. The breakdown of extended families and the rise of modern medicine have insulated most people in our society from death. Many people have no direct experience with death, and, partly as a result, they are afraid to talk about it. In 1900, two-thirds of those who died in the United States were under fifty, and most of them died at home in their own beds. Today, most Americans live until at least seventy-five, and many die in nursing homes and hospitals. Elaborate machines may prolong existence long after a person has stopped living a normal life.

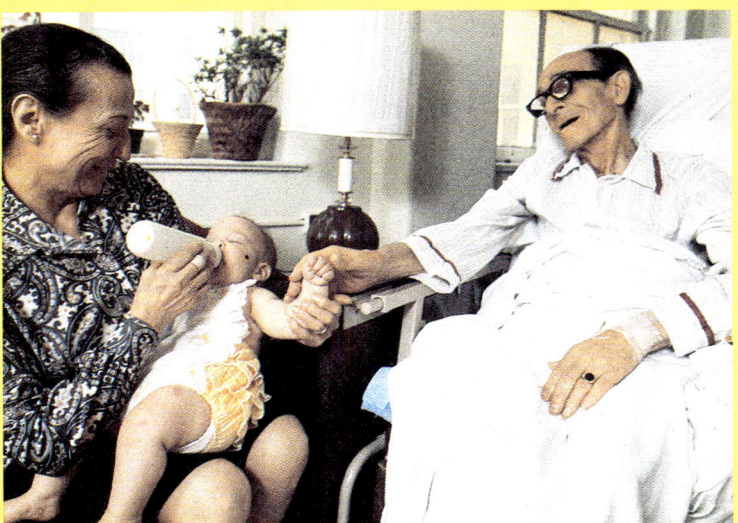

Figure 10.7
A hospice patient during a visit
with his family.

A new movement to restore the dignity of dying revolves around the concept of the hospice—usually a special place where terminally ill people go to die. The hospice is designed to make the patient's surroundings pleasant and comfortable—less like a hospital and more like a home. Doctors in hospices do not try to prolong life but to improve the quality of life. A key component of hospice care is the use of tranquilizers and other drugs to ease discomfort and relieve pain.

The patient in a hospice leads the most normal life he or she is able to and is taken care of as much as possible by family members. If it can be arranged, a patient may choose to die at home.

The first and most famous hospice facility was St. Christopher's Hospice in London, England, established in 1967 to treat terminally ill cancer patients. In 1974, the first hospice in the United States was established in New Haven, Connecticut, and the numbers have grown since.

Currently, there are hundreds of operational hospice programs in the United States. Although the availability of these programs is limited, a great deal of progress has been made in recent years. Some private insurance plans have added coverage for hospice care, and Medicare now pays hospice expenses. Most programs still depend on the help of a family member or friend to provide for the daily care of the dying person. Nonetheless, the hospice movement has helped to change many Americans' attitudes toward death.

During depression dying people are aware of the losses they are incurring (for example, loss of body tissue, loss of job, loss of life savings). Also, they are depressed about the loss that is to come: they are in the process of losing everything and everybody. Kübler-Ross suggests that it is helpful to allow such people to express their sadness and not to attempt to cover up the situation or force them to act cheerfully.

Finally, patients *accept* death. The struggle is over and they experience a sense of calm. At this point, they are tired and weak and sleep often. In some cases, the approach of death feels appropriate or peaceful. Patients may limit the number of people they will see and may not have much interest in matters of the world. They seem to become detached intentionally so as to make death easier.

Not all terminal patients progress through the stages Kübler-Ross describes. For example, a person may die in the denial stage because he or she is psychologically unable to proceed beyond it or because the course of the illness does not grant the necessary time to do so. Kübler-Ross notes that patients do not limit their responses to any one stage; a depressed patient may have recurring bursts of anger. She notes, too, that all patients in all stages persist in feeling hope. Even the most accepting and realistic patients leave open the possibility that they may live after all.

The Right to Die

In recent years, a great controversy has developed over the individual's right to control his or her own death. Diane, a woman with leukemia, chose not to undergo a painful course of chemotherapy that had little chance of succeeding. In addition, she wanted to avoid the long, painful dying process that doctors had told her she would experience. She decided to commit suicide and persuaded a doctor to provide her with the necessary pills (Altman, 1991). The doctor, who wrote about this case in a medical journal, is guilty of **euthanasia**. When an incurably ill person is killed, helped to commit suicide, or allowed to die by nonintervention or withdrawal of medical help, euthanasia is being committed.

Do people who suffer from terminal illnesses have a right to die when they choose? This controversial issue is further complicated by the fact that sick people often need help to take their own lives. In a recent case, a doctor in Michigan hooked up a suicide apparatus to a woman with Alzheimer's disease. The woman initiated her own death by pressing a button, but the doctor watched her as she did it. Was he performing an act of mercy or murder?

Those in favor of euthanasia argue that people have a right to die with dignity and to avoid as much pain as possible. Medical technology allows many people to be kept alive artificially with no apparent benefit to themselves. Is it necessary to keep people's bodies alive when it is clear they have no awareness or ability to experience life away from extremely restrictive hospital machinery?

People who are against euthanasia ask how one can be sure that a person really wants to die or that every hope or avenue for recovery is really gone. Once we start allowing euthanasia, people will become too casual about it. Perhaps doctors will stop exploring all possible avenues of recovery. Most major religious groups also oppose euthanasia.

It is clear that people on both sides of this controversy have raised legitimate issues. In a 1989 poll that asked whether the life of the terminally ill should be prolonged by machine, a majority said no (Papalia and Olds, 1989). Washington State is considering a law that would allow doctors to help patients die. Doctors, who have traditionally stood by their oath to heal, are recognizing the dilemma and discussing the issues surrounding euthanasia. One important factor is how well the doctor knows the patient. Is this a genuine decision to die, a passing expression of depression, or even a plea for reassurance that the sick person is still valued? The doctor who helped Diane insisted that she be counseled by a psychologist, and he interviewed members of her family. These procedures may be a way to ensure that a patient's request to die is legitimate (Altman, 1991).

To protect themselves, some individuals draw up **living wills** that outline their wishes in case they become incapacitated. (The majority of states have living will statutes.) In a living will, individuals might state that they do not want to be kept alive by artificial means if they become hopelessly paralyzed or comatose. They can also request medication that relieves pain, even if it contributes to an earlier death. Some people name a friend or relative to act on their behalf in making decisions about medical treatment if they are no longer capable (Papalia and Olds, 1989).

Euthanasia will continue to be a debated topic in the future. The issue of dying is being considered by more people at a younger age. Further experience with new medical technology and with the terminally ill who insist on controlling the way they die will help determine how our society deals with death and dying in the future.

CHAPTER REVIEW

KEY TERMS

- ageism
- crowded nest syndrome
- decremental model of aging
- display rules
- emotional experience
- emotional expression
- euthanasia
- generativity
- life events perspective
- living will
- menopause
- silent suicide
- stagnation
- thanatology

SUMMARY

1. Until recently psychologists knew very little about adulthood. Most studies and theories concentrated on childhood and adolescence. Recent work indicates that middle age involves many changes and important transitions. Part of a successful adjustment to middle age is the satisfactory fulfillment of specific developmental tasks.

2. The physical changes of middle age are slow and gradual. Strength and stamina decline, appearance changes, and the senses require increasingly more stimulation. Two of the most common health problems are heart disease and cancer.

3. The popular picture of dramatic physical changes at menopause and decreasing sexual desire in middle age is greatly exaggerated. Intellectual ability also remains fairly constant throughout middle age.

4. Daniel Levinson has proposed the following stages in the lives of adult males: entering the adult world (ages twenty-two to twenty-eight), the age-thirty crisis, settling down (mid-thirties to forty), the mid-life transition (ages forty to forty-five), and middle adulthood (ages fifty to sixty).

5. For many women, the "empty nest" syndrome—the feeling of loss experienced when children leave home—is not a reality. Women may view this period as one of the happiest in their lives. A trend opposite to the empty nest syndrome is the crowded nest syndrome. This occurs when grown children move back into their parents' home and the parent-child relationship must be reassessed.

6. Some women who have chosen family and home over a career feel dissatisfied with their lives when they reach mid-life. As more and more women have the opportunity to choose both, this may no longer be true.

7. Many of our beliefs about the aging process are based on the decremental model of aging, which holds that progressive physical and mental decline is inevitable with age. There are also many myths about old age that influence our views and treatment of the elderly.

8. The best predictor of happiness in old age is good health. And good health is related to the health of the person when he or she was younger.

9. The elderly face changes in many areas of their lives—retirement, death of spouse and friends, reduced income—but many old people manage to adjust and continue to be happy and active.

10. Elisabeth Kübler-Ross has identified five stages of psychological adjustment to death: denial, anger, bargaining, depression, and acceptance.

11. A hospice is a special place where terminally ill patients go to die. Quality of life is the main consideration in a hospice.

12. Euthanasia occurs when an incurably ill person is killed, helped to commit suicide, or allowed to die by nonintervention or withdrawal of medical help.

CHAPTER REVIEW

REVIEW QUESTIONS

1. In what ways are adulthood and adolescence similar stages of development?

2. What physical changes occur during adulthood? What are the more common health problems of adulthood?

3. What changes occur in intellectual abilities during adulthood? In what ways are adults better able to perform mental activities?

4. What are Levinson's stages of adulthood? What occurs in each?

5. What is the "mid-life transition"? What problems do men face during this transition?

6. List and summarize three mid-life problems adult women face.

7. Describe how the "decremental model of aging" leads to prejudiced attitudes toward the aged ("ageism").

8. What health problems do the elderly face? How many are able to lead normal lives? How many have a chronic illness? How does their sexual behavior change?

9. What kinds of life transitions or changes do the elderly face?

10. Describe the different levels of awareness at which terminally ill persons can view their condition. Which do you think is the best approach?

11. What are Kübler-Ross's five stages of psychological adjustment to death?

12. What is a hospice? How does a hospice differ from a typical hospital? What is one of the key components of hospice care?

13. What is euthanasia? What are some arguments in favor of euthanasia? What are some arguments against it?

ACTIVITIES

1. Interview an adult who is over fifty years old. Ask this person to describe himself or herself physically, socially, intellectually, and emotionally at the ages of twenty, thirty, forty, and fifty. Before the interview, list specific questions that would elicit this information. Ask which age was his or her favorite and why.

2. In this chapter, it is suggested that self-esteem is vulnerable when it is based on only one aspect of identity—physical attractiveness. List other aspects of identity on which one could base his or her self-esteem in order to strengthen it.

3. If someone were to ask you, "What can I do to stay mentally, emotionally, and physically young as long as possible?" what would you tell this person?

4. What provisions does your community make for its retired and elderly adults? How do you think these services could be improved to make the experience of old age a more fruitful and happier time? What services could the elderly provide to your community?

5. Death and dying have only recently become topics that are discussed openly. Given this growing openness, what changes do you see being made to make the adjustment to the prospect of dying less severe? What kinds of programs could hospitals and homes for the aged implement to help people make this adjustment?

6. List several controversial questions, such as "Do you believe in fighting for your country no matter what the circumstances?" Ask people of different age groups to respond to your questions. Do you notice differences in the levels of reasoning? Use the explanations contained in this chapter and your own thoughts to account for the differences.

Figure 11.1 Psychologists who study personality explore what makes people think, feel, and act differently.

Objectives: After studying this chapter, you should be able to
- identify the nature and aims of personality theory.
- compare and contrast the personality theories discussed in this chapter.

Instant Personality Analysis and Astrology

Suppose someone handed you an astrological reading and told you it was specially written for you. Would you believe it? According to several studies, you probably would.

Subjects who were shown general personality assessments, which could have been written for almost anyone, readily believed they were prepared just for them. Believers—both men and women alike—rated the accuracy of the description at approximately 4.5 on a scale of 1 to 5, with 5 being the highest rating.

Researchers also found that the more personal facts an individual believes are used to compile a personality description, the greater his or her faith in its accuracy. Thus, an individual who thinks a horoscope is based on the year, month, and day of birth is more likely to believe its description than someone who thinks no personal information was used at all.

Our willingness to accept general descriptions of ourselves as accurate may be due to the universal human failing of being a bit too gullible. This is especially true when the words we hear are filled with praise.

For more details, see C. R. Snyder and Randee Jane Shenkel, ''The P. T. Barnum Effect,'' *Psychology Today,* March 1975.

everyone recognizes that we need to grow and change, individually and collectively. But what are the proper goals of growth and change? How can we cope with the inevitable conflicts of life?

Personality psychologists attempt to answer these questions with systematic theories about human behavior. These theories are used to guide research; and research, in turn, can test parts of a theory to see whether they are right or wrong. Thus, while we all have our pet theories about why people act certain ways, formal personality theories try to make such ideas more scientific by stating them very precisely and then testing them.

Psychology is still a very young science, and these tests have just begun. There are now many conflicting theories of personality, each with its friends and foes. In this chapter, we will describe four major schools of thought among personality theorists.

Psychoanalytic theories, developed by Sigmund Freud and his followers, emphasize the importance of motives hidden deep in the unconscious. B. F. Skinner and the behaviorists study the way rewards and punishments shape our actions. Humanistic theorists, like Abraham Maslow and Carl Rogers, emphasize human potential for growth, creativity, and spontaneity. Finally, trait theorists, like Gordon Allport and Raymond Cattell, stress the importance of understanding basic personality characteristics such as friendliness and aggression.

Each of the theorists we will discuss has a different image of human nature. What they have in common is a concern with understanding the differences among people.

PSYCHOANALYTIC THEORIES

Charming, spacious, homelike 1 rm. apts. Modern kitchenette. Hotel service. Weekly rats available.

—from classified advertisement, *New York Times*

This advertisement was received and typeset by someone at the *Times*. The person who set the ad probably did not leave the "e" out of "rate" deliberately, but was it just an innocent mistake?

Slips like these are common. People usually laugh at them, even if they are meaningful. But sometimes they are disturbing. Everyone has had the experience of making some personal remark that hurt a friend and has later asked himself, "Why did I say that? I didn't mean it." Yet, when he thinks about it, he may realize that he was angry at his friend and wanted to "get back" at him.

Sigmund Freud: Psychosexuality and the Unconscious

It was Sigmund Freud who first suggested that the little slips that people make, the things they mishear, and the odd misunderstandings they have are not really mistakes at all. Freud believed there was something behind these mistakes, even though people claimed they were just accidental and quickly corrected themselves. Similarly, when he listened to people describe their dreams, he believed the dreams had some meaning, even though the people who dreamed them did not know what they meant.

Freud was a physician who practiced in Vienna in the early 1900s. Since he specialized in nervous diseases, a great many people talked to him about their private lives, their conflicts, fears, and desires. At that time most people thought, as many still do, that we are aware of all our motives and feelings. But Freud reasoned that if people can say and dream things without knowing their meaning, they must not know as much about themselves as they think they do. After years of study he concluded that some of the most powerful influences on human personality are things we are *not* conscious of.

Freud was the first modern psychologist to suggest that every personality has a large **unconscious** component. Life includes both pleasurable and painful experiences. For Freud, experiences include feelings and thoughts as well as actual events. Freud believed that many of our experiences, particularly the painful episodes of childhood, are forgotten or buried in the unconscious. But although we may not consciously recall these experiences, they continue to influence our behavior. For example, a child who never fully pleases his demanding mother or father may feel unhappy much of the time and will doubt his abilities to succeed and to be loved. As an adult, the person may suffer from feelings of unworthiness and low self-esteem, despite his very real abilities. Freud believed that unconscious motives and the feelings people experience as children have an enormous impact on adult personality and behavior.

Freud concluded that some of the most powerful influences on human personality are things we are not conscious of.

The Id, Ego, and Superego

Freud tried to explain human personality by saying that it was a kind of energy system—like a steam engine or an electric dynamo. The energy in human personality comes from two kinds of powerful drives, the life drives and the death drives. Freud theorized that all of life moves toward death, and that the desire for a final end shows up in human personality as destructiveness and aggression. But the life instincts were more important in Freud's theory, and he saw them primarily as erotic or pleasure-seeking urges.

By 1923 Freud had described what became known as the structural components of the mind: id, ego, and superego (Figure 11.2). Though Freud often spoke of them as if they were actual parts of the personality, he introduced and regarded them simply as a *model* of how the mind works. In other words, the id, ego, and superego do not refer to actual portions of the brain. Instead, they explain how the mind functions and how the instinctual energies are regulated.

In Freud's theory the **id** is the reservoir or container of the instinctual urges. It is the lustful or drive-ridden part of the unconscious. The id seeks immediate gratification of desires, regardless of the consequences.

The personality process that is mostly conscious is called the **ego**. The ego is the rational, thoughtful, realistic personality process. For example, if

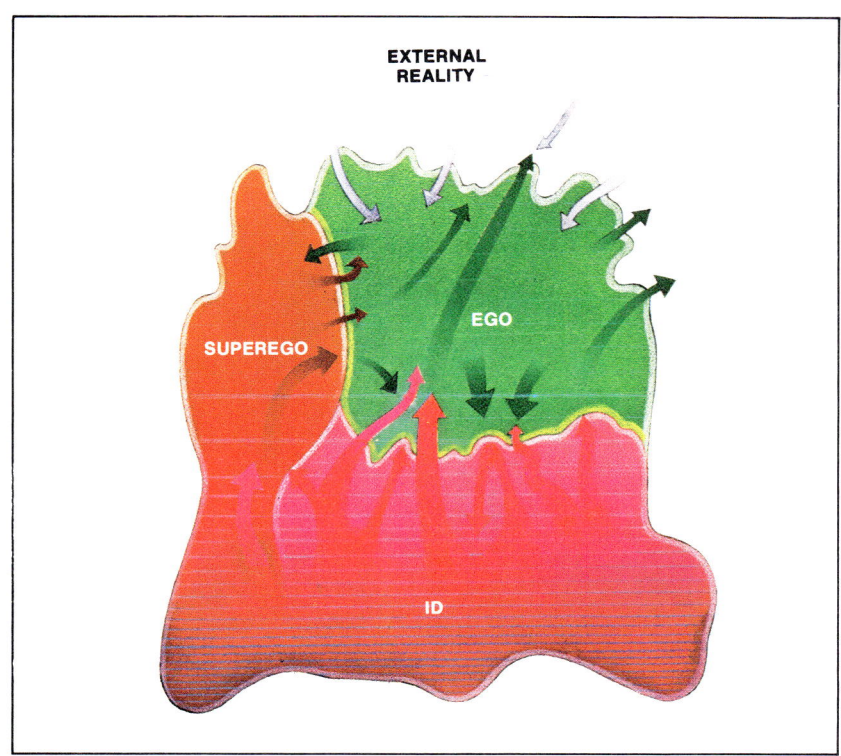

Figure 11.2
A visual interpretation of the Freudian theory of personality structure. The ego tries to balance the id's desires against the superego's demands and the realities of the world. In doing this it sometimes suppresses the irrational tendencies of the id, but it may also be able to deflect the id's energy into channels acceptable to both the superego and the outside world. These interactions and conflicts are represented by arrows in the figure.

a person is hungry, the id might drive her to seek immediate satisfaction by dreaming of food or by eating all the available food at once instead of keeping some of it for a later time. The ego would recognize that the body needs real food and that it will continue to need food in the future; it would use the id's energy to preserve some of the food available now and to look for ways of finding more.

Suppose you thought of stealing the desired food from someone else. The part of the personality that would stop you is called the **superego.** The id is concerned with what the person *wants* to do and the ego is concerned with planning what she *can* do; the superego is concerned with what she *should* do. It is the moral part of the personality, the source of conscience and of high ideals. But the superego can also create conflicts and problems. It is sometimes overly harsh, like a very strict parent. The superego, then, is also the source of guilt feelings which come from serious as well as mild deviations from what it defines as "right."

The id and the superego frequently come into conflict with each other. Because neither is concerned with reality, they may both come into conflict with the outside world as well. Freud saw the ego as part of the person that must resolve these conflicts. Somehow, the ego must find a realistic way to satisfy the demands of the id without offending the superego. If the id is not satisfied, the person feels an intolerable tension of longing or anger or desire. If the superego is not obeyed, the person feels guilty and inferior. And if outside reality is ignored, the person suffers such outcomes as starvation or dislike by other people (Freud, 1943).

Defense Mechanisms

The ego's job is so difficult that unconsciously all people resort to psychological defenses. Rather than face intense frustration, conflict, or feelings of unworthiness, people deceive themselves into believing nothing is wrong. If the demands of the id and the ego cannot be resolved, it may be necessary to distort reality. Freud called these techniques **defense mechanisms** because they defend the ego from experiencing anxiety about failing in its tasks (Figure 11.3). Freud felt that these defense mechanisms stem mainly from the unconscious part of the ego, and only ordinarily become conscious to the individual during a form of psychotherapy called psychoanalysis.

To some degree, defense mechanisms are necessary to psychological well-being. They relieve intolerable confusion, help people to weather intense emotional crises, and give individuals time to work out problems they might not be able to solve if they allowed themselves to feel all the pressures at work within them. However, if a person resorts to defense mechanisms all or most of the time, continually deceiving himself and others about his true feelings and aspirations, he will avoid facing and solving his problems realistically. A few of the defense mechanisms Freud identified are discussed below.

Displacement. Displacement occurs when the object of an unconscious wish provokes anxiety. This anxiety is reduced when the ego unconsciously

Figure 11.3
Some of the defense mechanisms in Freud's theory. Projection is a person seeing ridiculous attributes of his own personality as though they were possessed by others. Repression is shown by a woman who is not only concealing and restraining a monstrous impulse but also trying to conceal from herself the fact that she is doing so. The displacement of a widow's love from her lost husband and family onto her pets is another common mechanism.

shifts the wish to another object. The energy of the id is **displaced** from one object to another, more accessible, object. For example, if you wanted to hit your father but were afraid to, you might hit your kid brother instead. Your poor brother gets slapped around partly because he reminds you of your father and partly because he's not as likely to hit back.

Repression. When a person has some thought or urge that causes the ego too much anxiety, she may push that thought or urge out of consciousness down into the unconscious. This process is called **repression.** The person simply "forgets" the thing that disturbs her, or pushes it out of awareness without ever realizing it. For example, a grown woman whose father is meddling in her life may have the impulse to say "I hate you, Dad." But the woman may feel so anxious and afraid about having such an impulse that she will come to believe—without realizing what she is doing—that what she feels is not hatred. She replaces the feeling with apathy, a feeling of not caring at all. She says, "I don't hate you. I have no special feelings at all about you." Nevertheless, the feelings of anger and hostility remain in the unconscious and may show themselves in cutting remarks or sarcastic jokes, slips of the tongue, or dreams.

Reaction Formation. **Reaction formation** involves replacing an unacceptable feeling or urge with its opposite. For example, a divorced father may resent having his child for the weekend. Unconsciously, he feels it is terribly wrong for a father to react that way, so he showers the child with expressions of love, toys, and exciting trips. A woman who finds her powerful ambitions unacceptable may play the role of a weak, helpless, passive female who wants nothing more than to please the men in her life—unconsciously covering up her true feelings.

Projection. Another way the ego avoids anxiety is to believe that impulses coming from within are really coming from other people. For example, a boy who is extremely jealous of his girl friend but does not want to admit to himself that he is threatened by her independence may claim, "I'm not jealous—she's the one who's always asking where I've been, who was that girl I was talking to . . ." This mechanism is called **projection** because inner feelings are thrown, or projected, outside. It is a common mechanism, which you have probably observed in yourself from time to time. Many people, for example, feel that others dislike them, when in reality they dislike themselves.

Regression. **Regression** means going back to an earlier and less mature pattern. When a person is under severe pressure and his other defenses are not working, he may start acting in ways that helped him in the past. For example, he may throw a temper tantrum, make faces, cry loudly, or revert to eating and sleeping all the time the way he did as a small child. If you have ever been tempted to stick out your lower lip and pout when you know that you should really accept the fact that you cannot have your own way, you have experienced regression.

The recognition of the tremendous forces that exist in human personality and the difficulty of controlling and handling them was Freud's great contribution to understanding human life. After Freud, it became easier to understand why human life contains so much conflict. It is a matter, Freud thought, of a savage individual coming to terms with the rules of society. The id is the savage part, and the superego, the representative of society. In a healthy person the ego, the "I," is strong enough to handle the struggle (see Hall, 1954).

Freud was also the first psychologist to claim that infancy and childhood were critical times for forming a person's basic character structure. He felt that personality was well formed by the time the child entered school and that subsequent growth consisted of elaborating this basic structure. (We described Freud's theory of the stages of development in Chapter 8.)

Evaluating Freud's Contribution

Freud was the first major social scientist to propose a unified theory to understand and explain human behavior. No theory that has followed has been more complete or more complex. But his ideas were controversial when they were proposed at the turn of the century, and they are controversial today. Some psychologists treat Freud's writings as a sacred text—if Freud said it, it must be so. At the other extreme, many have accused Freud of being unscientific—of proposing a theory that is too complex ever to be proved true or false.

In 1977, Seymour Fisher and Roger Greenberg published a book *(The Scientific Credibility of Freud's Theories and Therapy)* that summarized more than fifty years of research on Freud's ideas. Some parts of his theory held up well. For example, Freud believed that the male homosexual had an unusually close and intense involvement with his mother, while his relationship with his father was more likely to be characterized by distance, coldness, and conflict. To test this idea one psychologist (Ullman, 1960) asked groups of heterosexual and homosexual prisoners to describe their parents. He found that homosexuals were more likely to say that their mothers gave them "too much" love and affection while their fathers gave "too little." Many other studies of homosexuals pointed in the same direction.

Other Freudian beliefs were not supported by evidence. For example, psychoanalysis (a form of therapy Freud proposed in which a person spends years examining the unconscious basis of his problems) seems to be no more effective than other forms of psychotherapy that are simpler, cheaper, and less time-consuming.

Fisher and Greenberg concluded: "When we add up the totals from our research, balancing the positive against the negative, we find that Freud has fared rather well. But like all theorists, he has proved in the long run to have far from a perfect score. He seems to have been right about a respectable number of issues, but he was also wrong about some important things" (396).

In Freud's Footsteps: Jung and Adler

Freud's revolutionary ideas attracted many followers, and a number of these psychoanalysts came to develop important theories of their own.

At one time, Carl Jung was Freud's closest associate. But when Freud and Jung started to argue about psychoanalytic theory, their personal relationship became strained. Finally, they stopped speaking to each other entirely, a mere seven years after they met.

Jung disagreed with Freud on two major points. First, he took a more positive view of human nature, believing that people try to develop their potential as well as to handle their instinctual urges. Second, he distinguished between the personal unconscious (which was similar to Freud's idea of the unconscious) and the **collective unconscious,** which is a storehouse of instincts, urges, and memories of the entire human species down

Figure 11.4
Carl G. Jung. One of the most mystical and metaphysical of the pioneer theorists, Jung has had, until recently, a wider acceptance in Europe than in America.

Figure 11.5
Alfred Adler. Adler's writings on psychotherapy offer more optimism and practicality than those of Freud or Jung. His intuitive and common-sense approach to human life has greatly affected the thinking of psychologists throughout this century.

through history. He called these inherited, universal ideas **archetypes.** The same archetypes are present in every person. They reflect the common experiences of humanity with mothers, fathers, nature, war, and so on.

Jung went on to identify the archetypes by studying dreams and visions, paintings, poetry, folk stories, myths, and religions. He found that the same themes—the "archetypes"—appear again and again. For example, the story of Jack and the Beanstalk is essentially the same as the story of David and Goliath. Both tell how a small, weak, good person triumphs over a big, strong, bad person. Jung believed such stories are common and easy to understand because the situations they describe have occurred over and over again in human history and have been stored as archetypes in the unconscious of every human being (Jung, 1963).

Like Jung, Alfred Adler was an associate of Freud who left his teacher in the early part of this century to develop his own approach to personality. Adler believed that the driving force in people's lives is a desire to overcome their feelings of inferiority. Classic examples are Demosthenes, who overcame a speech impediment by practicing speaking with pebbles in his mouth and became the greatest orator of ancient Greece; Napoleon, a short man who conquered Europe in the early 1800s; and Glenn Cunningham, an Olympic runner who lost his toes in a fire as a child and had to plead with doctors who wanted to amputate his legs because they thought he would never be able to use them again.

Everyone struggles with inferiority, said Adler. He describes a person who continually tries to cover up and avoid feelings of inadequacy as having an **inferiority complex** (a term he introduced). Children first feel inferior because they are so little and so dependent on adults. Gradually they learn to do the things that older people can do. The satisfaction that comes from even such simple acts as walking or learning to use a spoon sets up a pattern of overcoming inadequacies, a pattern that lasts throughout life. Adler called these patterns *"life styles."*

Adler believed that the way parents treat their children has a great influence on the styles of life they choose. Overpampering, in which the parents attempt to satisfy the child's every whim, tends to produce a self-centered person who has little regard for others and who expects everyone else to do what he or she wants. On the other hand, the child who is neglected by his or her parents may seek revenge by becoming an angry, hostile person. Both the pampered and the neglected child tend to grow up into adults who lack confidence in their ability to meet the demands of life. Ideally, said Adler, a child should learn self-reliance and courage from his or her father and generosity and a feeling for others from his or her mother (Adler, 1959).

Although Jung and Adler were the first major figures to break with Freud, many others followed. Erich Fromm's theory centered around the need to belong and the loneliness freedom brings. Karen Horney stressed the importance of basic anxiety, which a child feels because she is helpless, and basic hostility, a resentment of one's parents that generally accompanies this anxiety (Figure 11.6). She also attacked several basic beliefs of Freud, including his emphasis on the importance of penis envy in the development of women. Erik Erikson accepted Freud's basic theory, but

Horney on Basic Anxiety and Hostility

The typical conflict leading to anxiety in a child is that between dependency on the parents . . . and hostile impulses against the parents. Hostility may be aroused in a child in many ways: by the parents' lack of respect for him; by unreasonable demands and prohibitions; by injustice; by unreliability; by suppression of criticism; by the parents dominating him and ascribing these tendencies to love. . . . If

a child, in addition to being dependent on his parents, is grossly or subtly intimidated by them and hence feels that any expression of hostile impulses against them endangers his security, then the existence of such hostile impulses is bound to create anxiety. . . . The resulting picture may look exactly like what Freud describes as the Oedipus complex: passionate clinging to one parent and jealousy toward

the other or toward anyone interfering with the claim of exclusive possession. . . . *But the dynamic structure of these attachments is entirely different from what Freud conceives as the Oedipus complex. They are an early manifestation of neurotic conflicts rather than a primarily sexual phenomenon.*

From Karen Horney, *The Neurotic Personality in Our Time.* New York: Norton, 1939.

Figure 11.6
Karen Horney on basic anxiety and hostility.

outlined eight psychosocial stages (described in Chapter 8) that every person goes through from birth to old age. These and other neo-Freudians have helped to keep psychoanalytic theory alive and growing.

BEHAVIORAL THEORIES

American psychology has long been dominated by the study of human and animal learning. In the 1940s, Yale psychologists John Dollard and Neal Miller used learning theory to analyze Freud's ideas, but behaviorists did not endorse Freud. **Behaviorism** holds that the proper subject matter of psychology is objectively observable behavior. Behaviorists believe that as individuals differ in their learning experiences, they acquire different behaviors and hence different personalities.

B. F. Skinner: Radical Behaviorism

Although his radical behaviorism was not proposed as a theory of personality, B. F. Skinner has had a major impact on personality theory. Skinner saw no need for a general concept of personality structure. He focused instead on precisely what causes a person to act in a specific way. This is a very pragmatic approach, concerned less with understanding behavior than with predicting it and controlling it.

Consider the case of Fred, a college sophomore who has been rather depressed lately. Freud might seek the roots of Fred's unhappiness in events in his childhood. Skinner's approach would be more direct. First, Skinner would reject the vague label "depressed." Instead, he would ask

Figure 11.7
B. F. Skinner. Skinner's pioneering work in behavioral psychology has resulted in a number of new therapeutic techniques that have been markedly successful in treating certain kinds of problems.

exactly how Fred behaves. The answer might be that Fred spends most of the day in his room, cuts classes, and rarely smiles or laughs.

Next, Skinner would try to understand the **contingencies of reinforcement**. What conditions are maintaining these behaviors? What reinforces Fred for never leaving his room? One hypothesis is that Fred's girlfriend Ethel has unintentionally reinforced this behavior by spending a lot of time with Fred, trying to cheer him up. Perhaps she didn't pay much attention to him before he was depressed. Note that Skinner's approach immediately suggests a hypothesis that can be proved true or false. If paying attention to Fred encourages his moroseness, then ignoring him should decrease the likelihood of this behavior. So Ethel might try ignoring Fred for a few days. If he then starts leaving his room, she has discovered the contingencies of reinforcement that govern Fred's behavior. If not, she will know that the hypothesis is wrong and can try something else. Perhaps Fred is glued to the TV in his room all day. Take away the TV and you will find out whether that is the reinforcer.

At first, radical behaviorism may seem to imply that Fred is somehow faking his depression so that he can watch "Hollywood Squares," see more of his girlfriend, or whatever. Skinner did not make this assumption. Fred may be entirely unaware of the rewards that are shaping his behavior. In any case, Fred's feelings are beside the point. What matters is not what's going on inside Fred's head, but what he is doing. The point is to specify his behavior and then find out what causes it.

Skinner's approach has become very popular among psychologists, partly because it is so pragmatic. It is a very action-oriented, very American approach: don't get all agitated about what's wrong; just jump in and try to fix it. It is true that radical behaviorism often works. Skinnerians have applied the techniques to a wide range of behaviors, from teaching pigeons to play Ping-Pong to teaching severely retarded people to dress themselves and take part in simple activities once believed beyond their abilities.

Normal people's behavior, too, can be changed with rewards and punishments, as every parent knows. The success of radical behaviorists with normal people has been more limited, partly because our reinforcers are so complex. For example, in several studies juvenile delinquents have been placed in rehabilitation communities in which they are rewarded (with special privileges or food) for behaving in certain ways—taking classes, cleaning up their rooms, and so on. In one such study, Buehler, Patterson, and Furness (1966) found that delinquent girls reinforced each other for breaking the rules and talking back. Sometimes, peer approval can be a more powerful reinforcer than any reward a psychologist can offer.

Albert Bandura: Social Learning Theories

Skinner emphasized operant conditioning in his description and explanation of personality. However, according to Albert Bandura and his late colleague Richard Walters (1963), personality is acquired not only by direct reinforcement of behavior but also by *observational learning*, or imitation. In observational learning, a person acquires a new behavior by watching the actions of another person. For example, to teach a child how to hit a baseball with a bat, you could hand the child the bat and ball and reinforce him every time he used the bat and ball correctly (operant conditioning). However, you would probably demonstrate the correct way to hold the bat and swing at the ball instead because this way the child would acquire the behavior more quickly. Bandura and Walters believe that much of a young child's individual behavior and personality is acquired by exposure to specific everyday models.

Bandura found that the consequences to a model engaging in a particular behavior influence the observer's willingness to perform (but not necessarily acquire) that behavior. In one study (Bandura, 1965), three groups of children watched models engaging in behavior that was either rewarded, punished, or had no consequences. In a free play session afterward, the children imitated the rewarded model most and the punished and no-consequence models least. When the same children were later offered a reward for reproducing the behavior they had seen in the films, all three groups imitated the behaviors equally well.

In Bandura's view, people are capable of directing their own behavior by their choice of models. In part, when your parents object to the company you keep, they are trying to change the models you use. The most effective models are those who are the most similar to and most admired by the observer. Thus, you are more likely to learn new behaviors from your friends than from your parents' friends.

HUMANISTIC PSYCHOLOGY

One might look at **humanistic psychology** as a rebellion against the rather negative, pessimistic view of human nature that dominated personality theory in the first part of this century. As we have seen, psychoanalysts emphasized the struggle to control primitive, instinctual urges on the one hand, and to come to terms with the authoritarian demands of the superego or conscience on the other. The behaviorists, too, saw human behavior in mechanistic terms: our actions are shaped by rewards and punishments. Humanistic psychologists object to both approaches on the grounds that they demean human beings—Freud by emphasizing irrational and destructive instincts, Skinner by emphasizing external causes of behavior. In contrast, the humanists stress our relative freedom from instinctual pressures (compared to other animals) and our ability to create and live by personal standards.

Humanistic psychology is founded on the belief that all human beings strive for **self-actualization**—that is, the realization of their potentialities as unique human beings. Self-actualization involves an openness to a wide range of experiences; an awareness of and respect for one's own and other people's uniqueness; accepting the responsibilities of freedom and commitment; a desire to become more and more authentic or true to oneself; and an ability to grow. It requires the courage, in Kipling's words, "to trust

Interpersonal Theories of Personality. Most theories of personality consider the person as an individual. Some psychologists, however, regard personality as a function of a person's social environment. One of the first of these thinkers was Harry Stack Sullivan.

Sullivan's theories have been organized into a two-dimensional model. One dimension is *power,* which ranges from dominance at one end of the scale to submissiveness at the other. The second dimension is *friendliness,* which ranges from friendliness to hostility. Most behaviors can be described as a combination of these two dimensions. For example, "helpfulness" is a combination of dominance and friendliness; "trusting" is a combination of submissiveness and friendliness.

Researchers also noticed that a person's actions tend to elicit specific responses from other people. A behavior and its most likely response are said to be *complementary.* For example, most people will respond to a request for help (trusting) by offering advice (helping), regardless of how "helpful" they are as individuals. Thus, many behaviors result not simply from a person's personality but also from that person's social environment.

Improving Your Self-image

If your self-image can stand a boost, try taking these steps toward greater self-confidence. As you're reading this list, remember what humanistic personality theorists believe: a positive self-image is at the heart of successful adjustment.

- Base your personal goals on an honest appraisal of your strengths and weaknesses. Trying to be something you're not can only weaken your self-image.
- Don't let guilt and shame determine your goals. Let positive thinking guide your decision-making.
- Don't blame everything that goes wrong on yourself. Sometimes external events can play an equally important role.
- When others dismiss your views, keep in mind that events are interpreted in different ways by different people.
- When things go wrong, don't be too hard on yourself. Never think of yourself as a failure, stupid, or ugly.
- Accept criticism of the things you do, but don't allow people to criticize you as a person.
- Use your failures in a constructive way. They may be telling you to readjust your goals and start over in a new direction.
- Don't stay in a situation that makes you feel inadequate. If you can't change the situation, move on to something new.

Try these suggestions and you'll soon see that there's no better feeling than feeling good about yourself.

For more details, see Philip Zimbardo, *Shyness*, Reading, Mass.: Addison-Wesley, 1977.

Figure 11.8
Abraham Maslow. Maslow's work, as well as that of Carl Rogers and others, helped create a humanistic orientation toward the study of behavior by emphasizing growth and the realization of an individual's potential.

yourself when all men doubt you. . . .'' Humanists view this striving as a basic human instinct and the essence of human dignity.

Abraham Maslow: Growth and Self-Actualization

Abraham Maslow was one of the guiding spirits of the humanistic movement in psychology. He deliberately set out to create what he called "a third force in psychology" as an alternative to psychoanalysis and behaviorism. Maslow tried to base his theory of personality on studies of healthy, creative, self-actualizing people who fully utilize their talents and potential, rather than on studies of disturbed individuals. He criticized other psychologists for their pessimistic, negative, and limited conceptions of human beings. Where is the psychology, he asked, that deals with gaiety, exuberance, love, and expressive art to the same extent that it deals with misery, conflict, shame, hostility, and habit?

When Maslow decided to study the most productive individuals he could find—in history as well as in his social and professional circles—he was breaking new ground. The theories of personality we discussed earlier

---

Table 11.1 / Characteristics of Self-Actualized Persons

They are realistically oriented.	They identify with mankind.
They accept themselves, other people, and the natural world for what they are.	Their intimate relationships with a few specially loved people tend to be profound and deeply emotional rather than superficial.
They have a great deal of spontaneity.	Their values and attitudes are democratic.
They are problem-centered rather than self-centered.	They do not confuse means with ends.
They have an air of detachment and a need for privacy.	Their sense of humor is philosophical rather than hostile.
They are autonomous and independent.	They have a great fund of creativeness.
Their appreciation of people and things is fresh rather than stereotyped.	They resist conformity to the culture.
Most of them have had profound mystical or spiritual experiences although not necessarily religious in character.	They transcend the environment rather than just coping with it.

Source: Abraham Maslow, *Motivation and Personality* (New York: Harper & Row, 1954).

in this chapter were developed by psychotherapists after years of working with people who could not cope with everyday frustrations and conflicts. In contrast, Maslow was curious about people who not only coped with everyday problems effectively, but who also created exceptional lives for themselves, people like Abraham Lincoln, Albert Einstein, and Eleanor Roosevelt.

Maslow found that, although these people sometimes had great emotional difficulties, they adjusted to their problems in ways that allowed them to become highly productive. Maslow also found that such self-actualized individuals share a number of traits (Table 11.1). First, they *perceive reality accurately*, unlike most people who, because of prejudices and wishful thinking, perceive it rather inaccurately. Self-actualized people also *accept themselves*, other people, and their environments more readily than "average" people do. Without realizing it, most of us project our hopes and fears onto the world around us. Often we become upset with people whose attitudes differ radically from our own. We spend a good deal of time denying our own shortcomings and trying to rationalize or change things we do not like about ourselves. Self-actualizing individuals accept themselves as they are.

Secure in themselves, healthy individuals are more *problem-centered* than self-centered. They are able to focus on tasks in a way that people concerned about maintaining and protecting their self-image cannot. They are more likely to base decisions on ethical principles than on calculations of the possible costs or benefits to themselves. They have a strong sense of *identity with other human beings*—not just members of their family, ethnic group, or country, but all humankind. They have a strong *sense of humor*, but laugh with people, not at them.

Maslow also found that self-actualizing people are exceptionally *spontaneous*. They are not trying to be anything other than themselves. And they know themselves well enough to maintain their integrity in the face of opposition, unpopularity, and rejection. In a word, they are *autonomous*. They *value privacy* and frequently seek out solitude. This is not to say that they are detached or aloof. But rather than trying to be popular, they focus on deep, *loving relationships with the few people* to whom they are truly close.

Finally, the people Maslow studied had a rare ability to appreciate even the simplest things. They approached their lives with a *sense of discovery* that made each day a new day. They rarely felt bored or uninterested. Given to moments of intense joy and satisfaction, or "peak experiences," they got high on life itself. Maslow believed this to be both a cause and an effect of their creativity and originality (Maslow, 1970).

As indicated in Chapter 6, Maslow believed that to become self-actualizing a person must first satisfy his or her basic, primary needs—for food and shelter, physical safety, love and belonging, and self-esteem. Of course, to some extent the ability to satisfy these needs depends on factors beyond the individual's control. Still, no amount of wealth, talent, beauty, or any other asset can totally shield someone from frustration and disappointment. The affluent as well as the poor, the brilliant as well as the slow, have to adjust to maintain themselves and to grow.

Many psychologists have criticized Maslow's work. His claim that human nature is "good," for example, has been called an intrusion of subjective values into what should be a neutral science. His study of self-actualizing people has been criticized because the sample was chosen on the basis of Maslow's own subjective criteria. How can one identify self-actualized people without knowing the characteristics of such people? But then, if one knows these characteristics to begin with, what sense does it make to list them as if they were the results of an empirical study?

Despite such criticism, Maslow's influence has been great. He has inspired many researchers to pay more attention to healthy, productive people and has led many group leaders and clinicians to seek ways to promote the growth and self-actualization of workers, students, and clients in therapy.

Carl Rogers: Your Organism and Yourself

The people Carl Rogers counseled were "clients," not "patients." The word "patient" implies illness, a negative label that Rogers rejected. As a therapist, Rogers was primarily concerned with the roadblocks and detours on the path to self-actualization (or "full functioning," as he called it). Rogers believed that many people suffer from a conflict between what they value in themselves and what they learn other people value in them. He explained how this conflict develops this way: There are two sides or parts to every person. One is the **organism,** which is the whole of a person, including his or her body. Rogers believed that the organism is constantly struggling to become more and more complete and perfect. Anything that

Figure 11.9
Carl Rogers. Rogers's theories have had a considerable impact on modern psychology and on society in general. He has emphasized personal experience rather than drives and instincts.

furthers this end is good: The organism wants to become everything it can possibly be. For example, children want to learn to walk and run because their bodies are built for these activities. People want to shout and dance and sing because their organisms contain the potential for these behaviors. Different people have different potentialities, but every person wants to realize them, to make them real, whatever they are. It is of no value to be able to paint and not to do it. It is of no value to be able to make witty jokes and not to do so. Whatever you can do, you want to do—and to do as well as possible. (This optimism about human nature is the essence of humanism.)

Each individual also has what Rogers called a **self**. The self is essentially your image of who you are and what you value—in yourself, in other people, in life in general. The self is something you acquire gradually over the years by observing how other people react to you. At first, the most significant other person in your life is your mother (or whoever raises you). You want her approval or **positive regard**. You ask yourself, "How does she see me?" If the answer is, "She loves me. She likes what I am and what I do," you begin to develop positive regard for yourself.

But often this does not happen. The image you see reflected in your mother's eyes and actions is mixed. Whether or not she approves of you often depends on whether or not you spit up your baby food or do your homework on time. In other words, she places conditions on her love: *if* you do what she wants, she likes you. Young and impressionable, you accept these verdicts and incorporate **conditions of worth** into yourself. "When I use obscene language at the dinner table, I am bad." You begin to see yourself as good and worthy only if you act in certain ways. You've learned from your parents and from other people who are significant to you that unless you meet certain conditions you will not be loved.

Rogers's work as a therapist convinced him that people cope with conditions of worth by rejecting or denying parts of their organism that do not fit their self-concept. For example, if your mother grew cold and distant whenever you became angry, you learned to deny yourself the right to express or perhaps even feel anger. Being angry "isn't you." In effect, you are cutting off a part of your organism or whole being; you are allowing yourself to experience and express only part of your being.

The greater the gap between the self and the organism, the more limited and defensive a person becomes. Rogers believed the cure for this situation is **unconditional positive regard**. If significant others (parents, friends, a mate, perhaps a therapist) convey the feeling that they value you for what you are, in your entirety, you will gradually learn to grant yourself the same unconditional positive regard. The need to limit yourself declines. You will be able to accept your organism and become open to *all* your feelings, thoughts, and experiences— and hence to other people. This is what Rogers meant by **fully functioning**. The organism and the self are one: the individual is free to develop all his or her potentialities. Like Maslow and other humanistic psychologists, Rogers believed that self-regard and regard for others go together, and that the human potentials for good and for self-fulfillment outweigh the potentials for evil and despair (Rogers, 1951, 1961).

TRAIT THEORIES

Betsy spends many hours talking to other people, circulates freely at parties, and strikes up conversations while she waits in the dentist's office. Carl, though, spends more time with books than with other people and seldom goes to parties. In common-sense terms, we say that Betsy is friendly and Carl is not. Friendliness is a personality **trait** and some theorists have argued that studying such traits in detail is the best approach to solving the puzzle of human behavior.

One psychologist has defined a trait as "any relatively enduring way in which one individual differs from another" (Guilford, 1959). A trait, then, is a predisposition to respond in a certain way in many different kinds of situations—in a dentist's office, at a party, or in a classroom. More than any other personality theorists, trait theorists emphasize and try to explain the consistency of an individual's behavior in different situations.

Trait theorists generally make two basic assumptions about these underlying sources of consistency: every trait applies to all people (for example, everyone can be classified as more or less dependent) and these descriptions can be quantified (for example, we might establish a scale on which an extremely dependent person scores 1 while a very independent person scores 10).

Thus, every trait can be used to classify people. Aggressiveness, for example, is a continuum: a few people are extremely aggressive or extremely unaggressive, and most of us fall somewhere in the middle. We understand people by specifying their traits, and we use traits to predict people's future behavior. If you were hiring someone to sell vacuum cleaners, you would probably choose Betsy over Carl. This choice would be based on two assumptions: that friendliness is a useful trait for salespeople and that a person who is friendly in the dentist's office and at parties will be friendly in another situation—namely, in the salesroom.

Trait theorists go beyond this kind of common-sense analysis to try to discover the underlying sources of the consistency of human behavior. What is the best way to describe the common features of Betsy's behavior? Is she friendly, or socially aggressive, or interested in people, or sure of herself, or something else? What is the underlying *trait* that best explains her behavior?

Most (but not all) trait theorists believe that a few basic traits are central for all people. An underlying trait of self-confidence, for example, might be used to explain more superficial characteristics like social aggressiveness and dependency. If this were true, it would mean that a person would be dependent because he or she lacked self-confidence. Psychologists who accept this approach set out on their theoretical search for basic traits with very few assumptions.

Most trait theorists believe a few basic traits are central for all people.

This is very different from the starting point of other personality theorists we have considered. Freud, for example, began with a well-defined theory of instincts. When he observed that some people were stingy, he set out to explain this in terms of his theory. Trait theorists would not start by trying to understand stinginess. Rather, they would try to determine whether stinginess was a trait. That is, they would try to find out whether people who were stingy in one type of situation were also stingy in others. Then they might ask whether stinginess is a sign of a more basic trait like possessiveness: Is the stingy person also very possessive in relationships? Thus, the first and foremost question for the trait theorists is: What behaviors go together?

Instead of theories telling them *where* to look, trait theorists have complex and sophisticated methods that tell them *how* to look. These methods begin with the statistical technique of correlation (discussed in Chapter 19)—using one set of scores to predict another. If I know that someone talks to strangers in line at the supermarket, can I predict that he will be likely to strike up conversations in a singles bar? Such predictions are never perfect. Perhaps the reason Betsy is so outspoken in the dentist's office is that she's terrified, and jabbering to strangers is the only way she can distract herself from the image of a sixteen-foot drill. Sometimes, actions that look like manifestations of one trait may really reflect something else entirely.

Gordon Allport: Identifying Traits

Gordon W. Allport was one of the most influential psychologists of his day. Many of his ideas of personality are similar to those of humanistic psychology. For example, Allport emphasized the positive, rational, and conscious reasons why we act the way we do. But he is most famous for his pioneering work on traits (Allport, 1961).

A trait, Allport said, makes a wide variety of situations "functionally equivalent"; that is, it enables a person to realize that many different situations call for a similar response. Thus, traits are responsible for the relative consistency of every individual's behavior.

Allport provided a number of classification schemes for distinguishing among kinds of traits. For example, he was concerned with emphasizing the differences between two major ways of studying personality. In the nomothetic approach, researchers study large groups of people in the search for general laws of personality. This can be contrasted with the idiographic approach, in which one studies a particular person in detail, emphasizing his or her uniqueness. On the basis of this distinction, Allport defined common traits as those that apply to everyone and individual traits as those that apply more to a specific person.

An example of the latter is found in Allport's book *Letters from Jenny* (1965), which consists of 172 letters a woman whom Allport calls Jenny Masterson wrote to a friend. Jenny reveals herself in these letters (which she wrote between the ages of fifty-eight and seventy) as a complex and fiercely independent woman. In his preface to the book, Allport writes:

> To me the principal fascination of the Letters lies in their challenge to the reader (whether psychologist or layman) to "explain" Jenny—if he can. Why does an intelligent lady behave so persistently in a self-defeating manner?

Allport's own attempt to understand Jenny Masterson began with a search for the underlying traits that would explain the consistency of her behavior.

Raymond B. Cattell: Factor Analysis

More recent theorists have concentrated on what Allport called *common traits*, which they try to quantify in a precise, scientific manner. Their primary tool in this task has been an extremely sophisticated mathematical technique called **factor analysis** which describes the extent to which different personality variables are related.

Raymond B. Cattell has used factor analysis extensively to study personality traits. Cattell defines a trait as a tendency to react to related situations in a way that remains more or less stable. He distinguishes between two kinds of tendencies: surface traits and source traits. *Surface traits* are clusters of behavior that tend to go together. An example of a surface trait is altruism, which involves a variety of related behaviors such as helping a neighbor who has a problem or contributing to an annual blood drive. Other examples of surface traits are integrity, curiosity, realism, and foolishness. *Source traits* are the underlying roots or causes of these behavioral clusters—for example, ego strength, dominance, and submissiveness. Cattell believes that measuring surface and source traits will enable us to identify those characteristics that all humans share and those that distinguish one person from another.

Cattell (1965) discovered these traits by studying large numbers of people, using three basic kinds of data: life records, questionnaires, and objective tests. Life records include everything from descriptions of an individual (by people who have known him or her for some time) to school grades to records of automobile accidents. Questionnaire data are the individual's answers to a series of questions, whether or not these answers are truthful. (The fact that someone underrates himself or herself or tries to create a highly favorable impression may be significant.) Objective test data are a person's responses to tests designed to detect or prevent this type of "cheating."

Hans Eysenck: Two Dimensions of Personality

Using factor analysis of personality data similar to the type used by Cattell, Hans Eysenck (1970), an English psychologist, concluded that there are two basic dimensions of personality. The first dimension refers to the degree to which people have control over their feelings. At the emotionally stable end of the personality spectrum is a person who is easy-going, relaxed, well adjusted, and even-tempered. At the neurotic end of the spectrum is the moody, anxious, and restless person.

Eysenck's second dimension was actually identified years earlier by Carl Jung as *extroversion versus introversion.* **Extroverts** are sociable, outgoing, active, lively people. They enjoy parties and seek excitement. On the other end of the dimension are **introverts**, who are more thoughtful, reserved, passive, unsociable, and quiet.

CHAPTER REVIEW

KEY TERMS

- archetype
- behaviorism
- collective unconscious
- conditions of worth
- contingencies of reinforcement
- defense mechanisms
- displacement
- ego
- extrovert
- factor analysis

- fully functioning person
- humanistic psychology
- id
- inferiority complex
- introvert
- organism
- personality
- positive regard
- projection
- reaction formation

- regression
- repression
- self
- self-actualization
- superego
- trait
- unconditional positive regard
- unconscious

SUMMARY

1. Personality is that "something" that accounts for the differences among people and for the consistencies in an individual's behavior over time and in different situations.

2. Personality theories provide a way of organizing information about people's thoughts, feelings, and actions; explaining differences among people; exploring the whys of behavior; and determining methods for improving the quality of life.

3. Freudian theory centers around the unconscious and the important role it plays in an individual's personality. Energy from the id, or pleasure-seeking unconscious, is diverted into the ego, or rational part of the self, and the superego, or conscience.

4. Defense mechanisms are unconscious solutions to conflict situations. Stress and anxiety are reduced by denial, or distortion of reality. Some common defense mechanisms are displacement, repression, reaction formation, projection, and regression.

5. Later psychoanalysts proposed changes in Freud's theory. Jung believed that the collective unconscious is a universally shared inheritance of instincts, urges, and memories called

archetypes. Adler argued that the main motivating force in the development of personality is the effort to overcome feelings of inadequacy.

6. Skinner believed that psychologists should focus on the way rewards and punishments shape behavior. Another behaviorist, Bandura, feels that people learn through observation and imitation of the models they choose.

7. Humanistic theories of personality emphasize human dignity and potential. After studying highly productive people who fulfilled their capabilities, Abraham Maslow concluded that self-actualized people are not free of emotional problems. Rather, they adjust to their problems in ways that allow them to become highly productive.

8. Rogers suggested that full functioning depends on a person's opening the self to include all of the organism, shedding conditions of worth.

9. Trait theorists, like Allport and Cattell, believe that in time we will be able to explain and predict human behavior on the basis of a relatively small number of personality characteristics like friendliness and aggression. Eysenck believes that personalities range on a spectrum from extroversion to introversion.

REVIEW QUESTIONS

1. What functions do personality theories serve? Can you list the four major schools of thought among personality theorists?

2. According to Freud, what two factors have enormous impact on adult personality and behavior? What are the sources of the energy in the human personality? What are Freud's three structures of the personality? Can you match the words *can, want,* and *should* to these three structures?

3. What techniques do people use to defend against anxiety and to distort reality? What technique are you likely to be using if you pout? What technique might you be using if you think a teacher is angry at you because he or she gave a hard test but the teacher is not actually angry?

4. Who was the first major social scientist to propose a unified theory of human behavior? Who were two of his followers? How did they differ from him?

5. What name did Jung give to inherited, universal ideas? What term did Adler introduce?

6. What psychologist has had a major impact on personality theory without actually proposing a theory of personality? What was his approach called? Was he concerned about understanding behavior?

7. What branch of psychology developed in reaction to psychoanalytic theory and behaviorism? This theory was founded on what belief? Who were the men who founded this approach?

8. According to Rogers, there are two parts to every person. What are they? What situation creates a gap between these two parts? What is the cure for this situation?

9. What are the two basic assumptions behind trait theories? What is the foremost question for trait theorists? What are Gordon Allport's two major ways of studying personality? What tool did Raymond Cattell use to examine personality? Cattell distinguished two kinds of traits. What are they?

ACTIVITIES

1. List the qualities and traits that you think comprise the "healthy" or "actualized" person. If this is done in class, you can see how your ideas of health and actualization differ from those of the other class members.

2. What are the key features of your own personality? What are the key features of the personalities of each of your parents? Compare your personality with those of your parents. There will be both similarities and differences. Because one's parents are necessarily such highly influential forces in a child's development, it may be of greater interest to note the chief differences in personalities. Then try to identify the factors responsible for those differences.

For example, what key individuals or events have influenced or redirected the course of your life or changed your habits of living? How have society's institutions affected you?

3. Do some further reading on a particular personality theorist and arrange a class debate. A lively debate would be one between the behaviorists' position and the humanistic or existential approach.

4. The text contains a list of characteristics that Maslow found to be representative of people whom he described as "self-actualized." From among your acquaintances, choose a few whom you especially respect or admire for "doing

their own thing," people who achieve satisfaction by being who and what they are. Ask them to list what they see as their distinguishing personality characteristics. Compare their answers and your observations with Maslow's list. In addition, compare this information with Jung's idea of individuation and Rogers's fully functioning person. Do the theories adequately describe the characteristics you admire? Are they consistent with them?

5. Jung believed that people are unconsciously linked to their ancestral past. Can you think of any evidence for or against the "collective unconscious" Jung described? Which, if any, of your own experiences lend support to or deny this theory?

6. Make a collage that depicts your particular personality, using pictures and words from magazines and newspapers. For example, include your likes, dislikes, hobbies, personality traits, appearance, and so on.

7. Look and listen for "Freudian slips." Write them down and try to determine the reasons for each slip.

8. Listen to conversations of several friends, relatives, teachers, and so on. Try to identify their use of defense mechanisms and write down the circumstances surrounding their use. Try to listen to your own conversations and do the same for yourself. Why do you think people use defense mechanisms?

9. Select a newspaper or newsmagazine article that describes the activities or accomplishments of a person—for example, a popular sports figure, convicted criminal, politician, or business person. Then select a particular personality theory to describe the person's behavior and outlook on life. You may have to go beyond the material in the article to make a convincing argument for the theoretical view you have selected. Then, enter into a classroom discussion with other students who have selected different personality theories to explain the same individual's personality. How do these theoretical views of the person differ? Decide which view best explains the person's actions.

10. Develop your own theory of personality by answering the following questions. How does a person acquire a personality? What are the most important motivations for people? Why are people different? How can people change their personalities?

11. Read a weekly magazine that describes people and their lives and underline the adjectives used to describe the personalities of the people featured in the articles. Then make a list of these traits, noting how many times each trait or adjective was used in all of the magazine's articles. Are there some traits that appear more frequently than others? How important would you say these traits are in your own life? Are there characteristics that seem to be important to you but are not included in your list?

12. Think of a person you know well, someone you have had a chance to observe in a variety of social settings over a period of time. Describe that person in terms of his or her characteristic way of interacting with people. How do other people respond to this person? Does the person's behavior change depending on the setting? Explain your observations using a behavioral model of personality. What would you say are important reinforcers for this person?

Figure 12.1 Psychological testing reveals a great deal about a person in a very short time.

Objectives: After studying this chapter, you should be able to
• discuss the concept of IQ and list several IQ tests.
• explain the applications of aptitude tests, achievement tests, and interest tests.
• describe various test-taking strategies.
• identify and describe the use of personality tests and situational testing.

Psychological Testing

As a student, you are quite familiar with the use of tests to evaluate your academic performance. You may believe that you won't have to take any more tests when you finish school. However, testing has become an ever-present part of many people's lives in our culture. In order to apply for a job as mail carrier, fire fighter, lawyer, or electrician, a person must take a standard civil service or licensing exam. In these cases, the tests are designed to measure what skills and knowledge the person has acquired. Other tests are designed to assess more general characteristics of personality. For example, a psychologist may want to assess your personality to help you select a suitable career or deal with an emotional problem.

Whether the test is designed to measure mental abilities or personality characteristics, its usefulness and reliability depend on how well it is constructed. And then, only by relating scores to performance, can tests really be validated. What does it mean, for example, when a person scores high on standardized written intelligence tests but earns poor grades in school? Can you actually select a companion by a computerized matching of your personalities? Is it acceptable to screen job applicants by using personality tests or to place children in special education programs on the basis of intelligence testing? What general strategies are most useful in taking tests?

Over the years, psychologists have developed a wide range of tools for measuring individual differences in intelligence, interests, skills, achievements, knowledge, and personality patterns. The use of these testing mechanisms by educators, the military, industry, and mental health practitioners has raised some concerns. This chapter will describe the major types of tests that are currently being used and will discuss ways that test takers can deal with them.

Basic Characteristics of Tests
Test Reliability • Test Validity • Establishing Norms

Intelligence Testing
The Development of Intelligence Tests • The Uses and Meaning of IQ Scores • The Controversy over IQ • Family Size and IQ

Measuring Abilities and Interests
Aptitude Tests • Achievement Tests • Using Psychology: The SAT • Interest Tests

Test-Taking Strategies
Studying for a Test • Reducing Test Anxiety • Preparing Yourself for a Test • Using Psychology: Test-Taking Tips

Personality Testing
Objective Personality Tests • Projective Personality Tests

Situational Testing
Ethical Problems of Testing

The lure of tests is that they promise to make it possible to find out a great deal about a person in a very short time.

BASIC CHARACTERISTICS OF TESTS

All tests have one characteristic in common that makes them both fascinating and remarkably practical: they promise to make it possible to find out a great deal about a person in a very short time. Tests can be useful in predicting how well a person might do in a particular career; in assessing an individual's desires, interests, and attitudes; and in revealing psychological problems. One great virtue of standardized tests is that they can provide comparable data about many different individuals. Further, psychologists can use some tests to help people understand things about themselves more clearly than they did before.

One of the great dangers of testing, however, is that we tend to forget that tests are merely *tools* for measuring and predicting human behavior. We start to think of test results (for example, an IQ) as things in themselves. The justification for using a test to make decisions about a person's future depends on whether a decision based on test scores would be fairer and more accurate than one based on other criteria. The fairness and usefulness of a test depend on several factors: its reliability, its validity, and the way its norms were established.

Test Reliability

The term **reliability** refers to a test's consistency—its ability to yield the same result under a variety of different circumstances. There are three basic ways of determining a test's reliability. First, if a person retakes the test, or takes a similar test, within a short time after the first testing, does he or she receive approximately the same score? If, for example, you take a mechanical aptitude test three times in the space of six months and score

Figure 12.2
Two examples of group testing. Both school exams and aptitude tests can be considered psychological tests because both are intended to measure psychological variables (knowledge and skills).

65 in January, 90 in March, and 70 in June, then the test is unreliable. It does not produce a measurement that is stable over time (Figure 12.3).

The second measure of reliability is whether the test yields the same results when scored by different people. If both your instructor and a teaching assistant score an essay test that you have written, and one gives you a B while the other gives you a D, then you have reason to complain about the test's reliability. The score you receive depends more on the grader than on you. On a reliable test, your score would be the same no matter who graded your paper.

One final way of determining a test's reliability is to divide the test in half and score each half separately, to see whether the two scores are approximately the same. If a test is supposed to measure one quality in a person (for example, reading comprehension or administrative ability), then it should not have some sections on which the person scores high and others on which he or she scores low.

In checking tests for reliability, psychologists are trying to prevent chance factors from influencing a person's score. All kinds of irrelevant matters can interfere with a test. If the test taker is depressed because his pet goldfish is sick or angry that he had to miss his favorite "I Love Lucy" rerun to take the exam, or if a broken radiator has raised the temperature in the testing room to 114 degrees, he will probably score lower than if he is reasonably relaxed, comfortable, and content. No test can screen out all interferences, but a highly reliable test can do away with a good part of them.

Test Validity

A test may be reliable but still not be valid. **Validity** is the ability of a test to measure what it is supposed to measure (Figure 12.4). For example, a test that consists primarily of vocabulary lists will not measure aptitude for engineering. A history test will not measure general learning ability.

Determining the validity of a test is more complex than assessing its reliability. One of the chief methods for measuring validity is to find out how well a test *predicts* performance. For example, a group of psychologists design a test to measure management ability. They ask questions about management systems, attitudes toward employees, and so on. Will the people who score high on this test really make good managers?

Suppose the test makers decide that a good way to check the validity of the test is to find out how much a manager's staff improve in productivity in one year. If the staffs of those managers who scored high on the test produce more than the staffs of those managers who scored low on the test, the test may be considered valid. Corporations may then adopt it as one tool to use in deciding whom to hire as managers.

What if managers who are good at raising productivity are poor at decision making? It may be that this test measures talent for improving productivity, not general management ability. This is the kind of difficulty psychologists encounter in trying to assess the validity of a test. As the example shows, nothing can be said about a test's validity until the *purpose* of the test is absolutely clear.

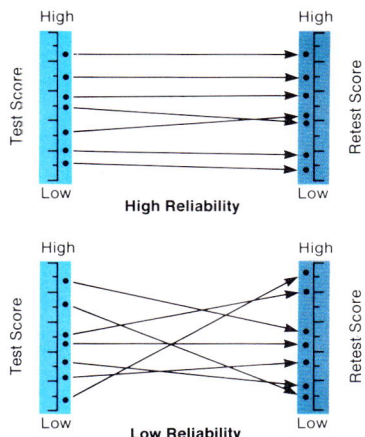

Figure 12.3

Test reliability. On the left, the test scores obtained by seven individuals are ordered on a scale. On the right, the corresponding scores on a second version of the same test, given at a later time, are ordered. In the upper diagram the two sets of scores correspond very closely. This pattern means the test is highly reliable. In the lower diagram, there is little relationship between the two. This scrambled pattern means the test has low reliability.

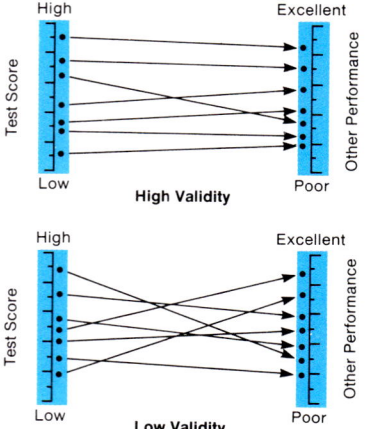

Figure 12.4
Test validity. Reliability and validity are assessed in exactly the same way, except that assessment of validity requires that test scores be compared to some other measure of behavior. The lower diagram might represent the comparison of scores on the "head size" test of intelligence (on the left) with school grades (on the right). The upper diagram might represent the result of comparing Stanford-Binet scores with school grades. The Stanford-Binet is a valid test for predicting school grades; the head size measurement is not.

Establishing Norms

Once a test result is obtained, the examiner must translate the score into something useful. Suppose a child answers thirty-two of fifty questions on a vocabulary test correctly. What does this score mean? If the test is reliable and valid, it means that the child can be expected to understand a certain percentage of the words in a book at the reading level being tested. In other words, the score predicts how the child will *perform* at a given level.

But a "raw" score does not tell us where the child stands in relation to other children at his or her age and grade level. If most children answered forty-five or more questions correctly, 32 is a low score. However, if most answered only twenty questions correctly, 32 is a very high score.

The method psychologists generally use to transform raw scores into figures that reflect comparisons with others is the **percentile system**, which bears some resemblance to what is called "grading on the curve." In the percentile system the scores actually achieved on the test are written down in order, ranging from the highest to the lowest. Each particular score is then compared with this list and assigned a percentile according to the percentage of scores that fall at or below this point. For example, if half the children in the above example scored 32 or below, then a score of 32 is at the fiftieth percentile. If 32 were the top score, it would be at the one-hundredth percentile. In the example given in Figure 12.5, a score of 32 puts the child in the seventy-fifth percentile, since only 25 percent of the children scored higher than she did.

When psychologists are designing a test to be used in a variety of schools, businesses, clinics, or other settings, they usually set up a scale for comparison by establishing norms. The test is given to a large representative sample of the group to be measured—for example, sixth graders, army privates, engineers, or perhaps the population as a whole. Percentiles are then established on the basis of the scores achieved by this standardization group. These percentiles are called the test's **norms**. Most of the intelligence, aptitude, and personality tests you will encounter have been provided with norms in this way. Your percentile on an aptitude test such as the

Figure 12.5
The meaning of percentile scores. The range of possible raw scores on a test is shown in relation to an idealized curve that indicates the proportion of people who achieved each score. The vertical lines indicate percentiles, or proportions of the curve below certain points. Thus, the line indicated as the 1st percentile is the line below which only 1 percent of the curve lies; similarly, 99 percent of the curve lies below the 99th percentile.

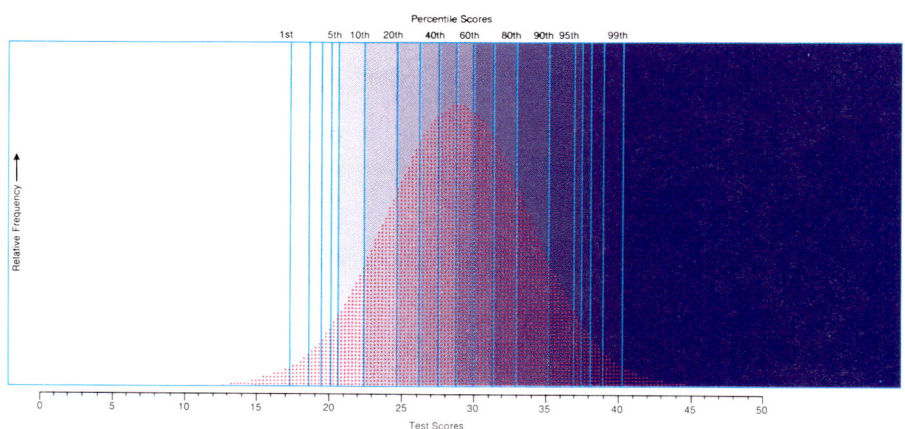

SAT, for example, reflects your standing among people of your age and grade who have taken these exams.

It should be remembered, however, that norms are not really standards—even though a norm group is sometimes misleadingly referred to as a "standardization group." Norms refer only to what has been found normal or average for some group of people. If Johnny can read at the fiftieth percentile level, that does not mean he has met some absolute standard for ability to read. It only means that he reads better than half the population (50 percent), and worse than the other half.

In summary, when you take a test and obtain your score, you should consider the following three questions in evaluating the results: (1) Do you think that if you took the same test or a similar test again, you would receive a similar score? (2) Does your performance on this test reflect your normal performance in the subject the test is designed to measure? (3) If you were to compare your score with those of your classmates, would it reflect your general standing within that group of people?

INTELLIGENCE TESTING

Among the most widely used and widely disputed tests in America today are those that are designed to measure "intelligence" and yield an "IQ" score. This section will describe some of the major intelligence tests and present some of the issues that surround them.

The Development of Intelligence Tests

Alfred Binet, a French psychologist, was the first to develop a useful intelligence test. In 1904 Binet was asked by the Paris school authorities to devise a means of picking out "slow learners" so they could be placed in special classes from which they might better profit. Binet was unable to define intelligence, but he believed it was reflected in such things as the ability to make commonsense judgments, to tell the meanings of words, and to solve problems and puzzles. Binet assumed that whatever intelligence was, it increased with age; that is, older children had more intelligence than younger children. Therefore, in selecting items for his test he only included items on which older children did better than younger children. By asking the same questions of many children, Binet was able to determine the average age at which a particular question could be answered. For example, he discovered that certain questions could be answered by most twelve-year-olds but not by most eleven-year-olds. If a child of eleven, or even nine, could answer these questions, he or she was said to have a *mental age* of twelve. If a child of twelve could answer the nine-year-old-level questions but not the questions for ten-year-olds and eleven-year-olds, he or she was said to have a mental age of nine. Thus a slow learner was one who had a *mental age* that was less than his or her *chronological age.*

The Stanford-Binet.   Binet's intelligence test has been revised many times since he developed it. The Binet test currently in widespread use in

Multiple   Intelligences? Many people believe that intelligence is primarily the ability to think logically. Psychologist Howard Gardner considers this view of intelligence to be inadequate, however, because it omits many other important skills. Gardner argues for a broader perspective that includes seven types of intelligence: (1) verbal ability; (2) logical-mathematical reasoning skills; (3) spatial ability, or the ability to find one's way around an environment and to form mental images; (4) musical ability, or the ability to create and perceive pitch and rhythm patterns; (5) body-kinesthetic ability, or skill at fine motor movements required for tasks such as gem cutting and surgery; (6) interpersonal skills, involving understanding the feelings of others; and (7) intrapersonal skills, or knowledge of oneself.

Gardner's research on the results of brain disease convinced him that humans possess these seven different and often unrelated intellectual capacities or "intelligences." Moreover, he argues that the biological organization of the brain affects one's strength in each of the seven areas.

Figure 12.6
Two tests on the Stanford-Binet being administered to a little boy. (top) The examiner has built a tower of four blocks and has told the child, "You make one like this." (bottom) The examiner shows the child the card with six small objects attached to it and says, "See all these things? Show me the dog," and so on.

the United States is a revision created at Stanford University: the Stanford-Binet Intelligence Test (Terman and Merrill, 1973). The Stanford-Binet, like the original test, groups test items by age level. To stimulate and maintain the child's interest, a variety of tasks are included, ranging from defining words to drawing pictures and explaining events in daily life. Children are tested one at a time. The examiner must carry out standardized instructions—at the same time putting the child at ease, getting him to pay attention, and encouraging him to try as hard as he can (Figure 12.6).

In the final scoring, the mental age indicates how high a level the person has reached. If his performance is as high as the average twelve-year-old's, he has a mental age of twelve. The **IQ**, or **intelligence quotient**, is called a quotient because it was originally computed by dividing mental age by actual (chronological) age and multiplying the result by 100 to eliminate decimals. (A nine-year-old with a mental age of twelve would have an IQ of 133.) Although the term "IQ" has stuck, the actual computation is now made on a basis similar to the percentile system.

The Wechsler Tests. Two other frequently used intelligence tests are the Wechsler Intelligence Scale for Children, or WISC+R, and the Wechsler Adult Intelligence Scale, or WAIS+R (Wechsler, 1981). The Wechsler tests differ from the Stanford-Binet in several important ways. For example, the Wechsler tests place more emphasis on performance tasks (such as doing puzzles) than does the Stanford-Binet, so that individuals who are not particularly skilled in the use of words will not be as likely to receive low IQ scores (Figure 12.7).

Moreover, in addition to yielding one overall score, the Wechsler tests yield percentile scores in several areas—vocabulary, information, arithmetic, picture arrangement, and so on. These ratings are used to compute separate IQ scores for verbal and performance abilities. This type of scoring provides a more detailed picture of the individual's strengths and weaknesses than a single score does.

Group Tests. The Wechsler and Stanford-Binet tests, because they are given individually, are costly and time-consuming to administer. During World War I, when the United States Army found that it had to test nearly two million men quickly, individual testing was a luxury the army could not afford. Thus paper-and-pencil intelligence tests, which could be given to large groups of people at the same time, were developed. Current group IQ tests, such as the Army Alpha and Beta tests, have proved to be convenient and effective and are used extensively in schools, employment offices, and many other institutions.

The Uses and Meaning of IQ Scores

In general, the norms for intelligence tests are established in such a way that most people score near 100. Out of one hundred people, seventeen will score above 115 and seventeen will score below 85. About three in one hundred score above 130, and three score below 70. This means that a score of

General Information
1. How many wings does a bird have?
2. How many nickels make a dime?
3. What is steam made of?
4. Who wrote "Paradise Lost"?
5. What is pepper?

General Comprehension
1. What should you do if you see someone forget his book when he leaves his seat in a restaurant?
2. What is the advantage of keeping money in a bank?
3. Why is copper often used in electrical wires?

Arithmetic
1. Sam had three pieces of candy and Joe gave him four more. How many pieces of candy did Sam have altogether?
2. Three men divided eighteen golf balls equally among themselves. How many golf balls did each man receive?
3. If two apples cost 15¢, what will be the cost of a dozen apples?

Similarities
1. In what way are a lion and a tiger alike?
2. In what way are a saw and a hammer alike?
3. In what way are an hour and a week alike?
4. In what way are a circle and a triangle alike?

Vocabulary
"What is a puzzle?"
"What does 'addition' mean?"

Figure 12.7
Test items similar to those included in the various Wechsler intelligence scales. (a) A sampling of questions from five of the verbal subtests. (b) A problem in block design, one of the performance subtests. (c) Another example of a performance subtest. The subject is asked to put together puzzle pieces to form a familiar object, such as a duck. (Test items courtesy the Psychological Corporation, New York)

130 places a person in the ninety-seventh percentile; a score of 70 places a person in the third percentile.

What do these scores mean? What do the tests measure? IQ scores seem to be most useful when related to school achievement: they are quite accurate in predicting which people will do well in schools, colleges, and universities. Critics of IQ testing do not question this predictive ability. They do wonder, however, whether such tests actually measure "intelligence." Most psychologists agree that intelligence is the ability to acquire new ideas and new behavior. Is success in school or the ability to take a test a real indication of such ability? Generally, IQ tests measure the ability to solve certain types of problems. But they do not directly measure the ability to pose those problems or to question the validity of problems set by others (Hoffman, 1962). This is only part of the reason why IQ testing is so controversial.

The Controversy over IQ

Much of the debate about IQ testing centers around one question: Do genetic differences or environmental inequalities cause two people to receive different scores on intelligence tests? Psychologists have found that genetics and environment are both important, although recent research suggests that genetic factors may wield the greater influence (Bouchard et al., 1990). What this means is that individuals may inherit a predisposition toward a general level of intelligence. However, the specific level that they achieve is greatly affected by their environment. No matter what contributions genetics and environment make to an individual's IQ, the measurement of intelligence must be free of bias. Tests should not discriminate against people because of their socioeconomic or cultural background.

One intelligence test, for example, includes the following question as a test of reasoning ability:

A symphony is to a composer as a book is to what?
paper   sculptor   author   musician   man

A. Davis (1951) found that 81 percent of children from well-off families, but only 51 percent of children from lower-class families, answered this correctly. When Davis rephrased the question in less "highbrow" terms, using everyday words and common experiences, the gap closed.

A baker goes with bread, like a carpenter goes with what?
a saw   a house   a spoon   a nail   a man

Fifty percent of the children from both income groups answered this question correctly. The first question measured experience in middle-class culture as well as reasoning; the second measured reasoning alone.

Such findings have led psychologists to develop knowledge-reduced or "culture-fair" tests that measure the basic thinking and reasoning abilities of individuals regardless of their backgrounds. Furthermore, tests in general are now carefully screened for items that might be biased against any particular group (AERA, APA, and NCME, 1985).

Family Size and IQ

It wasn't that long ago that nearly everyone came from a large family. Now most couples have just one, two, or three children. Can the size of a family influence how smart its children will be? More specifically, does your place in the birth order—whether you were born first or fifth—influence your intelligence?

Some psychologists say yes (Zajonc and Markus, 1975). In examining birth order, psychologists have found more firstborns among high-IQ achievers, graduate students, American presidents, members of Congress, and even astronauts launched into space. Moreover, large families seem to produce children with lower IQs; smarter children seem to come from smaller families.

The classic study of family size and IQ was conducted in the Netherlands. It was based on the military examinations of more than 386,000 Dutchmen. Researchers found that the brightest subjects came from the smallest families and had few, if any, brothers and sisters when they were born. Thus, the firstborn child in a family of two was usually brighter than the last child in a family of ten.

The effects of family size on intelligence may be explained by what a house full of children does to the home environment. It increases the amount of time a child spends with other children and decreases the amount of parental attention he or she receives. For example, a parent with one restless child is apt to sit and play with the child. The same parent with two or three restless children is more likely to ask them to play with each other. Some psychologists say that when a child interacts with an adult alone, the child learns more and therefore intelligence is enhanced. Researchers have also found that parents often expect more from their firstborn, which motivates such children to strive for a higher standard.

Not all psychologists agree that firstborns tend to be more intelligent (Bouchard and Segal, 1985). They say that the data need to be examined more closely for other possible explanations. For example, in industrialized nations most large families come from lower-socioeconomic backgrounds. Thus, environment, not family size or birth order, may be influencing intelligence. On the other hand, there may be genetic variations within families that also account for differences.

If firstborns have advantages in the area of intelligence, research has also shown that they may be more conforming and have poorer social skills than their younger siblings. Although more research needs to be done in this area, it is clear that such factors as birth order, the order in which boys and girls are born into a family, and the number of years that separate siblings probably have an effect on the development of intelligence, personality, and social relationships.

MEASURING ABILITIES AND INTERESTS

Intelligence tests are designed to measure a person's overall ability to solve problems that involve symbols such as words, numbers, and pictures. Psychologists have developed other tests to assess special abilities and experiences. These include aptitude tests, achievement tests, and interest tests.

Aptitude Tests

Aptitude tests attempt to discover a person's talents and to predict how well he or she will be able to learn a new skill. The General Aptitude Test Battery (GATB) is the most widely used of these tests (Figure 12.8). Actually, the GATB comprises nine different tests, ranging from vocabulary to manual dexterity. Test results are used to determine whether a person meets minimum standards for each of a large number of occupations. In addition to the GATB, there are aptitude tests in music, language, art, mathematics, and other special fields.

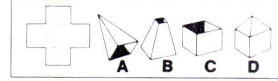

1. Which two words have the same meaning?
   (a) open   **(b)** happy   **(c)** glad   **(d)** green

2. Which two words have the opposite meaning?
   (a) old   **(b)** dry   **(c)** cold   **(d)** young

3. A man works 8 hours a day, 40 hours a week. He earns $1.40 an hour. How much does he earn each week?
   (A) $40.00   **(C)** $50.60
   (B) $44.60   **(D)** $56.00

4. At the left is a drawing of a flat piece of metal. Which object at the right can be made from this piece of metal?

Figure 12.8
The General Aptitude Test Battery (GATB) consists of a number of different kinds of tests. Samples of items testing verbal and mathematical skills (top) and manual skills (bottom) are shown here.

PSYCHOLOGY UPDATE

Adaptive Testing. Computers are often used to administer ability tests. One computer-based method is called adaptive testing. To understand adaptive testing, recall that in a standardized test everyone gets the same questions in the same order. With an adaptive test, however, the order of questions is changed by the computer as it *adapts* the test to the individual's performance.

If you are taking the test and answer several problems correctly, the computer will begin to challenge you with harder problems. If you miss a question, the computer will follow it with an easier problem, and so on. The purpose of this testing method is to measure your ability by finding the difficulty level where you correctly answer most but not all of the problems (70 percent correct, for example). Adaptive testing is more accurate than standardized testing, especially when test takers are either very high or very low in ability.

Achievement Tests

Whereas aptitude tests are designed to predict how well a person will be able to learn a new skill, **achievement tests** are designed to measure how much a person has already learned in a particular area. Such tests not only enable an instructor to assess a student's knowledge; they also help students to assess their progress for themselves.

The distinction between achievement and aptitude tests has become somewhat blurred in recent years. What psychologists had at first thought were tests of aptitude—defined as *innate* ability or talent—turned out to measure experience as well, so that in part they were achievement tests. On the other hand, achievement tests often turned out to be the best predictors of many kinds of occupational abilities, so that they were in some sense aptitude tests. Because of this overlap, psychologists have agreed that the distinction between the two types of tests rests more on purpose than on content. If a test is used to predict future ability, it is considered to be an aptitude test; if it is used to assess what a person already knows, it is an achievement test.

USING PSYCHOLOGY

The SAT

The tremendous success of mass testing to screen people for the army in World War I encouraged the College Board (a nonprofit membership association of schools and colleges) to develop objective tests to screen students for college admission. It developed a number of college entrance examinations, including the SAT (Scholastic Aptitude Test). This test, along with achievement and other tests, makes up the College Board's Admissions Testing Program. The American College Testing Program (ACT) offers another, similar series of admissions tests. The results of standardized tests are among several criteria that colleges use for selecting students.

More than one million high school students take the SAT every year. Juniors take the PSAT (Preliminary Scholastic Aptitude Test) to prepare them for the kinds of questions they will encounter on the SAT, for early admission to college, and for scholarship applications.

The three-hour SAT is a multiple choice test divided into six parts: two verbal parts, two parts on mathematics, a part on standard written English, and a part made up of "equating" questions. The verbal parts measure one's ability to use words. They include questions on vocabulary, sentence completions, word relationships (analogies and antonyms), and reading comprehension. The math parts measure one's grasp of elementary mathematical principles and determine how well and fast a person can solve problems. The Test of Standard Written English requires one to recognize mistakes in English grammar and usage. The "equating" questions are either new questions being tested for difficulty or old questions from former tests that are used to standardize scores so that students are not penalized if their particular SAT is more difficult than former SATs.

One does not pass or fail the SAT. One's score is compared with those of others who took similar tests over the years. Most colleges use these relative values as part of their assessment of a person's academic ability.

The average scores of students taking the SAT dropped gradually over the first ten years that national averages were recorded (beginning in 1972). There are many theories explaining this. One theory is that some schools lacked the traditionally strong emphasis on the basic academic skills. Another theory is that teachers were giving students higher grades than they gave in the past for comparable work, so students with lower capabilities were advancing through the grades. Between 1982 and 1986 there was an upward national trend in both math and verbal scores. However, since 1986, average verbal scores have been on the decline.

The fact that different teachers and schools grade comparable work differently is a major rationale for nationally standardized tests such as the SAT. Many studies have shown that SATs are a more accurate gauge of student ability than the opinions of the students' teachers (Stanley, 1976: 313).

The SAT is now being revised, and a new edition will be published in 1994 (Evangelauf, 1990). The major changes will include longer reading passages that test critical thinking skills such as analyzing and evaluating information, mathematical problems that require students to write in answers as opposed to choosing from a list of multiple choice responses, and an optional English test that requires an essay. Students will also be allowed to use calculators and have more time to answer each question.

Some educators welcome the changes as a better reflection of the kinds of skills that are valued in college. However, representatives of women's and minority groups have protested that these changes do not represent changes in basic biases against them in the SAT. Women and minorities have traditionally scored lower than white males on the test. According to the College Board, these differences in scores will not change with the revision.

Interest Tests

The instruments for measuring interests are fundamentally different from the instruments for measuring abilities. Answers to questions on an intelligence test indicate whether a person can, in fact, do certain kinds of thinking and solve certain kinds of problems. There are right and wrong answers. But the answers to questions on an interest or a personality test cannot be right or wrong. The question in this type of testing is not "How much can you do?" or "How much do you know?" but "What are you like?" and "What are you interested in?"

The essential purpose of an **interest test** is to determine a person's preferences, attitudes, and interests. The test taker's responses are compared to the responses given by people in clearly defined groups, such as professions or occupations. The more a person's answers correspond to those of people in a particular occupation, the more likely that person is to enjoy and succeed in that profession.

In constructing the widely used Strong Vocational Interest Inventory, for example, psychologists compared the responses of people who were successfully employed in different occupations to the responses of "people in general." Suppose most engineers said they liked the idea of becoming astronomers but would not be interested in a coaching job, whereas "people in general" were evenly divided on these (and other) questions. A person who responded as the engineers did would rank high on the scale of interest in engineering.

The Kuder Preference Record, part of which is shown in Figure 12.9, is based on the same principle. The purpose of these measures is to help people find the career that is right for them.

Figure 12.9
Items from the Kuder Preference Record (KPR), a test that works like the Strong Vocational Interest Inventory. The person taking the test is asked to pick from among three possible activities the one he or she would most like to do and the one he or she would least like to do. The test provides numerous sets of such alternatives.

		Most		Least
G.	Read a love story	●	G.	●
H.	Read a mystery	●	H.	●
I.	Read science fiction	●	I.	●
J.	Visit an art gallery	●	J.	●
K.	Browse in a library	●	K.	●
L.	Visit a museum	●	L.	●
M.	Collect autographs	●	M.	●
N.	Collect coins	●	N.	●
O.	Collect butterflies	●	O.	●
P.	Watch television	●	P.	●
Q.	Go for a walk	●	Q.	●
R.	Listen to music	●	R.	●

Admissions Test Scores

Every spring and winter, high school students go through an American rite of passage: they take their college entrance exams. How well they do influences what happens in their lives from that point on. The colleges they attend, the jobs they get, the people they marry are all affected, to some degree, by their scores.

Little wonder, then, that most students try to do everything they can to do well on the exams. Although no one has discovered a magic formula for getting the top grades, many students repeat exams such as the SAT, usually taking it first in the spring of their junior year and then in the winter of their senior year. According to Educational Testing Service, the writers of this test, one student in twenty will gain 100 points or more and about one in a hundred will lose 100 points or more. Generally speaking, the odds are with students to improve their scores. College admissions committees take this into account when they interpret the results.

Experts attribute this score gain to several factors. Students' knowledge has increased between their junior and senior years, and a round of practice helped take the jitters out of exam time. In sum, the students taking the test for the second time are a little older, a little smarter, and more experienced.

TEST-TAKING STRATEGIES

Many educators and psychologists have studied the way people prepare themselves for tests and the way they respond in a testing situation. These strategies can be useful in preparation for any kind of test, whether it is a midterm in biology, a civil service test, or a bar exam.

Studying for a Test

One of the differences between people who do well on tests or exams and those who do poorly is in the type and amount of studying they do. People who have developed good study habits often earn high grades and derive a general sense of accomplishment from their efforts. Knowing that they are adequately prepared for a test also reduces their anxiety. Like other skills, studying skills are acquired through practice and instruction.

Psychologists who study how people learn verbal or written material have shown that people master material better when they practice or rehearse the material several times. What this means is that the student who reads the assigned chapters for an exam several times will remember more of the material than the student who studies by reading the assigned chapters only once. In terms of studying, then, practice does make perfect. Furthermore, people's performance on a test will most likely improve if they

Figure 12.10
Taking a test: A number of factors, including the individual's mood and the physical setup of the room, can influence the results. A person can easily do poorly on one day in one setting and well on another day in different circumstances.

space their study time over several intervals rather than cram all the studying into one session. It would be better to study an hour a night for five nights than to cram all of the studying into five hours on the night before the exam. Cramming can sometimes be useful, but only when it is used as a reminder of what has previously been studied during spaced or distributed study sessions. When cramming is used as a substitute for planned study, test performance is not as good.

Psychological research also suggests that people should plan their study time so that they avoid studying materials that are similar to each other. Suppose, for example, that a student is studying for a French exam and at the same time she has Spanish and trigonometry work to do. Since French and Spanish are more similar than French and trigonometry, she should space her Spanish and French study time so that she reduces the possibility of one interfering with the other. She could do her Spanish assignment early in the day and set aside several short blocks of time in the late afternoon and evening to prepare for the French exam. In between the times set aside for studying French, she could do her trigonometry assignment, since this material is less likely to interfere with her memory of the French material.

Reducing Test Anxiety

One of the biggest problems that people have in preparing for or taking an exam or test is anxiety. As the time draws near to the test, people generally experience an increase in tension. While some people are able to keep their anxiety to a reasonable level, others are so panic stricken that they cannot perform well. Actually, a moderate amount of tension improves performance. A person who feels no tension at all is not as alert or attentive to details as he or she could be. When a person experiences a high level of tension, however, panic and disorganization set in and performance declines. Thus, a person who is too tense will need to calm down, while the noninvolved person may need to motivate himself or herself in order to do well on tests. Adequate preparation for a test helps reduce some of the anxiety people have. Beyond that, a person can learn specific techniques for reducing tension and relaxing before an exam. For example, allowing plenty of time to get to the testing setting and having a good night's sleep beforehand will help reduce anxiety.

Some people may be relatively relaxed when they enter an exam room but then suddenly find that they can't remember anything they had learned for the exam. Mental blocks occur when people temporarily panic. If you ever experience such a block, close your eyes and slowly take a few deep breaths and let your body relax. Sometimes this quick technique will be enough to free you from your mental block.

Since most tests are timed and many tests are designed to assess performance under pressure, one way you can reduce the stress of test taking is to manage the time you have during the exam. Know how much time you will have beforehand and be sure to have a watch so that you can keep track of the time. Divide your time so that you don't take too long on any one part. If you don't manage your time, you might discover that you have ten minutes left to complete the second half of the test.

Preparing Yourself for a Test

With the increase in the use of tests for job and college selection, a number of courses and books have been developed to help people prepare for specific exams. These courses usually have two goals. One is to familiarize the individual with testing strategies and to help the test taker develop a knowledge of testing procedures. The second goal is to provide specific instruction or coaching in the subject matter of the test.

If you have had no experience at all with machine-scored multiple choice exams, you may not be as confident as a more experienced test taker. Thus, a familiarity with the question format and with the special answer sheets can be useful. Many courses offer sample items on which you can practice. Sometimes the answer sheets can be confusing to the inexperienced test taker because of the various codes that are required to identify the person taking the test. Marking your answer correctly may also mean using a specific type of pencil, selecting an answer row, and completely filling in the space between two parallel lines or inside circles. When you do have to mark your answers in rows of circles or squares, make sure you are in the correct row. It's easy to skip one row accidentally and then place all subsequent answers in the wrong rows.

In addition to the actual mechanics of taking tests, you can learn how to read and answer multiple choice items. For example, learn to read all of the multiple choice options, not just the first one that seems right. You will probably improve your score if you don't spend too much time on puzzling items, especially since most tests are timed. Later, if time permits, you can

It is good practice to review and change your answers on a multiple choice test if you disagree with your first responses.

Fact. Although students often believe that their "first impression" is correct, this may not be the case. Studies show that students are likely to benefit from changing answers, especially if they are fairly confident that the new answer is the correct one.

USING PSYCHOLOGY

Test-Taking Tips

The following tips will help you perform better on tests. Some of them have to do with studying for the test, some with taking the test, and some with your answers on particular types of tests.

1. Outline a plan to decide how much and how long you will study. Use any practice material that is available for the test.

2. Make yourself familiar with the format of standardized tests—multiple choice, verbal analogy, and so on.

3. When preparing for an essay question, review the major ideas. For short answer tests, memorize material such as dates, events, and formulas.

4. Get plenty of sleep the night before the test. Always arrive at the testing place on time. Take a watch, but try not to focus on it.

5. Sit in a place where you will not be distracted by friends.

6. Read the instructions carefully and, if you are allowed to mark on the test, underline or circle key phrases in the directions. In essay questions, these might include "compare and contrast," "trace," "define," and "illustrate." Also underline important elements of a reading comprehension passage such as names, numbers, and dates so that you can locate them quickly. If the directions are not clear, ask any questions before the timing period begins.

7. Make sure you know what the penalty is for guessing.

8. Go through the test and plan how much time you will spend on each part. Answer the questions that are easy for you first, then concentrate on the harder ones if time permits.

9. For essay questions, always write an outline before you begin writing. Spend one-third to one-half of your time on the outline and the rest on the actual writing. If you run out of time, hand in the rest of the outline.

10. In a multiple choice test, read every possible answer before making your choice. In rankings, one of the answers in the middle is usually right. In true-false questions, answers with absolute qualifiers, such as "always" or "never" are often wrong. In an "all of the above" question, if you know that at least two answers are correct, choose "all of the above."

go back to difficult items and apply more specific strategies for deciding on the best answers. (See Test-Taking Tips box on page 306.)

Some organizations offer courses that provide coaching for specific tests. They vary in cost and quality. Some are very expensive and very intensive, sometimes involving daily study for a period of up to six months. There is debate among educators about the benefit of such courses. Often, the focus of coaching courses is on increasing a person's vocabulary and refreshing his or her knowledge of specific subjects such as trigonometry or advanced algebra. If a person has been out of school for a while, these courses may be helpful, but for a student who is currently taking English and mathematics courses, these programs may not prove beneficial.

PERSONALITY TESTING

Psychiatrists and psychologists use **personality tests** to assess personality characteristics and to identify problems. Some of these tests are **objective,** or forced choice—that is, a person must select one out of a small number of possible responses. Others are **projective**—they encourage test takers to respond freely, giving their own interpretations of various test stimuli.

Objective Personality Tests

The most widely used objective personality test is the Minnesota Multiphasic Personality Inventory (MMPI). The MMPI has no right or wrong answers. The test consists of 550 statements to which a person can respond "true," "false," or "cannot say." Items include "I like tall women"; "I wake up tired most mornings"; "I am envied by most people."

The items on the MMPI reveal habits, fears, delusions, sexual attitudes, and symptoms of mental problems. Although the statements that relate to a given characteristic (such as depression) are scattered throughout the test, the answers to them can be pulled out and organized into a single depression scale. There are ten such clinical scales to the MMPI.

In scoring the MMPI, a psychologist looks for patterns of responses, not a high or low score on all the scales. This is because the items on the test do not, by themselves, identify personality types. In creating the MMPI, the test makers did not try to think up statements that would identify depression, anxiety, and so on. Rather, they invented a wide range of statements about all sorts of topics; gave the test to groups of people already known to be well adjusted, depressed, anxious, and so on; and retained for the test those questions that discriminated among these groups—questions, for example, that people suffering from depression or from anxiety neurosis almost always answered differently from normal groups (Hathaway and McKinley, 1940). Many of the items on the MMPI may sound like sheer nonsense, but they work, and for many psychologists that's all that counts. One unique aspect of the MMPI is that it has a built-in "lie detector." If an individual gives a false response to one statement, he or she may be caught by a rephrasing of the same question at a later point.

The MMPI has proved useful in helping to diagnose various forms of mental disturbance and in providing data for personality research (Dahlstrom and Welsh, 1960). It has also been used—and misused—in employment offices to screen job applicants. A person who is trying to get a job is likely to give answers he or she thinks the employer would like to see—thereby falling into some of the traps built into the test. Administering the MMPI under such circumstances can produce misleading, even damaging results. Innocently trying to make a good impression, the job applicant ends up looking like a liar instead. As an aid to counseling and therapy, however, it can be a valuable tool.

Projective Personality Tests

Projective tests are open-ended examinations that invite people to tell stories about pictures, diagrams, or objects. The idea is that because the test material has no established meaning, the story a person tells must say something about his needs, wishes, fears, and other aspects of his personality. In other words, the subject will project his feelings onto the test items.

Perhaps the best-known and most widely discussed projective measure is the Rorschach ink-blot test, developed by Swiss psychiatrist Hermann Rorschach. Rorschach created ten ink-blot designs and a system for scoring responses to them. To administer the test, a psychologist hands the ink blots, one by one, to the subject, asking the person to say what he or she sees. The person might say that a certain area represents an airplane or an animal's head. This is the free-association period of the test. The psychologist then asks certain general questions in an attempt to discover what aspects of the ink blot determined the person's response (Figure 12.11).

There are a number of systems for scoring Rorschach responses. Some are very specific and concrete. For example, according to one system a per-

Figure 12.11
Ink blots similar to those used on the Rorschach test. In interpretations of a person's responses to the ink blots, as much attention may be paid to the style of the responses as to their content.

son who mentions human movement more often than color in the ink blots is probably introverted while an extrovert will mention color more than movement. Other systems are far more intuitive—for example, simply noting whether the person taking the test is open or hostile. Many researchers have criticized the Rorschach, charging that its scoring systems are neither reliable nor valid. But it continues to be widely used by therapists.

The second most widely used projective measure was developed by Henry Murray. The Thematic Apperception Test (TAT) consists of a series of twenty cards containing pictures of vague but suggestive situations. The individual is asked to tell a story about the picture, indicating how the situation shown on the card developed, what the characters are thinking and feeling, and how it will end.

As with the Rorschach, there are many different scoring systems. The interpreter usually focuses on the themes that emerge from the story and the needs of the main characters. Are they aggressive? Do they seem to have needs for achievement, love, or sex? Are they being attacked or criticized by another person, or are they receiving affection and comfort?

SITUATIONAL TESTING

The use of psychological tests for such things as job placement has become extremely controversial in recent years. Is there any direct relation between a person's responses to statements on the MMPI and his everyday behavior? Do a person's perceptions of an ink blot really tell whether she will be able to remain calm under pressure or to give and take orders efficiently? Many psychologists think not. They believe that the closer a test is to the actual situation the examiner wants to know about, the more useful the results will be. A test that measures an individual's performance in terms of emotional, attitudinal, and behavioral responses to "true life" situations is called a **situational test**. (An example is a test for a driver's license, requiring that the person actually drive.)

One of the first situational tests for job placement was developed by the Office of Strategic Services (OSS) during World War II (Office of Strategic Services Assessment Staff, 1948). The OSS wanted to evaluate candidates for assignment to military espionage, which requires a high degree of self-control and frustration tolerance. In order to judge the candidates, the OSS set up a three-day session of intensive testing during which candidates were required to live together in close quarters and were confronted with a number of complicated and frustrating problems.

In one procedure, a staff member instructed each candidate to build a certain type of cube with the help of two assistants. The helpers were actually psychologists who played prearranged roles. One was extremely lazy and passive, engaged in projects of his own, and offered no advice. The other interfered with the work by making impractical suggestions, harassing the candidate, and asking embarrassing questions. The "assistants" succeeded so well in frustrating the candidates that not one finished the construction. But by placing the candidates in situations similar to those

Figure 12.12
Using this airplane flight simulator, pilots are trained and tested before they are given the responsibility of flying a real airliner. None of the standard tests described in this chapter could predict accurately whether a pilot would panic in such a situation. (United Airlines photo)

they would encounter as agents, the examiners were able to predict how these men might respond to military intelligence work.

Similar logic underlies the current use of assessment centers (see Chapter 21). In an assessment center, a job applicant participates in a job simulation while being observed by trained evaluators. These assessments are valid selection instruments (Gaugler et al., 1987). Court decisions and federal regulations now stipulate that job-placement tests in many professions must be work related. Consequently, the use of situational tests is likely to increase in the years to come.

Ethical Problems of Testing

The widespread use of testing raises numerous ethical questions. We would all probably agree it is appropriate for the law to require that people pass driving tests before taking the wheel alone. But is it appropriate for a business organization to pry into an individual's fundamental beliefs and private fantasies before offering that person a job? Is it right for colleges to use attitude questionnaires in order to select their freshman classes? What does a student's attitude toward the opposite sex or freedom of the press have to do with whether or not she will be able to pass French 1A?

Such considerations lead to doubts about the use of tests in making major decisions about individual lives. Should people be denied a college education or be confined to a mental institution on the basis of test results? Should people be required to take tests at all, when many find it a traumatic, demanding experience of questionable value? The answers to these questions are not easy. Psychological tests, like other technological advances, have their uses and their limitations. But, as is the case with other technologies, they can be used effectively if people understand them.

CHAPTER REVIEW

KEY TERMS

- achievement test
- aptitude test
- intelligence quotient (IQ)
- interest test
- norms
- objective personality tests
- percentile system
- projective personality tests
- reliability
- situational test
- validity

SUMMARY

1. All tests are designed to find out a great deal about people in a relatively short time. Test scores are not ends in themselves; they are simply numbers indicating how a person responded to a particular situation.

2. Reliability is the ability of a test to yield the same results under a variety of circumstances. Validity is the extent to which a test measures what it is supposed to measure.

3. The percentile system is a method for ranking scores on a test. Standardization allows a test score to be interpreted in the light of the scores all people in a specified group achieved.

4. The first intelligence test was designed by Alfred Binet as a means of detecting slow learners. The test currently in widespread use is a revision of Binet's test, known as the Stanford-Binet. The results of this test yield an IQ score that is a measure of "mental age." The Wechsler intelligence tests differ from the Stanford-Binet in that they place more emphasis on performance tasks and yield a number of separate scores for different abilities.

5. IQ tests are good at predicting school performance, but whether they actually measure "intelligence" is difficult to say.

6. The classic study of family size and IQ was conducted in the Netherlands. Researchers found that the brightest subjects came from the smallest families and had few, if any, brothers and sisters when they were born.

7. Aptitude and achievement tests are virtually identical in content but serve different purposes. Aptitude tests are used to measure how well a person will be able to learn a new skill; achievement tests measure how much a person has already learned.

8. Many other psychological tests have no right or wrong answers; they attempt to find out what a person is like. Interest tests measure an individual's preferences for and attitudes toward different activities.

9. People who space their study time over several intervals are likely to do better on tests than those who rely on cramming at the last minute. A moderate amount of tension can improve test performance. Too much anxiety may produce panic.

10. Personality tests are used primarily as aids to psychotherapy. The MMPI is an objective (forced choice) personality test; the Rorschach ink blot test, and the Thematic Apperception Test are projective (open-ended) personality tests.

11. A situational test, such as a driver's examination, is designed to measure how well a person performs in specific "real life" situations.

12. Tests are the most objective measures of intelligence, aptitude or achievement, and personality that we have, and they are extremely useful tools. But, like any tool, they can be misused.

REVIEW QUESTIONS

1. What is one characteristic that all tests have in common?

2. In what ways can a test be useful?

3. What is test reliability? Describe three ways of assessing reliability.

4. What is test validity? How is the validity of a test determined?

5. What are norms?

6. An IQ test score is a poor predictor of musical ability. Does this mean the IQ test is not valid? Explain your answer.

7. How do psychologists compare scores obtained by different individuals?

8. Who was the first psychologist to develop an intelligence test? What is the name of the test he developed?

9. How was the first IQ test developed? How did Binet calculate the "intelligence quotient"? How is it calculated now?

10. How does the Stanford-Binet IQ test differ from the Wechsler IQ tests?

11. What are some ways you can prepare for taking a test besides studying a text and your notes? Give examples of ways to improve your general test-taking behavior.

12. What was the main finding of the study of family size and IQ in the Netherlands?

13. What is the difference between an aptitude test and an achievement test? Give an example of each type of test.

14. In what ways do interest tests differ from achievement tests? When are interest tests used?

15. What are the two basic types of personality tests? What are some of the differences between the types? Give an example of each type of test.

16. What distinguishes situational tests from other forms of tests previously discussed? What is the advantage of a situational test?

17. What are the advantages and disadvantages of using tests to make decisions?

ACTIVITIES

1. Can intelligence be learned? Try the following with two groups of subjects. Give one group a series of problems like the following example: "Is this statement true or false? If gyuks are jogins and kuulls are jogins, then gyuks are kuulls." Give the other group the same instructions but also explain the first example by translating gyuks, jogins and kuulls as cats, animals, and dogs. Then the statement will read, "If cats are animals and dogs are animals, then cats are dogs." The statement is obviously false. You can make up other examples. For instance, "If some chairs are made of wood, and some tables are made of wood, then chairs are tables." Experiment with a variety of such statements. Make some true and some false. Compare the results of the two groups. This is a question from an intelligence test. Can people learn to pass intelligence tests? Explain your answer.

2. The chapter discusses a wide range of devices used to measure intelligence, aptitudes, personality traits, and so on. Think about and write down the criteria by which you "test" others. How crucial are these "tests" in determining whether or not you decide to pursue a friendship? Think about the ways in which you "test" yourself. Are the criteria you use for yourself

the same as those you use for others? If not, what are the differences?

3. If you were asked to rate people on an intelligence scale of your own making, what criteria would you use, and how would you make your decision? What roles would such factors as memory, emotional maturity, creativity, morality, and intuition play in formulating your intelligence scale? How would you "test" for these factors?

4. Imagine that you work for an insurance company and are trying to find out how likely it is for people of different ages to be involved in accidents. What criterion do you use? The number of accidents per year? Accidents per thousand miles of driving? Discuss what is right or wrong with these and other criteria.

5. Some people consider psychological testing an invasion of privacy. Defend or refute the use of psychological testing. Discuss this issue with others—perhaps you can organize a discussion on the subject.

6. Call or write for one of the questionnaires available from a computer dating service (they usually place advertisements in the classified sections of newspapers). Fill out or just look over the questionnaire. Into what general categories do the questions seem to fall? What does the questionnaire seek to measure? Do you think this might be a useful way to obtain meaningful information about people?

7. Suppose you were asked to select the best person to be your instructor from among a group of applicants for the job. How would you go about making the selection? Devise a situational test to use in your assessment. What behaviors would you most want to evaluate in the applicants? Involve other students in your development of the situational test.

8. Go to your school career planning center and ask about the tests used to measure people's interests or abilities. What different tests are used in your school? How are they used? Look at the tests or inventories the office has on hand. Share what you learned about these measures with other students.

9. Organize a debate on the following hypothetical statement: People should be assigned to job and educational opportunities on the basis of their IQs. Divide the class into two teams, pro and con. How do you suspect that your life would be different in a culture that utilized this kind of placement?

10. Do you believe that test-taking strategies can make a major difference in how well a student performs on a test? Develop a ten-minute presentation on how to improve your test-taking skills. Give the presentation to your class. Be sure to include the following points: how to study more effectively, how to reduce test anxiety, and how to take the test itself.

11. Ask one of your instructors whether you can spend some time after class talking about how he or she makes up a test. How does the instructor decide the number and type of questions? Does he or she prefer objective or subjective questions? Does the instructor consider the validity or reliability of the test? How is the test scored? Are the tests ever graded on a curve?

12. Choose several adults you know—they may be relatives, instructors, or acquaintances. Interview them about the types of tests they have taken in their lives. Classify the various types of tests (for example, intelligence, personality, job-related). Ask whether they considered the test(s) fair. How do they feel about tests in general? Present your findings to the class, and lead a discussion about whether we rely too much on testing in our society.

UNIT 5

Adjustment and Breakdown

CHAPTER 13
Stress and Conflict

CHAPTER 14
Adjustment in Society

CHAPTER 15
Disturbance and Breakdown

CHAPTER 16
Therapy and Change

Figure 13.1 Stress is our perception of an inability to cope with a difficult situation or event.

Objectives: After studying this chapter, you should be able to
- identify various sources of stress.
- describe the psychological, behavioral, and physical reactions to stress.
- identify and explain the factors that influence reactions to stress.
- explain different strategies of coping with stress.

316

Stress and Conflict

John Stefano, an ambitious young bank clerk, works full-time and is also enrolled in a degree program at the local community college. Because of his busy schedule, he got behind in his studies and failed the final exam in accounting. John is worried that he may not be able to finish the program and earn his degree; he develops an unsightly rash. Sarah Mooney, also a student at the community college, learns that her parents cannot afford to help her with tuition next semester; her friends wonder why Sarah has suddenly become so bad tempered. Terry White has just heard that she's landed a terrific job. When she picks up the phone to tell her boyfriend the good news, she realizes that she has forgotten his number. John, Sarah, and Terry may all be suffering from **stress**.

What exactly is stress? There are many definitions, and even researchers in the field use the term in several ways. To some experts, stress is an *event* that produces tension or worry—failing a final exam, for instance. Others describe it as a person's physical or psychological *response* to such an event. Still other researchers regard stress as a person's *perception* of the event: a perceived difference between a demand placed upon a person and his or her ability to handle it or previous experience in coping with it (Mechanic, 1974; Wild and Hanes, 1976). This is the definition we shall use in this chapter—that is, we shall use the term "stress" to refer to a person's perception of his or her inability to cope with a certain tense event or situation.

To refer to the stress-producing event or situation, we shall use the term **stressor**, which is widely used in the field. It is important to note that an event that is a stressor for one person may not be for another. For example, traveling in an airplane may be a stressor for someone who has never flown, but not for a flight attendant. To discuss the body's response to a stressor, we shall use the term **stress reaction**.

Sources of Stress
Conflict Situations • Life Changes • Work • Everyday Sources of Stress

Reactions to Stress
Psychological Reactions • Behavioral Reactions • Physical Reactions • Factors Influencing Reactions to Stress

Coping with Stress
Psychological Coping Strategies • Modifying Physical Reactions to Stress • Behavioral Coping Strategies • A Lifelong Challenge

317

People who manage stress well are free from conflict.

Fiction. Conflict is an inevitable and unavoidable part of life. Conflicts can be a source of much stress. It is unrealistic to believe that anyone can eliminate all conflicts from his or her life. Rather, the key is learning to deal with conflicts when they occur. People who deal successfully with stress are usually good at coping with life's ever-present conflicts.

Many people think of stress only as a condition to be avoided. However, Hans Selye, the dean of stress researchers, has distinguished between two types of stress: negative stress, or **distress,** which stems from acute anxiety or pressure and can take a harsh toll on the mind and body; and positive stress, or **eustress,** which results from the strivings and challenges that are the spice of life (Selye and Cherry, 1978).

Stress, then, is a normal—even essential—part of life that goes hand in hand with working toward any goal or facing any challenge. In fact, as athletes gearing up for a game, executives meeting a deadline, and students cramming for an exam can testify, stress can spur us on to greater effectiveness and achievement. And whether we like it or not, we cannot escape stress; "complete freedom from stress," notes Selye (1974), "is death." But we can learn to cope with stress, so that it makes our lives interesting without overwhelming us.

SOURCES OF STRESS

Conflict Situations

In our daily lives, we often have to make difficult decisions between two or more options—for example, going to a movie with friends or staying home to study for tomorrow's exam. These alternatives tend to result from conflicting motives—say, the desire to socialize versus the desire to do well in school—and they are a major source of stress. Psychologists call these dilemmas **conflict situations** and divide them into four broad categories.

In an **approach-approach conflict,** the individual must choose between *two attractive alternatives.* For example, a high school senior has been accepted at two excellent colleges, and she must decide which one to attend. Such a conflict is generally easy to resolve. The student in this situation will find some reason to attend one college rather than the other—perhaps better climate or more courses in her intended major field. An approach-approach conflict normally does not produce a great deal of stress, since both choices are satisfying.

An **avoidance-avoidance conflict** occurs when an individual confronts *two unattractive alternatives.* Consider the case of a college graduate who has been unable to find a job after many months of searching. He is finally offered a position that has no future and does not pay well. Should he accept it, or should he continue to look for something better? Either course of action will be frustrating, and there is usually a high level of indecision and stress. The young man in this example may decide that one option is "the lesser of two evils," or he may try to escape the decision; for instance, he may register with a temporary-employment agency until he gets the "right" job, or he may apply to graduate school.

An individual who wants to do something but fears it at the same time is experiencing an **approach-avoidance conflict.** For example, a man wants to ask for a raise, but he is afraid he will be fired if he does. In cases like this, the degree of stress depends on the intensity of the desire or of the perceived threat. Resolution of this type of conflict is often very difficult and generally depends on the person's finding added reasons to choose one alternative over the other. The man in this example may learn that his boss thinks his work has been excellent, so he feels there is little risk of being fired if he asks for more money.

Probably the most common conflict situation is a **double approach-avoidance conflict,** in which the individual must choose between *two or more alternatives, each of which has attractive and unattractive aspects.* To use a simple illustration, a young woman working in Chicago cannot decide whether to spend her vacation in Paris or at her parents' home in North Carolina. She has never been to Paris, but the air fare and hotel bills will be more than she can really afford. Visiting her parents will be inexpensive and relaxing, but not very exciting. As in an approach-avoidance conflict, the degree of stress generated depends on the intensity of the attractions and repulsions. A double approach-avoidance conflict may be resolved in one of three ways: (1) finding new factors that make one option preferable—the young woman may hear about a reduced air fare to Paris; (2) finding a third alternative—she may decide to go to Quebec, which is closer and less expensive than Paris but still French in character; (3) choosing one of the alternatives in order to stop having to worry about the problem. In this last case, the person usually rationalizes his or her choice by emphasizing its good points and downplaying its drawbacks as well as the advantages of the other option; thus, the young woman may rationalize her decision to go to Paris by emphasizing that the trip will probably cost even more next year.

Life Changes

Among the most important sources of stress are major life changes—marriage, serious illness, a new job, moving away, and death in the family, for example. Common to most of these events is the separation of an individual from familiar friends, relations, or colleagues. Even marriage may involve breaking free from many longstanding ties.

Many stress researchers have concentrated on these life changes to determine how much stress they are likely to cause. One study (Thoits, 1978) differentiated between "isolating" events—death, divorce, and loss of job, for example—and "integrating" events, such as marriage, a new job, or birth of a child. It also analyzed events that involve a gain or a loss of prestige. This study found that isolating events and those that reduce prestige lead to higher levels of distress among all groups of people.

Two of the foremost life-change researchers are Thomas H. Holmes and Richard H. Rahe (1967), who developed a scale to measure the effects of forty-three common events, ranging from the death of a spouse to going on a vacation. Holmes and Rahe asked a cross-section of the population to rate each of these events on a scale of 1 to 100, with marriage randomly assigned a value of 50, on the basis of how much adjustment the event required. The figures they obtained form the basis of their Social Readjustment Rating Scale, which is shown in Table 13.1.

It is important to note that one life change can trigger others, thus greatly increasing the level of stress. For example, marriage (50 units) may be accompanied by a change in financial status (38 units), a change in living conditions (25 units), revision of personal habits (24 units), and a change in residence (20 units)—a combined total of 157 units.

Life changes are among the most important sources of stress.

Table 13.1 / Social Readjustment Rating Scale

Rank	Life Event	Mean Value
1	Death of spouse	100
2	Divorce	73
3	Marital separation	65
4	Jail term	63
5	Death of close family member	63
6	Personal injury or illness	53
7	Marriage	50
8	Fired at work	47
9	Marital reconciliation	45
10	Retirement	45
11	Change in health of family member	44
12	Pregnancy	40
13	Sex difficulties	39
14	Gain of new family member	39
15	Business readjustment	39
16	Change in financial state	38
17	Death of close friend	37
18	Change to different line of work	36
19	Change in number of arguments with spouse	35
20	Mortgage over $10,000	31
21	Foreclosure of mortgage or loan	30
22	Change in responsibilities at work	29
23	Son or daughter leaving home	29
24	Trouble with in-laws	29
25	Outstanding personal achievement	28
26	Wife begin or stop work	26
27	Begin or end school	26
28	Change in living conditions	25
29	Revision of personal habits	24
30	Trouble with boss	23
31	Change in work hours or conditions	20
32	Change in residence	20
33	Change in schools	20
34	Change in recreation	19
35	Change in church activities	19
36	Change in social activities	18
37	Mortgage or loans less than $10,000	17
38	Change in sleeping habits	16
39	Change in number of family get-togethers	15
40	Change in eating habits	15
41	Vacation	13
42	Christmas	12
43	Minor violations of the law	11

Rahe (1975) administered this scale to thousands of naval officers and enlisted men and found that the higher a man's score, the more likely he was to become ill. Men with scores below 150 tended to remain healthy, while about 70 percent of those with scores over 300 became sick. Researchers have since given the Holmes-Rahe scale to other groups of people and have found a relationship between high scores and a number of diseases.

The value assigned to a life change on the Holmes-Rahe scale is only a general indicator of its relative impact; it will not be true for every individual. Liem and Liem (1976) found that other factors can modify the effects of life-change stressors. In their study, psychological disturbances were lower among subjects who felt close to friends and received emotional support from them; physical symptoms were lower among subjects who had more money.

Some investigators (Hough, Fairbanks, and Garcia, 1976) have questioned the accuracy of the Holmes-Rahe scale. They point out that it examines only a small percentage of the enormous number of stressors and that it does not take into account cultural differences in what are regarded as stressors. Nevertheless, in spite of these problems and variations in individual stress reactions, the Holmes-Rahe scale is a useful guideline for measuring stress.

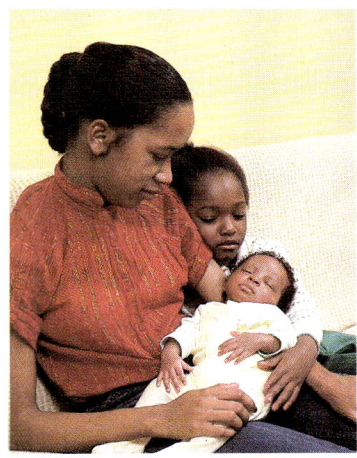

Figure 13.2
The birth of a child is a happy event, but it also creates stress for the baby's parents and siblings.

Work

Most people spend more time at work than they do at any other activity. Not surprisingly, then, work can be a prime source of stress, and there is a great deal of evidence to show that on-the-job stress affects the physical and mental health of many employees. The statistics are staggering: one study (Cooper and Marshall, 1976) estimated that cardiovascular disease, which is often linked to stress, accounts for 12 percent of worker absenteeism in the United States and adds up to an average loss of about $4 billion a year. Other physical and mental health problems that often stem from stress—migraine headaches, for example—resulted in a loss of 22.8 million work days in just one year.

What causes stress on the job? Researchers have identified more than forty factors that can be occupational stressors. We can group these factors into seven general categories.

1. *The nature of the job.* A worker may suffer stress reactions as a result of *working conditions* (temperature, humidity, noise, vibration, and lighting, for example) or *work overload* (a workload that is too heavy or too difficult); *underload* (too little work) can also be a stressor.
2. *Role in the organization.* An employee may suffer from *role ambiguity* or *role conflict.* Role ambiguity arises when the worker is unclear about what is expected of him or her. Role conflict occurs when the job demands that the worker do things that (a) he or she dislikes or disapproves of or (b) he or she thinks are beyond the scope of the job description. *Responsibility for other people* is another important role-related stressor. People in "white-collar" (managerial and professional) positions seem most likely to be victims of this type of stress.

Figure 13.3
Feeling responsible for other people is one source of on-the-job stress. In a hospital, where one wrong decision could mean the difference between life and death, this particular stressor may affect many employees.

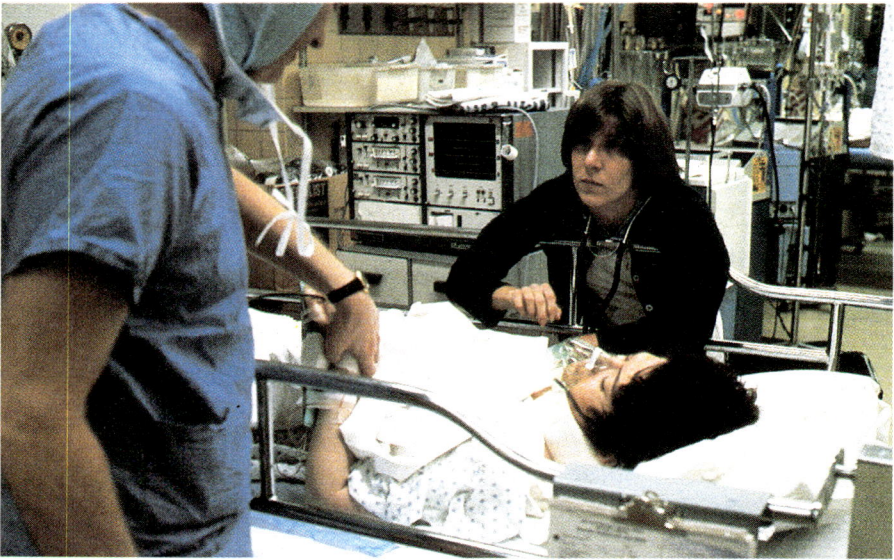

3. *Interpersonal relationships.* Research suggests that poor relationships between a worker and his or her superiors, subordinates, and colleagues may be stressful.
4. *Career development.* For many workers, especially those in the early phase of their careers, the desire to advance rapidly may be a stressor. For other workers, usually older ones, fear and frustration can result when they reach a "career ceiling," the point at which they can no longer advance within the organization.
5. *Organizational structure and climate.* An organization that does not encourage a sense of belonging, worker participation in decision making, and good communication within its ranks is likely to generate stress. Margolis *et al.* (1974) found that lack of participation is the most important and consistent signal of on-the-job stress and subsequent stress reactions.
6. *Family and outside activities.* The worker's life away from the job can cause stress on the job. Burke and Weir (1977) found that a close, supportive marriage—in which an employee can informally discuss job problems with his or her spouse—is likely to prevent or reduce on-the-job stress and increase both occupational and marital satisfaction. In contrast, a less successful marriage can intensify, if not create, stress at work.
7. *Miscellaneous.* As we have seen, life changes can be significant stressors. Many life changes are work-related—a change of jobs, unemployment, and retirement, for example (Cooper and Payne, 1979).

Everyday Sources of Stress

Some stressors—notably the life changes we have discussed—are major events. However, there are many minor sources of stress that we must confront and cope with either on an everyday basis (rush-hour traffic, for example) or only once in a while (say, running out of gas).

Frustration.   **Frustration** is a common source of everyday stress. It is the feeling of bafflement or disappointment that results when a person's progress toward a goal is blocked. It has a wide variety of causes—delays (a long checkout line at the supermarket), lack of resources (not enough money to buy a new record or clothes), physical limitations (running for a bus and missing it), accidents (breaking a glass), other people (someone breaks a date at the last minute), or institutional regulations (an overdue fine for returning a library book a day late).

Frustration is a daily occurrence; in fact, it would be possible for *all* of the examples given above to happen to one person in one day. Frustration is especially stressful when we feel that it has been caused by unreasonable circumstances (say, saving just enough money to buy a certain Father's Day present, only to learn that the store has raised its prices) or when the circumstances are unexpected. Constant frustration has been shown to cause stress reactions such as aggression, fantasy, and withdrawal.

Environmental Stressors.   As we have seen, environmental conditions such as noise may cause stress on the job, and these factors can have similar effects on the public at large. In fact, surveys have shown that Americans regard noise as one of the foremost irritants in their lives. Noise is particularly aggravating when it is loud, irregular, or uncontrollable. Constant exposure to unpleasant noise levels can lead to hearing loss and can interfere with learning. One study, for example, showed that children who lived in the lower, noisier floors of an apartment house built over a highway had a lower reading ability than did children living in the upper, quieter floors (Cohen *et al.*, 1973).

It has long been assumed that crowding is an environmental stressor, and indeed most people dislike certain high-density situations and can feel stress when other people get too close. Recent research on the long-term effects of crowding indicates, however, that its negative impact may have been overestimated.

For one thing, there is a positive side to crowding. Imagine, for example, that you and a friend go to a football game and find you are the only spectators in the stadium. You would probably feel quite peculiar, since we expect—and enjoy—the excitement of a cheering crowd in such a situation. The relationship between the actual density of a crowd and a person's feeling unpleasantly crowded is complex (Stokols, 1972). It depends largely on our ability to maintain a degree of privacy and distance from others. You may enjoy being part of a crowd at a rock concert, for example, but you may hate it when everyone shoves to get out.

Jonathan Freedman (1975) has concluded that the effects of crowding depend on the situation. If the situation is pleasant, crowding makes people feel better; if the situation is unpleasant, crowding makes them feel worse. In other words, being packed together *intensifies* people's reactions, but it does not *create* them.

Although there is overcrowding in many urban areas where there is also a high crime rate, we cannot state that crowding causes crime; other factors may be responsible. In fact, our modern urban life style is an extremely important stressor.

PSYCHOLOGY UPDATE

Hassles and Uplifts. In addition to the impact that major stressful events such as a divorce or death in the family can have, psychologists have studied the effects that relatively minor, day-to-day stressors can have on health. These more common stressors are called *hassles.* Examples of hassles include losing your car keys, being caught in a crowded elevator with a smoker, or being late for work because you were stuck in a traffic jam. Research has found a connection between hassles and health problems. It may be that hassles gradually weaken the body's defense system, making it harder to fight off potential health problems.

It has also been suggested that small, positive events—called *uplifts*—can protect against stress. Uplifts are things that make a person feel good, such as winning a few dollars in a lottery or doing well on an exam. Some psychologists claim that uplifts can have the opposite effect of hassles—they can reduce stress and protect a person's health.

Stress on the Battlefield.
Waiting for battle to begin is extremely stressful on wartime troops. In the Persian Gulf war, American troops spent five months camping in the desert before hostilities began. They were isolated, bored, and uninformed. In addition, most had never been in battle and were not prepared for the horror and carnage they were likely to see.

Mail from home provided the greatest relief from the stresses of waiting. Persian Gulf soldiers were inundated with cookies, candy, plastic Christmas trees, suntan oil, and other treats from family members back home. The military leased a cruise ship for troop furloughs. In addition, the soldiers were able to obtain news of the war from Armed Forces Radio.

The Army established a psychiatric ward in the desert where soldiers could come to talk about family problems and their own anxieties. Once battle commenced, the ward was used to treat battle fatigue.

The United States is now an urban nation, and more than one-half of our population lives on only 1 percent of the land. Not only are our cities crowded, but they also are nuclei of noise, soot, traffic, crime, and fear—all of which are stressors. Stanley Milgram (1970) describes urban living as "stimulus overload"; the individual is barraged by more inputs than he or she can deal with. As a result, Milgram says, people in cities tend to deal with each other more quickly, they ignore stimuli that do not directly concern them (a blind person trying to cross a busy street, for example), and they identify others only as roles (the tailor who does not have your suit ready, rather than Mr. Jones whose wife was rushed to the hospital last night). The result of these behaviors is a fast-paced, alienating, impersonal, and lonely environment. A steady push to achieve, another stressor, often stems from the pace and pressure of city life.

REACTIONS TO STRESS

A person who encounters a stressor that is intense or prolonged will react to it. There is a wide variety of stress reactions, and their effects range from beneficial to harmful. Many of these responses—physiological ones in particular—are inborn methods that our ancestors probably evolved to cope with stress effectively. And many responses to stress are automatic. Just as the body reacts to a cut by producing new tissue, it has means to heal the wounds of stress—crying, for example.

Coping mechanisms that worked for our remote ancestors are not necessarily successful in our modern technological society. But human beings are often slow to give up anything that is well established. We are more likely to depend solely on these ancient stress responses than to make conscious attempts to modify them or adopt others that we now know are more appropriate to our twentieth-century life style.

The ways in which different people react to stress vary considerably; each person's response is the product of many factors, some of which we shall discuss later in this section. Stress reactions may be physical, psychological, or behavioral, but these categories are not clear-cut. The human body is a *holistic* (integrated) organism; our physical well-being affects how we think and behave, poor mental health can trigger physical illness, and so on.

Regardless of the stressor, the body reacts with immediate arousal. The adrenal glands are stimulated to produce (a) hormones that increase the amount of blood sugar for extra energy and (b) adrenalin, which causes rapid heartbeat and breathing and enables the body to use energy more quickly. These responses are designed to prepare a person for self-defense. However, if stress persists for a long time, the body's resources are used up. The person becomes exhausted and, in extreme cases, dies.

Selye (1956) has identified three stages in the body's stress reaction: alarm, resistance, and exhaustion. In the *alarm* stage, the body mobilizes its "fight-or-flight" defenses: heartbeat and breathing quicken, muscles tense, the pupils dilate, and hormones that sustain these reactions are secreted. The person becomes exceptionally alert and sensitive to stimuli in

b

a

c

d

Figure 13.4
Our reactions to various events depend on our own personalities and attitudes as well as on the severity of the event itself. The man coping with the terminal illness of a loved one, the family facing the destruction of their home, the father facing a financial crisis at home, and the high school senior waiting for her college admissions interview are all experiencing various levels of stress.

the environment and tries to keep a firm grip on his or her emotions. For example, a hiker who confronts a rattlesnake on a mountain trail freezes in his tracks, is suddenly aware of every sound around him, and tries not to panic. If the alarm reaction is insufficient to deal with the stressor, the person may develop symptoms such as anxiety or gastrointestinal disturbance.

In the *resistance* stage, the person often finds means to cope with the stressor and to ward off, superficially at least, adverse reactions. Thus an airline passenger who recovers from the shock and frustration of losing her luggage may tell herself to keep calm when reporting its disappearance to airline officials, calling her insurance company, and so on. At this stage, the person may suffer psychosomatic symptoms, which result from strain that he or she pretends is nonexistent.

If exposure to the stressor continues, the individual reaches the stage of *exhaustion.* At this point, the adrenal and other glands involved in the "fight-or-flight" response have been taxed to their limit and become unable to secrete hormones. The individual reaches the breaking point: he or she becomes exhausted and disoriented and may develop delusions—of persecution, for example—in an effort to retain some type of coping strategy. A classic example of exhaustion is a mother who sits in the ruins of a bombed-out house rocking a dead baby as if nothing has happened. Soldiers in this condition have been known to wander aimlessly or fall asleep under fire (Toffler, 1970: 344–346).

Let us now examine some of the major psychological, behavioral, and physical reactions to stress. We shall discuss both short-term and long-term responses in each category.

Figure 13.5
A soldier subjected to extreme and prolonged stress may reach the stage that Hans Selye calls exhaustion and be unable to think clearly or act decisively.

Psychological Reactions

Short-Term Reactions.   Short-term psychological stress reactions may be either emotional or cognitive. The most common response to a sudden and powerful stressor is **anxiety**, which is a feeling of imminent but unclear threat. An employee whose boss passes by in the hall without saying hello may develop anxiety about her future on the job. **Anger** is likely to result from frustration. A college student who does not make the basketball team may fly into a rage when he goes to play his favorite CD and cannot find it. **Fear** is usually the reaction when a stressor involves real danger— a fire, for example. Fear directs the individual to withdraw or flee, but in severe cases he or she may panic or freeze and be unable to act. Common examples of short-term emotional stress reactions are overreacting to minor irritations, getting no joy from the daily pleasures of life, feeling hemmed in, and doubting one's own abilities.

Cognitive reactions include difficulty in concentrating or thinking clearly. A student who must give an oral presentation may worry about it but find himself unable to sit down and prepare for it. Another student wants to visit her father at work to surprise him with the news that she has been accepted in a highly selective corporate training program, but she cannot recall where her father's office is. Another type of cognitive stress reaction is unjustified suspicion or distrust of others.

Long-Term Reactions.   Prolonged stress, in combination with other factors, affects mental health. It does not necessarily cause mental illness, but it may contribute to the severity of mental illness. There is an increased likelihood of psychiatric disorder following a major life change, for example. Among attempted suicides, depressives, schizophrenics, and neurotics, there seems to be a definite link between stress and subsequent symptoms.

Behavioral Reactions

Short-Term Reactions.   Many short-term behavioral changes result from stress. A person may develop nervous habits (trembling or pacing, for example), gulp meals, smoke or drink more, or feel tired for no reason. There may be changes in his or her posture. He or she may temporarily lose interest in eating, grooming, bathing, and so on.

Some behavioral reactions are positive, however. In a tornado, for example, some people will risk their lives to help others. Such stressors often create attitudes of cooperation that override individual differences and disagreements.

Escape is another behavioral stress reaction, and it is often the best way to deal with frustration. For example, a woman who is on a bus that is caught in snarled traffic may get off and walk to her destination.

Long-Term Reactions.   While many people can endure great amounts of stress without marked behavioral responses, others may be seriously affected. Severe stress can be significant to the development of escapist personality styles—alcoholism, chronic unemployment, and attempted suicide, for example. It has also been noted as a contributing cause of aggressive personalities, delinquency, and criminal behavior. Moreover, people with high scores on the Holmes-Rahe scale appear to be more accident-prone than average.

Physical Reactions

Short-Term Reactions.   As we have mentioned, the physiological "fight-or-flight" response—accelerated heart rate and so on—is the body's immediate reaction to stress. This response is geared to prepare human beings to fight or run·from an enemy such as a savage animal or a band of warriors, and it was probably useful earlier in human history. But we cannot deal with most modern stressors—a financial problem, for instance—in this manner, and physical responses to stress are now generally inappropriate. In fact, prolonged physical arousal can cause health problems, including difficulty in breathing, insomnia, migraine headaches, urinary and bowel irregularities, muscle aches, sweating, and dryness of mouth.

Research is confirming that stress is a major cause of disease today.

Long-Term Reactions.   Evidence is mounting to confirm that stress is a major cause of illness today. We have already discussed the study by Rahe (1975), which found that most subjects who scored 150 or less on the Holmes-Rahe scale reported good health for the following year, while 70 percent of those with scores over 300 became sick. And one estimate (Schmale, 1972) holds that up to 80 percent of all disease today may have its origin in stress.

Emotional stress is very clearly related to such illnesses as peptic ulcers, hypertension, certain kinds of arthritis, asthma, and heart disease. Those who work in high-stress occupations may pay a high price. Air-traffic controllers, for example, who spend their days juggling the lives of hundreds of people on air routes where a minor error can mean mass death, are said to suffer from the highest incidence of peptic ulcers of any professional group (Cobb and Rose, 1973). Similarly, a student may come down with the flu on the day before an important exam, or a director may have an asthma attack on the opening night of a play.

Stress can be at least partly responsible for almost *any* disease, as shown by the scope of illnesses associated with high Holmes-Rahe scores. And stress can contribute to disease in several ways. Sometimes it can be the direct cause of illness; a migraine headache, for example, can be a physical reaction to stress. Stress may also contribute to illness indirectly. It may reduce our resistance to infectious disease by tampering with the immune defense system. Furthermore, stress can lower our resistance to disease if we react by neglecting our diet, not exercising, or smoking or drinking too much.

Animal studies suggest that psychological stress may contribute to some forms of cancer. One study involved a group of mice known to be vulnerable to cancer. Some of the mice were kept for 400 days in housing that exposed them to stressful noises made by people and animals. Other mice were kept in quieter housing. At the end of the period, 92 percent of the high-stress mice had developed cancer compared with only 7 percent of the low-stress animals (Anderson, 1982).

Some people smoke in order to reduce tension, but smoking increases their risk of lung and mouth cancer. Having any form of cancer is in itself a highly stressful occurrence. The degree to which a person is able to cope with this stress can be an important factor in his or her recovery (Taylor, 1983).

Factors Influencing Reactions to Stress

Personality Differences.   In some cases, the individual's personality may make him or her more vulnerable to stress. For example, two researchers have suggested that persons who exhibit a behavior pattern they call "Type A" are very likely to have coronary artery disease, often followed by heart attacks, in their thirties and forties. Those who do not have this pattern (Type B people) almost never have heart attacks before the age of seventy (Friedman and Rosenman, 1974).

The Type A person's body is in a chronic state of stress, with an almost constant flow of adrenalin into the bloodstream. This adrenalin apparently interacts with cholesterol or other chemical agents to block the coronary arteries, which lead to the heart. (It may be that high levels of adrenalin prevent the normal chemical breakdown of cholesterol in the blood.)

Type A people are always prepared for fight or flight. They have a great deal of "free-floating" hostility—that is, anger that has no real object or focus. They are extremely irritable, and one of the things that irritates Type A people most is delay of any kind. They become impatient waiting in line, always move and eat rapidly, often try to do two or three things at once (such as reading while eating), and feel guilty when they aren't doing *something*. They are also extremely competitive. In short, Type A people are always struggling—with time, other people, or both. Note that we have been describing an extreme version of the Type A personality. Most people respond to the world with Type A behavior at some times, but are not in a constant state of stress. According to Friedman and Rosenman, about half of the American white male population exhibits enough Type A behavior to bring on the high adrenalin and cholesterol levels that precede coronary disease.

Ray Rosenman has noted that modern society generally favors those who can achieve rapidly and aggressively; it therefore encourages Type A behavior. Thus, he believes, Type A behavior results from the interplay between personality and environmental conditions (Rosenman, in Dembroski, 1978).

Another personality trait that can affect the strength of a stress reaction is emotional expressiveness. Some recent research suggests that people who neither express nor admit to strong feelings of despair, depression, and anger are more likely to develop cancer than those who can give vent to their emotions. One study of cancer victims, for example, found that only 30 percent confessed to feeling discouraged about the future, even though many of these patients had tumors that were incurable (Plumb and Holland, 1977). However, the findings in this area have been mixed; some

Stress and Natural Disasters. A very stressful life event was experienced by the victims of the 1980 Mount Saint Helens volcanic eruption in the state of Washington.

One study looked at the effects of the eruption on the residents of Othello, Washington. The researchers compared data gathered from community records for a six-month period after the disaster with the same time the previous year. The records indicated large increases in alcohol abuse, domestic violence, and physical illnesses. The death rate increased by nearly 19 percent.

The long-lasting impact of the Mount Saint Helens disaster can be seen from the results of a three-year study that compared the residents of Castle Rock, Washington, which had been greatly affected by the volcano, with those living in another town that was not affected by the disaster. The adult residents of Castle Rock were nearly twelve times as likely to suffer from a psychiatric disorder. Many of the Castle Rock residents were suffering from posttraumatic stress, depression, and severe anxiety.

Are You Type A?

Are you high-strung, tense, always concerned about time? Then you might have a Type A personality. To find out for sure, ask yourself the following questions. Your answers will tell you whether you're giving your heart a hard time.

- Are you continually aware of time? Type A people live by the clock and measure their day in terms of how much they accomplish each minute.
- Are you always in a rush? Type A people do everything very quickly. They eat, move, walk, and talk at a speeded-up pace.
- Do you lose your patience when things take too long? Type A people get outraged when a sales clerk spends an extra minute ringing up a sale.
- Do you always try to do more than one thing at the same time? Type A people feel that one of the best ways to get more accomplished is to do two or more things at once.
- Do you tend to use nervous gestures to emphasize your point? Type A people express their tension by clenching their fists, pointing their fingers, and banging on the desk.
- Do you evaluate your life in terms of how much you accomplish rather than what you accomplish? Type A people emphasize such quantitative measures as the number of A's they got in school and the number of sales they made during the month.

If you answered yes to most of these questions, it may be time to slow down. Not because slower is better, but because slower is less taxing on your heart.

For more details, see Meyer Friedman and Ray Rosenman, *Type A Behavior and Your Heart.* New York: Knopf, 1974.

studies have found no strong connection between cancer and personality. The link remains an intriguing possibility that warrants further research.

Perceived Control over Stressors. In the late 1950s, psychologist Joseph Brady and his colleagues (1958) published the results of their classic (but now questioned) experiment on the effects of controlling stressful events. They linked two monkeys to a machine that gave them an equal number of shocks. One could prevent the shocks by pushing a lever and the other could not (Figure 13.6). The monkey who could control the shocks—later named the "executive monkey"—developed ulcers. Brady theorized that constant worry about when to press the lever produced higher levels of stress for the executive monkey than inability to act did for the powerless one.

Later attempts to achieve similar results with other animals were not successful. According to J. M. Weiss (1972), when Brady's research team

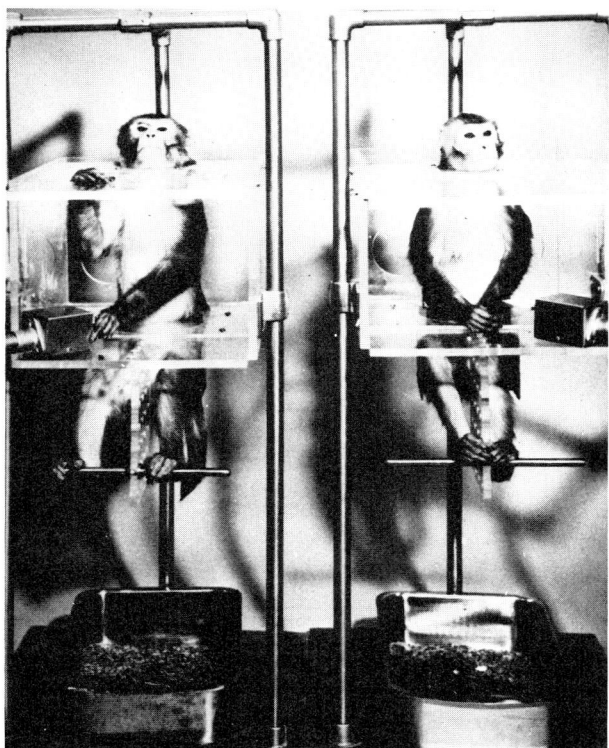

Figure 13.6
The "executive monkey" experiment. The monkey at the left, which could prevent shocks by pushing a lever, was the one that developed ulcers. The results of this study could not be duplicated, however. The accepted view today is that control over stressors helps to *prevent* physical disorders.

set up the original study, there was a bias in the selection of subjects. The monkeys who were selected to be the "executive monkeys" had shown themselves to be more likely to push the lever than the monkeys who were selected for the no-control situation. Thus, these monkeys may have been more reactive and hence possibly more prone to develop ulcers.

The accepted view today is that physical disorders are more likely when we do *not* have control over stressors. Most evidence to support this theory comes from experiments on animals. Weiss (1972), for example, gave two groups of rats identical electric shocks. In one group, a rat could avoid the shock by touching its nose to a panel; the other group had no control over the shocks. The group that could regulate the shocks developed far fewer ulcers than those that could not.

Subsequent experiments showed that feedback is also an important factor. Animals that responded to avoid shock and then heard a tone to signal that they had done the "right" thing suffered fewer ulcers than those that responded to avoid the shock but were given no feedback.

Weiss (1971) found that lack of feedback can harm human beings as well. His research showed that people develop ulcers when they have to make a very great many responses but receive no feedback about their effectiveness. This lack of feedback is a factor in role ambiguity, which we discussed earlier in the chapter.

Another study that used human subjects (Hokanson *et al.*, 1963) punished errors on cognitive tasks with mild electric shocks. Subjects who

Stress on the Home Front.
War creates tremendous
stresses not only on soldiers in
the field, but also on loved
ones back home. The Persian
Gulf war was particularly
stressful on military families
because more than 25,000 of
the armed forces sent to Saudi
Arabia were women.

The women soldiers were
forced to leave their children
behind with their husbands,
parents, or other family members. Husbands had to take
leave of absence from their
jobs or arrange for day care
for their children. Many children of troops in the Gulf suffered from nightmares and
loss of appetite.

One way that the husbands
and wives of combat troops
coped with wartime stresses
was to form support groups
among themselves so they
could talk about their problems and fears. Military bases
offered family members various kinds of help, such as psychological counseling and
financial support. Schools with
large numbers of military children also provided counseling
and special programs to help
students cope.

were allowed to take breaks when they wanted to showed less increase in blood pressure than did those who were assigned times for breaks. Such research supports the conclusion that we respond to a stressor more intensely when we cannot control it.

Social Support. Sidney Cobb (1976) has defined **social support** as information that leads someone to believe that he or she is cared for, loved, respected, and part of a network of communication and mutual obligation. He has found that social support can reduce both the likelihood and the severity of stress-related diseases.

Cobb's conclusion has been backed up by many other studies. A study of pregnant women (Nuckolls, Cassel, and Kaplan, 1972), for example, noted that 91 percent of those with high Holmes-Rahe scores and low social support experienced complications in pregnancy, as compared with only 33 percent of those with high Holmes-Rahe scores and high social support. (In fact, it is interesting to note that the high-stress and high-support group suffered fewer complications than did women who reported *low* Holmes-Rahe scores.) Another research team (Webb and Collette, 1975) showed that people who live alone are more likely to suffer serious illness or behavioral disorders due to stress than are people who live in families. As mentioned in Chapter 8, parents who physically abuse their children tend to be socially isolated. During periods of stress, they do not have a network of friends, co-workers, or church members to turn to. One of the preventive approaches to treating child abuse is to develop social support groups for people under financial, emotional, or psychological stress. In some communities, hot lines and volunteer family aides are available.

Some sources of social support can be especially helpful. One study of male blue-collar workers (Wells, 1977) reported that social support from wives and supervisors counteracted the health consequences of stress more effectively than did support from co-workers, friends, or relatives.

Amount of Stress. Throughout this chapter, we have emphasized that high amounts of stress can have serious effects on physical and mental health. However, as we noted earlier, *low* stress at work—underload—may trigger similar reactions. One group of researchers (Caplan *et al.*, 1975) studied more than 2,000 men in many different occupations. They found that as on-the-job boredom increases, so does the probability of psychological and physical complaints and illnesses. Assembly-line workers rated their jobs as most boring and suffered the most stress-related disorders. Accountants, engineers, and computer programmers reported average amounts of boredom. Professors and physicians expressed the lowest levels of boredom and had the fewest stress-related health problems.

Another study (Harrison, 1976), however, drew different conclusions. Work overload corresponded to greater job dissatisfaction in all the occupations under consideration. Underload, however, caused discontent mostly among white-collar workers; it had little effect on the job dissatisfaction of assembly-line workers. One possible explanation is that on-the-job gratification is more important to white- than to blue-collar workers, and underload does not allow for much job gratification (House, 1972).

a

b

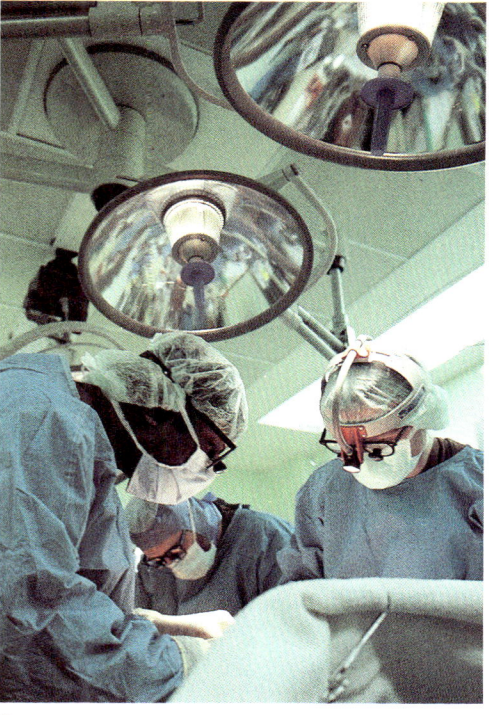

c

Figure 13.7
Low stress and boredom on the job can damage health as much as high stress can. One study found that assembly-line workers rated their jobs as most boring and suffered the most stress-related disorders. Computer programmers reported average levels of boredom. Physicians noted the least boredom and had the fewest stress-related complaints.

In spite of these somewhat inconsistent findings, we can basically describe the relationship between stress and health as a bell curve. At both extremes of the curve—very low and very high stress—illness is most probable. At the center of the curve, a person feels challenged without being overwhelmed; this is the point at which he or she is most likely to be healthy and effective.

COPING WITH STRESS

The best overall recommendation for coping with stress is to bring it under control before it is too late. Richard Rahe and Ransom J. Arthur (1968) have divided the process by which stress can cause disease into six stages:

1. *Perception of the situation.* The person is aware that something is challenging him or her.
2. *Psychological responses.* The person denies or minimizes the situation or represses its effects.
3. *Physiological responses.* The person undergoes the "fight-or-flight" reaction, which we have discussed.
4. *Protective behavior.* The person tried to deal with the situation.
5. *Signs of illness.* The person begins to act sick—staying home from work or school, for example.
6. *Frank disease.* A doctor confirms the illness, and the person is officially sick.

Rahe and Arthur believe that dealing with stress during the first four stages can generally—and relatively easily—prevent disease. If a person has reached the final two stages, though, the process is hard to stop or reverse.

To break the chain of events that can cause a stress-related disease, it is necessary for a person either to alter his or her awareness of the problem and of the potential consequences or, if stress is unavoidable, to modify its physical and psychological effects. Let us now look at some specific coping strategies that people use to combat stress.

Psychological Coping Strategies

Our interpretation or evaluation of an event—a process psychologists call **cognitive appraisal**—helps to determine its stress impact. Drugs can affect cognitive appraisal. For example, drinking may help to convince a man who has been fired that his troubles are not serious, or that he will enjoy unemployment, or that getting drunk is the best solution for the time being.

We can also try to influence our cognitive appraisals by means of psychological coping strategies, and stress reactions are more likely to occur when these strategies fail. Common coping mechanisms are **denial,** in which a person decides that the event is not really a stressor, and **intellectualization,** in which the person watches the situation from an emotionally detached standpoint.

Both denial and intellectualization can prevent physical reactions to stress. In one study (Lazarus *et al.*, 1965), three groups of subjects viewed a film that showed gruesome accidents at a sawmill. One group was told that the injuries were not real, but were staged by the actors (denial); a second group was advised that they were seeing an educational film about the importance of safety measures (intellectualization); the third group was told nothing. The levels of physical reaction were lower in the first two groups than in the third. Thus, if a person does not evaluate an event or situation as stressful, a stress reaction will not occur.

When a person knows that stress is unavoidable, though, **cognitive preparation** can be the most successful coping strategy. Irving Janis (1958) studied patients before and after surgery—which is a major stressor—to analyze the relationship between fear before the event and coping afterward. He found that patients who expressed a moderate amount of fear recovered most successfully; those who showed extreme fear or little or no fear before surgery did not cope as well following their operations. Janis believes that cognitive preparation, which he terms "the work of worrying," enables a person to rehearse possible outcomes mentally. In this way, he or she is better prepared for whatever does happen than is someone who has used denial or intellectualization beforehand.

Modifying Physical Reactions to Stress

Drugs.   Many people use drugs—both legal and illegal—as a way to reduce stress and the physical symptoms that accompany it, as well as tension, boredom, and depression. Physicians often prescribe mild sedatives (Valium, for example) for people who complain of stress. Some of these drugs may indeed relieve stress temporarily, but most do not. In addition, all of these drugs carry a risk of dangerous side effects, including physical dependence. If you must use drugs to cope with stress, do so only as a temporary measure to help you through a crisis. *Do not* use them to deal with normal, everyday stress.

Alcohol is the most widely used and abused drug today. It is a **depressant**, which means that it reduces the activity of the central nervous system. As a result, drinking will reduce tension quickly. However, research (for example, Miller, 1976) has demonstrated that the more often a person drinks to escape stress, the more dependent on alcohol he or she will become. Among chronic alcoholics in particular, drinking may actually *increase* depression or anxiety (Nathan and O'Brien, 1971). Alcoholism is a critical health problem in the United States; the National Institute on Alcohol Abuse and Alcoholism estimates that between nine and ten million adults in America are alcoholics or problem drinkers.

Tobacco is the second most commonly used drug. Many smokers claim that cigarettes relieve various stressors; they will smoke more at work, at parties, or when anxious or nervous. Studies (Silverstein, 1976; Perlick, 1977) indicate that smoking does not reduce anxiety or irritability, although *not* smoking tends to aggravate the smoker's stress reaction. Not only are cigarettes useless against stress, but they greatly increase the risk of lung cancer and a host of other major illnesses.

The most widely used illegal drugs, especially among young people, are marijuana and cocaine. Surveys indicate that the use of these drugs declined somewhat during the 1980s, but many people still use them to deal with stress (see Chapter 7).

Relaxation.   Many relaxation techniques have been developed to cope with stress. More than half a century ago, Dr. Edmond Jacobson devised a method called **progressive relaxation** to reduce muscle tension. This involves lying down comfortably and tensing and relaxing each major muscle group in turn. Jacobson later added exercises for mental relaxation in which a person conjures up images and then lets them go. **Meditation**, another relaxation technique, has been shown to counteract physical and psychological responses to stress (see Chapter 7). Experienced meditators quickly reach a mental state identical to that of Stage I sleep and are able to resume their activities feeling refreshed.

Biofeedback.   As Chapter 7 explained, **biofeedback** is a technique for bringing specific body processes—blood pressure and muscle tension, for example—under a person's conscious control. The subject is hooked up to an electronic device that measures the process he or she wants to regulate and plays that process back, in the form of either sounds or visual patterns. This feedback somehow enables many, though not all, people to learn to control various bodily responses. Biofeedback has been used most successfully to train tense people to relax.

Behavioral Coping Strategies

Controlling Stressful Situations.   There are several ways in which we can control our exposure to stressful events and thereby reduce levels of stress. As we have mentioned, escape or withdrawal, when possible, can be an effective coping strategy. A young woman who is not enjoying herself at a party, for example, can leave. When avoiding an event is not practical, controlling its timing may be helpful; you can try to space out stress-producing events so they do not occur at the same time. A couple who are planning to have a baby in the summer, for instance, may postpone looking for a new house until the following year.

Problem Solving.   Sometimes neither avoiding nor spacing events is possible. A high school senior may face a deadline for a college application and an important exam on the same day. In cases like this, problem solving, or confronting the matter head-on, can be the best way to cope. We often regard frustrations or conflicts as problems to be solved; in this way, the situation becomes a positive challenge rather than a negative setback. Problem solving involves a rational analysis of the situation that will lead to an appropriate decision. The student in our example may map out the remaining days to allocate specific times to work on the application and others to study for the test; he may also decide that he can gain more time for these activities by skipping band practice or postponing a date until the following weekend. Problem solving is a very healthy strategy that tends to sharpen insights and attention to detail and develop flexibility.

Exercise.   Physical exercise is another constructive way to reduce stress. It stimulates and provides an outlet for physical arousal, and it may burn off stress hormones. Continuous rhythmic exercise—running or swimming, for example—is not only effective against stress but also ideal for respiratory and cardiovascular fitness. One study of longshoremen (Paffenbarger and Hale, 1975) found that a high level of physical activity serves to protect against heart disease.

Support Groups and Professional Help.   We have discussed the positive role that social support plays in reducing stress. There are groups that operate beyond ordinary personal networks to help people with specific stress-related problems—Alcoholics Anonymous, Weight Watchers,

Figure 13.8
Physical exercise reduces stress, so find a way of introducing a regular exercise program into your schedule. You don't need to become an athlete: this man gets his exercise by walking to and from work every day.

crisis intervention centers, and so on. Professionals such as doctors, ministers, psychologists, and social workers can also be consulted when help is necessary.

Training. A situation can be stressful because we are unsure of our ability to deal with it; it may be new, unfamiliar, or dangerous. Training to prepare for such a situation can ease the stress. For instance, a person who is nervous about going to a friend's country club because she does not play tennis might take a few tennis lessons. Exposure to moderate stressors in a relatively safe but challenging environment allows a person to gain experience as well as confidence in his or her coping abilities; the Outward Bound program that trains young people in wilderness survival illustrates this strategy.

Improving Interpersonal Skills. A great deal of the stress we undergo today results from interpersonal relations. Developing skill in dealing with other people—family, friends, coworkers—is thus one of the best ways to manage stress. There are several advantages to being able to interact well with others: increased self-confidence and self-esteem, less chance of loneliness or interpersonal conflict, and development of social support systems.

A Lifelong Challenge

Although we have emphasized the problems and difficulties that stress can cause, we should not forget that stress is not necessarily "bad." As we have seen, too little stress can be as harmful as too much stress under some circumstances.

Throughout our lives, stress is a challenge that we will inevitably and repeatedly encounter. It is thus best to develop a range of coping strategies that we can apply to different situations, and it is important to learn when each strategy is most suitable. Coping strategies that are used inappropriately can actually increase stress.

Some people respond to setbacks in coping by learning *not* to try to cope at all. Psychologists call this condition **learned helplessness** (Seligman, 1975; see Chapter 2). In learned helplessness, a person suffers from an event or situation so severely or so often that he or she comes to believe that it is uncontrollable and that any effort to cope will fail. The person also begins to apply the same attitude to other situations; for example, a man who feels continually frustrated and thwarted on the job may give up trying to cope with difficulties in other areas of his life as well.

We *can* learn to cope if we try. Albert Ellis (1978) sums up perhaps the most positive way to deal with stress:

> I feel determined to strive to use whatever power I have to change the unpleasant stresses of life that I can change, to dislike but realistically accept those that I cannot change, and to have the wisdom to know the difference between the two.

KEY TERMS

- anger
- anxiety
- approach-approach conflict
- approach-avoidance conflict
- avoidance-avoidance conflict
- biofeedback
- cognitive appraisal
- cognitive preparation
- conflict situation

- denial
- depressant
- distress
- double approach-avoidance conflict
- eustress
- fear
- frustration
- intellectualization

- learned helplessness
- meditation
- social support
- stress
- stressor
- stress reaction
- progressive relaxation

SUMMARY

1. Stress is a perceived difference between a demand placed on a person and his or her ability to handle it or previous experience in coping with it. A stress-producing event or situation is called a stressor, and the body's response to it is termed a stress reaction. Stress can be constructive or destructive; it is a normal part of human life.

2. Conflict situations, which result from having to choose one of two options, are a major source of stress. The four basic types of conflict situations are approach-approach, avoidance-avoidance, approach-avoidance, and double approach-avoidance.

3. Life changes are among the most important sources of stress. Thomas Holmes and Richard Rahe have devised a scale that is a useful guide to how much stress various life changes are likely to cause.

4. On-the-job stress affects the physical and mental health of many workers. There are seven major categories of occupational stressors: the nature of the job, role problems, interpersonal relationships, career development, organizational structure and climate, family and outside activities, and miscellaneous.

5. Everyday sources of stress include frustrations and environmental stressors—noise, crowding, and the urban life style.

6. Hans Selye has identified three stages of stress reactions: alarm, resistance, and exhaustion.

7. Short-term psychological reactions to stress include anxiety, fear, anger, and cognitive disruptions. In the long term, stress may contribute to the severity of mental illness.

8. There are many short-term behavioral changes that result from stress; some are positive. Long-term behavioral reactions include escapist and aggressive personality styles.

9. Stress is a major cause of physical complaints and illnesses today; it can be at least partly responsible for almost *any* disease.

10. An individual's personality—notably the Type A pattern—may make him or her more vulnerable to stress. Other factors that can influence stress reactions include perceived control over stressors, social support, and amount of stress.

11. It is best to try to cope with stress before signs of illness develop. Coping strategies used to relieve stress may be physical, psychological, or behavioral in nature.

CHAPTER REVIEW

1. What is the most common conflict situation? In what ways can this conflict be resolved?

2. In what ways have researchers differentiated among life events?

3. What are two criticisms of the Holmes-Rahe scale?

4. Who identified three stages in the body's response to stress? What are the three stages?

5. To what illnesses is emotional stress clearly related? To what illnesses is stress at least partly related?

6. What are the negative effects of Type A behavior? Why do people exhibit Type A behavior?

7. How can emotional expressiveness affect the development of cancer? Are the research findings conclusive in this area?

8. What is the accepted view on the relationship between degree of control over stressors and its effect on physical disorders? Brady's famous study does not agree with the accepted view. How is this difference reconciled?

9. What is the best overall recommendation for coping with stress? When stress is unavoidable, what is the most successful coping strategy? Is worrying beneficial when a person faces an *unavoidable* stress?

10. What are five behavioral ways to cope with stress?

11. Is stress "bad"? Why or why not?

12. If a person does not learn to cope with stress, what condition may result?

ACTIVITIES

1. Study your own family, and try to identify stressors affecting each family member. Do these stressors result from the roles that family members have, from their ages, from their contacts with the outside world, from the ways that family members relate to each other, or from some other sources? Are there ways in which you contribute to family stress? Are there ways in which you do (or could) help reduce stress?

2. What are the major sources of stress in college? Can you pinpoint specific occasions, times, and events when many students seem to feel stressed? Are there any common elements in these? What might be done to alleviate stress in college?

3. The Holmes-Rahe "Social Readjustment Rating Scale" lists life events deemed to be stressful to adults. Assume your job is to develop a similar scale for teenagers only. In what ways would your scale be different? What would you add to or delete from the list?

4. Short-term reactions to stress often include physical responses—in other words, illnesses and other health problems. Ask a variety of people to give you examples of times when they have suffered from short-term health problems that they believe were associated with stress. You may have to prompt them with specific questions—for example: "Did you or your spouse get sick on your honeymoon?" "How did you feel on the first day of school this year?" "The last time you stayed home from school (or work) because of illness, was there anything stressful happening in your life?" Try to list a number of examples of stresses and corresponding health problems.

5. Observe a few cigarette smokers. Many smokers claim that cigarettes relieve stress. Do the smokers you observe seem to smoke more in stressful situations? What effect does the cigarette seem to have on the smoker? Do you believe smoking relieves tension and stress?

Figure 14.1 Adjustment is adapting to one's environment and coping with the stresses of life.

Objectives: After studying this chapter, you should be able to
- identify and describe different styles and types of marriages.
- explain the nature of parent-child interactions and conflicts.
- identify and discuss some of the issues related to adjustment to college life.
- explain various issues related to the work experience.

Adjustment in Society

The McCaslins and their five children live in a rural area of eastern Kentucky. The father is a tall, gangly man who broke his back several years ago while working in a local coal mine. He is not able to perform any kind of physical labor and has been unable to find any other kind of work. The coal company refused to give him a disability pension, and probably because he is living at home, his family has been denied welfare. Consequently, the family is forced to survive on garden vegetables and what little food they can buy with some assistance from relatives.

In spite of this hard, meager existence, they all work to maintain a close, loving relationship with one another. The father has strong ideas, talks a lot, and involves himself with his wife and children. The parents do not touch each other very much in front of strangers or their children, but "they give each other long looks of recognition, sympathy, affection, and sometimes anger or worse. They understand each other in that silent, real lasting way that defies . . . labels," writes psychiatrist Robert Coles (1971). Because they have learned to cope with the stresses of disability and poverty, we can say that the McCaslins are well adjusted.

By **adjustment**, psychologists mean the process of adapting to, as well as actively shaping, one's environment. When psychologists call a person well adjusted, they do *not* mean that he or she has managed to avoid stress, problems, and conflicts; as we saw in Chapter 13, such escape is impossible. They *do* mean that the person has learned to deal with frustration, disappointment, and loss and makes the most of himself or herself and available opportunities.

Psychologists who study adjustment try to understand not only how people cope with extreme hardship but also how they handle more ordinary experiences of life—for example, love and marriage, parent-child re-

Love and Marriage
Love • Marriage • Marital Problems and Divorce • Children and Divorce

Parent-Child Relationships
Sources of Parent-Adolescent Conflict • Parental Expectations • The Power Struggle: Escalating Conflict

College Life
Sources of Change • Coping with Change

The Work Experience
The First Job • Work Satisfaction and Dissatisfaction • Changing Careers • Comparable Worth

lationships, college, and work—that are potential sources of stress. Adjusting to each of these experiences involves unique challenges and difficulties, which we shall study in this chapter.

LOVE AND MARRIAGE

The idea of love without marriage is no longer shocking. The fact that a couple is developing a close and intimate relationship, or even living together, does not necessarily mean that they are contemplating marriage. Still, the idea of marriage without love remains heresy in Western thought. Marrying for convenience, companionship, financial security, or *any* reason that doesn't include love strikes most of us as immoral or at least unfortunate.

And this, according to psychologist Zick Rubin (1973), is one of the main reasons why it is difficult for many people to adjust to love and marriage. Exaggerated ideas about love may also help to explain the growing frequency of divorce. Fewer couples who have "fallen out of love" are staying together for the sake of the children or to avoid gossip than did so in the past. But let us begin at the beginning, with love.

Love

Some years ago Rubin (1973) covered the University of Michigan campus with requests for student volunteers. The top line of his posters—"Only dating couples can do it!"—attracted hundreds of students, so many that he had to turn most away. Those who remained—couples who had been going together for anywhere from a few weeks to six or seven years—filled out questionnaires about their feelings toward their partners and their same-sex friends. Their answers enabled Rubin to distinguish between liking and loving (see Figure 14.2).

Liking is based primarily on respect for another person and the feeling that he or she is similar to you. Loving is rather different. As Rubin writes, "There are probably as many reasons for loving as there are people who love. In each case there is a different constellation of needs to be gratified, a different set of characteristics that are found to be rewarding, a different ideal to be fulfilled" (228–229). However, looking beyond these differences, Rubin identified three major components of romantic love: *need, the desire to give,* and *intimacy.*

People in love feel strong desires to be with the other person, to touch, to be praised and cared for by their lover. Whether men and women look to their partners to fill leftover needs that were never satisfied in childhood, as many psychologists suggest, is debatable. But the fact that love is so often described as a longing, a hunger, a desire to possess, a sickness that only one person can heal, suggests the role need plays in romantic love.

Equally central is the desire to give. Love goes beyond the cost-reward level of human interaction. It has been defined as "the active concern for the life and growth of that which we love" (Fromm, 1956: 26), and as "that state in which the happiness of another person is essential to our own"

Figure 14.2
Distinguishing between liking and loving: a portion of Rubin's questionnaire.

Liking

1. *Favorable evaluation.*
   I think that _____ (my boyfriend or girlfriend) is unusually well adjusted.
   It seems to me that it is very easy for _____ to gain admiration.

2. *Respect and confidence.*
   I have great confidence in _____ 's good judgment.
   I would vote for _____ in a class or group election.

3. *Perceived similarity.*
   I think that _____ and I are quite similar to each other.
   When I am with _____, we are almost always in the same mood.

Loving

1. *Attachment.*
   If I could never be with _____, I would feel miserable.
   It would be hard for me to get along without _____.

2. *Caring.*
   If _____ were feeling badly, my first duty would be to cheer him (her) up.
   I would do almost anything for _____.

3. *Intimacy.*
   I feel that I can confide in _____ about almost anything.
   When I am with _____, I spend a good deal of time just looking at him (her).

(Heinlein, in Levinger and Snoek, 1972: 10). Without caring, need becomes a series of self-centered, desperate demands; without need, caring is charity or kindness. In love, the two are intertwined.

Need and caring take various forms, depending on individual situations. What all people in love share is intimacy—a special knowledge of each other derived from uncensored self-disclosure. Exposing your "true self" to another person is always risky. It doesn't hurt so much if a person rejects a role you are trying to play. But it can be devastating if a person rejects the secret longings and fears you ordinarily disguise, or if he or she uses private information to manipulate you. This is one of the reasons why

Figure 14.3
It is easy to think of love in a narrow context and consider only the sexual relationship that exists between a man and a woman. But this view omits the kinds of love that exist between children and grandparents, between people and their pets, between members of the same sex— particularly twins, and between parents and their children.

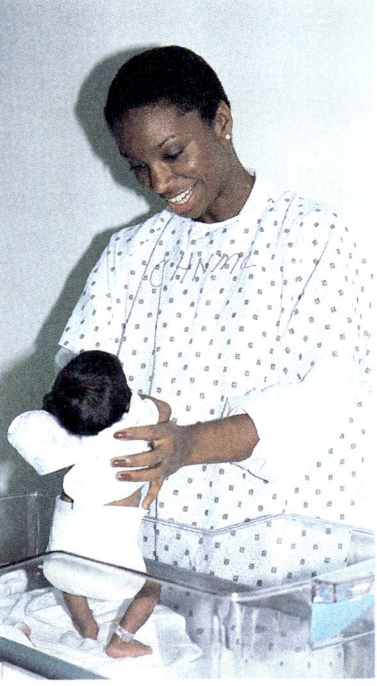

Triangular Theory of Love.
Love comes in many sizes and shapes. A theory that accounts for the many forms of love has been proposed by psychologist Robert Sternberg. Sternberg's triangular theory of love contends that love is made up of three parts: intimacy, passion, and commitment. The various combinations of these parts account for why love is experienced in many different ways.

Intimacy refers to the feeling part of love—as when we feel close to another. Passion is love's motivating aspect, which drives us to seek romance. Commitment is the thinking component of love—when we realize that a relationship is love and we desire to maintain the relationship over time.

Using Sternberg's model, we can see how different kinds of love are made up of different degrees of intimacy, passion, and commitment. The "love at first sight" felt on a first date has lots of passion but little commitment, whereas the love felt by a couple celebrating their fiftieth wedding anniversary has much intimacy and commitment but probably less passion.

love so often brings out violent emotions—the highs and lows of our lives.

Rubin conducted a number of experiments to test common assumptions about the way people in love feel and act. He found that couples who rated high on his "love scale" did, indeed, spend more time gazing into each other's eyes (while waiting for the experimenter) than other couples did. However, he was unable to prove that lovers sacrifice their own comfort for that of their partners.

Perhaps the most interesting discoveries in "love research" concern the differences between men and women. Rubin found that most couples were equal on the love scale: the woman expressed the same degree of love for her partner as he did for her. However, women tended to *like* their boy friends—to respect and identify with them—more than their boy friends liked them. Women also tended to love and share intimacies with their same-sex friends more often than men did with theirs.

This is not surprising. As Rubin suggests, women in our society tend to specialize in the social and emotional dimensions of life. However, the revelation that men are significantly more romantic than women is surprising. Men tended to agree with statements like "As long as they love each other, two people should have no difficulty getting along together in marriage," but disagree with unromantic statements like "One should not marry against the serious advice of one's parents." Women tended to take practical and social considerations more seriously. A full 72 percent of the women in the study were undecided about whether they would marry someone who possessed all the qualities they looked for in a mate but whom they did not love. In contrast, 65 percent of the men answered this question with a flat no.

A follow-up questionnaire, sent a year after Rubin's original study, indicated that when both a man and a woman are romantic, the relationship is likely to progress—that is, they become more intimate and committed to each other. The implication of this finding? That love is not something that happens *to* you; it is something you seek and create.

Marriage

A couple decides to make a formal and public commitment to each other. They marry. Will they "live happily ever after"? Their chances are good if they come from similar cultural and economic backgrounds, have about the same level of education, and practice (or fail to practice) the same religion. Their chances are better still if their parents were happily married, they had happy childhoods, and they maintain good relations with their families. All of these are good predictors of marital success. Study after study has shown that marital success tends to run in families, and particularly in families whose members marry "their own kind." This is the principle of homogamy: like marrying like (Arkoff, 1968: 467–474). What the statistics do not tell us is *how* couples who report they are satisfied with their marriages adjust to each other's hopes and demands, moods and quirks.

J. F. Cuber and Peggy Harroff (1965) found a wide range of adjustments in the upper-middle-class community they studied. Cuber and Harroff chose to study affluent families for two reasons: first, because they be-

Figure 14.4
Healthy adjustment to marriage seems to depend on whether the couple's needs are compatible, on whether their images of themselves coincide with their images of each other, and on whether they agree on what the roles of husband and wife should be.

lieved that too many marital studies focus on families in crisis; second, because such families represent the American ideal in many respects.

About one in six of the marriages they studied did in fact live up to the ideal. The couple enjoyed each other's company and spent a good deal of time together. At the same time, both husband and wife had a strong sense of individual identity and participated in separate activities. Cuber and Harroff called this a **vital marriage.** In a smaller number of **total marriages,** the husband and wife were deeply involved in each other's careers and hobbies, spent most of their time together, and seemed to live for each other.

More common were what the researchers labeled devitalized and passive-congenial marriages. **Devitalized marriages** had begun with passionate love affairs and high hopes for a life of marital bliss. Over the years the couple had drifted apart, but they still got along well enough to stay together. The couples who had worked out **passive-congenial marriages** had never been deeply involved with each other. For these individuals, marriage was a convenience. Living together and sharing responsibilities made it easier for both husband and wife to pursue individual interests. They had not been looking for a lifelong honeymoon and were content with their relationship.

Cuber and Harroff used the term **conflict-habituated marriage** to describe husbands and wives who spent most of their time fighting. These couples were always at each other's throats. But they did not see their battles as a reason for divorce. Indeed, the fighting seemed to bind them together.

Mirra Komarovsky's study of blue-collar marriages (1964) provides an interesting contrast. Nearly all the couples Komarovsky studied saw marriage as a utilitarian arrangement and had settled into passive-congenial relationships. In general these couples believed that males and females have different needs and interests. They thought it natural for a woman to feel closer to her female friends and relatives than to her husband; a husband closer to his male friends and relatives than to his wife. So long as the husband filled his role as breadwinner and the wife her role as home-maker and mother, both felt satisfied. There were some exceptions, some vital marriages, in the group studied. Komarovsky notes that the couples who enjoyed each other's company and shared leisure activities had higher levels of education and higher incomes than the other couples she interviewed (see Skolnick, 1973: 238–246).

Statistics on the reasons why couples file for divorce reveal a similar pattern. Lower-class couples are more likely to complain of lack of financial support, physical cruelty, or drinking; middle-class couples, of mental cruelty or incompatibility (Levinger, 1966).

Marital Problems and Divorce

In general, healthy adjustment to marriage seems to depend on three factors: whether the couple's needs are compatible; whether the husband's and wife's images of themselves coincide with their images of each other; and whether they agree on what the husband's and wife's roles in marriage are.

Conflict is likely to develop if the husband or wife has a deep need for achievement but the spouse is content with a leisurely, comfortable, undistinguished life. If a husband sees himself as sensitive and compassionate but the wife considers him crude and unfeeling, they are not likely to get along very well. Problems may erupt when a wife discovers that her husband expects her to quit her job when he finishes school and establishes himself in his career (something they may never have discussed). Similarly, a marriage may founder when a husband finds his wife devoting to their children the attention she once gave to him.

External factors may make it impossible for one or both to live up to their own role expectations. A man who is unemployed cannot be the good provider he wants to be and may take his frustrations out on his family, who constantly remind him of this. A woman trying to raise a family in a slum tenement cannot keep the kitchen with a broken sink clean, provide good meals for her family, or keep her children safe.

And often couples just grow apart: the husband becomes totally engrossed in his work or in a hobby; the wife, in her career, children, or community affairs. One day they wake up and realize that they stopped communicating years ago (see Arkoff, 1968: 469–487).

Let us suppose they are unable or unwilling to fill each other's needs and role expectations through accommodation or compromise. Perhaps they cannot face their problems. For example, many people have a taboo about discussing—much less seeking help for—sexual problems. Perhaps they have sought professional help, talked their difficulties out with each other and with friends, and come to the conclusion that they want more from life than their current marriage allows. For whatever reasons, they decide on divorce. What then?

In many ways, adjusting to divorce is like adjusting to death—the death of a relationship. Almost inevitably, divorce releases a torrent of emotions: anger (even if the person wanted a divorce), resentment, fear, loneliness, anxiety, and above all the feeling of failure. Both individuals are suddenly thrust into a variety of unfamiliar situations. A man may find himself cooking for the first time in years; a woman, fixing her first leaky faucet. Dating for the first time in five or ten years can make a formerly married person feel like an adolescent. Friends may feel they have to choose sides. Some divorcing people may find it unsettling to think of giving up on a marriage or being unattached and free to do whatever they like. One of the biggest problems may be time—the free time a person desperately wanted but now has no idea what to do with.

All of this adds up to what Mel Krantzler calls "separation shock." The shock may be greatest for individuals who saw divorce as liberation and did not anticipate difficult times. But whatever the circumstances, most divorced people go through a period of mourning that lasts until the person suddenly realizes that he or she has survived. This is the first step toward adjustment to divorce. Resentment of his or her former spouse and of the opposite sex in general subsides. The pain left over from the past no longer dominates the present. The divorced person begins calling old friends, making new ones, and enjoying the fact that he or she can base decisions on his or her own personal interests. In effect, the divorcee has begun to construct a new identity as a single person (Krantzler, 1973: 94–95).

Children and Divorce

Adjusting to divorce is usually far more difficult for children than for their parents. First, rarely do the children want the divorce to occur: the conflict is not theirs, but their parents'. Second, while the parents may have good reasons for the separation, the children (especially very young children) are unlikely to understand those reasons. Third, the children themselves rarely have any control over the outcome of the divorce. Such decisions as whom they will live with and how frequently they will be able to see the separated parent are out of their hands. Finally, children, especially young ones, can't muster as much emotional maturity as their parents to help them through such an overwhelming experience.

Adolescents experience special problems as a result of their parents' divorce, for their developmental stage already involves the process of breaking family ties. When that separation takes place before the adolescent is ready to play his or her own hand in it, the experience can be terribly unsettling. As one young person said, "[It was] like having the rug pulled out from under me" (Wallerstein and Kelly, 1974: 486).

Like their parents, most children do eventually come to terms with divorce. They learn to put some distance between themselves and their parents' conflict, and they learn to be realistic about the situation and make the best of it. Adjustment is made easier when parents take special care to explain the divorce and give children plenty of freedom to ask questions and express their feelings.

As common as divorce is in our society, luckily it is still a problem that

> **Adjusting to a divorce tends to be harder for children than for their parents.**

the majority of children don't have to cope with. But marital problems are not the only area of family conflict. Just as there are discrepancies between expectations and reality for husbands and wives, disillusionments and disagreements also exist between children and parents. Parents expect certain behaviors and attitudes from their children, but these expectations sometimes are not met. Children and their parents do often disagree. However, unlike married couples, children and parents cannot divorce. They must find other ways of resolving their conflicts.

PARENT-CHILD RELATIONSHIPS

The scene: Son enters living room, bouncing a basketball.

Mother: Get out of here with that. You'll break something!
Son: No, I won't!

(The ball hits a lamp.)

Mother: For crying out loud, you never listen to anything I say. You had to break something, didn't you? You're so stupid sometimes.
Son: You broke the washing machine. What does that make you?
Mother: Floyd, you know better than to be rude.
Son: You were rude first. You called me stupid.
Mother: I don't want to hear another word from you. Go to your room this minute!
Son: Quit trying to boss me around. I'm not a kid anymore.
Mother: To your room this instant!
Son: Go ahead, make me.

—Adapted from Haim G. Ginott, *Between Parent and Teenager* (1971).

As the scene above illustrates, conflict, whether between husband and wife or child and parent, is a process that can escalate with surprising quickness from contradictory desires to a bitter power struggle complete with name-calling. In our society, parent-child conflict is particularly common and explosive during adolescence. Adolescence is a period of inner struggles—goals versus fear of inability to accomplish them, desire for independence versus continued need for dependence, and idealized image of parents versus the realization that they are "only human." The adolescent thus needs parents who are sure of themselves, their identities, and their values. Such parents serve not only as models to follow or reject but also as sources of stability in a world that, to the adolescent, has become complicated and full of choices.

Sources of Parent-Adolescent Conflict

"The generation gap" is an expression we have all heard and used. It refers to a simple fact: adolescents and their parents tend to think differently about things. Some of the specific issues may change from one generation to the next. For example, in the days of World Wars I and II, many parents

Figure 14.5
Conflict and power struggles between parents and children are inevitable, especially when expectations of behavior or desires differ.

were upset and frightened because their sons wanted to run off and join the armed forces. But during the Vietnam War, parents were hurt and angered because some of their sons refused to "serve their country."

One of the most frequently discussed areas of disagreement between adolescents and their parents is sex. Parents accustomed to thinking of sex as something for married people are likely to find their children in active disagreement. In part as a result of the Pill, more young people are having sexual relations at a younger age than in the past. Equally significant, young people today tend to view premarital sex as equally acceptable for both men and women—a shift away from the old double standard (Smigel and Seiden, in LeFrancois, 1976: 316).

Another common area of disagreement is drugs. A recent survey of college students (Johnston, *10th National Survey of Drug Usage Among College Students*, 1990) found that 16.3 percent of the students had used marijuana in the past month and 2.8 percent had used cocaine. Some 76 percent of the students had drunk alcoholic beverages. Although this survey showed that the use of all three drugs had declined during the 1980s, drug use among adolescents remains a serious concern. Many parents may remember run-ins they had with their own parents over alcohol or drugs and dread similar conflicts with their children. However, parental concern usually prompts them to speak out.

The list of issues on which adolescents and parents can disagree could go on for pages, for it is seemingly endless. But there are other sources of conflict between parents and children of all ages.

Parental Expectations

In her book *Peoplemaking*, Virginia Satir describes a case from her experience as a family therapist:

> . . . [J]ust after Christmas . . . a young mother whom I will call Elaine came to see me. She was in a rage at her six-year-old daughter, Pam. It seems that Elaine had scrimped and saved many months to buy Pam a very fancy doll. Pam reacted with indifference to the doll her mother had worked so hard to get. Elaine felt very crushed and disappointed, inside. Outside she acted angry (1972: 205).

Elaine had done something many parents do. She had taken a childhood dream of her own (she never had a fancy doll when she was growing up) and projected it onto her daughter—who already had several dolls and really would have preferred a sled.

It is easy for parents to take their own unfulfilled dreams—not just for a little girl to have a doll but for a grown daughter or son to be a doctor or go to college—and wish for their child to fulfill them instead. It is also easy for parents to expect children to share their own interests and goals. Many fathers, for example, just assume that their sons will want to continue in the family business, whether or not the young man has ever expressed any such interest. But is is not always easy for parents to remember that because of different circumstances, different times, and different personalities, children frequently don't have the same dreams as their parents. If parents can't accept the difference between their own goals and those of their children, the result is likely to be hurt feelings and anger, leaving the child with the choice of either submission or rebellion.

The Power Struggle: Escalating Conflict

There is no question that there are many potential sources of conflict within the family. Fathers and mothers play different roles and have different expectations for themselves and each other. They also have values, goals, and expectations that they try to instill in their children—even though the effort may sometimes be reminiscent of putting a shoe on the wrong foot. Both children and adults may become stuck in their roles: parents sometimes forget how it felt to be a child, and children often have difficulty imagining what it is like to be a parent. Each family member experiences personal stresses, too, that relate to life outside the family, in jobs, school, or dating. All these pressures demand some understanding or at least tolerance from other members of the family.

As differences between family members persist, it may be difficult for individuals to keep trying to listen and understand each other's point of view. A father and son can argue the point of whether the motorcycle belongs in the garage or on the street just so many times before their words become a monotonous dialogue that no one listens to.

Instead of making a constructive effort to work out a solution to differences, parents and children, or wives and husbands, may take an easier but counterproductive route—that of blaming the other person, placing the entire responsibility for a problem on his or her shoulders. There are several ways of doing this. One is *judging*, or *criticizing*, accusing the other person of being at fault ("You're being selfish!"); another is *diagnosing*, or *psychoanalyzing*, by commenting on a person's possible psychological motives for an action ("You're taking it out on me because you had a rough day at work"). Other common tactics include teaching ("We don't put our elbows on the dinner table"); and *name-calling*, or *shaming*, humiliating another, thus making him or her feel ashamed, embarrassed, or guilty ("Don't you feel like a baby for storming around like that?") (Gordon, 1975: 113). In each instance, when one person tries to avoid responsibility for the conflict, the result is likely to be its escalation rather than its resolution.

In parent-child conflict the general pattern of family interactions also has a great deal to do with whether disagreements and disappointments reach the stage of war we witnessed earlier in the basketball episode. We saw in Chapter 9 that parents and children tend to relate to one another according to three general patterns. *Authoritarian parents* deal with their children (actually, deal *at* them) by making decisions for them. As one father put it, "You have to start early letting them know who's boss" (Gordon, 1975: 151). *Permissive parents* do just the opposite: they enforce only the guidelines their children will let them enforce. *Democratic parents* try to interact with their children in a way that will provide guidance but do not attempt to dominate the relationship.

Both dominant and permissive parents have good chances of develop-

Figure 14.6
When real communication is achieved in the family, family members are able to trust and be open with each other. They can be secure in the knowledge that they are understood.

ing a conflict-ridden relationship with their children. In the first case, as we have seen, children are bound to rebel as they grow up and learn to think for themselves; and in the second case, parents themselves may eventually feel like rebelling as their children keep testing their parents' limits. In democratic families, though, the chances for conflict to escalate are not so great. That is because these families try to depend on communication instead of power as a means of making decisions.

COLLEGE LIFE

We have been talking about the things that happen within the family, when children, wives, and husbands live together in the same household. But families don't stay together forever. Children grow up and leave home to set up new households and start their own families.

Growing up involves gaining a sense of autonomy (the ability to take care of oneself) and independence. Each person learns to make decisions, develop a value system, be responsible, and to care for himself or herself. Growing up is a process that starts long before an individual leaves home to live as a self-sufficient adult. But ultimately, it means separating from the family, both physically and emotionally.

For millions of young Americans, college is one of the first big steps toward this separation. College students are freer than they ever have been or may ever be again. This can be a personally liberating and stimulating

Figure 14.7
College life makes many demands on students away from home for the first time. Organizing one's time, meeting new people, and confronting ideas that challenge old assumptions all require adjustment.

experience. But it also requires adjustment. The emotional upheaval many freshmen feel has been called "college shock."

Peter Madison (1969) spent nearly ten years collecting data on how several hundred students adjusted to college. Each student provided a detailed life history and kept a weekly journal. Madison had classmates write descriptions of some of the students and tested and retested some at various points in their college careers. The results?

Madison found that many students approach college with high, and often unrealistic, aspirations. For example, Joan wanted to be an astronomer. She liked the idea of being different, and she considered astronomy an elite and adventuresome field. But she didn't know how many long, hard, unadventuresome hours she would have to spend studying mathematics to fulfill her dream. Sidney planned to become a physician for what he described as "humanitarian" reasons. But he had never thought about working in a hospital or watching people sicken and die.

These two students, like many others, based their goals on fantasy. They didn't have the experience to make realistic choices or the maturity to evaluate their own motives and needs. Their experiences during the first semesters of college led them to change both their minds and their images of themselves.

> **Many students approach college with unrealistically high expectations.**

Sources of Change

How does going to college stimulate change? First, college may challenge the identity a student has established in high school. A top student who does extremely well on the College Boards is likely to go to a top college. Nearly everyone there is as bright and competitive as she is. Within a matter of weeks the student's identity as a star pupil has evaporated; she may have to struggle to get average grades. Young people who excelled in sports, drama, or student politics may have similar experiences. The high school student-body president discovers two other high school presidents in his dormitory alone.

Second, whether students come from small towns or big cities, they are likely to encounter greater diversity in college than they ever have before—diversity in religious and ethnic backgrounds, family income levels, and attitudes. During his first semester, Bob dated a Catholic woman, a Jewish woman, and an Oriental woman; a history major, a music major, an English major, and a math major. Fred found that the students living in his house ranged from "grinds," who did nothing but study, to "liberals," who were involved in all sorts of causes; from athletes, who cared more about physical than intellectual competition, and business types, who saw college as a place to get vocational training and make contacts for future use, to guys who just wanted to have a good time.

A student who develops a close relationship with another, then discovers that the person holds beliefs or engages in behavior he or she has always considered immoral, may be badly shaken. If you come from a strict fundamentalist background, how do you reconcile the fact that a woman you have come to admire drinks heavily on occasion and thinks nothing of going to bed with a man on their first date? You are faced with a choice between abandoning deeply held values and giving up an important

Figure 14.8
After completing a year or two of college, students may find that the career goals they had as high-school seniors no longer suit their interests.

friendship. Madison (1969) calls close relationships between individuals who force each other to reexamine their basic assumptions **developmental friendships.** He found that developmental friendships in particular and student culture in general have more impact on college students than professors do.

However, if instructors and assigned books clarify thoughts that have been brewing in a student's mind, they can make all the difference. This was true of Sidney. Sidney did extremely well in the courses required for a pre-med student, but found he enjoyed his literature and philosophy classes far more. He began reading avidly. He felt as if each of the authors had deliberately set out to put all his self-doubts into words. In time Sidney realized that his interest in medicine was superficial. He had decided to become a doctor because it was a respected profession that would give him status, security, and a good income—and would guarantee his parents' love. The self-image Sidney had brought to college was completely changed.

Coping with Change

Madison found that students cope with the stress of going to college in several different ways. Some "tighten up" when their goals are threatened by internal or external change. They redouble their efforts to succeed in the field they have chosen and avoid people and situations that might bring their doubts to the surface. Bob, for example, stuck with a chemical-engineering program for three years, despite a growing interest in social science. By the time he realized that this was not the field for him, it was too late to change majors. He got his degree, but left college with no idea where he was heading.

Others avoid confronting doubt by frittering away their time, going through the motions of attending college but detaching themselves emotionally.

And some students manage to keep their options open until they have enough information and experience to make a choice. Sidney is an example. In June of his freshman year he wrote in his diary,

> I must decide between philosophy and medicine. If I have enough confidence in the quality of my thought, I shall become a philosopher; if not, a comfortable doctor. (quoted in Madison, 1969: 58)

By June of the following year he had decided.

> Sitting on a tennis court I had the very sudden and dramatic realization that my life was my own and not my parents', that I could do what I wanted and did not necessarily have to do what they wanted. I think I correlated this with dropping out of the pre-med program. Material values became less and less important from then on. (58)

Madison calls this third method of coping **resynthesis.** For most students this involves a period of vacillation, doubt, and anxiety. The student tries to combine the new and old, temporarily abandons the original goal, retreats, heads in another direction, retreats again—and finally reorganizes his or her feelings and efforts around an emerging identity. Thus Joan changed her major to psychology and found that she was now able to combine her desire to be a scientist with her interest in people.

THE WORK EXPERIENCE

For one person work means loading 70,000 pounds on his five-axle truck, driving alone for several hours a day, perhaps for several days, with only a few stops for food and fuel, talk, relief, and sleep. While he is alone in the cab, tension is constant: it is hard to brake suddenly carrying thousands of pounds, so he must always think ahead. The work is wearing, yet he likes the odd hours and the opportunity to be outside.

For another person work means spending eight or nine hours a day at an advertising agency, dealing with clients and supervising commercial writers. She earns good money, spends a great deal of time talking with people, and has plenty of opportunities to exercise her talents as a manager. All three are qualities she likes about her job. But she must also deal with deadlines and worry about whether millions of dollars worth of ads will sell the products or not—and, subconsciously, whether it's worth the effort if they do.

For a third person work means training severely handicapped children to use their muscles to grasp a spoon, to gesture in sign language, and perhaps to take a few steps. The job is often depressing and frustrating, but there are also moments of intense personal satisfaction when a child makes progress.

The point is, each person's work experience is different. Jobs are performed in different settings: offices, stores, schools, hospitals, mines, trucks. Some occupations have structured time schedules; others are more flexible. Some workers are self-employed; most must answer to one or

PSYCHOLOGY and YOU

Coping with Dorm Life. "I need my space," says the cartoon character Garfield the Cat in a TV commercial. Just as animals like their space, so do humans. We do better when we can control who moves in and out of our territory.

As the time approaches for college, you may be faced with choosing a dormitory. The most common types of dorms are the suite style, which consists of two or three double rooms in which four to six students share a common bathroom and lounge area, and the corridor style, which houses two to a room in a double-loaded corridor with a common bathroom.

Psychologists have found that corridor residents reported feeling more crowded and had impaired social relationships. They frequently avoided other people on their floor. Suite residents, in contrast, reported that most of their friends lived on the same floor. Corridor residents more often avoided eye contact with others. In addition, corridor residents were more competitive; suite dwellers were more cooperative. If you have a choice, it appears to be better to live in a suite-style dorm.

Figure 14.9
Each person's work experience is different; for some, work provides a means of self-expression. Few careers offer as much personal satisfaction as that of creative or performing artist. This photo shows the celebrated cellist and conductor Pablo Casals rehearsing with his orchestra.

more higher-ups. Some workers are "in it for the money"; for others, the job is a vehicle for more important personal satisfactions. Some workers do an entire task from beginning to end; others, like factory workers and copy editors, are only part of a larger process. And each person reacts differently to a job as a result of his or her own personality.

The First Job

For most people, getting their first full-time job is the major step into adulthood. It is exciting but frightening. Most students have vague notions about the world of work, pieced together from hearsay, brief glimpses during interviews, and the employer's sales pitch. The new secretary in publishing does not know what proofreaders and editors actually do. More important, she does not know what will be expected of her. Will the other workers accept her? The unknown is always frightening, and the first days and weeks on a job are often stressful. The ex-student finds herself completely exhausted at the end of the day.

Although some individuals receive training in job skills in school, few are taught all they will need to know in their first job: how to handle office politics, for instance, or cope with trivial problems, such as sending an overnight letter. Work also involves "psychological skills," such as common sense, an ability to deal with people, and an ability to cope with minor crises on a day-to-day basis. Few students are prepared for this.

In addition, the actual tasks a new employee is required to perform may be unexpected and disappointing. In school a student may have been writing papers about the world food crisis and the symbolist poets. At work in a publishing house she may find herself typing letters, filling out forms, and taking messages. She may get little or no feedback on her perform-

Figure 14.10
A young person's first job often requires a long period of adjustment. Hopes for an exciting, interesting job may have to be deferred until after serving an apprenticeship.

ance. A memo she spent hours writing may lie unread on her boss's desk. She dreamed of guiding young authors through their first novel, but in reality she rarely even meets an author. In short, she finds she is neither growing personally nor making a meaningful contribution to literature. The job falls considerably short of her expectations, in part because they were unrealistic to begin with (Coleman and Hammen, 1974: 351).

The "come-down" experience is common for almost any new worker, especially when he or she must start at the bottom of a job hierarchy. What kind of effect does it have? E. H. Schein (1968) found that half of one class of MIT graduates left their first jobs within three years—in part because they were not prepared for the work, in part because they were disillusioned.

Work Satisfaction and Dissatisfaction

The Ability to Adjust.   As a rule people do not become stars, editors, or company vice-presidents overnight. A young employee may know he could handle some things better than his boss does three weeks after taking a job. But if he becomes too impatient or if he makes the boss look foolish, he is likely to lose the opportunity to put his ideas into practice in the future. The emphasis here is on compromise: long-term personal goals should not be forsaken, but patience and an ability to tolerate frustration and delay are needed. A young woman may dream of becoming an actress, but waiting on tables may be the best job she can get. In this case, she will be happiest if she accepts waitressing as a short-term solution and uses her free time to come closer to achieving long-term goals.

Adjusting to work also means being able to take the good with the bad. No job, whether it be high-fashion model, corporation vice-president, or

People who are most satisfied with their work do the best job.

Fiction. In general, work satisfaction is not associated with how productive a person is on the job. People who dislike their jobs are often as productive as those with high levels of work satisfaction. However, work satisfaction is related to turnover. Employees who are unhappy with their jobs are the most likely to quit.

Figure 14.11
Many people continue to work after their retirement, but they are likely to change the kind of work they do. Someone who has worked in an office for many years, for instance, may relish the chance to work outdoors.

major-league baseball player, is all glamour. A model may have to pose in a bathing suit in 40-degree weather; a corporation vice president may have to deal with distasteful office politics and boring correspondence; a baseball player must attend practice sessions and stay away from liquor. As one chemist has stated: "Most of my job I do for free, because I enjoy it. The parts I don't like are what I do for the money."

Sources of Work Satisfaction. Some workers may seek high salaries, pleasant working conditions, and low-pressure jobs; others may be concerned only with finding personal fulfillment at work. Most workers, however, have both economic and personal goals. One study (Quinn et al., 1971) has identified five major sources of work satisfaction.

1. *Resources.* The worker feels that he or she has enough available resources—help, supplies, and equipment, for example—to do the job well.
2. *Financial reward.* The job pays well, offers good fringe benefits, and is secure.
3. *Challenge.* The job is interesting and enables the worker to use his or her special talents and abilities.
4. *Relations with coworkers.* The worker is on good terms professionally and socially with colleagues.
5. *Comfort.* Working conditions and related factors—hours, travel to and from the job, work environment, and so on—are attractive.

Changing Careers

The Department of Labor reported recently that in one twelve-month period, about one-third of all American workers (excluding farm workers and household workers) changed their occupations. Some theorists predict that in the future, people will change their **career** (by which they mean a vocation in which a person works at least a few years) several times in their lifetime.

As we saw earlier, people live longer today than ever before, and so they have a longer work life. It is not uncommon for a person to retire from one job at the age of sixty or sixty-five, then embark on a whole new career as a real estate salesperson, travel broker, writer, or consultant. Some employers (especially some local governments) have early-retirement programs that allow people to leave jobs with partial pay at a relatively young age; alumni of these programs have been especially good candidates for "second wind" careers. Many women also split their careers by stepping out of the job market to rear children and then reentering the work force for a second full career.

There is some evidence that people are changing careers because they are not so easily satisfied as they once were. There have been periods in our history, like the Great Depression, when work of any sort could attract and hold steady workers simply because of the great need for money. But times have changed. As we have seen, people want work that is psychologically as well as financially rewarding. If a person is unhappy at a job, changing careers may provide the answer, through better pay, better working conditions, or more interesting tasks. "Job shopping," or trying out several careers, is most common among people who have recently entered the labor force and are still trying to get a feel for the work that suits them best. This is one reason why most of the people who change occupations are under the age of thirty-five (Byrne, 1975: 54).

Does this mean you should forget about career training, since you probably will not stick with your first job? Not at all. You should acquire as many abilities and interests as you can—in and out of school; you should work to develop your interpersonal skills; and you should look at change as desirable and challenging. In these ways, more occupations will be open to you, and the better your chances of employment will be, both now and in the future.

Comparable Worth

Consider the following two cases. Susan is employed as a day-care supervisor for a state government. In order to qualify for this job, she needed three years of experience as well as college credit. In her job, she is responsible for not only the care and well-being of the children but also the supervision of several subordinates. Harry, also a state worker, is in charge of a storeroom and is responsible for supplying goods to various departments in his building as well as supervising several subordinates. In order to qualify for his job, Harry needed four years of experience. In terms of actual job demands, Harry's and Susan's jobs might seem to be quite comparable. However, Harry is paid more than Susan, despite the fact that Susan's job requires college credit. In theory, jobs of comparable training, skill, and importance should be compensated at the same rate. In practice, however, the market value of many jobs traditionally held by females is considerably lower than that of comparable jobs traditionally held by males. Moreover, as Juanita Kreps, Secretary of Labor in the Carter Administration, pointed out, "Many of the occupational groups in which women are concentrated pay low wages while requiring higher-than-average educational achievement" (Kreps, 1971: 40).

Many groups have been working hard to achieve equal pay for comparable work. The National Organization for Women has made the upgrading of traditionally female jobs one of its highest priorities. Labor unions have also been addressing the issue of pay equity. Delegates at the 1981 national convention of the AFL-CIO were urged to press for equal pay for comparable work in all future contract negotiations.

It may seem surprising that such demands were necessary. After all, the Civil Rights Act, passed by Congress in 1964, had included Title VII, which prohibits discrimination on the basis of sex in hiring, firing, terms of compensation, and work conditions. Moreover, the Equal Employment Opportunity Commission (EEOC) had been set up to enforce Title VII. The fact is that, for economic reasons, many employers are unwilling to raise salaries, especially if they are able to find workers who will accept the low wages that they do offer. It is up to the workers, therefore, to demand the wages to which they are entitled.

A 1981 Supreme Court decision opened the door for workers to bring lawsuits. However, it may be a while before standards of worth and job comparability are established.

CHAPTER REVIEW

SUMMARY

1. Adjustment is the process of adapting to, as well as actively shaping, one's environment.

2. There are three major components of romantic love: need, the desire to give, and intimacy. Love is not something that happens to you; it is something you seek and create.

3. Healthy adjustment in marriage depends on at least three factors: whether the couple's needs are compatible, whether their images of themselves coincide with their images of each other, and whether they agree on what their individual roles should be within the marriage.

4. Divorce is especially painful for children, but if they are treated with understanding and given the freedom to express their feelings of loss and anger, children do learn to adjust to their new family situation.

5. Adolescence is a difficult period for both teenagers and their families. Adolescents are questioning their parents' teaching and may begin to think differently about such issues as drugs and sex. Parents often have expectations for their adolescents—for example, the desire that a son become a lawyer or a daughter a musician—that are unacceptable to their children. These issues may result in conflict between parents and adolescents.

6. As family conflict escalates, many parents and children resort to counterproductive tactics of blaming the other person, such as judging, criticizing, diagnosing, psychoanalyzing, teaching, name-calling, or shaming, rather than trying to work out a reasonable solution to the problem. Relying on power (as authoritarian parents do), instead of open communication, to make family decisions is also likely to have negative results in resolving conflicts and to cause resentment and anger.

7. Students entering college meet people from many different backgrounds and are exposed to new ideas. Many students find that their career aspirations are unrealistic. They may also begin to question their own beliefs and behavior.

8. Some of the ways students cope with the stresses of college life include redoubling their efforts to maintain past choices, avoiding anything or anyone that could foster doubt, detaching themselves emotionally or dropping out, and resynthesizing their feelings and experiences.

9. A person's first full-time job is usually his or her first major step toward adulthood. Adjusting to work requires patience, toleration of frustration, and willingness to compromise. A first job usually involves tension in meeting the many unanticipated demands of the job and sometimes results in disappointment.

10. The most satisfying jobs provide adequate resources, financial reward, challenge, good relations with co-workers, and comfort.

11. Because of longer life spans and a greater demand for satisfying work, people today are more likely to have several careers in a lifetime. To meet this likelihood, people should acquire many varied interests and skills.

12. Male and female workers with comparable jobs do not always receive equal pay even though federal laws have been passed prohibiting sex discrimination. Sex discrimination in workers' salaries can result in lawsuits.

1. What do psychologists mean by "adjustment"? Give an example of an adjustment you have recently made.

2. In what ways are liking and loving different? What are three major components of liking and loving? How do males and females differ in their feelings of love?

3. What types of upper-middle-class marriages are described by Cuber and Harroff? What types of marriage did Komarovsky find in blue-collar workers?

4. What factors does marital happiness depend upon? What leads to marital conflict?

5. How do spouses react to divorce? How are children affected by divorce?

6. What are some common sources of parent-adolescent conflict?

7. How can parental expectations result in parent-child conflict? What are some of the counterproductive reactions to conflict displayed by parents and children?

8. How do authoritarian parents deal with their children? How about permissive parents? Democratic parents?

9. What are some of the new experiences and challenges that a student faces when entering college? How do students cope with stress at college?

10. What new challenges are faced in work? What factors determine how satisfied a person is with his or her work? What leads to career changes?

11. Why are people today more likely to have several careers in a lifetime? What are some things people can do to prepare themselves for more than one career?

ACTIVITIES

1. Pretend someone has just asked you, "How do I know if I'm in love?" How would you respond?

2. The idea of "romantic love" is fostered in fairy tales like "Cinderella" and "Sleeping Beauty" and in popular songs, novels, short stories, and TV commercials. Take examples from one or two of these areas, and discuss how they express the romantic ideal of falling in love with the perfect stranger.

3. Cuber and Harroff (1965) classify marriages as vital, total, devitalized, passive-congenial, or conflict-habituated. Study your family, neighbors, or friends, and discuss why you think their marriages fall into one of these five categories.

4. If any of the marriages of people you know have ended in divorce, make some notes on why you think this occurred. If some of these people are willing to talk about their experience, ask them how they adjusted to being divorced. What kind of problems did they have to deal with? What did they do to help their children adjust to the divorce?

5. The divorce rate has increased over the past several years. Some experts believe that one out of two marriages today will end in divorce. How do you account for this trend?

6. Write a short paper entitled "My Most Difficult Adjustment in Life." Relate an experience that required an adjustment, the feelings involved, and how you made the adjustment. What did you learn from this experience that could help you adjust to future changes in your life?

Figure 15.1 For psychologists, defining abnormality is neither simple nor sure.

Objectives: After studying this chapter, you should be able to
- distinguish between the concepts of normalcy and abnormality.
- identify behavioral patterns that psychologists classify as neurotic.
- explain the concept of psychosis and possible origins of psychosis.
- define "personality disorder" and explain how it differs from neurosis and psychosis.
- describe the problem of substance abuse in American society.

CHAPTER 15

Disturbance and Breakdown

A man living in the Ozark Mountains has a vision in which God speaks to him. He begins preaching to his relatives and neighbors, and soon he has the whole town in a state of religious fervor. People say he has a "calling." His reputation as a prophet and healer spreads, and in time he is drawing large audiences everywhere he goes. However, when he ventures into St. Louis and attempts to hold a prayer meeting, blocking traffic on a main street at rush hour, he is arrested. He tells the policemen about his conversations with God, and they hurry him off to the nearest mental hospital.

A homemaker is tired all the time, but she has trouble sleeping. The chores keep piling up because she has no energy. Applications for evening courses and "help wanted" clippings from the classified ads lay untouched in a drawer. She consults the family doctor, but he says she's in perfect health. One night she tells her husband that she's thinking of seeing a psychotherapist. He thinks this is ridiculous. According to him, all she needs is to get up out of her chair and get busy.

Who is right? The "prophet" or the policemen? The homemaker or her husband? It is often difficult to draw a line between "sanity" and "madness," normal and abnormal behavior. Behavior that some people consider normal seems crazy to others. Many non-Western peoples, along with religious fundamentalists in our own country, feel that having visions and hearing voices are important parts of a religious experience. Other people believe these are symptoms of mental disturbance. The man from the Ozarks was interviewed by psychiatrists, diagnosed as "paranoid schizophrenic," and hospitalized for mental illness. Had he stayed home, he could have been considered perfectly okay. Indeed, more than okay—special (Slotkin, 1955).

What Is Abnormal Behavior?
Deviation from Normality • Adjustment • Psychological Health • Is Mental Illness a Myth? • Using Psychology: Legal Definitions of Sanity

DSM-III-R: New Ways to Categorize Mental Illness

Further Aspects of Classification

Neurosis
Anxiety • Phobias • Obsessions and Compulsions • Somatoform Disorders • Dissociative Disorders • Depression • Suicide

Psychosis
Schizophrenia • Mood Disorders • Causes of Psychosis

Personality Disorders

Substance Abuse Disorders
Alcoholism

Behavior some people consider normal seems crazy to others.

WHAT IS ABNORMAL BEHAVIOR?

The man in our example was classified as mentally troubled because his behavior was so different from what other people felt was "normal." Yet the fact that a person is different does not necessarily mean that he or she is insane. Indeed, going along with the crowd may at times be self-destructive. Most readers—and most psychologists—would agree that a teenager who uses heroin because nearly everyone in his social circle does has problems.

In the case of the homemaker, she was the one who decided she was psychologically troubled, simply because she was so lethargic. Yet lethargy and even genuine depression are certainly not foolproof signs of psychological disturbance or of impending breakdown. Everyone feels low from time to time.

How, then, do psychologists distinguish the normal from the abnormal? There are a number of ways to define abnormality, none of which is entirely satisfactory. We will look at the most popular ways of drawing the line between normal and abnormal: the deviance approach, the adjustment approach, and the psychological-health model. Then we will look at the application of these methods in legal definitions of abnormality. Finally, we will consider the criticism that in all these models people are arbitrarily labeled mentally ill.

Figure 15.2
The line between normal and abnormal is a fine one and depends very much on the observer and the standard being used. What some people consider deviant, others may see as just a little odd.

Deviation from Normality

One approach to defining abnormality is to say that whatever most people do is normal. Abnormality, then, is any deviation from the average or from the majority. It is normal to bathe periodically, to express grief at the death of a loved one, and to wear warm clothes when going out in the cold because most people do so. Because very few people take ten showers a day, or laugh when a loved one dies, or wear bathing suits in the snow, those who do so may be considered abnormal.

However, the deviance approach, as commonly used as it is, has serious limitations. If most people cheat on their income-tax returns, are honest taxpayers abnormal? If most people are noncreative, was Shakespeare abnormal? Because the majority is not always right or best, the deviance approach to defining abnormality is not a generally useful standard.

Adjustment

Another way to distinguish normal from abnormal people is to say that normal people are able to get along in the world—physically, emotionally, and socially. They can feed and clothe themselves, work, find friends, and live by the rules of society. By this definition, abnormal people are the ones who fail to *adjust*. They may be so unhappy that they refuse to eat or so lethargic that they cannot hold a job. They may experience so much anxiety in relationships with others that they end up avoiding people, living in a lonely world of their own.

One criticism of this approach is that normal people may occasionally have problems coping or adjusting when they are faced with abnormal circumstances. For example, the death of a child may make a "normal" woman so unhappy that she wants to avoid all other people. Does that mean that she's abnormal?

Psychological Health

The terms "mental illness" and "mental health" imply that psychological disturbance or abnormality is like a physical sickness—such as the flu or tuberculosis. Although many psychologists are beginning to think that "mental illness" is different from physical illness, the idea remains that there is some ideal way for people to function psychologically, just as there is an ideal way for people to function physically. Some psychologists feel that the normal or healthy person would be one who is functioning ideally or who at least is striving toward ideal functioning. Personality theorists such as Carl Jung and Abraham Maslow (see Chapter 11) have tried to describe this striving process, which is often referred to as *self-actualization*. According to this line of thinking, to be normal or healthy involves full acceptance and expression of one's own individuality and humanness.

One problem with this approach to defining abnormality is that it is difficult to determine whether or not a person is doing a good job of actualizing himself or herself. How can you tell when a person is doing his or her best? What are the signs that he or she is losing the struggle? Answers to such questions must often be arbitrary.

Is Mental Illness a Myth?

The current definitions of abnormality are somewhat arbitrary. And this fact has led some theorists to conclude that labeling a person as "mentally ill" simply because his or her behavior is odd is cruel and irresponsible. The foremost spokesperson of this point of view is the American psychiatrist Thomas Szasz (1961).

Szasz argues that most of the people whom we call mentally ill are not ill at all. They simply have "problems in living"—serious conflicts with the world around them. But instead of dealing with the patient's conflict as something that deserves attention and respect, psychiatrists simply label him as "sick" and send him off to a hospital. The society's norms remain unchallenged, and the psychiatrist remains in a comfortable position of authority. The one who loses is the patient, who is deprived both of responsibility for his behavior and of his dignity as a human being. As a result, Szasz claims, the patient's problems intensify. Szasz's position is a minority stand. Most psychologists and psychiatrists would agree that a person who claims to be God or Napoleon is truly abnormal and disturbed.

The fact that it is difficult to define abnormality does not mean that no such thing exists. What it does mean is that we should be very cautious about judging a person to be "mentally ill" just because he or she acts in a way that we cannot understand. It should also be kept in mind that mild

Figure 15.3
The Madwoman, painted by Chaim Soutine in 1920. Many people believe that those who are mentally ill are always recognizable by their bizarre appearance and behavior—that they are somehow fundamentally different from the rest of us.

psychological disorders are extremely common. It is only when a psychological problem becomes severe enough to disrupt everyday life that it is thought of as "abnormality" or "illness."

USING PSYCHOLOGY

Legal Definitions of Sanity

When John Hinckley was tried for shooting President Ronald Reagan in 1981, he was found "not guilty by reason of insanity" and sent to a mental hospital. This widely publicized case raised some concern among psychiatrists and lawyers about the legal definition of sanity. The terms "sane" and "insane" are legal, rather than psychological, terms.

While there is no single definition of criminal insanity, the most widely used set of guidelines was developed by the American Law Institute in 1962. It emphasized that people are not responsible for their criminal acts if "as a result of mental disease or defect" they do not know that what they did was wrong or if they were unable to act differently. The guidelines also noted that "the terms 'mental disease or defect' do not include an abnormality manifested only by repeated criminal . . . conduct."

Figure 15.4
President Reagan waving to the crowd moments before he was shot by John Hinckley. Hinckley's attorney argued that his client was insane and could not be held responsible for the shooting.

It is often difficult to apply these guidelines to real people. As in the Hinckley case, expert witnesses are usually called on both sides. The defense lawyer maintains that his or her client is insane, and the prosecutor tries to prove the defendant sane. The jurors decide which set of expert witnesses is correct. A person who is judged insane may spend more time in a mental hospital than he or she would have spent in prison if judged sane.

Although an insanity defense generates publicity, this plea is used rarely and is usually unsuccessful. The courts judge people insane much more often for purposes of commitment to mental institutions.

Laws vary from state to state, but generally a person can be committed to a mental hospital if he or she is judged to be (1) mentally ill and (2) in need of treatment or dangerous to himself or herself or others.

In *formal commitment* proceedings, a friend or relative usually asks a judge to order a mental health examination. *Informal commitment* occurs when, for example, the police bring in a person who is acting wildly. In most states, a person can be held against his or her will for a specified period of time if two physicians (not necessarily psychiatrists) sign a certificate ordering the commitment.

Many mental patients have formed groups to protect their legal rights. As a result, the legal status of involuntary commitment procedures and patients' rights for treatment is likely to continue to change (Davison and Neale, 1978).

DSM-III-R: NEW WAYS TO CATEGORIZE MENTAL ILLNESS

For years psychiatrists have been trying to devise a logical and useful method for classifying emotional disorders. This is a difficult task, for psychological problems do not lend themselves to the same sort of categorizing that physical illnesses do. The causes and symptoms of psychological disturbances and breakdowns, and the cures for those breakdowns, are rarely obvious or clear-cut.

All of the major classification schemes have accepted the medical model—they assume that abnormal behavior can be described in the same manner as any physical illness. The physician diagnoses a specific disease when a person has certain specific symptoms.

In 1952, the American Psychiatric Association agreed upon a standard system for classifying abnormal symptoms, which it published in the *Diagnostic and Statistical Manual of Mental Disorders*, or **DSM**. This has been revised as the DSM-II (1968), the DSM-III (1980), and the DSM-III-R (1987).

The DSM-II was criticized as too vague: two psychologists often gave different diagnoses for the same patient. The DSM-III system required more concrete and specific symptoms for a diagnosis. As a result, its diagnoses were far more reliable. In DSM editions prior to DSM-III, disorders were classified not only by symptoms but also by assumed causes. This made consistent diagnoses difficult. Also, before the publication of DSM-III, it was difficult to assign multiple diagnoses.

The DSM-III-R (see Table 15.1) further refined the system of diagnoses and made it consistent with the International Classification of Diseases (ICD-9) system used by the World Health Organization for classifying all diseases. The DSM-IV, scheduled to be published in 1994, promises few major changes from DSM-III-R. One controversial addition, however, is the inclusion of premenstrual syndrome (PMS) as a distinct category.

The DSM-III-R emphasizes behavior patterns that have been found to occur in particular clusters rather than emphasizing the causes of various disorders. Furthermore, each diagnostic disorder is distinguished from other, similar diagnoses that a psychiatrist or psychologist may be considering.

Within each diagnostic category, the following four descriptions are included:

1. Essential features of the disorder—those that "define" the disorder
2. Associated features—features that are usually present
3. Diagnostic criteria—a list of symptoms (taken from the lists of essential and associated features) that must be present for the patient to be given this diagnostic label
4. Information on differential diagnosis—that is, how to distinguish this disorder from other disorders with which it might be confused

These more precise diagnostic criteria reduce the chances that the same patient will be classified as schizophrenic by one doctor and manic-depressive by another. Since researchers often rely on diagnostic labels to study underlying factors that may cause disorders, it is particularly important for their work that patients with similar symptoms be classified in the same diagnostic category.

The DSM-III-R also recognizes the complexity of classifying people on the basis of mental disorders. Often, a person may exhibit more than one disorder or may be experiencing other stresses that complicate the diagnosis. In early classification systems, it was difficult to give a patient more than one label. The DSM-III-R overcame this problem by using five major dimensions, or *axes*, to describe a person's mental functioning. Each axis reflects a different aspect of a patient's case. Because the DSM-III-R uses five axes to evaluate individuals, it is referred to as a multiple-axial system.

Axis I is used to classify current symptoms into explicitly defined categories. These categories range from disorders that are usually first evident in infancy, childhood, or adolescence (such as conduct disorders or autism) to substance-use disorders (such as alcoholism), to schizophrenic disorders.

Table 15.1 / Abbreviated List of DSM-III-R Categories

Disorders usually first evident in infancy, childhood, or adolescence
Mental retardation
Pervasive development disorders (for example, autism)
Specific developmental disorders (for example, reading disorder)
Attention deficit disorders
Disruptive behavior disorders
Anxiety disorders of childhood or adolescence
Eating disorders (for example, anorexia, bulimia)
Gender identity disorders (for example, transsexualism)
Elimination disorders (for example, bedwetting)

Organic mental disorders
Primary dementia of the Alzheimer type
Psychoactive substance-induced organic mental disorders (for example, alcohol intoxication, nicotine withdrawal)

Psychoactive substance use disorders

Schizophrenic disorders
Disorganized
Catatonic
Paranoid
Chronic undifferentiated

Delusional paranoid disorders

Mood disorders
Bipolar disorders
Major depression

Anxiety disorders
Phobic disorders
Anxiety disorders
Post-traumatic stress disorder

Somatoform disorders
Somatization disorder
Conversion disorder
Psychogenic pain disorder
Hypochondriasis

Dissociative disorders
Multiple personality disorder
Psychogenic amnesia
Psychogenic fugue
Depersonalization disorder

Sexual disorders
Paraphilias
Sexual dysfunctions

Sleep disorders

Impulse control disorders
(for example, kleptomania, pyromania, pathological gambling)

Adjustment disorders

Personality disorders
Paranoid
Schizoid
Schizotypal
Histrionic
Narcissistic
Antisocial
Borderline
Avoidant
Dependent
Compulsive
Passive-aggressive

Adapted from: *Diagnostic and Statistical Manual of Mental Disorders*, 3/E. Washington, D.C.: American Psychiatric Association, 1987.

Axis II is used to describe personality disorders or maladaptive traits such as compulsiveness, overdependency, or aggressiveness. Axis II is also used to describe specific developmental disorders for children, adolescents, and, in some cases, adults. Examples of developmental problems that would be classified under Axis II are language disorders, reading difficulties, and speech problems.

It is possible for an individual to have a disorder on both Axis I and Axis II. For example, an adult may have a major depression noted on Axis I and a compulsive personality disorder noted on Axis II. A child may have a conduct disorder noted on Axis I and a developmental language disorder on Axis II. In other cases, a person may be seeking treatment primarily for a condition noted on Axis I or Axis II alone. The use of both of these axes permits multiple diagnoses and allows the clinician flexibility in making provisional diagnoses when there is not enough information available on the patient to make a firm diagnosis.

Axis III is used to describe physical disorders or conditions that are potentially relevant to understanding or managing the person. In some cases,

Being Sane in an Insane Place

The doors slam shut. The hospital attendant turns the key. You are locked in a room with insane people. And they think you're insane too. They'll find out in no time, you tell yourself, but they don't. They keep you behind bars for your own good.

Despite our perception that psychiatric diagnosis is a science, it is quite possible for sane people to be institutionalized. The fact that it happened in the experiment we are about to describe suggests that psychiatric diagnosis is as much in the mind of the observer as it is in the behavior of the observed.

Eight people, including three psychologists, a pediatrician, and a homemaker, called twelve different psychiatric hospitals complaining that they heard voices. Beyond this symptom, the pseudopatients presented the facts of their lives as they actually were. Once they were admitted to the hospital, they went back to their ordinary behavior. They dropped their claims of hearing voices, spoke to other patients and staff as they would to people outside the hospital, and told everyone they were feeling fine.

The hospital staff was not at all suspicious of these changes. The staff members never suspected that the pseudopatients were sane. When these people were finally released, they were given the diagnosis of schizophrenia in remission. In the hospital's view, they were not sane nor had they ever been sane. Interestingly, many legitimate patients detected the experimenters' sanity and told them that they didn't belong.

For more details, see D. L. Rosenhan, "On Being Sane in Insane Places," *Science*, 179, January 1973.

a physical disorder may be causing the syndrome diagnosed on either Axis I or II. In other cases, the physical disorder may be important in the overall management of the individual, as in the case of a diabetic child with a conduct disorder.

Axis IV is a measurement of the current stress level at which the person is functioning. The rating of stressors is based on what the person has experienced within the past year. An eight-point code is used to describe stressors ranging from no apparent stressors to catastrophic levels of stress. The prognosis may be better for a disorder that develops following a severe stressor than for one that develops after no stressor or a minimal stressor.

Axis V is used to describe the highest level of adaptive functioning present within the past year. Adaptive functioning refers to three major areas: social relations, occupational functioning, and the person's use of leisure time. Social relations refer to the quality of a person's relationships with family and friends. Occupational functioning involves functioning as a worker, student, or homemaker and the quality of the work accomplished. Use of leisure time includes recreational activities or hobbies and the degree of involvement and pleasure a person has in them.

With DSM-II, a patient's diagnosis might have been simply "alcohol addiction." Under the new system, however, he or she might be diagnosed as follows:

Axis I: alcohol dependence
Axis II: avoidant personality disorder
Axis III: diabetes
Axis IV: loss of job, one child moved out of house, marital conflict
Axis V: fair

This offers a good deal more information about the patient—information that may be useful in devising a treatment program. Furthermore, this five-part diagnosis may be extremely helpful to researchers trying to discover connections among psychological disorders and other factors such as stress and physical illness.

FURTHER ASPECTS OF CLASSIFICATION

Before DSM-III was created in 1980, the two most commonly used diagnostic distinctions were neurosis and psychosis. **Neurosis** is a disorder in which severe anxiety reduces a person's ability to deal effectively with reality. **Psychosis** is a disorder in which a person is often unable to deal with reality at all and withdraws into a private world. Psychosis is not an advanced stage of neurosis. It is a distinct type of psychological disturbance. These two diagnostic terms were dropped in the new diagnostic classification scheme because it was felt that the range of disorders they described was too wide.

Even though the terms "neurosis" and "psychosis" have been replaced by more specific ones, they are still used by many psychologists and lay people. (In the DSM-III-R, some categories are alternatively defined as neurosis such as "anxiety disorder or anxiety neurosis.") Thus, this chapter will discuss symptoms and possible causes of several forms of neurosis and psychosis, as well as personality disorders and addiction to drugs.

As you read, you will probably feel that some of the descriptions could be applied to you at times. They probably could, but remember, a psychologically disturbed person is one who turns normal human quirks into extreme and distorted *patterns* of thought and behavior. When we speak of psychologically disturbed individuals, we are not talking about people who have their normal share of difficulties but rather about people who are hopelessly unhappy, whose minds are confused and chaotic, who have a difficult time doing the simple things in life, or who act in ways that are truly harmful to themselves or to other people.

NEUROSIS

The general term "neurosis" is used to refer to a variety of disorders that share certain characteristics, including feelings of anxiety and personal inadequacy and an avoidance of dealing with problems. Neurotic people often have unrealistic images of themselves. They are plagued by self-doubt and seem unable to free themselves of recurring worries and fears. Their emotional problems may be expressed in constant worrying, sudden mood swings, or a variety of physical symptoms (for example, headaches, sweating, muscle tightness, weakness, and fatigue). Neurotics often have difficulty forming stable and satisfying relationships. Even though their behavior may be self-defeating and ineffective in solving problems, neurotic people often refuse to give up their neurotic behaviors in favor of more effective ways of dealing with anxiety. In the DSM-III-R neurotic disorders are classified under the following three main headings: *anxiety disorders* such as *phobias*, *obsessions*, and *compulsions*; *somatoform disorders*; and *dissociative disorders*.

Anxiety

Once in a while, everyone feels nervous for reasons he or she cannot explain, but a severely neurotic person almost always feels this way. Neurotic **anxiety** is a generalized apprehension—a vague feeling that one is in danger. Sometimes, this anxiety blossoms into a full-fledged panic disorder, which may include choking sensations, chest pain, dizziness, trembling, and hot flashes. Unlike fear, which is a reaction to real and identifiable threats, anxiety is a reaction to vague or imagined dangers.

Some people experience a continuous, generalized anxiety. Fearing unknown and unforeseen circumstances, they are unable to make decisions or enjoy life. They may become so preoccupied with their internal problems that they neglect their social relationships. People who experience neurotic anxiety often have trouble dealing with their family and friends and fulfilling their responsibilities, and this adds to their anxiety. They are trapped in a vicious cycle. The more they worry, the more difficulty they have; the more difficulty they have, the more they worry.

Often, the experience of generalized anxiety is accompanied by physical symptoms: muscular tension, an inability to relax, a furrowed brow, and a strained face. Poor appetite, indigestion, diarrhea, and frequent urination are also commonly present. Because anxious people are in a constant state of apprehension, they may have difficulty sleeping or, once asleep, may wake up suddenly in the night. As a result, they may feel tired when they wake up in the morning.

Why are some people so anxious? According to Freudian psychoanalytic theory, anxiety is caused by unconscious desires and conflicts that are so disturbing that those who are affected cannot find any satisfying solution. These unresolved conflicts often persist on an unconscious level. Neurotically anxious people are more or less constantly afraid of emotions that they do not feel capable of handling. When something happens to bring the emotions closer to the surface, the fear becomes intense. For example, people who are unable to face or express feelings of anger may become tense and fearful when they see other people arguing or when hostile images flash into their minds, because they are reminded of emotions they are trying to deny.

According to social cognitive theorists, anxiety is due to an individual's unrealistic appraisal of actual dangers or threats. For example, an anxious person may react the same way to being in his own kitchen as he would to standing alone on a dark, deserted street corner. The person makes no distinction between the safety of home and that of a potentially more dangerous situation. Images of disaster haunt him equally in both situations.

Behaviorists, in contrast, view anxiety as a learned fear reaction much like Little Albert's rat phobia discussed in Chapter 2. However, in anxiety the reaction is not neatly confined to a specific object but is generalized to a wide class of situations. From a biological perspective, panic disorders may be caused by a congenitally sensitive autonomic nervous system (Ballenger, 1989). People with this condition are more responsive to fear arousal and consequently experience greater anxiety.

Phobias

When severe anxiety is focused on a particular object or situation, it is called a **phobia**. A phobia can focus on almost anything, including high places (acrophobia), enclosed spaces (claustrophobia), and darkness (nyctophobia). A person with a phobia has an intense, persistent, irrational fear of something.

Phobic individuals develop elaborate plans to avoid the situations they fear. For example, people suffering from an extreme fear of crowds (agoraphobia) may stop going to movies or shopping in large, busy stores. Some agoraphobics reach the point at which they will not leave their houses at all.

Phobias range in intensity from mild to extremely severe. Most people deal with their phobias by avoiding the thing they are frightened of. Thus

Figure 15.5
A person suffering from agoraphobia would fear going into a crowded shopping center such as this one.

a   b   c

Figure 15.6
An artist's representation of three phobias: (a) fear of heights, called acrophobia; (b) fear of enclosed spaces, called claustrophobia; and (c) fear of dirt, called mysophobia. (After Vassos, 1931)

Figure 15.7
A still from the film *The Caine Mutiny*, in which Humphrey Bogart played Captain Queeg, an individual who was obsessed with order. Any disruption of Queeg's routine sent him into panic and produced the compulsive behavior of continually rolling ball bearings in his hand. Queeg's behavior led his officers to label him "mentally ill" and to mutiny against him.

the phobias are learned and maintained by the reinforcing effects of avoidance. One common form of treatment for phobias involves providing the phobic person with opportunities to experience the feared object under conditions in which he or she feels safe.

Some psychologists explain certain phobias in terms of projection. What the people really fear is an impulse inside themselves. To avoid this fear, they unconsciously project it onto something outside themselves. For example, a woman who is terrified of heights may really be afraid of losing control and "letting go" to other wishes or feelings. By concentrating on avoiding heights, she is able to control other disturbing urges and push them out of her consciousness.

Obsessions and Compulsions

People suffering from acute anxiety may find themselves thinking the same thoughts over and over again. Such an uncontrollable pattern of thoughts is called an **obsession**. Or someone may repeatedly perform irrational actions. This is called a **compulsion**. The neurotic person may experience both these agonies together—a condition called *obsessive-compulsive neurosis*.

A compulsive person may feel compelled to wash her hands twenty or thirty times a day or to avoid stepping on cracks in the sidewalk when she goes out. An obsessive person may be unable to rid herself of unpleasant thoughts about death or of a recurring impulse to make obscene remarks in public. And the obsessive-compulsive may wash her hands continually *and* torment herself with thoughts of obscene behavior.

Everyone has obsessions and compulsions. Love might be described as an obsession; so might a hobby that occupies most of a person's spare time. Striving to do something "perfectly" is often considered to be a compulsion. But if the person who is deeply engrossed in a hobby or who aims for perfection enjoys this intense absorption and can still function effectively, he or she is usually not considered neurotic. Psychologists consider it a problem only when such thoughts and activities interfere with what a person wants and needs to do. Someone who spends so much time double-checking every detail of her work that she can never finish a job is considered more neurotic than conscientious.

Why do people develop obsessions and compulsions? Possibly because they serve as diversions from a neurotic person's real fears and their origins and thus may reduce anxiety somewhat. In addition, compulsions provide a disturbed person with the evidence that she is doing something well, even if it is only avoiding cracks on a sidewalk. Thus there is some logic in this apparently illogical behavior.

Somatoform Disorders

Neurotic anxiety can create a wide variety of physical symptoms for which there is no apparent physical cause. This phenomenon is known as a **somatoform disorder**, or hysteria. The term "hysteria" was more commonly used in Freud's time to refer to unexplainable fainting, paralysis, or deafness. Today the term "somatoform disorder" is preferred. There are two major types of somatoform disorders: *conversion reactions* and *hypochondriasis*.

Conversion Reactions. A **conversion reaction** is the conversion of emotional difficulties into the loss of a specific physiological function. Many people occasionally experience mild conversion reactions, as when someone is so frightened he or she cannot move, but a neurotic disorder is not simply a brief loss of functioning due to fright. It persists.

A conversion reaction results in a severe and prolonged handicap—the person literally cannot hear or speak or feel anything in his left hand or move his legs or exercise some other normal physical function (Figure 15.8). For example, a man might wake up one morning and find himself paralyzed from the waist down. The normal reaction to this would be panic. If the man is neurotic, however, he might accept the loss of function with relative calm. (This is one sign that a person is suffering from a psychological rather than a physiological problem.) Most psychologists believe that people suffering from conversion reactions unconsciously invent physical symptoms to gain freedom from unbearable anxiety. For example, a woman who lives in terror of blurting out things that she does not want to say may lose the power of speech. This "solves" the problem. Conversion reactions are comparatively rare.

Hypochondriasis. Conversion reactions must be distinguished from **hypochondriasis**, in which a person who is in good health becomes preoccupied with imaginary ailments. The hypochondriac spends a lot of time looking for signs of serious physical illness and often misinterprets minor aches, pains, bruises, or bumps as early signs of a fatal illness. Despite negative results in medical tests and physical evaluations, the hypochondriac

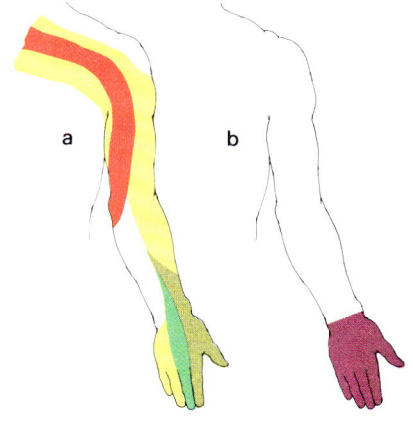

Figure 15.8
A patient who complained to a doctor that his right hand had become numb might be diagnosed as a neurotic suffering from a conversion reaction, depending on the exact pattern of the numbness. The skin areas served by different nerves in the arm are shown in (a). The "glove" numbness shown in (b) could not result from damage to these nerves.

PSYCHOLOGY UPDATE

Multiple Personality. The majority of people with multiple personality disorders have been abused as children (Bootzin and Acocella, 1988). In their attempts to distance themselves from the pain and trauma of abuse, they develop other personalities. Sherry, a twin who was abused as a child, first dealt with her feelings by believing that it was her sister who was the victim (Vitkus, 1988). For example, Sherry's mother had thrown a pot of boiling water on Sherry, causing second-degree burns on her body. However, Sherry maintained that it was her sister who had been scalded. In fact, Sherry only started to develop a second personality when she moved away from her sister. It is conceivable that Sherry would not have developed a multiple personality disorder if she had continued to live with her sister.

Psychologically healthy people may dissociate themselves from painful experiences simply by forgetting or blurring memories. This dissociation becomes abnormal when it forces another personality to emerge or causes undue anxiety.

typically continues to believe that a disease or malfunction exists. Hypochondriasis may also have its advantages. It allows a person to blame problems on an illness, and the person may succeed in getting the attention and care that a sick person usually receives.

Dissociative Disorders

Another form of neurotic behavior may take the form of a **dissociative reaction** in which the person experiences either a loss of memory or identity or exhibits two or more identities. These psychological phenomena fascinate many people, so we hear a good deal about amnesia and "split personalities." Actually, they are very rare.

Loss of memory, or *amnesia*, may be an attempt to escape from problems by blotting them out completely. Amnesiacs remember how to speak and usually retain a fund of general knowledge, but they may not know who they are, where they live and work, or who their family is (Levant, 1966). Other types of amnesia are caused by brain damage.

In **fugue**, another type of dissociative reaction, amnesia is coupled with active flight to a different environment. For example, a woman may suddenly disappear and "wake up" three days later in a restaurant 200 miles from home. She may actually establish a new identity—assume a new name, marry, take a job, and so forth—in a new place. She may repress all knowledge of a previous life. A fugue state may last for days or for decades. However long it lasts, the individual, when she comes out of it, will have no memory of what she has done in the interim. Fugue, then, is a sort of traveling amnesia, and it probably serves the same psychological function as amnesia: escape from unbearable conflict or anxiety.

In **multiple personality**, a third type of dissociative reaction, someone seems to have two or more distinct identities. Eve White, a young woman who sought psychiatric treatment for severe headaches and blackouts, has become a famous example. Eve White was a conscientious, self-controlled, rather shy person. However, during one of her therapy sessions, her expression—and her personality—suddenly changed. Eve Black, as she now called herself, was childlike, fun-loving, and irresponsible—the opposite of the woman who originally walked into the psychiatrist's office. Eve Black was conscious of Eve White's existence, but considered her a separate person. Eve White did not know about Eve Black, however, and neither was she conscious of Jane, a third personality that emerged during the course of therapy. (This case served as the basis for the book and film *The Three Faces of Eve*.) Some psychologists believe that this dividing up of the personality is the result of the individual's effort to escape from a part of himself or herself that he or she fears. The "secret self" then emerges in the form of a separate personality.

While cases like Eve and Sybil (a woman whose sixteen personalities were also described in a book and a movie) are fascinating, they are extremely rare and somewhat controversial. One researcher (Abse, 1966) reviewed the entire psychological literature and was able to find published accounts of only 200 people who supposedly suffered from any dissociative reaction.

Depression

Depression is a pattern of sadness, anxiety, fatigue, agitated behavior, and reduced ability to function and interact with others. It may also interfere with sleep patterns and the ability to concentrate. It ranges from mild feelings of uneasiness, sadness, and apathy to intense suicidal despair. Occasional depression, or dysthymia, is a common experience. Most of us feel depressed when someone we love dies, for example. And, from time to time, everyone feels "blue" for no apparent reason. However, when depression is chronic (that is, the person never seems to "snap out of it") or especially intense, it is considered a serious psychological problem.

According to Freudian theory, depression comes from a severe sense of loss coupled with some ambivalence toward the loss (Bootzin and Acocella, 1988). For example, a person may experience both positive feelings (love, caring) and negative feelings (relief, memories of some conflict) toward someone who just died. Guilt grows out of the positive feelings and anger directed toward oneself grows out of the negative feelings. These feelings produce a depression of despair and self-loathing.

The cognitive theories of Aaron Beck and Martin Seligman have often served as the basis for research on depression. Beck (1967) believes that depressed people draw illogical conclusions about themselves—they blame themselves for normal problems and consider every minor failure a catastrophe. A depressed man who failed his driver's test, for example, might consider himself hopeless as a result and conclude that he will never be able to get a car of his own. As described in Chapter 2, Martin Seligman (1975) believes that depression is caused by a feeling of learned helpless-

Figure 15.9
The pattern of major depression is a familiar one to therapists, but its causes are still a matter of debate. There are the Freudian theory of guilt and the need for self-punishment and the cognitive theories of Beck and Seligman.

Figure 15.10
A "suicide hot line." The man shown here is one of many trained volunteers who work at suicide prevention centers throughout the country.

ness. The depressed person learns to believe that he has no control over events in his life, that nothing he does makes any difference, and that it is useless to even try.

Suicide

Not all people who commit suicide are depressed, and not all depressed people attempt suicide. But many depressives do think about suicide, and some of them translate these thoughts into action.

People may take their lives for any number of reasons: to escape from physical or emotional pain (perhaps a terminal illness or the loneliness of old age), to end the torment of unacceptable feelings (such as homosexual fantasies), to punish themselves for wrongs they feel they have committed, or to punish others who have not perceived their needs (Mintz, 1968). In many cases we simply do not know why the suicide occurred.

But we do know that every year between 20,000 and 30,000 Americans end their lives—about one every thirty minutes. More women than men attempt suicide, but more men than women succeed. Suicide is most common among the elderly, but it also ranks as the third most common cause of death among college students. Contrary to popular belief, people who threaten suicide or make an unsuccessful attempt usually *are* serious. Studies show that about 70 percent of people who kill themselves threaten to do so within the three months preceding the suicide, and an unsuccessful attempt is often a trial run (Alvarez, 1970).

Anxiety, phobias, obsessions, compulsions, somatoform disorders, depression, and suicide—all are ways people use, in various combinations, to escape problems in themselves or the world in which they live. With the obvious exception of suicide, these neurotic reactions do not shut people off completely from daily life. Psychosis does.

PSYCHOSIS

A neurotic person is one who is emotionally crippled by anxiety but continues to function in life as best as he or she can. A psychotic person is one whose distorted perceptions and behavior reach such an irrational, fantastic, and fear-laden level that he or she withdraws completely from normal life. One might say that a neurotic person dreams in an unreal way about life, whereas a psychotic person lives life as an unreal dream.

Like neurosis, psychosis is not a single problem; it has no single cause or cure. Rather, it is a collection of symptoms indicating that an individual has serious difficulty trying to meet the demands of life. Two major categories of psychosis are *schizophrenia* and *mood disorders*.

Schizophrenia

Approximately half the patients in United States mental hospitals have been diagnosed as schizophrenic (Taube and Rednick, 1973). What distin-

Figure 15.11
These paintings were done by a male patient diagnosed as schizophrenic with paranoid tendencies. Both illustrations are characterized by the symbolism of watchful eyes, grasping hands, and the self as subject matter.

guishes this disorder from other types of psychological disturbance? **Schizophrenia** involves confused and disordered thoughts and perceptions.

Suppose a psychiatrist is interviewing a patient who has just been admitted to a hospital. The individual demonstrates a wide assortment of symptoms. He is intensely excited and he shows conflicting feelings, expressing extreme hostility toward members of his family and at the same time claiming that he loves them. One minute he is extremely aggressive, questioning the psychiatrist's motives and even threatening her. The next minute he withdraws and acts as if he does not hear anything she says. Then he begins talking again. "Naturally," he says, "I am growing my father's hair." Although all of the person's other behavior indicates psychological problems, this last statement would be the "diagnostic bell ringer." It reveals that the man is living in a private disordered reality.

Many schizophrenics experience **delusions** (false beliefs maintained in the face of contrary evidence) and **hallucinations** (sensations in the absence of appropriate stimulation). For example, a paranoid schizophrenic generally believes that others are plotting against him—contriving ways to confuse him, make him look ridiculous, perhaps to get rid of him. People are watching him constantly. His thoughts are being monitored. When he goes to the movies to escape, he finds—to his horror—that the film is all about him. The ticket taker and the man in the next row are in on the plot. These delusions are usually supported by hallucinations, in which his five senses detect the evidence of the plot. He may taste poison in his food, smell gas in his bedroom, or hear voices telling him why he has been singled out or what lies in store for him.

Often, schizophrenics withdraw from other people into a private world of fantasy. In *undifferentiated schizophrenia* individuals gradually lose interest in what happens around them, becoming increasingly apathetic, list-less, and noncommunicative. Such individuals may be able to hold menial jobs or may survive as "drifters," but their interpersonal contacts are few. *Catatonic schizophrenia* is an extreme form of withdrawal in which the person becomes totally unresponsive. She may maintain the same posture for hours, mute and seemingly oblivious to physical discomfort. The only sign of emotional life in a catatonic person may be periodic flare-ups, when the person becomes violent toward herself or others.

Other schizophrenics are active and busy, but their behavior and speech are incomprehensible to others. A schizophrenic person may repeat

Figure 15.12
A portrait of a "suicidal melancholic" done in England in the nineteenth century. This woman, only thirty-four when the portrait was made, suffered from the delusion that she would be murdered and eventually began to attempt suicide in order to escape the danger.

a bizarre gesture, whose meaning is known only to him, over and over. He may express inappropriate emotions—for example, giggling uncontrollably as he relates violent and morbid fantasies. He may invent words or repeat phrases as if they were magical incantations—for reasons known only to himself (Maher, 1972). The result is sometimes what psychologists call "word salad": a jumble of unconnected, irrational phrases.

It is as if the gears in the schizophrenic's mental machinery had slipped and the connections had gone haywire. One patient described the experience as losing the ability to focus his thoughts.

> "I can't concentrate. It's diversion of attention that troubles me. I am picking up different conversations. It's like being a transmitter. The sounds are coming through to me but I feel my mind cannot cope with everything. It's difficult to concentrate on any one sound."

Another told of being unable to organize his perceptions.

> "Everything is in bits. You put the picture up bit by bit into your head. It's like a photograph that's been torn to bits and put together again. You have to absorb it again. If you move it's frightening. The picture you had in your head is still there but it's broken up" (McGhie and Chapman, 1961).

Mood Disorders

Another common type of psychosis is one in which individuals are excessively and inappropriately happy or unhappy. Such **mood disorders** may take the form of high elation, hopeless depression, or an alternation between the two.

In a **manic reaction**, a person experiences elation, extreme confusion, distractibility, and racing thoughts. Often, the person has an exaggerated sense of self-esteem and engages in irresponsible behavior such as shopping sprees, insulting remarks, or the following type of behavior:

> On admission she slapped the nurse, addressed the house physician as God, made the sign of the cross, and laughed loudly when she was asked to don the hospital garb. This she promptly tore to shreds. . . . She sang at the top of her voice, screamed through the window, and leered at the patients promenading in the recreation yard (Karnash, 1945).

In **major depression**, the individual is overcome by feelings of failure, sinfulness, worthlessness, and despair. Major depression is a significant health problem in the United States (Bootzin and Acocella, 1988). Mental outpatient clinics see more people with depression than any other diagnosis. People from poor socioeconomic backgrounds are most likely to suffer from depression. And twice as many women as men are diagnosed as depressives. (See "More About Women and Depression.") We have already described depression as a form of neurosis. Psychotic depression differs from neurotic depression—just as psychosis in general differs from neuro-

Women and Depression. Surveys and official statistics show that women are twice as likely as men to suffer from depression. Does this indicate that depression has a sex-linked genetic component? Not necessarily. Researchers have found that women are more likely to report depressive symptoms.

First, in most cultures women show a greater awareness of their emotions than men do. Second, women are more likely to express their emotions to others, making them more likely than men to *report* that they feel depressed, even though the men may feel equally depressed. Third, women and men show different reactions to stress. Women often direct their frustrations inward, whereas men frequently react to their frustrations by showing aggression or drinking heavily.

In short, the sex differences in depression may say more about the way people deal with their feelings than about the causes of depression. With changing sex roles and increasing opportunities for women, this sex difference may decrease in the future.

sis in general—in that the psychotic has lost contact with reality. The neurotic depressive may feel chronically dejected, but she still knows how to get to the bank, how old her children are, and how to differentiate between fantasy and reality. The psychotic depressive has left reality behind and has moved into a bleak fantasy world constructed out of her despair. She is likely to claim that her children are dead, that she killed them, that the world is coming to an end, and that it is all her fault. Furthermore, the psychotic depressive may stop functioning altogether and descend into a stupor, not eating, not speaking, and not moving.

> The patient lay in bed, immobile, with a dull, depressed expression on his face. His eyes were sunken and downcast. Even when spoken to, he would not raise his eyes to look at the speaker. Usually he did not respond at all to questions, but sometimes, after apparently great effort, he would mumble something about the "Scourge of God" (Coleman, 1976).

In some cases, a patient will alternate between frantic action and motionless despair. Some theorists have speculated that these manic periods serve as an attempt to ward off the underlying hopelessness. Others believe that mania can be traced to a chemical imbalance in the brain. According to this view, some people are more likely to experience mood disorders because they are born with low levels of a specific brain chemical. (According to one current theory, the chemical is the neurotransmitter serotonin. This predisposing factor influences other brain chemicals. Low levels of the neurotransmitter norepinephrine are associated with depression; high levels with mania.)

Causes of Psychosis

Some people may inherit a predisposition or tendency to become psychotic.

There are many theories but very few facts about what causes psychosis. Psychologists think that their problems result from the interaction of several factors, but none of these factors is clearly understood.

Hereditary Factors.   There is some evidence that people may inherit a predisposition or tendency to become psychotic. Close relatives of schizophrenics, for example, are much more likely to become schizophrenic than are other people, even if they never come into contact with their schizophrenic relative (Rosenthal et al., 1971; Kety et al., 1971). However, even among close relatives with this predisposition, the risk is low and may depend on environmental factors (Nurnberger, Goldin, and Gershon, 1986). According to one theory, some people are born with a nervous system that gets aroused very easily and takes a long time to recover to normal (Figure 15.13). People like this might be particularly likely to get upset when they are stressed (Zubin and Spring, 1977). Thus a situation that might be only mildly upsetting to one person might cause a psychotic reaction in an acutely sensitive person. However, if this person is raised in a relatively simple, pressure-free environment, he might never develop psychological problems.

Figure 15.13
A child born with a biochemically unusual nervous system that reacts very strongly to stimulation may have pronounced hallucinations during an early childhood illness that has no lasting effect on most children. As he grows older, he may try to discuss his memories of that time with his parents. Being insecure themselves, they may become uneasy and respond in ways that make him feel he is wrong or bad in some way. His unusual biochemistry causes him to react very strongly to this rebuff, and he now has further troubling experiences he needs to make sense of. He then feels a conflict between his need to talk to his parents about these experiences and his fear of their cold response. He is well on the way to becoming psychologically disordered unless the links in this chain are somehow broken.

Biochemical Factors.   The proper working of the brain depends on the presence of the right amounts of many different chemicals, from oxygen to proteins. Some psychologists believe that psychosis is due largely to chemical imbalances in the brain. With depression, for example, abnormally low amounts of certain chemicals may disturb the transmission of electrical impulses from one brain cell to another.

Chemical problems may also be involved in schizophrenia. A number of researchers think that the basic problem in schizophrenia is that too much or too little of certain chemicals has "knocked out of kilter" the brain's mechanisms for processing information. As a result, the schizophrenic cannot organize his thoughts. When he tries to keep one thought at the center of his awareness, other thoughts—irrelevant ones—keep pushing in and interfering with his concentration (Wynne, Cromwell, and Matthyssee, 1978). In short, he experiences the kind of thought disturbance reported by the schizophrenic patients quoted earlier in this chapter.

Unusual concentrations of certain chemicals have in fact been found in the bodies of many schizophrenics. However, it is hard to tell whether these chemicals are the cause of schizophrenia or the result of it. They may even be caused by the fact that schizophrenics tend to live in hospitals, where they get little exercise, eat institutional food, and are generally given daily doses of tranquilizers. Living under such conditions, anyone—not just the schizophrenic person—might begin to show chemical imbalances.

The Double Bind.   Some theorists believe that many mental problems, particularly those that involve confused thoughts and isolation from other people, result from conflicts in communication. These psychologists believe that a child's ability to think and to communicate with others can be undermined if his or her parents repeatedly communicate contradictory messages. For example, a mother may resent her child and feel uncomfortable around him, yet also feel obligated to act lovingly toward him. She tells the child how much she loves him, but at the same time she stiffens whenever he tries to hug her. Thus the child is given one message in words and another in action.

As a result, the child is placed in an impossible situation. If he reaches out to his mother, she shows him (in her actions) that she dislikes this. If he avoids her, she tells him (in words) that she dislikes that. He wants very much to please her, but no matter what he does, it is wrong. He is caught in a *double bind*.

According to **double-bind theory**, a childhood full of such contradictory messages results in people perceiving the world as a confusing, disconnected place and believing that their words and actions have little significance or meaning. Consequently they may develop the kind of disordered behaviors and thoughts we have been describing.

Which of these theories is correct? At this point, we do not know. It may be that each is partially true. Perhaps the double bind is the result, not the cause, of having a disturbed family member. Perhaps people who inherit a tendency toward psychological disorders react more strongly to a double bind than others would. Perhaps people who are caught in a double bind are especially vulnerable to chemical imbalances. Or perhaps it takes a combination of all three factors—heredity, biochemical disorders, and conflict—to produce psychotic behavior (Meehl, 1962). Only further research will give us the answer.

PERSONALITY DISORDERS

Personality disorders are different from the problems we have been discussing. People with personality disorders generally do not suffer from acute anxiety; nor do they behave in bizarre, incomprehensible ways. Psychologists consider these people "abnormal" because they seem unable to establish meaningful relationships with other people, to assume social responsibilities, or to adapt to their social environment. This diagnostic category includes a wide range of self-defeating personality patterns, from painfully shy, lonely types to vain, pushy show-offs. In this section we focus on the **antisocial personality,** sometimes called the sociopath or psychopath.

Antisocial individuals are irresponsible, immature, emotionally shallow people who seem to court trouble. Extremely selfish, they treat people as objects—as things to be used for gratification and to be cast coldly aside when no longer wanted. Intolerant of everyday frustrations and unable to save or plan or wait, they live for the moment. Seeking thrills is their major occupation. If they should injure other people along the way or break social rules, they do not seem to feel any shame or guilt. It's the other person's tough luck. Nor does getting caught seem to rattle them. No matter how

Figure 15.14
Many psychologists would classify these gang members as antisocial individuals. Gangs are frequently dedicated to violence and destruction.

many times they are reprimanded, punished, or jailed, they never learn how to stay out of trouble. They simply do not profit from experience.

Many antisocial individuals can get away with destructive behavior because they are intelligent, entertaining, and able to mimic emotions they do not feel. They win affection and confidence from others whom they then take advantage of. This ability to charm while exploiting helped Charles Manson to dominate the gang of runaways whom he eventually led to committing the gruesome Tate-LaBianca murders in 1969.

If caught, antisocial individuals will either spin a fantastic lie or simply insist, with wide-eyed sincerity, that their intentions were utterly pure. Guilt and anxiety have no place in the antisocial personality. A fine example is that of Hugh Johnson, a con man caught after having defrauded people out of thousands of dollars in sixty-four separate swindles. When asked why he had victimized so many people, "he replied with some heat that he never took more from a person than the person could afford to lose, and further, that he was only reducing the likelihood that other more dangerous criminals would use force to achieve the same ends" (Nathan and Harris, 1975: 406–407).

How do psychologists explain such a lack of ordinary human decency and shame? According to one theory, the psychopath has simply imitated his or her own antisocial parents. Others point to lack of discipline or inconsistent discipline during childhood. Finally, some researchers believe that psychopaths have a "faulty nervous system." While most of us get very aroused when we do something that we've been punished for in the past, psychopaths never seem to learn to anticipate punishment.

SUBSTANCE ABUSE DISORDERS

In American society, substance abuse has become a major psychological problem. Millions of Americans depend so heavily on drugs that they hurt themselves physically, socially, and psychologically.

Substance abuse invariably involves **psychological dependence**. Users come to depend so much on the feeling of well-being they obtain from the drug that they feel compelled to continue using it. People can become psychologically dependent on a wide variety of drugs, including alcohol, caffeine, nicotine (in cigarettes), opium, marijuana, and amphetamines. When deprived of the drug, a psychologically dependent person becomes restless, irritable, and uneasy.

In addition to psychological dependence, some drugs lead to physiological **addiction**. A person is addicted when his system has become so used to the drug that the drugged state becomes the body's "normal" state. If the drug is not in the body, the person experiences extreme physical discomfort, just as he would if he were deprived of oxygen or of water.

Just as dependence causes a psychological need for the drug, addiction causes a physical need. Furthermore, once a person is addicted to a drug, he develops **tolerance;** that is, his body becomes so accustomed to the

Figure 15.15
A drug addict during one of the
stages of withdrawal.

drug that he has to keep increasing his dosage in order to obtain the "high" that he achieved with his earlier doses. With certain sleeping pills, for example, a person can rapidly develop a tolerance for up to fifteen times the original dose. Further, an addict must have his drug in order to retain what little physical and psychological balance he has left. If he does not get it, he is likely to go through the dreaded experience of withdrawal.

Withdrawal is a state of physical and psychological upset during which the body and the mind revolt against, and finally get used to, the absence of the drug. Withdrawal symptoms vary from person to person and from drug to drug. They range from a mild case of nausea and "the shakes" to hallucinations, convulsions, coma, and death.

Alcoholism

Although cocaine addiction seems to receive more attention in the media, this country's most serious drug problem is alcoholism. Somewhere between 8 and 12 million Americans are alcoholics. According to one recent estimate, 1.3 million teenagers and preteenagers have a serious drinking problem (Ray, 1978). Fifty percent or more of the deaths in automobile accidents each year can be traced to alcohol; in half of all murders either the killer or the victim has been drinking; and some 13,000 people die of liver damage caused by alcohol every year. In addition, the cost in human suffering to the alcoholic and his or her family is impossible to measure.

In small doses, alcohol might be called a social wonder drug. The first psychological function that it slows down is our inhibitions. Two drinks can make a person relaxed, talkative, playful, even giggly. (It is for this reason that many people consider alcohol a stimulant—it is really a depressant.) Some people believe drinking relieves stress. However, consumption of alcohol alone is not a particularly effective stress reducer. Alcohol must be accompanied by a distracting task, preferably a pleasant one, in order to affect the level of stress (Josephs and Steele, 1990).

As the number of drinks increases, the fun decreases. One by one, the person's psychological and physiological functions begin to shut down. Perceptions and sensations become distorted, and behavior may become obnoxious. The person begins to stumble and weave, speech becomes slurred (Pisoni and Martin, 1989), and reactions—to a stop sign, for example—become sluggish. If enough alcohol accumulates in the body, it leads to unconsciousness—and in some cases coma and death. It all depends on how much and how rapidly alcohol enters the bloodstream—which, in turn, depends on a person's weight, body chemistry, and how much he or she drinks how quickly (Figure 15.16).

Alcohol can produce psychological dependence, tolerance, and addiction. One researcher has outlined three stages of alcoholism. In the first stage, the individual discovers that alcohol reduces her tensions, gives her self-confidence, and reduces social pressures. Drinking makes her feel better. In the second stage, the beverage becomes a drug. The individual begins to drink so heavily that she feels she has to hide her habit. Thus she begins "sneaking" drinks. In this stage she may also begin to suffer from blackouts—she is unable to recall what happened during a drinking episode. In the final stage, she drinks compulsively, beginning in the morning. She becomes inefficient at work and tends to go on drinking sprees that may last for weeks. She is now an alcoholic, drinking continuously, eating infrequently, and feeling sick when deprived of her drug. Her health deteriorates rapidly (Jellinek, 1960).

The first step in treating the alcoholic is to see her through the violent withdrawal typical of alcohol addiction, and then to try to make her healthier. She may be given a variety of treatments—from drugs to psychotherapy. Alcoholics Anonymous, an organization for alcoholics that is run by people who have had a drinking problem, has been more successful than most organizations. There is no certain cure for alcoholism. As many alco-

FACT or FICTION

Alcoholism can lead to permanent memory loss.

Fact. Some alcoholics suffer from Korsakoff's syndrome, a form of amnesia in which they are unable to remember any newly acquired information. For example, even after years of treatment, one patient did not recognize his therapist and introduced himself whenever they met.

Figure 15.16
This chart shows the effects of alcohol on a 150-pound person. Because alcohol is diluted in the blood, a 200-pound man can usually tolerate more liquor than a 110-pound woman.

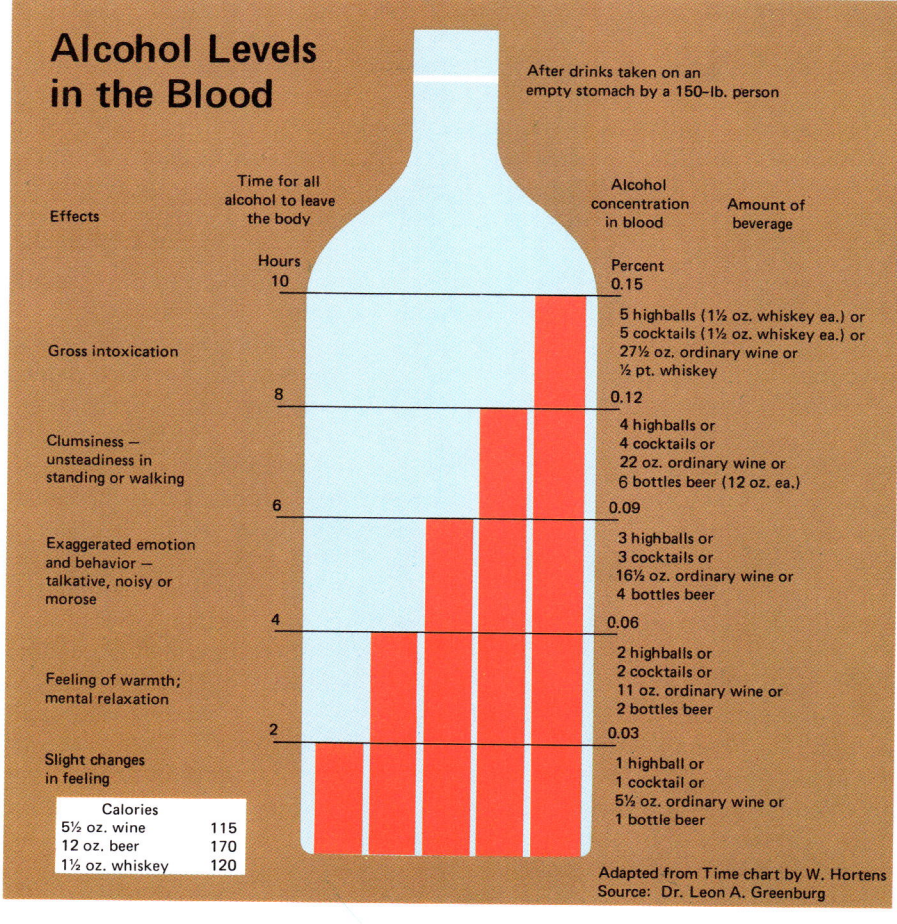

Alcohol Levels in the Blood

After drinks taken on an empty stomach by a 150-lb. person

Effects	Time for all alcohol to leave the body	Alcohol concentration in blood	Amount of beverage
	Hours	Percent	
	10	0.15	
Gross intoxication			5 highballs (1½ oz. whiskey ea.) or 5 cocktails (1½ oz. whiskey ea.) or 27½ oz. ordinary wine or ½ pt. whiskey
	8	0.12	
Clumsiness — unsteadiness in standing or walking			4 highballs or 4 cocktails or 22 oz. ordinary wine or 6 bottles beer (12 oz. ea.)
	6	0.09	
Exaggerated emotion and behavior — talkative, noisy or morose			3 highballs or 3 cocktails or 16½ oz. ordinary wine or 4 bottles beer
	4	0.06	
Feeling of warmth; mental relaxation			2 highballs or 2 cocktails or 11 oz. ordinary wine or 2 bottles beer
	2	0.03	
Slight changes in feeling			1 highball or 1 cocktail or 5½ oz. ordinary wine or 1 bottle beer

Calories	
5½ oz. wine	115
12 oz. beer	170
1½ oz. whiskey	120

Adapted from Time chart by W. Hortens
Source: Dr. Leon A. Greenburg

holics return to the bottle as heroin addicts return to the needle. One problem is that our society tends to encourage social drinking and to tolerate the first stage of alcoholism.

Because it is so difficult to overcome alcoholism, an effort is being made to heighten people's awareness of the dangers of alcohol abuse. Television commercials and newspaper advertisements are geared toward stopping young people from drinking. Along many roadsides, billboards have been erected to warn people of the dangers of drinking and driving. However, changing people's attitudes takes time. A 1988 study (Russ, Geller, and Leland, 1988) found that feedback devices in bars that let patrons know how intoxicated they were had little effect on people's intention to drive. Many people simply ignored the devices. More work needs to be done on how to prevent the abuse of alcohol and other harmful substances.

CHAPTER REVIEW

KEY TERMS

- addiction
- antisocial personality
- anxiety
- compulsion
- conversion reaction
- delusion
- depression
- dissociative reaction
- double-bind theory

- DSM
- fugue
- hallucinations
- hypochondriasis
- major depression
- manic reaction
- mood disorder
- multiple personality
- neurosis

- obsession
- personality disorder
- phobia
- psychological dependence
- psychosis
- schizophrenia
- somatoform disorder
- tolerance
- withdrawal

SUMMARY

1. There is no absolute list of symptoms of mental disorder. Most psychologists define normal behavior as the ability to cope with stress and conflict, and abnormal behavior as the failure to adjust to the stresses of life.

2. DSM-III-R is a system for classifying mental disorders. It contains precise diagnostic criteria, and uses five major axes to describe a person's mental functioning. DSM-III-R will be updated to include premenstrual syndrome.

3. Neurosis is a broad category of mental disorders, characterized by chronic anxiety. Severe neurotic anxiety may produce phobias, obsessions, compulsions, various somatoform disorders, and depression.

4. People commit suicide for many different reasons; not all suicidal individuals are depressed. Contrary to popular belief, people who threaten to kill themselves often do so.

5. Psychosis is a second category of mental disorders, characterized by behavior that is so incomprehensible to others as virtually to eliminate the individual's capacity to meet the demands of everyday life.

6. Schizophrenia is a type of psychosis in which a person's thoughts, emotions, and perceptions are confused and disconnected. Schizophrenics may experience delusions and hallucinations, withdraw into fantasies, and engage in bizarre behavior.

7. Mood disorders are another type of psychosis. They are characterized by excessive and inappropriate elation (manic behavior) or despair (major depression).

8. Major depression is a significant health problem in the United States. People from poor socioeconomic backgrounds are most likely to suffer from depression.

9. Psychosis may be caused by an inherited tendency to become disturbed, by biochemical imbalances, or by exposure to contradictory communications (the double bind), or—most likely—by combinations of these and other factors.

10. A personality disorder is an ongoing pattern of maladaptive behavior combined with an inability to establish appropriate relationships with other people and the environment. The antisocial personality is an example.

11. Substance abuse has become a major psychological problem in American society. Substance abuse leads to psychological dependence. Use of some drugs also leads to addiction, in which the person develops a physical need for the drug. America's most serious drug problem is alcoholism. An effort is being made to heighten people's awareness of the dangers of alcohol abuse. Some advertisements warn people of the dangers of drinking and driving.

REVIEW QUESTIONS

1. Describe three ways of defining abnormality. Describe one shortcoming of each definition.

2. What is the legal definition of insanity? Is pleading insanity highly successful as a means of defense in criminal cases?

3. What does Szasz mean by the phrase "problems in living"?

4. What system do psychologists use to classify abnormal behavior? In what ways is this system different from the one that preceded it? What are some of the advantages of the newer system?

5. What are some differences between neurosis and psychosis? What is the difference between symptoms (for example, depression) that a psychologically healthy person might experience from time to time and the symptoms of a psychologically disturbed person?

6. Describe the symptoms associated with anxiety. Give an explanation for the cause of anxiety.

7. How do phobias differ from normal fears? Give one explanation for the causes of phobias.

8. What is an obsession? What is a compulsion? Why do people develop obsessions and compulsions?

9. What do psychologists mean when they refer to someone as having a somatoform disorder?

10. What is a conversion reaction? What do psychologists believe causes a conversion reaction?

11. How do conversion reactions and hypochondriases differ?

12. What is fugue? What psychological function might it serve?

13. What is multiple personality? How common a disorder is it? What do psychologists think multiple personality may come from?

14. What is Freud's explanation for depression? Describe the more contemporary theories that explain the causes of depression.

15. What is schizophrenia? What are two common experiences of schizophrenics? Summarize two types of schizophrenic reactions.

16. What is a manic reaction? What is major depression? Both can be classified as what type of reaction?

17. What are the three major causes given for psychosis?

18. How do personality disorders differ from neuroses and psychoses?

19. How would you describe people who are classified as having antisocial personality disorders?

20. What are the differences between drug dependency, drug addiction, and drug tolerance?

21. What evidence is there that heavy drinking is a serious problem in America? Is alcohol a stimulant or a depressant? What are the stages of alcoholism? What can be done to help alcoholics?

ACTIVITIES

1. Formulate a definition of mental illness. Is your definition free of social values, or are values a necessary part of the definition?

2. Study a book of paintings and drawings by Vincent Van Gogh. Can you tell which were done when he was mentally healthy and which were done when he was suffering from severe psychological disorder? How?

3. It is thought that one of the conditions that produces mental disorders is overexposure to dou-

ble-bind situations. Everyone has faced these situations at various times. How many examples from your own experiences can you think of that illustrate various forms of the double-bind situation? How did you resolve the conflicts? Can you see patterns of behavior responses developing?

4. Whenever you dismiss certain people as "creeps," for example, you are really saying more about yourself than about the people you are labeling. For instance, people who are nervous in social gatherings usually cannot stand other people who are nervous in social gatherings. For a good indication of your own problems, make a list of people you don't like and the reason(s) why you don't like them. Take a hard, honest look at those traits you have written down and see how many of them apply to you as well.

5. Watch television for a week. Keep a journal of programs that have some psychological theme. What examples of mental breakdown are described? How common are they made to appear? Are simple solutions given? How is the psychologist or psychiatrist shown? Does this person have ready answers? What are they?

6. Cut out about fifteen pictures of people from magazines and paste them on a large piece of paper. Include among the pictures several of people with long or mussed up hair and untidy clothes. Ask several friends or classmates if they can determine which of the people in the pictures are mentally ill. How many select the

people with unkempt appearances? What conclusions can you draw from this experiment?

7. What are you afraid of? Do you fear high places, or water, or maybe snakes or spiders? Try to think back to when you first had these fears. Can you state rationally why you have each of your fears?

8. Read newspapers and newsmagazines for articles dealing with mental illness. Keep a record of the maladaptive behavior that is identified and who makes the diagnosis. In what contexts is mental illness discussed? Do the articles address legal issues? What can you learn about treatment of mental illness from your collection of articles?

9. Contact your local branch of Alcoholics Anonymous (listed in your phone book) and arrange to have a speaker come to your class to talk about the abuse of alcohol or drugs. Before the speaker comes, generate a list of questions or special issues that you and your classmates would like to have addressed. Give this list to the speaker to help organize the presentation.

10. What makes you anxious? Consider the times you have experienced a general apprehension and try to list the particular settings or situations in which you are most likely to feel this way. What ways have you developed to help you cope with anxiety? Are there times when anxiety has hindered your behavior? Are there times when anxiety has helped your behavior? If you answered the last two questions in the affirmative, how do you explain the difference?

Objectives: *After studying this chapter, you should be able to*
- explain the nature of psychotherapy and trace its historical development.
- cite the aims of psychoanalysis and describe its method of treatment.
- identify various forms of group therapy.
- discuss organic therapy and describe its main forms of treatment.
- identify recent trends in community mental health.

Therapy and Change

At certain times of transition and crisis in life, we may feel an urgent need to find someone trustworthy to share our doubts and problems with. A parent, relative, or close friend is often helpful in such times of need. But many psychological problems are too bewildering and complex to be solved in this way. When people become dissatisfied or distraught with life and suspect that the reason lies inside themselves, they are likely to seek help from someone with training and experience in such matters. People who have been trained to deal with the psychological problems of others include social workers, psychologists, and psychiatrists. The special kind of help they provide is called **psychotherapy**.

This chapter will present some of the major approaches to therapy and will describe what it is like to undergo therapy. It will explore various types of group therapy, probe the current situation in America's mental institutions, and touch on the trend toward community mental health.

WHAT IS PSYCHOTHERAPY?

Psychotherapy literally means "healing of the soul," and in early times psychological disturbances were often thought to represent some sort of moral or religious problem. Madmen were sometimes viewed as being inhabited by devils or demons, and treatment consisted of exorcism—the driving out of these demons by religious ceremonies or by physical punishment. Within the last two hundred years, however, views of psychological disorders have changed. Mental disorders have slowly come to be thought of as diseases, and the term "mental illness" is now popularly applied to many psychological problems.

What Is Psychotherapy?
Characteristics of Psychotherapy • What Makes a Good Therapist?

Kinds of Psychotherapy
Psychoanalysis • The Human Potential Movement • Gestalt Therapy • Rational-Emotive Therapy • Transactional Analysis • Behavior Therapy • Group Therapies

Does Psychotherapy Work?

Organic Therapy

Mental Institutions
Commitment • Conditions

Community Mental Health
Community Mental Health Centers • Using Psychology: Crisis Intervention Programs • The Rise of the Paraprofessional

Figure 16.2
Therapist and patient. Many people have a mental picture of therapy as taking place with the person lying on a couch while a middle-aged, bearded man sits taking notes in a chair. Nowadays therapists are more likely to talk to their patients in a face-to-face position and to use a variety of techniques rather than just a strict psychoanalytic approach.

The fact that psychological disturbance is seen as the symptom of a disease has helped to reduce the stigma associated with such problems, and it has done much to convince society that troubled people need care and treatment. Nevertheless many psychotherapists feel that the term "mental illness" has outlived its usefulness and that, in fact, it may now be doing more harm than good.

The trouble with letting a person think of herself as mentally ill is that she sees herself in a passive, helpless position. She sees her troubles as being caused by forces over which she has no control. By thinking of herself in this way, the person can avoid taking responsibility for her own situation and for helping herself change.

One of the functions of psychotherapy is to help people realize that they are responsible for their own problems and that, even more importantly, they are the only ones who can really solve these problems. This approach does not imply that people become disturbed on purpose or that no one should need outside help. People often adopt certain techniques for getting along in life that seem appropriate at the time but that lead to trouble in the long run. Such patterns can be difficult for the individual to see or change. The major task of the therapist, therefore, is to help people examine their way of living, to understand how their present way of living causes problems, and to start living in new, more beneficial ways. The therapist can be thought of as a guide who is hired by the individual to help her find the source of her problems and some possible solutions.

Characteristics of Psychotherapy

There are many different kinds of therapy, only a few of which will be described in this chapter. Each one is based on different theories about how human personality works, and each one is carried out in a different style. Some psychotherapists stick rigorously to one style and consider the others useless. Other psychotherapists pick and choose methods from many different kinds of therapy and use whatever works best. But whatever the style or philosophy, all types of psychotherapy have certain characteristics in common.

The primary goal of psychotherapy is to strengthen the patient's control over his or her life. People seeking psychotherapy feel trapped in behavior patterns. Over the years they have developed not only certain feelings about themselves, but behaviors that reinforce those feelings. Such people lack the freedom to choose the direction their lives will take. Their behavior and feelings make it impossible for them to reach their goals. For example, a man who is severely critical of himself may feel others are equally harsh in their judgments of him. Rather than risk feelings of rejection, he avoids social gatherings. A person who is uncomfortable meeting other people will, no doubt, feel lonely and rejected. His critical feelings about himself will be strengthened, and he may come to feel that he will remain unloved for life.

The aim of psychotherapy for such a person would be to free him of his burden of self-hate. With a more positive self-image, the man would not be locked into the cycle of avoidance, rejection, and despair. For perhaps the

How to be Assertive

It's hard to be assertive all the time in every situation. You may find it easy to ask a favor of a friend but impossible to make a similar request of a stranger. If you want to spread your assertiveness over more situations, try following these simple suggestions:

- Begin your attempts at developing assertiveness in the least threatening situations. Start with your brother, not your boss.
- Increase your nonverbal assertiveness. Stand erect, look a person straight in the eyes during conversation, eliminate nervous habits, smile.
- Work up to a difficult task in a series of gradual steps. If you're afraid to ask someone for a date, start by saying hello. Then gradually increase the time you spend talking to that person until you're comfortable enough to pop the question.
- If you're afraid to tell people how you feel when you disagree, start by expressing your opinion when you're asked. Once you feel confident in your ability to disagree, you're ready to volunteer your feelings.
- If you find it hard to begin a conversation with a person you've just met, try asking open-ended questions, listening carefully for any additional information the person gives and commenting on it, volunteering information about yourself, and giving compliments.

By following these suggestions, you probably won't increase your assertiveness overnight. But each day will bring you closer to your goal.

For more details, see R. L. Williams and J. D. Lang, *Toward a Self-Managed Life Style,* 2nd ed. Boston: Houghton Mifflin, 1979.

first time, he could feel in control of his life. His behavior would be based on *choice,* and not on the necessity that goes with fixed behavior patterns.

In order to change, it is necessary for the patient to achieve some *understanding* of his troubles. One of the first tasks of therapy, therefore, is to examine the patient's problem closely.

The man in our example will, in the course of his therapy, discover the origin of his self-critical, despairing feelings. He may also realize that, although these feelings developed from real situations, perhaps during his childhood, they no longer apply to his adult capabilities. Gradually the patient's view of himself will become more realistic.

Another major task of therapy is to help the patient find meaningful *alternatives* to his present unsatisfactory ways of behaving. The patient we have been discussing may look for ways to meet new people rather than avoid them.

One of the most important factors in effective treatment is the patient's belief or hope that he *can* change. The influence that a patient's hopes and expectations have on his improvement is often called the **placebo effect.** This name comes from giving medical patients *placebos*—harmless sugar

---

Table 16.1 / Kinds of Therapists

Psychiatrists are medical doctors who specialize in the treatment of mental illness. They generally take a post-M.D. residency in a mental institution. Because of their medical background, psychiatrists are the only group licensed to prescribe drugs.

Psychoanalysts are psychiatrists who have taken special training in the theory of personality and techniques of psychotherapy of Sigmund Freud, usually at a psychoanalytic institute. They must themselves be psychoanalyzed before they can practice.

Lay analysts are psychoanalysts who do not have degrees in medicine but who have studied with established psychoanalysts.

Clinical psychologists are therapists with a Ph.D. degree. They are the product of a three-to-four-year research-oriented program in the social sciences, plus a one-year predoctoral or postdoctoral internship in psychotherapy and psychological assessment.

Counselors generally have a master's or doctor's degree in counseling psychology. They usually work in educational institutions, where they are available for consultation about personal problems. They customarily refer clients with serious problems to psychiatrists or psychologists.

Psychiatric social workers are people with a graduate degree in psychiatric social work. They generally receive supervised practical training coupled with two years of courses in psychology.

Nonprofessionals include clergy, physicians, teachers, and others who dispense a great deal of advice despite the fact that they have had no formal training in therapy or counseling. Nevertheless, more troubled people turn to nonprofessionals than to professionals.

---

pills—when they complain of ailments that do not seem to have any physiological basis. The patients take the tablets and their symptoms disappear.

The placebo effect does not imply that problems can be solved simply by fooling the patient. It does demonstrate, however, the tremendous importance of the patient's attitude in finding a way to change. A patient who does not believe she can be helped probably cannot be. A patient who believes she can change and believes she has the power to change will find a way. Therapy goes beyond the placebo effect. It combines the patient's belief that she can change with hard work and professional guidance

What Makes a Good Therapist?

In American society, there are many people who practice psychotherapy. Some, like psychiatrists, are trained in psychology and medicine; others, like counselors and clergy, have considerably less formal training. The different kinds of professional therapists and the training that each goes through before practicing psychotherapy are shown in Table 16.1.

Before going to a professional therapist, most people first turn to a friend or other nonprofessional for help and advice. Sometimes, this is exactly what's needed. But professional therapists are likely to be more skillful in encouraging the person to examine uncomfortable feelings and problems. In the process of therapy, the patient may feel frustrated because he cannot push the burden of responsibility onto someone else the way he can with a friend.

The process of therapy is always difficult and upsetting, and patients often become heavily dependent on the therapist while they are trying to make changes. A patient may become angry or hurt, for example, if his therapist suddenly goes on vacation. The therapist, therefore, has to be careful not to betray the trust that the patient has placed in her. On the other hand, she must not let the patient lean on her or take out his problems on her. Patients often try to avoid their problems by using the therapist as a substitute parent or by blaming her for their misfortunes.

Whether psychotherapy will be beneficial to a person depends on both the patient and the therapist. Patients who get the most out of psychotherapy are people with high intelligence, a good education, and a middle-class background. Such people have much in common with most therapists, and this similarity seems to help. In addition, the people who benefit most from psychotherapy are those who have relatively mild problems about which they have considerable anxiety or depression. Severely disturbed, apathetic patients are much more difficult to change. Therapy will also be more effective with people who are introspective and who can withstand frustration. Therapy is neither easy nor fast; it demands as much from the patient as it does from the therapist.

Effective therapists share at least three common characteristics. First, they are reasonably *healthy*. A therapist who is anxious, defensive, and withdrawn will not be able to see his patient's problems clearly. A second important characteristic is a capacity for *warmth* and *understanding*. Troubled people are usually fearful and confused about explaining their problems. The therapist needs to be able to give the patient confidence that he is capable of caring and understanding. Finally, good therapists are *experienced* in dealing with people—in understanding their complexities, seeing through the games they play to trick the therapist and themselves, and judging their strengths and weaknesses. Only by having worked with many people can a therapist learn when to give support, when to insist that the patient stand on his own feet, and how to make sense of the things people say.

KINDS OF PSYCHOTHERAPY

Although there are many approaches to psychotherapy, only the three most influential approaches will be discussed here: psychoanalysis, the human potential movement, and behavior therapy. In addition to these types of individual therapy, several kinds of group therapy will be described.

Psychoanalysis

For a long time **psychoanalysis** was the only kind of psychotherapy practiced in Western society. It was this type of therapy that gave rise to the classic picture of a bearded Viennese doctor seated behind a patient who is lying on a couch.

Psychoanalysis is based on the theories of Sigmund Freud. According to Freud's views, psychological disturbances are due to anxiety about hidden conflicts between the unconscious components of one's personality. (Freud's theory of personality is described in Chapters 8 and 11.) One job of the psychoanalyst, therefore, is to help make the patient aware of the unconscious impulses, desires, and fears that are causing the anxiety. Psychoanalysts believe that if the patient can understand her unconscious motives, she has taken the first step toward gaining control over her behavior and freeing herself of her problems. Such understanding is called *insight.*

Psychoanalysis is a slow procedure. It may take years of fifty-minute sessions several times a week before the patient is able to make fundamental changes in her life. Throughout this time, the analyst assists his patient in a thorough examination of the unconscious motives behind her behavior. This task begins with the analyst telling the patient to relax and talk about everything that comes into her mind. This method is called **free association.** The patient may consider her passing thoughts too unimportant or too embarrassing to mention. But the analyst suggests that she express everything—the thought that seems most inconsequential may, in fact, be the most meaningful upon closer examination.

As the patient lies on the couch, she may describe her dreams, talk about her private life, or recall long-forgotten experiences. The psychoanalyst sits out of sight behind the patient and often says nothing for long periods of time. He occasionally makes remarks or asks questions that guide the patient, or he may suggest an unconscious motive or factor that explains something the patient has been talking about, but most of the work is done by the patient herself.

The patient is understandably reluctant to reveal painful feelings and to examine lifelong patterns that need to be changed, and as the analysis proceeds, she is likely to try to hold back the flow of information. This phenomenon—in fact, any behavior that impedes the course of therapy—is called **resistance.** The patient may have agreed to cooperate fully, yet she finds at times that her mind is blank, that she feels powerless and can no longer think of anything to say. At such times the analyst will simply point out what is happening and wait for the patient to continue. The analyst may also suggest another line of approach to the area of resistance. By analyzing the patient's resistances, both the therapist and the patient can understand how the patient deals with anxiety-provoking material.

Sooner or later, the analyst begins to appear in the patient's associations and dreams. The patient may begin feeling toward the analyst the way she feels toward some other important figure in her life. This process is called **transference.**

If the patient can recognize what is happening, transference may allow

Figure 16.3
The phenomena of resistance and transference. Here the patient's resistance is shown in the fact that he is seeing the therapist as a menacing dentist. At the same time, he is transferring: the "dentist" seems to him like an impersonal, frightening mother.

her to experience her true feelings toward the important person. But often, instead of experiencing and understanding her feelings, the patient simply begins acting toward the therapist in the same way she used to act toward the important person, usually one of her parents.

The therapist does not allow the patient to resort to these tactics. He remains impersonal and anonymous. He always directs the patient back to herself. The therapist may ask, for example, "What do you see when you imagine my face?" The patient may reply that she sees the therapist as an angry, frowning, unpleasant figure. The therapist never takes this personally. Instead, he may calmly say, "What does this make you think of?" Gradually, it will become clear to both patient and therapist that the patient is reacting to the neutral therapist as though he were a threatening father.

Through this kind of process, the patient becomes aware of her real feelings and motivations. She may begin to understand, for example, why she has trouble with her boss at work—she may be seeing her boss, her therapist, and indeed any man in a position of authority, in the same way that as a child she saw her father.

The Human Potential Movement

Humanistic psychology has given rise to several new approaches to psychotherapy, known collectively as the **human potential movement.** We discussed these schools of psychology in Chapter 11. To review, humanistic psychologists stress the actualization of one's unique potentials through personal responsibility, freedom of choice, and authentic relationships.

Client-centered Therapy.   **Client-centered therapy** is based on the theories of Carl Rogers (1951; see Chapter 11). The use of the term "client" instead of "patient" gives one an insight into the reasoning behind Rogers's method. "Patient" may suggest inferiority, whereas "client" implies an equal relationship between the therapist and the person seeking help.

     Client-centered therapists assume that people are basically good and

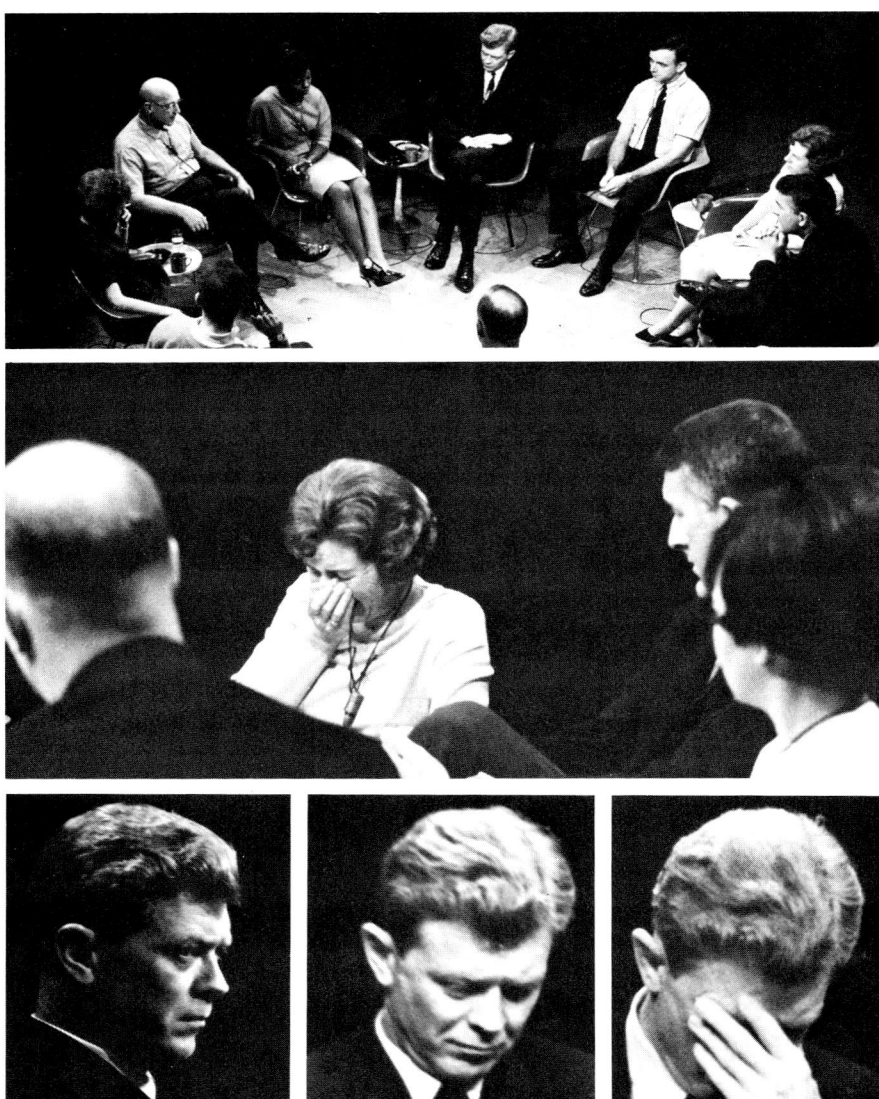

Figure 16.4
Carl Rogers is shown here *(on the left, top photograph)* leading an encounter group. Many encounter group leaders, including Rogers, feel that their role in the group is the same as that of any other member. Only if the group as a whole or any one of its members gets into trouble will the leader intervene to rescue the situation. Typically, other group members will exhibit leadership or therapeutic skills and the designated leader will remain in the background.

that they are capable of handling their own lives. Psychological problems arise when the true self becomes lost and the individual comes to view himself according to the standards of others. One of the goals of therapy, therefore, is to help the client to recognize his own strength and confidence so that he can learn to be true to his own standards and ideas about how to live effectively.

In the course of an interview, the client is encouraged to speak freely about intimate matters that may be bothering him. He is told that what he talks about is up to him. The therapist listens and encourages conversation but tries to avoid giving opinions. Instead, she tries to echo back as clearly as possible the feelings the client has expressed. She may try to extract the main points from the client's hesitant or rambling explanations. For example, a male client may tell a long story about an incident with his father, and the therapist may respond by saying, "This kind of thing makes you feel very stupid." The client may in turn say, "No, not stupid, angry. It's really he who is being stupid." And the therapist will say, "Oh, I see, you really feel angry at him when he acts this way." Between them, they form a clearer and clearer picture of how the client really feels about himself, his life, and the people around him.

Client-centered therapy is conducted in an atmosphere of emotional support that Rogers calls **unconditional positive regard.** As in psychoanalysis, the therapist never says that she thinks the client or what the client has said is good or bad. But she shows the client that she will accept anything that is said without embarrassment, reservation, or anger. Her primary responsibility is to create a warm and accepting relationship between herself and her client.

This acceptance makes it easier for the client to explore thoughts about himself and his experiences. He is able to abandon old values without fear of disapproval, and he can begin to see himself, his situation, and his relationships with others in a new light.

As he reduces his tensions and releases his emotions, the client feels that he is becoming a more complete person. He gains the courage to accept parts of his personality that he had formerly considered weak or bad, and, by recognizing his self-worth, he can set up realistic goals and consider the steps necessary to reach them. The client's movement toward independence signals the end of the need for therapy—he can assume the final steps to independence on his own.

Existential Therapy.   Like Rogers, all therapists in the human potential movement see their role as helping individuals to achieve self-determination. Existential therapists believe that for most people, freedom and autonomy are threatening. To acknowledge that you are a unique and independent person is to acknowledge that you are alone. Unconsciously many people avoid this realization, burying their feelings and desires. Therapists like Rollo May (1969) attempt to help patients overcome the fear of freedom, get in touch with their true feelings, and accept responsibility for their lives.

Viktor Frankl (1970) is also an existentialist, but approaches therapy

Carl Rogers and Unconditional Positive Regard. One of the fundamental aspects of Carl Rogers's client-centered therapy (also called "*person-centered therapy*") is to show the client unconditional positive regard. However, this ideal is difficult to reach in practice.

Rogers was not content merely to theorize about psychological processes. He believed in conducting research to verify his hypotheses. To that end he often recorded therapy sessions he conducted (with the client's permission, of course), so that his methods could be studied scientifically. One of his students, Charles Truax, did just that.

Truax analyzed Rogers's responses to a client during the course of therapy. He found that Rogers displayed frequent verbal and nonverbal reinforcements to statements that indicated optimism or self-assuredness. He provided relatively few reinforcements after the client complained of symptoms and frustrations.

It seems that there is a strong pull to support ideas we agree with and to ignore those we disagree with. Apparently, even the master of unconditional positive reinforcement is not immune from this motive.

somewhat differently. After listening to a patient express despair, he might ask, "Why don't you commit suicide?" Frankl is not being cruel or sarcastic. He is trying to help the individual find meaning in life. The patient's answer (whether it is "my husband and children," "my religion," or "my work") provides clues about what the person values.

In Frankl's view, feelings of emptiness and boredom are the primary source of emotional problems.

> Mental health is based on a certain degree of tension between what one has already achieved and what one still ought to accomplish, or the gap between what one is and what one should become. Such a tension is inherent in the human being and is therefore indispensable to mental well-being. . . . What people actually need is not a tensionless state but rather the striving and struggling for some worthy goal (1970: 165–166).

Frankl believes a therapist should help to open the patient's eyes to the possibilities in life and guide him or her toward challenges.

Gestalt Therapy

Developed by Fritz Perls in the 1950s and 1960s, **gestalt therapy** emphasizes the relationship between the patient and therapist in the here and now (Perls, Hefferline, and Goodman, 1965). Suppose that toward the middle of a session a patient runs out of problems to discuss and sits mute, staring blankly out the window. Instead of waiting for the patient to speak up, a gestalt therapist would say what he feels. "I can't stand the way you just sit there and say nothing. Sometimes I regret ever becoming a therapist. You are impossible. . . . There, now I feel better" (Kempler, 1973: 272). The therapist is not blowing off steam in an unprofessional way. He does this to encourage (by example) the patient to express his feelings, even if it means risking a relationship.

Gestalt therapy is based on the belief that many individuals are so concerned with obtaining approval that they become strangers to themselves. For example, an individual may always defer to authority figures, but he may be detached from the part of himself that has fantasies of rebelling. Neither part acknowledges the other. Gestalt therapists attempt to help a person fit the pieces together. (The word "gestalt" comes from the German word for "configuration.")

Rational-Emotive Therapy

Rational-emotive therapy (RET) is a form of therapy developed by Albert Ellis in the late 1950s (Ellis, 1973). Ellis believes that people behave in deliberate and rational ways, given their assumptions about life. Emotional problems arise when an individual's assumptions are unrealistic.

Supppose a man seeks therapy when a woman leaves him. He cannot stand the fact that she has rejected him. Without her his life is empty and miserable. She has made him feel utterly worthless. He must get her back. An RET therapist would not look for incidents in the past that are making the present unbearable for this man, as a psychoanalyst would. RET therapists do not probe; they reason. Like a spoiled child, the man is demanding that the woman love him. He expects—indeed, insists—that things will always go his way. Given this assumption, the only possible explanation for her behavior is that something is dreadfully wrong, either with him or with her.

What is wrong, in the therapist's view, is the man's thinking. By defining his feelings for the woman as need rather than desire, he—not she—is causing his depression. When you convince yourself that you need someone, you will in fact be unable to carry on without that person. When you believe that you cannot stand rejection, you will in fact fall apart when you encounter rejection.

The goal of rational-emotive therapy is to correct these false and self-defeating beliefs. Rejection is unpleasant, but it is not unbearable. The woman may be very desirable, but she is not irreplaceable. To teach the individual to think in realistic terms, the RET therapist may use a number of techniques: role playing (so that the person can see how his beliefs affect his relationships); modeling (to demonstrate other ways of thinking and acting); humor (to underline the absurdity of his beliefs); and simple persuasion. The therapist may also make homework assignments to give the man practice in acting more reasonably. For example, the therapist may instruct him to ask women who are likely to reject him out on dates. Why? So that he will learn that he can cope with things not going his way.

Ellis believes that the individual must take three steps to cure or correct himself. First, he must realize that some of his assumptions are false. Second, he must see that he is making *himself* disturbed by acting on false beliefs. Finally, he must work to break old habits of thought and behavior. He has to practice, to learn self-discipline, to take risks.

Transactional Analysis

Introduced by Eric Berne (1964) in the early 1950s, **transactional analysis** is both a theory of personality and a method of therapy. The central assumption of transactional analysis (often referred to as TA) is that people function and experience their world from one of three perspectives, or ego states. *Ego states* represent the ways people organize their thoughts, feelings, and actions. Sometimes adults think, feel, and act from a *child ego* state. For example, a man who has been stopped by a police officer for speeding may feel and act as he did when he was a boy and was caught doing something wrong by his parents. Other times, people may act, think, and feel like one of their parents, close friends, or teachers—from a *parent ego* state. For example, a person who acts in a judgmental and opinionated way is most likely functioning from the parent ego state.

The *adult ego* state represents people's thoughts, feelings, and behaviors that are rationally related to their experience of the present. Unlike reactions in the child or parent ego states (reactions that are shaped and sometimes distorted by past experiences with other people) reactions in the adult ego state allow people to deal effectively and responsibly with their everyday problems.

If a friend tells you "you should carry an umbrella today—it might rain," he or she is probably speaking from a parent ego state. If you say or think "Mind your own business," you are probably reacting from a child ego state. An adult ego state reaction would be to look around and see whether it looks like rain and act accordingly.

Berne believed that these three personality parts develop through people's interactions with significant people in their lives. Furthermore, he believed that while people are growing up they develop specific plans that define how they will act toward other people and how other people are expected to act toward them. People learn to "play games" or engage in predictable exchanges with other people to fit their life plan.

The goal of the TA therapist is to help people identify maladaptive transactions or strategies for living (usually from the parent or child ego state) and to help them develop more effective adult ego state responses. The TA therapist usually begins therapy by establishing a contract with the client. The contract states what the client wants to change and what the therapist will or will not do to help the client achieve his or her goal.

One woman sought TA therapy to help her deal with her relations with men. She found that on a first date with someone, she would always make a point of saying that she just wanted to be friends, but then she would act in a flirtatious way that gave the opposite impression. If the man made a pass at her, she would be outraged. By exploring and discussing her behavior with her therapist, she discovered that she had been playing games from her child ego state. This insight helped her recognize what she wanted in her relationships, and helped her learn how to behave. In most cases, transactional analysis focuses on the individual's assuming responsibility for his or her actions (see Holland, 1973).

Behavior Therapy

Behavior therapists believe a disturbed person has learned to behave in the wrong way.

Psychoanalysis and the human potential movement have sometimes been criticized for being "all talk and no action." In **behavior therapy** there is much more emphasis on action. Rather than spending large amounts of time going into the patient's past history or the details of his or her dreams, the behavior therapist concentrates on finding out what is specifically wrong with the patient's current life and takes steps to change it.

The idea behind behavior therapy is that a disturbed person is one who has *learned* to behave in the wrong way. The therapist's job, therefore, is to "reeducate" the patient. The reasons for the patient's undesirable behavior are not important; what is important is to change the behavior. To bring about such changes, the therapist uses certain conditioning techniques first discovered in animal laboratories. (The principles of conditioning are explained in Chapter 2.)

One technique used by behavior therapists is **systematic desensitization.** This method is used to overcome irrational fears and anxieties the patient has learned. The goal of desensitization therapy is to encourage people to imagine the feared situation while relaxing, thus extinguishing the fear response. For example, suppose a student is terrified of

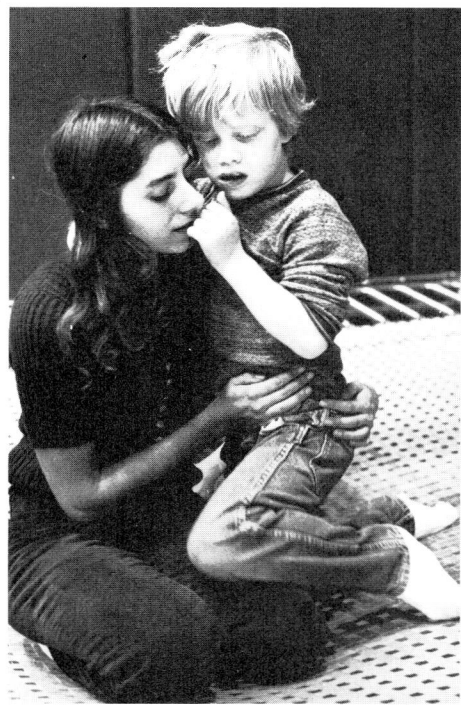

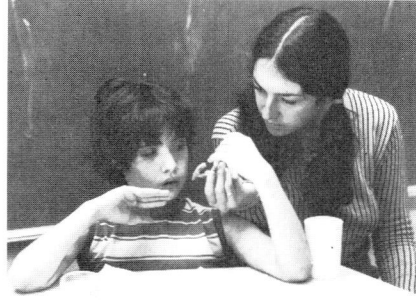

Figure 16.5
The behavior therapy approach to the treatment of autism involves the use of contingency management, also known as operant conditioning (see Chapter 2). The therapist is rewarding the child with affection (left) and with food (top right) for performing such desirable behaviors as coming toward the therapist and eating and drinking at the table. (bottom right) The therapists are introducing two autistic children to the experience of holding hands.

speaking in front of large groups of people—that, in fact, his stage fright is so tremendous that he is unable to speak when called upon in class. How would desensitization therapy effectively change this person's behavior?

The therapist might have the student make a list of all the aspects of talking to others that he finds frightening. Perhaps the most frightening aspect is actually standing before an audience, whereas the least frightening is speaking to a single other person. The patient ranks his fears in order, from the most frightening on down. First, the therapist begins teaching the patient to relax. As he relaxes, the patient tries to imagine as vividly as possible the least disturbing scene on his list. As he thinks about speaking to a single stranger, the student may feel a mild anxiety. But because the therapist has taught him how to relax, the patient is soon able to think about the experience without feeling afraid. The basic logic is that a person cannot feel anxious and relaxed at the same time. The therapist attempts to replace anxiety with its opposite, relaxation.

This procedure is followed step by step by the list of anxiety-arousing events. The patient finally reaches a point where he is able to imagine the situations that threaten him the most without feeling anxiety. Now the therapist starts to expose the person to real-life situations that have previously frightened him. Therapy finally reaches the point where the student is able to get up and deliver an unrehearsed speech before a full auditorium.

Another form of behavior therapy is called **contingency management.** In this method the therapist and patient decide what old, undesirable

behavior needs to be eliminated and what new, desirable behavior needs to appear (Figure 16.5). Arrangements are then made for the old behavior to go unrewarded and for the desired behavior to be reinforced. In its simplest form, contingency management consists of the therapist agreeing with the patient, "If you do X, I will give you Y." This form of agreement is similar to systems of reward that people often use on themselves. For instance, a college student may say to himself, "If I get a good grade on the exam, I'll treat myself to a great dinner." The reward is *contingent* (dependent) upon getting a good grade.

Contingency management is used in prisons, mental hospitals, schools, and army bases, as well as with individual patients. In these situations it is possible to set up whole miniature systems of rewards, called token economies. For example, psychologists in some mental hospitals select behavior they judge desirable. Patients are then rewarded for these behaviors with "hospital," or token, money. Thus if a patient cleans his room or works in the hospital garden, he is rewarded with token money. The patients are able to cash in their token money for things they want, such as candy or cigarettes, or for certain privileges, such as time away from the ward. These methods are successful in inducing mental patients, who often sit around doing nothing day after day, to begin leading active lives. They learn to take care of themselves and to take on responsibility instead of having to be cared for constantly.

In the past few years, behavior therapists have started experimenting with procedures to help people gain control over their own thoughts and actions. Chapter 2 describes some of these new techniques for cognitive behavior modification.

Group Therapies

In the forms of therapy described thus far, the troubled person is usually alone with the therapist. In **group therapy,** however, she is in the company of others. There are several advantages to this situation. Group therapy gives the troubled person practical experience with one of her biggest problems—getting along with other people. A person in group therapy also has a chance to see how other people are struggling with problems similar to her own, and she discovers what other people think of her. She, in turn, can express what she thinks of them, and in this exchange she discovers where she is mistaken in her views of herself and of other people and where she is correct.

Another advantage to group therapy is the fact that one therapist can help a large number of people. Most group-therapy sessions are led by a trained therapist who makes suggestions, clarifies points, and keeps activities from getting out of hand. In this way, her training and experience are used to help as many as twenty people at once.

Family Therapy.   Recently therapists have begun to suggest, after talking to a patient, that the entire family unit should work at group therapy. This method is particularly useful because the members of the group are all people of great importance in one another's lives. In **family therapy** it is

Figure 16.6
A group therapy session. Therapists use various techniques to get the members of the group to help one another see themselves and others more clearly.

Figure 16.7
A family therapy session. Here the therapist observes the interactions in a family in order to discern, describe, and treat the patterns that contribute to the disturbance of one or more of its members.

possible to untangle the twisted web of relationships that have led one or more members in the family to experience emotional suffering.

Often family members are unhappy because they are mistreating or are being mistreated by other family members in ways no one understands or wants to talk about. The family therapist can point out what is going wrong from an objective viewpoint and can suggest ways of improving communication and fairness in the family.

Not all group therapies are run by professionals, however. Some of the most successful examples are provided in nonprofessional organizations, such as self-help groups.

Self-Help Groups.   An increasing number of self-help groups have emerged in recent years. These voluntary groups, composed of people who share a particular problem, are conducted without the active involvement of a professional therapist. During regularly scheduled meetings, members of the group come together to discuss their difficulties and to provide support and possible solutions.

Self-help groups have been formed to deal with problems ranging from alcoholism, overeating, and drug addiction, to child abuse, widowhood, single parenting, adjusting to cancer, and gambling. The best known self-help group is Alcoholics Anonymous (AA) which was founded in 1930. Many self-help groups have based their organizations on the AA model in which individual members can call on other members for help and emotional support.

The purpose of Alcoholics Anonymous is "to carry the AA message to the sick alcoholic who wants it." According to AA, the only way for alcoholics to change is to admit that they are powerless over alcohol and that their lives have become unmanageable. Alcoholics must come to believe that only some power greater than themselves can help them. Those who think they can battle out the problem alone will not be successful.

Members of AA usually meet at least once a week to discuss the meaning of this message, to talk about their experiences with alcohol, and to

Figure 16.8
An encounter group session. The purpose of these groups is to provide experiences that will help people to live more intense lives; the methods used are intended to increase sensitivity, openness, and honesty.

describe the new hope they have found with AA. Mutual encouragement, friendship, and an emphasis on personal responsibility are used to keep an individual sober.

Encounter Groups.   The power of group interaction to affect and change people has given rise to the controversial **encounter group.** Encounter groups are primarily for people who function adequately in everyday life but who, for some reason, feel unhappy, dissatisfied, or stagnant.

The purpose of encounter groups (which are also known as T-groups or sensitivity training) is to provide experiences that will help people live more intense lives. Being in a small group (between five and fifteen people) for this express purpose is bound to teach an individual something about interpersonal relations. Techniques are often used in groups to overcome the restrictions people live by in everyday life. A typical exercise requires each person to say something to every other person and at the same time to touch him or her in some way. Such methods are intended to increase sensitivity, openness, and honesty.

Role playing is another common encounter-group technique. It is a form of theater in which the goal is to help people expose and understand themselves. A person may try acting out the role of a character in one of his dreams; another person may pretend to be herself as a child talking to her mother, played by another member. By switching roles and placing themselves in each other's situation, group members are better able to see themselves as others see them. Acting out a past experience or playing the role of another person can do much to bring out a person's hidden and true feelings (Back, 1972).

Regardless of the type of therapy, all groups require experienced leaders who are qualified to take responsibility for the group. In a few cases, people who have been unprepared for the intense emotional exposure that occurs in such groups have suffered long-lasting psychological distress from the experience.

DOES PSYCHOTHERAPY WORK?

In 1952 Hans Eysenck published a review of five studies of the effectiveness of psychoanalytic treatment and nineteen studies of the effectiveness of "eclectic" psychotherapy, treatment in which several different therapeutic approaches are combined. Eysenck concluded that psychotherapy was no more effective than no treatment at all. According to his interpretation of these twenty-four studies, only 44 percent of the psychoanalytic patients improved with treatment, while 64 percent of those given eclectic psychotherapy were "cured" or had improved. Most startling, Eysenck argued that even this 64-percent improvement rate did not demonstrate the effectiveness of psychotherapy, since it has been reported that 72 percent of a group of hospitalized neurotics improved *without* treatment. If no treatment at all leads to as much improvement as psychotherapy, the obvious conclusion is that psychotherapy is not effective. Eysenck (1966) vigorously defended his controversial position, which generated a large number of additional reviews and a great many studies of the effectiveness of psychotherapy.

One of the most thoughtful and carefully reasoned reviews was written by Allen Bergin (1971). Bergin made the following points in reply to Eysenck. First, he demonstrated that when some different but equally reasonable assumptions about the classification of patients were made, the effectiveness of psychoanalytic treatment was much greater than Eysenck had reported; perhaps as many as 83 percent of the patients improved or recovered. Second, he reviewed a number of studies which showed that the rate of improvement without treatment was only about 30 percent.

Bergin's review leads one to question the validity of Eysenck's sweeping generalization that psychotherapy is no more effective than no treatment at all. But much of Bergin's argument is based on differences of opinion about how patients should be classified. Precise criteria for "improvement" are difficult to define and to apply. The nature of "spontaneous remission" (sudden disappearance) of symptoms in persons who have not received formal psychotherapy is difficult to assess, for these people may have received help from unacknowledged sources—friends, relatives, religious advisers, family physicians. And if, as some researchers believe, the prime ingredient in therapy is the establishment of a close relationship, then "spontaneous remission" in people who have received continuing help from such sources is not spontaneous at all.

An analysis of nearly 400 studies of the effectiveness of psychotherapy, conducted by Mary Lee Smith and Gene V. Glass (1977), used elaborate statistical procedures to estimate the effects of psychotherapy. They found that therapy is generally more effective than no treatment and that on the average most forms of therapy have similar effects.

Will any therapy do for any client? Probably not. Smith and Glass (1977) were able to show that for some specific clients and situations, some forms of therapy would be expected to have a greater effect than others (Figure 16.9). For example, if the client is a thirty-year-old neurotic of average

Figure 16.9
Is psychotherapy effective? Researchers Lee and Glass think the answer is yes. People receiving each of the types of psychotherapy shown in this graph were compared with untreated control groups. The bars indicate the percentile rank the average treated person attained on outcome measures when compared to control subjects for each type of therapy. (Adapted from Smith and Glass, 1977)

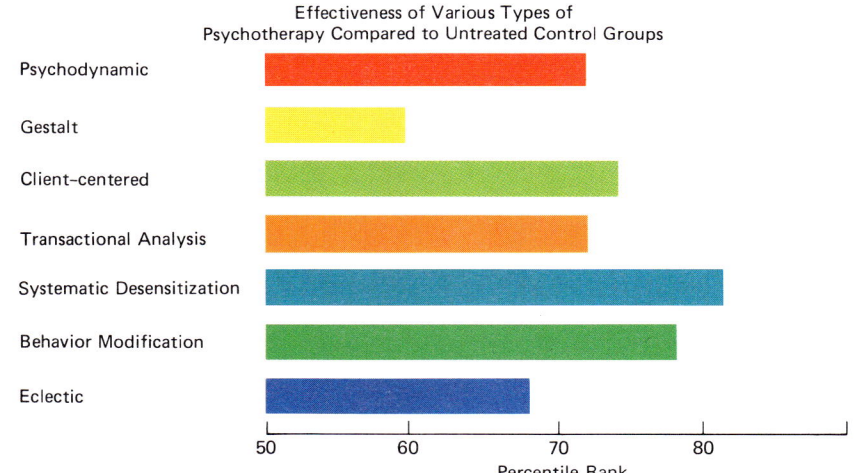

Effectiveness of Various Types of Psychotherapy Compared to Untreated Control Groups

intelligence seen in individual sessions by a therapist with five years of experience, psychodynamic therapy would be expected to have a greater effect than systematic desensitization. But in the case of a highly intelligent twenty-year-old with a phobia, systematic desensitization would be expected to have greater impact. However, these are educated guesses based on the interpretation of some complex statistical manipulations. Studies designed to answer these kinds of specific questions are now needed.

ORGANIC THERAPY

The various "talking" and "learning" therapies we have described so far in this chapter have been aimed primarily at patients who are still generally capable of functioning within society. But what of those people who are not capable of clear thinking or who are dangerous to themselves or others? For a long time the most common method of keeping dangerous or overactive psychotic patients in check was physical restraint—the strait jacket, wet-sheet wrapping, isolation. The patient was also calmed down by means of psychosurgery (see Chapter 5) and electroconvulsive shock. From the mid-1950s on, however, the use of drugs made it possible virtually to eliminate these forms of restraint.

Antipsychotic drugs (also known as major tranquilizers) are used in the treatment of schizophrenia. The most popular of these drugs are the phenothiazines, which include Thorazine (chlorpromazine) and Stelazine (trifluoperazine). Schizophrenic patients who take these drugs improve in a number of ways: they become less withdrawn, become less confused and agitated, have fewer auditory hallucinations, and are less irritable and hostile (Cole, 1964). Studies directly comparing phenothiazines with other forms of therapy suggest that these drugs are the most effective form of treatment now available for schizophrenia (May, 1968).

Although the patient who takes antipsychotic drugs is often improved enough to leave the hospital, he or she may have trouble adjusting to the outside world. Many patients now face the "revolving door" syndrome of going to a mental hospital, being released, returning to the hospital, being released again, and so on. Phenothiazines also have a number of unpleasant side effects, including a dry mouth, blurred vision, grogginess, constipation, and muscle disorders.

Another class of drugs, called *antidepressants* (including Elavil, Tofranil, and Parnate), make some depressed patients happier. Interestingly, they do not affect the mood of normal people. It is almost as if these drugs supply a chemical that some depressed people lack. Some of the antidepressants have such severe side effects that they can lead to death, so they must be given under close medical supervision.

Lithium is now widely used to return patients with mood disorders to a state of equilibrium in which extreme mood swings disappear. While all of the other drugs described here are synthetic, lithium is a natural chemical element. It, too, can lead to severe problems if it is not taken under proper medical supervision.

All About Valium

Valium is one of the most frequently prescribed brands of the drug diazepam. More than 25 million Americans use this minor tranquilizer to help them cope with the pressures in their lives. Approximately 80 percent of the Valium prescribed is consumed by ordinary people who have trouble dealing with today's fast-paced society. Only about 20 percent is taken by patients in hospitals and institutions.

Valium acts as a central nervous system depressant to reduce the amount of anxiety and arousal a person feels. It is also used for such varied purposes as the relief of muscle spasms, the emergency control of seizures, the control of hypertension, and the relief of anxiety and unwanted muscle spasms during labor. Most doctors believe that Valium serves these functions in a way that no other minor tranquilizer can.

Doctors who have analyzed the use and overuse of Valium agree, however, that it is a drug that can never be taken for granted and that it needs careful watching. Many people who use it could probably deal with their anxiety more effectively by determining and eliminating the source of the anxiety. If this is not effective, they might try other ways of handling stress, such as counseling, support groups, and exercise programs.

Commonly known as sedatives or mild tranquilizers, *anti-anxiety drugs* are used to reduce excitability and cause drowsiness. The most extensively used drugs of this kind are Miltown (meprobamate), Librium (chlordiazepoxide), and Valium (diazepam). Although these drugs came into widespread use in the 1970s, fewer people are using them now. Valium, however, continues to be one of the most widely prescribed drugs in the United States (see box).

While these drugs are effective for helping normal people cope with difficult periods in their lives, they are also prescribed for the alleviation of various neurotic symptoms, psychosomatic problems, and symptoms of alcohol withdrawal. The major effect of Valium, Librium, and Miltown is to depress the activity of the central nervous system. If the drugs are taken properly, the side effects are few and consist mainly of drowsiness. However, prolonged use may lead to dependency, and heavy doses taken along with alcohol can result in death.

"Shock treatment," as *electroconvulsive therapy* is commonly called, has proved extremely effective in the treatment of depression, though no one understands exactly how it works (Kalinowsky, 1975). It involves administering, over several weeks, a series of brief electrical shocks of approximately 70 to 130 volts. The shock induces a convulsion similar to an epileptic seizure. As it is now applied, electroconvulsive therapy entails very little discomfort for the patient. Prior to treatment, the patient is given a sedative and injected with a muscle relaxant to alleviate involuntary muscular contractions and prevent physical injury. Even with these improvements, however, electroconvulsive therapy is a drastic treatment and must be used with great caution. It is now used far less frequently than it was in the past.

MENTAL INSTITUTIONS

When the demands of everyday life cannot be met, the mentally disturbed person may face the prospect of institutionalization. There are institutions to handle many different social problems: prisons for criminals, hospitals for the physically ill, and mental institutions for people who are considered unable to function in normal society.

Commitment

The process of placing a person in a mental hospital is called *commitment*. It is estimated that two out of five mental patients are committed against their will. Involuntary commitment is a controversial legal and ethical issue. It has been argued that a committed mental patient has fewer rights than a convicted criminal.

Whether a person ends up in a mental hospital depends on a number of factors beyond his or her mental state. People with family and friends who are willing to care for them are less likely to be institutionalized. Money is also a factor. With budget cutbacks leading to more limited public facilities, it is now getting harder for a person to stay in a mental hospital for any length of time.

Conditions

The quality and cost of care in mental institutions vary greatly. There are more than 4,000 mental health facilities in the United States. About half of them offer inpatient care. Among these, private institutions offer more concentrated care and a better environment, but many of them are very expensive. The majority of people go to state mental hospitals or cheaper private institutions. The quality of treatment in these hospitals varies tremendously. It is possible, in fact, for a patient's condition to worsen or remain unchanged because the patient comes to depend on the hospital environment and loses social and vocational skills. When patients fail to improve, they remain institutionalized year after year. This situation exists because most public hospitals lack funds for adequate nursing staffs, equipment, and trained therapists. In many cases, the patients' day-to-day care is left to attendants who do little more than clean and feed the patients and keep order.

Ideally, a mental hospital should be a place where the patient is temporarily freed from social pressures he or she cannot bear. Limited and carefully planned demands should be made by a staff capable of under-

PSYCHOLOGY and YOU

The Mentally Ill Homeless: The Legacy of Deinstitutionalization. Homelessness is an increasing problem in the United States, and it is likely that you come into contact with the homeless at least occasionally. When you do, chances are good that you may be observing a person with a psychiatric disorder.

Recent surveys indicate that 30 to 40 percent of the homeless are mentally ill. This seems to be a direct result of deinstitutionalization.

Since the introduction of psychoactive drugs in the 1950s, the number of patients confined to mental institutions has steadily dropped. Unfortunately, most psychoactive drugs do not cure disorders. Rather, they merely control the more obvious symptoms of mental illness so that patients are no longer dangerous. Thus, there is no longer any reason to keep these people institutionalized.

A majority of mental inmates have been released from institutions, but they often find it impossible to hold steady jobs or to live on their own. In this way, the noble goal of deinstitutionalization has contributed to the problem of homelessness and has affected all our lives.

Figure 16.10
The traditional custodial mental hospital setting: a bare room, barred windows, a hospital gown. Such a setting contributes to the person's isolation and feeling of separation from the everyday world and can actually decrease the chances of recovery.

A mental hospital should be a place where a person is temporarily freed from social pressures he or she cannot bear.

standing and concern for the individual. Unfortunately, the reality of many state hospitals does not fit this ideal. Patients can become molded into a pattern of obedience, dependence, and conformity by a deadening routine of sleep, meals, Ping-Pong, and other ways of filling time (see Goffman, 1961).

As the patients become increasingly apathetic and resigned, they lose all ties with the outside world. In order to survive the boredom of each day, they rely on fantasy, dreams, and sleep, and they stop thinking about returning to outside life. Nevertheless, many patients welcome this routine—they prefer to be taken care of and to avoid the responsibilities of the outside world.

Individual and group psychotherapy are provided in mental hospitals, but this type of therapy is slow and expensive, and it does not work well with hospital patients, who are often beyond caring whether they improve or not. Partly as a result, mental hospitals tend to stress the organic treatments described above.

There are certain dangers inherent in the use of psychiatric drugs. They are often administered to make up for the lack of staff at mental hospitals. In many institutions it is common policy to administer a tranquilizer to every patient early in the morning, so that throughout the day there is very little activity among patients, thus reducing the workload required of an already overworked staff.

Most psychiatric drugs, when given in high doses over long periods, have undesirable side effects, such as extreme lethargy or peculiar losses of coordination. For such reasons, it is not uncommon for mental patients to flush some of their drugs down the toilet.

Figure 16.11
In a hospital where the goal is to restore the person to normal functioning, every effort is made to duplicate real settings and real situations and to involve the person in his or her treatment. This patient is meeting with her doctor to discuss her treatment and evaluate how she is doing and what should happen next.

COMMUNITY MENTAL HEALTH

Since the nineteenth century, extremely deviant behavior has been viewed as an illness to be treated by medical personnel in a hospital setting. Large mental hospitals were built in rural areas, where space could be obtained cheaply and patients could be concealed from the public, who thought them unsightly and dangerous. But the social isolation of patients, their removal from familiar surroundings and family life, often made later readjustment to society even more difficult. Released patients found themselves too far from the hospital for any supplementary care and too fragile to cope independently with the pressures of the outside world. Eventually it became apparent that if these patients were to make a successful return to the community, the community was going to have to provide some support.

Community Mental Health Centers

The Community Mental Health Centers Act of 1963 was designed to solve some of the problems faced by patients trying to reenter society. One mental health center was required for every 50,000 members of the U.S. population, to supply needed psychological services for the ex-patient attempting to function within the community. These centers were also supposed to educate community workers such as police, teachers, and clergy in the principles of preventive mental health, to train paraprofessionals, and to carry out research. A countrywide system of mental health centers

Figure 16.12
Halfway houses and community centers are part of a new movement to return as many people as possible to the community. This group of ex-hospital patients meets to discuss problems and help one another make the adjustment from inmate to functioning member of a community.

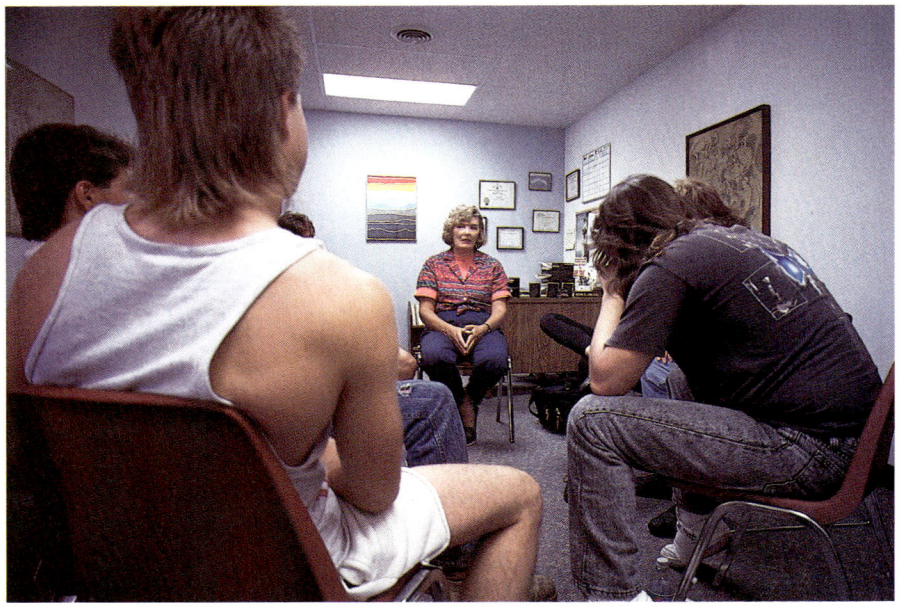

has not yet been achieved, and funding for existing centers has been cut back in many cities; but those centers that are in operation supply important services.

Outpatients can walk into a clinic and receive therapy once, twice, or several times a week, without leaving school, job, or family, and without feeling stigmatized as institutionalized mental patients. The centers also serve as a bridge between hospitalization and complete independence by giving care to patients after they are released from hospitals.

For the more severely disturbed, hospitalization can be provided within the community. Friends and family have easy access to patients, who feel less isolated and more accepted. Many centers have arrangements for day hospitals, in which patients take advantage of the hospital during the day and go home at night. Night hospitals work in a similar manner: patients may work or go to school during the day and spend the night at the hospital.

Many community mental health centers also maintain storefront clinics that are open around the clock to deal with such emergencies as acute anxiety attacks, suicide attempts, and bad drug trips. The centers may have teams of psychologically trained personnel on call to go to city hospital emergency rooms to deal with psychological traumas.

Mental health centers provide qualified personnel to serve as consultants to other community workers, such as teachers, police, and clergy, advising them on how to handle psychological problems in the classroom and within the community. Sensitivity workshops give instruction on such matters as how to intervene in potentially violent family quarrels, how to talk potential suicides out of jumping off a bridge, and how to keep truants from dropping out of school.

Halfway Houses. There are thousands of people who spend time in mental hospitals, prisons, and homes for delinquents and who, when finally released, are psychologically unprepared to return to life in society. They may be able to behave well under structured conditions, but they find the freedom and immensity of society confusing and overwhelming. Such people can ease back into society through halfway houses.

Halfway houses give their inhabitants the support they need in order to build enough confidence to reenter society. Unwritten rules and informal social pressures guide the members in their efforts to readjust to the larger world (Raush and Raush, 1968).

USING PSYCHOLOGY

Crisis Intervention Programs

A fairly new approach to mental health is the development of community-based crisis intervention programs, which help individuals and families deal with emergencies or highly stressful situations. Typically, during a period of emotional turmoil, people feel overwhelmed and cannot deal with their everyday affairs. The crises may be the death of a loved one, the loss of a job, a rape or mugging, a family breakup, or an attempted suicide. The intervention is generally short-term, lasting for no more than five or six sessions. It is like psychological first aid.

Crisis intervention counselors use four approaches. First, they provide general support by listening to the person's concerns and by providing encouragement and hope that the crisis will pass. Second, counselors help people assess their situation realistically; identify what they can do to help themselves; and look directly into their emotions, thoughts, and behavior to gain a clearer assessment of the problem. Third, counselors help individuals work out adaptive ways of coping with present and future crises. Fourth, counselors help people make some permanent changes in their lives. They may, for example, help people change jobs, move to a safer neighborhood, or establish stable friendships and support groups.

Crisis intervention may take the form of a telephone hot line. People who are in trouble can telephone at any time and receive immediate counseling, sympathy, and comfort. The best known of these systems is the Los Angeles Suicide Prevention Center, which was established in 1958. Similar hot lines have been set up for alcoholics, rape victims, battered women, runaway children, gamblers, sexually abused people, and lonely people who just need a shoulder to cry on or someone to listen to them. In addition to providing sympathy, hot line volunteers give information on community services that can help callers with their problems.

One type of hot line that has become available in recent years responds to issues and problems concerning AIDS (*Ac*quired *I*mmune *D*eficiency *S*yndrome). The National AIDS Hot Line is affiliated with the Centers for Disease Control in Atlanta. Its phones are answered twenty-four hours a day by information specialists who are trained to answer callers' questions and to use crisis intervention techniques. There are also many state AIDS hot lines. Some are staffed by medical personnel including physicians, nurses, and pharmacists. The reason for this is that some of the people who call in ask about symptoms they are experiencing. Counselors need to be able to answer effectively.

AIDS hot lines are not only for people who suspect they have AIDS. Since AIDS is an infectious and terminal disease, many people are confused and frightened about its spread. Hot lines encourage such people to call and ask questions about the disease. Can I get infected just by sitting next to someone with AIDS? If I do not know anyone with AIDS, should I still be concerned about the disease? These and other questions are answered by information specialists at the hot lines. The hot lines also provide referrals to treatment and assessment centers, counseling facilities, and support groups. People who call are not asked for their names. All callers remain anonymous. The National AIDS Hot Line number is 1-800-342-AIDS.

Figure 16. 13
Crisis intervention counselors are trained to deal with people who are going through critical periods in their lives. This counselor works in a shelter for battered women.

Hot lines are usually staffed by volunteers. After dealing with the immediate emotional turmoil over the telephone, the volunteer urges the caller to go to a community facility and meet with a crisis intervention counselor who can provide more assistance. If necessary, long-term help (more than five or six sessions) is set up so the person can develop more effective ways of coping.

Many of the people who staff the crisis intervention hot lines or community centers are not mental health specialists but have been trained to provide help to people who are going through crises. Even trained counselors and therapists require specialized skills to deal with their clients' emotional turmoil during an emergency.

Crisis intervention workers are taught to listen to and understand what people are saying, even when the situation may be highly emotional or chaotic. The skilled attention of a concerned listener sometimes helps a person in crisis become aware of feelings that contribute to his or her sense of panic.

In order to be effective in their helping role, crisis workers must learn how to deal with their own emotional reactions to common crisis situations through role-playing and other methods. By practicing their reactions beforehand, the trainees become more relaxed and less anxious in real-life crises. In addition, role playing allows the workers to become aware of their own feelings and biases.

The Rise of the Paraprofessional

Professionals who traditionally treat mental disorders have always been in short supply. Moreover, they tend to be white and middle class, which may inhibit free communication with nonwhite or poorly educated patients. To overcome both problems, increasing numbers of mental health workers called paraprofessionals are being trained. In a classic study, Margaret Rioch (1967) showed that homemakers with no previous psychological training but with well-balanced and sympathetic natures made excellent mental health counselors after two years of intensive training. In recent years, paraprofessionals have been providing a wide variety of mental health services, including interviewing, testing, and counseling. When they are carefully screened and trained and because they often are close in ethnic background to their clients, they have been effective.

Community mental health centers are now in a time of change. They were created when government spent freely to solve social problems. But many communities resisted the movement: people were frightened by the idea of living next door to mental patients. Community resistance, budgetary cutbacks, and controversy over the effectiveness of certain programs are all forces that will shape the future of community psychology.

CHAPTER REVIEW

KEY TERMS

- behavior therapy
- client-centered therapy
- contingency management
- encounter groups
- family therapy
- free association
- gestalt therapy
- group therapy
- human potential movement
- placebo effect
- psychoanalysis
- psychotherapy
- rational-emotive therapy
- resistance
- systematic desensitization
- transactional analysis
- transference
- unconditional positive regard

SUMMARY

1. Psychotherapy is used to help people realize that they are responsible for their own lives and that they can solve the problems that have been making them unhappy.

2. The primary goal of all patient-therapist relationships is to strengthen the patient's control of his or her life. The therapist helps the patient find meaningful alternatives to the patient's present, unsatisfactory ways of behaving.

3. Psychoanalysis is a form of therapy, based on the theories of Sigmund Freud, aimed at making patients aware of the unconscious impulses, desires, and fears that are causing anxiety. Psychoanalysts believe that if patients can achieve *insight*—that is, understand their unconscious motives—they may be able to gain control over their behavior and thus free themselves of recurring problems.

4. The forms of therapy known collectively as the human potential movement stress the actualization of an individual's potential through personal responsibility, freedom of choice, and authentic relationships.

5. Rational-emotive therapy, developed by Albert Ellis, attempts to correct an individual's self-defeating beliefs. Ellis believes that emotional problems arise when a person's assumptions about life are unrealistic.

6. Behavior therapy focuses on changing specific behaviors through conditioning techniques.

7. In group therapy a group of people meet with a single therapist. Each group member gains experience with one of his or her biggest problems—interacting with other people.

8. Organic therapy for severely disturbed patients includes antipsychotic drugs, antidepressant drugs, antianxiety drugs, lithium, and electroconvulsive therapy.

9. The quality of care in mental hospitals varies widely. Some patients may remain unchanged or actually get worse in mental hospitals.

10. The community mental health movement began as an attempt to return mental patients to their communities.

REVIEW QUESTIONS

1. What is psychotherapy and what is its goal? What two goals should the client achieve during therapy?

2. List some professionals who see persons with behavioral problems. What characteristics of the therapist have been found to increase effectiveness? What client characteristics are associated with favorable outcomes in therapy?

3. What is the goal of psychoanalysis? What does the therapist do to achieve this goal?

4. What is the goal of humanistic psychotherapy? What similarities are there between this type of therapy and psychoanalysis?

5. What is the goal of rational-emotive therapy (RET)? What steps does RET expect clients to take to solve a problem?

6. How does behavior therapy differ from the previously discussed therapies in its approach to correcting an individual's problem? Describe the behavioral therapeutic techniques of systematic desensitization and contingency management.

7. Describe three types of group therapy.

8. Describe the results of studies that have attempted to evaluate the effectiveness of psychotherapy.

9. What are the effects of antipsychotic drugs, antidepressants, and antianxiety drugs? When is each used? What are the side effects and dangers of each?

10. What are community mental health centers and how do they operate? What is a halfway house?

ACTIVITIES

1. On a sheet of paper draw a large thermometer ranging from 0 to 100 degrees. Think of the most fearful thing you can imagine, and write it down at the 100-degree mark. Write down the least fearful thing you can think of at the 0-degree mark. Continue to list your fears on the thermometer according to their severity. Have several friends make similar lists of their fears. Compare lists, looking for differences and similarities. Do you think any of your fears are based on conditioning? Can you think of a method of reconditioning that would remove the fear or make it less intense?

2. Ask several people in different businesses whether they would hire someone they knew had undergone psychotherapy. Do their responses indicate to you that society has matured to where it now understands and accepts emotional problems in the same way it accepts medical problems? Do you believe a person should be barred from high public office because he or she has sought psychotherapy?

3. Recommend a treatment for the following problems: compulsive overeating, inability to finish work, severe depression. Think of real examples as much as possible. How do the techniques you suggest resemble the therapies described in this chapter?

4. Begin assertiveness training by trying the following exercise. Engage a friend in a casual conversation. During part of the conversation, raise or lower your voice. Experiment with the amount of eye contact you have during the conversation. Try staring at your friend, then not making any eye contact at all. Change the rate of your speaking from very fast to very slow. What kind of reactions in your friend do you notice with each change? What new insights about yourself did you gain by doing this exercise?

5. Transactional analysis distinguishes between three different ways of experiencing ourselves: parent, adult, and child ego states. Think back to a recent crisis or difficult time you experienced. Then imagine your parents in the same situation. What would your mother or father do in that same situation? This represents a possible parent ego state reaction. Imagine how you would have reacted to the situation as a six-year-old. Your response to this reflects your child ego state reactions. How do you feel about the situation now? Your answer will most likely reflect your adult ego state. Which ego state helps you deal with the crisis most effectively?

Human Relations

CHAPTER *17*
Human Interaction

CHAPTER *18*
Attitudes and Social Influence

Figure 17.1 Interaction with others is a way of satisfying the needs we all have for respect, love, and affection.

Objectives: *After studying this chapter, you should be able to*
• describe the basic human need for interaction with others.
• summarize the research on nonverbal communication.
• discuss research and theory in the area of how we perceive others.
• explain the nature of groups and how they are held together.
• describe the interactive patterns within groups.

Human Interaction

People vary considerably in their need for social contact and in their desire and ability to be alone. You have probably heard tales of hermits and recluses who voluntarily isolate themselves, but most people would not welcome a solitary life. What is so important about being around other people? Why do people choose to interact with certain people and not with others? And what do psychologists know about human interaction? This chapter will answer these questions and provide insights into group interactions.

NEEDING OTHER PEOPLE

From infancy we depend on others to satisfy our basic needs. Throughout childhood and adolescence, we learn to associate close personal contact with the satisfaction of basic needs. As we mature and become adults, we seek personal contact for the same reason, even though we can now care for ourselves.

Being around other human beings, interacting with others, has become a habit that would be difficult to break. Moreover, we have developed needs for praise, respect, love and affection, the sense of achievement, and other rewarding experiences. And these needs, acquired through social learning, can only be satisfied by other human beings (Bandura and Walters, 1963).

Anxiety and Companionship

Social psychologists are interested in discovering what circumstances intensify our desire for human contact. It seems that we need to have other people around us most when we are afraid or anxious, and we also need company when we are unsure of ourselves and want to compare our feelings with other people's.

Needing Other People
Anxiety and Companionship
• Comparing Experiences and Reducing Uncertainty

Choosing Friends
Proximity • Reward Values

Personal Relationships
Parent-Child Relationships
• Love Relationships
• Nonverbal Communication

How People Perceive One Another
Implicit Personality Theory
• Personality Versus
Circumstance: Attribution
Theory

What Are Groups?
Interdependence • Common
Goals

How Groups Are Held Together
Norms • Ideology
• Commitment

Interactions Within Groups
Communication Patterns
• Leadership • Diffusion of
Responsibility • Using
Psychology: The Peer Group

Group Conflict Versus Cooperation
Social Traps

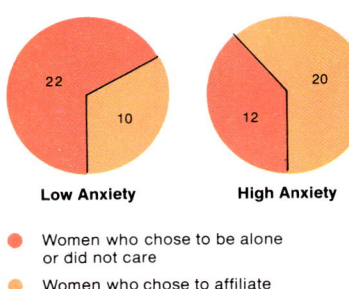

Low Anxiety   **High Anxiety**

● Women who chose to be alone
   or did not care
● Women who chose to affiliate

Figure 17.2
The results of Schachter's 1959 experiment about the effects of anxiety on affiliation.

Psychologist Stanley Schachter (1959) decided to test the old saying "Misery loves company." His experiment showed that people suffering from a high level of anxiety are more likely to seek out company than those who feel less anxious. He arranged for a number of college women to come to his laboratory. One group of women was greeted by a frightening-looking man in a white coat who identified himself as Dr. Gregor Zilstein of the medical school. Dr. Zilstein told each woman that she would be given electric shocks in order to study the effect of electricity on the body. He told the women, in an ominous tone, that the shocks would be extremely painful. With a devilish smile, he added that the shocks would cause no permanent skin damage. For obvious reasons, this group of women was referred to as the high-anxiety group.

The doctor was friendly to the other group of women, and told them that the shocks would produce only ticklish, tingling sensations, which they might even find pleasant. These women formed the low-anxiety group.

Zilstein told each subject that she would have to leave the laboratory while he set up the equipment. He then asked each woman to indicate on a questionnaire whether she wished to wait alone in a private room or with other subjects in a larger room. Most women in the low-anxiety group chose to wait alone. However, the overwhelming majority of high-anxiety women preferred to wait with others. Thus, the experiment demonstrated that high anxiety produces a need for companionship (Figure 17.2).

Comparing Experiences and Reducing Uncertainty

People also like to get together with one another to reduce their uncertainties about themselves. For example, when you get exams back, you probably ask your friends how they did. You try to understand your own situation by comparing it to other people's. You learn your strengths and weaknesses by asking: Can other people do it, too? Do they do it better or worse? Many individuals use the performance of others as a basis for self-evaluation. According to this theory, one of the reasons why the women in the shock experiment sought company was to find out how they should respond to Dr. Zilstein. Should they feel fear or anger, or should they take the whole thing in stride? One way to get this information was to talk to others.

Schachter conducted another experiment to test this idea. It was essentially the same as the Dr. Zilstein experiment, but this time *all* the women were made anxious. Half of them were then given the choice between waiting alone and waiting with other women about to take part in the same experiment. The other half were given the choice between waiting alone and passing the time in a room where students were waiting to see their academic advisers.

As you might expect, the women who had a chance to be with other women in the same predicament seized the opportunity. These women wanted to compare their dilemma with others. But most of the women in the second group chose to spend the time alone rather than with the unconcerned students. As the experimenter put it, "Misery doesn't love just any kind of company, it loves only miserable company."

Other researchers have shown that the more uncertain a person is, the more likely he or she is to seek out other people. Like Schachter, Harold Gerard and J. M. Rabbie recruited volunteers for an experiment. When the volunteers arrived, some of them were escorted to a booth and attached to a machine that was supposed to measure emotionality. The machine was turned on, and the subjects were able to see not only their own ratings but the ratings of three other participants as well. In each case the dial for the subject registered 82 on a scale of 100; the dials for the other participants registered 79, 80, and 81. (As you've undoubtedly guessed, the machine was rigged.) A second group of subjects was attached to a similar machine and was shown their own ratings but not those of other participants. A third group was not given any information about themselves or other participants in the experiment. When asked whether they wanted to wait alone or with other subjects, most of the people in the first group chose to wait alone. They had seen how they compared to others and felt they were reacting appropriately. However, most of the subjects in the other two groups, who had no basis for evaluating themselves, chose to wait with other people (Gerard and Rabbie, 1961).

Seeking company when you are frightened or uncertain about your feelings seems to work. People who choose to be in a group when they are afraid of an experimental procedure or lack information about how they compare to others are less anxious than those who "tough it out" and wait alone (Wrightsman, 1960).

CHOOSING FRIENDS

Most people feel they have a great deal of latitude in the friends they choose. Easy transportation, telephones, and the spare time available to most Americans would all seem to ease communication among them and, therefore, to permit them a wide range of individuals from whom to choose companions, friends, and lovers. But in fact, we rarely venture beyond the most convenient methods in making contact with others.

Proximity

Would it surprise you to learn that the most important factor in determining whether two people will become friends is **physical proximity**—the distance from one another that people live or work? In general, the closer two individuals are geographically to one another, the more likely they are to become attracted to each other. And it is more than just the opportunity for interaction that makes the difference.

Psychologists have found that even in a small two-story apartment building where each resident was in easy reach of everyone else, people were more likely to become close friends with the person next door than with anyone else (Figure 17.3). Psychologists believe that this is a result of the fears and embarrassments most people have about making contact with strangers. When two people live next door to one another, go to the same class, or work in the same place, they are able to get used to one

The single most important factor in choosing friends is physical proximity.

another and to find reasons to talk to one another without ever having to seriously risk rejection. To make friends with someone whom you do not see routinely is much more difficult. You have to make it clear that you are interested and thus run the risk of making a fool of yourself—either because the other person turns out to be less interesting than he or she seemed at a distance or because that person expresses no interest in you. Of course, it may turn out that both of you are very glad someone spoke up.

Reward Values

Proximity helps people make friends, but it does not ensure lasting friendship. Sometimes people who are forced together in a situation take a dislike to one another that develops into hatred. Furthermore, once people have made friends, physical separation does not necessarily bring an end to their relationship. What are the factors that determine whether people will like each other once they come into contact?

One reward of friendship is stimulation. A friend has **stimulation value** if she is interesting or imaginative or if she can introduce you to new ideas or experiences. A friend who is cooperative and helpful, who seems willing to give his time and resources to help you achieve your goals, has **utility value.** A third type of value in friendship is **ego-support value:** sympathy and encouragement when things go badly, appreciation and approval when things go well. These three kinds of rewards—stimulation, utility, and ego support—are evaluated consciously or unconsciously in every friendship. A man may like another man because the second man is a witty conversationalist (stimulation value) and knows a lot about gardening (utility value). A woman may like a man because he values her opinions (ego-support value) and because she has an exciting time with him (stimulation value).

Who Is Shy?

If you would rather disappear into the wallpaper than go to the class dance, you're shy. If you prefer to spend evenings at home instead of risking the possibility of meeting new people, you're shy too. But contrary to what you probably think, you are not alone. More than 80 percent of people questioned in one survey on shyness said they had been shy at some time in their lives. Out of this number, 40 percent said they felt shy now.

This does not mean that everyone is equally shy: There are degrees of shyness ranging from slight discomfort in some situations to sheer panic in all situations. Only 25 percent of the sample approached the far end of the scale, considering themselves to be chronically shy. An even smaller group—4 percent—said they were shy all the time in all situations.

If you are shy, it may give you some comfort to know that shyness is not a purely American trait. It is found to differing degrees in cultures throughout the world. In fact, right at this moment, 60 percent of Orientals would say they were shy too.

For more details, see Philip G. Zimbardo, *Shyness*. Reading, Mass.: Addison-Wesley, 1977.

By considering the three kinds of rewards that a person may look for in friendship, it is possible to understand other factors that affect liking and loving.

Physical Appearance. A person's physical appearance greatly influences others' impressions of him or her. People feel better about themselves when they associate with people others consider desirable. This is true of same-sex as well as opposite-sex relationships. Physical attractiveness influences our choice of friends as well as lovers.

In one study (Dion, Berscheid, and Walster, 1972), subjects were shown pictures of men and women of varying degrees of physical attractiveness and were asked to rate their personality traits. The physically attractive people were consistently viewed more positively than the less attractive ones. They were seen as more sensitive, kind, interesting, strong, poised, modest, and sociable, as well as more sexually responsive. It seems, therefore, that although we have all heard that "beauty is only skin deep," we act as if it permeates one's entire personality.

Homely people are generally viewed in an unfavorable light. Research has shown that obese adults, who in our culture are considered unattractive, are often discriminated against when they apply for jobs. Even homely children are targets of prejudice (Figure 17.4). An unattractive child is far more likely to be judged "bad" or "cruel" for a particular act of misbehavior than is a more attractive peer (Dion, Berscheid, and Walster, 1972).

Interestingly, psychologists have found that both men and women pay

How to Relate to People

If you're like most people, you want others to like you, but knowing exactly how to make them like you is not always that easy. Most psychologists believe that the principle of *reciprocal reinforcement* has a lot to do with how you get along with others. In simple terms, this principle states that people will like you if your behavior makes them feel good about themselves.

Here are some reinforcement techniques you can use to get a head start on winning and keeping friends:

- When you're talking to another person, try to spend at least 50 percent of the time listening to what the other person says. That may mean cutting down on your chatter, but the results will be well worthwhile.
- Be an active rather than a passive listener. By commenting directly on what the other person says, you will show that you are really interested in his conversation.
- Instead of focusing on your own accomplishments, ask questions about the person you are with. This tells him in no uncertain terms that you care about what he has done. The best time to talk about yourself is when the other person asks.
- Approval is one of the best reinforcers if it is used correctly, but another person is easily turned off if it is not sincere. Be sure to praise only those things the other person considers important and don't use an overlavish or repetitive approach.

For more details, see Robert L. Williams and James D. Long, *Toward a Self-managed Life Style,* 2nd ed. Boston: Houghton Mifflin, 1979.

much less attention to physical appearance when choosing a marriage partner or a close friend than when inviting someone to go to a movie or a party. But neither men nor women necessarily seek out the most attractive member of their social world. Rather, people usually seek out others whom they consider their equals on the scale of physical attractiveness (Levinger and Snoek, 1972).

Approval.   Another factor that affects a person's choice of friends is approval. All of us tend to like people who say nice things about us because they make us feel better about ourselves—they provide ego-support value.

The results of one experiment suggest that other people's evaluations of oneself are more meaningful when they are a mixture of praise and criticism than when they are extreme in either direction. No one believes that he or she is all good or all bad. As a result, one can take more seriously a person who sees some good points and some bad points. But when the good points come first, hearing the bad can make one disappointed and angry at the person who made them. When the bad points come first, the effect is opposite. One thinks, "This person is perceptive and honest. At

Figure 17.4
In cne experiment, adult women were shown reports about and photographs of children participating in a variety of antisocial behaviors. The adults tended not only to see the behaviors committed by the unattractive children as more generally antisocial, but to attribute a more inherently negative moral character to these children than to the attractive ones. (Adapted from Dion, 1972)

first she was critical but later she saw what I was really like" (Aronson and Linder, 1965).

Similarity.   People tend to choose friends whose backgrounds, attitudes, and interests are similar to their own. Nearly always, husbands and wives have similar economic, religious, and educational backgrounds.

There are several explanations for the power of shared attitudes. First, agreement about what is stimulating, worthwhile, or fun provides the basis for sharing activities. People who have similar interests are likely to do more things together and to get to know one another better.

Figure 17.5
These two men obviously enjoy each other's company. In addition to having stimulation value for each other, they probably provide considerable utility value: they may be able to give each other advice about business problems and opportunities.

Second, most of us feel uneasy around people who are constantly challenging our views, and we translate our uneasiness into hostility or avoidance. We are more comfortable around people who support us. A friend's agreement bolsters your confidence and contributes to your self-esteem. In addition, most of us are self-centered enough to assume that people who share our values are basically decent and intelligent (unlike others we know).

Finally, people who agree about things usually find it easier to communicate with each other. They have fewer arguments and misunderstandings; they are better able to predict one another's behavior and thus feel at ease with each other.

Complementarity—an attraction between opposite types of people—is not unusual, however. For example, a dominant person might look for a submissive mate. Still, most psychologists agree that similarity is a much more important factor. Although the old idea that opposites attract seems reasonable, researchers have not been able to verify it (Berscheid and Walster, 1978: 78–81).

PERSONAL RELATIONSHIPS

Your personal relationships with others bring meaning and substance to your everyday experiences. Knowing that you have loved ones who care about you and are willing recipients of your affection contributes to the quality of your life and your overall sense of well-being. Throughout life, you establish different kinds of personal relationships. Your first meaningful relationships were established within the family.

Parent-Child Relationships

Noted psychologist Erik Erikson, among others, believed that early and persistent patterns of parent-child interaction can influence people's later adult expectations about their relationships with the significant people in their lives. If a young infant's first relationship with a caregiver is loving, responsive, and consistent, the child will develop a trust in the ability of other people to meet his or her needs. This trusting, in turn, will encourage the person to be receptive to people. On the other hand, a child who has experienced unresponsive, inconsistent, or unaffectionate care in infancy will most likely be more wary or mistrustful of other people. Within the parent-child relationship, we learn how to manipulate others to have our needs met. A parent is likely to satisfy the wishes of a child who acts "good," that is, who does what the parent asks. The child may also learn to get attention by pouting or having temper tantrums.

As children develop and form relationships with people outside their family, they apply what they have learned about relationships. As a result of childhood experiences, an individual might, for example, believe that the only way to establish and maintain good relationships with friends is always to say what pleases them rather than speak the truth.

Your parents influence the quality of your adult relationships in other ways. They provide you with your first model of a marital relationship. As you watched your mother and father interacting with each other as husband and wife, you were most likely forming some tentative conclusions about the nature of relationships. Later on, you might use their example as a guide in selecting a future mate or in evaluating your relationships. If your parents have a happy marriage, you will most likely seek to duplicate it by imitating their patterns. If you believe their lives are unhappy or unfulfilled as a result of the nature of their relationship, you may try to create a very different type of relationship with a mate.

Love Relationships

While most people say that they love their parents, their friends, and maybe even their brothers and sisters, they attach a different meaning to *love* when referring to a boyfriend, girlfriend, or spouse. Love means different things to different people and within different relationships.

Psychologist Zick Rubin (1973) has distinguished between *like* and *love*. According to Rubin, liking usually involves respect or high regard for another person. Love usually involves liking plus three other elements: great attachment to and dependency on the person; a caring for or desire to help the person; and the desire for an exclusive, intimate relationship with the person. Other researchers (Berscheid, 1983; Davis, 1985; and Hatfield and Walster, 1981) have distinguished between two types of love. *Passionate love* is an intensely emotional and sexual fascination with a mate and a strong desire for exclusiveness. Feelings of excitement, anxiety, tenderness, and jealousy are all common in passionate love. Passionate love is what is commonly referred to as "romantic love" in which lovers long for their partners and seek to capture their affection. In contrast to the relatively short-lived passionate love is *companionate love*, which is defined as the affection we feel for those with whom our lives are deeply intertwined. People who share a mutual concern and care for each other and who have strong, frequent, and long-term interactions are likely to experience companionate love. Friendship, understanding, and the willingness to make sacrifices for each other are characteristic of companionate love.

Falling in Love. The differences between passionate and companionate love can be further examined by reviewing the development of each type of love. Psychologists Ellen Berscheid and Elaine Walster (1974) maintain that three criteria must be met for passionate love to occur. First, there must be a culturally held expectation that one will fall in love or be smitten by passionate desire for a person. People who believe in "love at first sight" or "falling head over heels in love" are likely to experience it. Second, there must be an appropriate "love object," someone who is "right."

The third criterion is the presence of an emotional arousal, which the person interprets as love. This emotional arousal can be experienced in a number of different ways, ranging from sexual arousal to anxiety or anger. In fact, the source of a person's emotional arousal or love feelings

Figure 17.6
What makes people fall in love? Is there such a thing as love at first sight? Does romantic love endure? Romance has inspired poets, painters, and playwrights through the ages. Psychologists are also interested in learning more about what causes people to fall in and out of love.

PSYCHOLOGY and YOU

Love and Separation. Suppose you were involved in a serious romance and your partner had to move away. What would happen to your relationship?

Psychologists have studied couples who endure many different types of separation: college students who separate during vacations, college students who attend different schools, traveling executives and their spouses, military couples separated by active tours of duty, and prisoners of war and their families. Two findings consistently emerge from these studies: (1) all separations are stressful; and (2) strong relationships generally endure separations, whereas weak relationships generally do not. In fact, some college students report that they use separations (during the summer break or a semester abroad) specifically to test the strength of their relationships. On the other hand, people dissatisfied with their relationships often seek separations by accepting jobs requiring frequent travel or requesting transfers to new locations.

Will your relationship survive a separation? The answer depends more on the strength of your relationship than on the separation itself.

may not even be the loved one, but another source. Suppose, for example, you have a frightening or unsettling experience. To calm yourself down, you think about your boyfriend or girlfriend. According to Berscheid and Walster's theory, the emotional arousal you have experienced from the fright will channel itself into what feels like romantic love. Similarly, if you are going on a date and are anxious or excited about going to a new place, you may interpret the emotional arousal you feel as love for your date.

The onset of romantic or passionate love is fairly swift and sudden. It is quite fragile compared with companionate love. Passionate love, marked by strong, emotional upswings, rarely lasts long. Some passionate love relationships turn into longer lasting companionate love relationships.

The development of companionate love is less dramatic than that of passionate love. It begins as a mutual attraction between two people and changes as they build their relationship together. The development of a more intimate relationship may be stable and uneventful, stable but increasingly satisfying, or unstable and conflict-ridden. There are many variations in relationship patterns. Relationships that seem unstable often find stability, and seemingly unchanging relationships sometimes deteriorate into separation.

The development of a close companionate relationship is influenced by the degree to which each person is willing to reveal personal and private information about himself or herself. Couples who are willing to trust each other and who communicate their feelings and ideas freely are likely to have a close relationship that endures. Ordinarily, the more personal information a person discloses to a companion, the more personal information the companion is likely to disclose in return. This mutual disclosure serves to deepen the relationship.

Nonverbal Communication

Central to the development and maintenance of a relationship is the willingness to communicate aspects of yourself to others. Communication involves at least two people: a person who sends a message and a person who receives it. The message sent consists of an idea and some emotional component. Messages are sent verbally and nonverbally. "I like to watch you dance" is a verbal message; a warm smile is an example of **nonverbal communication.**

Although most people are aware of what they are saying verbally, they are often unaware of their nonverbal messages. They are more aware of the nonverbal messages when they are on the receiving end of them. You have probably heard someone say, "It doesn't matter," speaking in a low voice and looking away; the unspoken message is "My feelings are hurt." You do not need to be told in so many words that a friend is elated or depressed, angry or pleased, nervous, or content. You sense these things. People communicate nonverbally not only through facial expressions but also through their use of space and body language (posture and gestures).

Personal Space. Anthropologist Edward T. Hall became acutely aware of the importance people attach to space when he found himself backing away from a colleague he particularly liked and respected. The associate was not an American, which led Hall to wonder whether people from different cultures had different ideas about the proper distance at which to hold an informal conversation. He decided to pursue the question.

After much observation, Hall concluded that Americans carry a two-foot "bubble" of privacy around them. If another person invades this bubble, we feel slightly threatened, imposed upon, and generally uncomfortable. For Germans, the bubble of privacy is much larger; for Arabs, much smaller (Hall, 1959). Thus, an Arab man talking to a German man, for example, may try to establish his accustomed talking distance and move closer. The German may conclude that the Arab is "pushy." When the German moves back to what he feels is a normal distance, the Arab may take this as a sign of coldness and conclude that the man is aloof.

Hall observed Americans to see how we use space to communicate our feelings about other people and to define relationships. He found that Americans usually allow only intimates (husbands and wives, other family members, and close friends) to come closer than two feet, a point at which touching is almost inevitable. When we are forced to stand very close to non-intimates, as in a crowded elevator, we try to hold our bodies immobile and avoid eye contact.

When we maintain a distance of four feet or so, we are essentially putting the other person "at arm's length." People who work together generally observe this boundary. When we want to hold people off, consciously or unconsciously, we create a four- to seven-foot bubble between us and them. Sometimes, we use social distance to show status. An executive of a large corporation may put visitors' chairs nine feet from his or her desk to create the impression of status, but many executives are aware of this form of communication and will try to counter the impression by placing the chairs closer than four feet.

If you go to an uncrowded beach, you will probably settle down between twelve and twenty-five feet from other people (Figure 17.7). If you arrange a room for a speaker, you will probably leave this same twelve- to twenty-five feet of space between the podium and the first row of seats. Hall calls this "public distance" and suggests it provides a sense of safety. At twelve feet, an alert person can take defensive action if threatened. At the same time, twelve feet or more does not invite personal communication. To talk, two people would have to move closer (Hall, 1966). The ways in which people use space to communicate will become clear if you keep this scheme in mind. If you put your beach towel five feet from another person's when there is plenty of empty space, you're issuing an invitation. If you step back when someone at a party comes within two feet, you're discouraging further intimacy even though you may not be aware of the nonverbal message you're sending.

Body Language.   The way you carry your body also communicates information about you. This is your **body language.** If you stand tall and erect, you convey the impression of self-assurance. If you sit and talk with your arms folded and legs crossed, you communicate that you are protecting yourself. When you unfold your arms and stretch out, you may be saying that you are open to people.

Figure 17.7
"Public distance" at the beach. People place themselves between 12 and 25 feet apart, a signal that no direct personal communication is desired.

Figure 17.8
Body language: The postures we adopt and the gestures we make convey messages. Like all other kinds of behavior, how we use our bodies is governed by social rules.

One group of researchers found that women who adopt an open body position are better liked and are listened to more closely than women who assume a closed position. A number of students were given a questionnaire that measured their opinions on everything from the legalization of marijuana to the custom of tipping. A few weeks later, they were invited back and asked to evaluate a certain other student's responses to the same questions. Some subjects were shown a slide of this female student sitting in a closed position; others saw a slide of her sitting in a neutral or open position. A high percentage of those who saw the open-looking picture indicated that they liked her and changed many of their opinions to agree with hers when they filled out the questionnaire a second time. On the other hand, the group that saw the closed-looking picture tended to stick with their original responses (McGinley, LeFevre, and McGinley, 1975).

Although the use of body language is often unconscious, many of the postures we adopt and gestures we make are governed by **social rules** (Figure 17.8). These rules are very subtle. For example, your teacher or boss is much more likely to touch you than you are to touch him or her. Touching is considered a privilege of higher status.

There are cultural differences in body language, just as there are in the use of space. For example, Americans move their heads up and down to show agreement and shake them back and forth to show disagreement. The Semang of Malaya thrust their heads sharply forward to agree and lower their eyes to disagree, while the Dayak of Borneo agree by raising their eyebrows and disagree by bringing them together.

You do not have to go to Borneo to observe cultural variations in nonverbal communication. In a field study conducted in hospitals, airports, and fast-food restaurants, LaFrance and Mayo (1976) found that American blacks and whites use eye contact in very different ways. Although people of both races looked at each other for the same proportion of time during a conversation, the timing was different. Blacks tend to look at their partner when they are speaking, and to look away while listening; whites do just the opposite. These unconscious differences may sometimes make blacks and whites uncomfortable when they talk to each other.

HOW PEOPLE PERCEIVE ONE ANOTHER

It takes people very little time to make judgments about one another. From one brief conversation, or even by watching a person across a room, you may form an impression of what someone is like. And first impressions influence the future of a relationship. If a person *seems* interesting, he or she becomes a candidate for future interaction. A person who seems to have nothing interesting to say—or much too much to say—does not. We tend to be sympathetic toward someone who seems shy; to expect a lot from someone who impresses us as intelligent; to be wary of a person who strikes us as aggressive.

Forming an impression of a person is not a passive process in which certain characteristics of the individual are the input and a certain impression is the automatic outcome. If impressions varied only when input varied, then everyone meeting a particular stranger would form the same impression of him or her. This, of course, is not what happens. One individual may judge a newcomer to be "quiet," another may judge the same

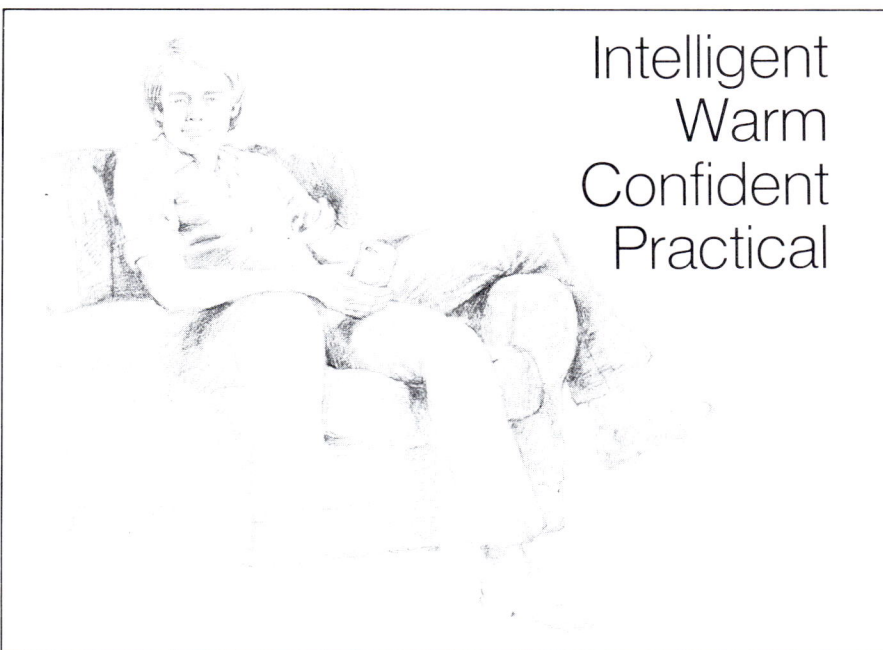

Figure 17.9
What is your impression of this person? Do you think you would like him? What do you think of the way he is dressed? What sort of expression does he have on his face? When you have formed an impression, turn to the drawing in Figure 17.10 and do the same.

person to be "dull," and still another person may think the person "mysterious." These various impressions lead to different expectations of the newcomer and to different patterns of interaction with him or her.

Implicit Personality Theory

One reason different people tend to develop different impressions of the same stranger is that we each have our own **implicit personality theory**—our own set of assumptions about how people behave and what traits or characteristics go together. When you meet someone who seems unusually intelligent, you may assume she is also active, highly motivated, conscientious, and so on. Another person in the group may have an altogether different "theory" about highly intelligent people—that they are unrealistic, boastful, insensitive, and the like. Whatever the person does provides "evidence" for both theories. You are impressed by how animated she becomes when talking about her work; the other person is impressed by how little attention she pays to other people. Both of you are filling in gaps in what you know about the person, fitting her into a type you carry around in your head.

Experiments indicate that our impressions are strongly influenced by a few traits (Figures 17.9, 17.10). For example, one researcher invited a guest lecturer to a psychology class. Beforehand all the students were given a brief description of the visitor. The descriptions were identical in all traits but one. Half the students were told that the speaker was cold, the other half that he was warm. After the lecture the researcher asked all the students to evaluate the lecturer. Reading their impressions, you would hardly

Intelligent
Cold
Confident
Practical

Figure 17.10
If your impressions of this person are different from your impressions of the person in Figure 17.9, the difference must be due to the change in a single word—the illustrations are otherwise identical.

know that the two groups of students were describing the same person. The students who had been told he was cold saw a humorless, ruthless, self-centered person. The other students saw a relaxed, friendly, concerned person. Changing one word—substituting "warm" for "cold"—had a dramatic impact on the audience's perception of the lecturer. It also affected their behavior. Students in the "warm group" were warm themselves, initiating more conversations with the speaker than did the students in the other group (Kelley, 1950).

Stereotypes. The line between applying implicit personality theories to people (as the students did) and thinking in stereotypes is a very thin one. A **stereotype** is a set of assumptions about people in a given category. The belief that Jews are clannish or that students who wear suits are not to be trusted are examples. Stereotypes are based on half-truths and nontruths, and tend to blind us to differences among people and to the way individuals actually behave.

Implicit personality theories are useful because they help us to predict with *some* degree of accuracy how people will behave. Without them, we would spend considerable energy observing and testing people to find out what they are like, whether we want to pursue a relationship with them, and so on. Like stereotypes, the assumptions we make about people from our first impressions tend to weaken as we get to know them better.

Personality Versus Circumstance: Attribution Theory

First impressions and the decision to pursue or abandon a relationship depend in large part on the situations in which we observe people. Suppose you walk into a library and find a man pacing back and forth. You sit down. He continues to pace for what seems like hours. The chances are you would want to avoid this man. He seems like an extremely unhappy and nervous person. But suppose the setting is the waiting room for a maternity ward. Your feelings about him would be entirely different (Rubin, 1973: 100–101).

The conclusions we draw about people thus vary according to whether we attribute their actions to personal qualities (such as general nervousness) or to the situation or role in which they find themselves (such as an expectant father). In recent years, many social psychologists have become interested in **attribution theory**—the attempt to understand how we interpret people's actions (Shaver, 1975). One key step involves deciding, as we did in the case of the pacing man, whether behavior is a result of personal qualities or external pressure (Figure 17.11).

Another important issue involves motive and intent: "What did he hope to accomplish by that?" If a new friend, for example, starts off your day by telling you that the sweater you just bought is hideous, you can interpret that as an attempt to be helpful or as an act of hostility. Your opinion of this person will depend on the motive you accept.

Of course, some actions are more revealing than others. Some behavior is so common that it reveals very little about personality. If a bank teller cashes your check without comment and gives you a half smile, you prob-

---

PSYCHOLOGY UPDATE

Stereotyping Bias in Psychiatric Diagnosis. Psychiatric professionals are trained to be objective observers of human behavior, but they are not immune to stereotyping their patients. Researchers have identified biases involving several groups, including the mentally retarded, the elderly, and people of low socioeconomic status (SES).

Mentally retarded people were consistently *underdiagnosed*; that is, they were not given a diagnosis when their symptoms indicated that a disorder in fact existed. Specifically, retarded patients frequently showed symptoms of depression, anxiety, and other disorders, but these problems were rarely diagnosed.

Frequently people of low SES and elderly patients were *overdiagnosed*, that is, given diagnoses that were not warranted by their behavior. In the absence of clear symptoms, some low-SES patients were falsely labeled as schizophrenic. Often physical and cognitive deterioration expected of elderly patients was labeled depression or dementia (disorganized thinking).

These findings have prompted psychiatric professionals to take a closer look at the symptoms of these patients and the conditions that may contribute to their problems.

Figure 17.11
Who attributes what to whom? In this first part of an experiment, actors A and B were talking while observers C and D watched B and A, respectively. Both actors later rated their own behavior in terms of personal characteristics about themselves or characteristics of the situation. Observers C and D similarly rated each of their target actors. The results showed that actors attributed their own behavior more to situational factors than to enduring personality factors. Observers, however, saw the actors' behavior more in terms of personality factors. (Adapted from Storms, 1973)

> **How we interpret another's behavior depends just as much on how we perceive it as on what it is.**

ably will not be able to tell much about her personality. But if she greets you with a warm hello (even though you've never laid eyes on this person in your life) and proceeds to get you in a long discussion of the weather, politics, and football, you might infer a great deal more about her personality. According to one theory (Jones and Davis, 1965), behavior that is unexpected or unusual and that can most plausibly be explained by only one motive provides the most important clues to a person's real nature.

In one study investigating attribution theory, a group of researchers asked subjects to watch three individuals take a test, and to evaluate their intelligence at various points during the test and after it was finished. *All* three individuals answered fifteen of thirty questions correctly. However, one started out well but then did poorly; the second did poorly at first but then improved; the third alternated between right and wrong answers, showing no pattern. Most subjects indicated that they thought the first individual was more intelligent than the others, although they all received the same score (Jones *et al.*, 1968). Why? Because once you have committed yourself to a judgment about a person (as subjects were required to do), changing your evaluation means admitting you made a mistake. Most of us find this somewhat hard to do. The subjects in this experiment clung to their original evaluation rather than admit a mistake.

The point is that we all actively perceive other people's actions. And what we conclude about other people depends not just on what they do, but also on our interpretations. This is true not just when we deal with individuals, but also when we react to groups.

WHAT ARE GROUPS?

What do the Rolling Stones, the St. Stanislaus Parish Bowling Team, the National Association for Retired Midgets, and Argentina have in common?

Each can be classified as a **group.** In general, the features that distinguish a group from a nongroup are interdependence and shared goals.

Interdependence

All the people in the world who have red hair and freckles make up a category of people, but they are not a group. The people in this collection are not interdependent. Interdependence occurs when any action by one of them will affect or influence the other members or when the same event will influence each one. For instance, in groups of athletes, entertainers, or roommates, each member has a certain responsibility to the rest of the group; if he or she does not fulfill his or her responsibility, the other members will be affected. For the athletes, the consequence may be losing the game; for the entertainers, a bad show; for the roommates, a messy apartment.

In small groups, members usually have a direct influence on one another: one person yells at another, smiles at him, or passes him a note. In larger groups, the influence may be indirect. The interdependence between you and the president of the United States is not a result of personal contact. Nevertheless, one of the things that make the people of the United States a group is the fact that the president's actions affect you and that your actions, together with those of many other Americans, affect him.

Common Goals

Group members become interdependent because they see themselves as sharing certain common goals. Groups are usually created to perform tasks

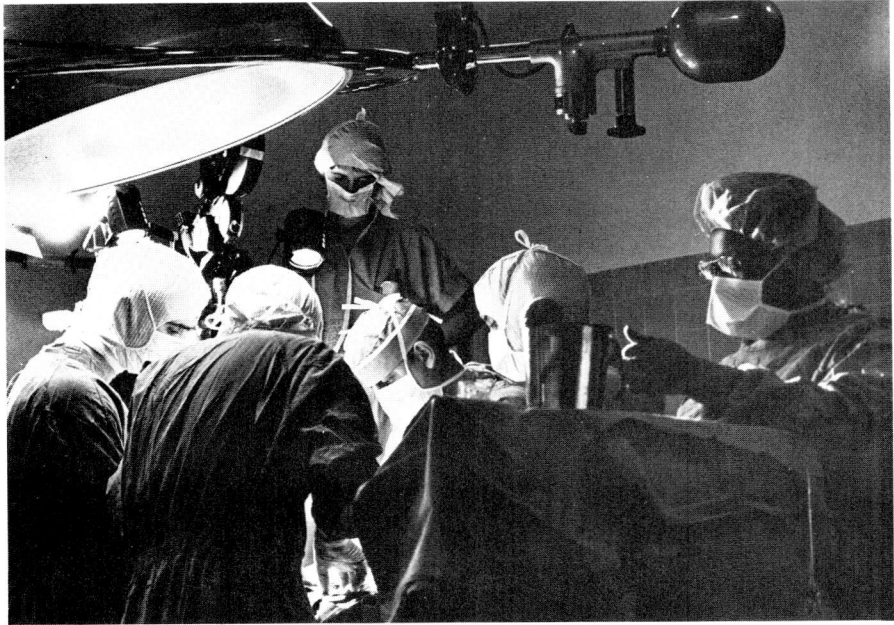

Figure 17.12
A task-oriented group. Whether or not the doctors and nurses in this surgical team are friendly outside the operating room does not matter; their main purpose as a group is to do a certain job.

or to organize activities that no individual could handle alone. Members of a consumer group, for example, share the common goal of working for consumer protection. Members of ethnic and religious groups desire to perpetuate a common heritage or set of beliefs.

The purposes groups serve are of two general kinds: **task functions,** those directed toward getting some job done; and **social functions,** those directed toward filling the emotional needs of members. In most groups, task and social functions are naturally combined and cannot easily be separated.

Political parties, teams of surgeons, and crews of construction workers are all task-oriented groups (Figure 17.12). Although social interactions occur within each of these groups, their main purpose is to complete a project or achieve some change in the environment. Social functions are emphasized in more informal, temporary groups. When people take walks together, attend parties, or participate in conversations, they have formed a group to gain such social rewards as companionship and emotional support. But again, every group involves both task and social functions, at least to some degree.

HOW GROUPS ARE HELD TOGETHER

The factors that work to hold groups together—that increase cohesiveness—include the attitudes and standards they share, and their commitment to them.

Norms

One way in which groups keep their members going in the same direction is by developing group norms. **Norms** are rules for the behavior and attitudes of group members. These rules are not necessarily rigid laws. They may be more like tendencies or habits. But group members are expected to act in accordance with group norms and are punished in some way if they do not. If a college student shaved her hair off, her friends would not hesitate to say something about it. And strangers might point and giggle—simply because she violated the norm that hair should be a certain length and style. Thus, the punishment may take the form of coldness or criticism from other group members. If the norm is very important to the group, a member who violates it may receive a more severe punishment or may be excluded from the group.

Ideology

For a group to be cohesive, members must share the same values. In some cases, people are drawn together because they discover they have common ideas, attitudes, and goals—that is, a common **ideology.** In other instances, people are attracted to a group because its ideology provides them with a new way of looking at themselves and interpreting events, and a new set of goals and means for achieving them. The civil rights movement of the sixties, for example, provided, among other things, an explanation of black oppression in America and the hope that something could be done to change things. Similarly, the gay rights movement of the eighties focused on the rights of homosexuals. Leaders, rallies, books and pamphlets, slogans, and symbols all help to popularize an ideology, win converts, and create feelings of solidarity among group members.

Commitment

Cohesiveness will be high if members are committed to their group. One factor that increases individual commitment is the requirement of personal sacrifice. If a person is willing to pay money, endure hardship, or undergo humiliation to belong to a group, he or she is likely to stick with it. For example, college students who undergo embarrassing initiation rites to join sororities or fraternities tend to develop a loyalty to the group that lasts well beyond their college years.

Another factor that strengthens group commitment is participation. When people actively participate in group decisions and share the rewards of the group's accomplishments, their feeling of membership increases—they feel that they have helped make the group what it is. For example, social psychologists have compared groups of workers who participate in decisions that affect their jobs with other workers who elect representatives to decision-making committees or workers who are simply told what to do. Those who participate have higher morale and accept change more readily than the other workers (Coch and French, 1948).

The processes that hold a group together must work both ways. The individual must be responsive to the norms of the group, subscribe to its ideology, and be prepared to make sacrifices in order to be a part of it. But the group must also respond to the needs of its members. It cannot achieve cohesiveness if its norms are unenforceable, if its ideology is inconsistent with the beliefs of its members, or if the rewards it offers do not outweigh the sacrifices it requires.

INTERACTIONS WITHIN GROUPS

Providing an individual with values and a sense of identity is only one aspect of the group's meaning to him or her. The particular part he or she plays in the group's activities is also important. Each group member has certain unique abilities and interests, and the group has a number of different tasks that need to be performed. The study of the parts various members play in the group, and of how these parts are interrelated, is the study of *group structure*.

There are many different aspects to group structure: the personal relationships between individual members, such as liking relationships and trusting relationships; the rank of each member on a particular dimension, such as power, popularity, status, or amount of resources; and the roles

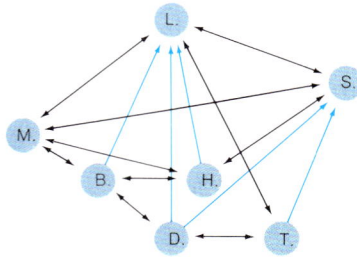

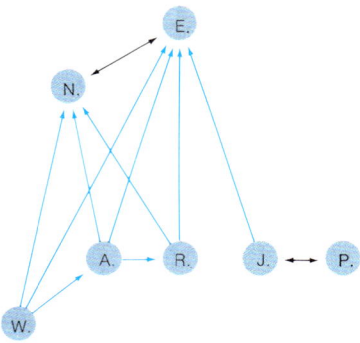

Figure 17.13
Sociograms showing patterns of friendship choices within two groups. The blue arrows indicate liking that is not returned; the black arrows indicate a two-way friendship. The more a person is liked, the higher in the pattern he or she appears. The pattern of the bottom group shows a hierarchical structure, with E and N clearly the leaders. The sociogram of the top group indicates strong group cohesiveness, with even D and T, the two least-liked members, clearly tied in to the group and having friends who like them.

various members play. (A few typical group roles are leader, joker, and the silent member.)

Communication Patterns

One technique psychologists use to analyze group structure is the **sociogram.** All members of a group are asked to name those people with whom they would like to interact on a given occasion or for a specific purpose, those they like best, and so on. For example, the members may be asked with whom they would like to go to a party, to discuss politics, to spend a vacation, or to complete an organizational task. Their choices can then be diagramed, as shown in Figure 17.13. Sociograms can help psychologists predict how that individual is likely to communicate with other group members.

Another way to discover the structure of a group is to examine the communication patterns in the group—who says what to whom, and how often.

One experiment on communication patterns was done by Harold Leavitt in 1951. He gave a card with several symbols on it to each person in a group of five. (Leavitt put each person in a separate room or booth and allowed the members to communicate only by written messages.) In this way he was able to create the networks shown in Figure 17.14. Each circle represents a person; the lines represent open channels. Subjects placed in each position could exchange messages only with the persons to whom they were connected by channels.

The most interesting result of this experiment was that the people who were organized into a "circle" were the slowest at solving the problem but the happiest at doing it. In this group everyone sent and received a large number of messages until someone solved the problem and passed the information on. In the "wheel," by contrast, everyone sent a few messages to one center person, who figured out the answer and told the rest what it was. These groups found the solution quickly, but the people on the outside of the wheel did not particularly enjoy the job.

Following the experiment, the members in each group were asked to identify the leader of their group. In the centralized groups (wheel, Y, and chain), the person in the center was usually chosen as the group leader. But in the circle network half the group members said they thought there was no real leader, and those who did say there was a leader disagreed on who that leader was. Thus a centralized organization seems more useful for task-oriented groups, whereas a decentralized network is more useful in socially oriented groups.

Leadership

All groups, whether made up of gangsters, soldiers, workers, or politicians, have leaders. A leader embodies the norms and ideals of the group and represents the group to outsiders. Within the group, a leader initiates action, gives orders, makes decisions, and settles disputes. In short, a leader is one who has a great deal of influence on the other members of the group.

Most of us think of leadership as a personality trait. To an extent this is true. Leaders tend to be better adjusted, more self-confident, more energetic and outgoing, and slightly more intelligent than other members of their group (Gibb, 1969). However, the nature of the group in part determines who will lead. Different circumstances call for different kinds of leaders. A group that is threatened by internal conflict requires a leader who is good at handling people, settling disputes, soothing tempers, and the like. A group that has a complex task to perform needs a leader with special experience to set goals and plan strategies for achieving them (Fiedler, 1969).

Within a group there may be two kinds of leaders, then. They are easy to tell apart by the things they say. One kind, the **social leader,** tends to make encouraging remarks, to break any tension with a joke, to solicit the reactions of others to whatever is going on. The other, the **task leader,** takes over when it is time to convey information, give opinions, or suggest how to do something. This leader is bossier and is not reluctant to disagree and press for a particular idea or course of action even if it creates tension in the group. A task leader usually has special knowledge or skills, and so different people may fill this role, depending on what the group is doing. The social leader is likely to be the same person, whatever the group does, because the need for promoting cohesion is always there. The social leader usually commands the loyalty of the group (Bales, 1958).

FACT or FICTION

Fiction. Often group decisions are more daring than the choice any individual member would make on his or her own. This process is known as *risky shift*. Psychologists believe that risky shift occurs because of a diffusion of responsibility—when no individual will be held accountable for the group's decision.

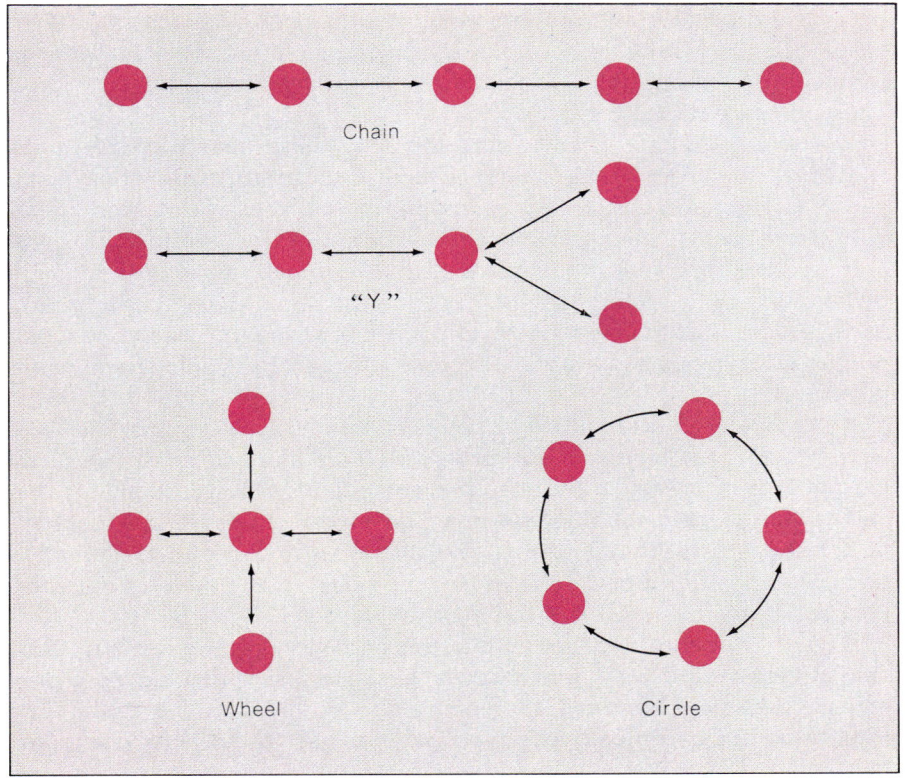

Chain

"Y"

Wheel

Circle

Figure 17.14
Harold Leavitt's communication network.

Figure 17.15
Lee Iacocca was fired from his job at one automobile company, yet he went on to become the Chairman of the Board of the Chrysler Corporation. Iacocca's leadership skills were put to the test at Chrysler, and he is widely credited with having steered his company away from bankruptcy to success.

There are many ways in which a person can acquire enough influence to become the leader of a group. Three of the most common are expertise, charisma, and power.

An expert directs the group's activity because he or she has the knowledge that the group needs to achieve its goals. For example, a ship's captain must know how to run a ship and how to meet an emergency at sea. Many leaders also possess a strong emotional appeal, or **charisma.** President John F. Kennedy was a striking example of a political leader with a charisma that aroused strong feelings among both followers and enemies. Influence can also come from the power to control rewards and punishments. A president of a company can give raises and promotions; he can also fire or demote people. He is a leader not because members like him, but because he owns the most shares in the company or because he has been appointed by those who own shares.

For whatever reason a member becomes a leader, the way he or she leads will affect the structure of his or her group and the roles other members play. A powerful leader may make all the important decisions for the group and assign relatively unimportant tasks to other members. A more democratic leader may try to involve as many members as possible in the decision-making process.

Diffusion of Responsibility

Sometimes, several people are faced with a common problem although they have no leader and may not even see themselves as a group. There have been many famous examples of muggings, rapes, and murders that were committed in public while a large group of people watched without intervening or calling for help.

Psychologists have tried to find out why these people didn't act by studying artificial crises. In one experiment, college students were asked to participate in a discussion of personal problems. They were asked to wait in separate rooms. Some were told that they would be communicating with only one other person; others were given the impression that they would be talking with five other people. All communication, the psychologist told each student, was to take place over microphones so that everyone would remain anonymous and thus would speak more freely. Each person was to talk in turn.

In reality, there were no other people—all the voices the subjects heard were on tape. As the discussion progressed, the subject heard one of the participants go into what sounded like an epileptic fit. The victim began to call for help, making choking sounds. The experimenters found that most of the people who thought they were alone with the victim came out of their room to help him. But of those who believed there were four other people nearby, less than half did anything to help.

The experimenters suggested that this behavior was the result of **diffusion of responsibility.** In other words, because several people were present, each subject assumed someone else would help. The researchers found that in experiments where people could see the other participants, the same pattern emerged. In addition, bystanders reassured one another that it would not be a good idea to interfere. These findings on diffusion of responsibility suggest that the larger the crowd or group of bystanders, the more likely any given individual is to feel that he or she is not responsible for whatever is going on (Darley and Latané, 1968).

Another influence that inhibits action is the tendency to minimize the *need* for any response. To act, you must admit that an emergency exists. But you may not know exactly what is going on when you hear screams or loud thumps upstairs. You are likely to wait before risking the embarrassment of rushing to help where help is not needed or wanted. It is easier to persuade yourself that nothing needs to be done if you look around and see other people behaving calmly. Not only can you see that they think nothing is wrong, but you can see that not doing anything is entirely proper. You are able to minimize the need to act and shift any responsibility to those around you.

USING PSYCHOLOGY

The Peer Group

In the early years of a child's life, parents play an important and influential role. As children grow older, however, the influence of their peers becomes increasingly strong. Peer groups are made up of people who have similar interests, frequent contact, and a mutual influence on each other. Peer interactions are different from parent-child or teacher-student interactions in that peer interactions are usually initiated for companionship and amusement, whereas parent or teacher interactions are more often based on a need for protection, care, or instruction (Damon, 1983). People generally choose their peer groups, whereas they do not choose their parents, siblings, or teachers.

Research on infants and preschool children indicates that peer interactions through play help children develop important social skills. By the time children reach school age, they spend almost as much of their time with peers as they do with their parents. By the second grade, most children have at least three or four good friends among their same-sex peers (Reisman and Shorr, 1978). During the transition from childhood to adolescence, peers become the central focus of attention. The peer group remains a major source of socialization during adolescence and young adulthood. Unlike peer groups in grade school, which are made up primarily of same-sex friends of the same age, adolescent and adult peer groups consist of members of both sexes and include a wider range of ages.

The peer group serves a number of important functions in a person's life. To begin with, peers provide companionship—people to spend time with and talk to. The way peers provide this closeness changes with development.

Sociologist Dexter Dunphy (1963) has observed the changes in the way teenagers in an urban setting spend time with each other. In early adolescence, teenagers spend most of their time with same-sex friends in cliques of three or four people. Then, these friendships expand to include additional same-sex friends. By the mid-teens, these friendships have evolved into organized crowds in which cliques engage in group-to-group interaction. The crowds soon include both sexes and include social activities such as dances and parties. By late adolescence, people begin to date within these crowds and to form more intimate relationships. By young adulthood, the peer crowd has disintegrated, to be replaced by loosely organized groups of couples.

Another important psychological feature of peer groups is peer acceptance. Peer friendships and peer group acceptance are compelling forces. The extent to which you are liked and accepted by your peers can affect the way you feel about yourself as well as the way your peers treat you. In an effort to be accepted and admired, members of peer groups conform to the standards and values of the group.

In adolescence, conformity to peer group standards generally increases with age, but the level of conformity depends on the tasks or behavior demanded. If a person is uncertain about an issue or has mixed feelings, he or she is more likely to go along with the group opinion. In matters involving a firm personal conviction, however, the older adolescent is more likely to take an individual stand, even when the opinion conflicts with peer group standards.

Peer group influence is generally strongest in matters of personal preference and taste. Peers shape a teenager's preference for music, hairstyles, clothes, recreation, and choice of friends. Peers are also much more influential than parents or teachers in shaping sexual attitudes and behavior. The use of drugs and alcohol is heavily influenced by peer group activities.

While parents, older adults, and teachers are more likely than peers to influence a person's political views and academic and career choices, the socioeconomic status of the peer group does influence an adolescent's vocational plans. For example, lower-class teenagers with middle-class friends generally aspire to higher-status careers. One reason for this influence may be that people seek out others who share their goals and values. Parents of any class who encourage their

Figure 17.16
Peer groups are an important part of a teenager's life. Group members are likely to dress alike, talk alike, and share similar interests and goals.

children to do well in school and to aspire to high-status careers also influence their children's choice of friends based on these values.

Peer group affiliation can encourage adolescents to become more independent of their parents. Peers provide an opportunity for people to try out or discuss new behaviors that are not encouraged or are discouraged by parents. For example, most parents do not discuss or encourage adolescents' sexuality, but peers readily exchange ideas and information on this subject. Family ties become less intense as adolescents identify with their peer group and try out new behaviors and ideas.

The shift in interest toward the peer group helps to encourage a separateness between parent and adolescent. Sometimes, the pressure to conform to peer group standards instead of parental standards results in overt rebellion and antisocial behavior. For most people, however, independence from parents is achieved without extreme disruption. Most adolescents and young adults accept their parents' values as their own once they establish independence.

The influence of peers can sometimes produce unpleasant effects. While almost everyone wants to be accepted and liked by peers, not everyone is. Some people experience peer rejection or neglect. Usually the people who achieve high peer status (those liked by a number of peers) are friendlier, more physically attractive, more socially outgoing, cooperative, and do better in school (Dodge, 1983). As a rule, the unpopular people lack the social skills necessary for acceptance and often engage in socially undesirable actions such as aggressive and antagonistic behavior. People who are neglected or rejected by their peers may withdraw and feel very lonely and isolated. Frequently they are shy and unhappy and lack self-confidence. Some individuals go to extreme lengths to please a group in order to earn acceptance or avoid rejection. This desire to please can, in turn, lead to further disruptive behavior. Adolescents who try to adjust to a peer group whose views oppose those held by their families may also face considerable conflict and stress (Newman, 1982).

Adolescents derive more than just "fun" from participating in their peer group activities. Peer groups satisfy an emotional need—the need to belong. The members of a peer group feel a bond that distinguishes "us" from "them." It is somewhat paradoxical that this way of finding out who "we" are helps the individual find out who he or she is.

The negative aspect of peer group unity is the prejudicial nature of the "in group" and the tendency to discredit members of the "out group." The positive side of this unity is the security and strength that it gives, for example, to minorities dealing with prejudices from a majority. In this way, peer groups serve the same psychological function as support groups.

GROUP CONFLICT VERSUS COOPERATION

Conflicts between groups are a fact of everyday life: some level of hostility exists between women and men, young and old, workers and bosses, blacks and whites, Catholics and Protestants, students and teachers. Why do these conflicts exist, and why do they persist? In the next chapter, we discuss prejudice, discrimination, and related issues. But first let us consider the findings of a group of psychologists who created a boys' camp in order to study intergroup relations. The camp at Robber's Cave offered all the usual activities, and the boys had no idea that they were part of an experiment.

From the beginning of the experiment, the boys were divided into two separate groups. The boys hiked, swam, and played baseball only with members of their own group, and friendships and group spirit soon developed. After a while the experimenters (working as counselors) brought the groups together for a tournament. The psychologists had hypothesized that when these two groups of boys were placed in competitive situations, where one group could achieve its goals only at the expense of the other, hostility would develop. They were right.

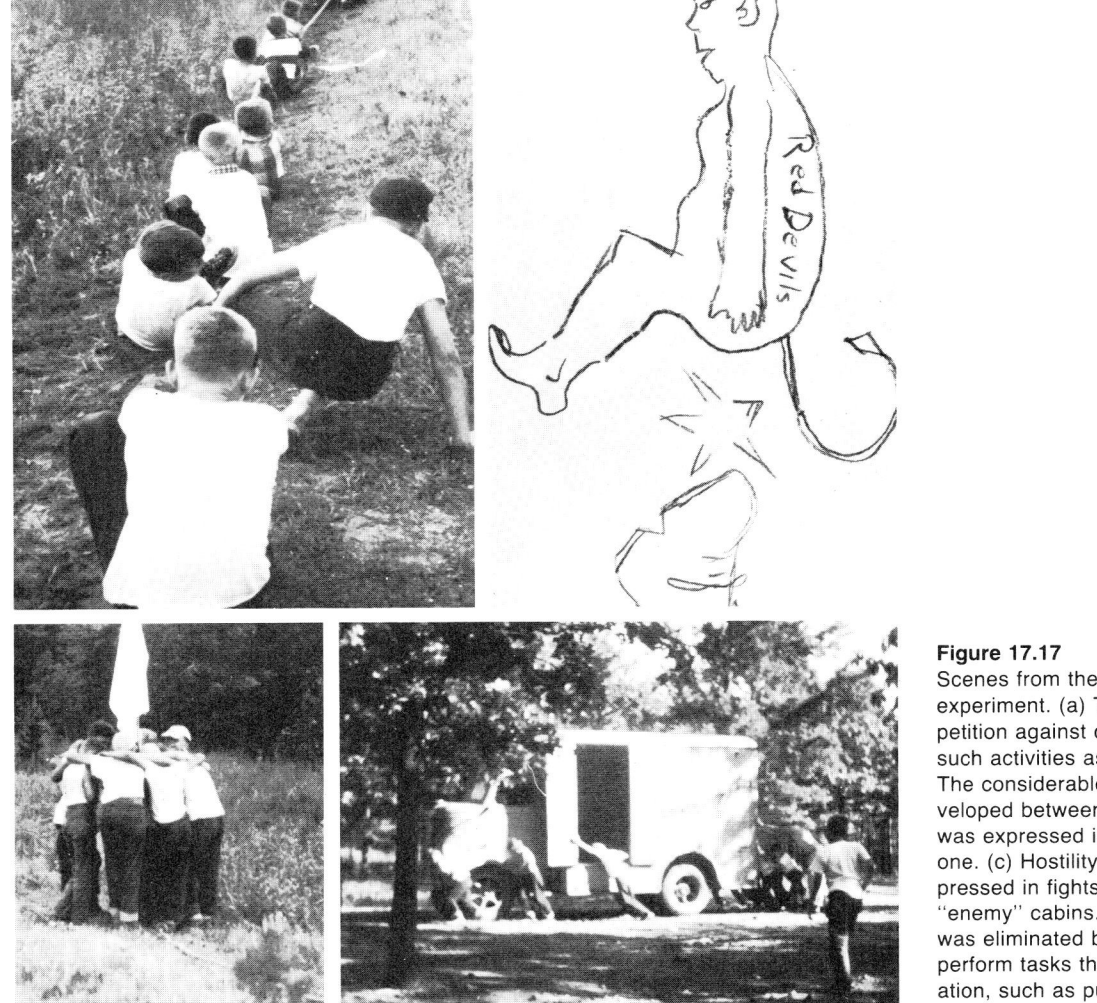

Figure 17.17
Scenes from the Robber's Cave experiment. (a) The boys in competition against one another in such activities as tug-of-war. (b) The considerable hostility that developed between the two groups was expressed in drawings like this one. (c) Hostility was also expressed in fights and in raids on "enemy" cabins. (d) The hostility was eliminated by having the boys perform tasks that needed cooperation, such as pushing a truck that supplied food to the camp.

Although the games began in a spirit of good sportsmanship, tension mounted as the tournament continued. Friendly competition gave way to name-calling, fistfights, and raids on enemy cabins. The psychologists had demonstrated the ease with which they could produce unity within the two boys' groups and hatred between them. The experimenters then tried to see what might end the conflict and create harmony between the two groups. They tried to bring the groups together for enjoyable activities, such as a movie and a good meal. This approach failed. The campers shoved and pushed each other, threw food and insults, and generally used the opportunity to continue their attacks.

Next, the psychologists deliberately invented a series of "emergencies" so that the boys would either have to help one another or lose the chance to do or get something they all wanted. For instance, one morning someone reported that the water line to the camp had broken. The boys were told that unless they worked together to find the break and fix it, they would all have to leave camp. By afternoon, they had jointly found and fixed the damage. Gradually, through such cooperative activities, intergroup hostility and tensions lessened. Friendships began to develop between individuals of the opposing groups, and eventually the groups began to seek out occasions to mingle. At the end of the camp period, members of both groups requested that they ride home together on the same bus.

The results of this experiment were striking. A group of boys from identical backgrounds had developed considerable hostility toward each other, simply because they were placed in competition. The crucial factor in eliminating group hostility was cooperation (Sherif et al., 1961).

Social Traps

The question of conflict is not confined just to small groups. It applies to large communities too, but then the possibility of a social trap is greater. A social trap occurs when individuals in a group decide not to cooperate. Instead, they act selfishly and create a bad situation for all.

An illustration of the social trap can be seen in the way Americans have responded to the problems of pollution. We know that automobile exhaust pollutes the air. We know that one way to reduce air pollution is to carpool or use public transportation. Yet the driver who commutes 30 miles a day, alone, and who knows that he or she is polluting the air, thinks: "Yes, I know my car exhaust is bad. But I am only one person. If I stop driving, it won't make any difference." As long as we fall into that social trap, we shall continue to destroy our environment.

Psychologists have been exploring ways to overcome social traps such as this one. One approach is to use laws to bring about behavior changes, such as the law requiring special exhaust systems in cars. Another way to change people's behavior is to educate them concerning the issues and also to communicate the idea that "Yes, you do make a difference." By publicizing the problems and solutions, and organizing groups to act, individuals begin to feel that what they do does have an impact. And their actions are reinforced by the group. In this way, people find it more beneficial to cooperate than to act in a purely selfish manner.

CHAPTER REVIEW

KEY TERMS

- attribution theory
- body language
- charisma
- complementarity
- diffusion of responsibility
- ego-support value
- group
- ideology

- implicit personality theory
- nonverbal communication
- norms
- personal space
- physical proximity
- social functions
- social leader
- social rule

- sociogram
- stereotype
- stimulation value
- task functions
- task leader
- utility value

SUMMARY

1. Social psychologists have found that people need other people most when they are afraid, anxious, unsure of themselves, or want to compare their feelings to the feelings of others in the same situation.

2. The most important factor in determining whether two people will become friends is physical proximity.

3. Some of the rewards found in friendships are stimulation, utility, and ego support. These are evaluated consciously or unconsciously in every friendship. Other factors that affect a person's choice of friends are physical appearance, approval, and similarity.

4. Body language—gestures, positions, and movements of the body—communicates information about an individual. Much of it is unconscious, and many gestures are governed by social rules.

5. In forming impressions of other people, each person has his or her own implicit personality theory—a set of assumptions about how people behave and what traits or characteristics go together.

6. The conclusions we draw about people vary according to whether we attribute their actions to personal qualities or to the situation in which we find them.

7. Groups are aggregates of people who are interdependent—that is, the actions of any one group member will affect or influence other members. Group members become interdependent because they see themselves as sharing common goals.

8. The two primary purposes of groups are to perform task functions and to perform social functions.

9. Group structure is the way in which individuals fit together into a whole unit. The way people interact in a group is studied through the use of sociograms and the analysis of communication patterns. An important element in the group's structure is leadership. A leader is the person who exerts the most influence in a group.

10. Diffusion of responsibility is similar to mob action in that people in a crowd seem to feel they are not responsible for whatever is going on. In a crisis, people often refrain from acting because they minimize the emergency, because they expect other people to act, or because they do not want to be "different."

11. The peer group is a major source of socialization during adolescence and young adulthood. Peer groups provide companionship and shape an individual's preferences and tastes. They also satisfy a person's emotional need to belong.

12. Group conflict can be broken down when members of hostile groups need to cooperate.

REVIEW QUESTIONS

1. In what situations do we want to be with other people?

2. Is the saying "Misery loves company" accurate?

3. What is the most important factor in determining the start of a friendship? Why is this an important factor?

4. What are the three kinds of rewards in a friendship?

5. At what stage of a relationship is physical attractiveness of a partner an important concern? Are you likely to ask a very attractive person for a date?

6. Which person is likely to make a better impression on you—one who praises you first and then criticizes you or someone who points out your faults and then discusses your good points?

7. In general, are you likely to choose as a friend a person who is similar to you or a person who complements your strengths and weaknesses?

8. Compare passionate and companionate love.

9. How far would you stand from someone to indicate that you would like to talk to that person?

10. What theory do you use when you form an impression of a stranger? If that judgment is based on the stranger's similarity to other people in a given category, what set of assumptions are you using?

11. If you want people to think that you are smart, should you try to do your best on the first, second, or last test in a class? What theory does this illustrate?

12. What features distinguish a group from a nongroup? What are the purposes of a group?

13. What factors work to hold a group together? What factors increase the commitment of a person to the group?

14. What technique do psychologists use to study group structure? In what types of group structures will a leader be easily recognized?

15. What are the two kinds of group leaders? Which type will command the loyalty of the group? What are three ways to become a group leader?

16. What are two factors that inhibit group action?

17. If you wanted to reduce conflict between two opposing groups of students, what kinds of activities would you ask them to participate in?

ACTIVITIES

1. We may think that stereotyping does not influence us. Watch a television program about (a) a detective, (b) a black family, (c) an independent woman. What character traits does each have? Do we laugh at some of these characterizations when they do not fit the stereotypes? Which stereotypes do we not laugh at?

2. How do you analyze new instructors at the beginning of a term? On what do you base your impressions? How do your impressions affect how you behave toward each instructor? Have you ever changed your mind after getting the "wrong impression" about someone?

3. Conduct an experiment on personal space by going to the library and sitting at a table with another person. After a few minutes begin to "invade" his or her space by placing your books and papers across the imaginary line that divides the space between the two of you. Carefully observe the person's behavior. Describe his or her reactions to your encroachments.

4. Describe several situations in which you either "put on an act" or disguised your true feeling regarding a person or situation. Did your deception occur consciously or unconsciously? How did others react?

5. List in detail the main things you look for when you choose close friends. What are your reasons for rejecting certain people as either close friends or acquaintances?

6. Write down the first ten or fifteen words or phrases that come to mind when you ask yourself, "Who am I?" Now categorize these items as either physical traits, psychological characteristics, or group affiliations. How much of your self-concept is built on your identification with groups?

7. In the groups to which you belong (clubs, your college, and so on), you have undoubtedly had leaders or people with influence over you. Pick a few such leaders and try to analyze the sources of their influence. Are they experts? Do they have charisma? Are they socially attractive? How much power do they have? How have they obtained it?

8. Ask one male and one female to reverse sex roles and discuss the following contentions. (1) Men need liberation as much as women. (2) Men are at least as vain as women. (3) Women do not mind being dominated as long as they are loved and cared for. (4) Women can never be as competent as men, or men as women in which of the following occupations: scientist, child rearer, politician, construction worker, nurse, airplane pilot?

9. People tend to see other people's behavior as determined by personality traits, while they see their own behavior as a function of the situation they are in. To demonstrate this phenomenon, you will need the help of a friend. Give your friend a sheet of paper and ask him or her to list the following traits across the top of the sheet: sincere, conscientious, aggressive, friendly, independent, and mature. Then have your friend list the following names of people

down the left-hand side of the paper: the president, a public figure he or she dislikes, himself or herself, the name of a neighbor he or she hardly knows, and his or her best friend. Then ask your friend to fill in the chart by rating each person on each trait, giving a plus if the person has the trait listed across the top, a minus if the person does not have the trait, and a zero if it depends on the situation. When your friend is finished, sum up the number of pluses, minuses, and zeros for each person, including himself or herself. If your friend is like most people, you will notice that more traits, both positive and negative, were assigned to other people. Share your observations with your friend.

10. Friendship and love are often combined in personal relationships, yet loved ones and friends are often selected for different reasons and we often act differently toward each one. Think of people whom you consider your friends. What type of behavior do you expect from them? What do you do with them that you can't do with people you do not call friends? Be as specific as you can. Do different friends fulfill different roles in your life? Think of someone you love now or loved at one time. How would you describe this person? What are or were your expectations of him or her? In what ways do you act similarly toward your loved one and friends? Share your ideas and insights with a classmate, friend, or loved one and get reactions.

11. Have you ever been jealous of a boyfriend, girlfriend, sibling, friend, or parent? Recall a time when you were jealous of another person. What was the nature of your relationship with this person? How did you feel about yourself? What made you feel jealous? What effect did your responses to the jealousy have on your relationship with the person? Ask several of your friends (both male and female) to respond to these questions. Compare your experience of jealousy with your friends' reactions. Do you notice any similarities? Are there differences between your male and female friends' jealous reactions? If you had it to do over again within the relationship, would you respond the same way?

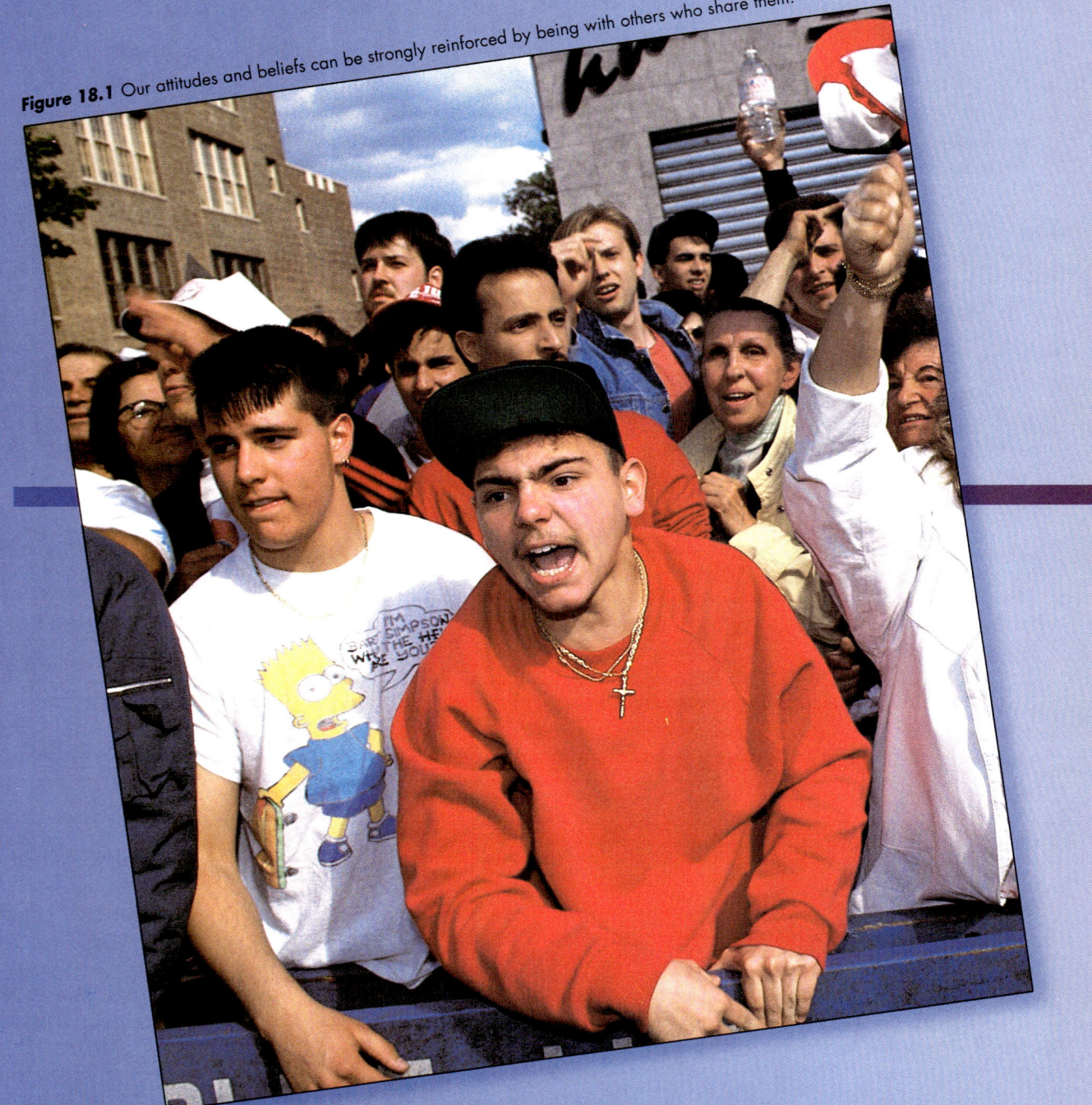

Figure 18.1 Our attitudes and beliefs can be strongly reinforced by being with others who share them.

Objectives: *After studying this chapter, you should be able to*
- trace the origin of attitudes.
- describe the concept of prejudice.
- identify and explain the sources of attitude change.
- explain the persuasion process.
- describe how social influences affect behavior.

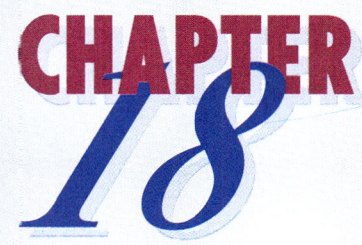

CHAPTER
18

Attitudes and Social Influence

Are you convinced that vitamin C is the best cure for the common cold? Should the United States have gone to war with Iraq? How do you feel about atheism, patriotism, and the Los Angeles Rams? Each of us has a wide variety of opinions, attitudes, and beliefs. We may feel that some of them are worth dying for, while others aren't worth the time it takes to explain them.

This chapter is about our attitudes, opinions, and beliefs—where they come from, how they form, and how they change. It is also about the subtle and complex relationships between what we think, what we say, and what we do.

WHERE ATTITUDES COME FROM

An **attitude** is a predisposition to respond in particular ways to specific things. It has three main elements: (1) a belief or opinion about something, (2) feelings about that thing, and (3) a tendency to act toward that thing in certain ways. For example, what is your attitude toward the senators from your state? Do you *believe* they are doing a good job? Do you *feel* you trust or distrust them? Would you *act* to vote for them?

We all have very definite beliefs, feelings, and responses to things about which we have no firsthand knowledge. Where do these attitudes come from? The culture in which we grew up, the people who raised us, and those with whom we associate—our peers—all shape our attitudes.

Culture. Culture influences everything from our taste in food to our attitudes toward human relationships and our political opinions. For example,

Where Attitudes Come From

Attitude Formation
Compliance • Identification • Internalization

Prejudice
Stereotypes and Roles • Oppression • The Authoritarian Personality • Prejudice and Discrimination • Scapegoating • Integration

Cognitive Consistency and Changing Attitudes

Attitudes and Actions
Doing Is Believing • Self-fulfilling Prophecy • Practical Implications

Persuasion
The Communication Process • The Sleeper Effect • The Inoculation Effect • Using Psychology: Promoting Energy Conservation

Social Influence
Brainwashing • Group Pressure to Conform • Obedience to Authority

457

most (if not all) Americans would consider eating grubs, curdled milk spiced with cattle blood, or monkey meat disgusting. Yet in some parts of the world these are considered delicacies. Some Americans believe eating meat is essential for good health. Hindus consider our relish for thick, juicy steaks and hamburgers disgusting.

Almost all Americans would agree that in polygamous societies, where a man is allowed to have more than one wife, women are oppressed. But women in polygamous societies feel nothing but pity for a woman whose husband hasn't acquired other wives to help with the work and to keep her company.

Most of us would also agree that parents who interfere in their children's choice of a marriage partner are behaving outrageously and that a person should be able to marry the person he or she loves. However, in some parts of India, parents choose husbands for their daughters, and the girls are relieved not to have to make such an important choice:

> "We girls don't have to worry at all. We know we'll get married. When we are old enough our parents will find a suitable boy and everything will be arranged. We don't have to go into competition with each other.... Besides how would we be able to judge the character of a boy? ... Our parents are older and wiser, and they aren't deceived as easily as we would be. I'd far rather have my parents choose for me" (Mace and Mace, 1960: 131).

The list of culturally derived attitudes is endless. Indeed, it is only by traveling and reading about other ways of life that we discover how many of the things we take for granted are *attitudes*, not facts.

Parents.   There is abundant evidence that all of us acquire many basic attitudes from our parents. How else would you account for the finding that 80 percent of a national sample of elementary school children favored the same political party as their fathers (Hess and Torney, 1967), and 76 percent of high school seniors in a nationwide sample also preferred the same party as both their parents (Jennings and Niemi, 1968)? Parental influence wanes as children get older, of course. A sample of college students selected the same party as their father only 50 to 60 percent of the time (Goldsen *et al.*, 1960). Despite the decline, this study still suggests significant parental influence even after a person has become an adult.

Peers.   It is not surprising that parental influence declines as children get older and are exposed to many other sources of influence. In a now classic study, Newcomb (1943) questioned and requestioned students at Bennington College about their political attitudes over a period of four years. Most of the young women came from wealthy, staunchly conservative families. In contrast, most Bennington faculty members were outspoken liberals. Newcomb found that many of the students were "converted" to the liberal point of view. In 1936, 54 percent of the juniors and seniors supported Franklin D. Roosevelt and the New Deal—although praising Roosevelt to their families would have produced about the same reactions as praising

Karl Marx to Ronald Reagan. Indeed, nearly 30 percent of the students favored Socialist or Communist candidates. Newcomb contacted the subjects of his study twenty-five years after they had graduated, and found that most had maintained the attitudes they had acquired in college. One reason was that they had chosen friends, husbands, and careers that supported liberal values (Newcomb *et al.*, 1967). People tend to adopt the likes and dislikes of groups whose approval and acceptance they seek.

Figure 18.2
Scenes from Bennington College at the time Newcomb was there; Newcomb himself is shown on the left. The marked change in reference groups experienced by Bennington students is shown in a remark by one subject: "Family against faculty has been my struggle here."

ATTITUDE FORMATION

Having suggested where attitudes come from, we can now look at how they develop. The three main processes involved in forming or changing attitudes are compliance, identification, and internalization (Kelman, 1961).

If you praise a certain film director because everyone else does, you are complying. If you find yourself agreeing with everything a friend you particularly admire says about the director, you are identifying with the friend's attitudes. If you genuinely like the director's work and, regardless of what other people think, regard it as brilliant, you are expressing an internalized attitude.

Compliance

One of the best measures of attitude is behavior. If a man settles back into "his chair" after dinner, launches into a discussion of his support of the women's movement, then shouts to his wife—who is in the kitchen washing the dishes—to bring more coffee, you probably wouldn't believe what he had been saying. His actions speak louder than his words. Yet the same man might hire women for jobs he has always considered "men's work" because the law requires him to do so. And he might finally accept his wife's going to work because he knows that she, their children, and many of their friends would consider him old-fashioned if he didn't.

People often **comply** with the wishes of others in order to avoid discomfort or rejection and to gain support. As one Bennington student who professed to be a liberal explained,

> "It's very simple, I was so anxious to be accepted that I accepted the liberal complexion of the community here. I just couldn't stand out against the crowd . . ." (Newcomb, 1943: 132).

But under such circumstances, attitudes do not really change. Social pressure often results in only temporary compliance. Later in this chapter, however, we shall see that compliance can sometimes affect one's beliefs. We shall also discuss in detail how group pressure can lead to conformity.

Identification

One way in which attitudes may really be formed or changed is through the process of **identification.** Suppose you have a favorite uncle who is everything you hope to be. He is a successful musician, has many famous friends, and seems to know a great deal about everything. In many ways you identify with him and copy his behavior. One night, during an intense conversation, your uncle announces he is an atheist. At first you are confused by this statement. You have had a religious upbringing and have always considered religious beliefs as essential. However, as you listen to your uncle, you find yourself starting to agree with him. If a person as knowledgeable and respectable as your uncle holds such beliefs, perhaps you should, too. Later you find yourself feeling that atheism is acceptable. You have adopted a new attitude because of your identification with your uncle.

Identification occurs when a person wants to define himself or herself in terms of a person or group, and therefore adopts the person's or group's attitudes and ways of behaving. Identification is different from compliance because the individual actually believes the newly adopted views. But because these attitudes are based on emotional attachment to another person or group rather than the person's own assessment of the issues, they are fragile. If the person's attachment to that person or group fades, the attitudes may also weaken. Thus, one Bennington student ultimately rejected the liberal point of view:

> "Family against faculty has been my struggle here. As soon as I felt really secure I decided not to let the college atmosphere affect me too much. Everytime I've tried to rebel against my family I've found how terribly wrong I am, and I've very naturally kept to my parents' attitudes" (Newcomb, 1943: 124).

For this student, identification with the college community was only temporary.

Internalization

Internalization is the wholehearted acceptance of an attitude; it becomes an integral part of the person. Internalization is most likely to occur when an attitude is consistent with a person's basic beliefs and values and supports his or her self-image. The person adopts a new attitude because he or she believes it to be right—not because he or she wants to be like someone else.

Internalization is the most lasting of the three sources of attitude formation or change. Your internalized attitudes will be more resistant to pressure from other people because your reasons for holding these views have nothing to do with other people: They are based on your own evaluation of the merits of the issue. A Bennington student put it this way:

"I became liberal at first because of its prestige value; I remain so because the problems around which my liberalism centers are important. What I want now is to be effective in solving the problems" (Newcomb, 1943: 136).

As this example suggests, compliance or identification may lead to the internalization of an attitude. Often the three overlap. You may support a political candidate in part because you know your friends will approve, in part because someone you admire speaks highly of the candidate, and in part because you believe his or her ideals are consistent with your own.

PREJUDICE

Prejudice literally means prejudgment. It means deciding beforehand what a person will be like instead of withholding judgment until it can be based on his or her individual qualities. To hold stereotypes about a group of people is to be prejudiced about them. Prejudice is not necessarily negative—whites who are prejudiced against blacks are often equally prejudiced in favor of whites, for example.

Stereotypes and Roles

Prejudice is strengthened and maintained by the existence of stereotypes and roles. A stereotype is an oversimplified, hard-to-change way of seeing people who belong to some group or category. Black people, scientists, women, Mexicans, and the rich, for example, have often been seen in certain rigid ways rather than as individuals. A role is an oversimplified, hard-to-change way of acting. Stereotypes and roles can act together in a way that makes them difficult to break down. For example, many whites once had a stereotype of blacks, believing them to be irresponsible, superstitious, and unintelligent. Whites who believed this expected blacks to act out a role that was consistent with a stereotype. Blacks were expected to be submissive, deferential, and respectful toward whites, who acted out the

PSYCHOLOGY and YOU

Protest Demonstrations. At the start of the Persian Gulf war, thousands of people marched in antiwar demonstrations in American cities. Some carried signs that said "No blood for oil," or "No corpses for crude."

The antiwar demonstrators marched because they believed that the war was morally wrong or that it was not worth the loss of American lives. Others feared that they or their friends or family members would be called upon to fight. By demonstrating, the protesters both publicly declared their own stand on the war and hoped to persuade others to adopt their point of view.

The protests helped stimulate public debate about whether the war was necessary and the causes were just. The demonstrators also reflected the divisions and doubts among the American public over the war. In America's last major conflict, the Vietnam war, the American public largely supported the conflict at first. But years of antiwar demonstrations gradually changed public opinion about the war to widespread opposition to it.

Figure 18.3
These lines from James Baldwin's novel *Nobody Knows My Name* express the impossible dilemma of being black in a white world and the way it feels to try to break free of the roles and stereotypes that are part of that situation.

role of the superior, condescending parent. In the past, many blacks and whites accepted these roles and looked at themselves and each other according to these stereotypes. In the past three decades, however, many blacks and whites have worked to step out of these roles and drop these stereotypes, and to some extent they have been successful.

Stereotypes are also preserved in the communications media, which have traditionally portrayed American Indians as villains, Italians as greasy gangsters, Jews as misers, and teenagers as car-crazy rock fans. Many of these stereotypes are changing now, but new ones have replaced them. For example, doctors on television are usually heroes, housewives are charming idiots, and so on. A critical look at television programs and movies reveals a great deal about what is widely believed in American society.

Oppression

Group conflict often involves the oppression of one group by another. It is not hard to see how such domination gives rise to feelings of hostility on the part of the oppressed group. In addition, the powerful group stereotypes the oppressed group because it wants to justify its unfair actions and because it wants to stop the oppressed group from fighting back.

This is called a master-slave relationship, for obvious reasons. The present relationship between blacks and whites in America is a result of the fact that at one time blacks were literally the slaves and whites were literally the masters. The oppression of blacks by whites has lessened only gradually. Psychologists are learning that the master-slave relationship exists between other groups, too. For example, the freedom of women has been restricted by men.

The Authoritarian Personality

The most extreme forms of racial oppression were practiced by European Fascists in the 1930s and 1940s. One group of researchers (Adorno *et al.,* 1969) tried to analyze this phenomenon by studying the kinds of people who are attracted to the ideas of racial superiority. They found that highly prejudiced people share a number of traits which they called the **authoritarian personality.** These people tend to have inflexible ideas about themselves and others. Highly conventional, they view differences with suspicion and hostility, and like the sense of security that comes from a very structured authority. They tend to glorify their own qualities and upbringing, despite the fact that their fathers were inclined to be punitive and exacted obedience and unquestioning loyalty through harsh discipline.

The researchers who originally uncovered the relationships among prejudice, personality traits, and upbringing believed that punitive parents create insecure and hostile children. As adults, these people fear their own aggressiveness and cannot admit their own fears and shortcomings. It is easier to claim that others are inferior than to recognize one's own shortcomings. The authoritarian person falls back on the use of stereotypes about others to keep from facing his or her own inadequacies.

This is not the only interpretation of highly prejudiced people, however. The link may be simpler: authoritarian parents teach their views to their children. Or perhaps prejudice and authoritarianism may actually be characteristics of lower social standing rather than quirks of personality.

Prejudice and Discrimination

We can see, then, that there are many possible causes for prejudice. Psychologists have found that people tend to be prejudiced against those less well-off than themselves—they seem to justify being on top by assuming that anyone of lower status or income must be inferior. People who have suffered economic setbacks also tend to be prejudiced—they blame others for their misfortune.

Prejudice also arises from "guilt by association." People who dislike cities and urban living, for example, tend to distrust people associated with cities, such as Jews and blacks. Also, people tend to be prejudiced *toward* those they see as similar to themselves and *against* those who seem different.

Whatever the original cause, prejudice seems to persist. One reason is that children who grow up in an atmosphere of prejudice conform to the prejudicial norm—at first because their parents do and later with the personal conviction that it is the right way to be. Children are socialized into the prejudicial culture of their parents; that is, they encounter numerous forces that induce them to conform to the thoughts and practices of their parents and other teachers, formal and informal.

Prejudice, which is an attitude, should be distinguished from **discrimi-**

Figure 18.4
After the assassination of Martin Luther King in 1968, a third-grade teacher gave her students a lesson in discrimination. On the basis of eye color the teacher divided the class into two groups and favored one group (the blue-eyed children the first day) with privileges. The next day she reversed the situation, favoring the brown-eyed children. On the day they were favored, the blue-eyed children reportedly "took savage delight" in keeping "inferiors" in their place and said they felt "good inside," "smarter," and "stronger." On that day, one child drew the picture shown on the right. The next day, the same child, now one of the "inferiors," drew the picture on the left. The children who had felt "smart" and "strong" on their favored day became tense, lacked confidence, and did badly at their work on the day they were discriminated against. They said they felt "like dying" and "like quitting school."

nation, the unequal treatment of members of certain groups. It is possible for a prejudiced person not to discriminate. He or she may recognize his or her prejudice and try not to act on it. Similarly, a person may discriminate, not out of prejudice, but in compliance with social pressures. Personal discrimination may take the form of refusing to rent to black people or allowing only men to frequent a particular club or paying Mexican-Americans substandard wages.

Scapegoating

One of the most popular theories to explain prejudice is the scapegoat theory (Allport, 1954; Hovland and Sears, 1940). According to this view, prejudice and the associated discrimination are the result of displaced aggression. When people are prevented from achieving their goals, they often react by being aggressive. When there is no obvious target for their aggression, they displace their frustration onto other people who are not responsible for the problem but who cannot strike back or cause them social disapproval. The target of displaced aggression is called a **scapegoat.**

Blacks in this country have been the scapegoats for the economic frustrations of lower-income white Americans who felt exploited and powerless themselves. The anger they felt could not be expressed on an appropriate target (say, the government), so instead they directed their hostility toward those whom they viewed as less powerful than themselves, the blacks. Between 1882 and 1930, the number of lynchings per year in southern states varied according to the price of cotton. When prices were low, indicating economic hard times, the number of lynchings increased (Hovland and Sears, 1940).

Integration

Centuries of racial prejudice in the United States and throughout the world seem to indicate that racial hatred poses an extremely complicated problem. One barrier to cooperation between the races is segregation. In one research project, a group of psychologists reasoned that if people of different races had the opportunity to meet as equals, they might come to recognize that their prejudices had no basis. Therefore, they interviewed people who had been placed in integrated and segregated buildings of a housing project just after World War II. The results of the interviews showed clearly that the amount and type of contact between black and white neighbors greatly influenced their opinions toward each other.

In the integrated buildings more than 60 percent of the white house-wives reported having "friendly relations" with blacks. In the segregated buildings less than 10 percent reported friendships, and more than 80 percent reported no contact at all. In the integrated buildings, two out of three white women expressed a desire to be friendly with blacks. In the segregated buildings only one in eleven expressed such a desire. Similar effects occurred in the attitudes of black women toward whites.

The integrated housing situation gave the housewives a chance to have contact with one another and to interact informally and casually. The housewives were likely to encounter each other in the elevators, hallways, and laundry room. In this informal climate they did not have to worry that trying to strike up a conversation might be misinterpreted. In contrast, contact in the segregated buildings would have to be more deliberate and might be considered suspicious (Deutsch and Collins, 1951).

Contact does not always reduce prejudice, however. Studies of schools that were integrated after the 1954 Supreme Court decision show mixed results. While some students became less prejudiced after a semester in an integrated school, others became *more* prejudiced than they had been before integration (Campbell, 1958). One exception was a community that voluntarily integrated its schools before the 1954 ruling. Children in that community were significantly less prejudiced than children in a similar community with all-white schools (Singer, 1964).

Why does contact reduce intergroup hostility in some instances but not in others? Several factors seem to be involved. First, the need to cooperate forces people to abandon negative stereotypes. Second, contact between people who occupy the same status is more likely to break down barriers than contact between people who do not perceive themselves as equals. Frequent contact with a white landlord is not likely to change a black person's stereotype of whites; nor is the relationship between a white executive and a black chauffeur likely to change the white person's stereotype of blacks. The housewives in the integrated buildings were social equals: they had about the same incomes, lived under similar conditions, faced the same problems, and so on.

Finally, when social norms support intergroup cooperation, people are likely to turn contacts into friendships. Presumably parents and teachers in the community that voluntarily desegregated its schools wanted to break down racial barriers. In accepting integration, the children were conforming to group norms. So were the young people whose communities integrated their schools only after they were required to do so by law. Those whose families and friends approved of integration were open to interracial friendships; those whose families and friends opposed desegregation kept their distance.

COGNITIVE CONSISTENCY AND CHANGING ATTITUDES

Many social psychologists have theorized that people's attitudes change because they are always trying to get things to fit together logically inside their heads. Holding two opposing attitudes can create great conflict in an individual, throwing him or her off balance. A socialist who inherits ten million dollars, a doctor who smokes, and a parent who is uncomfortable with children all have one thing in common: they are in conflict.

According to Leon Festinger (1957) people in such situations experience cognitive dissonance (Figure 18.5). **Cognitive dissonance** is the uncomfortable feeling that arises when a person experiences contradictory or conflicting thoughts, beliefs, attitudes, or feelings. To reduce dissonance, it is necessary to change one or both of the conflicting attitudes. Our newly rich socialist, for example, believes that wealth should be shared, but he or she may also be opposed to paying thousands in taxes to the government or contributing to traditional charities. (There might also be a strong temptation to buy fine clothes and a vacation home.) One solution is for the person to give all the money to CARE and forget any reservations regarding capitalist charities. Alternatively, the person could decide that a mere ten million dollars can't do much to stamp out poverty anyway, so he or she might as well hire an expensive tax lawyer and enjoy it.

Some people attempt to evade dissonance by avoiding situations or exposure to information that would create conflict. For example, they may make a point of subscribing to newspapers and magazines that uphold their political attitudes, of surrounding themselves with people who share the same ideas, and of attending only those speeches and lectures that support their views. It is not surprising that such people get quite upset when a piece of conflicting information finally does get through.

The process of dissonance reduction does not always take place consciously, but it is a frequent and powerful occurrence. In fact, remarkably long-lasting changes in attitudes were produced in an experiment in which students were made aware that their emphasis on freedom was inconsistent with their indifference to equality and civil rights. In the initial forty-minute session, students ranked a number of values by importance to themselves—including the key variables "freedom" and "equality." They were also asked to express their attitudes toward civil rights. The students then compared their answers with a table of typical answers, which was interpreted for them by the researchers. The researchers said that the typical tendency to rank freedom high and equality low not only showed

Figure 18.5
An example of cognitive dissonance. Mary has a positive attitude toward Bill and a negative attitude toward certain clothing styles. She can maintain both attitudes until a situation arises in which they are brought into conflict. Then she is faced with a state of dissonance that can be reduced only by a change in attitude. Mary may decide she really does not care so much for Bill; she may decide she really likes the clothes; or she may decide that Bill's ''poor taste'' is a minor fault.

that students in general are "much more interested in their own freedom than in other people's" but also that such rankings are consistent with a lack of concern for civil rights. Finally, students were asked whether their results left them satisfied or dissatisfied. The control group, who did not receive the researchers' explanation, simply filled out their rankings and went home, oblivious to any inconsistencies in attitude they might have expressed.

Three to five months after the initial test, the researchers sent out a solicitation for donations or memberships on NAACP stationery, to test whether students tested would act on the values they expressed. They received many more replies from students in the experimental group than in the control group. They concluded that the test had somehow made the first group of students more receptive to civil-rights issues. On tests fifteen to seventeen months later, changes in attitude were much more likely in subjects who had been dissatisfied with what they had been told about the results of their original test than in subjects who had not been dissatisfied.

This suggests that cognitive dissonance spurred changes in attitudes toward civil rights.

This is a powerful and lasting impact from a simple forty-minute session and a few follow-up tests. One of the researchers was disturbed by the implications, for "If such socially important values as equality and freedom can be altered to become more important to human subjects, they can surely be altered to also become less important. Who shall decide . . ." (Rokeach, 1971: 458).

ATTITUDES AND ACTIONS

Social psychologists have discovered several interesting relationships between attitudes and actions. Obviously, your attitudes affect your actions: if you like Fords, you will buy a Ford. Some of the other relationships are not so obvious.

Doing Is Believing

If you speak and act as if something is true, you yourself may come to believe it.

It turns out, for example, that if you like Fords but buy a Chevrolet for some reason (perhaps you can get a better deal on a Chevy), you will end up liking Fords less. In other words, actions affect attitudes.

In many instances, if you act and speak as though you have certain beliefs and feelings, you may begin to *really* feel and believe this way. For example, people accused of a crime have, under pressure of police interrogation, confessed to crimes they did not commit. They have confessed in order to relieve the pressure; but having said that they did the deed, they begin to believe that they really *are* guilty.

One explanation for this phenomenon comes from the theory of cognitive dissonance. If a person acts one way but thinks another, he or she will experience dissonance. To reduce the dissonance, the person will have to change either the behavior or the attitude. A similar explanation is that people have a need for **self-justification**—a need to justify their behavior.

In an experiment that demonstrated these principles, subjects were paid either one dollar or twenty dollars to tell another person that a boring experiment in which they both had to participate was really a lot of fun. Afterward, the experimenters asked the subjects how they felt about the experiment. They found that the subjects who had been paid twenty dollars to lie about the experiment continued to believe that it had been boring. Those who had been paid one dollar, however, came to believe that the experiment had actually been fairly enjoyable. These people had less reason to tell the lie, so they experienced more dissonance when they did so. To justify their lie, they had to believe that they had actually enjoyed the experiment (Festinger and Carlsmith, 1959).

The phenomenon of self-justification has serious implications. For example, how would you justify to yourself the fact that you had intentionally injured another human being? In another psychological experiment, subjects were led to believe that they had injured or hurt other subjects in some way (Glass, 1964). The aggressors were then asked how they felt about the victims they had just harmed. It was found that the aggressors had convinced themselves that they did not like the victim of their cruelty. In other words, the aggressors talked themselves into believing that their defenseless victims had deserved their injury. The aggressors also considered their victims to be less attractive after the experiment than before—their self-justification for hurting another person was something like, "Oh well, this person doesn't amount to much, anyway."

Self-Fulfilling Prophecy

Another relationship between attitudes and actions is rather subtle—but extremely widespread. It is possible, it seems, for a person to act in such a way as to make his or her attitudes come true. This phenomenon is called **self-fulfilling prophecy.** Suppose, for example, you are convinced that you are a bad cook. Every time you go into the kitchen, you start thinking poorly of yourself. Because you approach the task of baking a cake with great anxiety, you fumble the measurements, pour in too much milk, leave out an ingredient, and so on. As a result, your cake is a flop. You thus confirm that you *are* a bad cook.

Self-fulfilling prophecies can influence all kinds of human activity. Suppose you believe that people are basically friendly and generous. Whenever you approach other people, you are friendly and open. Because of your smile and positive attitude toward yourself and the world, people like you. Thus your attitude that people are friendly produces your friendly behavior, which in turn causes people to respond favorably toward you. But suppose you turn this example around. Imagine that you believe people are selfish and cold. Because of your negative attitude, you tend to avert your eyes from other people, to act gloomy, and to appear rather unfriendly. People think your actions are strange and, consequently, they act coldly toward you. Your attitude has produced the kind of behavior that makes the attitude come true.

Practical Implications

The psychological findings related to self-justification and self-fulfilling prophecy show that there is truth in the saying "Life is what you make it." What you do affects you directly, and it affects the way the world acts toward you. The fact that all people tend to justify their actions by changing their attitudes has several practical consequences. If you give in to pressure and act against your better judgment, you will be undermining your own beliefs. The next time you are in a similar situation, you will find it even harder to stand up for what you believe in because you will have begun to wonder whether you believe it yourself. If you want to strengthen your convictions about something, it is a good idea to speak and act on your beliefs at every opportunity. If you do make a mistake and act against your beliefs, you should admit that you are wrong and not try to justify yourself.

The phenomenon of self-fulfilling prophecy shows that the way the

Behavioral Confirmation. The text describes how beliefs can change actions through processes such as self-justification and the self-fulfilling prophecy. Our expectations can also affect other people's actions. This process is called *behavioral confirmation.*

For example, suppose you are led to believe that another person is friendly and outgoing. To find out more about that person, you would most likely ask that person questions an outgoing person would answer. "What kinds of things do you do with your friends?" "What do you do to have fun?"

Most likely you would get answers that describe the person's outgoing activities. Even a shy person who has only a few friends will think of some outgoing things, though probably not as many as an extroverted person would.

Furthermore, by discussing these activities, the person will actually start to *feel* and *act* more outgoing than he or she usually does. In this way the person's behavior will start to confirm your initial impression, even if that impression was not particularly accurate.

world seems to you may be a result of your own actions. Other people, who act differently, will have different experiences and produce different effects. When you find the world unsatisfactory, remember that to some extent, you are creating it. When you find the world a joyful place, remember, too, that it is making you happy partly because you believe that it can.

PERSUASION

Persuasion is a direct attempt to influence attitudes through the medium of communication. At one time or another everyone engages in persuasion. When a smiling student who is working her way through college by selling magazine subscriptions comes to the door, she attempts to persuade you that reading *Newsweek* or *Sports Illustrated* or *Ms.* will make you better informed and give you lots to talk about at parties. Parents often attempt to persuade a son or daughter to conform to their values about life. Similarly, some young people try to persuade their parents that all their friends' parents are buying them home computers. In each case, the persuader's main hope is that by changing the other person's attitudes he or she can change that person's behavior as well.

The Communication Process

Enormous amounts of time, money, and effort go into campaigns to persuade people to change their attitudes and behavior. Some succeed on a grand scale; others seem to have no effect. One of the most difficult questions social psychologists have tried to answer is: What makes a persuasive communication effective?

Figure 18.6
Successful advertising. This advertisement presents a powerfully emotional picture and headline to shock readers into attention and arouse their concern. It then gives some hard facts to further involve them in the subject matter.
Readers might have ignored the ad if it had simply said, ''Doctors need to know about current issues relevant to the medical profession. Subscribe to *Medical World News.*''

Sex in Advertising

Pick up any newspaper or magazine and you'll see dozens of scantily-clad beauties and rugged, sensual he-men trying to sell products in the best way they know how. As they drape themselves over automobiles and puff provocatively on their cigarettes, they tell consumers that sex and their product are a package deal.

This may sound like a message few of us could resist, but according to recent findings, our will power is stronger than advertisers think. Research has shown that sexy ads get readers' attention, but the wrong audience actually reads the message. More women than men read the ads in which a sexy woman appears, and more men than women read ads showing attractive men.

Researchers have also found that sex does not increase product recall, and may in fact get in the way of remembering a brand name. In one study, subjects were shown some ads containing sexy pictures and some without. One week after seeing the ads, subjects could remember more about the "nonsexy" products than they could about the "sexy" ones.

Results like these are sure to change at least some advertisers' approaches. But it will take a lot more than this to convince others that sex is not the advertiser's best friend.

For more details, see Duane P. Schultz, *Psychology in Use.* New York: Macmillan, 1979.

The communication process can be broken down into four parts. The **message** itself is only one part. It is also important to consider the **source** of the message, the **channel** through which it is delivered, and the **audience** that receives it.

The Source.   How a person sees the source, or originator, of a message may be a critical factor in his or her acceptance or rejection of it. The person receiving the message asks himself or herself two basic questions: Is the person giving the message trustworthy and sincere? Does he or she know anything about the subject? If the source seems reliable and knowledgeable, the message is likely to be accepted.

Suppose, for example, that you have written a paper criticizing a poem for your English class. A friend who reads the paper tells you about an article that praises the poem and asks you to reconsider your view. The article was written by Agnes Stearn, a student at a state teachers college. You might change your opinion—and you might not. But suppose your friend tells you the same positive critique was written by T. S. Eliot. The chances are that you would begin to doubt your own judgment. Three psychologists tried this experiment. Not surprisingly, many more students changed their minds about the poem when they thought the criticism was written by T. S. Eliot (Aronson, Turner, and Carlsmith, 1963).

A person receiving the message also asks: Do I like the source? If the communicator is respected and admired, people will tend to go along with

Figure 18.7
Winston Churchill, in a speech to the British House of Commons in 1940. Churchill's long record as a soldier (in India, South Africa, and in World War I) and as a political leader made him a source whose knowledge and trustworthiness were beyond question by the time he was needed to lead the fight against Hitler.

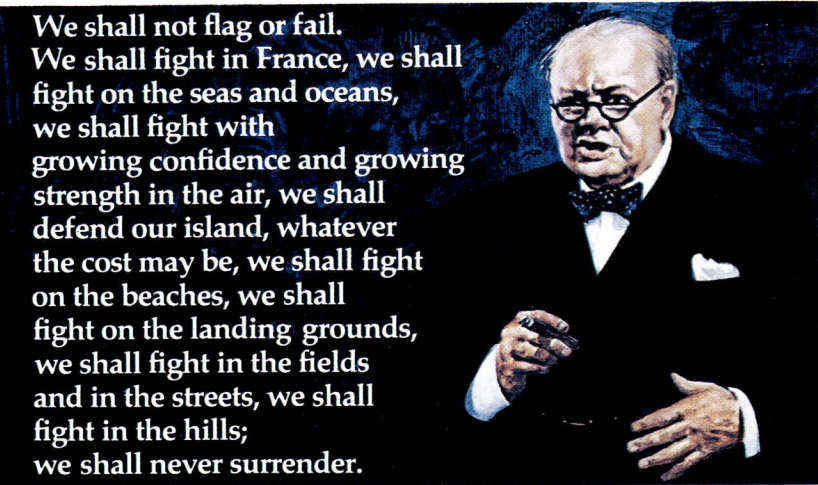

Figure 18.7
Winston Churchill, in a speech to the British House of Commons in 1940. Churchill's long record as a soldier (in India, South Africa, and in World War I) and as a political leader made him a source whose knowledge and trustworthiness were beyond question by the time he was needed to lead the fight against Hitler.

the message, either because they believe in his or her judgment or because they want to be like him or her. The identification phenomenon explains the frequent use of athletes in advertisements. Football players and Olympic champions are not (in most cases) experts on deodorants, electric razors, or milk. Indeed, when an athlete endorses a particular brand of deodorant on television, we all know he or she is doing it for the money. Nevertheless, the process of identification makes these sales pitches highly effective.

Similarly, people are much more likely to respond favorably to a physically attractive source than to one who does not make a good appearance. In the 1960 presidential campaign Richard Nixon apparently lost many votes as a result of his poor appearance on a televised debate with John F. Kennedy. During the 1968 campaign Nixon was coached on how to present a likable image to the camera. His campaign managers filmed him in informal settings, hired people to applaud and crowd around him, encouraged him to joke and smile more often, and even used make-up to erase the shadows that gave many people the impression that he had "shifty eyes" (McGinniss, 1970). Nixon, of course, won that campaign.

However, attempts to be friendly and personal can backfire. When a group of college students who opposed the war in Southeast Asia visited homes in the surrounding community in the hope of persuading townspeople to support their cause, they succeeded in further alienating residents. Why? Apparently the townspeople perceived the students as radicals and resented the invasion of their privacy (Nesbitt, 1972). When people dislike the individual or group delivering a message, they are likely to respond by taking the opposite point of view. This is known as the **boomerang effect.**

As the students' failure to persuade townspeople of the wrongfulness of the war suggests, people are more apt to agree with those who are *similar* to them (or who resemble what they would like to be) than with those who are not.

The Message.   Suppose two people with opposing viewpoints are trying to persuade you to agree with them. Suppose further that you like and trust both of them. In this situation the message becomes more important than the source. The persuasiveness of a message depends on the way in which it is composed and organized as well as on the actual content.

Should the message arouse emotion? Are people more likely to change their attitudes if they are afraid or angry or pleased? The answer is yes, but the most effective messages combine emotional appeal with factual information and argument. A communication that overemphasizes the emotional side of an issue may boomerang. If the message is too upsetting, it may force people to mobilize their defenses. For example, showing pictures of accident victims to people who have been arrested for drunken driving may convince them not to drive when they've been drinking. But if the film is so bloody that people are frightened or disgusted, they may also stop listening to the message. On the other hand, a communication that includes only logic and information may miss its mark because the audience does not relate the facts to their personal lives.

When presenting an argument, is it more effective to present both sides of an issue or only one side? For the most part, a two-sided communication is more effective because the audience tends to believe that the speaker is objective and fair-minded. A slight hazard of presenting opposing arguments is that they might undercut the message or suggest that the whole issue is too controversial to make a decision about.

People usually respond positively to a message that is structured and delivered in a dynamic way. But a communication that is forceful to the point of being pushy may produce negative results. People generally resent being pressured. If listeners infer from a message that they are being left with no choice but to agree with the speaker's viewpoint, they may reject an opinion for this reason alone.

The Channel.   Where, when, and how a message is presented also influences the audience's response. In general, personal contact is the most effective approach to an audience. For example, in one study in Ann Arbor, Michigan, 75 percent of voters who had been contacted personally voted in favor of a change in the city charter. Only 45 percent of those who had received the message in the mail and 19 percent of those who had only seen ads in the media voted for the change (Eldersveld and Dodge, 1954).

However, as we saw earlier, personal contact may boomerang: people may dislike the communicator or feel that they are being pressured. Besides, you can reach a great many more people through mailings and radio and television broadcasts than you can in person.

There is some evidence that television and films are more effective media of persuasion than printed matter. People tend to believe what they see and hear with their own senses (even if they know the information has been edited before it is broadcast). In one experiment, 51 percent of people who had watched a film could answer factual questions about the issue in question—compared to 29 percent of those who had only seen printed material. And more of the people who had viewed the film altered their viewpoints than did people who had read about the issue (Hovland,

PSYCHOLOGY and YOU

The Anchoring Effect. Most research on persuasion focuses on large efforts such as political and advertising campaigns. How can you, as an individual, persuade others?

One technique is *anchoring.* When people make judgments under conditions of uncertainty, they are often swayed by suggestions of what is appropriate. One study asked two groups of subjects how many African countries were in the United Nations. One group was asked, "Is it more or less than 65?" The other group was asked, "Is it more or less than 15?" On the average, the first group estimated about 40, the second group about 25. The suggested number serves as an anchor, or starting point, for people's estimates.

Examples of anchors are common. When street performers begin their acts, they often line their hats with dollar bills. People selling cars and houses start with a high price.

We've got over 300 good, steady jobs.

Jobs in construction, transportation, communications, computers.

Jobs for photographers, printers, truck drivers, teachers, typists, TV cameramen and repairmen. Cooks, electricians, medical aides, meteorologists. Motor and missile maintenance men.

Jobs for young men. And young women.

Jobs in Europe, Hawaii, Panama, Alaska. And just about any place in the States.

We'll train you to do the jobs. Train you well, in good schools, under excellent instructors, with the best equipment obtainable.

And you get full pay while you train.

You also get unusually good fringe benefits, including a chance to continue your education. In many cases at our expense. In all cases with at least 75% of your tuition paid.

And if you qualify we'll give you your choice of training. We'll put it in writing, before you sign up.

Today's Army wants to join you.

Figure 18.8
Audiences change from generation to generation, so the means of persuading them must also change. Attitudes toward the armed services, for example, have changed markedly since World War I, thus requiring army recruiters to alter their approach.

Lumsdaine, and Sheffield, 1949). But the most effective channel also depends in part on the audience.

The Audience. The audience includes all those people whose attitudes the communicator is trying to change. Being able to persuade people to alter their views depends on knowing who the audience is and why they hold the attitudes they do (Figure 18.8).

Suppose, for example, you are involved in a program to reduce the birth rate in a population that is outgrowing its food supply. The first step would be to inform people of various methods of birth control as well as how and where to obtain them. However, the fact that people know how to limit their families does not mean that they will do so. To persuade them to use available contraceptives, you need to know why they value large families. In some areas of the world, people have as many children as they can because they do not expect most babies to survive early childhood. In this case you might want to tie the family-planning campaign to programs of infant care. In some areas, children begin working at odd jobs at an early age and bring in needed income. In this case, you might want to promote an incentive system for families who limit themselves to two or three children.

If the people are not taking advantage of available means of birth control, you will want to know who is resisting. Perhaps men believe fathering a child is a sign of virility. Perhaps women consider motherhood an essential element of femininity. Perhaps both sexes see parenthood as a symbol of maturity and adulthood (see Coale, 1973). Knowing who your audience is and what motivates them is crucial.

One way to maximize the chances of persuasion is to capitalize on the audience's emotional needs. For example, one advertising researcher was able to help the Red Cross collect blood donations from men by analyzing their fears. He thought that men associated loss of blood with weakness and loss of manliness. He suggested that the Red Cross publish ads telling prospective donors how manly they were and offer donors pins shaped like drops of blood as medals for bravery. The campaign worked: blood donations from men increased sharply (Dichter, 1964).

The Sleeper Effect

Changes in attitudes are not always permanent. In fact, efforts at persuasion usually have their greatest impact immediately and then fade away. However, sometimes people seem to be persuaded by a message after a period of time has elapsed. This curious **sleeper effect** has been explained in several ways.

One explanation of the delayed-action impact depends on the tendency to retain the message but forget the source. As time goes by, a positive source no longer holds power to persuade nor does a negative source undercut the message. When the source is negative and the memory of the source fades, the message then "speaks for itself" and more people may accept it (Kelman and Hovland, 1953).

Perhaps the original message also sensitizes people to subsequent information and events that reinforce the ideas. Repetition is a valuable tool, and the sleeper effect may simply be the result of hearing or reading similar messages from a number of different sources (Middlebrook, 1974).

It may also be that it simply takes time for people to change their minds. As the message "sinks in," attitudes change more. A dramatic example of this was the experiment mentioned earlier in which students who were made aware of inconsistencies in their values concerning civil rights changed their ideas more after fifteen to seventeen months than after three weeks.

The Inoculation Effect

What can you do to resist persuasion? Research has shown that people can be educated to resist attitude change. This technique can be compared to an inoculation (McGuire, 1970). Inoculation against persuasion works in much the same way as inoculation against certain diseases. When a person is vaccinated he is given a weakened or dead form of the disease-causing agent, which stimulates his body to manufacture defenses. Then, if that person is attacked by a more potent form of the agent, his defenses make him or her immune to infection. Similarly, a person who has resisted a mild attack on her beliefs is ready to defend herself against an onslaught that might otherwise have overwhelmed her.

The **inoculation effect** can be explained in two ways: it motivates the person to defend her beliefs more strongly, and it gives her some practice in defending those beliefs. The most vulnerable attitudes you have, therefore, are the ones that you have never had to defend. For example, you

People expect other people to think like they do.

Fact. Common sense tells you that people are unique and hold different values and attitudes. Yet we often expect other people to think and act like we do and are surprised when they do not. This process is called the *false consensus effect.*

The most vulnerable attitudes are those you have never had to defend.

might find yourself hard put to defend your faith in democracy or in the healthfulness of beefsteak if you have never had these beliefs questioned.

USING PSYCHOLOGY

Promoting Energy Conservation

Americans use—and waste—more energy than any other people on earth. The fuel crisis, ad campaigns on the need to conserve energy, and the steadily rising cost of gasoline, oil, and electricity have hardly made a dent in our rate of energy use. How can Americans be persuaded to conserve energy?

Three psychologists attempted to answer this question with an extremely simple experiment (Kohlenberg, Phillips, and Proctor, 1976). The demand for electricity tends to peak in the morning and again in the late afternoon, when people take showers and use vacuum cleaners, washing machines, and other electrical appliances. Unlike other forms of energy, electricity cannot be stored. Power companies therefore have to maintain generators that are in full use for only a few hours each day. One solution to the growing demand for electricity is to build more generators. The other solution is to change people's habits, cutting back the peak demand.

Kohlenberg and his colleagues tried three techniques for convincing volunteer families to reduce their electricity use during peak periods. The first was to provide information. Researchers explained the problem, asked the families to try to cut back, and suggested how they might do so. Monitors installed in each house indicated that this approach had little or no effect. (Considering that all the families were conservation-minded, this was surprising.)

Next, the researchers tried feedback. A bulb that lit up whenever the family approached peak consumption levels was placed in each house. Immediate and direct evidence of electricity overuse was expected to help the families cut back. Although somewhat more effective than information alone, feedback did not break the families' habits of electricity use.

Finally, the researchers gave the experimental households an incentive. Families would earn twice the amount of their electricity bill if they reduced their peak use 100 percent, the full amount if they cut back 50 percent, and so on. This strategy worked. None of the families reduced their peak use 100 percent, but all did cut back. A follow-up revealed that all returned to the convenience of using appliances during peak hours after the incentive was removed.

What this simple experiment demonstrated was that campaigns to reduce the use of electricity during peak periods are largely ineffective. However, if power companies were to provide incentives—say, reduced rates for families that cut back during the peaks—they might save themselves the cost of building and maintaining partially used plants.

SOCIAL INFLUENCE

Brainwashing

The most extreme means of changing attitudes involves a combination of psychological gamesmanship and physical torture, aptly called **brainwashing.** The most extensive studies of brainwashing have been done on Westerners who had been captured by the Chinese during the Korean War and subjected to "thought reform." Psychiatrist Robert Jay Lifton interviewed several dozen prisoners released by the Chinese, and, from their accounts, he outlined the methods used to break down people's convictions and introduce new patterns of belief, feeling, and behavior (1963).

The aim in brainwashing is as much to create a new person as to change attitudes. So the first step is to strip away all identity and subject the person to intense social pressure and physical stress. Prison is a perfect setting for this process. The person is isolated from social support, is a number not a name, is clothed like everyone else, and can be surrounded by people who have had their thoughts "reformed" and are contemptuous of "reactionaries." So long as the prisoner holds out, he is treated with contempt or exhorted to confess by his fellow prisoners. He is interrogated past the point of exhaustion by his captors, and is humiliated and discomfited by being bound hand and foot at all times, even during meals or elimination. Any personal information the prisoner uses to justify himself is turned against him as evidence of his guilt.

At some point, the prisoner realizes that resistance is impossible; the pressures are simply intolerable. Resistance gives way to cooperation, but only as a means of avoiding any more demoralization. The prisoner is rewarded for cooperating. Cooperation involves confessing to crimes against the people in his former way of life.

Throughout the process his cell mates are an integral part of the brainwashing team, berating him at first, then warming to him after his confession. For most of his waking hours, the prisoner is part of a marathon group therapy session built on Marxist ideology. The prisoner is asked not only to interpret his current behavior that way but also to reinterpret his life before capture. Guilt is systematically aroused and defined by Marxist standards. What the prisoner does is to learn a new version of his life, and his confession, provided at first to get some relief from the isolation and pain, becomes more elaborate, coherent, and ideologically based. And with every "improvement" in his attitudes, prison life is made a little more pleasant. Finally, by a combination of threat, peer pressure, systematic rewards, and other psychological means, the prisoner comes to believe his

PSYCHOLOGY and YOU

Psychological Warfare. Psychological warfare refers to any activities and techniques designed to demoralize enemy troops and persuade them to give up the fight. Both sides used psychological warfare extensively in the Persian Gulf war.

As American troops waited in the Saudi Arabian desert for the war to begin, an Iraqi radio announcer nicknamed "Baghdad Betty" tried to persuade them that they would be crushed by Iraqi might. After the war started, Iraq forced captured Allied pilots to denounce the war on TV.

The Allied forces dropped leaflets on Iraqi soldiers and issued false reports of Iraqi defections in an attempt to convince Iraqi soldiers to surrender. In addition, underground radio stations broadcast war news into Iraq. Allied forces also armed resistance fighters in Iraqi-occupied Kuwait so they could wage a secret war against Iraq. No one knows how effective psychological warfare is, but military leaders consider it an essential part of modern warfare.

confession. But as one survivor recalled, "it is a special kind of belief . . . you accept it—in order to avoid trouble—because every time you don't agree, trouble starts again" (Lifton, 1963: 31). These techniques appear to succeed only as long as the person remains a prisoner.

It's hard to say just where persuasion ends and brainwashing begins. (Some researchers believe that brainwashing is just a very intense form of persuasion.) Drawing this line has become particularly important to the courts—from the much publicized case of Patty Hearst in 1977 to lawsuits over deprogramming members of religious cults.

Margaret Thaler Singer (1979) has studied over 300 former members of religious cults. Many had joined during periods of depression and confusion. The cults offered structure and gave life meaning: they provided friends and ready-made decisions about marriage and careers, dating and sex. Being cut off from the outside world and intensive indoctrination into a new ideology often increased the new member's sense of commitment.

When people become dissatisfied and quit, many have trouble readjusting to the world they left behind. Among the problems Singer has observed are depression, loneliness, indecisiveness, passivity, guilt, and

Figure 18.9
Members of the Hare Krishna cult.

blurring of mental activity. The average person takes six to eighteen months to return to normal.

Group Pressure to Conform

Most Americans claim they would never become supporters of Hitler if they had lived in Germany during World War II. Yet a nation of Germans did. Under pressure from others, individuals at least complied with the prevailing attitudes. Everyone conforms to group pressure in many ways. Have you ever come home and surprised your parents by wearing the latest fad in clothing? Possibly the conversation that followed went something like this:

"How can you go around looking like that?"

"But everyone dresses like this."

Psychologist Solomon Asch (1952) designed a famous experiment to test conformity to pressure from one's peers. He found that people may conform to other people's ideas of the truth, even when they disagree. The following is what you would have experienced if you had been a subject in this experiment.

You and seven other students meet in a classroom for an experiment on visual judgment. You are shown a card with one line on it. You are then shown another card containing three lines and are asked to pick the one that is the same length as the first line. One of the three is exactly the same length and is easy to determine. The other two lines are obviously different (Figure 18.10). The experiment begins uneventfully. The subjects announce their answers in the order in which they are seated in the room. You happen to be seventh, and one person follows you. On the first comparison, every person chooses the same matching line. The second set of cards is displayed, and once again the group is unanimous. The discriminations seem easy, and you prepare for what you expect will be a rather boring experiment.

On the third trial, there is an unexpected disturbance. You are quite certain that line 2 is the one that matches the standard. Yet the first person in the group announces confidently that line 1 is the correct match. Then, the second person follows suit and he, too, declares that the answer is line 1. So do the third, fourth, fifth, and sixth subjects. Now it is your turn. You are suddenly faced with two contradictory pieces of information: the evidence of your own senses tells you that one answer is clearly correct, but the unanimous and confident judgments of the six preceding subjects tell you that you are wrong.

The dilemma persists through eighteen trials. On twelve of the trials, the other group members unanimously give an answer that differs from what you clearly perceive to be correct. It is only at the end of the experimental session that you learn the explanation for the confusion. The seven other subjects were all actors, and they had been instructed to give incorrect answers on those twelve trials (Figure 18.11).

How do most subjects react to this situation? Asch found that almost one-third of his fifty subjects conformed at least half the time. These conformers he called the "yielders." Most yielders explained to Asch afterward

Figure 18.10
These two cards were shown to subjects in one trial of Asch's experiment on conformity. The actual discrimination is easy.

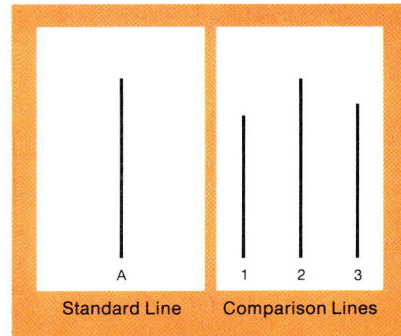

Standard Line   Comparison Lines

Figure 18.11

Photographs taken during Asch's experiment on conformity. Subject 6 is the only real subject; the others are confederates of the experimenter (seen at the right in the first photograph). The subject listens to the others express identical judgments that differ from his own. He is in a dilemma: does he express the judgment he knows to be correct and risk being different from the group, or does he conform to the group's judgment?

that they knew which line was correct but that they yielded to group pressure in order not to appear different from the others. Asch called those who did not conform "independents." They gave the correct answer despite group pressure. Why so much conformity? According to one theory, most children are taught the overriding importance of being liked and of being accepted. Conformity is the standard means of gaining this approval.

One of the most important findings of Asch's experiment was that if even one person failed to conform to the group's judgment, the subject was able to stick to his own perceptions. It seems that it is hardest to stand alone. Later researchers have shown that, under some conditions, a minority view can come to win over the larger group (Moscovici, 1976).

Obedience to Authority

The influence other people have on your attitudes and actions is considerable. Sometimes this influence is indirect and subtle; at other times it is quite direct. People may simply tell you what to believe and what to do. Under what conditions do you obey them?

Everyone in this society has had experiences with various authorities, such as parents, teachers, police officers, managers, judges, clergymen, and military officers. **Obedience** to these authorities can be either useful or destructive. For instance, obeying the orders of a doctor or firefighter in an emergency would be constructive. Psychologists are more interested, however, in the negative aspects of obedience. They know from such cases in history as German Nazism and American atrocities in Vietnam that individuals frequently obey irrational commands. In fact, people often obey authority even when obedience goes against their conscience and their whole system of morality.

The most famous investigation of obedience was conducted in 1963 by social psychologist Stanley Milgram. The experiment was set up as follows. Two subjects appeared for each session. They were told that they would be participating in an experiment to test the effects of punishment on memory. One of the subjects was to be the "teacher" and the other, the "learner." (In reality, the learner was not a volunteer subject; he was Milgram's accomplice.) The teacher was to read a list of words into a microphone for the learner, who would be in a nearby room, to memorize. If the learner failed to recite the list back correctly, the teacher was to administer an electric shock. The alleged purpose of the experiment was to test whether the shock would have any effect on learning. In actuality, however, Milgram wanted to discover how far the teacher would follow his instructions; how much shock would he be willing to give a fellow human being?

As the experiment began, the learner continually gave wrong answers, and the teacher began to administer the prescribed shocks from an impressive-looking shock generator. The generator had a dial that ranged from 15 volts, which was labeled "Slight Shock," to 450 volts, which was labeled "Danger: Severe Shock." After each of the learner's mistakes, the teacher was told to increase the voltage by one level, thus increasing the severity of the shock. The teacher believed that the learner was receiving these shocks because he had seen the learner being strapped into a chair in the other room and had watched electrodes being attached to the learner's hands. In reality, however, the accomplice was receiving no shocks at all from the equipment.

As the experiment progressed, the learner made many mistakes and the teacher had to give increasingly severe shocks. At 300 volts the learner

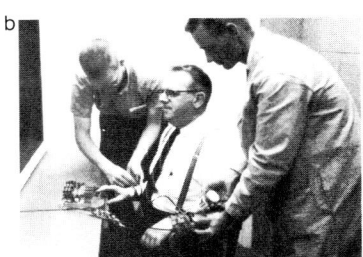

Figure 18.12
Stanley Milgram's experiment on obedience. (a) The fake "shock generator" used by the "teacher." (b) The "learner" is connected to the shock apparatus. (c) Milgram explains the procedure to the "teacher." (d) This subject refuses to shock the "learner" any further and angrily arises in protest. (e) Milgram explains the truth about the experiment. (© 1965 by Stanley Milgram. From the film *Obedience*. Distributed by New York University Film Library.)

pounded on the wall in protest and refused to provide any further answers. At this point the experimenter instructed the subject to treat the absence of an answer as a wrong answer and to continue the procedure. The experiment ended either when the maximum 450 volts was administered or when the teacher refused to administer any more shocks. If at any point the teacher indicated that he wanted to stop, the experimenter calmly told him to continue: "Whether the learner likes it or not," the experimenter asserted, "you must go on until he has learned all the word pairs correctly."

Before Milgram began this study, he had checked with forty psychiatrists in order to get their predictions. These experts thought that most people would not continue beyond the 150-volt level and that only one in one thousand would actually give the highest shock. Yet in Milgram's experiments more than half of the forty subjects gave the full shock!

These subjects were not sadists. Many of them showed signs of extreme tension and discomfort during the session, and they often told the experimenter that they would like to stop. But in spite of these feelings, they continued to obey the experimenter's commands. They were ordinary men—salesmen, engineers, postal workers—placed in an unusual situation.

What accounts for this surprisingly high level of obedience? Part of the answer is that the experimenter represents a legitimate authority. People assume that such an authority knows what he is doing, even when his instructions seem to run counter to their own standards of moral behavior.

Milgram's subjects could have walked out at any time—they had nothing to lose by leaving. Nevertheless, social conditioning for obeying legitimate authorities is so strongly ingrained that people often lack the words or the ways to do otherwise. Simply getting up and leaving would have violated powerful unwritten rules of acceptable social behavior.

Subsequent experiments showed that there were three ways in which subjects could be helped to resist authority in this situation. One was the removal of the physical presence of the experimenter. Even more effective was putting the subject face-to-face with his victim. The third and most effective variation of the experiment was to provide other "teachers" to support the subject's defiance of the experimenter (Milgram, 1964).

Another experiment that caused ordinary people to act in extraordinary ways was performed by Philip Zimbardo and his colleagues in the early 1970s. Zimbardo randomly divided male volunteers, who were mostly college students, into two groups: "prisoners" and "prison guards." He sent both groups to live in a simulated "prison" set up in the basement of a Stanford University building. He gave the "guards" instructions simply to maintain order. Within two days, most of the "guards" had become intoxicated with power; they acted cruelly toward the prisoners, often without any reason. At the same time, the "prisoners" began showing signs of extreme stress, often acting subdued and depressed. The emotional reactions were so extreme that the two-week experiment was ended after only six days. It seems that the prison environment was much stronger than individual personalities. Although the subjects in this experiment were emotionally mature and stable, the roles these individuals adopted dramatically changed the way they acted. There may be other situations in everyday life that may cause us and those around us to act in ways we do not expect.

KEY TERMS

- attitudes
- audience
- authoritarian personality
- boomerang effect
- brainwashing
- channel
- cognitive dissonance

- compliance
- discrimination
- identification
- inoculation effect
- internalization
- message
- obedience

- persuasion
- prejudice
- scapegoat
- self-fulfilling prophecy
- self-justification
- sleeper effect
- source

SUMMARY

1. An attitude is an enduring set of beliefs, feelings, and tendencies to act toward people or things in predisposed ways. Culture, parents, peers, and personal experience shape a person's attitudes.

2. The processes involved in attitude formation include compliance (acting as though one has a certain attitude in order to avoid discomfort or rejection and win approval), identification (the adoption of new attitudes as a result of a strong emotional attachment to another person or group), and internalization (the incorporation of attitudes into a person's belief system).

3. Prejudice is a judgment of people on the basis of stereotypes. Prejudice seems to have a number of causes, and it is perpetuated by social institutions. Discrimination is the unequal treatment of people.

4. People have a need for cognitive consistency—that is, a need to fit their attitudes together into a nonconflicting set of beliefs. People who simultaneously hold two or more opposing attitudes experience cognitive dissonance. In order to reduce dissonance, they change one or more of the attitudes.

5. People's actions affect their attitudes. People often justify actions that go against their beliefs by changing their beliefs. Self-fulfilling prophecy is the phenomenon of acting in such a way as to make one's attitudes come true.

6. Persuasion is a direct attempt to change attitudes and behavior through the process of communication.

7. Four components of the communications process are the source, the message, the channel, and the audience. For attitude change to occur, the source must be trustworthy and sincere, the message should combine fact and emotional arousal, the channel should be appropriate to the message, and the audience must be receptive.

8. The effects of persuasion are usually short-lived. However, a "sleeper effect," in which attitudes change more as time passes, can occur.

9. People can be educated to resist persuasion by hearing a mild attack on their beliefs. This spurs them to defend their attitudes more strongly and gives them practice in their defense. The inoculation effect helps people resist stronger attacks on their beliefs that may follow.

10. The most extreme means of attitude change is called brainwashing. First, identity is destroyed and the will to resist is broken. Then intensive indoctrination is combined with rewards for compliance. New attitudes are drilled into the subject. The effects seem to diminish once the victim returns to his former life.

11. Asch's experiment showed that conformity to pressure from peers may be so strong that people will question or deny their own senses.

12. One of the strongest ways in which social influence is exerted is through authority. Obedience to authority can be either useful or destructive. Milgram's experiment showed that social conditioning produces such a strong tendency toward obeying legitimate authorities that people may easily be induced to do harm to others against their conscience or better judgment.

REVIEW QUESTIONS

1. What is an attitude? What are the three elements of an attitude?

2. What are the three processes involved in changing an attitude? Which process is based on emotional attachment to another person? Which process is the most lasting and has nothing to do with other people?

3. Can prejudice be defined as a negative judgment toward another group of people? What is the name given by researchers to prejudiced persons who share a number of traits in common? According to these researchers, why do these people use stereotypes? Can a person discriminate against another person without being prejudiced?

4. What factors are important in reducing intergroup hostility through integration?

5. What is the name Leon Festinger gave to the uncomfortable feelings that arise when a person experiences conflicting thoughts, beliefs, attitudes, or feelings?

6. What cognitive act are people engaging in when they convince themselves that they did not like the victim of their aggressive act? Actions can affect attitudes and attitudes can affect actions. What is this latter phenomenon called?

7. What are the four parts of the communication process? What two questions do people ask themselves about the source of a communication? If you listen to the argument of a person whom you dislike and then take the opposite point of view, what effect has just taken place?

8. What will be the effect on a listener if you use a very emotional appeal or if you pressure her to adopt your point of view?

9. How can the sleeper effect be explained? The inoculation effect?

10. What are the steps used to brainwash a person?

11. What percentage of people were "yielders" in Solomon Asch's conformity experiments? Why do people conform? What event will reduce conformity?

12. What are the three ways in which subjects were helped to resist the authoritative experimenter in Stanley Milgram's experiment?

ACTIVITIES

1. Collect magazine ads of ten different brands of cigarettes. Using a scale of 0 to 10, have subjects rate the cigarettes as being weak or strong—0 being the weakest and 10 being the strongest. Have different subjects rate the same brands on the same scale for masculinity or femininity—0 being the most feminine and 10 being the most masculine. Now average your scores. What conclusions can you draw from your results? (From Sol Gordon, *Psychology and You,* New York: Oxford Book Company, 1972, p. 452.)

2. Collect samples of advertising that depict various techniques of persuasion—identification, social approval, fear of disaster, and so on. Analyze each ad on the basis of effectiveness and what type of person it might appeal to.

3. Do researchers have the right to fool their subjects, even in the name of science? Consider, for example, the effects on Milgram's subjects of believing they had harmed a fellow subject by obliging the order of a stranger. Do you think this experiment was valuable for allowing the subjects to realize the extent of their conformity? If you answered the first question no and the second yes, how would you reconcile these two conflicting attitudes?

4. Choose some issue on which you have a strong opinion. If you were given an unlimited budget, how would you go about persuading people to agree with you? Describe the sources you would employ, the channels you would use, the content of your message, and the audience you would try to reach.

5. To what extent does advertising influence your choice of foods? Find several people who prefer butter to margarine. Ask them why they prefer butter. If they say it tastes better, then ask them to participate in an experiment to test their claims. Get several brands of both butter and margarine and spread them lightly on the same kind of crackers or toast. Blindfold your subjects and provide them with a glass of water to rinse their mouths whenever they wish. Ask them to identify the samples. Run through the series about four times, varying the order of presentation. Try similar experiments with people who prefer certain brands of milk, cola, or coffee.

6. One of the primary objectives of advertising is to get the viewers/listeners to remember the product. To what extent do you think familiarity with brand names influences your choices in the market? How many television commercials do you find obnoxious? Do you find that you remember the products advertised in "obnoxious" commercials better than you remember products that appear in less offensive advertisements? Do you think there is a possibility that some commercials are deliberately offensive?

7. Experiments have shown that enforced integration in housing has resulted in less interracial hostility. What is your opinion of legally enforcing racial integration in housing, employment, and schools?

8. Make a list of ten or more nationalities, religions, races, and occupations. Have friends or family members list five things that come to mind when these groups are mentioned. What are your conclusions?

9. Parents have an early influence on their children's attitudes and beliefs. Check the degree of similarity between your parents' views and your view on selected issues. First, generate a list of ten of your beliefs on issues such as political affiliation, nuclear energy, mandatory retirement, equal pay, and paternity leave. Then ask one of your parents whether he or she agrees with your statements. Use a five-point scale ranging from 1 (strongly agree) to 5 (strongly disagree). Notice the similarity or dissimilarity between your beliefs and those of your parents.

10. Research psychologists seek to understand and control human behavior; their overall goal is to promote healthy psychological development of individuals. Through their efforts, however, they have identified a variety of tools that are effective in socially controlling people through persuasion. Organize a class debate to answer the question, "Is it ethically acceptable for people to use techniques of psychological control to sell merchandise?" Gather support for your views and present them to your class.

11. A stereotype is a shorthand, overly simplified description of a group of people, which influences attitudes. People can acquire stereotypes from their social interactions with others, from watching television, or from elsewhere. Examine the stereotypes that have emerged about teenagers by asking a group of adults to describe teenagers. Have them complete the open-ended statement, "Teenagers are . . . ," as many times as they can. Ask at least eight to give you responses. Then compile the statements and see whether you can pick out stereotypes of teenagers. How might adults' stereotyped views of teenagers affect the way they act toward them? How can stereotypes be changed?

Psychological Research

CHAPTER *19*
Research Methods

CHAPTER *20*
Statistical Evaluation

CHAPTER *21*
Psychology: Approaching the
Twenty-First Century

Figure 19.1 Psychologists' research findings help us better understand our behaviors, perceptions, and attitudes.

Objectives: *After studying this chapter, you should be able to*
- explain the process of psychological research.
- identify and describe the different types of psychological research.
- describe some of the methodological hazards of psychological research.

Research Methods

In this chapter we go behind the scenes to see how psychologists learn about what they don't already know. We poke into laboratories where they are conducting experiments, follow them on surveys, and expose some of the research problems psychologists have.

The surprise is that psychologists do what most people do in everyday life—only more carefully and more systematically. When you turn on the television and the picture is out of focus, you *experiment* with different knobs and dials until you find the one that works. When you ask a number of friends about a movie you are thinking of seeing, you are conducting an informal *survey*. Of course, there is more to doing scientific research than turning dials at random or asking friends what they think. Over the years psychologists, like other scientists, have transformed these everyday techniques for gathering and analyzing information into more precise tools.

As described in Chapter 1, researchers must begin by asking a specific question about a limited topic. The next step is to look for evidence.

Gathering Data
Samples • Correlations and Explanations • Experiments • Naturalistic Observation • Case Studies • Surveys • Longitudinal Studies • Cross-cultural Studies

Traps in Doing Psychological Research and How to Avoid Them
The Self-fulfilling Prophecy • The Double-Blind Procedure • Observer Effects

Conclusions

GATHERING DATA

How do psychologists collect information about the topic they've chosen to study? The method a researcher uses partly depends on the research topic. For example, a social psychologist who is studying the effects of group pressure is likely to conduct an experiment. A psychologist who is interested in personality theories might begin with intensive case studies of individuals. But whatever approach to gathering data a psychologist selects, he or she must make certain basic decisions in advance.

Samples

Suppose a psychologist wants to know how the desire to get into college affects the attitudes of high-school juniors and seniors. It would be impossible to study every junior and senior in the country. There are just too many. Instead, the researcher would select a **sample,** a relatively small group out of the total **population** under study (in this case, all high-school juniors and seniors).

Choosing a sample can be tricky. A sample must be *representative* of the population a researcher is studying. For example, if you wanted to know how tall American men are, you would want to make certain that your sample did not include a disproportionately large number of professional basketball players. This sample would be *biased;* it would not represent American men in general.

The editors of *Literary Digest* learned about sample bias the hard way. Before the 1936 presidential election, the magazine conducted a massive telephone survey to find out whether voters favored Franklin Roosevelt or Alf Landon. Based on the results of this poll, the *Digest* predicted that Landon would win by a landslide. However, when the votes were counted on election night, it was Roosevelt who won by a landslide. What went wrong? The magazine had only questioned people who appeared on their subscription rolls or who were listed in the telephone book. In those Depression days, conservatives usually subscribed to this magazine, and only the affluent could afford the luxury of a telephone. And these people tended to be Republicans. The *Digest*'s sample did not represent the views of American voters; it was biased toward Landon.

There are two ways to avoid a biased sample. One is to take a purely

Figure 19.2
A survey researcher interviewing a family that is part of the *sample*, the relatively small group selected from the total population under study, for an experiment.

random sample, so that each individual within the scope of the research has an *equal chance* of being represented. For example, a psychologist might choose every twentieth name on school enrollment lists for a study of schoolchildren in a particular town. Random sampling is like drawing names or numbers out of a hat while blindfolded.

The second way to avoid bias is deliberately to pick individuals who represent the various subgroups in the population being studied. For example, the psychologist doing research on schoolchildren might select students of both sexes, of varying ages, of all social classes, and from all neighborhoods. This is called a **stratified sample.**

The size of the sample may also be important. If the sample is too small, the results will be meaningless. For example, a pollster who wants to know what Democrats think about a particular candidate will have to question a relatively large number of people. Why? Because Democrats vary considerably in their political attitudes. Northern and southern, rural and urban, male and female Democrats often disagree. If the pollster interviews only six of the millions of Democrats in the country, the results will not reflect these differences. In most general surveys aimed at large populations, the researcher questions about a thousand people. However, a sample of one hundred may be sufficient *if* those one hundred individuals represent the population as a whole. Indeed, if Democrats were all of one mind, it would only be necessary to interview one!

Sampling techniques apply to the collection of data as well as to the choice of subjects for study. A psychologist who wants to learn how children react to their first years at school might observe them every tenth day (a random sample). Alternatively, he or she might select typical experiences and spend several weeks observing them when they arrive at school, playing alone and in groups, with and without supervision, at different activities inside and outside. This would be a stratified sample of observations.

Correlations and Explanations

A researcher may simply want to observe people or other animals and record these observations in a descriptive study. More often, however, researchers want to examine the *relationship* between two sets of observations—say, between students' grades and the number of hours they sleep.

Scientists use the word **correlation** to describe the degree of relatedness between two sets of data (Figure 19.3). Sometimes the relationship is quite close. For example, there is a **positive correlation** between IQ scores and academic success. High IQ scores tend to go with high grades; low IQ scores tend to go with low grades. On the other hand, there is a **negative correlation** between smoking cigarettes and living a long, healthy life. The more a person smokes, the fewer years he or she may live. In this case, a high rank on one measure tends to go with a low rank on the other.

Establishing a correlation is useful because it enables scientists to make relatively accurate *predictions.* Knowing there is a positive correlation between IQ and academic success, you can predict that a person with a high IQ will do well in school. You won't be right all the time: some people with high IQs do poorly in school. But you will be right most of the time.

Figure 19.3
This series of drawings shows a correlation between the woman's sadness and the man's anger. But is one causing the other? Not necessarily. The woman's sadness may be causing the man's anger; his anger may be causing her sadness; or they may both be responding to a third factor.

Similarly, you might predict that a person with high grades has a high IQ. Here, again, you will be right more often than you will be wrong.

But people often confuse correlations with explanations. Instead of looking at a correlation as a comparison of two things, they think of it as a cause-and-effect relationship. Some years ago, for example, medical researchers discovered a high correlation between cancer and drinking milk. It seemed that the number of cancer cases was increasing in areas where people drink a lot of milk (such as New England) but that cancer was rare in areas where they do not (such as Ceylon). These data suggested to many people that milk causes cancer.

However, when researchers analyzed these data further they found a third factor was involved. Cancer usually strikes people in middle age or later. As a result, cancer is more common in places where people enjoy a high standard of living and live longer than in places where people tend to die at an earlier age. Thus drinking milk is related to cancer, but only because they are both related to a high standard of living. Milk does not cause cancer, but they may be correlated.

As this example illustrates, a correlation between two things may or *may not* indicate a cause-and-effect relationship. Suppose you were told there is a positive correlation between the number of Popsicles sold by ice-cream vendors at swimming pools and the number of people admitted to hospitals for heat stroke. Would you conclude that Popsicles cause heat stroke? To test their hypotheses about cause-and-effect relationships, researchers must turn to experiments.

Experiments

Why would a researcher choose experimentation over other research methods? Because it enables the investigator to *control* the situation and to decrease the possibility that unnoticed, outside factors will influence the results.

This is why, for example, social psychologists Kenneth Gergen, Mary Gergen, and William Barton (1973) put groups of six and seven student volunteers who did not know each other in a dark room for an hour, told them they could do whatever they liked, then photographed their activities with infrared cameras and recorded their conversations (Figure 19.4). What was the purpose of this experiment? To test the hypothesis that a group of

Figure 19.4
The Gergen, Gergen, and Barton experiment. The experimental group was placed in a dark room (darkness is the independent variable), and the amount of talking, moving, and touching was recorded. A control group was placed in an identical room, but with normal light. Again talking, moving, and touching were measured.

strangers left alone in a dark room will do and say things they would not do and say in a lighted room. Darkness provides a cloak of anonymity. The researchers thought that if people can't see each other, they won't worry about being recognized after the experiment and so will be uninhibited. The experiment was designed to prove or disprove this hypothesis. This is the main purpose of psychological studies and experiments—to develop a **hypothesis** or refine and test previous ones.

In designing and reporting experiments, psychologists think in terms of **variables**—that is, conditions and behaviors that are subject to variation or change. In the experiment we are describing, the two significant variables were the amount of light in the room and the amount of conversation, movement, and touching in each of the groups. There are two types of variables: independent and dependent. The **independent variable** is the one experimenters deliberately control so they can observe its effects. Here, the independent variable is the amount of light in the room. The **dependent variable** is the one that researchers believe will be affected by the independent variable. Here, conversation, movement, and touching were the dependent variables. The researchers thought darkness would influence these behaviors.

Of course, there is always a chance that the very fact of participating in an experiment will change the way people act. For this reason, Gergen, Gergen, and Barton put similar groups of students in a lighted room, told them they could do whatever they liked, and photographed and recorded their behavior. Subjects such as these form the **control group.** Subjects who undergo the **experimental treatment**—here, turning off the lights—are called the **experimental group.**

A control group is necessary in all experiments. Without it, a researcher cannot be sure the experimental group is reacting to what he or she thinks it is reacting to—a change in the independent variable. By comparing the way control and experimental groups behaved in this experiment, the researchers could determine whether darkness did in fact influence behavior and how.

What were the results of this experiment? In the lighted room students remained seated (about three feet apart) for most of the hour and kept up a continuous conversation. No one touched anyone else. In the dark room, the students moved around. Although conversation tended to slack off after half an hour or so, there was a great deal of touching—by accident and on purpose. In fact, half of the subjects in the experimental group found themselves hugging another person. Thus the researchers' hypothesis was supported. Anonymity does to some extent remove inhibitions against letting conversation die out and against touching, even hugging a stranger.

Replication. The results of this experiment do not constitute the final word on the subject, however. Psychologists do not fully accept the results of their own or other people's studies until they have been **replicated**—that is, duplicated by at least one other psychologist with different subjects. Why? Because there is always a chance that some unnoticed factor in the original experiment was atypical. For example, perhaps the subjects in the experimental group just happened to be naturally very outgoing.

Confounds. When psychologists design experiments, they want the experimental group and the control group to differ *only* in the independent variable. Anything else that differs between the experimental group and the control group is a *confound*.

There are many examples of confounds. In studies of therapeutic effectiveness, for instance, the experimental group (patients who receive the treatment procedure) is usually compared to a wait-list control group (patients who remain on the treatment waiting list for the duration of the study). While these two groups differ in the treatment they receive, they differ in other ways as well. The experimental group receives attention from the research staff, a feeling of belonging to a specified group, and a knowledge of contributing to science. These factors are all confounds, and any of them may affect their behavior. To address these confounds, researchers often run "attention control groups" that receive the same treatment as the experimental group except for the actual therapy.

**Controlled experiments
are better than
naturalistic observation.**

Fiction. Many psychologists
prefer the greater degree of
control that is possible in experiments. However, this control comes at the price of
environmental realism, what
psychologists term *ecological
validity*. Psychology needs
many types of studies, including experiments and natural
observations, to prosper as a
science.

One example will illustrate why replication is so important. In the mid-
1960s, Neal Miller and Leo DiCara (1967) stunned the psychological and
medical world by reporting that they had trained rats to control their heart
rates. (Before the experiment, researchers believed that animals had no
control over the autonomic nervous system.) But all attempts to replicate
Miller and DiCara's study failed—including their own. What went wrong?
To date, no one has found the answer.

Sometimes, a second researcher purposely changes one or more variables of the original study. For example, he or she may use middle-aged
people instead of college students as subjects. The goal is to find out
whether the conclusions drawn from the original study apply to people in
general, or to just one segment of the population.

Experimentation is sometimes impossible for practical or ethical reasons. Suppose a psychologist suspects that normal visual development in
humans depends on visual experience as well as on physical maturation.
An ideal way to test this hypothesis would be to raise an experimental
group of infants in total darkness, thus depriving them of visual experience, and a control group of infants under similar conditions but with
normal lighting. Such an experiment would be impossible, of course. But
most ethical problems are not this clear-cut. In the last few years, the
American Psychological Association and the United States government
have developed a number of guidelines and regulations to ensure that the
rights of people who take part in experiments are protected.

Researchers also need to understand the way people and animals behave naturally, when they are not conscious of being the subjects of an
experiment. To obtain such information, a psychologist uses **naturalistic
observation.**

Naturalistic Observation

One of the most direct ways to learn about psychology is to listen and
watch—observing how humans and animals behave, without interfering.
For example, a social psychologist might join a commune or participate in
a therapy group to study how leadership develops in these settings. A
developmental psychologist might position himself or herself behind a
two-way mirror to watch youngsters at play (Figure 19.5). Ethologists
(scientists who specialize in studying animal behavior) often spend years
observing members of a species before even considering an experiment.
The cardinal rule of naturalistic observation is to avoid disturbing the
people or animals you are studying, by concealing yourself or by acting as
unobtrusively as possible. Otherwise, you may observe a performance
produced for the researcher's benefit rather than natural behavior.

Case Studies

A **case study** is an intensive investigation of an individual or group. Many
case studies focus on a particular disorder, such as schizophrenia, or a
particular experience, such as being confined to prison. And most combine
long-term observation (by one or more researchers), self-reports (such as

Figure 19.5
Naturalistic observation, sometimes done through a one-way window or mirror, is a useful technique for studying teaching methods and classroom interactions because the observer does not distract the students or the teacher and perhaps cause them to alter their behavior.

diaries, tapes of therapy sessions, or perhaps artwork), and the results of psychological tests.

   In the hands of a brilliant psychologist, case studies can be a powerful research tool. Sigmund Freud's theory of personality development, discussed in Chapter 11, was based on case studies of his patients. Jean Piaget's theory of intellectual development, described in Chapter 8, was

Figure 19.6
Jean Piaget's theories of intellectual development grew partly from case studies of his own children. Here, Piaget observes children playing in a park near his home.

based in part on case studies of his own children. By itself, however, a case study does not prove or disprove anything. The sample is too small, and there is no way of knowing if the researcher's conclusions are correct. For example, a researcher might conduct intensive case studies of families that include an individual diagnosed as schizophrenic. On the basis of these studies she might conclude that a particular kind of interaction produced schizophrenia. However, unless she studies families that do *not* include schizophrenic individuals and finds that they interact differently, she has no way of proving her conclusion. In other words, what is missing from case studies is a control group. The researcher might study a million families that include a schizophrenic person and find similar patterns. But unless she compares these families to others, she cannot be certain that normal families are different.

What, then, is the value of case studies? They provide a wealth of descriptive material that may generate new hypotheses which researchers can then test under controlled conditions with comparison groups.

Surveys

Surveys may be impersonal, but they are the most practical way to gather data on the attitudes, beliefs, and experiences of large numbers of people. A survey can take the form of interviews, questionnaires, or a combination of the two.

Interviews allow a researcher to observe the subject and modify questions if the subject seems confused by them. On the other hand, questionnaires take less time to administer and the results are more uniform. Questionnaires also eliminate the possibility that the researcher will influence the subject by unconsciously frowning at an answer he or she does not like. Of course, there is always a danger that subjects will give misleading answers in order to make themselves "look good." One way to detect this is to phrase the same question in several different ways. A person who says yes, she believes in integration, but no, she would not want her child to marry someone of another race, is not as free of prejudice as the first answer implied.

Perhaps the most famous survey of recent times is the Kinsey report on sexuality. Alfred Kinsey and his staff questioned over 10,000 men and women about their sexual attitudes and behavior—a radical thing to do in the 1940s. The results shocked many people, much as Masters and Johnson's observational studies of human sexual behavior did in the late 1960s.

Longitudinal Studies

Longitudinal studies cover long stretches of time. The psychologist studies and restudies the same group of subjects at regular intervals over a period of years to determine whether their behavior and feelings have changed, and if so, how (Figure 19.7). For example, Lewis Terman followed over a thousand gifted children from an early age to adulthood. He found that they were generally taller, heavier, and stronger than youngsters with average IQs. In addition, they tended to be active socially and to mature

Figure 19.7
The results of a longitudinal study. Kagan and Moss wanted to find out how much continuity there is between individual's behavior in childhood and their behavior as adults. They found the correlations shown here. Traditional sex roles had a strong influence on whether a childhood behavior pattern died out or survived into adulthood. (After Kagan and Moss, 1962)

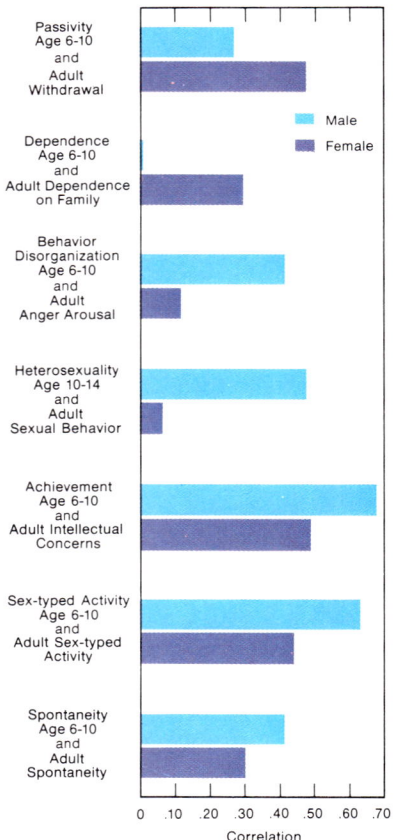

faster than average children. (So much for the stereotype of the skinny, unpopular bookworm.) As adults, they were less likely than people with average intelligence to become involved in crime, to depend on alcohol or drugs, or to develop severe mental illnesses. Some people have said that geniuses are crazy. This study indicates that they are more adaptive, creative, and adjusted than people of normal intelligence (Terman, 1916; Terman and Merrill, 1937).

Longitudinal studies are time-consuming and precarious; subjects may disappear in mid-study. But they are an ideal way to examine consistencies and inconsistencies in behavior over time.

Cross-cultural Studies

Cross-cultural studies are just what the term suggests: comparisons of the way people in different cultures behave, feel, and think. The primary purpose of such research is to determine whether a behavior pattern is universal or reflects the way children are raised and the experiences adults have in a particular culture. For example, Lawrence Kohlberg studied the development of moral reasoning by presenting American, Mexican, and Taiwanese boys age seven and older with a series of dilemmas. (For example, if a man's wife is dying, should he steal a drug that he cannot afford to save her life?) He found that some children in all three societies progress through six stages of moral awareness, from fear of punishment to an inner sense of justice (see Chapter 8). However, the percentage of those in each society who reached stage six varied. Thus although certain values appear to be universal, cultural differences do affect the development of moral reasoning (see Kohlberg and Kramer, 1969).

All the methods for gathering information we've described have advantages and disadvantages; no one technique is better than the others for all purposes. The method a psychologist chooses depends on what he or she wants to learn. It also depends on practical matters such as the amount of money available for research and the kind of training the researcher has had.

TRAPS IN DOING PSYCHOLOGICAL RESEARCH AND HOW TO AVOID THEM

In describing the methods and statistical techniques psychologists use, we have made research appear much simpler and much more straightforward than it actually is. Science is a painstaking, exacting business. Every researcher must be wary of numerous pitfalls that can trap him or her into mistakes. In this section we look at some of the most common problems psychological researchers confront and how they cope with them.

The Self-fulfilling Prophecy

Psychologists are only human, and like all of us they prefer to be right. No matter how objective they try to be in their research, there is always a

---

PSYCHOLOGY UPDATE

Cross-cultural studies of obedience. Chapter 18 ends with a discussion of Stanley Milgram's experiments on obedience. Recall that in his original study, over half of the subjects (26 of 40, or 65 percent) administered the highest level of shock.

Researchers at Swarthmore College hypothesized that Milgram's findings were due, in part, to the fact that his subjects were mostly middle-aged, working-class men. Most had probably served in the military during World War II and thus had experience taking orders and obeying authority. Young, liberal, highly educated Swarthmore students would obey less. Surprisingly, 88 percent of the Swarthmore undergraduates administered the highest level of shock!

Eventually, Milgram's experiment was conducted in Germany and Japan. To no one's surprise, the German and Japanese subjects showed a high rate of obedience—over 80 percent in both groups.

When Milgram began his study, he doubted that any subject would administer the highest level of shock. Imagine his surprise when he learned that the 65 percent rate he found was the lowest of any group.

Figure 19.8
The Red Queen's fatalistic attitude is likely to be confirmed if she behaves in this way. This common phenomenon is called self-fulfilling prophecy.

chance that they will find what they want to find, unwittingly overlooking contrary evidence. This is what we mean by the self-fulfilling prophecy.

Researchers have shown how the self-fulfilling prophecy works in an experiment with experimenters (Rosenthal and Rosnow, 1969). The task was to administer the Wechsler Intelligence Scale for Children to twelve youngsters. Each child was tested by two experimenters, one of whom administered the odd-numbered questions, the other the even-numbered questions. With each child, one of the experimenters was told beforehand that the subject was above average in intelligence. The other was told the subject was below average. The results? The youngsters scored an average of 7.5 points higher on the half of the test administered by the experimenter who had been told they were bright. Thus the experimenters found what they expected to find: the prophecy that a given child would achieve a relatively high score was self-fulfilling.

The Double-Blind Procedure

One way to avoid the self-fulfilling prophecy is to use the double-blind technique. Suppose a psychologist wants to study the effects of a particular tranquilizer. She might give the drug to an experimental group and a placebo (a harmless substitute for the drug) to a control group. The next step would be to compare their performances on a series of tests. This is a *single-blind* experiment. The subjects are "blind" in the sense that they do not know whether they have received the tranquilizer or the placebo.

As a further guarantee of objectivity, the researcher herself doesn't know who takes the drug or the placebo. (She may ask the pharmacist to number rather than label the pills.) *After* she scores the tests, she goes back to the pharmacist to learn which subjects took the tranquilizer and which took the placebo. This is a **double-blind experiment.** Neither the subjects nor the experimenter know which subjects received the tranquilizer. This eliminates the possibility that the researcher will unconsciously find what she expects to find about the effects of the drug.

Observer Effects

Psychologists, like everyone else, are complex people, with attitudes, feelings, and ideas of their own, and their reactions to different subjects may distort the results of a study. Researchers may unknowingly react differently to male and female subjects, short and tall subjects, subjects who speak with an accent or who remind them of someone they particularly dislike. These attitudes, however subtly expressed, may influence the way subjects behave.

In addition, subjects may behave differently than they would otherwise just because they know they are being studied. The presence of an observer may cause them to change their behavior, just as the presence of a photographer can transform a bunch of unruly children into a peaceful, smiling group. Under observation, people are apt to try to please or impress the observer—to act as they think they are expected to act. The use of a control group helps to correct for this, but it does not totally eliminate the "observer effect."

Finally, a researcher may not have the equipment to study a subject adequately. For example, psychologists would never have been able to identify the stages of sleep (see Chapter 7) if the electroencephalograph had not been invented. Psychology is a relatively young science, and the tools and techniques psychologists possess may not be equal to the questions they ask.

CONCLUSIONS

What distinguishes psychologists and other scientists from nonscientists is nagging skepticism. Scientists do not believe that they have any final answers or that they ever will. But they do believe they can learn more about feelings and behavior if they persist in asking questions and studying them systematically. Do people actually behave like that? Does this method work? Does that way of thinking help? When the answer is yes, scientists do not stop asking questions. It is always possible that the next answer will be no or that it is yes for some people and no for others. Hence it is essential for researchers to *invite* criticism by publishing detailed accounts of their methods as well as their results.

The reason why *students* of psychology need to understand research methods is simple. You wouldn't vote for a political candidate simply because she promised to do something you agreed with. You'd want to know whether she had delivered on past campaign promises, whether she was indebted to special-interest groups, and whether she was an effective bargainer in the legislature. You wouldn't buy a new brand of soap because the company claimed that "tests prove" it is good for your skin. You'd want to know what the tests were, who conducted them, and why other companies make the same claim.

You shouldn't accept what you read about psychology just because a psychologist says so. (The "experts" often disagree.) To evaluate psychological studies for yourself, you need to understand research methods.

It is also important to understand what psychologists do once they have completed their studies. They must organize the information they have obtained in order to draw conclusions. For example, how were the researchers Kagan and Moss able to create the graph presented as Figure 19.7 in this chapter? How did researchers determine that youngsters scored an average of 7.5 points higher on the test administered by experimenters who thought they were bright? What does it mean when reports say that 9 out of 10 dentists recommend that their patients chew a certain type of gum, or, as reported in a recent newspaper article, that 5 to 10 percent of the general population suffers from a dissociative disorder (see Chapter 15)? How do researchers come up with these numbers? In Chapter 20 we will discuss the tools that psychologists use to formulate percentages, create graphs, and derive correlations to prove their hypotheses. We hope that with this information you will become more informed "consumers" of psychology.

CHAPTER REVIEW

KEY TERMS

- case study
- control group
- correlation
- cross-cultural studies
- dependent variable
- double-blind technique
- experimental group
- experimental treatment

- hypothesis
- independent variable
- longitudinal studies
- naturalistic observation
- negative correlation
- population
- positive correlation
- random sample

- replication
- sample
- statistics
- stratified sample
- survey
- variable

SUMMARY

1. The first step in psychological research is generating testable ideas.

2. The next step is to select a sample of the population relevant to a study. A random sample (the equivalent of picking subjects while blindfolded) or stratified sample (one that mirrors variations in the population as a whole) helps a researcher avoid bias.

3. Although some research is purely descriptive, more often studies are designed to investigate the degree of association or correlation between two phenomena. But neither a positive nor a negative correlation should be mistaken for a cause-and-effect relationship.

4. Psychologists often use experiments to test hypotheses about cause-and-effect relationships. The researchers observe the effects of the independent variable (the condition they manipulate) on the dependent variable (the condition they think will change) in an experimental group. They then compare the reactions of the experimental group to those of a control group that has not been exposed to the experimental treatment.

5. Psychologists do not accept the results of an experiment until it has been replicated by another researcher using different subjects.

6. Other methods for gathering data on behavior and feelings include
   a. naturalistic observation—watching and recording behavior without intruding on the actors;
   b. case studies—intensive investigations of individuals or groups that convey the quality of behavior and experiences;
   c. surveys—gathering data from a large number of people through face-to-face interviews or questionnaires;
   d. longitudinal studies—studying and restudying the same group of subjects over a period of years;
   e. cross-cultural studies—comparing the way people from different cultures behave and feel.

7. Psychological research is full of traps. The self-fulfilling prophecy (which the double-blind procedure is designed to eliminate), observer effects, and inadequate tools may distort the results.

8. Statistics are the mathematical computations researchers perform on the data they collect in research.

9. Careful collection and analysis of data do not provide "final answers." Science is based on insatiable curiosity and persistent questioning.

CHAPTER REVIEW

REVIEW QUESTIONS

1. What is the name given to a relatively small group selected from the total population? What is an important quality of this selected group?

2. What are the two ways that a biased sample can be avoided?

3. What word do scientists use to describe the relationship between two sets of data? How is this relationship useful? Does it indicate a cause-and-effect relationship?

4. What is the main purpose of an experiment?

5. What is the name of the variable that experimenters can control? Which variable is affected by the other?

6. What is the name given to the group that receives the special treatment?

7. What is an intensive investigation of an individual or group called?

8. On what method of experimentation was Freud's theory of personality based?

9. What is the most practical way to gather data on the attitudes, beliefs, and experiences of large numbers of people? How can this method obtain data?

10. What type of studies obtain data from people at regular intervals over a span of several years?

11. What is the main purpose of a cross-cultural study?

12. What is the name given to the tendency of researchers to find what they want to find despite evidence to the contrary? How can this tendency be avoided in experiments?

ACTIVITIES

1. Measurement is the assignment of numbers to observations. Psychologists face many problems in trying to measure behaviors and feelings. For example, how might the following factors be measured: (1) the number of people in a room, (2) height, (3) the proportion of votes a candidate will receive, (4) hunger, (5) love, (6) liberty. What makes each phenomenon difficult or easy to measure? What can you predict from this exercise regarding the difficulties of measuring such things as personality and intelligence?

2. Several theories are presented below. How could you attempt to disprove each one? Are there any that could not be disproved?
   a. A person will remember an unfinished task.
   b. Love reduces hate.
   c. You can raise blood pressure by making a subject anxious.
   d. Motivation increases learning.
   e. Making a rat hungry will cause the rat to require less training to find its way through a maze.

3. Select a particular area of psychological investigation that is of interest to you. Go to a main branch or university library and by utilizing the card catalog, bibliographical references, and journals or magazines, see how far your research takes you. You may find that, like looking up a word in the dictionary, one thing leads to another, which leads to another, and so on.

4. Look through a popular magazine such as *Time, Newsweek,* or *Psychology Today.* Read an article about a scientific experiment and try to determine whether the results presented correspond to the data given. What approach to obtaining data was used? Did the experiment contain a control group? What were the dependent and independent variables?

5. Based on the information in this chapter, design your own research experiment. If you decide to carry out your design, write a research report according to the style presented in the chapter and present your findings to the class.

Figure 20.1 Statistics enables large amounts of research data to be organized in a concise, meaningful way.

Objectives: *After studying this chapter, you should be able to*
- define descriptive and inferential statistics.
- cite specific research methods used to organize and summarize data.
- compare the three measures of central tendency.
- explain statistical significance.

Statistical Evaluation

How many times have you been told that, in order to get good grades, you have to study? A psychology student named Kate has always restricted the amount of TV she watches during the week, particularly before a test. She has a friend, though, who does not watch TV before a test but who still does not get good grades. This fact challenges Kate's belief. Although Kate hypothesizes, or guesses, that among her classmates those who watch less TV get better grades, she decides to conduct a survey to test the validity of her hypothesis. Kate asks fifteen students in her class to write down how many hours of TV they watched the night before their weekly psychology quiz and how many hours they watched on the night after the quiz. To make her study more interesting, Kate collects additional data. She has her subjects check off familiar products on a list of twenty brand-name items that were advertised on TV the night before the quiz. Kate also asks her subjects to give their height.

When the data is turned in, Kate finds herself overwhelmed with the amount of information she has collected. Her data are presented in Figure 20.2. How can she organize it all so that it makes sense? How can she analyze it to see whether it supports or contradicts her hypothesis? The answers to these questions are found in **statistics**, a branch of mathematics that enables researchers to organize and evaluate the data they collect. In this chapter we will explore the statistical procedures that help psychologists make sense out of the masses of data they collect.

Descriptive Statistics
Distributions of Data
• Measures of Central Tendency • Measures of Variability • Correlation Coefficients

Inferential Statistics
Probability and Chance • Statistical Significance

Statistics and You

DESCRIPTIVE STATISTICS

When a study such as Kate's is completed, the first task is to organize the data in as brief and clear a manner as possible. For Kate, this means that she must put her responses together in a logical format. When she does

FIGURE 20.2
Kate's data: number of hours of TV watched before and after the quiz, grade on quiz, number of products recognized, and height in inches.

Before	After	Grade*	Products	Height
0.0	1.5	5	2	71
0.5	2.5	10	4	64
0.5	2.5	9	6	69
1.0	2.0	10	14	60
1.0	2.5	8	10	71
1.0	1.5	7	9	63
1.5	3.0	9	7	70
1.5	2.5	8	12	59
1.5	2.5	8	9	75
1.5	3.0	6	14	60
2.0	3.0	5	13	68
2.5	2.5	3	17	65
2.5	3.5	4	10	72
3.0	3.0	0	18	62
4.0	4.0	4	20	67

* Highest grade possible is 10.

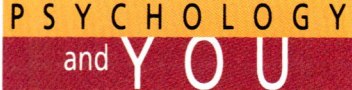

PSYCHOLOGY and YOU

Baseball Statistics. Let us look at how statistics are used in one of our most popular sports, baseball. A batting average is the number of hits per official "at bats" (walks do not count). If a player has a batting average of .250, it means that he gets a hit every fourth time at the plate.

The earned run average represents the number of runs a pitcher allows per 9 innings of play. Consider the pitcher who pitches 180 innings in a season and allows 60 runs. On the average, this pitcher allows one run every 3 innings (180 innings divided by 60 runs). One run every 3 innings equals 3 runs every 9 innings, so the earned run average is 3. The next time you watch your favorite sport, think about the part that statistics plays in it.

this, she is using **descriptive statistics**, the listing and summarizing of data in a practical, efficient way, such as graphs and averages. In this section we will discuss the different forms of descriptive statistics.

Distributions of Data

One of the first steps that researchers take to organize their data is to create frequency tables and graphs. Tables and graphs provide a rough picture of the data. Are the scores bunched up or spread out? What score occurs most often? Frequency distributions and graphs provide researchers with their initial "peek" at the data.

Frequency Distributions. Kate is interested in how many hours of TV her subjects watched the night before and the night after the quiz. She uses the numbers of hours of TV viewing as categories, and then she counts how many subjects reported each category of hours before and after the quiz. She has created a table called a frequency distribution (see Figure 20.3). A **frequency distribution** is a way of arranging data so that we know how often a particular score or observation occurs.

What can Kate do with this information? A commonly used technique is to figure out percentages. This is done simply by dividing the frequency of subjects within a category by the total number of subjects. So, before the quiz, about 13 percent of her subjects (2 divided by 15) watched TV for 2.5 hours. On the night after the quiz, 40 percent of her subjects watched 2.5 hours of TV (6 divided by 15). You are familiar with the use of percentages; test grades are often expressed as percentages (the number of correct points divided by 100). Sometimes frequency distributions include a column giving the percentage of each occurrence.

Graphs. It is often easier to visualize frequency information in the form of a graph. Since Kate is most interested in how much TV her classmates watched the night before their psychology quiz, she decides to graph the results. The graph of the "before the quiz" frequency distribution shown in Figure 20.4 is called a histogram. You are probably familiar with bar graphs. **Histograms** are very similar to bar graphs except that histograms are always vertical, and the bars touch. The X axis, which runs horizontally, lists the number of hours of TV watched, and the Y axis, which runs vertically, is the number of people, or frequency. The height of each bar represents the number of people who reported watching a particular amount of TV. The highest bar shows the number of hours reported most frequently (1.5), and the lowest bar shows the number of hours reported least frequently. In this case, no one reported watching TV for 3.5 hours the night before the quiz. The graph also shows that few people watched more than 2 hours of TV.

Another kind of graph is the frequency polygon or frequency curve. Figure 20.5 is a **frequency polygon**. It shows the same information presented in the histogram. The X axis and Y axis are exactly the same. Instead of drawing boxes, however, a mark is placed on the graph where the midpoint of the top of each histogram bar would be. Then the marks are connected with straight lines.

Frequency polygons are useful because they provide a clear picture of the shape of the data distribution. Another important feature is that more than one set of data can be graphed at the same time. For example, Kate might be interested in comparing how much TV was watched the night before the quiz with the amount watched the evening after the quiz. As shown in Figure 20.6, she can graph the "after quiz" data using a different kind of line. The comparison is obvious; in general, her subjects watched more TV on the night after the quiz than on the night before the quiz.

The Normal Curve. Imagine that Kate could measure how much TV everyone in Chicago watched one night. If she could graph that much information, her graph would probably look something like Figure 20.7. A few people would watch little or no TV, a few would have the TV on all day, while most would watch a moderate amount of TV. Therefore, the graph

FIGURE 20.3
Frequency distribution: number of hours of TV viewing on the nights before and after the quiz.

Hours	Frequency Before*	Frequency After*
0.0	1	0
0.5	2	0
1.0	3	0
1.5	4	2
2.0	1	1
2.5	2	6
3.0	1	4
3.5	0	1
4.0	1	1
Total	15	15

* Number of students.

FIGURE 20.5
Frequency polygon: number of hours of TV watched the night before the quiz.

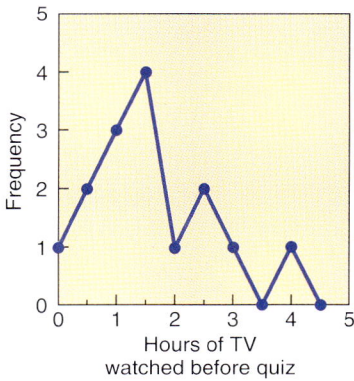

FIGURE 20.4
Histogram: number of hours of TV watched the night before the quiz.

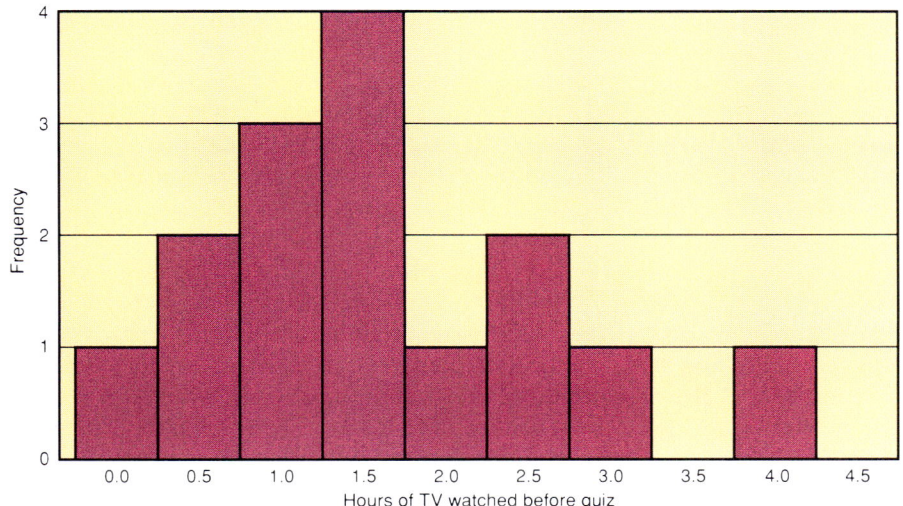

FIGURE 20.7
Normal curve: if a line is drawn down the middle of the curve, one side of the curve is a mirror image of the other side.

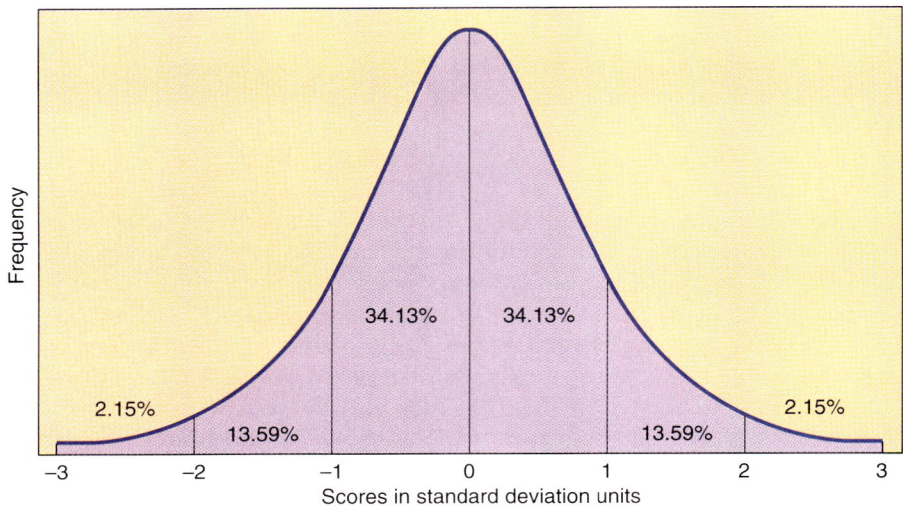

would be highest in the middle and taper off toward the tails, or ends, of the distribution, giving it the shape of a bell. (The standard deviation units shown in Figure 20.7 will be explained later in this chapter.)

This curve is special. It is called the **normal curve** (or bell-shaped curve). Many variables, such as height, weight, and IQ, fall into such a curve if enough people are measured. The normal curve is symmetrical. This means that if a line is drawn down the middle of the curve, one side of the curve is a mirror image of the other side. It is an important distribution because of certain mathematical characteristics. We can divide the curve into sections and can predict how much of the curve, or what percentage of cases, falls within each section. We shall return to this idea later and discuss the importance of the information shown on the curve.

Many curves are not "normal" because scores pile up on one end of the distribution. These are called **skewed distributions** (see Figures 20.8a and 20.8b). Take a look at Figure 20.5 again. Most of the students fell in the lower range of the distribution (they did not watch much TV), and so it is positively skewed (the tail of the distribution points to the right, or positive, end of the *X* axis). If everyone in your class takes a graduate-school statistics exam, the distribution of grades will also be positively skewed, since most of you will probably get low scores (Figure 20.8a). On the other hand, if everyone in your class takes a sixth-grade math test, most will get high scores, and so the graph will be skewed in the other direction, or negatively skewed (Figure 20.8b).

Measures of Central Tendency

Most of the time, researchers want to do more than organize their data. They want to be able to summarize information about the distribution into statistics. One of the most common ways of summarizing is to use a measure of **central tendency**—a number that describes something about the "average" score. We shall use Kate's quiz grades (refer back to Figure 20.2) in the examples below.

FIGURE 20.6
Frequency polygons: number of hours of TV watched on the nights before and after the quiz.

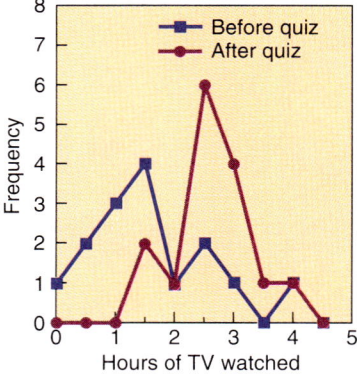

The Mode. The **mode** is the most frequent score. In a graphed frequency distribution, the mode is the peak of the graph. The most frequently occurring quiz grade is 8; that is, the most students, in this case three, got a score of 8. Distributions can have more than one mode. The data for height presented in Figure 20.2 has two modes: 60 and 71. Distributions with two modes are called "bimodal."

The mode is the simplest statistic to figure out, but it gives the least amount of information. For example, in the distribution 1, 2, 3, 4, 10, 10, the mode is 10. Most of the scores, though, are below 5, so the mode does not provide an accurate portrait of the "average" score. However, if you just want to identify the most frequent score, or observation, the mode is the measure to use.

The Median. When scores are put in order from least to most, the **median** is the middle score. Since the median is the midpoint of a set of values, it divides the frequency distribution into two halves. Therefore, 50 percent of the scores fall below the median, and 50 percent fall above the median. For an odd number of observations, the median would be the exact middle value. Here are the psychology quiz grades, in order: 0, 3, 4, 4, 5, 5, 6, 7, 8, 8, 8, 9, 9, 10, 10. The median is 7. As the middle score it divides the distribution in half: There are seven scores above it and seven scores below it. With an even number of observations, the median would be the midpoint between the two most central scores.

The median does not reflect the value of all the scores in a distribution. If the highest score in a data set were a few points higher, the median would stay the same. Regardless of the numerical value, the highest score represents only a score above the median. If we change the highest quiz grade from 10 to 20, the median remains the same.

The Mean. The **mean** is what most people think of as an "average" and is the most commonly used measure of central tendency. To find the mean, you add up all the scores and then divide by the number of scores you add. Here are some simple symbols that will be helpful in expressing the mean.

$$X = \text{an individual observation (score)}$$
$$N = \text{the total number of observations}$$
$$\Sigma = \text{"the sum of" (the Greek capital letter sigma)}$$
$$\overline{X} = \text{the mean}$$

The mean is calculated from the following formula:

$$\overline{X} = \frac{\Sigma X}{N}$$

which reads: The mean equals the sum of the scores on variable X divided by the total number of observations. For the quiz grades, the sum of the scores is 96, and the number of scores is 15. The mean equals 96 divided by 15, to give us a mean quiz grade of 6.4.

$$\overline{X} = \frac{96}{15} = 6.4$$

FIGURE 20.8
Skewed distributions. (a) A positively skewed distribution. (b) A negatively skewed distribution.

a

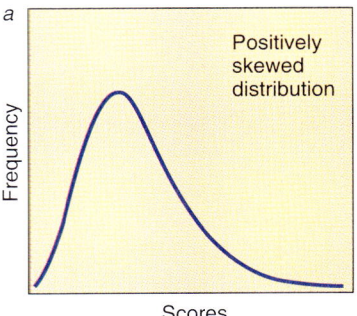

Positively skewed distribution

b

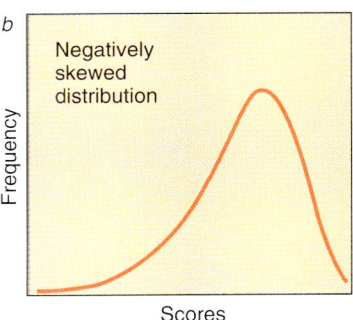

Negatively skewed distribution

The mean can be considered the balance point of the distribution, like the middle of a seesaw, since it does reflect all the scores in a set of data. If the highest score in a data set is shifted higher, the mean will shift upward also. If we change the highest quiz grade from 10 to 20, the mean changes from 6.4 to 7.1.

This change is not very dramatic because we are working with small numbers. Let us take another example. Five people are randomly chosen at a local shopping mall and are asked their annual incomes. Their answers are: $18,000, $20,000, $25,000, $26,000, and $100,000. The mean income for this group is $41,400! This mean is not very descriptive of most of the incomes. The median, on the other hand, is $25,000—a more accurate portrait of an "average." In skewed distributions, the mean is always pulled toward the most extreme scores. (See Figures 20.8a and 20.8b.) Annual income is positively skewed because a small percentage of the population has extremely high incomes. An "average annual income" that is computed as a mean will be pulled toward these high incomes and will not be as representative of the general population's income as the median.

Measures of Variability

Distributions differ not only in their "average" score but also in terms of how "spread out" or how variable the scores are. Figure 20.9 shows two distributions drawn on the same axis. Each is symmetrical and each has the same mean. However, the distributions differ in terms of their variability. Measures of **variability** provide an index of how spread out the scores of a distribution are.

Two commonly used measures of variability are the range and the standard deviation. To compute the **range**, subtract the lowest score in a data set from the highest score. The highest quiz grade is 10 and the lowest is 0, so the range is 10. Like the mode, the range uses only a small amount of information, and it is used only as a crude measure of variability.

The **standard deviation** (SD) is a better measure of variability because, like the mean, it uses all the data points in its calculation. It is the most widely used measure of variability. The standard deviation is like (but not exactly like) an "average" distance of every score to the mean of the scores. This distance is called a "deviation" and is written: $X - \overline{X}$ (which means a score minus the mean). Scores above the mean will have a positive deviation, and scores below the mean will have a negative deviation. The size of the "average" deviation depends on how variable, or spread out, the distribution is. If the distribution is very spread out, deviations tend to be large. If the distribution is bunched up, deviations tend to be small.

To figure out this "average" distance, deviations cannot simply be added up and then divided by the number of observations. The negative and positive deviations cancel each other out, and the sum of deviation scores is always 0. The traditional way that mathematicians get around this problem is to square each deviation (to make them all positive). These squared deviations are then averaged. To compensate for the fact that the

FIGURE 20.9
Two distributions with the same mean and different standard deviations.

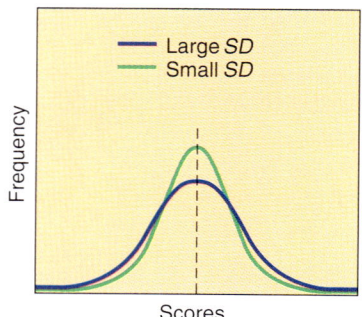

deviations are squared, the square root is taken. The formula for the standard deviation is:

$$\text{Standard deviation} = \sqrt{\frac{\text{sum of (score} - \text{mean)}^2}{\text{number of scores}}}$$

or

$$SD = \sqrt{\frac{\Sigma(X - \bar{X})^2}{N}}$$

The mean is subtracted from each score, resulting in a deviation. Each deviation is squared, then all of the squared deviations are added together. This sum is divided by the number of scores. When the square root is taken, the result is the standard deviation. Calculation of the quiz grades' standard deviation is shown in Figure 20.10.

The standard deviation is a measure of distance, describing an "average" distance of every score to the mean. The larger the standard deviation, the more spread out the scores are. Look back at Figure 20.6, where the hours of TV watched before and after the quiz are graphed into two frequency polygons. You can easily see that the observations for the "before" polygon are more spread out than those for the "after" polygon. The standard deviation for "before" is 1.06 and for "after" is 0.67.

The standard deviation does more than summarize information about a data set. When a set of measurements is distributed in the shape of the normal curve, researchers are able to interpret scores by looking at their distance from the mean using the standard deviation as the unit of measurement. In other words, the standard deviation is used to carve up the normal curve into sections. Return to Figure 20.7, where the normal curve is pictured. The numbers on the X axis represent standard deviation units. About 34 percent of the curve lies between the mean and one standard deviation above the mean. Since the curve is symmetrical, the same amount lies between the mean and one standard deviation below the mean. Over 99 percent of the curve lies between –3 and +3 standard deviation units. Only a few standard deviation units are pictured in Figure 20.7.

When a teacher "grades on the curve," it means that there is no absolute standard that equals an A, B, C, etc. The grade a person gets depends on what everyone else gets. If the teacher uses the normal curve to determine the grades, he or she would first compute the mean and standard deviation of the set of test scores. The teacher might then decide that scores above +2 standard deviations receive an A, while those below –2 standard deviations receive an F. Between +1 and +2 standard deviations, the grade will be B; and scores between –1 and –2 standard deviations receive a D. All scores between –1 and +1 standard deviations receive a C. With this system, it is possible for everyone in a class to score between 80 and 100 on an exam, yet most of the students will still get Cs, Ds, and Fs. On the other hand, the entire class can score below 50 on an exam and some students will still get As and Bs.

FIGURE 20.10

Calculations of the standard deviation: grades on quiz

X (Score)	$\bar{X}$	$(X - \bar{X})$	$(X - \bar{X})^2$
0	6.4	–6.4	40.96
3	6.4	–3.4	11.56
4	6.4	–2.4	5.76
4	6.4	–2.4	5.76
5	6.4	–1.4	1.96
5	6.4	–1.4	1.96
6	6.4	–0.4	0.16
7	6.4	+0.6	0.36
8	6.4	+1.6	2.56
8	6.4	+1.6	2.56
8	6.4	+1.6	2.56
9	6.4	+2.6	6.76
9	6.4	+2.6	6.76
10	6.4	+3.6	12.96
10	6.4	+3.6	12.96
		$\Sigma(X-\bar{X})$ = 0	$\Sigma(X-\bar{X})^2$ = 115.6

$$SD = \sqrt{\frac{115.6}{15}} = \sqrt{7.71} = 2.78$$

FIGURE 20.11
Scatterplot of hours of TV before quiz
and number of products recognized
($r = 0.85$)

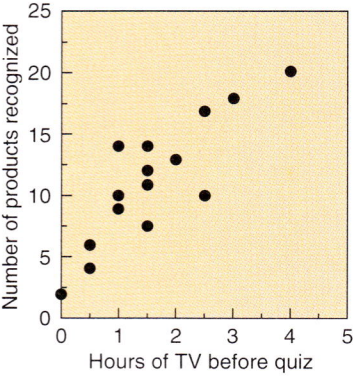

Correlation Coefficients

As discussed in Chapter 19, a **correlation coefficient** describes the direction and strength of the relationship between two sets of observations. While there are many types of correlation coefficients, the most commonly used measure is the Pearson correlation coefficient (r). A coefficient with a plus (+) sign indicates a **positive correlation**. This means that as one variable *increases*, the second variable also *increases*. For example, the more you jog, the better your cardiovascular system works. A coefficient with a minus (–) sign indicates a **negative correlation**; as one variable *increases*, the second variable *decreases*. For example, the more hours a person spends at an after-school job, the fewer hours are available for studying. Correlations can take any value between +1 and –1 including 0. An r near +1 or –1 indicates a strong relationship (either positive or negative), while an r near 0 indicates a weak relationship. Generally, an r from 0.60 to 1.0 indicates a strong correlation, from 0.30 to 0.60 a moderate correlation, and from 0 to 0.30 a weak correlation. A correlation of 1.0 indicates a perfect relationship between two variables and is rare in real-life data.

Using correlations, Kate can analyze a number of variables she measured. She uses the data presented in Figure 20.2 to look at the relationship between hours of TV viewing the night before the exam and three variables: number of products recognized, exam grade, and height.

To get an idea of how her data looks, Kate draws some scatterplots. A **scatterplot** is a graph of subjects' scores on the two variables, and it demonstrates the direction of the relationship between them. Figures 20.11, 20.12 and 20.13 illustrate the different kinds of correlations Kate looks at. Note that each point represents one person's score on two variables.

Kate first looks at hours of TV viewing and number of products recognized. She finds that students who watch more TV can identify more products that were advertised on TV. A positive correlation results in a scatterplot in which the points generally tend to cluster on a diagonal from lower left to upper right (Figure 20.11).

She next considers hours of TV and quiz grades. Her original hypothesis was that students who watched more TV would not do as well on the quiz as students who watched less TV. The points on her scatterplot generally tend to cluster on a diagonal from upper left to lower right. This means that, in general, students who watched less TV did better on the next day's quiz than students who watched more TV. This is an example of a negative correlation (Figure 20.12).

Where there is little or no relationship between two variables, the points in the scatterplot do not seem to fall into any pattern. Not surprisingly, Kate finds that TV viewing and height are not related (Figure 20.13)!

Having established that a relationship is either positive or negative, it is also important to note how closely the cluster in the scatterplot approximates a straight line. The stronger the *linear* relationship between two variables, the more closely the points in the scatterplot tend to cluster along a straight line (whether positive or negative) and the higher is the correlation. Data fitting a perfect +1.00 or –1.00 correlation will fall on a straight line. While TV viewing is related strongly to both grades and products identified, Kate finds that the correlation between TV viewing and product identification is higher.

FIGURE 20.12
Scatterplot of hours of TV before quiz
and grade on quiz ($r = 0.69$)

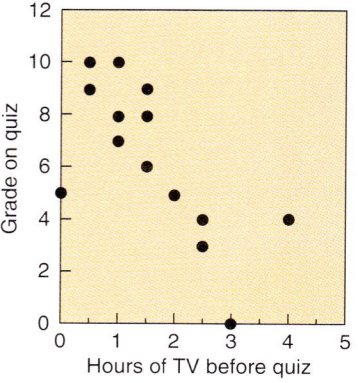

While a correlation tells us something about the relationship or association between two variables, it does not tell us whether one variable *causes* the other. For example, we are all aware that before major holidays, the American Automobile Association predicts, correctly, that more people will be involved in automobile accidents during the holiday period. Does this mean that holidays cause auto accidents? A closer look at the data reveals that holidays and accidents are related to a third variable: the dramatic increase in the number of people who travel during a holiday. Since there are many more people on the roads, the number of accidents increases because the number of people has increased. So, auto accidents and holidays can be correlated, but one does not necessarily cause the other.

To go back to Kate's question, does viewing TV itself cause poorer performance on a quiz? Probably not. Perhaps students who watch more TV have less time to study, and the lack of studying is what affects test grades. Maybe better students are not interested in TV. No matter how high a correlation coefficient is, it tells us nothing about causes.

However, correlations are useful for a different purpose. If two variables are shown to be related, one variable can be predicted from knowledge of the other. Why did you take the SATs before going to college? Because your score told admissions officers something about how well you would do in your first year of college. The correlation is not perfect. Some students do poorly on standardized tests like the SATs but excel in college. Others have no problems with the SATs but flunk out before the end of the first semester of college. The accuracy of prediction can be increased if other variables are used in combination to predict a single variable (like first-year grades). So, in addition to your SATs, your high school grades, extracurricular activities, and letters of recommendation were considered.

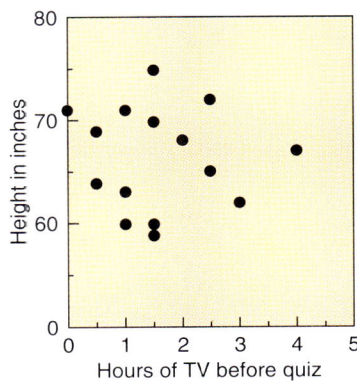

FIGURE 20.13
Scatterplot of hours of TV before quiz and height in inches ($r = -0.06$)

INFERENTIAL STATISTICS

The purpose of descriptive statistics is to describe the characteristics of a sample. But psychologists are interested only in the information they collect from their subjects. They want to make generalizations about the population from which the subjects come. To make such generalizations, we need the tools of inferential statistics. Using **inferential statistics**, researchers can determine whether the data they collect support their hypotheses, or whether their results are merely due to chance outcomes.

Probability and Chance

If you toss a coin in the air, what is the probability that it will land with heads facing up? Since there are only two possible outcomes, heads or tails, the probability of heads is 0.50. If you toss a coin ten times, you would expect five heads and five tails. What if in nine flips you toss nine heads and no tails? What is the probability that your next toss will be heads? It will

Meta-Analysis. The results of one study cannot provide definite answers to a research question. Studies must be replicated, or repeated. Many studies have looked at the relationship between psychological factors and coronary heart disease (CHD). Some studies have linked heart disease with "Type A" personality (a hurried, impatient workaholic); others have not found this relationship, or have linked CHD with different personality variables. How can conclusions be drawn if numerous studies result in contradictory findings? A statistical technique, *meta-analysis*, can be used to integrate and organize the results of studies. The number of subjects and the size of the effects reported in each study are combined into an "average" effect. A meta-analysis of personality factors and CHD concluded that the stereotyped "Type A" individual is not necessarily the most likely to suffer from heart disease. People at most risk may be those who experience negative emotions such as depression, anger, or anxiety. Other researchers have criticized this meta-analysis, some using meta-analyses of their own. Even a technique like meta-analysis may not provide final answers.

still be 50–50. Each toss has the same probability, if the coin is fair, no matter how many times you toss it. Each toss is independent of the other.

Let's go back to the normal curve pictured in Figure 20.7. The Stanford-Binet, a widely used IQ test described in Chapter 12, has a mean of 100 and a standard deviation of 15. If you choose one person at random walking through your local mall, what is the probability that the person's IQ is between 100 and 115 (between the mean and one standard deviation above the mean)? We know that, with a normally distributed variable, about 34 percent of the population lies between the mean and one standard deviation above the mean. We could say, then, that the probability of randomly choosing a person (or of choosing a person by chance) with such an IQ is about 0.34 (or 34 chances out of 100). What is the probability of choosing a person who has an IQ above 130 (two standard deviations above the mean)? Now the probability goes down to about 0.02 (2 chances out of 100). This would certainly be a rare event!

Let us say that a new diet has been developed and a researcher wants to test its effectiveness. She takes twenty equally overweight people, puts ten of them on the new diet and a program of exercise for three months, and has the other group follow the program of exercise without the diet. At the end of the three months, she finds that, on the average, the diet group lost 10 pounds more than the nondiet group. Is her diet a success? Is her 10-pound difference a real difference (due to the diet), or is it the result of chance? Researchers face this problem whenever they do research: Are the results strong enough to have confidence in them? This is where probability comes in.

Statistical Significance

The normal curve is one of many distributions used by psychologists to evaluate the results of their studies. For example, Kate wants to know if her classmates watch more TV than the "average American." Since daily TV viewing is probably normally distributed, she can compare her results to the normal distribution, if she knows the population's mean number of TV viewing hours. There is a distribution to use when two groups are compared (as in the diet example), a distribution when three or more groups are studied, and a distribution for correlations. All inferential statistics are associated with a distribution. Therefore, all possible outcomes or results are associated with a probability, just as with the normal curve. When psychologists evaluate the results of their studies, they ask: Could the results be due to chance? What researchers really want to know is whether the results are extreme enough so that they are more likely to be due to the variables being studied.

The problem is that this question cannot be answered with a yes or no. This is why researchers use some guidelines to evaluate probabilities. Many researchers say that if the probability that their results were due to chance is less than 0.05 (5 chances out of 100), then they are confident that the results are not due to chance. Some researchers want to be even more sure, and so they use 0.01 as their level of confidence. When the probability of a result is 0.05 or 0.01 (or whatever level the researcher sets), we say that the result is **statistically significant**. It is important to remember that probability tells us how *likely* it is that an event or outcome is due to chance, but not whether the event is *actually* due to chance.

STATISTICS AND YOU

You may never conduct psychological experiments, but statistics can still be useful to you. A basic knowledge of statistics and research principles can help you to become a better consumer and critical thinker.

Look at the backs of some major fashion magazines. There will be advertisements for products that "guarantee" thicker hair, freedom from wrinkles, and huge weight losses in "just two weeks!" Or check the psychology section of a large bookstore. Shelves of books are devoted to self-help—how to achieve the perfect relationship, how to get out of bad relationships, how to find inner talents, how to raise your children. On TV, a trusted actor, who has become famous playing a doctor, makes commercials praising a particular product and is perceived as an "expert." Are any of the claims made for these products, diets, and methods valid?

An advice columnist asks her readers to write in stating whether they would remarry their current spouse if they had the chance. Over 75 percent of the women who respond say that they would not remarry the same person. Before we conclude that most women are trapped in unhappy marriages, let us ask what other information we need. We do not know how many people read this column, and we do not know what proportion of the readers actually responded to the columnist's request. It is very possible that people who are unhappy in their marriages are more motivated to respond than are those who are happily married, so our distribution of responses is skewed.

Whenever you see the results of a "survey" in the media, always ask yourself: "How many people were surveyed? Who was surveyed?" If the survey reports that 40 percent of respondents agree with a statement, ask yourself: "Does that mean that 60 percent disagreed? Did 60 percent have no opinion?" A product is advertised as being 34 percent more effective. Ask yourself: "More effective than what? Another product? No product?"

Finally, just because an "expert" makes a statement or claim, it does not necessarily mean that the claim is true. If you ask a group of psychologists which method of psychotherapy is most effective, many answers will be given. Each psychologist may strongly defend a particular method while claiming that the others do not work as well. You should always ask yourself: "Were studies done to test the effectiveness of these methods? What data support these claims?"

Statistics are used by researchers to organize, summarize, and evaluate data. Advertisers use statistics to sell products, "experts" use statistics to support their conclusions. You can use your knowledge of statistics to become a better-informed citizen.

FACT or FICTION

A statistically significant result always represents an important finding.

Fiction. Many statistical tests are affected by sample size. A small difference between groups may be magnified by a large sample and may result in a statistically significant finding. However, the difference may be so small that it is not a meaningful difference.

CHAPTER REVIEW

KEY TERMS

- central tendency
- correlation coefficient
- descriptive statistics
- frequency distribution
- frequency polygon
- histogram
- inferential statistics

- mean
- median
- mode
- negative correlation
- normal curve
- positive correlation
- range

- scatterplot
- skewed distribution
- standard deviation
- statistically significant
- statistics
- variability

SUMMARY

1. Statistics is a branch of mathematics that enables researchers to organize and evaluate the data they collect.

2. Descriptive statistics is the listing and summarizing of data in a practical, efficient way, such as in graphs or averages. There are several different forms of descriptive statistics, including distributions of data, measures of central tendencies, measures of variability, and correlation coefficients.

3. Frequency distribution is a way of arranging data so that we know how often a particular score or observation occurs. Histograms and frequency polygons are often used to illustrate frequency.

4. One of the most common ways of summarizing information about distribution as statistics is by using a measure of central tendency.

5. Measures of central tendency include the mode, the median, and the mean. The mode is the most frequent observation. The median is the middle score when scores are ranked in ascending or descending order. It divides the frequency distribution into two halves. The mean is commonly thought of as an "average."

6. Measures of variability provide an index of how spread out the scores of a distribution are. Two commonly used measures of variability are the range and the standard deviation. The range is the difference between the highest and lowest scores of a set. The standard deviation is like an average distance of every score to the mean of the scores.

7. A correlation coefficient describes the direction and strength of the relationship between two sets of observations. A correlation may be positive or negative.

8. While a correlation tells us something about the relationship or association between two variables, it does not tell us whether one variable causes the other. However, one variable can be predicted from knowledge of another.

9. Researchers use inferential statistics to determine whether the data they collect support their hypotheses or whether their results are due to chance outcomes.

10. Probability is the likelihood of an event or response occurring. Probability does not tell us whether the event is actually due to chance.

11. Statistics can be used for many purposes. You can use statistics to become a better-informed consumer. Statistics could help you determine the likelihood that the claims for diets advertised on television are valid.

CHAPTER REVIEW

1. What statistics are used to organize and summarize data? Give two examples of the methods researchers use to make sense of their data.

2. What are histograms and frequency polygons?

3. What is the normal curve? What properties make it important in statistics?

4. What is a skewed distribution? Give an example of when a skewed distribution of scores is likely to occur.

5. What are the three measures of central tendency? What does each measure?

6. What is the preferred measure of central tendency? What is the best measure of central tendency for a skewed distribution? For the normal distribution?

7. What do measures of variability tell researchers? What are two common measures of variability? Which one is more useful?

8. What does a correlation coefficient measure? What does the size of the correlation tell us? Describe the two types of correlation.

9. How are inferential statistics and descriptive statistics different?

10. What does it mean when the results of a study are labeled "statistically significant"?

ACTIVITIES

1. Look through newspapers and magazines and cut out or photocopy several graphs. Write a short paper that includes each graph. For each example, state what type of graph it is, what the X axis and Y axis represent, and what information or conclusions you draw from the graphic presentation. Compare your evaluation of the graph to the results presented in the text of the article from which the graph came. How would you improve the presentation of information?

2. Coin tossing can demonstrate some of the concepts illustrated in this chapter. If you toss four coins at once, there are five possible outcomes: (1) four heads, (2) three heads and one tail, (3) two heads and two tails, (4) one head and three tails, and (5) four tails. Create a table with these possible outcomes. Give coins to four friends. Have them toss the coins once. Note the outcome by drawing a slash next to it on your table. Your friends will need to toss their coins ninety-nine more times. Each time you should note the outcome on your table. Draw a bar graph of the results after 25 tosses, 50 tosses, 75 tosses, and 100 tosses. What you should find in each graph is that your friends will make a few tosses resulting in four heads or four tails and many tosses of two heads and two tails. You should notice that as the number of tosses increases, your graph begins to look more like a normal curve. What do you think would happen if you could toss coins 1,000 times? 10,000 times? What might you suspect if your results did not come out as expected?

3. Collect weights from twenty women and twenty men. Create a frequency distribution for each group. Since there are likely to be many different weights, group them in five-pound intervals before counting. For example: 110–114, 115–119, 120–124, 125–129, etc. Graph your data for men and women separately as frequency polygons on the same axis. Compute means, medians, modes, ranges, and standard deviations for women and men separately. How are the two distributions alike? How are they different? What would a frequency polygon look like if you combined the data for women and men into one sample? Write an essay summarizing your results.

Figure 21.1 Psychologists' understanding of human behavior has many applications—including wartime strategies.

Objectives: *After studying this chapter, you should be able to*
- identify and describe new areas of research in biological psychology.
- identify and describe post-traumatic stress disorder.
- explain the role psychology has played in education reform.
- identify and describe ways in which psychology is used to improve the workplace.
- explain the role psychology can play in issues of war and peace.

Psychology: Approaching the Twenty-First Century

The next century will no doubt bring remarkable changes in society and people's life-styles. There are already indications of what may be in store: movies and television feature computers that think, make decisions, and even converse; goggles that help the blind to see; long-range sensors that can spy at great distances; and surgery without incisions. Although such things may seem fantastic, many are already in the works, and most involve psychology in one way or another.

Psychology will play an important role in shaping the health and happiness of humankind in the coming years. People will live longer and be healthier than ever before. Working closely with health professionals, biological psychologists are using technological advances to learn more about the function of the human brain and to develop genetically engineered drugs. To help people deal with the complexity, challenges, and stresses of modern living, psychologists are studying such diverse issues as improving our educational system and dealing with the changing roles of women. Psychology will continue to play an important role in the world of work—in the design of the workplace, for example, and in personnel assessment. Finally, psychology will be involved in global issues, such as limiting the damages of war and promoting peace on our planet.

Biological Psychology
New Cameras of Brain Research • New Drug Technology

Psychology and the New Stressors of Life
Post-Traumatic Stress Disorder • Changing Roles for Women • Educational Reform

Psychology and Work
Design of the Workplace • Stressors in the Workplace • Intelligent Machines • Personnel Assessment

War and Peace
Psychology and War • Peace Psychology

BIOLOGICAL PSYCHOLOGY

In 1989 President George Bush signed a declaration naming the 1990s the "Decade of the Brain." Supported by numerous organizations, including the American Psychological Association, this declaration should help focus research on the brain—adding to our knowledge of how the brain works, how it becomes diseased, and how it can be healed. There has already been much progress in these areas. Working together, people from such diverse fields as medicine, neuroscience, and psychology may someday unlock the remaining secrets of this complex organ.

517

As you have already learned, the brain and nervous system play a principal role in controlling behavior. Other systems, such as the endocrine system, also play an important part in behavior. Biological psychologists continue to increase knowledge of the brain, nervous system, and endocrine system. They do so by investigating the answers to such questions as how people remember pain, how parts of the brain cooperate and communicate, how the brain creates new circuits and changes old ones, and, of course, what roles the brain and hormones play in mental illness. Their research is an important step in answering questions about how the brain influences healing and whether damage to the brain can be repaired (Markowitsch, 1986).

New Cameras of Brain Research

Until recently, most knowledge of the brain came from studies that compared damage to the brain and nervous system through injuries, strokes, and surgery. Two of the earliest studies identified links between specific areas of the brain and specific behaviors. In these nineteenth-century studies, Broca and Wernicke examined the brains of deceased individuals (Hothersall, 1990). Today, technology makes it possible to learn much about the brain from live patients.

Two important devices, the electroencephalogram (EEG) and the positron emission tomography (PET) scan have helped improve our understanding of the brain. The EEG measures electrical activity in the brain through electrodes placed on an individual's scalp and forehead. Although an EEG allows researchers to create maps of general brain activity, it does not reveal accurate locations of activity.

The **positron emission tomography scan**, or **PET scan**, however, does allow psychologists and other doctors to look inside the brain and observe activity as it happens. For example, a PET scan can show which areas of the brain are utilizing a certain kind of sugar; it is also used to observe which areas of the brain are active while a person is reading a book. Because PET scans identify areas of the brain that exhibit abnormal activity, they are important diagnostic tools to detect damage. Recently, biological psychologists using the PET scan have discovered that the cerebral cortex, a part of the brain typically associated with higher brain functions, is involved in the experience of pain. Earlier, it was thought that only lower brain centers were involved (Wheeler, 1991). This better understanding of pain has benefited specialists who treat people who suffer chronic pain.

Other devices have also helped improve our understanding of the brain. Computer technology has made it possible to create a three-dimensional picture of the brain, called a **CAT scan**. In a CAT scan, a computer creates a picture of the brain by putting together a number of X-ray images. These images help experts locate lesions and other damage and can help therapists devise treatments for relearning lost skills such as speech, emotional response/interpretation, and even walking. A CAT scan reveals only the bone masses and tissue density of body organs. Unlike the PET scan, it cannot show what is actually happening at any particular moment. One concern with CAT scans is the possible danger of overexposure to X rays.

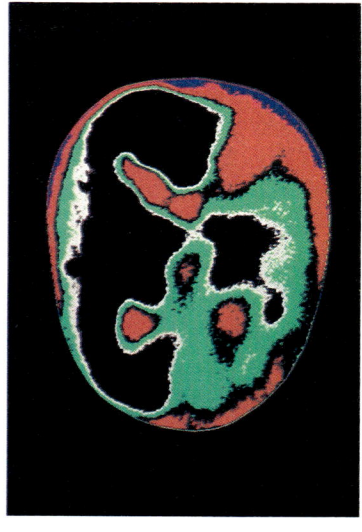

Figure 21.2
In the past, scientists had to learn about the brain and behavior by studying the brains of deceased individuals. Today, MRI and other advanced systems allow scientists to study the brains of living persons.

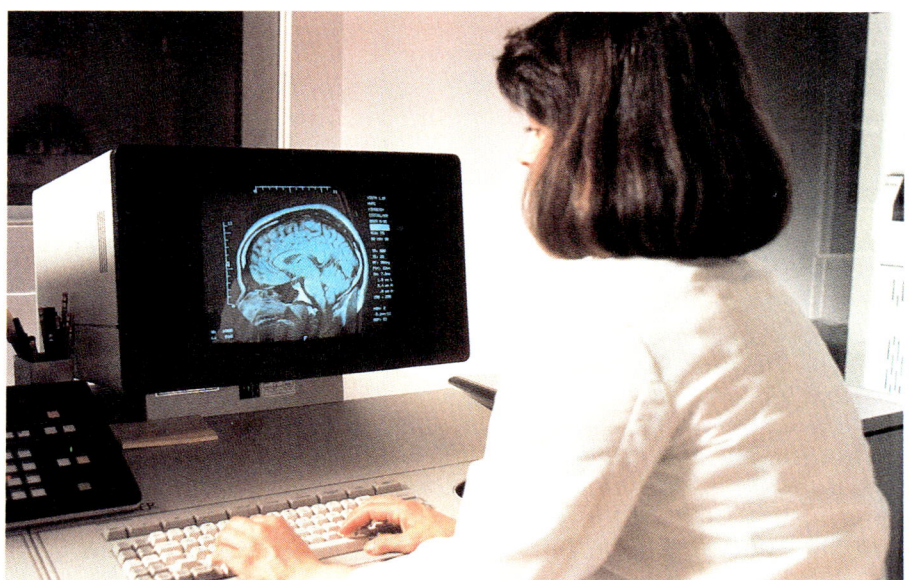

Figure 21.3
A technician operating an MRI scanner. MRI uses the magnetic field of molecules and cells in the body to produce pictures of different tissues and bone structures.

Another relatively new method of examining body tissue and bone structure is **magnetic resonance imaging (MRI)**. MRI uses the magnetic field of molecules and cells in the body to construct precise images that are far more accurate than those of a CAT scan. Every tissue and bone in the body has its own magnetic property. An MRI scanner can sense these properties through the use of powerful magnets and radio waves. A computer then analyzes the patterns to construct a picture. Like the CAT scan, MRI is limited to producing pictures of different tissues and bone structures. Unlike the CAT scan, however, it is completely safe.

Techniques are being developed that will make it possible to compare the results of PET scans, CAT scans, and MRI with results from psychological tests such as the Minnesota Multiphasic Personality Inventory (MMPI) and the Rorschach (see Chapter 12). Such methods will improve the ability to diagnose and treat mental illness, help victims of disease and injury, and add to our knowledge of the links between the brain and behavior (Moses, 1990). Improved knowledge about the brain and the accurate images that technology can now produce are paving the way for two exciting developments: the creation of new drug technologies and the transplantation of tissues into the brain. Like many other aspects of research, progress in these new areas requires the cooperation of psychologists and experts in a variety of disciplines.

New Drug Technology

One new technology involved in drug development is **gene therapy**, which involves manipulating individual genes to change certain traits. This method is already being tested in cancer research. First, tissue is taken from a patient's body—usually from the cancer tumor itself. Using genetic

PSYCHOLOGY UPDATE

Prozac, the Wonder Drug. In recent years, a drug called Prozac has been used as an antidepressant. This new wonder drug appeared to have fewer side effects than other antidepressant drugs. Yet only a short time after its release, many people began to question its safety. Some Prozac users experienced anxiety, tremors, behavioral changes, weight loss, and many other troubling symptoms. Many of those users have legal claims against its maker because of the unexpected side effects. Perhaps the most alarming of the alleged side effects was an increase in suicidal thoughts—and this from a drug used for depression, a disorder that tends toward suicidal thoughts!

Before Prozac's side effects were generally known, the drug was being considered for use in the treatment of drug addiction, obesity, and obsessive compulsive disorder (Chapter 15).

Fortunately, all new drugs do not carry this much hidden risk. However, almost all drugs have side effects (Cowley, 1990; Toufexis, 1990).

material from this tissue, researchers "program" white blood cells to identify and destroy the tumor. Another approach is to use the tissue to create antibodies that will attack only the cancerous tissue and nothing else (Ames and Crandall, 1990). Genetically engineered drugs currently are used only in the area of cancer treatment. However, researchers believe that it may be possible to design drugs that can help the mentally ill by compensating for hormone deficiencies and reduced activity of neurotransmitters. These drugs would work like estrogen replacement therapy for women whose ovaries have been removed (the ovaries produce estrogen). The goal of this type of drug therapy is to restore the balance of a missing chemical in the body or the brain.

Drug therapies are also being developed to deal with drug abuse. This is already being done with a drug that helps alcoholics stop drinking. Taken daily, the drug Antabuse causes nausea if alcohol is drunk; thus the person taking Antabuse avoids drinking alcohol (Peachy and Naranjo, 1983). Several drugs, such as fluoxetine, desipramine, and carbamazepine, are currently being studied for their ability to help cocaine addicts. Most psychologists recognize that finding a single drug "cure" for any addiction in unlikely. Treatment of addiction may be helped with drug therapy, but real success also requires behavioral therapy to help change people's habits (Adler, 1991).

Advances in biological psychology are particularly dramatic because of the detailed images they provide and the important results they can produce. The new technologies of PET scans, CAT scans, and MRI and the realm of new drug therapies represent exciting frontiers for psychology.

PSYCHOLOGY AND THE NEW STRESSORS OF LIFE

Everyone faces stress in his or her life. In today's world, daily stressors are increasing, especially among young people. Violence in society, environmental problems, changing social roles, and wars are some of the stress-producing situations that people must face each day. The next century promises to produce even greater stressors as the world and society change. Psychologists are hard at work trying to identify and solve the stress-related problems that exist now and that may arise in the future.

Post-Traumatic Stress Disorder

The survivors of a 1984 sniper attack at an inner-city school in Los Angeles continued to experience sleep and learning disturbances fourteen months after the attack (DeAngelis, 1991a). These symptoms are among those found in post-traumatic stress disorder. Usually associated with extreme or prolonged cases of severe stress, **post-traumatic stress disorder (PTSD)** produces symptoms of insomnia, anxiety, recurrent dreams, and difficulty in concentration. Earthquakes, hurricanes, serious accidents, the threat or experience of violence, and war all have the potential to cause this disorder.

Figure 21.4
Post-traumatic stress disorder is often the result of extreme or prolonged stress. The disorder reached epidemic proportions among veterans of the Vietnam War.

Loss or the fear of loss in time of war has led to many cases of PTSD. The first significant PTSD epidemic occurred among veterans of the Vietnam War. About 15 percent of Vietnam veterans reported recurring flashbacks and nightmares about the traumatic events they experienced during the war. These flashbacks and dreams, which led to insomnia and an inability to concentrate, interfered with the normal aspects of life (Roberts, 1988). For many of these veterans, the post-traumatic stress disorder lasted fifteen years or more; some are still suffering from it.

The nation's experience with the Vietnam War led to anxiety about the Persian Gulf War. However, there was also a sense of optimism that with proper planning, the mistakes of Vietnam would not be repeated. Military psychologists have since developed strategies to prevent or lessen the likelihood of PTSD. Knowledge gained from a wide range of traumatic and extreme stress situations has been used to prepare soldiers for the experience of war (Blank, 1982). Psychologists have found that the best way of coping with the experience of war involves practice and preparation. If a soldier is prepared and knows what to expect, then he or she usually feels safer and better able to perform duties effectively. Several things have changed since the Vietnam War that will improve the chances of soldiers avoiding postwar stress. Unlike in the Vietnam War, soldiers today are trained as units and are deployed and returned as units. This group training and deployment allows soldiers to share the psychological pressure and provide each other with psychological support. Military psychologists, considering the prevention of stress to be like the prevention of any illness, call their programs "stress inoculation."

It is impossible to avoid stress completely; it is a pervasive and natural component of life that can arise from many situations. The rapid and unpredictable changes that await us in the twenty-first century will only increase the possibility of stress. Psychologists now have the skills to help people cope with it.

Changing Roles for Women

In their roles as mothers, women have the greatest influence on children and their life success. As women's self-confidence and self-reliance increase, so too should the self-confidence and self-reliance of their children. This in turn should have a positive effect on the family and society (Freiberg, 1991a; Gelles and Straus, 1989).

A recent study showed that *severe* family violence decreased by about 4 percent nationwide between 1975 and 1985 (Gelles and Straus, 1989). One reason for this decrease may be the changing roles of men and women within the family: more women today are working and bringing in salaries to help support the family, and more men are taking on greater responsibilities at home with children and chores. This decrease in family violence is only one of the many positive results of the changing roles of women.

On the negative side, as the roles of women expand to include more responsibilities and to meet increasingly higher expectations, the results will be greater stress and stress-related psychological and physical illness (Freiberg, 1991a). Cancer and heart disease, two stress-related illnesses, have already begun to increase. Many women will have to find ways to cope with being "supermoms," and families will have to find ways to negotiate the new and changing roles women have before them.

Educational Reform

Several of the stress-related problems discussed previously—indiscriminate violence, post-traumatic stress disorder, and the new pressures on women—can be addressed through the educational system. In both inner-city and suburban schools, efforts are currently underway to make education more appropriate to the specific ethnic and cultural backgrounds of the students, a concept called **multiculturalism**. It is thought that by being more relevant to the students, education can also be more accessible. The role of psychology in these efforts is to help teachers learn how to be more sensitive to individuals who differ from the norm.

Psychology has played an important role in the design of various new educational reform measures. One new approach, called progressive learning, uses the performance of each individual student as a measure of learning rather than comparing the individual to some group "norm." In this approach, problem areas as well as special skills can be recognized and instructional programs designed to meet the needs of the individual student. For example, if a child has difficulty with addition, individualized activities can be designed to present the material at an appropriate pace. Another educational approach, which has been in place for several years, is that of magnet schools. The magnet schools approach, used principally in large school systems, allows students to attend a school that addresses special needs or interests. One school, for example, may have special programs to encourage the performing arts; another may emphasize science and technology. Giving students a choice of programs encourages success. Magnet schools can also help break down racial and economic barriers because student populations are not drawn from narrow geographic locations.

Why is educational reform so important? The average worker today can expect to change jobs at least four times in his or her working lifetime. As the pace of innovation and technological change continues to increase into the next century, this rate of job change will no doubt increase as well. Education can help workers prepare to meet the challenge. Schooling must encourage flexibility as well as provide the basic skills needed to utilize current and future technologies. The creation of meaningful and effective strategies to educate and retrain people will continue to be a major challenge for psychologists and educators. Working together, they can prepare today's children for a productive work life in the twenty-first century.

PSYCHOLOGY AND WORK

Business is governed by the simple motives of profit and productivity. If any change can be made that will increase either, an individual or company somewhere will attempt to make it. One specialized area of research in psychology is industrial and organizational psychology. This field includes personnel, management processes, and organizational behavior (how organizations act as a whole). Industrial and organizational (I/O) psychologists study **human factors engineering**, which is concerned with how humans interact with their environment. Psychologists use this knowledge to design more efficient tools, machines, and work spaces.

Design of the Workplace

Recently, the 3M company built a new office building in Austin, Texas. The company had realized that many good ideas resulted from informal brainstorming during coffee breaks and casual discussion. 3M wanted to encourage this process in its new building by incorporating design elements that would facilitate the exchange of ideas. For that reason, hallways throughout the building open into "nodes," or special spaces, where employees can meet either on purpose or incidentally during the day. Psychologists have studied and contributed to the design of the work environment by creating such spaces and others that encourage specific activities. Research supports the idea that the characteristics of an office space, such as having a window or corner office, can be very rewarding and add to a person's job satisfaction (Greenberg, 1988).

While some buildings may be designed to encourage productive behavior, others may have basic flaws that make work more difficult. Industrial and organizational psychologists attempt to find ways to "cure" the problems brought on by flawed work spaces and working conditions. While many of these problems are psychological, "sick buildings" can also cause health problems. In a condition known as **sick-building syndrome**, work-

Psychologists help design airplanes.

Fact. Psychologists involved in human factors engineering help airplane designers determine the best locations for instruments in the cockpit. This helps the pilot achieve the greatest efficiency with minimal error. Human factors have become very important in the design of today's extremely complicated military planes.

ers develop symptoms such as eye irritation, headaches, and mental fatigue as a result of poor air quality (Freiberg, 1991b).

Stressors in the Workplace

While it is clear that well-designed work spaces can improve productivity, the major improvements will come from the redesign or restructure of work itself. Sick-building syndrome has been experienced in buildings with no known air-quality problems. In one study of workers in healthy buildings, those who experienced sick-building type symptoms tended to have more job dissatisfaction and to work more with computer video terminals (Freiberg, 1991a). Therefore, psychologists must determine how much of the syndrome is caused by the work space problems and how much is caused by job stress. They must then develop methods for dealing with the work space and also the well-being of the worker.

Figure 21.5
A major concern of many working parents is child care during working hours. Soon, more parents will be able to choose between child care at home or in the workplace.

As job stressors increase, productivity and health problems will continue to worsen. Among job-related stressors, concerns about job security is probably near the top of the list. Other factors that contribute to excessive stress are a concern for doing the job well, worry over meeting deadlines, the amount of repetition in a job, and a poor match of skills and job. A wide variety of possible solutions for job-related stress are already being tested. For example, one source of stress for many working parents concerns the care of their children while they are at work. To reduce this stress, some companies sponsor summer camp programs to take care of their employees' children during summer vacation. Many have instituted day-care centers in or near their office buildings to provide year-round support. To help ease the burden on working parents, some companies offer job-sharing, flexible hours, and work-at-home programs. Cross-training programs or educational programs to teach new skills are provided by some companies to help reduce the stress caused by boring and repetitive tasks. A common seminar topic today for all levels of corporate positions is stress management. In stress management, simple relaxation techniques are taught to help individuals improve their ability to cope with stress. Finally, the use of careful selection processes by employers can help reduce stress by improving the chance that an employee will be placed in a job that is appropriately matched to skills and ability. Both I/O psychologists and personnel psychologists have been instrumental in implementing new ways to relieve job stress.

Intelligent Machines

In recent years, automobile manufacturers have adopted production methods that depend heavily upon robots and computer-monitored work. Quality control is shared between humans and computers in an increasing number of industries. Both products and manufacturing methods are being revolutionized in many industries as they come under the control of microprocessor chips. The psychological fields of artificial intelligence and human factors engineering are involved in many of these changes. **Artificial intelligence** refers to the simulation of human thought processes by computer programming.

Contrary to one popular view, computers do not eliminate jobs; they create new ones. While a computer can analyze vast amounts of information quickly, someone must evaluate the results and respond to them. The same is true for robotic manufacturing. For example, an automobile manufacturer may use robotic painters for consistency and quality control, but the robot itself requires a great deal of maintenance and monitoring. Therefore, machines take over some human jobs, and humans become responsible for monitoring the machines. Unfortunately, the workers whose jobs have been replaced are not usually trained as robotics engineers. I/O psychologists work to help individuals who have been displaced by machines. On a practical level, they help displaced workers seek retraining so the workers can learn new skills and return to work as soon as possible. In addition, these individuals need counseling to help them cope with the sense of loss or failure that can accompany a job layoff.

Computers can recognize faces.

Fact. Researchers at the Salk Institute have created a computer program that converts pictures of faces into small units called pixels and further reduces these to about forty bits of information. The computer then "recognizes" features in the patterns of information. So far, the computer can distinguish male from female, and it is working on different emotional expressions.

Figure 21.6
Increasingly, automobile manufacturers are relying on robots in their production plants. Artificial intelligence, human factors engineering, and I/O psychology are three psychological fields involved in this development.

While the stressors of the future workplace pose a great challenge to psychology, psychological research in the field of artificial intelligence will play an important role in creating the workplace itself. Psychologists are studying how human beings make decisions, solve problems, and become experts. Slowly, they and scientists from other fields, such as computer science, are beginning to design computers that can duplicate some of these complex human processes. So-called **expert systems**—computer programs that can apply specific rules to a situation and make choices according to the preset rules—are already being applied in such areas as banking, pharmaceutical quality control, and the stock market. Of course, these systems are not error free. For example, when the Dow Jones Industrial Average of the stock market fell 508 points in October 1987, some analysts blamed the rapid fall on computerized trading programs that determine when to buy or sell stock. Since these programs operate much more rapidly than human brokers, many sell orders were complete before a "chain reaction" of selling could be stopped. Some people have questioned the extent to which these computer programs were responsible for the plunge in prices. Nevertheless, new rules concerning computer trading are being established to prevent a similar possibility in the future. As the twenty-first century begins, computers may both create new rules and programs and correct ineffective rules and program flaws.

Personnel Assessment

As new systems are introduced in the workplace, workers, managers, and executives will need a variety of skills to deal with them. Along with technical expertise, they will need flexibility and strong interpersonal skills to help them survive in a rapidly changing workplace. Psychologists in the educational and I/O fields are looking for better ways to identify and measure the skills and abilities of employees.

For more than forty years, general skills tests, such as the **General Aptitude Test Battery (GATB)**, have been used to measure basic manual and computational skills (basic math is extremely important in almost every job today). Such kinds of tests, however, do not reveal anything about a person's ability to solve simple problems, communicate with fellow workers, or assume leadership responsibilities.

An approach to testing called the **assessment center method** has recently become quite popular. It is based on the situational tests developed for the military in World War II (see Chapter 12). In this method, highly trained observers, called assessors, rate the performance of individuals in simulated work situations (Miner, 1988). For example, these simulations may require the individual to prepare responses to subordinates' concerns or to develop a plan for solving a manufacturing or scheduling problem. With this method, the responses of army officers, police chiefs, airplane pilots, senior executives, and others can be tested before they are actually placed in real-life situations. The assessment center method has become

Figure 21.7
The assessment center method, which puts individuals into simulated work situations, is used to test and train airline pilots.

an important training tool because it can simulate the challenges and problems that an individual will encounter in an actual work situation. After evaluation, the assessors and trainee can then devise strategies for strengthening weak skills and further strengthening strong ones.

Personnel decisions in the future will continue to rely on the ability of I/O psychologists to discover ways of measuring and assessing the skills of potential employees. Changes in the workplace, greater use of computers and computer technologies, increased stress, and new demands for employee cooperation will all be part of the coming century. The smart companies of the future will continue to look for better ways to find the right workers for the jobs available.

WAR AND PEACE

Just as psychology will play an important role in shaping life, health, and work in the next century, it will also continue to play a role in the politics of war and peace. There are three broad areas in which psychology can make a contribution. First, it can provide people with the knowledge to understand an enemy. Second, it can provide new technologies and techniques that improve or expand the limits of human performance. Research into vision, artificial intelligence, and decision making, for example, may have valuable military applications. Finally, the study of conflict resolution and social cooperation contributes to efforts toward peace.

Psychology and War

The role of psychology in war is not limited to the work of psychologists in helping soldiers deal with traumatic stress. Knowledge of the enemy—how it makes decisions, how it controls its forces, and the kinds of tactics that it may employ—is useful in developing military strategies. Understanding the personalities of the enemy's leadership can also be important. It can help military planners anticipate enemy reaction and thus is a crucial part of any military plan. In the Persian Gulf War, for example, President Bush and other senior officials regularly received detailed psychological profiles of Saddam Hussein prepared by psychiatrists and psychologists.

In the same war, reference was sometimes made to "psych ops," the military term for psychological operations. This refers to the use of psychology to confuse and unnerve the enemy. Psychology can be used in wartime to devise strategies for undermining the enemy's combat effectiveness. Such strategies might include the use of subtle "disinformation" to confuse the enemy or the use of intense bombing to demoralize enemy troops. In the Persian Gulf War, the possibility that Iraq might employ chemical weapons created a certain atmosphere of terror and influenced the coalition partners' decision making. On the one hand, the chemical weapons threat made the United States and its allies reluctant to engage in a land battle. On the other hand, it made Saddam Hussein appear to be a wicked person and thus made the war more acceptable to many people.

An important tool of war is propaganda—information that is prepared and released in such a way that it influences people's attitudes, feelings, and judgments. Propaganda is useful for uniting people against a common enemy, as well as for confusing the enemy. When America's leaders began comparing Saddam Hussein to Adolf Hitler, the American people quickly identified him as one of the worst evils of the twentieth century. At the same time, this comparison conveyed a certain message to Israel and the Soviet Union, whose peoples suffered greatly at the hands of the Nazis.

In the future, the ability to judge world opinion and manipulate individual fears will no doubt become increasingly accurate; and this will affect the way psychology is applied to war. At the same time, the increased deadliness of warfare makes it increasingly important to apply psychology toward the quest for peace.

Peace Psychology

The thought that psychology is so involved with war has deeply concerned psychologists for decades. Psychology is supposed to help people live better lives, not wage war more successfully. Of course, psychology does have an important role in the pursuit of peace. That role includes contributions to diplomacy and statesmanship—helping diplomats better understand how to negotiate with others and helping leaders understand the attitudes and expectations of leaders from other countries.

In their study of decision making, psychologists have noted errors of **groupthink**, a decision-making process identified in groups operating under pressure or in time of crisis. Groupthink leads to premature decisions based upon incomplete evidence, as well as to a high degree of commitment to group decisions and a tendency to ignore any information that suggests possible failure. This groupthink phenomenon is thought to have been the cause of President Kennedy's disastrous decision to undertake the Bay of Pigs operation in 1961. Apparently, the solidarity of Kennedy's advisers, as well as their own desires to preserve their power and remain in the inner circle, led to their failure to criticize the decision to invade Cuba. Kennedy, for his part, could not be expected to criticize views that confirmed his own. Such errors of thinking, which can lead to faulty, and potentially dangerous, decisions can be avoided when the processes involved are better understood (Janis, 1972).

The characteristics of leadership are a major focus of the psychological study of peace. This is partly because leadership involves the holding and exercising of power and partly because leadership is required to achieve peace. The desire for power has often led nations to war. For the last few decades, it has also led nations to build huge arsenals of weapons that can be used in offensive aggression, provide defense against aggression, and ultimately secure the power of the nation and its leader. As part of these military arsenals, nuclear weapons have dramatically changed the international balance of power. Because of the potential for devastation, the only meaningful defense against nuclear attack is to prevent any nation from using nuclear weapons. Anything less could have catastrophic results. Nuclear weapons policy has thus stressed deterrence—to deter the enemy

Figure 21.8
Depicting Saddam Hussein as an evil man made it easier to justify U.S. involvement in the Persian Gulf War. Psychology is an important part of any war strategy.

Figure 21.9
World leaders need the support of their people in their efforts to promote peace. Psychology can play a major role in this by encouraging an attitude of tolerance toward other nations.

from using nuclear weapons by having more of them. Psychology can help address this situation and others in two ways. First, psychology can help improve our understanding of leaders and supporters, and knowing how they interact can help prevent errors of decision making such as groupthink. Second, psychology can devise ways of converting the desire for power to less confrontational modes, such as the expression of human compassion or cooperation. However, reaching the goal of eliminating violence is still far in the future (Frank, 1986).

Attitudes toward others are another factor that can be related to peace. Biases toward people from cultures that differ from our own can work against peaceful relations. Psychology, because it promotes an attitude of tolerance and acceptance of others, can therefore play an important role in working toward peace. Chances for peace depend upon people tolerating the views of others. Changes in relations between the United States and the Soviet Union serve as an example of what can happen when attitudes change. For more than forty years, the Soviet Union was seen as America's great enemy, an "evil empire" in the words of Ronald Reagan. In recent years, the attitudes of the two nations' leaders and people have changed, and the nations have become partners in peace.

Nuclear weapons, international terrorism, and regional wars still dominate people's fears about the future of world peace. Psychologists must translate these fears into motivations toward peace. To do so, they continue to study the ways people misperceive others, the methods of resolving international conflict, the errors that lead to bad decision making, and other aspects of human behavior that lead to misunderstanding, aggression, and violence. As much as any topic discussed in this chapter, the goal of peace is one of the major obligations of the application of psychology to the human condition. As with many other aspects of the future, this effort will require that psychologists work together with experts in other disciplines to achieve this crucial goal.

CHAPTER REVIEW

KEY TERMS

- artificial intelligence
- assessment center method
- CAT scan
- expert systems
- gene therapy
- General Aptitude Test Battery (GATB)

- groupthink
- human factors engineering
- magnetic resonance imaging (MRI)
- multiculturalism
- positron emission tomography scan (PET scan)

- post-traumatic stress disorder (PTSD)
- sick-building syndrome

SUMMARY

1. Biological psychologists investigate the relationship between the brain and behavior using PET scans, CAT scans, and MRI. These methods produce precise pictures of brain structure and activity.

2. In the future, gene therapy may be used to treat cancer, certain types of mental illness, and possibly drug addiction.

3. Violence, war, accidents, and natural disasters can lead to post-traumatic stress disorder. PTSD has been experienced by many veterans of the Vietnam War. Military psychologists have since devised methods to prevent or lessen the likelihood of PTSD.

4. Women's changing roles will increase the stress in their lives. Increased stress has already contributed to greater rates of heart disease and cancer among women.

5. Education will play an important role in preparing individuals for the twenty-first century. A number of reforms, such as progressive learning and magnet schools, are currently being tried. Education can help people meet the challenges presented by frequent job changes.

6. Industrial/organizational psychologists study personnel issues, management processes, and organizational behavior. Psychologists have contributed to improvements in building designs and to methods for reducing workplace stress.

7. Psychologists study the factors involved in job satisfaction and improved performance and then try to use this knowledge to improve working conditions.

8. Artificial intelligence will change the way much work is performed. Computers have the potential to increase the quality of work and the productivity of the individual worker. Computers do not eliminate jobs; they create new ones.

9. Psychologists are studying the ways humans make decisions and solve problems, and are developing expert systems—computer programs that can duplicate some complex human processes.

10. New personnel assessment tools, such as the assessment center method, help employers place people in jobs that are more appropriate to their individual skills and interests.

11. Psychologists deal with issues of war through analysis of the enemy and the devising of strategies that will be useful against the enemy. Such strategies might include disinformation and propaganda.

12. The study of leadership contributes to the study of peace, and psychologists hope to attain the goal of world peace through better understanding of conflicts and of people's attitudes toward others.

REVIEW QUESTIONS

1. Why are PET scans and MRI preferred over EEGs and CAT scans? What kind of information do these newer technologies provide?

2. How is gene therapy used to create new drugs? What are some possible uses for these new drugs?

3. What is post-traumatic stress disorder?

4. Are veterans of the Persian Gulf War as likely to suffer post-traumatic stress disorder as were the veterans of the Vietnam War? Why or why not?

5. What are some of the new stressors facing women today and in the future?

6. What are some advantages of the progressive learning model in education? How might progressive learning differ from the traditional approach?

7. What are some of the issues that industrial and organizational psychologists study?

8. What is sick-building syndrome?

9. What are some possible solutions for reducing job-related stress?

10. What is the assessment center method, and what are some of its advantages?

11. In what way can psychologists help in understanding issues related to war and peace?

ACTIVITIES

1. Biological psychology, like medicine, assumes that human biology has a powerful influence over human behavior. Consider how you view this connection. How much of your behavior is influenced by your biology? How much is influenced by other factors? What are some of those other factors?

2. Consider whether stress is increasing or decreasing in your life. What are you doing to cope with stress? What aspects of the future do you think will cause the most stress in your life? Why?

3. Look around your house or apartment and count the number of electronic appliances and other pieces of electronic equipment. Compare this to the number of devices your grandparents had. What differences have these devices made in your life? Now consider what technologies will be available to your grandchildren. How might this affect them?

4. Ask several of your friends who have applied for jobs recently to describe the hiring process they went through. Were their interviews structured? Did they have to take tests? If so, what types of tests were they? Did the tests seem appropriate to the nature of the job? Did your friends think the hiring process was fair?

5. Look through the politics section of several newsmagazines and observe the number of times the articles refer to a leader's personality, the way he or she makes decisions, and other psychological references. Do these references seem relevant to understanding the person's behavior? How has this person's psychological profile influenced his or her effectiveness as a leader?

How to Write a Research Paper

Because psychology is a discipline based on research and experimentation, it is quite likely that you will be assigned a research paper in the course of your studies. A research paper is a long, formal essay that includes information gathered from several sources. The prospect of writing a paper usually stimulates much thought—and perhaps much anxiety. You may have questions such as, "How do I find a good topic?" "How will I decide which issues to discuss?" "Where can I find psychology sources in the library?" and "How will I be able to write clearly about a subject as complex as psychology?"

This appendix is intended to help you deal with these issues. The process of writing a paper is straightforward when you follow certain steps. These steps include choosing a topic, creating a preliminary outline, doing research at the library, taking notes and revising the outline, and writing the paper. The last step is formatting the paper, or following guidelines for acceptable style and form.

Among the first considerations are what kind of research paper your instructor requires, how long it should be, what types of references are acceptable, what the desired format is, and when the paper is due. If you are unclear about any of these matters, ask your instructor to clarify what is expected. It is important for you to get a clear sense of your assignment before you start. Otherwise, you may end up wasting time trying to do something that is not expected, and ultimately, you will not fulfill your class requirements. It is also a good idea to start work on your paper as soon as possible. This will give you more time to prepare and to use source materials in the library.

Choosing a Topic
Creating a Preliminary Outline
Doing Research at the Library
Using the Catalog System
• Using Source Materials
Taking Notes and Revising the Outline
Writing the Paper
Formatting the Paper
Following General Guidelines
• Following Style Guidelines

CHOOSING A TOPIC

If your instructor does not assign a topic, you will have to choose your own subject. One way to do this is to examine your interests within the field of psychology. If you are interested in psychotherapy, for instance, you may elect to write about one particular form of psychotherapy, or you could

533

compare two or three types. The important thing is to choose a subject general enough to enable you to find sufficient information, yet narrow enough for you to explore your ideas fully. A good place to start is your textbook. Scanning the table of contents and major headings within the chapters may help you choose a topic suitable for your research paper. You can narrow your general subject by checking resources in the library. While you work on developing the topic, remember that it is important to choose one that interests you.

CREATING A PRELIMINARY OUTLINE

Once you have selected a topic and before you start your research, write a preliminary outline. A preliminary outline consists of the major headings you think you will include in your paper. You may know little about your topic, but it does not matter how rough the outline is at this point. What is important is that you force yourself to think about your subject. Suppose you decide to write about adolescents and drugs. Your outline might look like the one shown in Figure A.1. Although the outline will probably be brief and may not reflect the final paper, it will help organize your thoughts and give you a starting point from which to work.

Figure A.1
Preliminary outline.

```
                    ADOLESCENTS AND DRUGS


        I.   Introduction

       II.   Characteristics of adolescents who take drugs

      III.   Reasons for drug abuse

       IV.   Types of popular drugs

        V.   Amounts taken, where, and when

       VI.   Treating drug abuse

      VII.   Conclusion
```

DOING RESEARCH AT THE LIBRARY

Modern libraries have grown more sophisticated in recent years. Most now have computerized catalog and search systems that make finding source material much easier than it used to be. However, librarians are still available to help you locate whatever you need. Do not hesitate to ask them for assistance. In this section, we will discuss some basic aspects of the catalog system and the types of references that will be most helpful to you.

Using the Catalog System

The traditional card catalog system is a collection of cards arranged in alphabetical order and stored in drawers. Books are listed by subject, author (last name first), and title. For example, information on the title *General Psychological Theory* by Sigmund Freud would be found on a subject card under "Psychoanalysis," on an author card under "Freud," and on a title card under *General Psychological Theory*. Each card would include useful information such as the book's location in the library and the year the book was published.

The computer card catalog system provides similar information but is much easier to access than the traditional system. The computer card catalog system is located on computer terminals in the library. The program is user friendly, telling you exactly what to do. Computer card catalog systems differ from library to library, so if you aren't sure how to use one, ask the librarian.

The titles in any catalog system appear with a call number, which refers to either the Dewey Decimal System (usually used in small and medium-sized libraries) or the Library of Congress Classification System (usually found in large libraries). Regardless of the system used in your library, each book has a unique number that enables you to find it. Some books have special letters in front of their call numbers to designate a specific category. For example, reference books have an "R" in front of their call numbers. These books are usually grouped together on the main floor of the library. They cannot be taken out; you may use them only in the library.

When you find specific books dealing with your general subject in the catalog system, be sure to write down the author, title, and call number. If you do not record enough information, you may not be able to locate a title. Recording all of the information the first time around can save you a good deal of time later.

Sometimes it is useful to browse through the section in the library where the books that interest you are located. This enables you to see the variety of books available on a general subject. By examining the different titles on the shelves, you may be able to find more references, and this may also help you narrow your topic area.

Using Source Materials

There are two categories of printed source materials. Primary sources are those that report directly on a subject and convey the writer's own observations, reactions, theories, or conclusions. Secondary sources are derivative. They usually involve the compilation or interpretation of primary source materials. For example, books by Piaget or Freud on their theories are primary sources. In contrast, a book by someone else that describes Piaget's or Freud's theories is a secondary source. An experiment reported by its creators is a primary source, whereas your textbook, which tells you about others' experiments, is a secondary source. Other secondary sources include newspaper articles and abstracts published in various psychology journals. Each type of source material has its advantages. Reading a primary source gives you the opportunity to form your own opinions about the material. A secondary source allows you to see how someone else views the material, and it may provide certain insights. Instructors usually ask their students to use a combination of both kinds of source materials. Make sure you know what your instructor requires.

In addition to books, you will find that periodicals, which include magazines and journals, are a good source of information. The advantage of using periodicals is that they are often more up-to-date than the books you find. Most current periodicals are available in bound form in the library. Older issues are usually put on microfilm. Magazine and journal articles are referenced in several places in the library.

Perhaps the most important periodical reference source for the field of psychology is *Psychological Abstracts*, a collection of abstracts, or summaries, of professional journal articles in psychology and related behavioral and social sciences. *Psychological Abstracts* is published monthly by the American Psychological Association and is available in most college libraries. The articles are arranged according to subject, and an annual index of abstracts organized by subject and author is also available. By reading the summary of an article, you can get an idea of what the article is about and decide whether it would be useful for you to read the entire article. Full bibliographical information is also included.

Another periodical reference is the *Readers' Guide to Periodical Literature*. Published bimonthly, quarterly, and yearly, it lists articles in popular magazines and journals, such as *Time*, *Newsweek*, and *Psychology Today*. The articles are listed by subject and author. Titles of all the magazines included, along with their abbreviations, are given at the beginning of the book. When you find articles you want to read, copy all of the bibliographical information given. Then ask the librarian how to go about finding the appropriate periodicals in your particular library.

Periodical listings may also be computerized. One system, called Info-Trac, includes periodicals such as the *Journal of the American Medical Association* and *Psychology Today*, as well as the *New York Times Index* (a guide to feature articles and news stories in that newspaper). Like the computerized book catalog, InfoTrac is user friendly. You simply type in your topic, and the screen will show you all the subheadings under that category.

As you look through the book and periodical catalogs, be discriminating in the references you decide to use. For example, there may be a dozen books on Piaget. It would be unrealistic to try to read all of them. Basically, there are two criteria on which to base your choice. First, try to use books that have been recommended, either in your textbook's bibliography or by your instructor. Second, unless you know a book is a classic, choose the most current books (usually those published within the last five years), which are likely to cover new developments in the field.

TAKING NOTES AND REVISING THE OUTLINE

Once you have chosen your source materials and located them in the library, you are ready to begin reading them, taking notes, and revising your outline. When you are ready to begin this process, make sure that you are in a quiet, comfortable place and that you have all the necessary materials such as a pen or pencil, note cards, and paper. Students waste a lot of time when they are not fully organized.

Before you begin to take notes, remember that when you sit down to write your paper, your notes will be all you have to use. The books and periodicals will be back in the library. Therefore, your notes must be clear, concise, and complete. Remember, however, that it is impractical to take notes on every sentence or paragraph you read. You must decide what's important as you do your research.

When taking notes, use two types of cards, either two different colors or two different sizes. Use one set of cards for your bibliography. Each of these cards should contain full bibliographical information for one book or periodical (we will talk more about bibliographical form in the section on style later in this appendix). Number each bibliography card so that when you take notes from a source you need only put the number of the bibliographical card and the page number on your note cards.

Use the other type of cards for taking notes. Each note card should begin with the number of the reference, the page number from which you are taking the notes, and a heading taken from your outline. For example, suppose you are writing a paper based on the outline in Figure A.1. One major heading to use on your note cards would be "Types of popular drugs." As you gather more information, you may want to add other headings to your preliminary outline, headings such as "Alcohol," "Peer pressure," and "Family problems." In fact, taking notes and revising your outline go on simultaneously. As you learn more about your subject, you should amend your outline and possibly narrow your topic. For example, because there is so much information on adolescents and drugs, it would be better to narrow the subject of your paper to a specific abused substance. Figure A.2 shows a final outline that focuses on alcohol.

In writing your notes, you can use direct quotations, or you can rewrite a passage to communicate the basic ideas. Take special care to avoid plagiarism, which is using other people's words or thoughts without giving them proper credit. In effect, plagiarism is stealing other people's work and pretending it is your own. For example, if you were to copy a direct quotation from a book or periodical to use in your paper, you would need to put it in quotation marks and give credit to its source. If you wanted to present it as your own, you would have to do more than change some of the words and delete some of the phrases. Otherwise, it would be considered plagiarism.

Figure A.2
Final outline.

```
                    ADOLESCENTS AND ALCOHOL

    I.   Introduction
         A. How many adolescents abuse alcohol
         B. Why focus on alcohol

   II.   How alcohol is abused
         A. Amount
         B. Where it is abused
         C. How it is procured

  III.   Characteristics of adolescents who abuse alcohol
         A. Depression
         B. School problems
         C. Anger
         D. Impulsiveness

   IV.   Reasons for alcohol abuse
         A. Peer pressure
         B. Family problems
         C. Poor role models

    V.   Treating alcohol abuse
         A. Media advertising
         B. Recognizing early warning signs
         C. Organizations
            1. AA (Alcoholics Anonymous)
            2. S.A.D.D. (Students Against Drunk Driving)
         D. Residential programs

   VI.   Conclusion
         A. The situation as it is
         B. What the future can bring
```

You can avoid using too many direct quotations in your paper by paraphrasing statements from a source. However, in most cases, you must still cite that source. We will discuss the form for citing sources in the last section of this appendix.

On the other hand, when you introduce new examples or new ideas (those that originate with you), no citations are necessary. Similarly, widely known facts and widely shared ideas carry no citations. For example, you could write, "Adults use conditioning to shape a child's development." Although this exact sentence may appear in one of the many books on child development, the statement is considered a piece of general information. Simply stating it does not constitute plagiarism.

Sometimes it is difficult to decide whether or not you need to cite a source. When in doubt, cite it.

As you learn more about your subject, taking notes becomes easier and less time-consuming. For example, information often appears in more than one source. In that case, you need only write it down once. This will help you limit your number of references. Furthermore, once you have narrowed your topic, you no longer have to read materials on other subjects. It is easier to concentrate on the references that deal with your specific topic.

When you finish taking notes, organize your note cards by headings. Then organize the headings according to your outline. Now you are ready to begin writing.

WRITING THE PAPER

When you start writing the paper, there are a number of simple rules to follow. First, keep in mind that writing also involves rewriting. Do not expect your first draft to be your final draft. If you do, you may sit for a very long time in front of a blank piece of paper trying to write the "perfect" sentence. It is more important to get your ideas on paper. You can polish your prose later.

Write as simply and directly as possible. Think about the points you want to make before you get caught up in difficult psychological terms. Your introduction should state simply what the paper is about and the ways in which you are going to amplify your topic. The body of the paper should illuminate the points you said you would make in your introduction. Develop each point into a paragraph. Finally, the conclusion should reflect the accomplishment of what you set out to present.

Once you have finished your first draft, it is often helpful to put aside your paper for a day or two. Being "too close" to a paper can make it difficult to see its strengths and weaknesses. Come back to it after you have distanced yourself from the subject for a while. This will help you evaluate its quality and make improvements. In the final draft, improvements usually take the form of clarifying any vague or ambiguous statements, correcting spelling and grammatical errors, and generally refining your style. It is helpful to keep some writers' references close at hand. You can use a thesaurus to find synonyms and antonyms, and a dictionary will help you with spelling and the use of precise language. You can also use a guide for writers to get tips on how to write effectively.

FORMATTING THE PAPER

Your instructor will undoubtedly have many term papers to read. In order to communicate your ideas, it is important to present them in a clear, legible manner. In this section we will discuss how to format your paper.

Following General Guidelines

Research papers should be typed and double-spaced on white paper with neat margins. Begin the paper with a title page that includes the title of the paper, your name, the course name and section number, and the date. All pages should be numbered except for the title page and page 1 of the text. If you do not have access to a typewriter or word processor, find out whether you can rent one or use one in a library.

Following Style Guidelines

Papers in psychology usually follow the style of the *Publication Manual of the American Psychological Association* (APA), Third Edition. This manual includes tips on everything from organizing your manuscript to specific word usage. All of the information on research papers in this appendix reflects APA style. You can locate the APA manual in the reference section of your library. In this section, we will review how to cite references in your paper and how to compile a reference list according to APA style.

Citing References in Text. When you cite a reference in the text of your paper, you need to use the name of the author and the date of publication.

Suppose you were using some material from the second edition of *History of Psychology* by David Hothersall, which was published in 1990. You might write:

> According to Hothersall (1990), psychology's past includes both successes and failures.

or

> The *History of Psychology* (Hothersall, 1990) includes both successes and failures.

In either case, you give credit to the source. In the first citation, the author's name is included in the text so only the date of publication appears in parentheses. In the second citation, you want your reader to know the name of the source, so you put the author's name and publication date in parentheses right after the title.

When the information you are presenting is not the result of paraphrasing very general ideas from another source or widely known facts, you may also need to include a page number as shown in Figure A.3, citation 1. If you are including a direct quotation, you must cite the page number (see Figure A.3, citation 2).

When there are two authors, always list both authors (see Figure A.3, citation 3). When there are more than two authors and fewer than six authors, list all the authors in the first citation. In subsequent citations, list the first author followed by "et al." (see Figure A.3, citation 4). When there are six or more authors, list the first author followed by "et al." in all citations, including the first.

Citation 1: Citation with page number

Whiskey making was a deeply rooted folk custom in the subsistence economy of colonial America (Fellmann, 1991, p. 215).

Citation 2: Citation for a direct quotation

"Both man and society change, and, as they do, 'human nature' changes with them" (Szasz, 1961, p. 7).

Or

According to Szasz (1961, p. 7), "both man and society change, and, as they do, 'human nature' changes with them."

Citation 3: Journal article, two authors

One study (Cooper & Marshall, 1976) estimated that cardiovascular disease accounts for 13 percent of worker absenteeism in the United States.

Citation 4: Journal article, more than two and fewer than six authors

First citation: In a study by Hokanson, DeGood, Forrest, and Brittain (1963), errors on cognitive tasks were punished with mild electric shocks.

Or

In one study (Hokanson, DeGood, Forrest, & Brittain, 1963), errors on cognitive tasks were punished with mild electric shocks.

Later citation of the same article: We need more studies like the one by Hokanson et al. (1963).

Citations indicate that the information and conclusions you are presenting are substantiated and properly credited. The form of a citation gives the reader enough information to look up the full reference in your reference list.

Compiling a Reference List. When you put together a reference list, include only the references that you cited in your paper. References should appear with the last name of each author first, followed by a comma, then initials for first and middle names. References should be arranged in alphabetical order according to the name of the first author, then the name of second author, and so on.

An entry that is authored by one author comes before an entry by that author and others. Thus, "Lamb, M. E." comes before "Lamb, M. E., & Bornstein, M. H." Entries by the same author(s) are ordered by copyright/publication date, with the earliest one first: Sroufe, L. A. (1979) precedes Sroufe, L. A. (1983).

Figure A.4
Types of reference list entries.

1. **Book**

    Sroufe, L. A., & Cooper, R. G. (1988). <u>Child</u> <u>development</u>: <u>Its</u>
    <u>nature</u> <u>and</u> <u>course.</u> New York: McGraw-Hill.

2. **Article/chapter in an edited book**

    Offer, D., Ostrov, E., & Howard, K. I. (1984). Epidemiology
    of mental health and mental illness among adolescents. In J.
    Call (Ed.), <u>Significant</u> <u>advances</u> <u>in</u> <u>child</u> <u>psychiatry</u> (pp.
    231-264). New York: Basic Books.

3. **Journal article**

    Zigler, E. (1987). Formal schooling for four-year olds? No.
    <u>American</u> <u>Psychologist,</u> 42, 254-260.

4. **Magazine article**

    Rosen, R. D. (1982, November). Self-help smorgasbord. <u>Psychology</u>
    <u>Today,</u> pp. 24-33.

5. **Newspaper article**

    Schuchman, M. (1991, February 21). Psychological help for chil-
    dren in urban combat. <u>The</u> <u>New</u> <u>York</u> <u>Times,</u> p. 39.

Examples of actual reference list entries are shown in Figure A.4. Use the exact punctuation indicated. Capitalize only the first letter of journal articles and book titles and their subtitles. For books, include author name(s), copyright date, book title, place of publication, and publisher. This information can be found on the front and back of the book's title page. For an article or chapter in an edited book, list the elements in this order: the author(s) of the chapter/article, the title of the chapter/article, then "In" followed by the name of the editor of the book, with first initial(s) first, then last name, the book title, page numbers of the chapter/article, place of publication, and publisher.

The information that you need for journal articles will be listed in the reference catalogs. This is why it is important to have accurate bibliography cards. For a journal article, list the author(s), year of publication, title of the article, title of the journal, the volume number (journals are organized in volumes), and the page numbers. The listings for magazine and newspaper articles are similar to those for journal articles. As shown in Figure A.4, however, they include the year, month, and—where appropriate—day of publication, but they do not include the volume number.

Careers in Psychology

Everyone knows what the baker and the boxer do for a living, but the work of psychologists is not so clearly defined. Not that one has to look far to find a psychologist. The media regularly call on psychologists to give expert opinion on everything from the next target of a serial killer to the impact a war will have on young TV viewers. The local bookstore carries dozens of self-help books written by psychologists. Watch TV, and chances are that one of the talk shows will have a psychologist on its panel.

WHAT IS A PSYCHOLOGIST?

Popular images give many people a mistaken notion that psychology is really "shrinkology" and that all psychologists try to analyze other people's personalities and conduct therapy in their spare time. Psychologists are often stereotyped as clinicians or counselors. In fact, there are numerous subfields in which psychologists are involved primarily in scientific research. Many psychologists have neither counseled patients nor practiced psychotherapy.

Psychologists have studied the distorted images that people have of them and their profession. Webb and Speer (1985) asked people to write essays about psychologists, psychiatrists, and scientists. They found that there was a strong correlation between the way people viewed psychiatrists and psychologists but a low correlation between the popular views of psychologists and scientists. Psychologists were seen as "tender-minded clinicians preoccupied with psychological abnormality" (Webb and Speer, 1985).

The majority of psychologists in the United States are interested in clinical issues, such as studying abnormal behavior and conducting psychotherapy. However, a large and very diverse group of psychologists hold jobs in other areas.

What Is a Psychologist?
Becoming a Psychologist

Specialty Areas in Psychology
Physiological Psychology
• Experimental Psychology
• Developmental Psychology
• Social Psychology • Clinical Psychology

Applications of Psychology to Careers and Professions
Psychology Applied to the Military • Psychology Applied to Education • Psychology Applied to Medical Settings • Psychology Applied to Legal Issues • Psychology Applied to Business and Organizations

543

Figure B.1
People with a master's degree in psychology can find employment in different fields. They can work for the government, or they can work in schools administering and interpreting psychological tests.

Becoming a Psychologist

Most of the jobs psychologists hold require a doctoral degree. To earn this, a candidate must have an undergraduate degree and then devote four to six years to intense study and research in one of the specialty areas of psychology. Doctoral programs are offered at major universities and at a few professional psychology schools. Between 1979 and 1988, 31,522 candidates were awarded psychology doctorates in the United States (Rosenzweig, 1991). There are two kinds of doctoral degrees: the Ph.D. (doctor of philosophy), which requires an independent research project known as the doctoral dissertation in addition to course work, and the Psy.D. (doctor of psychology), which emphasizes course work and practical training and does not require a doctoral dissertation. Most recipients of the Psy.D. degree specialize in clinical and counseling psychology.

Many psychology programs, particularly those in the clinical and counseling areas, also require students to spend a year of psychological internship, during which they learn the practice of psychology in a supervised setting. All fifty states have licensing or certification requirements for psychologists who set up a clinical practice. Obtaining a license may involve further supervised experience and a licensing exam.

Some people who want to be psychologists lack the money, time, aptitude, or patience required to obtain a doctoral degree. Can they still be psychologists? The answer is a resounding yes. Many people work as psychologists after having earned a master's (M.A. or M.S.) degree. Typically, the master's degree involves several years of course work beyond an undergraduate degree and may also require a research project or paper known as the master's thesis.

Today master's programs in psychology are very popular, and graduates have found employment in a variety of fields. Some work as school psychologists, administering and interpreting psychological tests; others work for the government, teach at community colleges, or work in rehabilitation counseling (Wortman and Loftus, 1985).

Although relatively few people who take a basic psychology course decide to become professional psychologists, psychology is often chosen as a major at the undergraduate level. More than 2,000 colleges and universities in the United States offer a four-year bachelor of arts (B.A.) or bachelor of science (B.S.) degree in psychology (Rosenzweig, 1991). Although a B.A. or B.S. degree in psychology might not be sufficient to obtain a job in a psychological setting, it could lead to a job such as a psychological technician, administrative aide, or research assistant in a correctional institution or rehabilitation program. In addition, some people with undergraduate degrees in psychology work in such areas as advertising and personnel, where their training in psychology has a practical application (Wortman and Loftus, 1985). Of course, more advanced degrees usually enable a person to earn a higher salary and enjoy greater career opportunities.

SPECIALTY AREAS IN PSYCHOLOGY

The types of career specialties psychologists choose are so different that you may wonder what they have in common. In most cases, the answer is *behavior*. Regardless of their specialty, psychologists are united by their interest in understanding behavior.

At one time, the world of psychology was so simple that one person could be an expert in many, if not all, its specialty fields. However, today's world is so complex that no one person can know all there is to know about behavior. To deal with this explosion of psychological knowledge, psychologists specialize in one area of the study of behavior. The American Psychological Association (APA), which was founded in 1892, now includes more than 100,000 members, associates, fellows, and affiliates (Strickland, 1988) and has forty-five divisions (American Psychological Association, 1990).

Physiological Psychology

Perhaps the most "scientific" of psychology's specialty areas is physiological psychology. A *physiological psychologist* believes that most or all psychological events are the result of a basic biological or chemical process. Many physiological psychologists conduct research on the functioning of the nervous system and study the way in which brain cells communicate with one another. Study of the brain and its chemical messengers is the focus of many physiological psychologists.

One area of study in which recent advances have been made is that of brain damage following serious head injuries. Physiological psychologists hope that a better understanding of the effects of head injuries on the brain will help psychologists treat or prevent the devastating effects of head trauma.

Experimental Psychology

When the field of psychology was founded more than a hundred years ago, experimental psychology was its primary area. Although less popular as a career choice today, experimental psychology has played an important role in establishing psychology as a scientifically based field. *Experimental psychologists* use the scientific method (for example, controlled laboratory experiments) to study basic facets of behavior, including sensation, perception, learning, memory, problem solving, motivation, emotion, thinking, and language.

In the past decade, computers that can function in a way that imitates human intelligence have appeared. These computers perform complex tasks, such as playing chess, that require a form of reasoning. Such developments in artificial intelligence have encouraged experimental psychologists to devote more attention to the study of complex human mental processes, including reasoning, memory, and problem solving. Psychologists interested in these areas are called *cognitive psychologists*. Because the ideas of cognitive psychology have become so influential, some have said that psychology has undergone a "cognitive revolution."

Developmental Psychology

Many people are attracted to psychology because they want to help individuals with psychological problems. *Developmental psychologists*, on the other hand, are interested in the factors that influence growth and development. Because developmental psychologists study changes in behavior, their interests can involve many subfields of psychology, such as social, personality, cognitive, and physiological psychology.

At one time, developmental psychologists focused primarily on the behavior of infants and young children. This focus has now broadened to a

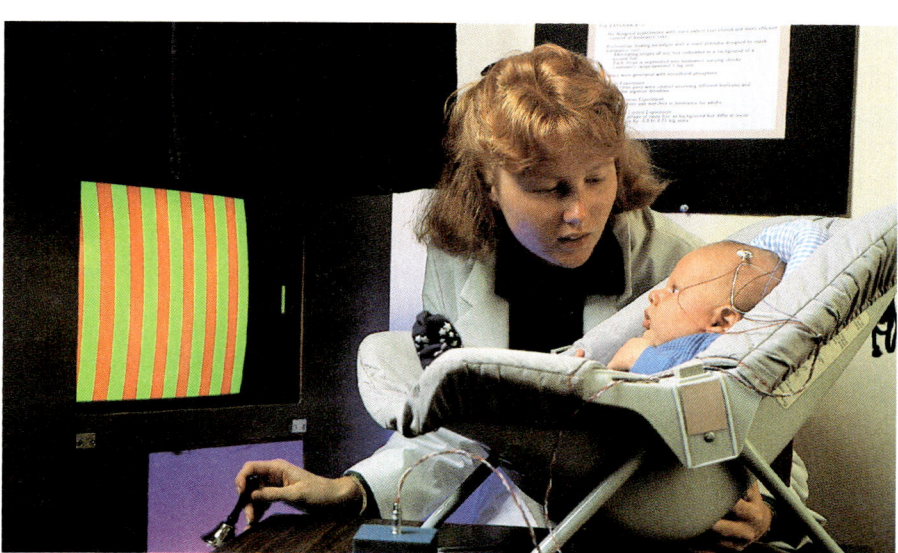

Figure B.2
Many developmental psychologists concentrate on infant and child behavior in order to predict behavior in the future. These psychologists are concerned with the factors that influence growth and development.

CAREERS IN PSYCHOLOGY   **547**

life-span approach in which development is studied from conception to death.

However, many developmental psychologists continue to concentrate on infant and child behavior. For example, developmental psychologists have recently devised intelligence, or IQ, tests for infants as young as six months (Kolata, 1989). The tests make it possible to identify babies who are at risk of doing poorly in school, as well as those who are likely to be above average in intelligence. Early identification allows intervention with low-IQ individuals so that their future academic performance can be enhanced.

Social Psychology

"No man is an island," the poet John Donne wrote, meaning that human beings need others to survive and prosper. *Social psychologists* study the influence of other people on our behavior. These psychologists conduct research on how people's behavior is affected by the actual or imagined presence of others (Tedeschi, Lindskold, and Rosenfeld, 1985). They attempt to answer such questions as whether individuals will harm others if they are ordered to, what the nature of attitudes is, and how we change our actions in public to impress others (Giacalone and Rosenfeld, 1989). One social psychologist, Zick Rubin, has even attempted to study a topic many psychologists have found elusive—love. Rubin (1970) distributed a questionnaire to several hundred dating couples at the University of Michigan. Their answers led him to conclude that love can be reduced to three core components: attachment, caring, and intimacy.

Because much of human behavior is affected by social situations, social psychologists often work closely with psychologists in other specialties. For instance, there is a good deal of overlap between social psychology and personality psychology. *Personality psychologists* study individual differences in behavior—the impact of traits such as self-esteem, aggressiveness, and shyness. However, since these and other traits are affected by the presence of other people, social and personality psychologists often study similar phenomena. Because the social dynamics of the workplace can affect productivity, social psychologists also study behavior in organizations (Giacalone and Rosenfeld, 1989).

Clinical Psychology

Clinical psychologists specialize in the assessment and treatment of people who have adjustment, emotional, or other psychological problems. Most clinical psychologists are trained to conduct and understand psychological research as well as to apply the findings of research.

Clinical psychology is now the most popular career area for psychologists. Over one-third of all new psychology doctorates in the United States are awarded in clinical psychology (Rosenzweig, 1991). Most clinical psychologists work in hospitals, clinics, or their own private practice.

Clinical psychology is often confused with the related areas of psychiatry and counseling psychology. Although both clinical psychologists and psychiatrists attempt to diagnose and treat abnormal behavior, there are basic differences between them. An old joke goes: "Question: What's the difference between a psychiatrist and a clinical psychologist?" "Answer: about $50 an hour!" This joke reflects the fact that psychiatrists frequently have more prestige and earn more money than clinical psychologists (Kingsbury, 1987). Clinical psychologists are trained in a psychology graduate program and typically receive a Ph.D. degree. Psychiatrists attend medical school, receive an M.D. degree, and specialize in psychiatry during their internship and residency. Traditionally, only psychiatrists have been able to dispense drugs and to hospitalize patients.

Whereas clinical psychologists deal with "abnormal" populations, such as schizophrenics, *counseling psychologists* deal with those who have less severe psychological problems or with "normal" populations, such as college students. For example, a student might seek the advice of a counseling psychologist to help her make a career decision or deal with a difficult relationship.

APPLICATIONS OF PSYCHOLOGY TO CAREERS AND PROFESSIONS

Psychology has had a dramatic impact on many other fields. Although you may not become a psychologist, you will undoubtedly encounter applications of psychology in your field of work—whether you go into the military, education, medicine, law, or business.

Psychology Applied to the Military

The U. S. military, with its vast array of personnel and its multitude of jobs, makes extensive use of psychologists. Every new recruit must take an aptitude test developed by psychologists to determine whether the recruit is qualified for military service and what type of job he or she is suited for. Civilian research psychologists employed by the military often interpret and grade these tests (Driskell and Olmstead, 1989). Currently, the military applies psychology in areas such as human performance, morale, selection and classification, and training.

One particularly important application of psychology in the military is in the area of training. On any given day, as many as 200,000 military people receive some form of training (Halff, Holland, and Hutchins, 1986). The military uses training techniques developed by psychologists who have done research on ways to enhance learning.

The need to test and classify military personnel has been most urgent during wartime. During both world wars, military psychology flourished, and about 25 percent of American psychologists were involved with the military. By the end of World War I, more than 1,700,000 inductees had been given intelligence tests that psychologists had developed. During World War II, psychologists helped classify large numbers of newly enlisted troops in an effort to utilize their skills effectively. Social psychologists conducted a series of "American Soldier" studies on soldiers' attitudes, and the army used the information gathered in this study in formulating subsequent policy (Driskell and Olmstead, 1989). Today many military psychologists are also involved in clinical and health issues related to the stressful environments military personnel face.

Psychology Applied to Education

You probably had your first encounter with a psychologist while in grade school. Most students are given IQ or other tests at a very young age. For more than half a century, *school psychologists* have administered IQ and achievement tests to schoolchildren (Bardon, 1983). More recently, school psychologists began to focus on the mental health of students and often assess and counsel students suffering from psychological problems.

Psychology has also been applied to education through the efforts of *educational psychologists*. These psychologists conduct research on such topics as classroom learning, teacher-student relationships, and the components of effective teaching.

Psychology Applied to Medical Settings

The expression "Don't worry, be happy" may be more than a catchy song lyric. We now know that psychological factors such as worry and stress are related to disease and illness. While the medical profession used to concentrate primarily on physical causes of illness, they now study as well how psychological factors can make you sick. This rapidly growing area is called health psychology. *Health psychologists* investigate the role that psychological variables, such as stress and anxiety, play in health and disease. They also do research on how people learn and maintain bad health habits. For example, although doctors often assume that patients follow their advice, health psychologists have found that 93 percent of patients do not strictly adhere to their medical treatment regimens (Taylor, 1990).

As a student, you probably worry about your grades or feel stress when a major paper or project is due. Health psychologists Stephanie Booth-Kewley and Howard Friedman found that personality traits associated with being "neurotic" (anxiety, pessimism, sadness, and hostility) can make a person susceptible to a number of illnesses (Goleman, 1988).

If your personality can be a cause of disease, can changes in your life-style lessen illness? Some recent research suggests that drastic changes in life-style and diet can reverse clogged arteries, a condition associated with coronary heart disease. One study found that the combination of one hour of yoga and meditation, exercise, and a strict vegetarian diet reduced the levels of arterial blockage in individuals who had had heart attacks. Researchers found that eighteen of the twenty-two people in this radical treatment program had reduced the level of blockage in their coronary arteries. Conversely, ten out of nineteen in the group that received standard medical treatment (reduced dietary fats, moderate exercise, and no smoking) experienced increased blockage. Only six out of nineteen in the standard treatment group showed a reduction of coronary artery blockage.

Figure B.3
Psychology is applied in many facets of the military. It is particularly important in the area of training, where it is used to enhance learning.

Thus, it appears that the psychological variable may have made a difference (Goleman, 1989).

Psychology Applied to Legal Issues

American society seems to be occupied more and more with legal actions. If you have a close encounter with the legal system, chances are that you will see the influence of psychology. *Forensic psychologists* conduct research on various aspects of crime and the criminal justice system, such as jury size and the impact of eyewitness testimony. Psychologists also work for police departments, working up psychological profiles of suspected criminals and counseling potential suicide victims. Moreover, psychologists counsel inmates in prisons, serve as consultants to parole boards, provide expert testimony in trials, and work as researchers in state and federal justice agencies (Oskamp, 1988). Psychologists are called to testify for either the prosecution or the defense, usually on matters relating to the mental competence of a defendant and the extent of psychological damage suffered by victims (Loftus and Monahan, 1980).

Psychology Applied to Business and Organizations

Work plays a central role in our lives. In addition to providing financial security, work offers people an opportunity to reach their potential and do something creative and constructive with their lives. Many older people, who have looked forward to retirement for years, return to some sort of work even though they do not have to.

You may still be in the process of formulating your career goals. The factors that have an impact on what career you ultimately choose and how successful you will be are of interest to *industrial/organizational (I/O) psychologists*. In addition to focusing on careers, I/O psychologists study employee morale, productivity, training methods, and ways to enrich jobs. I/O psychologists also design many of the performance appraisal systems that businesses use to evaluate their employees.

A subfield of I/O psychology is personnel psychology. *Personnel psychologists* deal with the issues of hiring, assigning, and promoting people. If you have ever been given a test while applying for a job, it is likely that an I/O or personnel psychologist designed it. Surveys have found that about 40 percent of small companies give employment tests as part of the job selection process and that about 60 percent of large companies use some testing in selection. If you are not a good test taker, do not despair—most companies that use tests as part of the selection process do not disqualify people solely on the basis of their test performance (Tenopyr, 1981).

As you might expect, a business that is successful in recruiting new employees and proficient in placing, training, and evaluating those whom it hires is likely to be an efficient organization. This efficiency may result in savings of millions of dollars. If the preceding organizational tasks are not handled well, however, productivity can be affected and profits reduced. For that reason, I/O psychologists are much in demand by private industry. They are also among the highest-paid psychologists.

Glossary

absolute threshold: The lowest level of physical energy that will produce a sensation in half the trials.

accommodation: In Piaget's theory of cognitive development, the adjustment of one's scheme for understanding the world to fit newly observed events and experiences.

achievement test: An instrument used to measure how much an individual has learned in a given subject or area.

adaptation: In sensation, an adjustment of the sensitivity of sensory receptors of the brain in response to prolonged stimulation.

addiction: An altered psychological state in the body that causes physical dependence on a drug.

adjustment: The process of adapting to, as well as actively shaping, one's environment.

ageism: Prejudice against the old.

anal stage: According to Freud, the stage at which children associate erotic pleasure with the elimination process.

androgynous: Combining or confusing traditionally male and female characteristics.

anger: The irate reaction likely to result from frustration.

antisocial personality: A personality disorder characterized by irresponsibility, shallow emotions, and lack of conscience.

anxiety: A vague, generalized apprehension or feeling that one is in danger.

applied science: Discovering ways to use scientific findings to accomplish practical goals.

approach-approach conflict: A situation in which the individual must choose between two attractive alternatives.

approach-avoidance conflict: A situation in which the individual wants to do something but fears it at the same time.

aptitude test: An instrument used to estimate the probability that a person will be successful in learning a specific new skill or skills.

archetype: According to Jung, an inherited idea, based on the experiences of one's ancestors, that shapes one's perception of the world.

artificial intelligence: The simulation of human thought processes by computer programming.

assessment center method: A testing method in which highly trained observers called assessor rate the performance of individuals in simulated work situations.

assimilation: In Piaget's theory of cognitive development, the process of fitting objects and experiences into one's schemes for understanding the environment.

asynchrony: The condition during the period of adolescence in which the growth or maturation of bodily parts is uneven.

attitudes: Predispositions to act, think, and feel in particular ways toward particular things.

attribution theory: A theory that tries to understand how we interpret people's behavior.

audience: In the communication process, the person or persons receiving a message.

auditory nerve: The nerve that carries impulses from the inner ear to the brain, resulting in the sensation of sound.

authoritarian families: Families in which parents are the "bosses."

authoritarian personality: A personality type characterized by rigid thinking; denial and projection of sexual and aggressive drives onto others; respect for and submission to authority; prejudice regarding people unlike himself or herself.

autonomic nervous system: Part of the peripheral nervous system that controls internal biological functions such as heart rate and digestion.

aversive control: The process of influencing behavior by means of aversive, or unpleasant, stimuli.

avoidance-avoidance conflict: A situation in which the individual must choose between two unattractive alternatives.

avoidance conditioning: The training of an organism to remove or withdraw from an unpleasant stimulus before it starts.

basic science: The pursuit of knowledge about natural phenomena for its own sake.

behavior modification: The systematic application of learning principles to change people's actions and feelings.

behavior therapy: A form of therapy aimed at changing undesirable behavior through conditioning techniques.

behaviorism: The school of psychology that holds that the proper subject matter of psychology is objectively observable behavior—and nothing else.

binocular fusion: The process of combining the images received from the two eyes into a single, fused image.

biofeedback: The process of learning to control bodily states with the help of machines that provide information about physiological processes.

body language: Nonverbal communication through gestures, positions, and movements of the body.

boomerang effect: A change in attitude or behavior opposite to the one desired by the persuader.

brainwashing: The most extreme form of attitude change, accomplished through peer pressure, physical suffering, threats, rewards for compliance, manipulation of guilt, intensive indoctrination, and other psychological means.

Cannon-Bard theory: A theory introduced by psychologists Cannon and Bard that attributed emotion to the simultaneous activity of the brain and "gut" reactions.

career: A vocation in which a person works at least a few years.

case study: An intensive investigation of an individual or group, usually focusing on a single psychological phenomenon.

CAT scan: A device that uses a computer to create a picture of the brain by putting together a number of X-ray images that reveal the bone mass and tissue density of body organs.

central nervous system (CNS): The brain and spinal cord.

central processing: The second stage of information processing—storing (in memory) and sorting (by thought) information in the brain.

central tendency: A number that describes something about the "average" score of a distribution.

cerebellum: A lower portion of the brain which controls posture and balance and regulates the details of motor commands from the cerebral cortex.

cerebral cortex: The gray mass surrounding the subcortex, which controls most of the higher brain functions, such as reading and problem solving.

cerebrum: The inner part of the brain, in front of and above the cerebellum.

channel: In the communication process, the means by which a message is transmitted from the source to the audience.

charisma: A leader's strong emotional appeal that arouses enthusiasm and loyalty.

chunking: The process of grouping pieces of information for easier handling.

classical conditioning: A learning procedure in which a stimulus that normally elicits a given response is repeatedly preceded by a neutral stimulus (one that usually does not elicit the response). Eventually, the neutral stimulus will evoke a similar response when presented by itself.

client-centered therapy: A form of therapy aimed at helping clients recognize their own strengths and gain confidence so that they can be true to their own standards and ideas about how to live effectively.

cognitive appraisal: The interpretation of an event that helps to determine its stress impact.

cognitive dissonance: The uncomfortable feeling that arises when a person experiences contradictory or conflicting thoughts, attitudes, beliefs, or feelings.

cognitive preparation: The coping strategy in which the person mentally rehearses possible outcomes.

collective unconscious: According to Jung, that part of the mind that contains inherited instincts, urges, and memories common to all people.

color blindness: Complete or partial inability to distinguish colors, resulting from malfunction in the cones.

complementarity: The attraction that often develops between opposite types of people because of the ability of one to supply what the other lacks.

compliance: A change of behavior in order to avoid discomfort or rejection and gain approval; a superficial form of attitude change.

compulsion: The impulsive and uncontrollable repetition of an irrational action.

concept: A label for a class of objects or events that share common attributes.

conditioned reinforcer: A stimulus that increases the frequency of a response because it has become a signal for a stimulus which is reinforcing.

conditioned response (CR): In classical conditioning, the learned response to a conditioned stimulus.

conditioned stimulus (CS): In classical conditioning, a once-neutral stimulus that has come to elicit a given response after a period of training in which it has been paired with an unconditioned stimulus (UCS).

conditions of worth: Rogers's term for the conditions a person must meet in order to regard himself or herself positively.

cones: Receptor cells in the retina sensitive to color. Because they require more light than rods to function, they are most useful in daytime vision.

confabulation: The act of filling in memory with statements that make sense but that are, in fact, untrue.

conflict-habituated marriage: A marriage in which the partners spend most of their time fighting.

conflict situations: The situation in which a person must choose between two or more options that tend to result from conflicting motives.

conformity: Compliance to group standards.

consciousness: A state of awareness, including a person's feelings, sensations, ideas, and perceptions.

conservation: The principle that a given quantity does not change when its appearance is changed. The discovery of this principle between the ages of five and seven is important to the intellectual development of the child.

constancy: The tendency to perceive certain objects in the same way, regardless of changing angle, distance, or lighting.

contingencies of reinforcement: Skinner's term for the occurrence of a reward or punishment following a particular behavior.

contingency management: A form of behavior therapy in which undesirable behavior is not rewarded, while desirable behavior is reinforced.

control group: In an experiment, a group of subjects that is treated in the same way as the experimental group, except that the experimental treatment is not applied.

conversion reaction: A form of hysteria characterized by the conversion of emotional difficulties into a loss of a specific body function.

corpus callosum: A band of nerves that connects the two hemispheres of the cortex and carries messages back and forth between them.

correlation: The degree of relatedness between two sets of data.

correlation coefficient: A statistic that describes the direction and strength of the relationship between two sets of observations.

creativity: The capacity to use information and/or abilities in such a way that the results are new, original, and meaningful.

critical periods: Times when specific environmental influences are most likely to affect development.

cross-cultural studies: Acquiring comparable data from two or more cultures for the purpose of studying cultural similarities and differences.

crowded nest syndrome: A condition that may occur when grown children move back into their parents' home, necessitating the reassessment of the parent-child relationship.

decibel: A measure of the physical intensity of sound, which is lawfully related to the sensation of loudness.

decremental model of aging: This holds that progressive physical and mental decline is inevitable with age.

defense mechanisms: According to Freud, certain specific means by which the ego unconsciously protects itself against unpleasant impulses or circumstances.

delusion: A false belief that a person maintains in the face of contrary evidence.

democratic families: Families in which adolescents participate in decisions affecting their lives.

denial: A coping mechanism in which a person decides that the event is not really a stressor.

dependent variable: In an experiment, the factor that is not controlled by the experimenters but changes as a result of changes in the independent variable.

depressant: A drug that reduces the activity of the central nervous system.

depression: A pattern of sadness, anxiety, fatigue, insomnia, underactivity, and reduced ability to function and to work with others.

descriptive statistics: The listing and summarizing of data in a practical, efficient way, such as by means of graphs and averages.

designer drugs: Hallucinogens that are illegally manufactured psychoactive compounds that are manipulated for the consumer; each batch varies in strength and purity.

developmental friendship: The type of friendship in which the partners force one another to re-examine their basic assumptions and perhaps adopt new ideas and beliefs.

developmental psychology: The study of changes that occur as individuals mature.

devitalized marriage: A marriage, originally based on love, in which the partners no longer attempt or expect passion or bliss, but get along well enough to remain together.

difference threshold: The smallest change in a physical stimulus that produces a change in sensation in half the trials.

diffusion of responsibility: The tendency of the presence of others to lessen an individual's feelings of responsibility for his or her actions or failure to act.

directed thinking: Systematic, logical, goal-directed thought.

discrimination: (1) The ability to respond differently to similar but distinct stimuli. (2) The unequal treatment of individuals on the basis of their race, ethnic group, class, sex, or membership in another category, rather than on the basis of individual characteristics.

displacement: The redirection of desires, feelings, or impulses from their proper object to a substitute.

display rules: Societal conventions or rules that govern what people think.

dissociative reaction: A form of hysteria in which a person experiences a loss of memory or identity, or exhibits two or more identities.

distress: The type of stress that stems from acute anxiety or pressure.

double approach-avoidance conflict: A situation in which the individual must choose between two or more alternatives, each of which has attractive and unattractive aspects.

double-bind theory: A theory that states that a childhood full of contradictory messages from parents (double bind) results in people perceiving the world as a confusing, disconnected place and believing that their words and actions have little meaning.

double-blind technique: A research technique in which neither the subjects nor the experimenter know which subjects have been exposed to the experimental treatment.

drive reduction theory: A theory formulated by psychologist Clark Hull that states that physiological needs drive an organism to act in random or habitual ways until its needs are satisfied.

DSM: Published and updated by the American Psychiatric Association, the *Diagnostic and Statistical Manual of Mental Disorders* is the standard system for classifying abnormal symptoms.

effectors: The cells that work the muscles, internal glands, and organs.

ego: According to Freud, the part of the personality that is in touch with reality. The ego strives to meet the demands of the id and the superego in socially acceptable ways.

ego-support value: The ability of a person to provide another person with sympathy, encouragement, and approval.

eidetic memory: The ability to remember with great accuracy visual information on the basis of short-term exposure; also called "photographic memory."

electrode: A type of wire used by scientists to detect the minute electrical changes that occur when neurons fire.

electroencephalograph (EEG): A machine used to record the electrical activity of large portions of the brain.

emotional experience: What we actually feel inside ourselves at any time.

emotional expression: The way we externalize our emotions.

encounter groups: A type of therapy for people who function adequately in everyday life but who feel unhappy, dissatisfied, or stagnant; aimed at providing experiences that will help people increase their sensitivity, openness, and honesty.

endocrine system: A chemical communication system, using hormones, by which messages are sent through the bloodstream to particular organs of the body.

escape conditioning: The training of an organism to remove or terminate an unpleasant stimulus.

ethology: The study of animal behavior in its natural environment.

eustress: Positive stress, which results from the strivings and challenges that are the spice of life.

euthanasia: The act of killing or permitting the death of an incurably ill person.

experimental group: The group of subjects to which an experimental treatment is applied.

experimental treatment: The manipulation of an independent variable in an experiment designed to observe its effects.

expert systems: Computer programs that can apply specific rules to a situation and make choices according to preset rules.

extinction: The gradual disappearance of a conditioned response because the reinforcement is withheld or because the conditioned stimulus is repeatedly presented without the unconditioned stimulus.

extrasensory perception (ESP): An ability to gain information by some means other than the ordinary senses (such as taste, hearing, vision, and so on).

extrovert: An outgoing, active person who directs his or her energies and interests toward other people and things.

factor analysis: A complex statistical technique used to identify the underlying reasons variables are correlated.

family therapy: A form of therapy aimed at understanding and improving relationships that have led one or more members in a family to experience emotional suffering.

fear: The usual reaction when a stressor involves real danger.

feature extraction: The identification and analysis of specific features of a sensory input.

feedback: Information received after an action as to its effectiveness or correctness.

figure-ground: The division of the visual field into two distinct parts, one being the object or objects, the other the background or space between objects.

fixed action patterns: Patterns of behavior that are inflexible. Such responses are common to many animal species, but not to humans.

fixed-interval schedule: A schedule of reinforcement in which a specific amount of time must elapse before a response will elicit reinforcement.

fixed-ratio schedule: A schedule of reinforcement in which a specific number of correct responses is required before reinforcement can be obtained.

free association: A method used by psychoanalysts to examine the unconscious. The patient is instructed to say whatever comes into his or her mind.

frequency distribution: An arrangement of data that indicates how often a particular score or observation occurs.

GLOSSARY

frequency polygon: A line graph that indicates how often a particular score or observation occurs.

frontal lobes: The lobes located in the front of the brain, which control intellect and personality.

frustration: The feeling of bafflement or disappointment that results when a person's progress toward a goal is blocked.

fugue: A rare dissociative reaction in which complete or partial amnesia is combined with a move to a new environment.

fully functioning person: Rogers's term for an individual whose organism and self coincide, allowing him or her to be open to experience, to possess unconditional positive regard, and to have harmonious relations with others.

fundamental needs: In Maslow's hierarchy-of-needs theory, these are the biological drives that must be satisfied in order to maintain life.

gene therapy: A new technology in drug development that involves manipulating individual genes to change certain traits.

generalization: Responding similarly to a range of similar stimuli.

generativity: According to Erikson, the desire, in middle age, to use one's accumulated wisdom to guide future generations.

General Aptitude Test Battery (GATB): A general skills test used to measure basic manual and computational skills.

genital stage: According to Freud, the stage during which an individual's sexual satisfaction depends as much on giving pleasure as on receiving it.

Gestalt: In perception, the experience that comes from organizing bits and pieces of information into meaningful wholes.

gestalt therapy: A form of therapy that emphasizes the relationship between the patient and therapist in the here and now. The aim is to encourage the person to recognize all sides of his or her personality.

grasping reflex: An infant's clinging response to a touch on the palm of his or her hand.

group: An aggregate of people characterized by shared goals and a degree of interdependence.

group therapy: A form of therapy in which patients work together with the aid of a group leader to resolve interpersonal problems.

groupthink: A decision-making process identified in groups operating under pressure or in a time of crisis that leads to premature decisions.

hallucinations: Sensations or perceptions that have no direct external cause.

hallucinogens: Drugs that often produce hallucinations.

histogram: A graph similar to a bar graph that indicates how often a particular score or observation occurs.

homeostasis: The tendency of all organisms to correct imbalances and deviations from their normal state.

hormones: Chemical substances that carry messages through the body in the blood.

human factors engineering: An area of I/O psychology that studies how humans interact with their environment and uses this knowledge to design more efficient tools, machines, and work spaces.

human potential movement: An approach to psychotherapy that stresses the actualization of one's unique potentials through personal responsibility, freedom of choice, and authentic relationships.

humanistic psychology: An approach to psychology that stresses the uniqueness of the individual; focuses on the value, dignity, and worth of each person; and holds that healthy living is the result of realizing one's full potential.

hypertension: Unhealthy levels of high blood pressure.

hypnosis: An altered state of consciousness resulting from a narrowed focus of attention and characterized by heightened suggestibility.

hypochondriasis: A preoccupation with imaginary ailments, on which a person blames other problems.

hypothalamus: A small area deep inside the brain that regulates the autonomic nervous system and other body functions.

hypothesis: An educated guess about the relationship between two variables.

id: According to Freud, that part of the unconscious personality that contains our needs, drives, and instincts as well as repressed material. The material in the id strives for immediate satisfaction.

identification: (1) The process by which a child adopts the values and principles of the same-sex parent. (2) The process of seeing oneself as similar to another person or group, and accepting the attitudes of another person or group as one's own.

identity crisis: According to Erikson, a time of storm and stress during which adolescents worry intensely about who they are.

ideology: The set of principles, attitudes, and defined objectives for which a group stands.

illusions: Perceptions that misrepresent physical stimuli.

image: A rough representation of specific events or objects; the most primitive unit of thought.

implicit personality theory: A set of assumptions each person has about how people behave and what personality traits or characteristics go together.

imprinting: A process in which some species form attachments to other organisms or to objects very early in life.

independent variable: In an experiment, the factor that is deliberately manipulated by the experimenters to test its effect on another factor.

inferential statistics: The use of statistical methods to determine whether research data support a hypothesis or whether results were due to chance.

inferiority complex: According to Adler, a pattern of avoiding feelings of inadequacy and insignificance rather than trying to overcome their source.

innate behavior: Behavior that is part of one's biological inheritance.

inoculation effect: A method of developing resistance to persuasion by exposing a person to arguments that challenge his or her beliefs so that he or she can practice defending them.

input: The first stage of information processing—receiving information through the senses.

insight: The sudden realization of the solution to a problem.

instinct: A behavior pattern that is inborn rather than learned.

intellectualization: A coping mechanism in which the person watches the situation from an emotionally detached standpoint.

intelligence quotient (IQ): Originally, a measure of a person's mental development obtained by dividing his or her mental age (the score achieved on a standardized intelligence test) by his or her chronological age and multiplying by 100; now, any standardized measure of intelligence based on a scale in which 100 is defined to be average.

interest test: An instrument designed to measure a person's preferences, attitudes, and interests in certain activities.

internalize: To incorporate the values, ideas, and standards of others as a part of oneself.

introspection: A method of self-observation in which subjects report on their thoughts and feelings.

introvert: A reserved, unsociable person who is preoccupied with his or her inner thoughts and feelings.

James-Lange theory: A theory formulated by psychologists James and Lange that suggests that emotions are the perception of bodily changes.

kinesthesis: The sense of movement and body position, acquired through receptors located in and near the muscles, tendons, and joints.

laissez-faire families: Families in which children have the final say; permissive families.

latency stage: According to Freud, the stage at which sexual desires are pushed into the background and the child becomes involved in exploring the world and learning new skills.

lateral hypothalamus (LH): The part of the hypothalamus that produces hunger signals.

learned helplessness: The condition in which a person suffers from a situation so severely or so often that he or she comes to believe that it is uncontrollable and that any effort to cope will fail.

learning: A lasting change in behavior that results from experience.

lens: A flexible, transparent structure in the eye that, by changing its shape, focuses light on the retina.

life events perspective: A perspective in which adult development is more closely linked to significant events than to the passage of time.

living will: A will that outlines one's wishes with regard to medical treatment if one becomes incapacitated.

lobes: The different regions into which the cerebral cortex is divided.

long-term memory: Information storage that has unlimited capacity and lasts indefinitely.

longitudinal studies: Repeatedly gathering data on the same group of subjects over a period of time for the purpose of studying consistencies and change.

LSD: An extremely potent psychedelic drug that produces hallucinations and distortions of perception and thought.

magnetic resonance imaging (MRI): A method of examining body tissue and bone structure that uses the magnetic field of molecules and cells in the body to construct precise images.

major depression: A common mood disorder in which the individual is overcome by feelings of failure, sinfulness, worthlessness, and despair.

manic reaction: A psychotic reaction characterized by extreme elation, agitation, confusion, disorientation, and incoherence.

marijuana: The dried leaves and flowers of Indian hemp (*Cannabis sativa*) that produce an altered state of consciousness when smoked or ingested.

mean: The arithmetic average.

median: The score that divides a distribution of observations in half; the middle score.

meditation: Focusing of attention on an image, thought, bodily process, or external object with the goal of clearing one's mind and producing an "inner peace."

memory: The complex mental function of storage and retrieval of what has been learned or experienced.

menarche: The first menstrual period.

menopause: The biological event by which a woman's production of sex hormones is sharply reduced.

message: In the communication process, the actual content transmitted from the source to the audience.

mnemonic devices: Methods for remembering items by relating them to information already held in the brain.

mode: The most frequent score in a distribution of observations.

mood disorder: A common type of psychosis in which individuals are excessively and inappropriately happy or unhappy.

motion parallax: The apparent movement of stationary objects relative to one another that occurs when the observer changes position. Near objects seem to move greater distances than far objects.

motor cortex: The portion of the brain located in the front of the somatosensory cortex, which controls body movement.

multiculturalism: The concept of education being made more appropriate to the specific ethnic and cultural backgrounds of students.

multiple personality: A rare condition in which one person shows two or more separate consciousnesses with distinct personalities.

narcolepsy: A disorder in which a person may fall asleep at any moment.

naturalistic observation: Studying phenomena as they occur in natural surroundings, without interfering.

near-death experience: A type of hallucination caused by a close brush with death or the belief that death is near.

negative correlation: A correlation indicating that as one variable increases, the second variable decreases.

negative reinforcement: Increasing the strength of a given response by removing or preventing a painful stimulus when the response occurs.

nerve fibers: The slender threadlike pieces of nerve cells through which messages are sent to and from the brain.

neurons: The long, thin cells that constitute the structural and functional unit of nerve tissue, along which messages travel to and from the brain.

neurosis: A psychological disturbance characterized by prolonged high levels of anxiety. Neurotics often suffer from unrealistic self-images and have difficulty forming satisfying, stable relationships.

neurotransmitters: The chemicals released by neurons which determine the rate at which other neurons fire.

neutral stimulus: A stimulus that does not initially elicit a response.

nondirected thinking: The free flow of images and ideas, occurring with no particular goal.

nonverbal communication: The process of communicating through the use of space, body language, and facial expression.

normal curve: A symmetrical, bell-shaped curve with known mathematical properties.

norms: (1) Shared standards of behavior accepted by and expected from group members. (2) Standards of comparison for test results developed by giving the test to large, well-defined groups of people.

obedience: A change in attitude or behavior brought about by social pressure to comply with people perceived to be authorities.

object permanence: A child's realization, developed between the ages of one and two, that an object exists even when he or she cannot see or touch it.

objective personality tests: Forced-choice tests (in which a person must select one of several answers) designed to study personal characteristics.

obsession: An uncontrollable pattern of thoughts.

obstructive sleep apnea: A common form of sleep apnea caused by the collapse of the upper airways during sleep.

Oedipal conflict: According to Freud, a boy's wish to possess his mother sexually, coupled with hostility toward his father. Correspondingly, girls desire their fathers sexually and feel hostile toward their mothers. In order to reduce his or her fear of punishment from the same-sex parent, the child begins to identify with the parent of the same sex.

olfactory nerve: The nerve that carries smell impulses from the nose to the brain.

operant conditioning: A form of conditioning in which a certain action is reinforced or punished, resulting in corresponding increases or decreases in the likelihood that similar actions will occur again.

optic nerve: The nerve that carries impulses from the retina to the brain.

oral stage: According to Freud, the stage at which infants associate erotic pleasure with the mouth.

organism: Rogers's term for the whole person, including all of his or her feelings, thoughts, and urges as well as body.

out-of-body experience: Also known as a metachoric; a type of hallucination in which a person's entire perceptual world changes and the person reports leaving the body to look at a scene from a completely different and very real perspective.

output: The final stage of information processing—acting on the basis of information.

parapsychology: The systematic study of ESP and other unusual phenomena.

parasympathetic nervous system: The system that works to conserve energy and enhance the body's ability to recuperate after strenuous activity.

passive-congenial marriage: A marriage based on convenience, in which the partners live together and share responsibilities in order to make it easier to pursue individual interests.

PCP: A hallucinogen and central nervous system depressant also known as angel dust.

percentile system: A system for ranking test scores that indicates the percentage of scores lower and higher than a given score.

perception: The organization of sensory information into meaningful experiences.

perceptual inference: The process of assuming, from past experience, that certain objects remain the same and will behave as they have in the past.

peripheral nervous system (PNS): A network of nerves branching out from the spinal cord that conducts information from the bodily organs to the central nervous system and takes information back to the organs.

permissive families: Families in which children have the final say; laissez-faire families.

personal space: The space between two people that communicates their feelings about one another and defines the relationship.

personality: The sum total of physical, mental, emotional, and social characteristics that distinguish one person from another.

personality disorder: A psychological disturbance characterized by lifelong maladaptive patterns that are relatively free of anxiety and other emotional symptoms.

persuasion: The direct attempt to influence attitudes through the communication process.

phallic stage: According to Freud, the stage at which children associate sexual pleasure with their genitals.

phobia: A form of severe anxiety in which a person focuses on a particular object or situation.

physical proximity: The physical nearness of one person to another person.

pitch: The sensation associated with a sound's frequency; the "highness" or "lowness" of a sound.

pituitary gland: The center of control of the endocrine system which secretes a large number of hormones.

placebo effect: The influence that a patient's hopes and expectations have on his or her improvement during therapy.

polygraph: A machine used to measure physiological changes, particularly in lie detection.

population: The total group of subjects from which a sample is drawn.

positive correlation: A correlation indicating that as one variable increases, the second also increases.

positive regard: Rogers's term for viewing oneself in a positive light, because of positive feedback received from interaction with others.

positron emission tomography scan (PET scan): A technological device that allows psychologists and others to look inside the brain and observe activity as it occurs.

post-traumatic stress disorder (PTSD): A condition associated with extreme or prolonged cases of severe stress and characterized by symptoms of insomnia, anxiety, recurrent dreams, and difficulty concentrating.

posthypnotic suggestion: A suggestion made during a hypnotic trance that influences the subject's behavior after the trance is ended.

prejudice: Preconceived attitudes toward a person or group that have been formed without sufficient evidence and are not easily changed.

primary reinforcers: Natural rewards.

proactive interference: The hampering of recall of newly learned material by the recall of previously learned material.

progressive relaxation: Lying down comfortably and tensing and relaxing each major muscle group in turn.

projection: Ascribing one's own undesirable attitudes, feelings, or thoughts to others.

projective personality tests: Unstructured tests of personality in which a person is asked to respond freely, giving his or her own interpretation of various ambiguous stimuli.

psychiatry: A medical specialty that involves the study, diagnosis, and treatment of mental disorders.

psychoactive drugs: Drugs that interact with the central nervous system to alter a person's mood, perception, and behavior.

psychoanalysis: A form of therapy aimed at making patients aware of their unconscious motives so that they can gain control over their behavior and free themselves of self-defeating patterns.

psychological dependence: Use of a drug to such an extent that a person feels nervous and anxious without it.

psychological needs: In Maslow's hierarchy-of-needs theory, these include the need to belong and to give and receive love, and the need to acquire esteem through competence and achievement. If these needs are frustrated, it will be difficult for the person to strive for fulfillment of the next level in the hierarchy—*self-actualization needs.*

psychology: The study of mental processes and the behavior of organisms.

psychophysics: The study of the relationships between sensory experiences and the physical stimuli that cause them.

psychosis: A psychological disturbance characterized by a breakdown in the ability to accurately perceive reality. Psychotics are unable to relate to other people and to function in everyday life.

psychosurgery: Brain surgery aimed at changing a person's thoughts or actions.

psychotherapy: A general term for treatment used by social workers, psychologists, and psychiatrists to help troubled individuals overcome their problems. The goal of psychotherapy is to break the behavior patterns that lead to unhappiness.

puberty: Sexual maturation; it is the biological event that marks the end of childhood.

punishers: Negative consequences that decrease the likelihood of a behavior occurring again.

pupil: The opening in the iris that regulates the amount of light entering the eye.

random sample: A sample that gives an equal chance of being represented to every piece of data within the scope of the research.

range: A measure of variability; the lowest score in a distribution subtracted from the highest score.

rational-emotive therapy: A form of therapy aimed at changing unrealistic assumptions about oneself and other people. It is believed that once a person understands that he or she has been acting on false beliefs, self-defeating thoughts and behaviors will be avoided.

rationalization: A process whereby an individual seeks to explain an often unpleasant emotion or behavior in a way that will preserve his or her self-esteem.

reaction formation: Replacing an unacceptable feeling or urge with its opposite.

recall: The type of memory retrieval in which a person reconstructs previously learned material.

receptors: Cells whose function it is to gather information and send messages to the brain.

recognition: The type of memory retrieval in which a person is required to identify an object, idea, or situation as one he or she has or has not experienced before.

recombination: Mentally rearranging the elements of a problem in order to arrive at a novel solution.

referred pain: The sensation of pain in an area away from the actual source; most commonly experienced with internal pain.

regression: A return to an earlier stage of development or pattern of behavior in a threatening or stressful situation.

reinforcement: Immediately following a particular response with a reward in order to strengthen that response.

reliability: The ability of a test to give the same results under a variety of different circumstances.

REM sleep: The period of sleep during which the eyes dart back and forth (rapid eye movement) and dreaming usually occurs.

replication: Repetition of an experiment and achievement of the same results.

representational thought: The intellectual ability of a child to picture something in his or her mind.

repression: The exclusion from conscious awareness of a painful, unpleasant, or undesirable memory.

resistance: The reluctance of a patient to reveal painful feelings and to examine long-standing behavior patterns.

response chains: Learned responses that follow one another in sequence, each response producing the signal for the next.

resynthesis: The process of combining old ideas with new ones and reorganizing feelings in order to renew one's identity.

reticular activating system: The system in the brain that screens incoming messages, blocking out some signals and letting others pass.

retina: The innermost coating of the back of the eye, containing the light-sensitive receptor cells.

retinal disparity: The differences between the images on the two retinas.

retrieval: The process of obtaining information that has been stored in memory.

retroactive interference: The hampering of recall of learned material by the recall of other material learned more recently.

rods: Receptor cells in the retina that are sensitive to light, but not to color. Rods are particularly useful in night vision.

role taking: An important aspect of children's play that involves assuming adult roles, thus enabling the child to experience different points of view firsthand.

rooting reflex: An infant's response toward the source of touching that occurs anywhere around his or her mouth.

rule: A statement of the relationship between two or more concepts; the most complex unit of thought.

sample: The small portion of data, out of the total amount available, that a researcher collects.

scapegoat: A person (or group of people) who becomes the target of another person's displaced anger or aggression.

scatterplot: A graph used to demonstrate the direction of the relationship between variables.

schizophrenia: A group of psychoses characterized by confused and disconnected thoughts, emotions, and perceptions.

selective attention: Focusing one's awareness on a limited segment of the total amount of sensory input one is receiving.

self: Rogers's term for one's experience or image of oneself, developed through interaction with others.

self-actualization: The humanist term for realizing one's unique potential.

self-actualization needs: The top of Maslow's hierarchy of needs. These include the pursuit of knowledge and beauty, or whatever else is required for the realization of one's unique potential. Before these needs can be satisfied, people must first meet their *fundamental* and *psychological needs*.

self-fulfilling prophecy: A belief, prediction, or expectation that operates to bring about its own fulfillment.

self-justification: The need to rationalize one's attitude and behavior.

sensation: The result of converting physical stimulation of the sense organs into sensory experience.

sensitive period: A specific time during which individuals are most receptive to certain environmental influences.

sensory storage: The momentary storage of sensory information at the level of the sensory receptors.

set: A habitual strategy or pattern of problem solving.

sex identity: One's biological inheritance; it includes genetic traits and may include some sex-linked behaviors.

sex role: Defined partly by genetic makeup, but mainly by the society and culture in which the individual lives, it is a description of how a person with a given sex identity is supposed to behave.

shaping: A technique of operant conditioning in which the desired behavior is "molded" by first rewarding any act similar to that behavior and then requiring closer and closer approximations to the desired behavior before giving the reward.

short-term memory: Memory that is limited in capacity to about seven items and in duration to about twenty seconds.

sick-building syndrome: A condition in which workers develop symptoms such as eye irritation, headaches, and mental fatigue as a result of poor air quality.

signal-detection theory: The study of mathematical relationships between motivation, sensitivity, and sensation.

signals: In operant conditioning, behavioral cues (or stimuli) that are associated with reward or punishment.

silent suicide: Suicide through nonviolent means such as self-starvation or noncompliance with medical regimens.

situational test: A simulation of a real situation designed to measure a person's performance under such circumstances.

skewed distribution: A distribution of scores in which most observations pile up at one end rather than in the middle.

sleep apnea: A disorder in which a sleeping person stops breathing for ten seconds or more.

sleeper effect: The delayed impact on attitude change of a persuasive communication.

social functions: In groups, those functions directed toward satisfying the emotional needs of members.

social leader: The leader within a group who promotes group cohesion and commands group loyalty.

social learning theory: Bandura's view of human development, emphasizing interaction.

social rule: Any agreement among members of society about how people should act in particular situations; also called a *norm*.

social support: Information that leads someone to believe that he or she is cared for, loved, respected, and part of a network of communication and mutual obligation.

socialization: The process of learning the rules of behavior of the culture within which an individual is born and will live.

sociobiology: The study of the biological basis of social behavior.

sociogram: A diagram representing relationships within a group.

somatic nervous system: The half of the peripheral nervous system that controls voluntary movement of skeletal muscles.

somatoform disorder: A mental disorder marked by physical symptoms for which there is no apparent physical cause.

somatosensory cortex: An area of the brain, within the cerebral cortex, that receives information from the skin and muscles.

source: In the communication process, the person or group from which a message originates.

species-specific behavior: Behavior that is characteristic of a particular animal species.

spinal cord: The bundle of nerves that run down the length of the back and transmit most messages back and forth between the body and the brain.

stagnation: According to Erikson, a discontinuation of development and a desire to recapture the past, characteristic of some middle-aged people.

standard deviation: A measure of variability that describes an average distance of every score from the mean of the scores.

statistically significant: A description of studies that indicates the results were probably not due to chance.

statistics: The branch of mathematics concerned with summarizing and making meaningful inferences from collections of data.

stereopsis: The use by the visual system of retinal disparity to give depth information, providing a three-dimensional appearance to the world.

stereotype: A set of assumptions about people in a given category based on half-truths and non-truths.

stimulation value: The ability of a person or subject to interest or to expose you to new ideas and experiences.

stratified sample: A sample that includes representatives of subgroups or variations of the population being studied.

stress: A person's perception of his or her inability to cope with a certain tense event or situation.

stress reaction: The body's response to a stressor.

stressor: A stress-producing event or situation.

subcortex: The part of the brain where all messages are first received and that, together with the spinal cord, controls and coordinates vital functions and reflex actions. It is sometimes called the "old brain."

sublimation: The process of redirecting sexual impulses into learning tasks that begins at about the age of five.

subliminal advertising: The unsuccessful attempt to influence people with messages that are below normal thresholds of detection.

superego: According to Freud, the process of the personality that inhibits the socially undesirable impulses of the id. The superego may cause excessive guilt if it is overly harsh.

survey: A relatively large sampling of data, obtained through interviews and questionnaires.

symbol: An abstract unit of thought that represents an object, event, or quality.

sympathetic nervous system: The system that prepares the body for dealing with emergencies or strenuous activities.

synapses: The gaps that occur between individual nerve cells.

systematic desensitization: A technique used by behavior therapists to help a patient overcome irrational fears and anxieties. The goal is to teach the person to relax so that he or she will not feel anxious in the presence of feared objects.

task functions: In groups, those functions directed toward getting a job done.

task leader: The leader within a group who takes over when the group must accomplish something.

telegraphic speech: The kind of speech used by young children. Words are left out, but the meaning is still clear.

thalamus: The portion of the brain that sorts incoming impulses and directs them to various parts of the brain. It also relays messages from one part of the brain to another.

thanatology: The study of death and dying.

thyroid gland: The gland in the endocrine system that produces several hormones, including thyroxin.

token economy: A form of conditioning in which desirable behavior is reinforced with tokens, which can be accumulated and exchanged for various rewards.

tolerance: Physical adaptation to a drug, so that a person needs an increased dosage in order to produce the original effect.

total marriage: A marriage in which both partners are deeply involved in each other's careers and hobbies, spend most of their time together, and seem to live for each other.

trait: A tendency to react to a situation in a way that remains stable over time.

transactional analysis: A form of therapy aimed at helping clients become more flexible by discovering the scripts they play and replay in their lives.

transfer: The effects of past learning on the ability to learn new tasks.

transference: The process, experienced by the patient, of feeling toward an analyst or therapist the way he or she feels toward some other important figure in his or her life.

unconditional positive regard: In client-centered therapy, the atmosphere of emotional support provided by the therapist. The therapist shows the client he or she accepts anything said and does not become embarrassed or angry.

unconditioned response (UCR): In classical conditioning, an organism's automatic (or natural) reaction to a stimulus.

unconditioned stimulus (UCS): A stimulus that elicits a certain response without previous training.

unconscious: According to Freud, the part of the mind that contains material we are unaware of, but that strongly influences conscious processes and behaviors.

utility value: The ability of a person or subject to help another achieve his or her goals.

validity: The ability of a test to measure what it is intended to measure.

variability: A measurement that provides an index of how spread out scores of a distribution are.

variable: In an experimental situation, any factor that is capable of change.

variable-interval schedule: A schedule of reinforcement in which varying amounts of time must elapse before a response will obtain reinforcement.

variable-ratio schedule: A schedule of reinforcement in which a variable number of responses are required before reinforcement can be obtained.

ventromedial hypothalamus (VMH): The part of the hypothalamus that produces feelings of fullness as opposed to hunger, and causes one to stop eating.

vestibular system: Three semicircular canals located in the inner ear and connected to the brain by the vestibular nerve. They regulate the sense of balance.

vital marriage: A marriage in which both partners have a strong sense of individual identity and participate in separate activities.

Weber's law: The principle that the larger or stronger a stimulus, the larger the change required for an observer to notice a difference.

withdrawal: The symptoms that occur after a person discontinues the use of a drug to which he or she had become addicted.

Bibliography

AARONSON, BERNARD, AND OSMOND, H. *Psychedelics: The Uses and Implications of Hallucinogenic Drugs*. Garden City, N.Y.: Doubleday, 1970.

ABRAMSON, LYN Y., SELIGMAN, MARTIN E. P., AND TEASDALE, JOHN D. "Learned Helplessness in Humans: Critique and Reformulation." *Journal of Abnormal Psychology* 87 (1978): 49–74.

ABSE, D. W. *Hysteria and Related Mental Disorders*. Baltimore: Williams & Wilkins, 1966.

ADAMS, JACK A. *Human Memory*. New York: McGraw-Hill, 1967.

ADELMANN, P. K., ANTONUCCI, T. C., CROHAN, S. E., AND COLEMAN, L. E. "Empty Nest, Cohort, and Employment in the Well-Being of Midlife Women." *Sex Roles* 20 (1989): 173–89.

ADLER, ALFRED. *What Life Should Mean to You*. New York: Putnam, 1959 (paper).

ADLER, TINA. "Study Looks for Drug to Treat Coke Addicts." *APA Monitor* 22 (February 1991): 8.

ADORNO, T. W., ET AL. *The Authoritarian Personality*. New York: Norton, 1969 (paper).

AHLSKOG, J. ERIC, AND HOEBEL, BARTLEY G. "Overeating and Obesity from Damage to a Noradrenergic System in the Brain." *Science* 182 (1973): 166–69.

AHRENS, R. "Beitrag zur Entwicklung des Physiognomie-und Mimikerkennens." *Z. exp. angew. Psychol.* 2 (1954): 412–54.

ALEXANDER, B. K. "The Disease and Adaptive Models of Addiction: A Framework Evaluation." *Journal of Drug Issues* 17 (1987): 47–66.

ALLPORT, GORDON. *The Nature of Prejudice*. Garden City, N.Y.: Doubleday, 1954 (paper).

_____ . *Pattern and Growth in Personality*. New York: Holt, Rinehart & Winston, 1961.

_____ , ED. *Letters from Jenny*. New York: Harcourt, Brace & World, 1965.

ALTMAN, L. K. "More Physicians Broach Forbidden Subject of Euthanasia." *New York Times*, 12 March 1991, C3.

ALVAREZ, A. *The Savage God: A Study of Suicide*. New York: Random House, 1970.

AMERICAN EDUCATION RESEARCH ASSOCIATION, AMERICAN PSYCHOLOGICAL ASSOCIATION, AND NATIONAL COUNCIL ON MEASUREMENT IN EDUCATION. *Standards for Educational and Psychological Testing*. Washington, D.C.: American Psychological Association, 1985.

AMERICAN LAW INSTITUTE. *Model Penal Code: Proposed Official Draft*. Philadelphia: American Law Institute, 1962.

AMERICAN PSYCHIATRIC ASSOCIATION. *Diagnostic and Statistical Manual of Mental Disorders*. 2d ed. Washington, D.C.: American Psychiatric Association, 1968.

_____ . *Diagnostic and Statistical Manual of Mental Disorders*. 3d ed. Washington, D.C.: American Psychiatric Association, 1987.

AMERICAN PSYCHOLOGICAL ASSOCIATION. *Publication Manual of the American Psychological Association*. 3d ed. Washington, D.C.: American Psychological Association, 1983.

_____ . Officers, boards, committees, and representatives. *American Psychologist* 45 (1990): 848–68.

AMES, KATRINE, AND CRANDALL, REBECCA. "On the Trail of an Elusive Killer." *Newsweek,* 26 November 1990, 68.

AMES, R. "Physical Maturing Among Boys as Related to Adult Social Behavior: A Longitudinal Study." *California Journal of Educational Research* 8 (1957): 69–75.

ANASTASI, ANNE. *Psychological Testing.* 3d ed. New York: Macmillan, 1968.

ANDERSON, A. "How the Mind Heals." *Psychology Today* 16 (December 1982): 51–56.

ANGIER, N. "Deaf Babies Use Their Hands to Babble, Researcher Finds." *New York Times,* 22 March 1991, 1, B6.

ANGOFF, W. H., AND DYER, H. S. "The Admissions Testing Program." In *The College Boards Admissions Testing Program,* edited by W. H. Angoff, 1–13. New York: College Entrance Examination Board, 1971.

ANTHONY, J. "The Reactions of Adults to Adolescents and Their Behavior." In *Adolescence: Psychological Perspectives,* edited by G. Caplan and S. Lebovici. New York: Basic Books, 1969.

ARIETI, SILVANO, ED. *American Handbook of Psychology.* 3 vols. New York: Basic Books, 1959.

ARKOFF, ABE. *Adjustment and Mental Health.* New York: McGraw-Hill, 1968.

ARNHEIM, RUDOLPH. *Art and Visual Perception: A Psychology of the Creative Eye.* Berkeley: University of California Press, 1974.

ARNOLD, MAGDA B. *Emotion and Personality.* New York: Columbia University Press, 1960.

_____ , ED. *Feelings and Emotions: The Loyola Symposium.* New York: Academic Press, 1970.

ARONSON, E., AND LINDER, D. "Gain and Loss of Esteem as Determinants of Interpersonal Attractiveness." *Journal of Experimental Social Psychology* 1 (1965): 156–71.

ARONSON, E., TURNER, J., AND CARLSMITH, M. "Communicator Credibility and Communicator Discrepancy as Determinants of Opinion Change." *Journal of Abnormal and Social Psychology* 67 (1963): 31–36.

ARONSON, E., ET AL. "Busing and Racial Tension: The Jigsaw Route to Learning and Liking." *Psychology Today* 9 (February 1975): 43–50.

ASCH, S. *Social Psychology.* New York: Prentice-Hall 1952.

_____ . "Effects of Group Pressure upon the Modification and Distortion of Judgments." In *Basic Studies in Social Psychology,* edited by J. Proshansky and B. Seidenberg, 393–401. New York: Holt, Rinehart & Winston, 1965.

ASH, P., AND KROEKER, L. P. "Personnel Selection, Classification, and Placement." In *Annual Review of Psychology,* 481–507. Palo Alto, Calif.: Annual Reviews, 1975.

ATKINSON, JOHN W., ED. *Motives in Fantasy, Action, and Society.* Princeton, N.J.: Van Nostrand, 1958.

ATKINSON, JOHN W., AND FEATHER, NORMAN T. *A Theory of Achievement Motivation.* New York: Wiley, 1966.

AVERILL, J. "Studies on Anger and Aggression: Implications for Theories of Emotion." *American Psychologist* 38 (1983): 1145–60.

BACHRACH, A. J. *Psychological Research: An Introduction.* 2d ed. New York: Random House, 1965.

BACK, KURT W. *Beyond Words: The Story of Sensitivity Training and the Encounter Movement.* New York: Basic Books, 1972.

BAKAL, D. A. *Psychology and Medicine: Psychological Dimensions of Health and Medicine.* New York: Springer, 1979.

BALDWIN, ALFRED A. *Theories of Child Development.* New York: Wiley, 1967.

BALES, R. F. "Task Roles and Social Roles in Problem-Solving Groups." In *Readings in Social Psychology,* 3d ed., edited by E. Maccoby, T. M. Newcomb, and E. L. Hartley, 347–447. New York: Holt, Rinehart & Winston, 1958.

BALLENGER, J. C. "Toward an Integrated Model of Panic Disorder." *American Journal of Orthopsychiatry* 59 (1989): 284–93.

BALTES, P. B., AND SHAIE, K. W. "Aging and IQ: The Myth of the Twilight Years." In *Readings in Aging and Death: Contemporary Perspectives,* edited by S. H. Zarit. New York: Harper & Row, 1977.

BALTES, P. B., SOWARKA, D., AND KLIEGL, R. "Cognitive Training Research on Fluid Intelligence in Old

Age: What Can Older Adults Achieve by Themselves?" *Psychology and Aging* 4 (1989): 217–21.

BANDURA, ALBERT. "The Stormy Decade: Fact or Fiction?" *Psychology in the Schools* 1 (1964): 224–31.

———. "Influence of Models' Reinforcement Contingencies on the Acquisition of Imitative Responses." *Journal of Personality and Social Psychology* 1 (1965): 589–95.

———. "Analysis of Modeling Processes." In *Psychological Modeling: Conflicting Theories*, edited by A. Bandura, 1–62. Chicago: Aldine-Atherton, 1971.

BANDURA, ALBERT, AND WALTERS, R. H. *Social Learning Personality Development*. New York: Holt, Rinehart & Winston, 1963.

BARBER, T. X. "Measuring 'Hypnotic-like' Suggestibility With and Without 'Hypnotic Induction': Psychometric Properties, Norms, and Variables Influencing Response to the Barber Suggestibility Scale (BSS)." *Psychological Reports* 16 (1965): 809–44.

BARD, PHILIP. "On Emotional Expression After Decortication with Some Remarks of Certain Theoretical Views: Part I." *Psychological Review* 41 (1934): 309–29. "Part II." 41 (1934): 424–49.

BARDON, J. I. "Psychology Applied to Education: A Specialty in Search of an Identity." *American Psychologist* 38 (1983): 185–96.

BARROW, G. M., AND SMITH, P. A. *Aging, Ageism and Society*. St. Paul, Minn.: West, 1979.

BATESON, GREGORY. *Steps to an Ecology of Mind*. San Francisco: Chandler, 1972.

BAUER, M. "Near-Death Experiences and Attitude Change." *Anabiosis* 5 (1985): 39–47.

BAUM, ANDREW, AND VALINS, STUART. *Architecture and Social Behavior*. Hillsdale, N.J.: Erlbaum, 1977.

BECK, AARON T. *Depression: Causes and Treatment*. Philadelphia: University of Pennsylvania Press, 1967.

BECK, J. "MDMA: The Popularization and Resultant Implications of a Recently Controlled Psychoactive Substance." *Contemporary Drug Problems* 13 (1986): 23–63.

BEEBE-CENTER, J. G. "Standards for the Use of Gust Scale." *Journal of Psychology* 28 (1949): 411–19.

BELLUGI, U., AND BROWN, R., EDS. *The Acquisition of Language*. Chicago: University of Chicago Press, 1970.

BELSKY, J. "The Determinants of Parenting: A Process Model." *Child Development* 55 (1984): 83–96.

BEM, DARYL J. *Beliefs, Attitudes and Human Affairs*. Belmont, Calif.: Brooks/Cole, 1970.

BEM, SANDRA. "Androgyny vs. the Little Lives of Fluffy Women and Chesty Men." *Psychology Today* 8 (September 1975): 59–62.

BENSON, HERBERT. *The Relaxation Response*. New York: Avon, 1975.

BENSON, HERBERT, AND WALLACE, ROBERT KEITH. "Decreased Drug Abuse with Transcendental Meditation: A Study of 1862 Subjects." In *Drug Abuse: Proceedings of the International Conference*, edited by C. J. D. Arafonetis. Philadelphia: Lea & Febiger, 1972.

BERGIN, ALLEN E. "The Evaluation of Therapeutic Outcomes." In *Handbook of Psychotherapy and Behavior Change: An Empirical Analysis*, edited by Allen E. Bergin and Sol L. Garfield. New York: Wiley, 1971.

BERNARD, H. W., AND HUCKINS, W. C. *Dynamics of Personal Adjustment*. 3d ed. Boston: Holbrook Press, 1978.

BERNARD, JESSIE. *The Future of Marriage*. New York: Bantam, 1973 (paper).

BERNE, ERIC. *Games People Play*. New York: Grove Press, 1964.

BERNE, ERIC, AND WALSTER, A. "A Little Bit of Love." In *Foundations of Interpersonal Attraction*, edited by T. L. Huston. New York: Academic Press, 1974.

BERSHEID, E. "Emotion." In *Close Relationships*, edited by H. H. Kelley. New York: Freeman, 1983.

———. "Physical Attractiveness." In *Advances in Experimental Social Psychology*, edited by Leonard Berkowitz. New York: Academic Press, 1974.

———. *Interpersonal Attraction*. 2d ed. Reading, Mass.: Addison-Wesley, 1978.

BISCHOF, L. *Adult Psychology*. New York: Harper & Row, 1969.

BLACKMORE, S. J. *Beyond the Body: An Investigation of Out-of-the-Body Experiences*. London: Heinemann, 1982a.

_____ . "Where Am I? Perspectives in Imagery and the Out-of-Body Experience." *Journal of Mental Imagery* 11 (1982b): 53–56.

BLANK, A. "Stresses of War: The Example of Vietnam." In *Handbook of Stress: Theoretical and Clinical Aspects,* edited by L. Goldberger and S. Breznitz, 631–43. New York: Free Press.

BOOTZIN, R. R., AND ACOCELLA, J. *Abnormal Psychology: Current Perspectives.* 5th ed. New York: McGraw-Hill, 1988.

BOTWINICK, J. *Aging and Behavior.* 2d ed. New York: Springer, 1978.

BOUCHARD, T. J., LYKKEN, D. T., MCGUE, M., SEGAL, N. L., AND TELLEGEN, A. "Sources of Human Psychological Differences: The Minnesota Study of Twins Reared Apart." *Science* 250 (1990): 223–28.

BOUCHARD, T. J., AND SEGAL, N. L. "Environment and IQ." In *Handbook of Intelligence,* edited by B. B. Wolman. New York: Wiley, 1985.

BOWER, G. "Mood and Memory." *American Psychologist* 36 (1981): 129–48.

BOWERS, K. *Hypnosis for the Seriously Curious.* Monterey, Calif.: Brooks/Cole, 1976.

BOWLBY, J. *Child Care and Growth of Love.* 2d ed. Baltimore: Penguin, 1965.

BOYD, J., AND WEISSMAN, M. "The Epidemiology of Psychiatric Disorders of Middle Age: Depression, Alcoholism, and Suicide." In *Modern Perspectives in the Psychiatry of Middle Age,* edited by J. G. Howels. New York: Brunner/Mazel, 1981.

BRACKBILL, YVONNE, ET AL. "Arousel Level in Neonates and Preschool Children Under Continuous Auditory Stimulation." *Journal of Experimental Child Psychology* 4 (1966): 177–88.

BRADY, JOSEPH V. "Ulcers in 'Executive' Monkey." *Scientific American* 199 (October 1958): 95–100.

BRANT, B. A., AND OSGOOD, N. J. "The Suicidal Patient in Long-Term Care Institutions." *Journal of Gerontological Nursing* 16 (1990): 14–18.

BREAN, HERBERT. "Hidden Sell Technique Almost Here." *Life,* 31 March 1958, 102–14.

BRECHER, E. M. *The Sex Researchers.* New York: New American Library, 1971.

BRECHER, E. M., AND THE EDITORS OF CONSUMER REPORTS. *Licit and Illicit Drugs.* Boston: Little, Brown, 1972.

BRITTAIN, C. V. "Adolescent Choices and Parent-Peer Cross Pressures." *American Sociological Review* 28 (1963): 385–91.

_____ . "A Comparison of Urban and Rural Adolescence with Respect to Peer Versus Parent Compliance." *Adolescence* 4 (1969): 59–68.

BROOK, J. S., GORDON, A. S., BROOK, A., AND BROOK, D. W. "The Consequences of Marijuana Use on Intrapersonal and Interpersonal Functioning in Black and White Adolescents." *Genetic, Social, and General Psychology Monographs* 115 (1989): 349–69.

BROWN, J. A. C. *Techniques of Persuasion.* Baltimore: Penguin, 1963.

BROWN, ROGER. *A First Language: The Early Stages.* Cambridge, Mass.: Harvard University Press, 1973.

BRUNER, JEROME S., GOODNOW, JACQUELINE J., AND AUSTIN, GEORGE A. *A Study of Thinking.* New York: Wiley, 1956 (paper).

BUCKHOUT, ROBERT. "Eyewitness Testimony." *Scientific American* 231, no. 6 (1974): 23–31.

BUDZYNSKI, T. H., ET AL. "EMG Biofeedback and Tension Headache: A Controlled Outcome Study." *Psychosomatic Medicine* 35 (1973): 484–96.

BUEHLER, R. E., PATTERSON, G. R., AND FURNESS, R. M. "The Reinforcement of Behavior in Institutional Settings." *Behavior Research and Therapy* 4 (1966): 157–67.

BURKE, R. J., AND WEIR, T. "Marital Helping Relationships: The Moderators Between Stress and Well-Being." *Journal of Psychology* 95 (1977): 121–30.

BUTLER, R. N. "Psychiatric Evaluation of the Aged." *Geriatrics* 18 (1963): 220–32.

CAHALAN, D. "Subcultural Differences in Drinking Behavior in U.S. National Surveys and Selected European Studies." In *Alcoholism: New Directions in Behaviorial Research and Treatment,* edited by P. E. Nathan, G. A. Marlatt, and T. Loberg. New York: Plenum, 1978.

CAMPBELL, E. "Some Social Psychological Correlates of Direction in Attitude Change." *Social Forces* 36 (1958): 335–40.

CANNON, WALTER B. *Bodily Changes in Pain, Hunger, Fear and Rage.* New York: Appleton-Century-Crofts, 1929.

CAPLAN, GERALD. *Principles of Preventive Psychiatry.* New York: Basic Books, 1965.

CAPLAN, R. D., COBB, S., FRENCH, J. R. P., VANHARRISON, R., AND PINNEAU, R. *Job Demands and Worker Health: Main Effects and Occupational Differences.* Washington, D.C.: National Institute for Occupational Safety and Health, 1975.

CARRINGTON, P. *Releasing: The New Behavioral Science Method for Dealing with Pressure Situations.* New York: Morrow, 1984.

CATTELL, R. B. *The Scientific Analysis of Personality.* Baltimore: Penguin, 1965.

CHANCE, PAUL. "Telepathy Could Be Real." *Psychology Today* 9 (February 1976): 40–44, 65.

CHAND, I. P., CRIDER, D. M., AND WILLETS, F. K. "Parent-Youth Disagreement as Perceived by Youth: A Longitudinal Study." *Youth and Society* 6 (1975): 365–75.

CHOROVER, S. L. "Big Brother and Psychotechnology II: The Pacification of the Brain." *Psychology Today* 7 (May 1974): 59–69.

CHUKOVSKY, K. *From Two to Five.* Berkeley: University of California Press, 1963.

COALE, A. J. "The Demographic Transition Reconsidered." Paper presented at the International Population Conference, Liège, Belgium, 1973.

COBB, SYDNEY. "Social Support as a Moderator of Life Stress." *Psychosomatic Medicine* 38 (September-October 1976): 300–14.

COBB, SYDNEY, AND ROSE, ROBERT. "Hypertension, Peptic Ulcers, and Diabetes in Air Traffic Controllers." *Journal of the American Medical Association* 224 (1973): 489–92.

COCH, L., AND FRENCH, J. R. P., Jr. "Overcoming Resistance to Change." *Human Relations* 1 (1948): 512–32.

COFER, C. N. *Motivation and Emotions.* Glenview, Ill.: Scott, Foresman, 1972.

COHEN, A. R. *Attitude Change and Social Influence.* New York: Basic Books, 1964.

COHEN, H., AND FILIPCZAK, J. *A New Learning Environment.* San Francisco: Jossey-Bass, 1971.

COHEN, S., GLASS, D., AND SINGER, J. "Apartment Noises, Auditory Discrimination and Reading Ability in Children." *Journal of Experimental Social Psychology* 9 (1973): 407–22.

COLE, J. O. "Phenothiazine Treatment in Acute Schizophrenia: Effectiveness." *Archives of General Psychiatry* 10 (1964): 246–61.

COLEMAN, JAMES C. *Abnormal Psychology and Modern Life.* 5th ed. Glenview, Ill.: Scott, Foresman, 1976.

———. *Contemporary Psychology and Effective Behavior.* 4th ed. Glenview, Ill.: Scott, Foresman, 1979.

COLEMAN, JAMES C., AND HAMMOND, CONSTANCE L. *Contemporary Psychology and Effective Behavior.* Glenview, Ill.: Scott, Foresman, 1974.

COLEMAN, J. S. *The Adolescent Society.* New York: Free Press, 1961.

COLES, R. "Life in Appalachia: The Case of Hugh McCaslin." In *Life at the Bottom,* edited by G. Armstrong, 26–42. New York: Bantam, 1971 (paper).

CONGER, J. J. *Adolescence and Youth: Psychological Development in a Changing World.* New York: Harper & Row, 1973.

Congressional Quarterly Weekly Report, June 13, 1981, 1049.

COOPER, CARY L., AND MARSHALL, JUDI. "Occupational Sources of Stress: A Review of the Literature Relating to Coronary Heart Disease and Mental Ill Health." *Journal of Occupational Psychology* 49 (March 1976): 11–28.

COOPER, CARY L., AND PAYNE, R., EDS. *Stress at Work.* New York: Wiley, 1979.

CORSINI, RAYMOND J., ED. *Current Psychotherapies.* Itasca, Ill.: Peacock, 1973.

COWLEY, GEOFFREY. "The Promise of Prozac." *Newsweek,* 26 March 1990, 38.

COX, T. *Stress.* Baltimore: University Park, 1978.

CREWS, F., AND SCHOR, S. *The Borzoi Handbook for Writers.* 2d ed. New York: McGraw-Hill. 1989.

CRONBACH, LEE J. *Essentials of Psychological Testing.* 3d ed. New York: Harper & Row, 1970.

CUBER, J. F., AND HARROFF, P. *Sex and the Significant American.* Baltimore: Penguin, 1965.

CULLITON, B. J. "Psychosurgery: National Commission Issues Surprisingly Favorable Report." *Science* 194 (1976): 299–301.

DACEY, J. S. *Adolescents Today.* Santa Monica, Calif.: Goodyear, 1979.

DAHLSTROM, WILLIAM GRANT, AND WELSH, GEORGE, S. *An MMPI Handbook: A Guide to Use in Clinical Practice and Research.* Minneapolis: University of Minnesota Press, 1960.

DAMON, W. *Social and Personality Development*. New York: Norton, 1983.

DARLEY, J. M., AND LATANE, B. "Bystander Intervention in Emergencies: Diffusion of Responsibility." *Journal of Personality and Social Psychology* 8 (1968): 377–83.

DARWIN, CHARLES. *The Expression of Emotions in Man and Animals*. Chicago: University of Chicago Press, 1967. (Originally published 1872.)

DAVIS, A. "Socio-Economic Influences upon Children's Learning." *Understanding the Child* 20 (1951): 10–16.

DAVIS, K. "Near and Dear: Friendship and Love Compared." *Psychology Today* 19 (February 1985): 22–30.

DAVISON, GERALD C., AND NEALE, JOHN M. *Abnormal Psychology: An Experimental Clinical Approach*. 2d ed. New York: Wiley, 1978.

DE ANGELIS, TORI. "Living with Violence: Children Suffer and Cope." *APA Monitor* 22 (January 1991a): 27–28.

———. "Role of Psychologist in Gulf Is Demanding." *APA Monitor* 22 (February 1991b): 1, 19.

DE BONO, EDWARD. *New Think: The Use of Lateral Thinking in the Generation of New Ideas*. New York: Basic Books, 1968.

DEIKMAN, ARTHUR J. "Experimental Meditation." *Journal of Nervous and Mental Disease* 136 (1963): 329–73.

DELGADO, J. M. R. *Physical Control of the Mind*. New York: Harper & Row, 1969.

DEMENT, W. *Some Must Watch While Some Must Sleep*. New York: Norton, 1976.

DEMENT, W., AND WOLPERT, E. "Relation of Eye Movements, Bodily Mobility, and External Stimuli to Dream Content." *Journal of Experimental Psychology* 55 (1958): 543–53.

DENNIS, W. "Creative Productivity Between the Ages of Twenty and Eighty Years." *Journal of Gerontology* 21 (1966): 1–8.

DENNIS, WAYNE. "Causes of Retardation Among Institutional Children: Iran." *Journal of Genetic Psychology* 96 (1960): 47–59.

DEUTSCH, M., AND COLLINS, M. *Interracial Housing: A Psychological Evaluation of a Social Experiment*. Minneapolis: University of Minnesota Press, 1951.

DICHTER, ERNEST. *Handbook of Consumer Motivations*. New York: McGraw-Hill, 1964.

DION, K. L., BERSCHEID, E., AND WALSTER, E. "What Is Beautiful Is Good." *Journal of Personality and Social Psychology* 24 (1972): 285–90.

DIXON, N. F. *Subliminal Perception: The Nature of a Controversy*. London: McGraw-Hill, 1971.

DODGE, K. "Behavioral Antecedents of Peer Social Status." *Child Development* 54 (1983): 1379–86.

DODGE, K., AND HAMMEN, CONSTANCE L. *Contemporary Psychology and Effective Behavior*. Glenview, Ill.: Scott, Foresman, 1974.

DRISKELL, J. E., AND OLMSTEAD, B. "Psychology and the Military: Research Applications and Trends." *American Psychologist* 44 (1989): 43–54.

DU BOIS, PHILIP H. "Review of Scholastic Aptitude Test." In *The Seventh Mental Measurements Yearbook*, edited by O. K. Buros, 646–48. Highland Park, N.J.: Gryphon Press, 1972.

DUNCKER, KARL. "On Problem Solving." Translated by L. S. Lees. *Psychological Monographs* 58, no. 270 (1945).

———. *The Mechanism of the Mind*. New York: Simon & Schuster, 1969.

DUNPHY, D. "The Social Structure of Urban Adolescent Peer Groups." *Sociometry* 26 (1963): 230–46.

DWYER, JOHANNA, AND MAYER, JEAN. "Psychological Effects of Variations in Physical Appearance During Adolescence." *Adolescence* (1968–1969): 353–68.

EDITORS OF THE LITERARY DIGEST. "Landon, 1,293,669; Roosevelt, 972,897." *Literary Digest* 122 (October 1936): 5–6.

EDWARDS, J. N., AND BRAUBURGER, M. B. "Exchange and Parent-Youth Conflict." *Journal of Marriage and the Family* 35 (1973): 101–07.

EKMAN, PAUL, FRIESEN, WALLACE V., AND ELLSWORTH, PHOEBE. *Emotion in the Human Face: Guidelines for Research and an Integration of Findings*. Elmsford, N.Y.: Pergamon, 1972.

ELDERSVELD, S., AND DODGE, R. "Personal Contact or Mail Propaganda? An Experiment in Voting Turnout and Attitude Change." In *Public Opinion and Propaganda*, edited by D. Katz et al., 532–42. New York: Dryden Press, 1954.

ELKIND, D., AND WEINER, I. B. *Development of the Child*. New York: Wiley, 1978.

ELLIS, ALBERT. "Rational-Emotive Therapy." In *Current Psychotherapies,* edited by R. Corsini, 167–206. Itasca, Ill.: Peacock, 1973.

_____ . "What People Can Do for Themselves to Cope with Stress." In *Stress at Work,* edited by C. L. Cooper and R. Payne. New York: Wiley, 1978.

ERIKSON, ERIK. *Childhood and Society*. New York: Norton, 1950.

_____ . *Identity: Youth and Crisis*. New York: Norton, 1968.

ERLEMEIR, N. "Suizidalitat im Alter" (Suicide in Old Age). *Zeitschrift fur Gerontologie* 21 (1988): 267–76.

ERON, L., HUESMANN, L. R., BRICE, P., FISCHER, P., AND MERMELSTEIN, R. "Age Trends in the Development of Aggression, Sex Typing, and Related Television Habits." *Developmental Psychology* 19 (1983): 71–77.

ESTABROOKS, G., ED. *Hypnosis: Current Problems*. New York: Harper & Row, 1962.

EVANGELAUF, J. "College Board to Revise Entrance Exam; Says New Version Will Be More Useful." *Chronicle of Higher Education,* 7 November 1990, A1, A33, A34.

EVANS, N. "Women's Development Across the Life Span." *New Directions for Student Services* 29 (1985): 9–27.

EYSENCK, HANS J. "The Effects of Psychotherapy: An Evaluation." *Journal of Consulting Psychology* 16 (1952): 319–24.

_____ . *The Dynamics of Anxiety and Hysteria*. London: Routledge & Kegan Paul, 1957.

_____ . *The Effects of Psychotherapy*. New York: International Science Press, 1966.

_____ . *The Structure of Human Personality*, London: Methuen, 1970.

FARADAY, ANN. *The Dream Game*. New York: Harper & Row, 1974.

FEIL, N. "Resolution: The Final Life Task." *Journal of Humanistic Psychology* 25 (1985): 91–105.

FESTINGER, L. *A Theory of Cognitive Dissonance*. Stanford, Calif.: Stanford University Press, 1957.

FESTINGER, L., AND CARLSMITH, J. M. "Cognitive Consequences of Forced Compliance." *Journal of Abnormal and Social Psychology* 58 (1959): 203–10.

FIEDLER, F. E. "Style or Circumstance: The Leadership Enigma." *Psychology Today* 2 (1969): 38–43.

FISCHER, KURT W. *Piaget's Theory of Learning and Cognitive Development*. Chicago: Markham, 1973a.

_____ . *The Organization of Simple Learning*. Chicago: Markham, 1973b.

FISHER, S., AND GREENBERG, R. P. *The Scientific Credibility of Freud's Theories and Therapy*. New York: Basic Books, 1977.

FITCH, V. "The Psychological Tasks of Old Age." *Naropa Institute Journal of Psychology* 3 (1985): 90–106.

FITTS, P. M., AND POSNER, M. I. *Human Performance*. Belmont, Calif.: Brooks/Cole, 1967.

FITTS, WILLIAM H. *The Experience of Psychotherapy*. Princeton, N.J.: Van Nostrand, 1965.

"Five Antidotes for Job Tension." *Supervisory Management* 14 (1969): 32–34.

FIXX, JAMES. *The Complete Book of Running*. New York: Random House, 1977.

FLACK, R. "The Liberated Generation: An Exploration of the Roots of Student Protest." *Journal of Social Issues* 23 (1967): 52–57.

FLAVELL, JOHN H. *The Developmental Theory of Jean Piaget*. Princeton, N.J.: Van Nostrand, 1963.

FLEXNER, L. "Dissection of Memory in Mice with Antibiotics." *Proceedings of the American Philosophical Society* 111 (1967): 343–46.

FLOOD, J. F., BENNETT, E. L., AND ORME, A. E. "Relation of Memory Formation for Controlled Amounts of Brain Protein Synthesis." *Physiology and Behavior* 15 (1975): 97–102.

FOULKES, DAVID. *The Psychology of Sleep*. New York: Scribner's, 1966.

FOX, L. JUNGBERG. "Effecting the Use of Efficient Study Habits." In *Control of Human Behavior,* vol. 1, edited by R. Ulrich, T. Stachnik, and J. Mabry. Glenview, Ill.: Scott, Foresman, 1966.

FRAM, D. H., AND STONE, N. *National Institute on Drug Abuse: Research Monograph Series* 64 (1986): 237–51.

FRANCIS, G. J., AND MILBOURN, G. *Human Behavior in the Work Environment: A Managerial Perspective*. Santa Monica, Calif.: Goodyear, 1980.

FRANK, JEROME. "The Drive for Power and the Nuclear Arms Race." *American Psychologist* 42 (1986): 337–44.

FRANKL, VIKTOR. *Man's Search for Meaning: An Introduction to Logotherapy*. New York: Clarion, 1970.

FREEDMAN, JONATHAN L. *Crowding and Behavior*. San Francisco: Freeman, 1975.

FREIBERG, PETER. "Experts Urge Changes in Work, Not the Worker." *APA Monitor* 22 (January 1991a): 23–24.

_____. "At Work, Nobody Knows the Troubles Women See." *APA Monitor* 22 (January 1991b): 24–25.

FREUD, SIGMUND. *An Outline of Psychoanalysis*. Edited and translated by James Strachey. New York: Norton, 1949. (Originally published 1940.)

_____. *A General Introduction to Psychoanalysis*. Translated by Joan Riviere. Garden City, N.Y.: Garden City Publishing, 1943.

FRIEDMAN, MEYER, AND ROSENMAN, RAY. *Type A Behavior and Your Heart*. New York: Knopf, 1974.

FRIER, R. C. "PCP: A Relook at the Chemistry, Intoxication, Psychosis and Treatment." *Psychiatric Forum* 14 (1989): 52–57.

FROMM, ERICH. *Man for Himself: An Inquiry into the Psychology of Ethics*. New York: Holt, Rinehart & Winston, 1947.

_____. *The Art of Loving*. New York: Harper & Row, 1956.

FURN, B. G. "Adjustment and the Near-Death Experience: A Conceptual and Therapeutic Model." *Journal of Near-Death Studies* 6 (1987): 4–19.

FURTH, HANS. *Piaget and Knowledge*. Englewood Cliffs, N.J.: Prentice-Hall, 1969.

GALTON, SIR FRANCIS. *Hereditary Genius: An Inquiry into Its Laws and Consequences*. London: Macmillan, 1869.

GARCIA, JOHN, AND KOELLING, R. A. "The Relation of Cue to Consequence in Avoidance Learning." *Psychonomic Science* 4 (1966): 123–24.

GARDNER, R. A., AND GARDNER, B. T. "Teaching Sign Language to a Chimpanzee." *Science* 165 (1969): 644–72.

GAUGLER, B. B., ROSENTHAL, D. B., THORNTON, G. C., III, AND BENTSON, C. "Meta-Analysis of Assessment Center Validity." *Journal of Applied Psychology* 72 (1987): 439–511.

GAZZANIGA, MICHAEL S. "The Split Brain in Man." *Scientific American* 217 (August 1967): 24–29.

GELDARD, FRANK A. *The Human Senses*. 2d ed. New York: Wiley, 1972.

GELLES, RICHARD, AND STRAUS, MURRAY. *Intimate Violence*. New York: Simon & Schuster, 1989.

GELMAN, R., AND BAILLERGEON, R. "A Review of Piagetian Concepts." In *Handbook of Child Psychology: Cognitive Development*, edited by J. H. Flavell and E. M. Markman. New York: Wiley, 1983.

GERACI, J. B. "Comments on Betty Furn's 'Adjustment and the Near-Death Experience.'" *Journal of Near-Death Studies* 6 (1987): 28–29.

GERARD, H. B., AND RABBIE, J. M. "Fear and Social Comparison." *Journal of Abnormal and Social Psychology* 62 (1961): 586–92.

GERGEN, KENNETH J., GERGEN, MARY M., AND BARTON, WILLIAM H. "Deviance in the Dark." *Psychology Today* 7 (October 1973): 129, 130.

GERST, M. S. "Symbolic Coding Processes in Observational Learning." *Journal of Personality and Social Psychology* 19 (1971): 9–17.

GHISELIN, B., ED. *The Creative Process*. New York: New American Library, 1952 (paper).

GIBB, C. "Leadership." In *The Handbook of Social Psychology*, vol. 4, 2d ed., edited by G. Lindsey and E. Aaronson. Reading, Mass.: Addison-Wesley, 1969.

GIBSON, E. J., AND WALK, R. D. "The Visual Cliff." *Scientific American* 202 (1960): 64–71.

GINSBURG, HERBERT, AND OPPER, SYLVIA. *Piaget's Theory of Intellectual Development: An Introduction*. Englewood Cliffs, N.J.: Prentice-Hall, 1969.

GLACALONE, R. A., AND ROSENFELD, P., EDS. *Impression Management in the Organization*. Hillsdale, N.J.: Erlbaum.

GLASS, D. C. "Changes in Liking as a Means of Reducing Cognitive Discrepancies Between Self-Esteem and Aggression." *Journal of Personality* 32 (1964): 531–49.

GLASS, RICHARD. "Mental Health and Mental Illness." In *1991 Medical and Health Annual*, 337–41. Chicago: Encyclopaedia Britannica, 1990.

GOFFMAN, ERVING. *Asylums*. Garden City, N.Y.: Doubleday, 1961 (paper).

GOLANN, S. E., AND EISENDORFER, C., EDS. *Handbook of Community Mental Health*. New York: Appleton-Century-Crofts, 1972.

GOLDEN, F. "Clever Kanzi." *Discover,* March 1991, 20.

GOLDSEN, R., ET AL. *What College Students Think*. Princeton, N.J.: Van Nostrand, 1960.

GOLEMAN, D. "Who's Mentally Ill?" *Psychology Today* 11 (January 1978): 34–41.

_____. "Study Affirms Link of Personality to Illness." *New York Times,* 19 January 1988, C1, C6.

_____. "Life-Style Shift Can Unclog Ailing Arteries, Study Finds." *New York Times,* 14 November 1989, C1, C12.

GOODENOUGH, FLORENCE L. "Expression of the Emotions in a Blind-Deaf Child." *Journal of Abnormal and Social Psychology* 27 (1932): 328–33.

GREEN, DAVID M., AND SWETS, JOHN A. *Signal Detection Theory and Psychophysics.* New York: Wiley, 1966.

GREENBERG, JERALD. "Equity and Workplace Status: A Field Experiment." *Journal of Applied Psychology* 73 (1988): 606–13.

GREENBLATT, MILTON, ET AL., EDS. *Drugs and Social Therapy in Chronic Schizophrenia.* Springfield, Ill.: Charles C. Thomas, 1965.

GREGORY, R. L. *The Intelligent Eye.* New York: McGraw-Hill, 1970 (paper).

_____. *Eye and Brain.* 3d ed. New York: McGraw-Hill, 1978.

GRINSPOON, LESTER. *Marijuana Reconsidered.* Cambridge, Mass.: Harvard University Press, 1970.

Guilford, J. P. *Personality.* New York: McGraw-Hill 1959.

GUILLEMINAULT, C. "Obstructive Sleep Apnea Syndrome: A Review." *Psychiatric Clinics of North America* 10 (1987): 607–21.

GUSTAVSON, C. R., ET AL. "Coyote Predation Control by Aversive Conditioning." *Science* 184 (1974): 581–83.

HAAN, N., AND DAY, D. "A Longitudinal Study of Change and Sameness in Personality Development: Adolescence to Later Adulthood." *International Journal of Aging and Human Development* 5 (1974): 11–39.

HABER, R. N. "How We Remember What We See." *Scientific American* 222 (1970): 104–12.

HALACY, D. R., JR. *Man and Memory.* New York: Harper & Row, 1970.

HALFF, H. M., HOLLAND, J. D., AND HUTCHINS, E. L. "Cognitive Science and Military Training." *American Psychologist* 41 (1986): 1131–39.

HALL, CALVIN S. *A Primer of Freudian Psychology.* Cleveland: World, 1954 (paper).

HALL, CALVIN S., AND LINDZEY, GARDNER. *Theories of Personality.* 3d ed. New York: Wiley, 1978.

HALL, CALVIN S., AND VAN DE CASTLE, R. L. *The Content Analysis of Dreams.* New York: Appleton-Century-Crofts, 1966.

HALL, EDWARD T. *The Silent Language.* Garden City, N.Y.: Doubleday, 1959.

_____. *The Hidden Dimension.* Garden City, N.Y.: Doubleday, 1966.

HALL, G. STANLEY. "The Moral and Religious Training of Children." *Princeton Review,* January 1882, 26–48.

_____. *Adolescence.* New York: Appleton, 1904.

HANCOCK, E. "Age or Experience?" *Human Development* 28 (1985): 274–80.

HARKINS, E. B. "Effect of Empty Nest Transition on Self-Report of Psychological and Physical Well-Being." *Journal of Marriage and the Family* 40 (1978): 549–56.

HARLOW, HARRY F. "The Formation of Learning Sets." *Psychological Review* 56 (1949): 51–65.

_____. "The Development of Affectional Patterns in Infant Monkeys." In *Determinants of Infant Behavior,* edited by B. M. Foss, 75–100. New York: Wiley, 1961.

HARLOW, HARRY F., AND ZIMMERMAN, R. R. "Affectional Responses in the Infant Monkey." *Science* 140 (1959): 421–32.

HARRIS, B. "Whatever Happened to Little Albert?" *American Psychologist* 34 (1979): 151–60.

HARRIS, C. S. *Fact Book on Aging: A Profile of America's Older Population.* Washington, D.C.: National Council on the Aging, 1978.

HARRISON, R. V. "Job Demands and Worker Health: Person-Environment Misfit." Doctoral dissertation, University of Michigan, 1976. *Dissertation Abstracts International,* 37, 1035B (University Microfilms no. 76–19, 150).

HARTUP, W. W. "Peer Interaction and Social Organization." In *Carmichael's Manual of Child Psychophysiology,* vol. 3, edited by P. H. Mussen. New York: Wiley, 1970.

HASSAN, R., AND CARR, J. "Changing Patterns of Suicide in Australia." *Australian and New Zealand Journal of Psychiatry* 23 (1989): 226–34.

HASSETT, JAMES. *A Primer of Psychophysiology.* San Francisco: Freeman, 1978a.

———. "Teaching Yourself to Relax." *Psychology Today* 12 (August 1978b): 28–40.

———. "Caution: Meditation Can Hurt." *Psychology Today* 12 (November 1978c): 125–26.

HASSETT, JOHN. "Checking the Accuracy of Pupil Scores in Standardized Tests." *English Journal* 67 (October 1978): 30–31.

HASTORF, ALBERT H., SCHNEIDER, DAVID J., AND POLEFKA, JUDITH. *Person Perception*. 2d ed. Reading, Mass.: Addison-Wesley, 1979.

HATFIELD, E., AND WALSTER, G. *A New Look at Love*. Reading, Mass.: Addison-Wesley, 1981.

HATHAWAY, STARKE R., AND MCKINLEY, JOHN CHARNLEY. "A Multiphasic Personality Schedule (Minnesota): I. Construction of the Schedule." *Journal of Psychology* 10 (1940): 249–54.

HAVIGHURST, R. J. *Developmental Tasks and Education*. 3d ed. New York: McKay, 1972.

HAYS, WILLIAM L. *Statistics for Psychologists*. New York: Holt, Rinehart & Winston, 1963.

HEBB, D. O. "What Psychology Is About." *American Psychologist* 29 (1974): 71–79.

HELD, R., AND HEIN, A. "A Movement-Produced Stimulation in the Development of Visually Guided Behavior." *Journal of Comparative Physiology and Psychology* 56 (1963): 606–13.

HENNING, HANS. "Die Qualitätenreihe des Geschmacks." *Zeitschrift für Psychologie* 74 (1916): 203–19.

HERNÁNDEZ-PEÓN, R. "Reticular Mechanisms of Sensory Control." In *Sensory Communication*, edited by W. A. Rosenblith, 497–520. New York: Wiley, 1961.

HERRNSTEIN, RICHARD. "I.Q." *Atlantic* 228 (1971): 43–64.

HERRON, JEANNINE. "Southpaws: How Different Are They?" *Psychology Today*, March 1976, 50–56.

HESS, R., AND TORNEY, J. *The Development of Political Attitudes in Children*. Chicago: Aldine, 1967.

HIGGINS-TRENK, A., AND GAITE, A. J. H. "Elusiveness of Formal Operational Thought in Adolescents." *Proceedings of the Seventy-Ninth Annual Convention of the American Psychological Association*. Washington, D.C.: American Psychological Association, 1971.

HILGARD, E. R. *Hypnotic Susceptibility*. New York: Harcourt Brace Jovanovich, 1965.

———. *Divided Consciousness*. New York: Wiley, 1977.

HIROTO, D. S. "Locus of Control and Learned Helplessness." *Journal of Experimental Psychology* 102 (1974): 187–93.

HOCHBERG, JULIAN. *Perception*. Englewood Cliffs, N.J.: Prentice-Hall, 1964 (paper).

HOFFMAN, BANESH. *The Tyranny of Testing*. New York: Collier, 1962 (paper).

HOKANSON, J. E., DEGOOD, D. E., FORREST, M. S., AND BRITTAIN, T. M. "Availability of Avoidance Behaviors for Modulating Vascular-Stress Responses." *Journal of Personality and Social Psychology* 67 (1963): 60–68.

HOLBORN, HAJO. *A History of Modern Germany 1850–1945*. New York: Knopf, 1969.

HOLDEN, C. "Identical Twins Reared Apart." *Science* 207 (1980): 1323–28.

HOLLAND, GLEN A. "Transactional Analysis." In *Current Psychotherapies*, edited by R. Corsini, 353–400. Itasca, Ill.: Peacock, 1973.

HOLMES, D. L., AND MORRISON, F. J. *The Child: An Introduction to Developmental Psychology*. Monterey, Calif.: Brooks/Cole, 1979.

HOLMES, T. H., AND RAHE, R. H. "The Social Readjustment Scale." *Journal of Psychosomatic Research* 11 (1967): 213.

HONIG, W. H., ED. *Operant Behavior: Areas of Research and Application*. New York: Appleton-Century-Crofts, 1966.

HORN, J. L. "The Aging of Human Abilities." In *Handbook of Developmental Psychology*, 847–70. Englewood Cliffs, N.J.: Prentice Hall, 1982.

HORNER, MATINA S. "Femininity and Successful Achievement: A Basic Inconsistency." In *Feminine Personality and Conflict*, edited by J. Bardwick, E. M. Douvan, M. S. Horner, and D. Gutman. Belmont, Calif.: Brooks/Cole, 1970.

———. "Towards an Understanding of Achievement-Related Conflicts in Women." *Journal of Social Issues* 28 (1972): 157–75.

HORROCKS, J. E., AND BENIMOFF, M. "Isolation from the Peer Group During Adolescence." *Adolescence* 2 (1967): 41–52.

HOTHERSALL, DAVID. *History of Psychology*. 2d ed. New York: McGraw-Hill, 1990.

HOUGH, R. L., FAIRBANKS, D. T., AND GARCIA, A. M. "Problems in the Ratio Measurement of Life Stress." *Journal of Health and Social Behavior* 17 (1976): 70–82.

HOUSE, J. S. "The Relationship of Intrinsic and Extrinsic Work Motivation to Occupational Stress and Coronary Heart Disease Risk." Doctoral dissertation, University of Michigan, 1972. *Dissertation Abstracts International*, 33, 2514–A (University Microfilms no. 72–29094).

HOVLAND, C., LUMSDAINE, A., AND SHEFFIELD, F. *Experiments on Mass Communication*. Princeton, N.J.: Princeton University Press, 1949.

HOVLAND, C., AND SEARS, R. "Minor Studies of Aggression: Correlation of Lynching with Economic Indices." *Journal of Psychology* 9 (1940): 301–10.

HRABA, J., AND GRANT, G. "Black Is Beautiful: A Reexamination of Racial Preference and Identification." *Journal of Personality and Social Psychology* 16 (1970): 398–402.

HUBEL, DAVID H., AND WIESEL, TORSLEN N. "Receptive Fields, Binocular Interaction, and Functional Architecture in the Cat's Visual Cortex." *Journal of Physiology* 160 (1962): 106–54.

HULL, CLARK. *Principles of Behavior: An Introduction to Behavior Theory*. New York: Appleton-Century-Crofts, 1943.

HURLOCK, E. B. *Developmental Psychology: A Life-Span Approach*. 5th ed. New York: McGraw-Hill, 1980.

HUSTON, A., ET AL. "Communicating More Than Content: Formal Features of Children's Television Programs." *Journal of Communication* 31 (1981): 32–48.

INHELDER, BAERBEL. "Memory and Intelligence in the Child." In *Studies in Cognitive Development*, edited by D. Elkind and J. F. Flavell, 337–64. New York: Oxford University Press, 1969.

INHELDER, BAERBEL, AND PIAGET, J. *The Early Growth of Logic in the Child*. New York: Harper & Row, 1964.

IRWIN, H. J. "Out-of-Body Experiences and Attitudes to Life and Death." *Journal of the American Society for Psychical Research* 82 (1988): 237–51.

IZARD, CARROLL, E. *The Face of Emotion*. New York: Appleton-Century-Crofts, 1971.

_____. *Patterns of Emotions: A New Analysis of Anxiety and Depression*. New York: Academic Press, 1972.

JAMES, WILLIAM. *The Principles of Psychology*. Vol. 2. New York: Holt, 1890.

JAMIESON, A. O. "Obesity and Sleep Disordered Breathing." *Annals of Behavioral Medicine* 10 (1988): 107–12.

JANIS, IRVING. *Psychological Stress*. New York: Academic Press, 1958.

_____. *Victims of Groupthink: A Psychological Study of Foreign Policy Decisions and Fiascoes*. Boston: Houghton Mifflin, 1972.

JELLINEK, ELVIN M. *The Disease Concept of Alcoholism*. New Brunswick, N.J.: Hillhouse Press, 1960.

JENNINGS, M., AND NIEMI, R. "The Transmission of Political Values from Parent to Child." *American Political Science Review* 62 (1968): 169–84.

JOHNSON, E. S., AND WILLIAMSON, J. B. *Growing Old: The Social Problems of Aging*. New York: Holt, Rinehart & Winston, 1980.

JOHNSTON, L. D., BACHMAN, J. G., AND O'MALLEY, P. M. *Monitoring the Future: Questionnaire Responses from the Nation's High School Seniors*. 1978 vol. Ann Arbor: University of Michigan, Institute for Social Research, 1980.

JOHNSTON, LLOYD. *10th National Survey of Drug Usage Among College Students*. Ann Arbor: University of Michigan, Institute for Social Research, 1990.

JONES, EDWARD E., AND DAVIS, KEITH E. "From Acts to Dispositions: The Attribution Process in Person Perception." In *Advances in Experimental Social Psychology*, vol. 2, edited by Leonard Berkowitz, 219–66. New York: Academic Press, 1965.

JONES, EDWARD E., ET AL. "Internal States or Emotional Stimuli: Observers' Attitude Judgments and the Dissonance of Theory-Self-Presentation Controversy." *Journal of Experimental Social Psychology* 4 (1968): 247–69.

JONES, F. H. "A Four-Year Follow-Up of Vulnerable Adolescents." *Journal of Nervous and Mental Disease* 159 (1974): 20–39.

JONES, M. C. "The Elimination of Children's Fears." *Journal of Experimental Psychology* 29 (1924): 383–90.

_____. "Psychological Correlates of Somatic Development." *Child Development* 36 (1965): 899–911.

_____. "Albert, Peter, and John B. Watson." *American Psychologist*, August 1974, 581–83.

JOSEPHS, R. A., AND STEELE, C. M. "The Two Faces of Alcohol Myopia: Attentional Mediation of Psychological Stress." *Journal of Abnormal Psychology* 99 (1990): 115–26.

JOURARD, SIDNEY, M. *The Transparent Self*. 2d ed. Princeton, N.J.: Van Nostrand, 1971 (paper).

JOUVET, MICHEL. "The Stages of Sleep." *Scientific American* 216 (1967): 62–72.

JUNG, CARL G. *Memories, Dreams, Reflections*. Edited by Anna Jaffe and translated by Richard and Clara Winston. New York: Pantheon, 1963.

KALINOWSKY, L. B. "The Convulsive Therapies." In *Comprehensive Textbook of Psychiatry*, edited by A. M. Freedman, H. I. Kaplan, and B. J. Saddocks. Baltimore: Williams & Wilkins, 1975.

KALISH, RICHARD A. "Attitudes and Aging: Myths and Realities." In *The Later Years: Social Applications of Gerontology*, edited by R. A. Kalish. Monterey, Calif.: Brooks/Cole, 1977.

KANDEL, D. B., AND LESSER, G. S. "Parental and Peer Influences on Educational Plans of Adolescents." *American Sociological Review* 34 (1969): 213–23.

————, AND ————. "The Role of Parents and Peers in Adolescent Marijuana Use." *Science* 181 (1973): 1067–70.

KAPLAN, B., ED. *The Inner World of Mental Illness*. New York: Harper & Row, 1964 (paper).

KARNASH, L. J. *Handbook of Psychiatry*. St. Louis: Mosby, 1945.

KELLEY, H. H. "The Warm-Cold Variable in First Impressions of Persons." *Journal of Personality* 18 (1950): 431–39.

KELMAN, H. C. "Processes of Opinion Change." *Public Opinion Quarterly* 21 (1961): 57–78.

KELMAN, H. C., AND HOVLAND, C. I. "'Reinstatement' of the Communicator in Delayed Measurement of Opinion Change." *Journal of Abnormal and Social Psychology* 48 (1953): 327–35.

KEMPLER, WALTER. "Gestalt Therapy." In *Current Psychotherapies*, edited by R. Corsini, 251–86. Itasca, Ill.: Peacock, 1973.

KETY, S. S., ET AL. "Mental Illness in the Biological and Adoptive Families of Adopted Schizophrenics." *American Journal of Psychiatry* 128, no. 3 (1971): 302–06.

KIMMEL, D. C. *Adulthood and Aging*. 2d ed. New York: Wiley, 1980.

KINGSBURY, STEVEN J. "Cognitive Differences Between Clinical Psychologists and Psychiatrists." *American Psychologist* 42 (1987): 152–56.

KINSEY, ALFRED C., POMEROY, WARDELL B., AND MARTIN, CLYDE E. *Sexual Behavior in the Human Male*. Philadelphia: Saunders, 1948.

KINSEY, ALFRED C., ET AL. *Sexual Behavior in the Human Female*. Philadelphia: Saunders, 1953.

KISKER, GEORGE. *The Disorganized Personality*. New York: McGraw-Hill, 1964.

KLAPPER, J. T. *The Effects of Mass Communications*. New York: Free Press, 1960.

KLEINMAN, P. H., WISH, E. D., DEREN, S., AND RAINONE, G. "Daily Marijuana Use and Problem Behaviors Among Adolescents." *International Journal of the Addictions* 23 (1988): 87–107.

KLEITMAN, NATHANIEL. "Patterns of Dreaming." *Scientific American* 203 (November 1960): 82–88.

————. *Sleep and Wakefulness*. Rev. ed. Chicago: University of Chicago Press, 1963.

KLINEBERG, OTTO. "Emotional Expression in Chinese Literature." *Journal of Abnormal and Social Psychology* 33 (1938): 517–20.

KLÜVER, H., AND BUCY, P. C. "Psychic Blindness and Other Symptoms Following Bilateral Temporal Lobectomy in Rhesus Monkeys." *American Journal of Physiology* 119 (1937): 532–35.

KOENIG, PETER. "Field Report on Psychological Testing of Job Applicants: They Just Changed the Rules on How to Get Ahead." *Psychology Today* 8 (June 1974): 87–96.

KOESTLER, ARTHUR. *The Act of Creation*. New York: Macmillan, 1964.

KOFFKA, K. *Principles of Gestalt Psychology*. New York: Harcourt Brace Jovanovich, 1963.

KOHLBERG, LAWRENCE. "The Child as Moral Philosopher." *Psychology Today* 2 (September 1968): 25–30.

KOHLBERG, LAWRENCE, AND KRAMER, R. "Continuities and Discontinuities in Child and Adult Moral Development." *Human Development* 12 (1969): 93–120.

KOHLBERG, LAWRENCE, AND TUNEL, E. *Research in Moral Development: The Cognitive-Developmental Approach*. New York: Holt, Rinehart & Winston, 1971.

KOHLENBERG, ROBERT, PHILLIPS, THOMAS, AND PROCTOR, WILLIAM. "A Behavioral Analysis of Peaking in

Residential Electrical Energy Consumers." *Journal of Applied Behavioral Analysis* 9 (1976): 13–18.

KÖHLER, WOLFGANG. *The Mentality of Apes*. New York: Harcourt, 1925.

KOLATA, G. "Infant I.Q. Tests Found to Predict Scores in School." *New York Times*, 4 April 1989, C1, C8.

_____ . "Alzheimer's Researchers Close in on Causes." *New York Times*, 26 February 1991, C1, C7.

KOLB, D. A. "Changing Achievement Motivation." In *Behavior Change*, edited by R. Schwitzgabel and D. A. Kolb. New York: McGraw-Hill, 1973.

KOMAROVSKY, M. *Blue-Collar Marriage*. New York: Random House, 1964.

KRAMER, M. "Statistics of Mental Disorders in the United States: Some Urgent Needs and Suggested Solutions." *Journal of the Royal Statistical Society,* Series A, 132 (1969): 353–407.

KRANTZLER, MEL. *Creative Divorce*. New York: Evans, 1973.

KREPS, J. *Sex in the Marketplace: American Women at Work*. Baltimore: Johns Hopkins University Press, 1971.

KÜBLER-ROSS, ELISABETH. *On Death and Dying*. New York: Macmillan, 1969.

LA FRANCE, MARIANNE, AND MAYO, CLARA. "Racial Differences in Gaze Behavior During Conversations: Two Systematic Observation Studies." *Journal of Personality and Social Psychology* 33 (1976): 547–52.

LAHEY, B. B., AND CIMINERO, A. R. *Maladaptive Behavior: An Introduction to Abnormal Psychology*. Glenview, Ill.: Scott, Foresman, 1980.

LAING, R. D. *The Politics of Experience*. New York: Pantheon, 1967.

LAING, R. D., AND ESTERSON, AARON. *Sanity, Madness, and the Family*. 2d ed. New York: Basic Books, 1971.

LANGE, CARL G., AND JAMES, WILLIAM. *The Emotions*. Edited by Knight Dunlap and translated by I. A. Haupt. Baltimore: Williams & Wilkins, 1922.

LASHLEY, KARL S. *Brain Mechanisms and Intelligence*. Chicago: University of Chicago Press, 1929.

LAZARUS, R. S., ET AL. "The Principle of Short-Circuiting of Threat: Further Evidence." *Journal of Personality* 3 (1965): 622–35.

LEAVITT, H. J. "Some Effects of Certain Communication Patterns on Group Performance." *Journal of Abnormal Social Psychology* 46 (1951): 38–50.

LEE, ALFRED M., AND LEE, ELIZABETH. *The Fine Art of Propaganda*. New York: Farrar, Straus, & Giroux, 1939.

LERNER, R. M., AND KNAPP, J. R. "Actual and Perceived Intrafamilial Attitudes of Late Adolescents and Their Parents." *Journal of Youth and Adolescence* 4 (1975): 17–36.

LERNER, R. M., AND SPANIER, G. B. *Adolescent Development: A Life-Span Perspective*. New York: McGraw-Hill, 1980.

LEVANT, OSCAR. *The Memoirs of an Amnesiac*. New York: Bantam, 1966 (paper).

LEVINGER, GEORGE. "Sources of Dissatisfaction Among Applicants for Divorce." *American Journal of Orthopsychiatry* 36 (1966): 803–07.

LEVINGER, GEORGE, AND SNOEK, J. DIDRICK. *Attraction in Relationship: A New Look at Interpersonal Attraction*. Morristown, N.J.: General Learning Press, 1972.

LEVINSON, DANIEL J. "Living with Dying." *Newsweek*, 1 May 1978, 52–61.

LEVINSON, DANIEL J., ET AL. *The Seasons of a Man's Life*. New York: Knopf, 1978.

LIEBERT, R., SPRAFKIN, J., AND DAVIDSON, E. *The Early Window: Effects of Television on Children and Youth*. 2d ed. New York: Pergamon, 1982.

LIEM, J. H., AND LIEM, R. "Life Events, Social Supports, and Physical and Psychological Well-Being." Paper presented at the annual meeting of the American Psychological Association, Washington, D.C., 1976.

LIFTON, ROBERT JAY. *Thought Reform and the Psychology of Totalism: A Study of "Brainwashing" in China*. New York: Norton, 1963 (paper).

_____ . *Home from the War*. New York: Simon & Schuster, 1973.

LINDNER, ROBERT. *The Fifty-Minute Hour*. New York: Bantam, 1954.

LINGEMAN, RICHARD R. *Drugs from A to Z*. New York: McGraw-Hill, 1974.

LITTENBERG, R., TULKIN, S., AND KAGAN, J. "Cognitive Components of Separation Anxiety." *Developmental Psychology* 4 (1971): 387–88.

LOEHLIN, JOHN C., LINDZEY, GARDNER, AND SPUHLER, J. N. *Race Differences in Intelligence*. San Francisco: Freeman, 1975.

LOFTUS, E., AND MONAHAN, J. "Trial by Data: Psychological Research as Legal Evidence." *American Psychologist* 35 (1980): 270–83.

LOFTUS, ELIZABETH. "Reconstructing Memory: The Incredible Eyewitness." *Psychology Today* 8, no. 7 (1974): 116–19.

_____. *Eyewitness Testimony*. Cambridge, Mass.: Harvard University Press, 1979.

LOGUE, ALEXANDRA. "Waiter, There's a Phobia in My Soup." *Psychology Today* 12 (1978): 36.

LORAYNE, HARRY, AND LUCAS, JERRY. *The Memory Book*. New York: Ballantine, 1974 (paper).

LORENZ, KONRAD Z. *Studies in Animal and Human Behavior*. Translated by Robert Martin. 2 vols. Cambridge, Mass.: Harvard University Press, 1972.

LORENZ, SARAH. *Our Son, Ken*. New York: Dell, 1969 (paper).

LOVAAS, O. I., ET AL. "Establishment of Imitation and Its Use for the Development of Complex Behavior in Schizophrenic Children." *Behavior Research and Therapy* 5 (August 1967): 171–81.

LUCE, GAY GAER, AND SEGAL, JULIUS. *Sleep*. New York: Coward, McCann & Geoghegan, 1966.

LURIA, A. R. *The Mind of a Mnemonist*. New York: Basic Books, 1968.

LYKKEN, DAVID T. "Psychology and the Lie Detector Industry." *American Psychologist* 29 (1974): 725–39.

MACCOBY, ELEANOR, AND MASTERS, JOHN C. "Attachment and Dependency." In *Manual of Child Psychology,* vol. 2, edited by Paul H. Mussen, 159–260. New York: Wiley, 1970.

MACE, D., AND MACE, V. *Marriage: East and West*. New York: Doubleday, 1960.

MACKAY, CHARLES. *Extraordinary Popular Delusions and the Madness of Crowds*. New York: Farrar, Straus, & Giroux, 1932.

MADISON, PETER. *Personality Development in College*. Reading, Mass.: Addison-Wesley, 1969.

MAHER, BRENDAN. "The Shattered Language of Schizophrenia." In *Readings in Psychology Today,* 2d ed., 549–53. Del Mar, Calif.: CRM Books, 1972.

MAJERES, R. L. "Semantic Connotations of the Words 'Adolescent,' 'Teenager,' and 'Youth.'" *Journal of Genetic Psychology* 129 (1976): 57–62.

MALATESTA, C. Z., AND KALNOK, M. "Emotional Experience in Younger and Older Adults." *Journal of Gerontology* 39 (1984): 301–08.

MARANON, GREGORIO. "Contribution à l'étude de l'action emotive de l'adrenaline." *Review Français d'Endocrinologie* 2 (1952): 141–47.

MARCIA, J. E. "Development and Validation of Ego Identity Status." *Journal of Personality and Social Psychology* 3 (1966): 551–58.

MARGOLIS, B. L., KROES, W. H., AND QUINN, R. P. "Job Stress: An Unlisted Occupational Hazard." *Journal of Occupational Medicine* 16 (1974): 654–61.

MARKOWITSCH, HANS. "Physiological and Comparative Psychology: Current Research Interests." *American Psychologist* 41 (1986): 1301–05.

MARLATT, G., AND ROHSENOW, D. "The Think-Drink Effect." *Psychology Today* 15 (December 1981): 60–70.

MARLER, PETER. "On Animal Aggression: The Roles of Strangeness and Familiarity." *American Psychologist* 31, no. 3 (March 1976): 239–46.

MASLOW, ABRAHAM. *Motivation and Personality*. 2d ed. New York: Harper & Row, 1970 (paper).

MASTERS, WILLIAM H., AND JOHNSON, VIRGINIA E. *Human Sexual Inadequacy*. Boston: Little, Brown, 1970.

MASTERSON, J. F. *The Psychiatric Dilemma of Adolescence*. Boston: Little, Brown, 1967a.

_____. "The Symptomatic Adolescent Five Years Later: He Didn't Grow Out of It." *American Journal of Psychiatry* 123 (1967b): 1338–45.

MAY, P. R. A. *Treatment of Schizophrenia: A Comparative Study of Five Treatment Methods*. New York: Science House, 1968.

MAY, ROLLO. *Existential Psychology*. 2d ed. New York: Random House, 1969.

McCARLEY, ROBERT W. "Where Dreams Come From: A New Theory." *Psychology Today* 12 (December 1978): 54–65.

McCLELLAND, D. C. *The Achieving Society*. Princeton, N.J.: Van Nostrand, 1961.

_____. "Need Achievement and Entrepreneurship: A Longitudinal Study." *Journal of Personality and Social Psychology* 1 (1965): 389–92.

McCLELLAND, D. C., AND HARRIS, T. G. "To Know Why Men Do What They Do: A Conversation with David C. McClelland." *Psychology Today* 4 (January 1971): 35–39.

McCLELLAND, D. C., AND WINTER, D. G. *Motivating Economic Achievement*. New York: Free Press, 1969.

McCLELLAND, D. C., ET AL. *The Achievement Motive*. New York: Appleton-Century-Crofts, 1953.

McCONNELL, J. V. "Cannibalism and Memory in Flatworms." *New Scientist* 21 (1964): 465–68.

McCOY, K. *Coping with Teenage Depression*. New York: Mosby, 1982.

McGHIE, A., AND CHAPMAN, J. "Disorders of Attention and Perception in Early Schizophrenia." *British Journal of Medical Psychiatry* 34 (1961): 103–16.

McGINLEY, HUGH, LeFEVRE, RICHARD, AND McGINLEY, PAT. "The Influence of a Communicator's Body Position on Opinion Change in Others." *Journal of Personality and Social Psychology* 31 (1975): 686–90.

McGINNISS, JOE. *The Selling of the President, 1968*. New York: Pocket Books, 1970 (paper).

McGUIRE, W. J. "A Vaccine for Brainwash." *Psychology Today* 3 (February 1970): 36–39, 62–64.

McINTOSH, J. L., AND HUBBARD, R. W. "Indirect Self-Destructive Behavior Among the Elderly: A Review with Case Examples." *Journal of Gerontological Social Work* 13 (1988): 37–48.

McKENZIE, S. C. *Aging and Old Age*. Glenview, Ill.: Scott, Foresman, 1980.

MEAD, MARGARET. *Coming of Age in Samoa*. New York: Morrow, 1961.

MECHANIC, D. "Discussion of Research Programs on Relationships Between Stressful Life Events and Episodes of Physical Illness." In *Stressful Life Events: Their Nature and Effects*, edited by B. S. Dohrenwend and B. P. Dohrenwend. New York: Wiley, 1974.

MEEHL, PAUL M. "Schizotaxia, Schizotype, Schizophrenia." *American Psychologist* 17 (1962): 827–32.

MEYER, W. J., AND DUSEK, J. B. *Child Psychology: A Developmental Perspective*. Lexington, Mass: Heath, 1979.

MIDDLEBROOK, P. N. *Social Psychology and Modern Life*. 2d ed. New York: Knopf, 1980.

MIKULAS, WILLIAM L. *Behavior Modification*. New York: Harper & Row, 1978.

MILGRAM, STANLEY. *Obedience to Authority*. New York: Harper & Row, 1964.

———. "The Experience of Living in Cities." *Science* 167 (1970): 1461–68.

MILLER, GEORGE A. "The Magical Number Seven, Plus or Minus Two: Some Limits on Our Capacity for Processing Information." *Psychological Review* 63 (1956): 81–97.

MILLER, GEORGE A., GALANTER, EUGENE, AND PRIBRAM, KARL H. *Plans and the Structure of Behavior*. New York: Holt, Rinehart & Winston, 1960.

MILLER, GERALD R., AND FONTES, NORMAN E. "Trial by Videotape." *Psychology Today* 12 (May 1979): 92–101.

MILLER, L. K. "Behavioral Principles and Experimental Communities." In *Behavior Modification: Principles, Issues, and Applications*, edited by W. E. Craighead, A. E. Kazdin, and M. J. Mahoney. Boston: Houghton Mifflin, 1976.

MILLER, L. K., AND SCHNEIDER, R. "The Use of a Token System in Project Headstart." *Journal of Applied Behavior Analysis* 3 (1970): 213–20.

MILLER, NEAL E., AND DI CARA, LEO. "Instrumental Learning of Heart Rate Changes in Curarized Rats: Shaping and Specificity to Discriminative Stimulus." *Journal of Comparative and Physiological Psychology* 63 (1967): 12–19.

MILLER, NEAL E., AND DWORKIN, B. R. "Visceral Learning: Recent Difficulties with Curarized Rats in Significant Problems for Human Research." In *Cardiovas Psychophysiology*, edited by Paul A. Obrist et al. Chicago: Aldine-Atherton, 1974.

MILLER, S., AND SELIGMAN, M. "The Reformulated Model of Helplessness and Depression: Evidence and Theory." In *Psychological Stress and Psychopathology*, edited by N. W. Newfield. New York: McGraw-Hill, 1982.

MINER, J. B. "Psychological Testing and Fair Employment Practices." *Personnel Psychology* 27 (1974): 49–62.

———. *Organizational Behavior: Performance and Productivity*. New York: Random House, 1988.

MINTZ, R. S. "Psychotherapy of the Suicidal Patient." In *Suicidal Behaviors*, edited by H. L. P. Resnik. Boston: Little, Brown, 1968.

MITLER, M. M., NELSON, S., AND HAJDUKOVIC, R. *Psychiatric Clinics of North America* 10 (1987): 593–606.

MORSE, M. L., VENECIA, D., AND MILSTEIN, J. "Near-Death Experiences: A Neurophysiological Explanatory Model." *Journal of Near-Death Studies* 8 (1989): 45–53.

MOSCOVICI, SERGE. *Social Influence and Social Change*. New York: Academic Press, 1976.

MOSES, SUSAN. "Neuropsychologist Wins NAMI Award." *APA Monitor* 21 (September 1990): 5.

MOWRER, O. H., AND MOWRER, M. "Enuresis: A Method for Its Study and Treatment." *American Journal of Orthopsychiatry* 8 (1938): 436–59.

MUNNS, M. "The Values of Adolescents Compared with Parents and Peers." *Adolescence* 7 (1972): 519–24.

MURRAY, HENRY A., ET AL. *Exploration in Personality*. New York: Oxford University Press, 1934.

MUSSEN, PAUL H., CONGER, JOHN J., AND KAGAN, JEROME. *Child Development and Personality*. 4th ed. New York: Harper & Row, 1974.

———, ———, AND ———. *Essentials of Child Development and Personality*. New York: Harper & Row, 1980.

NARAJANO, C., AND ORNSTEIN, R. *On the Psychology of Meditation*. New York: Viking, 1971.

NATHAN, P. E., AND HARRIS, S. L. *Psychopathology and Society*. New York: McGraw-Hill, 1975.

NATHAN, P. E., AND O'BRIEN, J. S. "An Experimental Analysis of the Behavior of Alcoholics and Nonalcoholics During Prolonged Experimental Drinking: A Necessary Precursor of Behavior Therapy?" *Behavior Therapy* 2 (1971): 455–76.

NEISSER, ULRIC. *Cognitive Psychology*. New York: Appleton-Century-Crofts, 1967.

NESBITT, P. "The Effectiveness of Student Canvassers," *Journal of Applied Psychology* 2 (1972): 252–58.

NEUGARTEN, BERNICE, ET AL. "Women's Attitudes Toward the Menopause." *Vita Humana* 6 (1963): 140–51.

NEWCOMB, T. *Personality and Social Change*. New York: Dryden Press, 1943.

NEWCOMB, T., ET AL. *Persistence and Change: Bennington College and Its Students After 25 Years*. New York: Wiley, 1967.

NEWMAN, G., AND NICHOLS, C. R. "Sexual Activities and Attitudes in Older Persons." *Journal of the American Medical Association* 173 (1960): 33–35.

NEWMAN, OSCAR. *Defensible Space*. New York: Macmillan, 1972.

NEWMAN, P. "The Peer Group." In *Handbook of Developmental Psychology*, edited by B. B. Wolman. Englewood Cliffs, N.J.: Prentice-Hall, 1982.

NOGRADY, H., MCCONKEY, K. M., AND PERRY, C. "Enhancing Visual Memory: Trying Hypnosis, Trying Imagination and Trying Again." *Journal of Abnormal Psychology* 94 (1985): 195–204.

NUCKOLLS, K., CASSEL, J., AND KAPLAN, B. H. "Psychological Assets, Life Crisis, and the Prognosis of Pregnancy." *American Journal of Epidemiology* 95 (1972): 431–44.

NURNBERGER, J. I., JR., GOLDIN, L. R., AND GERSHON, E. S. "Genetics of Psychiatric Disorders." In *The Medical Basis of Psychiatry*, edited by G. Winokur and P. Clayton. Philadelphia: Saunders, 1986.

OFFICE OF STRATEGIC SERVICES ASSESSMENT STAFF. *Assessment of Men*. New York: Holt, Rinehart & Winston, 1948.

OLDS, J., AND OLDS, M. E. "Drives, Rewards and the Brain." In *New Directions in Psychology II*, edited by F. Barron et al. New York: Holt, Rinehart & Winston, 1965.

OLSON, M. "The Incidence of Out-Of-Body Experiences in Hospitalized Patients." *Journal of Near-Death Studies* 6 (1988): 169–74.

ORLANSKY, J. "An Assessment of Lie Detection Capability." In *Use of Polygraphs and "Lie Detectors" by the Federal Government*. House Report No. 198, Eighty-ninth Congress, First Session. Washington, D.C.: U.S. Government Printing Office, 1965.

ORNE, MARTIN T. "The Nature of Hypnosis: Artifact and Essence." *Journal of Abnormal and Social Psychology* 58 (1959): 277–99.

ORNSTEIN, ROBERT. *The Psychology of Consciousness*. 2d ed. New York: Harcourt Brace Jovanovich, 1977.

OSKAMP, S. "Nontraditional Employment Opportunities for Applied Psychologists." *American Psychologist* 43 (1988): 484–85.

PAFFENBARGER, RALPH S., JR., AND HALE, WAYNE E. "Work Activity and Coronary Heart Mortality." *New England Journal of Medicine* 292 (March 1975): 545–50.

PALMORE, ERDMAN. "What Can the USA Learn from Japan About Aging?" In *Readings in Aging and Death: Contemporary Perspectives*, edited by S. H. Zarit. New York: Harper & Row, 1977.

PAPALIA, D. E., AND OLDS, S. W. *Human Development*. 4th ed. New York: McGraw-Hill, 1989.

"Parents on the Brink of Child Abuse Get Crisis Aid." *New York Times,* 17 April 1983, 1, 29.

PARKE, R., AND LEWIS, N. "The Family in Context: A Multilevel Interactional Analysis of Child Abuse." In *Parent-Child Interaction: Theory, Research and Prospect,* edited by R. W. Henderson. New York: Academic Press, 1980.

PARKE, R., AND SLABY, R. "Aggression: A Multilevel Analysis." In *Handbook of Child Psychology.* Vol. 14, *Socialization, Personality and Social Development,* 4th ed., edited by P. H. Mussen and M. E. Hetherington. New York: Wiley, 1983.

PATCH, VERNON D. "Methadone." *New England Journal of Medicine* 286 (1972): 43–45.

PAVLOV, IVAN P. *Conditioned Reflexes.* Translated by G. V. Anrep. London: Oxford University Press, 1927.

PAYKEL, E. S. "Life Stress and Psychiatric Disorder: Applications of the Clinical Approach." In *Stressful Life Events: Their Nature and Effects,* edited by B. S. Dohrenwend and B. P. Dohrenwend. New York: Wiley, 1974.

PEACHY, J. E., AND NARANJO, C. A. "The Use of Disulfiram and Other Alcohol-Sensitizing Drugs in the Treatment of Alcoholism." *Research Advances in Alcohol and Drug Problems* 7 (1983): 397–431.

PEARL, D., BOUTHILET, L., AND LAZAR, J., EDS. *Television and Behavior: Ten Years of Scientific Progress and Implications for the Eighties.* Vols. 1 and 2. Washington, D.C.: U.S. Government Printing Office, 1982.

PENFIELD, WILDER. "Consciousness, Memory, and Man's Conditioned Reflexes." In *On the Biology of Learning,* edited by Karl H. Pribram. New York: Harcourt Brace Jovanovich, 1969.

PENFIELD, WILDER, AND RASMUSSEN, THEODORE. *The Cerebral Cortex of Man.* New York: Macmillan, 1950.

PERLICK, D. "The Withdrawal Syndrome: Nicotine Addiction and the Effects of Stopping Smoking in Heavy and Light Smokers." Ph.D. diss., Columbia University, 1977.

PERLS, FRITZ, HEFFERLINE, R. F., AND GOODMAN, P. *Gestalt Therapy.* New York: Dell, 1965.

PEROUTKA, S. J., NEWMAN, H., AND HARRIS, H. "Subjective Effects of 3,4–methylenedioxymethamphetamine in Recreational Users." *Neuropsychopharmacology* 1 (1988): 273–77.

PETERSON, LLOYD R. AND PETERSON, MARGARET. "Short-Term Retention of Individual Verbal Items." *Journal of Experimental Psychology* 58 (1959): 193–98.

PIAGET, JEAN. *The Language and Thought of the Child.* London: Routledge & Kegan Paul, 1926.

PILBEAM, DAVID. "An Idea We Could Live Without—The Naked Ape." *Discovery* 7, no. 2 (Spring 1972): 63–70.

PISONI, D. B., AND MARTIN, C. S. "Effects of Alcohol on the Acoustic-Phonetic Properties of Speech: Perceptual and Acoustic Analyses." *Alcoholism: Clinical and Experimental Research* 13 (1989): 577–87.

PLUMB, M. M., AND HOLLAND, J. "Comparative Studies of Psychological Function in Patients with Advanced Cancer. I. Self-Reported Depressive Symptoms." *Psychosomatic Medicine* 39 (1977): 264–76.

POCS, OLLIE, ET AL. "Is There Sex After 40?" *Psychology Today* 10 (June 1977): 54–57.

PRADHAN, S. N. "Phencyclidine (PCP): Some Human Studies." *Neuroscience and Biobehavioral Reviews* 8 (1984): 493–501.

PROSHANSKY, H., AND NEWTON, P. "The Nature and Meaning of Negro Self-Identity." In *Social Class, Race and Psychological Development,* edit d by M. Deutsch, J. Kate, and A. R. Jensen. New York: Holt, Rinehart & Winston, 1968.

"Psychokinetic Fraud." *Scientific American* 238 (September 1974): 68, 72.

QUINN, R., SEASHORE, S., KAHN, R., MANGIONE, T., CAMPBELL, D., STAINES, G., AND MCCULLOUGH, M. *Survey of Working Conditions.* Washington, D.C.: U.S. Government Printing Office, 1971.

RABKIN, LESLIE, ED. *Psychopathology and Literature.* San Francisco: Chandler, 1966.

RAFT, D., AND ANDRESEN, J. J. "Transformations in Self-Understanding After Near-Death Experiences." *Contemporary Psychoanalysis* 22 (1986): 319–46.

RAHE, R. H. "Life Changes and Near-Future Illness Reports." In *Emotions: Their Parameters and Measurement,* edited by L. Levi. New York: Raven Press, 1975.

RAHE, R. H., AND ARTHUR, R. J. "Life Change Patterns Surrounding Illness Experience." *Journal of Psychosomatic Research* 11 (1968): 341–45.

RAUSH, HAROLD L., AND RAUSH, CHARLOTTE. *The Halfway House Movement: A Search for Sanity*. New York: Appleton-Century-Crofts, 1968.

RAY, OAKLEY. *Drugs, Society, and Human Behavior*. 2d ed. St. Louis: Mosby, 1978.

REED, J. G., AND BAXTER, P. M. *Library Use: A Handbook for Psychology*. Washington, D.C. : American Psychological Association, 1983.

REID, D. W., HAAS, G., AND HAWKINGS, D. "Locus of Desired Control and Positive Self-Concept of the Elderly." *Journal of Gerontology* 32 (1977): 441–50.

REISMAN, D., GLAZER, N., AND DENNEY, R. *The Lonely Crowd*. New Haven, Conn.: Yale University Press, 1953 (paper).

REISMAN, J., AND SHORR, S. "Friendship Claims and Expectations Among Children and Adults." *Child Development* 49 (1978): 913–16.

REPPUCCI, N. D., AND SAUNDERS, J. T. "Social Psychology of Behavior Modification." *American Psychologist* 29 (1974): 649–60.

REYNOLDS, G. S. *A Primer of Operant Conditioning*. Glenview, Ill.: Scott, Foresman, 1968.

RHINE, JOSEPH B. *Extra-Sensory Perception*. Boston: Bradon, 1964.

RHINE, LOUISA E. *Hidden Channels of the Mind*. New York: Apollo, 1961 (paper).

RICE, F. P. *The Adolescent: Development, Relationships, and Culture*. Boston: Allyn & Bacon, 1978.

RICE, M. "The Role of Television in Language Acquisition." *Developmental Review* 3 (1983): 221–24.

RIGTER, H., VAN RIEZE, H., AND WIED, D. D. "The Effects of ACTH and Vasopressin Analogues on CO_2–Induced Retrograde Amnesia in Rats." *Physiology and Behavior* 13 (1974): 381–88.

RILEY, V. "Psychoneuroendocrine Influences on Immunocompetence and Neoplasia." *Science* 212 (1981): 1100–09.

ROB, M., REYNOLDS, I., AND FINLAYSON, P. F. "Adolescent Marijuana Use: Risk Factors and Implications." *Australian and New Zealand Journal of Psychiatry* 24 (1990): 47–56.

ROBERTS, G. A., AND OWEN, J. H. "The Near-Death Experience." *British Journal of Psychiatry* 153 (1988): 607–17.

ROBERTS, L. "Vietnam's Psychological Toll." *Science* 241 (1988): 159–61.

ROGERS, CARL. *Client-Centered Therapy*. Boston: Houghton Mifflin, 1951.

_____ . *On Becoming a Person*. Boston: Houghton Mifflin, 1961.

ROGERS, D. *The Psychology of Adolescence*. 3d ed. Englewood Cliffs, N.J.: Prentice-Hall, 1977.

_____ . *The Adult Years: An Introduction to Aging*. Englewood Cliffs, N.J.: Prentice-Hall, 1979.

ROKEACH, M. "Long-Range Experimental Modification of Values, Attitudes, and Behavior." *American Psychologist* 26 (1971): 453–59.

ROLLINS, B. C., AND FELDMAN, H. "Marital Satisfaction over the Family Life Cycle." *Journal of Marriage and the Family* 32 (1970): 20–28.

ROSENMAN, R. H. In *Coronary-Prone Behavior*, edited by T. M. Dembrowski, S. M. Weiss, J. L. Shields, S. G. Haynes, and M. Feinleib. New York: Springer, 1978.

ROSENTHAL, D. *Genetic Theory and Abnormal Behavior*. New York: McGraw-Hill, 1970.

ROSENTHAL, D., ET AL. "The Adopted-Away Offspring of Schizophrenics." *American Journal of Psychiatry* 128, no. 3 (1971): 307–11.

ROSENTHAL, ROBERT. *Environmental Effects in Behavioral Research*. New York: Appleton-Century-Crofts, 1966.

ROSENTHAL, ROBERT, AND ROSNOW, R. L., EDS. *Artifact in Behavioral Research*. New York: Harper & Row, 1963.

ROSENZWEIG, R. R. "Training in Psychology in the United States." *Psychological Science* 2 (1991): 16–18.

RUBIN, I. "Sex over 65." In *Advances in Sex Research*, edited by H. G. Beigel. New York: Harper & Row, 1963.

RUBIN, ZICK. "Measurement of Romantic Love." *Journal of Personality and Social Psychology* 16 (1970): 265–73.

_____ . *Liking and Loving*. New York: Holt, Rinehart & Winston, 1973.

RUMBAUGH, DUANE M., GILL, TIMOTHY V., AND VON GLASERSFELD, E. C. "Reading and Sentence Completion by a Chimpanzee." *Science* 182 (1973): 731–33.

RUSS, N. W., GELLER, E. S., AND LELAND, L. S. "Blood-Alcohol Level Feedback: A Failure to Deter Impaired Driving." *Psychology of Addictive Behaviors* 2 (1988): 124–30.

SAAVENDRA-AGUILAR, J. C., AND GOMEZ-JERIA, J. S. "A Neurobiological Model for Near-Death Experiences." *Journal of Near-Death Studies* 7 (1989): 205–22.

SAHAKIAN, WILLIAM S. *Psychology of Learning.* Chicago: Markham, 1970.

SALK, LEE. "Mother's Heartbeat as an Imprinting Stimulus." *Transactions of the New York Academy of Sciences* 24 (1962): 753–63.

SARASON, I. G., AND SARASON, B. R. *Abnormal Psychology.* 3d ed. Englewood Cliffs, N.J.: Prentice-Hall, 1980.

SARBIN, I., AND COE, W. *Hypnosis: A Social Psychological Analysis of Influence Communication.* New York: Holt, Rinehart & Winston, 1972.

———, and ———. "Hypnosis and Psychopathology: Replacing Old Myths with Fresh Metaphors." *Journal of Abnormal Psychology* 88 (1979): 506–26.

SATIR, VIRGINIA. *Peoplemaking.* Palo Alto, Calif.: Science and Behavior, 1972.

SAUL, S. *Aging: An Album of People Growing Old.* New York: Wiley, 1974.

SAVAGE-RUMBAUGH, S., ET AL. "Spontaneous Symbol Acquisition and Communication by Pygmy Chimpanzees." *Journal of Experimental Psychology: General* 115 (1986): 211–35.

SCARF, M. *Unfinished Business: Pressure Points in the Lives of Women.* New York: Ballantine, 1980.

SCHACHTER, STANLEY. *The Psychology of Affiliation.* Stanford, Calif.: Stanford University Press, 1959.

———. *Emotion, Obesity, and Crime.* New York: Academic Press, 1971.

———. "Second Thoughts on Biological and Psychological Explanations of Behavior." In *Cognitive Theories in Social Psychology,* edited by L. Berkowitz. New York: Academic Press, 1978.

SCHACHTER, STANLEY, AND LATANÉ, B. "Crime, Cognition, and the Autonomic Nervous System." In *Nebraska Symposium on Motivation,* edited by M. Jones. Lincoln: University of Nebraska Press, 1964.

SCHACHTER, STANLEY, AND SINGER, JEROME. "Cognitive, Social, and Physiological Determinants of Emotional State." *Psychological Review* 69 (1962): 379–99.

SCHEIN, E. H. "The First Job Dilemma." *Psychology Today* 1 (1968): 26–37.

SCHMALE, A. "Giving Up as a Final Common Pathway to Changes in Health." *Advances in Psychosomatic Medicine* 8 (1972): 20–40.

SCHNAIBERG, A., AND GOLDENBERG, S. "From Empty Nest to Crowded Nest: The Dynamics of Incompletely Launched Young Adults." *Social Problems* 36 (1989): 251–69.

SCHREIBER, FLORA RHETA. *Sybil.* New York: Warner, 1973.

SCHULMAN, JAY, ET AL. "Recipe for a Jury." *Psychology Today* 6 (May 1973): 37–44.

SCHULTES, R. E. *Hallucinogenic Plants.* New York: Golden Press, 1976.

SCHWARTZ, A. N., AND PETERSON, J. A. *Introduction to Gerontology.* San Francisco: Holt, Rinehart & Winston, 1979.

SCHWARTZ, G. E., DAVIDSON, R., AND MAER, F. "Right Hemisphere Lateralization for Emotion in the Human Brain: Interactions with Cognition." *Science* 190 (1975): 286–88.

SCOTT, WILLIAM, AND WERTHEIMER, MICHAEL. *Introduction to Psychological Research.* New York: Wiley, 1962.

SEARS, ROBERT, MACCOBY, ELEANOR, AND LEVIN, HARRY. *Patterns of Child Rearing.* New York: Harper & Row, 1957.

SELIGMAN, MARTIN E. P. *Helplessness.* San Francisco: Freeman, 1975.

SELYE, HANS. *The Stress of Life.* New York: McGraw-Hill, 1956.

———. *Stress Without Distress.* Philadelphia: Lippincott, 1974.

SELYE, HANS, AND CHERRY, L. "On the Real Benefits of Eustress." *Psychology Today* 11 (March 1978): 60–70.

SERDAHELY, W. J. "A Pediatric Near-Death Experience: Tunnel Variants." *Omega: Journal of Death and Dying* 20 (1990): 55–62.

SHAPIRO, DAVID. "Preface." In *Biofeedback and Self-Control 1972,* edited by D. Shapiro et al. Chicago: Aldine-Atherton, 1973.

SHAPIRO, EVELYN, ED. *PsychoSources: A Psychology Resource Catalog.* New York: Bantam, 1973 (paper).

SHAVER, KELLY G. *An Introduction to Attribution Processes.* Cambridge, Mass.: Winthrop, 1975.

SHAVER, PHILLIP. "Questions Concerning Fear of Success and Its Conceptual Relatives." *Sex Roles* 2 (1976): 305–20.

SHEEHY, GAIL. *Passages*. New York: Dutton, 1976.

SHEHAN, K. C. L., BERARDO, D. H., AND BERARDO, F. M. "The Empty Nest Is Filling Again: Implications for Parent-Child Relationships." *Parenting Studies* 1 (1984): 67–73.

_____, _____, and _____ . "Study Finds Men's Brains Deteriorate at Greater Rate." *New York Times*, 2 April 1991, C2.

SHERIF, MUZAFER, ET AL. *Intergroup Conflict and Cooperation: The Robber's Cave Experiment*. Norman, Okla.: Institute of Group Relations, 1961.

SHOR, R. E., AND ORNE, M. T., EDS. *The Nature of Hypnosis*. New York: Holt, Rinehart & Winston, 1965.

SIFFRE, MICHEL. "Six Months Alone in a Cave." *National Geographic* 147 (March 1975): 426–35.

SILVERMAN, J. "When Schizophrenia Helps." *Psychology Today* 4 (September 1970): 62–65.

SILVERSTEIN, B. "An Addiction Explanation of Cigarette-Induced Relaxation," Ph.D. diss., Columbia University, 1976.

SIMON, W., AND GAGNON, J. H., EDS. *The Sexual Scene*. Chicago: Transaction Books, 1970.

SINGER, D. "The Impact of Interracial Classroom Exposure on the Social Attitudes of Fifth Grade Children." Unpublished study, 1964.

SINGER, J., AND SINGER, D. "Psychologists Look at Television: Cognitive, Developmental, Personality and Social Policy Implications." *American Psychologist* 38 (1983): 826–34.

SINGER, J. N. "Job Strain as a Function of Job and Life Stress," Ph.D. diss., Colorado State University, 1975.

SINGER, MARGARET T. "Coming Out of the Cults." *Psychology Today* 12 (January 1979): 72–82.

SKINNER, B. F. *The Behavior of Organisms*. New York: Appleton-Century-Crofts, 1961.

_____ . *Walden Two*. New York: Macmillan 1962. (Originally published 1948.)

_____ . *Beyond Freedom and Dignity*. New York: Knopf, 1971.

_____ . *About Behaviorism*. New York: Knopf, 1974.

_____ . "Intellectual Self-Management in Old Age." *American Psychologist* 39 (1983): 239–44.

SKINNER, B. F., AND VAUGHN, M. E. *Enjoy Old Age*. New York: Norton, 1983.

SKOLNICK, ARLENE. *The Intimate Environment*. Boston: Little, Brown, 1973.

SLOTKIN, J. J. "Culture and Psychopathology." *Journal of Abnormal and Social Psychology* 51 (1955): 269–75.

SMITH, MARY LEE, AND GLASS, GENE V. "Meta-Analysis of Psychotherapy Outcome Studies." *American Psychologist* 32 (1977): 752–60.

SNELLGROVE, L. *Psychological Experiments and Demonstrations*. New York: McGraw-Hill, 1967.

SNYDER, SOLOMON H. *Madness and the Brain*. New York: McGraw-Hill, 1973.

SPANOS, N. P., AND MORETTI, P. "Correlates of Mystical and Diabolical Experiences in a Sample of Female University Students." *Journal for the Scientific Study of Religion* 27 (1988): 105–16.

SPERLING, G. "The Information Available in Brief Visual Presentations." *Psychological Monographs* 74, no. 11 (1960).

SPERRY, ROGER W. "Changing Concepts of Consciousness and Free Will." *Perspectives in Biology and Medicine* 20, no. 1 (Autumn 1976): 9–19.

SPITZER, R. L., ENDICOTT, J., AND ROBINS, E. "Research-Diagnostic Criteria: Rationale and Reliability." *Archives of General Psychiatry* 35 (1978): 773–82.

SROUFE, L. A., COOPER, R. G., AND MARSHALL, M. E. *Child Development: Its Nature and Course*. New York: McGraw-Hill, 1988.

STANFORD, M. W. "Designer Drugs: Medical Aspects and Clinical Management." *Alcoholism Treatment Quarterly* 4 (1988): 97–125.

STANFORD, R. G. "The Out-of-Body Experience as an Imaginal Journey: The Developmental Perspective." *Journal of Parapsychology* 51 (1987): 137–55.

STANLEY, JULIAN C. "Test Better Finder of Great Math Talent Than Teachers Are." *American Psychologist* 31 (1976): 313–14.

STEINBERG, L., BELSKY, J., AND MEYER, R. *Infancy, Childhood, & Adolescence*. New York: McGraw-Hill, 1991.

STERNBACH, R. A., GUSTAFSON, L. A., AND COLIER, R. L. "Don't Trust the Lie Detector." *Harvard Business Review* 40 (1962): 127–34.

STEVENS, S. S. "The Surprising Simplicity of Sensory Metrics." *American Psychologist* 17 (1962): 29–39.

STEVENS-LONG, J. *Adult Life Developmental Processes*. Palo Alto, Calif.: Mayfield, 1979.

STEVENSON, I., COOK, E. W., AND McCLEAN-RICE, N. "Are Persons Reporting 'Near Death Experiences' Really Near Death? A Study of Medical Records." *Omega: Journal of Death and Dying* 20 (1990): 45–54.

STOKOLS, D. "On the Distinction Between Density and Crowding: Some Implications for Future Research." *Psychological Review* 79 (1972): 275–78.

STONE, ALAN, AND STONE, SUE. *The Abnormal Personality Through Literature*. Englewood Cliffs, N.J.: Prentice-Hall, 1966.

STRICKLAND, B. R. "Clinical Psychology Comes of Age." *American Psychologist* 43 (1988): 104–07.

STROMEYER, C. F. "Eidetikers." *Psychology Today* 4 (1970): 76–80.

SUE, S., SMITH, R. E., AND CALDWELL, C. "Effects of Inadmissible Evidence on the Decisions of Simulated Jurors." *Journal of Applied Social Psychology* 3 (1973): 345–53.

SURWIT, R. S., SHAPIRO, D., AND GOOD, M. I. "Comparison of Cardiovascular Feedback, Neuromuscular Feedback, and Meditation in the Treatment of Borderline Essential Hypertension." *Journal of Consulting and Clinical Psychology* 46 (1978): 252–63.

SWEETLAND, J. *Occupational Stress and Productivity*. Work in America Institute Studies in Productivity. Scarsdale, N.Y.: Work in America Institute, 1979.

SZASZ, THOMAS. *The Myth of Mental Illness*. New York: Dell, 1967.

———. *The Age of Madness*. Garden City, N.Y.: Doubleday Anchor, 1973 (paper).

TART, C. T., ED. *Altered States of Consciousness*. 2d ed. New York: Wiley, 1972.

TAUBE, C. A., AND REDNICK, R. *Utilization of Mental Health Resources by Persons Diagnosed with Schizophrenia*. DHEW Publication No. (HSM) 72–9110. Rockville, Md.: National Institute of Mental Health, 1973.

TAYLOR, S. "Adjustment to Threatening Events." *American Psychologist* 38 (1983): 1161–73.

TAYLOR, S. E. "Health Psychology: The Science and the Field." *American Psychologist* 45 (1990): 40–50.

TEDESCHI, J. T., LINDSKOLD, S., AND ROSENFELD, P. *Introduction to Social Psychology*. St. Paul, Minn.: West, 1985.

TENOPYR, M. L. "The Realities of Employment Testing." *American Psychologist* 36 (1985): 1120–27.

TERMAN, LEWIS M. *The Measurement of Intelligence*. Boston: Houghton Mifflin, 1916.

TERMAN, LEWIS M., AND MERRILL, MAUD A. *Measuring Intelligence*. Boston: Houghton Mifflin, 1937.

———, and ———. *Stanford-Binet Intelligence Scale: Manual for the Third Revision. Form L-M*. Boston: Houghton Mifflin, 1973.

TERRACE, H. "How Nim Chimpsky Changed My Mind." *Psychology Today*, November 1979, 65–76.

THOITS, P. "Life Events, Social Isolation and Psychological Distress," Ph.D. diss., Stanford University, 1978.

THOMPSON, RICHARD F. "The Search for the Engram." *American Psychologist* 31 (1976): 209–27.

———, ED. *Physiological Psychology*. San Francisco: Freeman, 1971.

TIMIO, M., AND GENTILI, S. "Andreosympathetic Overactivity Under Conditions of Work Stress." *British Journal of Preventive and Social Medicine* 30 (1976): 262–65.

TOFFLER, ALVIN. *Future Shock*. New York: Bantam, 1970 (paper).

TOUFEXIS, ANASTASIA. "Warnings About a Miracle Drug: Reports of Suicide Attempts in Prozac Users Raise Doubts About the Popular Antidepressant." *Time*, 30 July 1990, 54.

TRESEMER, DAVID. "Current Trends in Research on 'Fear of Success.'" *Sex Roles* 2 (1976a): 211–16.

———. "The Cumulative Record of Research on 'Fear of Success.'" *Sex Roles* 2 (1976b): 217–36.

TROTTER, R. "Baby Face." *Psychology Today* 17 (August 1983): 15–20.

TURNER, J. S., AND HELMS, D. B. *Contemporary Adulthood*. Philadelphia: Saunders, 1979.

TYLER, LEONA E. *The Psychology of Human Differences*. 3d ed. New York: Appleton-Century-Crofts, 1965.

———. "Human Abilities." In *Annual Review of Psychology,* 177–206. Palo Alto, Calif.: Annual Reviews, 1975.

ULLMAN, P. "Parental Participation in Child Rearing as Evaluated by Male Social Deviates." *Pacific Sociological Review* 3 (1960): 89–95.

U.S. DEPARTMENT OF HEALTH, EDUCATION, AND WELFARE. "Leading Causes of Death in Middle Age, as Percentage of Total Deaths Between Ages 45 and 64." In *Vital Statistics of the United States, 1968.* Vol. 2, Part B: *Mortality.* Rockville, Md.: U.S. Department of Health, Education, and Welfare, 1971.

VALENSTEIN, ELLIOT. *Brain Control: A Critical Examination of Brain Stimulation and Psychosurgery.* New York: Wiley, 1973.

VALVO, ALBERTO. *Sight Restoration After Long-Term Blindness: The Problems and Behavior Patterns of Visual Rehabilitation.* New York: American Foundation for the Blind, 1971.

VAN HARRISON, R. "Person-Environment Fit and Job Stress." In *Stress at Work,* edited by C. L. Cooper and R. Payne. New York: Wiley, 1978.

VICTOR, MAURICE, AND ADAMS, RAYMOND D. "Opiates and Other Synthetic Analgesic Drugs." In *Harrison's Principles of Internal Medicine,* edited by M. M. Wintrobe et al., 677–81. New York: McGraw-Hill, 1970.

VITKUS, J. *Casebook in Abnormal Psychology.* New York: McGraw-Hill, 1988.

WADE, NICHOLAS. "Sociobiology: Troubled Birth for a New Discipline." *Science* 191 (19 March 1976): 1151–55.

WALD, G. "The Receptors of Color Vision." *Science* 145 (1964): 1007–16.

WALLACE, B. C. "Relapse Prevention in Psychoeducational Groups for Compulsive Crack Cocaine Smokers." *Journal of Substance Abuse* 6 (1989): 229–39.

WALLACE, ROBERT KEITH. "Physiological Effects of Transcendental Meditation." *Science* 167 (1970): 1751–54.

WALLERSTEIN, J., AND KELLY, J. "The Effects of Parental Divorce: The Adolescent Experience." In *The Child in His Family: Children at Psychiatric Risk,* edited by J. Anthony and C. Koupernik, 479–505. New York: Wiley, 1974.

WASHBURN, S. L. "Human Behavior and the Behavior of Other Animals." *American Psychologist* 33 (May 1978): 405–18.

WATSON, DAVID L., AND THARP, RONALD G. *Self-Directed Behavior: Self-Modification for Personal Adjustment.* Monterey, Calif.: Brooks/Cole, 1972.

WATSON, JOHN B. *Behaviorism.* New York: Norton, 1970. (Originally published 1924.)

WATSON, JOHN B., AND RAYNER, ROSALIE. "Conditioned Emotional Reactions." *Journal of Experimental Psychology* 3 (1920): 1–14.

WEBB, A. R., AND SPEER, J. R. "The Public Image of Psychologists." *American Psychologist* 40 (1985): 1063–64.

WEBB, S. D., AND COLLETTE, J. "Urban Ecological and Household Correlates of Stress-Alleviative Drug Use." *American Behavioral Scientist* 189 (1975): 750–69.

WEBB, WILSE B. *Sleep: The Gentle Tyrant.* Englewood Cliffs, N.J.: Prentice-Hall, 1975.

WEBER, ERNST H. *De Pulse, Resorptione, Audito et Tactu.* Leipzig: Kohler, 1834.

WECHSLER, D. *WAIS-R Manual: Wechsler Adult Intelligence Scale—Revised.* New York: Psychological Corporation, 1981.

WEIL, ANDREW. *The Natural Mind.* Boston: Houghton Mifflin, 1972.

WEIL, ANDREW, ZINBERG, N., AND NELSEN, J. M. "Clinical and Psychological Effects of Marijuana in Man." *Science* 162 (1968): 1234–42.

WEISS, J. M. "Influence of Psychological Variables on Stress-Induced Pathology." In *Physiology, Emotion and Psychosomatic Illness* (Ciba Foundation Symposium 8). New York: American Elsevier, 1972.

WEISS, JAY M. "Effects of Coping Behavior in Different Warning-Signal Conditions on Stress Pathology in Rats." *Journal of Comparative and Physiological Psychology* 77 (1971): 1–13.

WELLS, J. A. "Differences in Sources of Social Support in Conditioning the Effect of Perceived Stress on Health." Paper presented at the annual meeting of the Southern Sociological Association, Atlanta, 1977.

WHEELER, DAVID. "Research Notes: Pain Centers Located in Cerebral Cortex." *Chronicle of High Education,* 20 March 1991, A12.

WHEELIS, ALLEN. *The Desert.* New York: Basic Books, 1970.

WHITE, BURTON L. "Child Development Research: An Edifice Without a Foundation." *Merrill-Palmer Quarterly of Behavior and Development* 15 (1969): 49–79.

WHITE, ROBERT. "Motivation Reconsidered: The Concept of Competence." *Psychological Review* 66 (1959): 297–333.

———. *The Abnormal Personality*. New York: Ronald Press, 1964.

———. *Lives in Progress: A Study of the Natural Growth of Personality*. New York: Holt, Rinehart & Winston, 1976.

WHITE, ROBERT, RIGGS, MARGARET M., AND GILBERT, DORIS C. *Case Workbook in Personality*. New York: Holt, Rinehart & Winston, 1976.

WILD, B. S., AND HAYNES, C. A. "A Dynamic Conceptual Framework of Generalized Adaptation to Stressful Stimuli." *Psychological Reports* 38 (1976): 319–34.

WILL, GEORGE F. "A Good Death." *Newsweek,* 9 January 1978, 72.

WILLIAMSON, J. G., EVANS, L., AND MUNLEY, A. *Aging and Society*. New York: Holt, Rinehart & Winston, 1980.

WILSON, EDWARD O. *Sociobiology: A New Synthesis*. Cambridge, Mass.: Harvard University Press, 1975a.

———. "Human Decency Is Animal." *New York Times Magazine,* 12 October 1975b, 38–49.

WOLFE, JOHN B. "Effectiveness of Token-Rewards for Chimpanzees." *Comparative Psychological Monographs* 12 (1936): whole no. 5.

WOLMAN, BENJAMIN B., ED. *Handbook of Clinical Psychology*. New York: McGraw-Hill, 1965.

———, ED. *Handbook of General Psychology*. Englewood Cliffs, N.J.: Prentice-Hall, 1973.

WOOLFOLK, ROBERT L. "Psychophysiological Correlates of Meditation." *Archives of General Psychiatry* 32 (1975): 1326–33.

WORTMAN, C. B., AND LOFTUS, E. F. *Psychology*. 2d ed. New York: Knopf, 1985.

WRIGHT, J., AND HUSTON, A. "A Matter of Form: Potentials of Television for Young Viewers." *American Psychologist* 38 (1983): 835–43.

WRIGHTSMAN, L. S. "Effects of Waiting with Others on Changes in Level of Felt Anxiety." *Journal of Abnormal and Social Psychology* 61 (1960): 216–22.

WRIGHTSMAN, L. S., SIGELMAN, C. K., AND SANFORD, F. H. *Psychology: A Scientific Study of Human Behavior*. 5th ed. Monterey, Calif.: Brooks/Cole, 1979.

WYNNE, L., CROMWELL, R., AND MATTHYSSE, S., EDS. *Nature of Schizophrenia: New Approaches to Research and Treatment*. New York: Wiley, 1978.

YOUNG, T. J. "PCP Use Among Adolescents." *Child Study Journal* 17 (1987): 55–66.

ZAJONC, R. B., AND MARKUS, G. B. "Birth Order and Intellectual Development." *Psychological Review* 82 (1975).

ZARIT, S. H., ED. *Readings in Aging and Death: Contemporary Perspectives*. New York: Harper & Row, 1977.

ZIMBARDO, F. G. *Psychology and Life*. 10th ed. Glenview, Ill.: Scott, Foresman, 1979.

ZIMBARDO, F. G., EBBESEN, E. B., AND MASLACH, C. *Influencing Attitudes and Changing Behavior*. 2d ed. Reading, Mass.: Addison-Wesley, 1977.

ZUBIN, J., AND MONEY, J., EDS. *Contemporary Sexual Behavior: Critical Issues in the 1970s*. Baltimore: Johns Hopkins University Press, 1973.

ZUBIN, J., AND SPRING, BONNIE. "Vulnerability: A New View of Schizophrenia." *Journal of Abnormal Psychology* 86 (1977): 103–26.

Photo Credits

Index

abnormal behavior, 4–5, 7, 44, 93–95, 364–366
Abramson, Lyn Y., 39
Abse, D. W., 376
absolute threshold, 109, 114
accommodation, 188, 189
achievement, 139–143
achievement tests, 299, 300
Acocella, J., 376, 377, 381
active awake state, 186
active sleep, 158, 159
adaptive testing, 300
addiction, 385
Adelmann, P. K., 252
Adelson, Joseph, 239
adjustment, 340–361
Adler, Alfred, 276, 520
admissions test, 295, 300–301, 303, 353
adolescence, 218–241, 244, 247, 248
"adolescent rebellion," 234
Adorno, T. W., 463
adrenal glands, 95
adrenalin, 95, 151–152, 159
adult ego, 403
adulthood, 243–252, 276, 522
advertising, 470, 471
ageism, 253
age-thirty crisis, 248–249
aggression, 36–37, 93, 99, 100, 203–205, 208, 209, 211, 213, 269, 284
aging process, 245, 253
agoraphobia, 373
"aha" experience, 75
Ahlskog, J. Eric, 134
Ahrens, R., 123
AIDS (Acquired Immune Deficiency Syndrome), 418
Ainsworth, Mary, 198, 199
airplane design, 523
air traffic controllers, 113–114
alcohol, 157, 167, 168–169, 173–174, 187, 349, 371, 385, 520
abuse of, 44, 335, 387–388, 412
Alcoholics Anonymous (AA), 336, 408
Alexander, B. K., 172
Allport, Gordon, 269, 285–286, 464
alpha waves, 158
Altman, L. K., 261
altruism, 98–100
Alvarez, A., 378
Alzheimer's disease, 254, 261
American Association for the Advancement of Science, 99
American Psychiatric Association, 367
American Psychological Association, 211
Ames, Adelbert, 126, 225
Ames, Katrine, 520
amnesia, 376

amphetamines, 161, 167, 168–169, 172, 385
Amytal, 168–169
anagrams, 141
anal stage (Freud), 204
anchoring effect, 473
Anderson, A., 329
Andresen, J. J., 166
androgyny, 231–232
angel dust, 171–172
Angier, N., 196
anorexia nervosa, 134
Antabuse, 520
Anthony, J., 221
anti-anxiety drugs, 412
antidepressants, 168–169, 411, 520
antipsychotic drugs, 411
antisocial personality, 384–385, 431
anxiety, 162, 276, 277, 327, 378, 404–405, 425–427
anxiety disorders, 372–373
applied science, 9
approach-approach conflict, 318
approach-avoidance conflict, 318–319
approval, 430–431
aptitude tests, 292, 294, 299, 300
archetype, 276
Arkoff, Abe, 344, 346
Army Alpha test, 296
Army Beta test, 296
Arnold, Magda, 152–153
Arnold's theory, 152–153
Aronson, Elliot, 431, 471, 472
arousal, 138
Arthur, Ransom J., 333–334
artificial intelligence, 525, 526
Asch, Solomon, 479–480
assertiveness, 395
assessment center method, 310, 527
assimilation, 188, 189
association areas, 85
astrology, 269
asynchrony, 223
attachment, 198–200
attitudes, 457–477
attribution theory, 439–440
audience, 471, 474–475
auditory nerve, 117
authoritarian family, 234, 236, 237, 351–352
authoritarian personality, 463
autism, 405
autonomic nervous system, 83, 494
autonomy, 206–207
Averill, James, 147
aversive control, 34–37
avoidance-avoidance conflict, 318
avoidance conditioning, 35
Awareness of Dying (Glaser/Strauss), 257–258
axes, 368, 370–371

Back, Kurt W., 409
Bahrick, Harry P., 65
Bahrick, Phyllis O., 65
Baillergeon, R., 193
balance, 119
Bales, R. F., 445
Ballenger, J. C., 373
Baltes, P. B., 247, 257
Bandura, Albert, 208, 228–229, 239, 278–279, 425
Barber, Theodore, 164
barbiturates, 168–169
Bard, Philip, 148
bark, 85
Barton, William, 492–493
baseball statistics, 504
basic science, 9, 10, 16
Bauer, M., 166
Beck, Aaron, 172, 377
bedwetting, 27, 158
Beebe-Center, J. G., 117
behavior, 4, 5–7, 9, 13, 14, 96–97
behavioral confirmation, 469
behavioral reactions, to stress, 327–328, 336–337
behaviorism, 14–15, 40, 101, 157, 277, 406
personality theory, 269, 277–279, 280
behavior modification, 9, 43–44, 47, 406, 410
behavior therapy, 404–406
bell and pad device, 27
bell-shaped curve, 506
Belsky, J., 185, 192, 201
Bem, Sandra, 231–232
Bem Sex Role Inventory, 232
Benimoff, 237
Bennett, E. L., 60
Bennington College experiment, 458–459, 460, 461
Benson, Herbert, 176, 177
Benzedrine, 168–169
Berardo, D. H., 252
Berardo, F. M., 252
Bergin, Allen, 410
Berne, Eric, 403, 404
Berscheid, Ellen, 429, 432, 433–434
Beyond Freedom and Dignity (Skinner), 14
bias, in samples, 490–491
Binet, Alfred, 295
binocular fusion, 116
biochemical factors, of psychosis, 383
biofeedback, 174–175, 176, 177, 336
biological motivation, 133–138, 143, 144, 145
biological psychology, 12, 517–520
biopsychologists, 12
birth, 185–188
birth defects, 185
Bischof, L., 247

Blackmore, S. J., 165, 166
Blank, A., 521
blindness, 124, 146
blind spot, in eye, 114
blood pressure, 161, 175, 176–177, 245, 254
"Bobo" doll, 208
body language, 435–437
body sensations, 119
body temperature, 118, 119, 134, 135, 175
Bonaparte, Napoleon, 276
boomerang effect, 472
Bootzin, Richard R., 160, 376, 377, 381
Botwinick, J., 246, 247
Bouchard, Thomas, 103, 298, 299
Bower, Gordon, 66–67
Bowers, K., 165
Boyd, J., 252
Brady, Joseph, 330–331
brain, 60, 81–95, 96, 107, 120, 163
brain damage, 81, 85, 86, 88, 94, 245, 295, 518
brain mapping, 85, 89
brain research, 89–95, 517–519
brainstem, 84
brainwashing, 477–479
brain waves (EEG), 55, 88, 91, 157, 158, 159, 174, 175
Branberger, M. B., 237
branching system, 45
Brant, B. A., 255
Brittain, C. V., 238
Broadbent, D. E., 54
Broca, Pierre Paul, 518
Brook, A., 170
Brook, D. W., 170
Brook, J. S., 170
Brown, J. A. C., 109
Brown, Roger, 196
Bruner, Jerome S., 226
Bucy, P. C., 93
Budzynski, Thomas, 175
Buehler, R. E., 278
bulimia, 134
Burke, R. J., 322
Butler, R. N., 253, 255
Byrne, James L., 359

caffeine, 167, 168–169, 176, 385
California Personality Inventory (CPI), 286
Campbell, David, 465
cancer, 92, 170, 245, 254, 260, 328–333, 492, 522
Cannon, Walter B., 148–149
Cannon-Bard theory, 148–149
Caplan, R. D., 332
carbamazepine, 520
career, 358
Carlsmith, M., 468, 471
Carr, J., 254
cartoons, 211, 213
Casals, Pablo, 356

case study, 12, 494–496
Cassel, J., 332
castration anxiety, 205
CAT scan, 518, 519, 520
catatonic schizophrenia, 380
Cattell, Raymond B., 269, 286
central nervous system (CNS), 83, 161, 412, 518
central processing, 53, 56–60, 69–75
central tendency, 506–508
cerebellum, 84
cerebral cortex, 84–85, 86
cerebral dominance, 87–89
cerebrum, 84, 85
chaining, 41–42
Chance, Paul, 128
Chand, I. P., 238
channel, 471, 473–474
Chapman, J., 381
charisma, 446
chemical senses, 117–118
Cherry, L., 318
child abuse, 201–202, 376
child development, 16, 182–217, 226, 274, 447, 497
child ego, 403
Chimp-O-Mat, 33–34, 46
China, psychology in, 14
chlordiazepoxide, 412
chloro-hydrocarbons, 168–169
chlorpromazine, 411
Chomsky, Noam, 194
chronological age, 295, 296
Chukovsky, K., 188
chunking, 57–58
Churchill, Winston, 472
cingulotomy, 95
civil rights, 466–468
Civil Rights Act (1964), 359
classical conditioning, 23–29, 30, 42, 43, 44
client-centered therapy, 400–401, 410
clinical psychology, 9, 15–16, 396
clique, 237–238
closed awareness, 258
closure, 120
Coale, A. J., 474
Cobb, Sydney, 328, 332
cocaine, 168–169, 172, 173, 335, 349, 520
Coch, L., 443
cochlea, 116
codeine, 168–169
Coe, W., 165
cognitive appraisal, 334
cognitive development, 4, 188–193, 196, 225–226, 495–496
cognitive-developmental approach, to child development, 212–214
cognitive development stages, 189–193, 225–226, 495–496
cognitive dissonance, 466–468

cognitive preparation, 334–335
cognitive theories, 151–153
Cohen, H., 46, 323
cohorts, 244
Cole, J. O., 411
Coleman, James C., 357, 382
Coleridge, Samuel Taylor, 74–75, 162
Coles, Robert, 341
Colier, R. L., 150
collective unconscious, 275
college life, 352–355
Collette, J., 332
Collins, M., 465
color blindness, 115
commitment, 413
common traits, 286
communication, 444, 445, 470–475
community mental health, 415–419
Community Mental Health Centers Act (1963), 415
community psychology, 16
companionate love, 433
comparable worth, 359
complementarity, 432
complementary (Sullivan), 279
compliance, 459–460
compulsion, 372, 374–375, 378
computer-assisted instruction (CAI), 44–46
computers, 525–526
concept, 69–70
concrete operational stage (Piaget), 189, 190, 192–193
conditioned reflex, 14
conditioned reinforcer, 33
conditioned response (CR), 24, 25, 26, 28
conditioned stimulus (CS), 24, 25, 26, 27, 28, 29
conditioning. see specific type
conditions of worth, 283
cones, 112, 114, 115
confabulation, 63
conflict situation, 318–319, 336, 348–352, 450–453, 462–463, 466
conformity, 238, 448, 479–480
confound, 493
Conger, J. J., 224, 236
consciousness, 12, 157, 158, 164
altered states of, 156–181
conservation, 192–193
constancy, 124–125
contingency management, 405–406
continuous reinforcement schedule, 31
control group, 493, 498
conversion reaction, 375
Cook, E. W., 166
Cooper, Cary L., 321, 322
Cooper, R. G., 198
Corbit, John D., 139

corpus callosum, 87, 93
correlation, 285, 491–492
correlation coefficients, 510–511
cortex, 85
counseling psychology, 15–16, 396
Cowley, Geoffrey, 520
crack, 168–169, 172, 187
cramming, 304
Crandall, Rebecca, 520
creativity, 72–75, 86, 282
Crichton, Michael, 94
Crick, Francis, 163
Crider, D. M., 238
crisis intervention program, 417–419
critical periods, 184–185
Cromwell, R., 383
cross-cultural studies, 497
cross-sectional studies, 244
crowded nest syndrome, 252
crystallized intelligence, 257
Cuber, J. F., 344–345
Culliton, B. J., 95
cults, 478
culture, behavior and, 100, 147, 202, 214, 221, 226, 231, 252, 435, 436–437, 457–458, 497
Cunningham, Glenn, 276

Dahlstrom, William Grant, 308
Damon, W., 447
Darley, J. M., 447
Darwin, Charles, 13, 96–97, 98, 101, 145–146
data gathering, 9, 489–497, 503, 504
datura, 170
Daumier, Honoré, 164
Davidson, E., 209
Davidson, R., 89
Davis, A., 298
Davis, Keith, 433, 440
Davison, Gerald C., 367
Day, D., 228
day care, 199–200, 524, 525
daydreams, 157, 165
deafness, 146, 196
De Angelis, Tori, 520
death, 254, 257–261, 347
De Bono, Edward, 70, 74
decibel, 117
decision processing, 59
decremental model of aging, 253
defense mechanisms, 272–274
Deikman, Arthur J., 175
Delgado, J. M. R., 92
delirium, 157
delta waves, 158
delusions, 379
Dembroski, T. M., 329
Dement, W., 160, 161, 162
Demerol, 168–169
democratic family, 234, 236, 351
Demosthenes, 276
denial, 334

Dennis, Wayne, 10, 184, 247
dependent variable, 493
depressants, 168–169, 171, 173, 335
depression, 39–40, 47, 232–233, 252, 254, 258, 260, 261, 377–378, 381
treatment of, 12, 95, 411, 412, 520
depth perception, 122, 123, 124
Deren, S., 170
Descartes, René, 11
descriptive statistics, 503–511
designer drugs, 172
desipramine, 520
detection thresholds, 113–114
Deutsch, M., 465
development, 7, 213–214
see also specific types
developmental friendships, 354
developmental psychology, 16, 183
development stages, 4
devitalized marriage, 345
Dexedrine, 168–169
diabetes, 245, 254
diastolic pressure, 176, 177
diazepam, 412
dibenzapines, 168–169
DiCara, Leo, 494
Dichter, Ernest, 475
difference threshold, 110–112
diffusion of responsibility, 446–447
Dion, K. L., 429, 431
directed thinking, 70–71
discrimination, 25, 33
prejudice and, 463–464
disinhibition, 43
displacement, 272–273
display rules, 255
dissociative disorder, 372, 376
distress, 318
distributions, of data, 504–506
divorce, 346–348
dizygotic twins, 101
dizziness, 119
Dodge, K., 450
Dodge, R., 473
Dollard, John, 277
dorm life, 355
double approach-avoidance conflict, 319
double-bind theory, 383–384
double-blind experiment, 498
Douvan, Elizabeth, 239
dread, 162
dream analysis, 12, 162, 276
dreams, 12, 158, 159, 161–163, 165, 166, 270, 274
drive reduction theory, 136–138
drug therapies, 519–520
DSM-III-R, 367–372
dualism, 11
duct glands, 95

ductless glands, 95
Duncker, Carl, 72, 74
Dunphy, Dexter, 448
Dvorine Pseudo-Isochromatic
    Plates, The, 115
Dwyer, Johanna, 223, 225

eating, act of, 107, 134–135, 141,
    143, 145
eating disorders, 134
ecological validity, 494
"ecstasy," 172
education, 14–15, 44–46, 211,
    522–523, 525
educational psychology, 16
Edwards, J. N., 237
effectors, 82
ego, 271, 272, 273
ego states, 403
ego-support value, 428, 430
eidetic memory, 63–64
Einstein, Albert, 281
Ekman, Paul, 146
Elavil, 168–169, 411
Elderveld, S., 473
electroconvulsive therapy, 412–413
electrode, 90
electroencephalograph (EEG),
    88, 90–91, 157, 158, 159, 175,
    499, 518
Ellis, Albert, 337, 402, 403
Ellsworth, Phoebe, 146
emotion, 4, 42, 96, 139, 145–153,
    162, 381
emotional development, 197–200,
    255
emotional experience, 255
emotional expression, 255
empiricism, 11
employment, 239, 251, 256,
    321–322, 355–359, 523–528
empty nest syndrome, 251–252
encounter group, 400, 408, 409
endocrine glands, 95
endocrine system, 95–96, 145, 518
energy conservation, 476–477
Enjoy Old Age (Skinner), 257
entering the adult world, 248
environmental stressors, 323–324
environment versus heredity, 13,
    98–103, 183, 184, 297–299
epilepsy, 87, 91, 92
Erikson, Erik, 205–207, 227–229,
    250, 276–277, 432
Erlemeir, N., 254
Eron, L., 209
escape conditioning, 35
ethics, 26, 128, 310, 494
ethnicity, 187, 209, 211
ethnography, 172
ethology, 97–98, 494
eustress, 318
euthanasia, 261
Evangelauf, J., 301
Evans, N., 244

evolution, 100
exercise, 336
existential therapy, 401–402
exocrine glands, 95
experiment, 489, 492–494
experimental group, 493, 498
experimental psychology, 16
experimental treatment, 493
expert systems, 526
explanation, 492
*Expression of the Emotions in Man
    and Animals, The* (Darwin), 145
extinction, 26–27, 30, 32
extrasensory perception (ESP),
    108, 126–128
extrovert, 286, 309
eye, 112
eyewitness testimony, 61–62, 63
Eysenck, Hans, 286, 409–410
Eysenck Personality Inventory
    (EPI), 286

face recognition, 122–123, 525
facial expressions, 146, 147
factor analysis, 286
Fairbanks, D. T., 321
false consensus effect, 475
family, 234–237, 251, 298–299
family therapy, 406–408
fear, 145, 153, 162, 211, 404–405
    of success, 142–143
fear response, 26
feature extraction, 54, 55–56
feedback, 37, 331, 388, 476
Feil, Naomi, 255–256
Feldman, H., 250
female development, 244,
    251–252, 276, 522
Festinger, Leon, 466, 468
fetal alcohol syndrome, 187
fetus, 185
Fiedler, F. E., 445
"fight or flight" reaction, 149,
    324, 334
figure-ground perception, 121
Filipczak, J., 46
filter model, of input, 54, 55
financial resources, 256
Finlayson, P. F., 170
firstborn, 298–299
Fisher, Seymour, 275
Fitch, V., 255
five robust factors, 286
fixed action patterns, 97
fixed-interval reinforcement
    schedule, 32
fixed-ratio reinforcement
    schedule, 31
flexibility, 73, 74
Flexner, L., 60
Flood, J. F., 60
fluid intelligence, 257
fluoxetine, 520
forensic psychology, 15

forgetting, 64–66
formal commitment, 367
formal operational stage (Piaget),
    189, 190, 225–226
Fox, L. J., 49
Fram, D. H., 172
frames, 44
Frank, Jerome, 530
Frankl, Viktor, 401–402
fraternal twins, 101, 102
free association, 12, 398
Freedman, Daniel G., 187
Freedman, Jonathan, 323
Freiberg, Peter, 522, 524
French, J. R. P., Jr., 443
frequency curve, 505
frequency distribution, 504, 505
frequency polygon, 505, 506
Freud, Sigmund, 13, 66, 207, 373,
    375, 377, 396
    on dreams, 162–163
    personality theory, 12, 284,
        398, 495
    psychosexual development
        theory, 203–205, 269–277, 279
Friedman, Meyer, 329, 330
friendship, 354, 427–432
Frier, R. C., 171
Friesen, Wallace, 146
Fromm, Erich, 276, 342
frontal lobe, 86, 87, 94
frontal lobotomy, 94, 95
frustration, 323
fugue, 376
fully functioning person, 282, 283
functional fixedness, 72
fundamental needs (Maslow), 143
Furn, B. G., 166
Furness, R. M., 278

Gage, Phineas, 86
Gaite, A. J. H., 226
Galton, Francis, 13, 101
gangs, 384
Garcia, A. M., 321
Garcia, John, 29
Gardner, B. T., 194–195
Gardner, Howard, 295
Gardner, R. A., 194–195
Gaugler, B. B., 310
Geldard, Frank A., 109
Geller, E. S., 388
Gelles, Richard, 522
Gelman, R., 193
gender differences, 100, 150, 381
General Aptitude Test Battery
    (GATB), 299, 527
generalization, 25, 33
generativity, 250, 251
gene therapy, 519–520
genital stage (Freud), 205
Geraci, J. B., 166
Gerard, Harold, 427
Gergen, Kenneth, 492–493

Gergen, Mary, 492–493
Gershon, E. S., 382
Gestalt, 120
gestalt therapy, 402, 410
Gibb, C., 445
Gibson, E. J., 122, 124
Ginott, Haim G., 348
Ginsburg, Herbert, 191
Glaser, Barney, 258
Glass, Gene V., 410, 469
globality, 39, 40
glutamate, 94
Goffman, Erving, 414
Golden, F., 195
Goldenberg, S., 252
Goldin, L. R., 382
Goldsen, R., 458
Gomez-Jeria, J. S., 167
Good, M. I., 177
Goodenough, Florence L., 146
Goodman, P., 402
Gordon, A. S., 170
Gordon, Thomas, 351
Gould, Stephen, 99
grammar, 194
Grant, G., 237
graphs, 504–505
grasping reflex, 186
Green, D., 113
Greenberg, Roger, 275, 523
Gregory, R. L., 121, 124
group, 16, 440–452, 462–463,
    479–480
group testing, 292, 296, 300–301
group therapy, 406–409, 414
groupthink, 529
Guilford, J. P., 284
Guilleminault, C., 161
Gur, Ruben, 245
Gustafson, L. A., 150
Gustavson, C. R., 29

Haan, N., 228
habits, 136
Hajdukovic, R., 161
Haldane, J. B. S., 98
Hale, Wayne E., 336
halfway houses, 416, 417
Hall, Calvin, 12, 161, 274
Hall, Edward T., 434–435
Hall, G. Stanley, 219, 221
hallucinations, 157, 161,
    165–166, 170–172, 379, 383
hallucinogens, 168–169, 170–172
Hammen, Constance L., 357
Hancock, E., 244
handedness, 87, 89, 90
Hanes, C. A., 316
Harkins, E. B., 252
Harlow, Harry, 38–39, 138,
    197–198
Harris, B., 26
Harris, C. S., 253
Harris, H., 172
Harris, S. I., 385

Harris, T. G., 142
Harrison, R. V., 332
Harroff, Peggy, 344–345
Hartup, W. W., 237
hashish, 167, 168–169
Hassan, R., 254
Hassett, James, 118, 150, 176, 177, 188
hassles, 323
Hatfield, E., 433
Hathaway, Starke R., 307
Havighurst, Robert J., 222, 239, 244
headaches, 175, 321
head injuries, 94
health, 145, 246, 250, 254, 332–333
hearing, 109, 112, 114, 116, 117, 121, 146, 196, 244
heart disease, 245, 246, 254, 336, 512, 522
Hefferline, R. F., 402
Hein, A., 123
Held, R., 123
Helms, D. B., 245
Henning, Hans, 117
Hereditary Genius (Galton), 101
heredity, 13, 382
    versus environment, 13, 98–103, 183, 184, 297–299
Hernández-Peón, R., 55
heroin, 168–169
Herron, Jeannine, 89
Hess, R., 458
Higgins-Trenk, A., 226
Hilgard, Ernest R., 164
Hinckley, John, 366–367
Hippocrates, 81
Hiroto, D. S., 39
histograms, 505
Hitler, Adolf, 472, 529
Hoebel, Bartley G., 134
Hoffman, Banesh, 297
Hokanson, J. E., 331–332
Holden, C., 103
Holland, G. A., 404
Holland, J., 329
Holmes, Thomas H., 319, 320, 321, 328, 332
homelessness, 413
homeostasis, 134
homosexuality, 275
hormones, 95, 134, 159, 223
Horn, John, 257
Horner, Matina, 142–143
Horney, Karen, 276, 277
hospice, 259–260
hostility, 276, 277, 327, 451–452
Hothersall, David, 518
Hough, R. L., 321
House, J. S., 332
Hovland, C., 464, 473, 475
Hraba, J., 237
Hubbard, R. W., 254, 255
Hubel, David H., 90
Hull, Clark, 136–137, 138

human-animal relationship, 96–101
human factors engineering, 523, 526
human interaction, 424–455
humanistic psychology, 15, 143, 399–400
    personality theory, 269, 279–283, 285
human potential movement, 269, 399–402, 404
hunger, 134–135, 141, 143
Hussein, Saddam, 528, 529
Huston, A., 211
Huxley, Aldous, 109
hydrocarbons, 168–169
hypertension, 176, 177, 245, 254
hypnosis, 66, 157, 163–165, 166
hypochondriasis, 375–376
hypothalamus, 92, 95, 134–135, 149
hypothesis, 8–9, 278, 492–493, 503
hysteria, 375

Iacocca, Lee, 446
id, 271, 272, 273, 274
identical twins, 101
identification, 205, 459, 460, 472
identity achievement adolescents, 228
identity confused adolescents, 228
identity crisis, 227
identity crisis theory, 227–229
identity diffused adolescents, 228
identity foreclosure adolescents, 228
identity formation, 227–229
identity moratorium adolescents, 228
ideology, 442–443
illusions, 125–126
image, 69, 70
imaginary playmates, 213
imitation, 43, 207–208, 278–279
implicit personality theory, 438–439
impressions, 437–440
imprinting, 185
incentives, 476, 477
incus, 116
independence, 206–207, 236, 249, 449
independent variable, 492, 493
industrial and organizational (I/O) psychology, 16, 523, 525–528
infants, 147, 185–188
inferential statistics, 511–513
inferiority complex, 276
informal commitment, 367
information processing, 53, 59, 107, 108
inhalants, 168–169
Inhelder, Baerbel, 63, 225
inherited traits, 13

inhibition, 83
innate behavior, 145–147, 300
inoculation effect, 475–476
input, 53–56, 59
Inquiries into Human Faculty and Its Development (Galton), 13
insight, 75, 398
insomnia, 160, 161
instinct, 14, 97–98, 101
integration, 465–466
intellectual development, 247, 256–257
intellectualization, 334
intelligence, 295, 297, 298–299
intelligence tests, 13, 247, 257, 291, 294, 295–299
interdependence, 441
interest tests, 299, 302
interference, 65–66, 68
intermittent reinforcement schedule, 31
internality, 39, 40
internalization, 205, 459, 461
interneurons, 82
interpersonal skills, 337, 351, 430
interpersonal theories, 279
interval reinforcement schedule, 31, 33
introspection, 11
introvert, 286, 309
involuntary acts, of nervous system, 83
IQ (intelligence quotient), 101, 292, 295, 296–299
Irwin, H. J., 166
Izard, Carroll, 146–147, 148

Jacobson, Edmond, 335
James, Henry, 12
James, William, 12, 147–148, 187
James-Lange theory, 148
Jamieson, A. O., 161
Janis, Irving, 334–335, 529
Japan, old age in, 256
Jellinek, Elvin M., 387
Jennings, M., 458
Johnson, Hugh, 385
Johnson, Virginia, 246, 496
Johnston, Lloyd, 349
Jones, Edward E., 225, 440
Jones, F. H., 239
Jones, Mary Cover, 26
Jordan, Michael, 98
Josephs, R. A., 387
Jung, Carl G., 275–276, 286, 365
juvenile delinquents, 278

Kagan, Jerome, 496, 499
Kaimowitz, Gabe, 93
Kalinowsky, L. B., 412
Kalisy, Richard A., 256
Kalnok, M., 255
Kandel, D. B., 238
Kanzi, 195
Kaplan, B. H., 332

Karnash, L., 381
Keeler, Leonarde, 150
Kelley, H. H., 439
Kelly, J., 347
Kelman, H. C., 459, 475
Kempler, Walter, 402
Kennedy, John F., 446, 472, 529
Kennedy, Robert, 66
Kety, Seymour, 382
Kimmel, D. C., 247
kinesthesis, 114, 119
King, Martin Luther, Jr., 464
Kinsey, Alfred C., 246, 496
Kipling, Rudyard, 279–280
kissing, 6
Kleinman, P. H., 170
Kleitman, Nathaniel, 163
Kliegl, R., 257
Klineberg, Otto, 147
Klüver, H., 93
Knapp, J. R., 239
knowledge, 11, 46, 188–189
Koelling, R. A., 29
Koffka, K., 120
Kohlberg, Lawrence, 213–214, 226–227, 497
Kohlenberg, Robert, 476
Köhler, Wolfgang, 75
Kohut, Heinz, 272
Kolata, G., 254
Kolb, D. A., 141
Komarovsky, Mirra, 345–346
Korsakoff's syndrome, 387
Kramer, R., 497
Krantzler, Mel, 347
Kreps, Juanita, 359
Kubla Khan (Coleridge), 162
Kübler-Ross, Elisabeth, 258, 260
Kuder Preference Record (KPR), 302

LaFrance, Marianne, 437
LaFrancois, Guy, 349
laissez-faire family, 234, 236, 351
Landon, Alf, 490
Lang, J. D., 395
language acquisition device (LAD), 194
language development, 40–41, 87, 88, 89, 192, 193–197
Lashley, Karl, 60
Lashley jump stand, 35
Latané, B., 447
latency stage (Freud), 205
lateral hypothalamus (LH), 134–135
lateral thinking, 74
lay analysts, 396
Lazarus, R. S., 334
leadership, 444–446, 530–531
learned behavior, 4, 14, 145–147, 404
learned helplessness, 39–40, 47, 337, 377–378

learned laziness, 39–40
learning, 14, 22–51, 147, 247
learning theory, 277
Leavitt, Harold, 444, 445
Lees, Harriet, 87
LeFevre, Richard, 436
Leland, L. S., 388
lens, 115
Lerner, R. M., 239
lesioning, 90, 93
Lesser, G. S., 238
Letters from Jenny (Allport), 285
Levant, Oscar, 376
Levinger, G., 343, 346, 430
Levinson, Daniel, 243, 248–251
Lewis, N., 201
Lewontin, Richard, 99
Librium, 168–169, 412
Liebert, R., 209
lie detection, 149–151
Liem, J. H., 321
Liem, R., 321
life changes, 319–321, 322
life events perspective, 244
life records, 286
life review process, 255–256
life situation, 254–256
"life styles," 276
Lifton, Robert Jay, 477, 478
like (emotion), 342, 343
Lincoln, Abraham, 281
Linder, D., 431
Lindzey, Gardner, 12
linear system, 45
lithium, 168–169, 411
Little Albert, 26, 373
living wills, 261
lobes, 85
lobotomy, 94, 95
Locke, John, 11
Loftus, Elizabeth, 61, 62
Long, James D., 137, 430
long-term memory, 56, 58–59, 60, 65
longitudinal study, 244, 496–497
Lorayne, Harry, 69
Lorenz, Konrad, 98, 185, 197
Lovaas, O. I., 41
love, 145, 342–344, 433–434
LSD (lysergic acid diethylamide), 167, 168–169, 170–171
Lucas, Jerry, 69
Lumsdaine, A., 474
Luria, A. R., 64
Lykken, David T., 149
lynchings, 464

Maccoby, Eleanor, 198
Mace, D., 458
Mace, V., 458
Madison, Peter, 353, 354, 355
Maer, F., 89
magnetic resonance imaging (MRI), 518, 519, 520

Maharishi Mahesh Yogi, 175
Maher, Brendan, 381
Majeras, R. L., 220
major depression, 381–383
Malatesta, C. Z., 255
male development theory, 248–251
malleus, 116
mandrake, 170
manic reaction, 381
Manson, Charles, 385
mantra, 175
MAO inhibitors, 168–169
Marcia, James, 228
Margolis, B. L., 322
marijuana, 167, 168–169, 170, 335, 385
"marketplace orientation," 214
Markowitsch, Hans, 518
Markus, G. B., 298
Marlatt, G., 174
Marler, Peter, 100
marriage, 248, 249, 250, 252, 254, 319, 342, 344–347, 430, 431, 458
Marshall, Judi, 321
Marshall, M. E., 198
Martin, C. S., 387
Maslow, Abraham, 15, 143–145, 269, 280–282, 283, 365
Maslow's Hierarchy of Needs, 143–145
master-slave relationship, 462–463
Masters, John C., 198
Masters, William, 246, 496
Masterson, J. F., 239
masturbation, 205
Matata, 195
matter (dualism), 11
Matthyssee, S., 383
May, Rollo, 15, 401
Mayer, Jean, 223, 225
Mayo, Clara, 437
McCarley, Robert W., 163
McClean-Rice, N., 166
McClelland, David, 140–143
McClintock, Martha, 118
McCoy, Kathleen, 232, 233
McGhie, A., 381
McGinley, Hugh, 436
McGinley, Pat, 436
McGinnis, Joe, 472
McGuire, W. J., 475
McIntosh, J. L., 254, 255
McKinley, John Charnley, 307
Mead, Margaret, 219, 222, 229
mean, 507–508
Mechanic, D., 316
median, 507
meditation, 157, 165, 175–177, 335
Meehl, Paul M., 384
Melzack, Ronald, 112
memory, 4, 52–69, 86, 92, 257, 387
menarche, 223
menopause, 245–246

mental age, 295, 296
mental disorders, 102, 165, 239, 308, 365–371, 439, 520
  treatment of, 411–413, 414, 519
mental institutions, 413–414
mentally retarded, 439
mental practice, 38
mentor, 249
meprobamate, 412
Merrill, Maud A., 296, 497
mescaline, 168–169, 170, 172
message, 471, 473
"messianic complex," 226
meta-analysis, 512
metachoric experience, 165–166
Methedrine, 168–169
Meyer, R., 185, 192
Michael, Richard, 118
mid-life transition, 249–251
middle adulthood (Levinson), 251
Middlebrook, P. N., 475
migraine headaches, 175
Milgram, Stanley, 324, 481–482, 497
Miller, George, 58
Miller, L. K., 46, 335
Miller, Neal, 277, 494
Miller, S., 39
Milstein, J., 167
Miltown, 412
mind (dualism), 11
Mind of a Mnemonist, The (Luria), 64
Miner, J. B., 527
Minnesota Multiphasic Personality Inventory (MMPI), 307–308, 309, 519
Mintz, R. S., 378
Mitler, M. M., 161
mnemonic devices, 6, 64, 68–69
mode, 507
modeling, 23, 42–49, 208, 279
Money, J., 230
monozygotic twins, 101
mood-dependent recall, 66–67
mood disorders, 378, 381–382, 411
moral development, 213–214, 226–227, 497
Moretti, P., 166
morphine, 168–169
Morse, M. L., 167
Moscovivi, Serge, 480
Moses, Susan, 519
Moss, H., 496, 499
mother-love experiment, 138, 197–198
motion parallax, 124
motion sickness, 108, 119
motivation, 96, 268, 269, 439
  biological, 133–138, 143, 144, 145
  signal-detection theory and, 113–114
  social, 139–145
motor cortex, 85, 86, 87

motor development, 184
Mowrer, Mollie, 27, 28
Mowrer, O. Hobart, 27, 28
Muller-Lyer illusions, 125
multiculturalism, 522
multiple choice test, 305
multiple personality, 376
Munns, M., 238
Murray, Henry, 139, 309
muscular control, 175, 177
mutual pretense awareness, 258

naps, 160
Naranjo, C. A., 520
narcissism, 272
narcolepsy, 160, 161
narcotics, 168–169
Nathan, P. E., 335
Nathan, P. W., 385
natural disasters, 329
naturalistic observation, 494, 495
natural selection, theory of, 98
nature versus nurture, 13, 98–103, 183, 184, 297–299
Neale, John M., 367
near-death experiences, 166–167
negative afterimage, 125
negative correlation, 491, 510
negative reinforcement, 34, 35, 36
Nelson, S., 161
Nembutal, 168–169
neodissociation theory, 164
nerve cells, 82–83
nerve damage, 85
nerve fibers, 82
nervous system, 81–89, 95, 107
Nesbitt, P., 472
Neugarten, Bernice, 245
neurons, 82–83, 90–91, 92, 94
neurosis, 371–378, 412, 520
neurotransmitters, 83, 170
neutral stimulus, 24, 26, 28, 42
"new brain," 84, 85
Newcomb, T., 458–459, 460, 461
Newman, H., 172
Newman, P., 450
Newton, Isaac, 73–74
Newton, P., 237
Nicassio, Perry M., 160
Niemi, R., 458
nightmares, 162
Nim Chimpsky, 195
nitrous oxide, 168–169
Nixon, Richard, 472
nondirected thinking, 70, 71, 74–75
nonobservable behavior, 7
nonverbal communication, 434–437
normal curve, 505–506, 512
norms, 4, 294–295, 442
noticeable difference, 110–112
NREM (non-REM) sleep, 159, 160
Nuckolls, K., 332
Nurnberger, J. I., Jr., 382

obedience, 480–481, 497
obesity, 135–136, 161
objective personality tests, 286, 307–308
object permanence, 190–191
O'Brien, J. S., 335
observable behavior, 7, 10–11, 14–15, 47
observational learning, 43, 278–279
observer effect, 498–499
obsession, 372, 374–375, 378, 520
obstructive sleep apnea, 161
Oedipal conflict, 204–205, 277
Offir, Carol Wade, 93
old age, 243, 244, 253–257
"old brain," 84, 91, 92, 93
Olds, J., 92
Olds, M. E., 92
Olds, S. W., 246, 254, 261
olfactory nerve, 117
Olson, M., 166
open awareness, 258
operant conditioning, 23, 29–37, 42, 43, 44, 194, 208, 278, 279, 404, 405
opium, 168–169, 385
Opper, Sylvia, 191
oppression, 462–463
optic nerve, 114, 115
oral stage (Freud), 204
organic therapy, 411–413, 414
organism, 282–283
Orlansky, J., 151
Orme, A. E., 60
Osgood, N. J., 255
Otis, Leon, 176
out-of-body experience (OBE), 165–166
output, 53, 59, 60–69
Outward Bound, 337
Owen, J. H., 166, 167

Paffenbarger, Ralph S., Jr., 336
pain, 92, 95, 112, 118, 119, 259, 261
Palmore, Erdman, 256
panic disorders, 372–373
panic reaction, 171
Papalia, D. E., 246, 254, 261
paralysis, 84, 87
paraprofessionals, 419
parapsychology, 108, 126–128
parasympathetic nervous system, 83
parental expectations, 350
"parental instinct," 98
parent-child relationship, 36, 138, 185, 197–198, 235, 252, 348–352, 432–433, 449, 458
parent ego, 403
parietal lobes, 86
Parke, R., 201, 202
Parnate, 411

Passages: Predictable Crises of Adult Life (Sheehy), 248, 251
passive-congenial marriage, 345, 346
passive-habituated marriage, 345
Pasteur, Louis, 128
Patterson, G. R., 278
Pavlov, Ivan, 14, 23–27, 28, 43
Payne, R., 322
PCP (phencyclidine), 168–169, 171–172
peace, 529–530
Peachy, J. E., 520
Pearl, D., 211
peer group, 234, 237–239, 278, 447–450, 458–459, 477, 479–480
Penfield, Wilder, 92
penis envy (Freud), 205, 276
Peoplemaking (Satir), 350
percentile system, 294–295, 296
perception, 4, 107–108, 120–126
perceptual compensation, 126, 127
perceptual inference, 121–122
Percodan, 168–169
performance tasks, 296
peripheral nervous system (PNS), 83, 84
Perlick, D., 335
Perls, Fritz, 402
permissive family, 234, 236, 351–352
Peroutka, S. J., 172
personal development, 222–232
personality, 4, 13–14, 86, 269
    adolescence and, 227–229, 247, 248
    adulthood and, 247–252
    stress and, 329–330
    theories, 266–289, 437–440
personality disorders, 384–385
personality psychology, 16
personality tests, 13, 16, 291, 294, 307–309
personality trait theory, 268, 269, 284–286, 445
personal relationships, 432–437
personal space, 434–435, 436
personal unconscious, 275
person-centered therapy, 401
personnel assessment, 527–528
persuasion, 470–476, 478
Peter (case study), 26
phallic stage (Freud), 204
phantom limb pain, 112
phenobarbital, 168–169
phenothiazines, 411
phenylketonuria (PKU), 103
phenylthiocarbamide (PTC), 118
pheromones, 118
Phillips, Thomas, 476
phobias, 372, 373–374, 378
photographic memory, 63–64
physical appearance, 429–431, 472
physical changes:
    during adolescence, 223–225

during adulthood, 244–246
during old age, 244, 253
physical proximity, 427–428
physical reactions, to stress, 328–329, 335–336
physiological psychology, 12, 89–90
physiology, 3, 11
    of emotions, 147–149, 151
    of motivation, 133–138, 143, 144, 145
Piaget, Jean, 188–193, 212, 225, 495–496
Pilbeam, David, 100
pilot training, 310, 527
Pines, Maya, 213
Pisoni, D. B., 387
pitch, 117
pituitary gland, 95, 134
placebo effect, 395–396
play, 212–213, 279
"pleasure center," 91, 92
Plumb, M. M., 329
Pocs, Ollie, 246
polygraph, 149–151
Ponzo illusion, 125
population, 490
positive correlation, 491, 510
positive regard, 283
positron emission tomography (PET) scan, 91, 518, 519, 520
posthypnotic suggestion, 164
post-traumatic stress disorder (PTSD), 520–521
practical application, of psychology, 5, 6–7, 9, 10
practice, 30, 37–38
Pradhan, S. N., 172
predictions, 491
prefrontal lobotomy, 94
prejudice, 461–466, 530
Preludin, 168–169
"premature affluence," 239
preoperational stage (Piaget), 189, 190, 192
Pressey, S. L., 44
pressure, 118, 119
primary reinforcer, 33, 34
Principles of Psychology (James), 12, 147
proactive interference, 65–66
probability, 511–512
problem solving, 71–74, 336
Proctor, William, 476
programmed instruction, 44–46
progressive relaxation, 335
projection, 273, 274
projective personality tests, 140, 307, 308–309
prompt, 44
propaganda, 529
Proshansky, H., 237
prospagnosia, 61
protest demonstrations, 461
Prozac, 520

psilocybin, 168–169, 170
psychedelic drugs, 170
psychiatric social worker, 396
psychiatrist, 15, 396
psychiatry, 15
psychoactive drugs, 157, 167–174, 187, 335, 349
psychoanalysis, 272, 279, 396, 398–399, 404
    personality theory, 268–277, 280
psychobiologist, 157
psychodynamic therapy, 410
psychological dependence, 385
psychological needs (Maslow), 144
psychological reactions, to stress, 327
psychological tests, 14, 290–313
psychological warfare, 477
psychologists, 15–17
psychology, 5–7, 9–15
psychopath, 384
psychophysics, 108, 111
psychosexual development theory (Freud), 204–205, 284
psychosexuality theory of personality (Freud), 269–277
psychosis, 371–372, 378–384
psychosocial development theory (Erikson), 205–207, 277
psychosurgery, 93–95, 411
psychotherapy, 15, 268, 275, 276, 281, 392–421
puberty, 221, 223, 224, 229
"public distance," 435, 436
public opinion, 16
punishers, 34, 35
punishment, 30, 35–37, 42, 207, 269, 278, 279
"punishment center," 92
pupil (eye), 115

questionnaires, 286
quiet alert state, 186
quiet sleep, 158, 159
Quinn, R., 358

Rabbie, J. M., 427
radial behaviorism, 277–278
Raft, D., 166
Rahe, Richard H., 319, 320, 321, 328, 332, 333–334
Rainone, G., 170
random sample, 491
range, 508
Rasmussen, Theodore, 92
rational-emotive therapy (RET), 402–403
rationalization, 225–226
ratio reinforcement schedule, 31, 33
Raush, Charlotte, 417
Raush, Harold L., 417
raw scores, 294
Ray, Oakley, 387

Rayner, Rosalie, 26
reaction formation, 274
Reagan, Ronald, 253, 366, 530
recall, 63–64
receptors, 82, 83, 106, 112
reciprocal reinforcement, 430
recognition, 61
recombination, 73–75
recording, 90–91
Rednick, R., 378
referred pain, 119
reflexes, 186, 189
regression, 274
rehearsal, 57, 59
reinforcement, 14, 30–33, 34, 46,
    207, 278
Reisman, J., 447
relaxation, 158, 163, 175, 176,
    335, 405, 525
Relaxation Response, The
    (Benson), 176
reliability, 292–293, 294
religion, hallucinogens and, 171
REM (rapid eye movement)
    sleep, 158–159, 160, 161, 163
replication, 128, 493–494, 512
representational thought, 191
repression, 66, 273–274
research, 7–9, 488–501
resistance, 398, 399
response, 14, 24
response chains, 41–42
response patterns, 41–42
resynthesis, 355
reticular activating system, 86
retina, 114, 115, 116
retinal disparity, 116, 124
retirement, 254, 358
retrieval, 61
retroactive interference, 65–66
rewards, 30, 42, 47, 207, 269,
    278, 279
reward values, 428–432
Reynolds, I., 170
Rhine, J. B., 127
Rice, F. P., 235
Rice, M., 220
rigidity, 72, 73
Rioch, Margaret, 419
risk taking, 139
risky shift, 445
Ritalin, 168–169
Rob, M., 170
Robber's Cave experiment,
    451–452
Roberts, G. A., 166, 167
rods, 112, 114, 115
Rogers, Carl, 15, 269, 280,
    282–283, 400, 401
Rogers, D., 238, 251
Rohsenow, D., 174
Rokeach, M., 468
roles, 213, 403, 461–462
Rollins, B. C., 250
Roosevelt, Eleanor, 281

Roosevelt, Franklin D., 490
rooting reflex, 186
Rorschach, Hermann, 308
Rorschach ink-blot test, 308–309,
    519
Rose, Robert, 328
Rosenhan, D. L., 370
Rosenman, Ray, 329, 330
Rosenthal, D., 102, 382
Rosenthal, Robert, 498
Rosnow, R. L., 498
Rubin, Zick, 342, 344, 433, 439
rule, 70
Russ, N. W., 388

Saavendra-Aguilar, J. C., 167
sample, 490–491
sanity, 366–367, 370
Sarbin, I., 164
SAT (Scholastic Aptitude Test),
    295, 300–301, 511
Satie, Virginia, 350
Savage-Rumbaugh, S., 195
scapegoat, 464
Scarf, Maggie, 252
scatterplot, 510, 511
Schachter, Stanley, 135–136,
    151–152, 426, 427
Schachter-Singer experiment,
    151–152
Schaie, K. W., 247
Schein, E. H., 357
schemes, 188–189
schizophrenia, 12, 102, 378–381,
    383, 411
Schmale, A., 328
Schnaiberg, A., 252
Schneider, R., 46
Schultes, R. E., 170
Schultz, Duane P., 471
Schwartz, Gary E., 89, 177
Scientific Credibility of Freud's
    Theories and Therapy, The
    (Fisher/Greenberg), 275
scientific method, 8–9
Sears, R., 464
Seasons of a Man's Life, The
    (Levinson), 243
Seconal, 168–169
Segal, N. L., 299
Seiden, R., 349
seizures, 93
selective attention, 54–55
selective memory problems, 61
self (Rogers), 283
self-actualization, 279–282, 283,
    365
self-actualization needs, 144–145
self-control, 47–48
self-esteem, 228, 238, 254, 280,
    283, 284
self-fulfilling prophecy, 225,
    469–470, 497–498
self-help group, 336–337, 408–409
self-justification, 468–469

self-observation, 11, 272
Seligman, Martin, 39–40, 47,
    337, 377–378
Selye, Hans, 318, 324–325, 326
senility, 60
sensation, 107, 108–114
senses, 112, 114–119, 244, 254
sensitive period, 185
sensorimotor stage, 189–192
sensory adaptation, 112–113
sensory experience, 108
sensory storage, 56–57, 64
separation, 434
separation anxiety, 198
"separation shock," 347
Serdahely, W. J., 166
set, 71–72
sex, 118, 229–232, 245, 246, 250,
    349, 471, 496
sex identity, 230
sex roles, 207, 209, 229, 230–232,
    496
sexual abuse, 201, 202
sexual maturation, 223
shaping, 6, 40–41
Shapiro, David, 174, 177
Shaver, Kelly G., 439
Sheehy, Gail, 248, 251
Sheffield, F., 474
Shehan, K. C. L., 252
Shenkel, Randee Jane, 269
Sherif, Muzafer, 452
"shock treatment," 412–413
Shorr, S., 447
short-term memory, 56–58, 59, 64
shyness, 429
sick-building syndrome, 523–524
signal-detection theory, 113–114
signals, 33–34
sign language, 194, 195, 196
sign stimulus, 97–98
silent suicide, 255
Silverstein, B., 335
similarity, 431–432
Singer, Dorothy G., 211, 213, 465
Singer, Jerome L., 151, 211, 213
Singer, Margaret Thaler, 478–479
Sirhan Sirhan, 66
situational test, 309–310
size constancy, 125
skewed distributions, 506, 507
skills, learning of, 40–42
Skinner, B. F., 14–15, 30, 40, 43,
    44, 194, 257, 269, 277–278, 279
Skinner box, 29
skin senses, 112, 114, 118–119
Skolnick, Arlene, 346
Slaby, R., 202
sleep, 157–162, 163, 176, 253, 499
sleep apnea, 160–161
sleep disorders, 160–161
sleeper effect, 475
sleepwalking, 158
Slotkin, J. J., 363
smell, 66, 112, 114, 117–118

Smigel, E. O., 349
smiles, 34
Smith, Mary Lee, 410
smoking, 164, 168–169, 177, 187,
    245, 329, 335, 385
Snoek, J. Didrich, 343, 430
Snyder, C. R., 269
social development:
    during adolescence, 234–239
    during adulthood, 247–252
    in children, 447
social function group, 4, 5, 442
social influence, 477–482
socialization, 200, 202–208
social leader, 445
social learning theories, 212, 229
    of development, 207–208
    of personality, 278–279
social motivation, 139–145
social psychology, 16
Social Readjustment Rating
    Scale, 319, 320, 328, 332
social rules, 436
social support, 332
social traps, 452
sociobiology, 98–101
Sociobiology: A New Synthesis
    (Wilson), 98
sociogram, 444
sociopath, 384
Socrates, 44
Solomon, Richard L., 139
somatic nervous system, 83
somatoform disorders, 372,
    375–376, 378
somatosensory cortex, 85, 86
"Son of Sam," 62
sound waves, 117
source, 471–472
source traits, 286
Soutine, Chaim, 365
Sowarka, D., 257
spatial learning, 43, 87, 88, 295
species-specific behaviors, 97
speech development, 88, 196
Sperling, G., 56–57
Sperry, Roger, 157
spinal cord, 83, 84
split-brain surgery, 87, 88, 93
Spock, Benjamin, 253
spontaneous recovery, 26–27
"spontaneous remission," 410
Sprafkin, J., 209
Spring, Bonnie, 382
SQ3R, 67
Sroufe, L. A., 198
stability, 39, 40
Stage I sleep, 158, 159, 335
Stage II sleep, 158, 159
Stage III sleep, 158, 159
Stage IV sleep, 158, 159
stagnation, 250, 251
standard deviation (SD), 506,
    508–509, 512

standardization group, 295
Stanford, M. W., 172
Stanford, R. G., 166
Stanford-Binet Intelligence Test, 294, 295–296, 512
Stanley, J., 301
stapes, 116
state-dependent memory, 66–67
statistical significance, 512–513
statistics, 502–515
Steele, C. M., 387
Steinberg, L., 185, 192
Stelazine, 411
stereopsis, 116
stereotypes, 97, 98, 187, 209, 211, 231, 243, 246, 252–255, 439, 461–462
Sternbach, R., 150
Sternberg, Robert, 344
Stevens, S. S., 111
Stevens-Long, J., 252, 254
Stevenson, I., 166
stimulants, 168–169
stimulation:
    in brain research, 90, 92
    in child development, 10
stimulation value, 428, 431
stimulus, 14, 24
    sensation and, 108–109, 110–114
Stokols, D., 323
Stone, N., 172
storefront clinics, 416
storm and stress, 221–222, 227
stratified sample, 491
Strauss, Anselm, 258
Strauss, Murray, 522
stress, 245, 316–339, 354, 434, 524–525, 526
"stress inoculation," 521
stress management, 330–332, 333–337, 525
stressor, 316, 322, 520–526
    environmental, 323–324
stress reaction, 316, 324–333
stroke, 87, 94, 177, 254
Strong Vocational Interest Inventory, 302
structured group, 5
study skills, 48–49, 67, 292, 303–307
subcortex, 84, 93, 95
sublimation, 205
subliminal advertising, 109–110
subliminal perception, 110
substance abuse, 165, 176, 385–388
    treatment programs, 172, 520
success, fear of, 142–143
sucking reflexes, 186, 187
suicide, 232–233, 239, 254–255, 261, 378
Sullivan, Harry Stack, 279
superego, 271, 272, 274, 279
surface traits, 286

survey, 489, 496, 513
Surwit, R. S., 177
suspected awareness, 258
sweat glands, 95
Swets, John A., 113
symbol, 69–70, 163, 191, 192, 194, 196
sympathetic nervous system, 83, 149
synapse, 60, 82, 83
systematic desensitization, 404–405, 410
systolic pressure, 176, 177
Szasz, Thomas, 365

tabula rasa, 11
Tandy, Jessica, 253
Tart, Charles, 128, 157
task function group, 5, 441, 442
task leader, 445
taste, 114, 117–118
taste aversions, 27–29
Taube, T. A., 378
Taylor, S., 329
tear glands, 95
Teasdale, John D., 39
telegraphic speech, 196
telepathy, 127–128
television programs, 209–211, 213
temperature changes, 118, 119, 134, 135, 175
temporal lobe, 92
tension headaches, 175
10th National Survey of Drug Usage Among College Students (Johnston), 349
Terman, Lewis, 296, 496–497
terminal illness, 257–261
Terminal Man, The (Crichton), 94
Terrace, Herbert, 195
tetrahydrocannabinol (THC), 167
thalamus, 83, 86, 148–149
thalidomide, 185
thanatology, 258
Thematic Apperception Test (TAT), 140–141, 309
theory, 9, 269–277
therapists, 394, 396–397
Thoits, P., 319
Thompson, Richard, 60
Thorazine, 411
thought, 69–75, 188–193, 212, 225–226
thought reform, 477
threshold, 108–109
thyroid gland, 95
thyroxin, 95, 134
Tinbergen, Niko, 97–98
Toffler, Alvin, 326
Tofranil, 168–169, 411
token economy, 46–47, 406
tolerance, 385–386
tongue display acts, 98
Torney, J., 458
total marriage, 345

touch, 85, 114
Toufexis, Anastasia, 520
traits, 13, 268, 269, 284–286, 445
tranquilizers, 411
transactional analysis (TA), 403–404, 410
Transcendental Meditation (TM), 175
transfer, 37
transference, 398–399
Traux, Charles, 401
Tresemer, David, 143
triangular theory of love, 344
trifluoperazine, 411
Trotter, R., 146
tumors, 91
Turner, J., 471
Turner, J. S., 245
Tursky, Bernard, 177
twins, 101–103, 343
Type A personality, 329, 330, 512

Ullman, P., 275
unconditional positive regard, 283, 401
unconditioned response (UCR), 24, 26, 27
unconditioned stimulus (UCS), 24, 25, 26, 27, 42
unconscious mind, 12–13, 109–110, 269–277
undifferentiated schizophrenia, 379–380
Unfinished Business (Scarf), 252
unstructured group, 5
uplifts, 323
utility value, 428, 431

Valenstein, Elliot, 94
validity, 293, 294
Valium, 168–169, 335, 412
Valvo, Alberto, 124
Van de Castle, R. L., 161
variable-interval reinforcement schedule, 32–33
variable-ratio reinforcement schedule, 31–32
variability, 508–509
variables, 493
Vaughn, M. E., 257
Venecia, D., 167
ventromedial hypothalamus (VMH), 135
vestibular system, 114, 119
vision, 108, 112, 114, 115–116, 121, 123–124, 146, 187–188, 244
visual cliff apparatus, 122, 124
visual sensitivity, 112
vital marriage, 345
Vitkus, J., 376
voluntary acts, of nervous system, 83

Wade, Nicholas, 99
waking state, 186
Wald, G., 115
Walden Two (Skinner), 14
Walk, R. D., 122, 124
walking, 184
Wallace, Robert Keith, 172, 175, 176
Wallerstein, J., 347
Walster, Elaine, 429, 432, 433–434
Walters, R. H., 208, 425
Walters, Richard, 278, 279
war, 324, 326, 332, 348–349, 461, 472, 477, 521, 528–531
Washburn, S. L., 99
Washoe, 194–195
Watson, John B., 14, 26, 101
weaning, 204
Webb, S. D., 332
Webb, Wilse B., 161
Weber, Ernst H., 111
Weber's law, 111
Wechsler, David, 296
Wechsler intelligence scales, 247, 296, 297, 498
weight, 135–136, 137, 161, 164
Weight Watchers, 336
Weir, T., 322
Weiss, J. M., 330–331
Weissman, M., 252
Wells, J. A., 332
Welsh, George S., 308
Wernicke, Carl, 518
Wheeler, David, 518
White, Burton, 10
Wiesel, Torslen N., 90
Wild, B. S., 316
Willers, F. K., 238
Williams, R. L., 137
Williams, Robert L., 395, 430
Wilson, Edward O., 98, 99–100, 101
Winter, D. G., 142
Wish, E. D., 170
withdrawal, 386
Wittinger, Roy P., 65
Wolfe, John B., 33–34
Wolpert, E., 162
Woolfolk, Robert L., 176
workplace design, 523–524
Wright, J., 211
Wrightsman, L. S., 427
Wundt, Wilhelm, 11–12
Wynne, L., 383

yoga, 175
Young, T. J., 171

Zajonc, Robert B., 298
Zarlt, S. H., 256
Zimbardo, Philip G., 280, 429, 482
Zimmerman, Robert F., 138
Zubin, Joseph, 230, 382